Winchelsea
Poor Law Records
1790 - 1841

Newgate March 2⁰ 1827

Gentleman I am sorry to inform you of
my unfortunate case I am confined in newgate
under sentence of death and the expence of my
trial has reduced me to go to the parish for relief
and the parish I dwelt in last was St Saviours Parish
Southwark they have relieved my wife by whom there
is 2 Children 1 is 2 years old the other 4 months
the parish of St Saviours sent the officer this day and I
have gaind no other settlement, not being 12 Months
at one place since I left winchelsea I have paid no
taxes since I left Winchelsea, my wife brother has
offered to keep my wife and 2 children for 5 ⅌ week
if you gentlemen think it proper to pay it as it out
her power to do any thing with a Child 2 months
and in a bad state of health, Please to send answer
by Return of post as this parish will be forced to
bring the family home begining of the next week
if you gentlemen think proper allow that sum
it will save her friend and the parish great
expence My wife brother lives at Minster
Isle of Shefsey Kent Please to direct Governors of
I am Gent Your unfortunate J Eagles St Saviours Parish
Humble serv J Eagles Southwark London

John Eagles' first letter from the Newgate condemned cell

PAR 511/35/1/260 transcribed as (**181**)
reproduced by arrangement with the County Archivist

Winchelsea
Poor Law Records
1790 - 1841

Edited by
Malcolm Pratt

SUSSEX RECORD SOCIETY
VOLUME 94
Issued to members of the Society for the year 2011

Published 2012 by
Sussex Record Society
Barbican House,
High Street,
Lewes,
East Sussex, BN7 1YE
© Sussex Record Society and Malcolm Pratt 2012
ISBN 978 0 85445 076 3

Printed by Hobbs the Printers Ltd., Totton, Hampshire

SUSSEX RECORD SOCIETY

Volumes issued by the Society

Vol. 1 *Marriage Licences at Lewes, 1586-1642*
Vol. 2 *Sussex Fines, 1190-1248*
Vol. 3 *Post Mortem Inquisitions, 1558-1583*
Vol. 4 *Ecclesiastical Returns for East Sussex, 1603; Sussex Poll Book, 1705;*
  Sussex MSS in the Harleian MSS; Bishop Praty's Register, 1438-1445.
Vol. 5 *West Sussex Protestation Returns, 1641-1642*
Vol. 6 *Marriage Licences at Lewes, 1670-1732*
Vol. 7 *Sussex Fines, 1249-1307*
Vol. 8 *Bishop Rede's Register, 1397-1415 (Pt.1)*
Vol. 9 *Marriage Licences at Chichester 1575-1730*
Vol. 10 *Subsidy Rolls, 1296, 1327 and 1332*
Vol. 11 *Bishop Rede's Register, 1397-1415 (Pt. I)*
Vol. 12 *Marriage Licences at Chichester (peculiars), 1579-1730*
Vol. 13 *Cuckfield Parish Register, 1598-1699*
Vol. 14 *Post Mortem Inquisitions, 1485-1649*
Vol. 15 *Bolney Parish Register, 1541-1812*
Vol. 16 *Star Chamber Proceedings, 1500-1558*
Vol. 17 *Ardingly Parish Register, 1558-1812*
* Vol. 18 *Angmering Parish Register, 1562-1687*
Vol. 19 *Sussex Manors and Advowsons, etc., 1509-1833, A-L*
Vol. 20 *Sussex Manors and Advowsons, etc., 1509-1833, M-Z*
Vol. 21 *Horsham Parish Register, 1541-1635*
Vol. 22 *Cowfold Parish Register, 1558-1812*
Vol. 23 *Sussex Fines, 1308-1509*
Vol. 24 *East Grinstead Parish Register, 1558-1661*
Vol. 25 *Marriage Licences at Lewes, 1771-1837, A-L*
Vol. 26 *Marriage Licences at Lewes, 1772-1837, M-Z*
Vol. 27 *Preston Manor Court Rolls, 1562-1702*
Vol. 28 *Sussex Apprentices and Masters, 1710-1752*
Vol. 29 *Abstracts of Documents relating to the Dobell family, 16th-18th cents.*
Vol. 30 *Glynde Parish Register, 1558-1812*
Vol. 31 *Thirteen Custumals of the Sussex Manors of the Bishop of Chichester, c.1256-1374*
Vol. 32 *Sussex Marriage Licences at Chichester, 1731-1774*
Vol. 33 *Sussex Inquisitions (from Bodleian Library), 1541-1616*
Vol. 34 *The Book of John Rowe, Steward to Lord Bergavenny, 1622*
Vol. 35 *Marriage Licences at Chichester, 1775-1800, with Index covering Licences, 1731-1800*
Vol. 36 *Sussex Chantry Records, 1535-1652*
Vol. 37 *Hastings Rape Records, 1387-1474*
Vol. 38 *Chartulary of Lewes Priory (Pt. I), 11th-I4th cents.*
* Vol. 39 *The Buckhurst Terrier, 1597-1598*
Vol. 40 *Chartulary of Lewes Priory (Pt. II), I2th-I4th cents.*
Vol. 41 *Transcripts of Sussex Wills up to 1560, Vol.1 Albourne -Chichester*
Vol. 42 *Transcripts of Sussex Wills up to 1560, Vol.2 Chiddingly -Horsham*
Vol. 43 *Transcripts of Sussex Wills up to 1560, Vol.3 Horsted Keynes –Pyecombe*
Vol. 44 *Records of the Barony and Honour of the Rape of Lewes, 1265-1466*
Vol. 45 *Transcripts of Sussex Wills up to 1560, Vol.4 Racton -Yapton*
Vol. 46 *Chichester Cathedral Chartulary, I3th-I6th cents.*
Vol. 47 *Survey of Robertsbridge Manor, 1567-1570*
* Vol. 48 *The Town Book of Lewes, 1542-1701*
Vol. 49 *Churchwardens' Presentments, (Pt. I), Archdeaconry of Chichester, 1621-1628, 1664-1670*

Vol. 50 *Churchwardens' Presentments, (Pt. II), Archdeaconry of Lewes, 1674-1677*
Vol. 51 *Record of Deputations of Gamekeepers, 1781-1928*
Jubilee Volume *Sussex Views from the Burrell Collection*
Vol. 52 *Chapter Acts, Chichester, 1472-1544 (The White Act Book)*
Vol. 53 *The Manor of Etchingham cum Salehurst, 1597-1865*
Vol. 54 *Quarter Sessions Order Book, 1642-1649*
Vol. 55 *Ministers' Accounts of the Manor of Petworth, 1347-1353*
Vol. 56 *Lay Subsidy Rolls, 1524-1525*
Vol. 57 *Custumals of Sussex Manors of the Archbishop of Canterbury, 1285-1330*
Vol. 58 *Chapter Acts, Chichester, 1545-1642*
Vol. 59 *Chartulary of Boxgrove Priory, l2th-14th cents.*
Vol. 60 *Custumals of the Manors of Laughton, Willingdon and Goring, 1292-1338*
* Vol. 61 *A Catalogue of Sussex Estate and Tithe Award Maps (Pt. I), 1606-1884*
Vol. 62 *Minutes of the Common Council of the City of Chichester, 1783-1826*
Vol. 63 *The Book of Bartholomew Bolney, 15th cent.*
Vol. 64 *Rye Shipping Records, 1566-1590*
Vol. 65 *Cellarers' Rolls of Battle Abbey, 1275-1513*
Vol. 66 *A Catalogue of Sussex Maps, (Pt. II) 1597-1958*
Vol. 67 *Estate Surveys of the Fitzalan Earls of Arundel, 14th cent.*
Vol. 68 *The Journal of Giles Moore of Horsted Keynes, 1655-1679*
Vol. 69 *The Town Book of Lewes, 1702-1837*
Vol. 70 *The Town Book of Lewes, 1837-1901*
* Vol. 71 *Accounts of the Roberts Family of Boarzell, 1568-1582*
Vol. 72 *Printed Maps of Sussex, 1575-1900*
* Vol. 73 *Correspondence of the Dukes of Richmond and Newcastle, 1724-1750*
Vol. 74 *Sussex Coroners' Inquests, 1485-1558*
* Vol. 75 *The Religious Census of Sussex, 1851*
Vol. 76 *The Fuller Letters, 1728-1755*
Vol. 77 *East Sussex Land Tax, 1785*
* Vol. 78 *Chichester Diocesan Surveys, 1686 and 1724*
* Vol. 79 *Saint Richard of Chichester*
Vol. 80 *The Ashdown Forest Dispute, 1876-1882*
* Vol. 81 *Sussex Schools in the 18th century*
* Vol. 82 *West Sussex Land Tax, 1785*
* Vol. 83 *Mid Sussex Poor Law Records, 1601-1835*
* Vol. 84 *Sussex in the First World War*
Vol. 85 *Sussex Depicted: Views and Descriptions 1600-1800*
* Vol. 86 *Sussex Shore to Flanders Fields: E. Heron–Allen's Journal of the Great War*
* Vol. 87 *East Sussex Parliamentary Deposited Plans, 1799-1970*
Vol. 88 *Sussex Cricket in the 18th century*
* Vol. 89 *East Sussex Coroners' Records, 1688-1838*
* Vol. 90 *The Durford Cartulary*
* Vol. 91 *Sussex Clergy Inventories, 1600-1750*
* Vol. 92 *Records of the Manor of Mote in Iden, 1442-1551, 1673*
* Vol. 93. *East Sussex Church Monuments, 1530-1830*

Volumes marked with an asterisk can be obtained from the Hon. Secretary, Sussex Record Society, Barbican House, Lewes, East Sussex, BN7 IYE. Prices can be found on the Society's website (www.sussexrecordsociety.org)

CONTENTS

Acknowledgements ix

Introduction xi

Winchelsea Poor Law Records - Part I People 1

Winchelsea Poor Law Records - Part II Topics 229

Appendix A: Leading Winchelsea Residents and Officials 297

Appendix B: The Poor 315

Appendix C: Naval and Army Recruitment 319

Appendix D: The Poor Rate 329

Appendix E: Additional Documents 339

Index of Persons 347

Index of Places 367

Index of Subjects 373

ILLUSTRATIONS

John Eagles' first letter from the condemned cell at Newgate Frontispiece

The settlement examination of Cornelius Clarke 39

Apprenticeship arrangements for Daniel Edwards 71

The removal order of Joseph Ronalds and family 151

The Barrack Houses 225

Map of Winchelsea with key 226 & 227

The pre-1894 parishes of eastern Sussex 228

Winchelsea Court Hall, 1850 259

Winchelsea Poor Law Records 1790 – 1841

Dedicated to the memory of

Dr Roy Hunnisett

from whose original idea this
volume grew

ACKNOWLEDGEMENTS

I must first record my debt to my friend and mentor, Roy Hunnisett. He took a great and supportive interest in my earlier books about Winchelsea, and was one of the first to recognise the value of, and to enthuse about, the sequence of letters on which this book is based. Invaluably he also suggested how they could be published in this way, enhanced by additional relevant material. Sadly he did not live to see the work completed.

Perhaps the most delightful moment which I associate with the whole project was receiving a letter, totally unexpectedly, from a direct descendant of the book's principal character, Charles Arnett, Winchelsea's first professional assistant overseer. Philip Emerson, a resident of Cuckfield in West Sussex, is Arnett's great-great-great grandson. Philip has provided much information about his ancestor and has allowed me to have a copy of his quite outstanding family history research which uses Charles Arnett's life as its starting point. I very greatly appreciate Philip's interest and support.

Peter Macleod has used his exceptional skills to prepare my text for the printer. When he volunteered for this task I doubt if he realised that it would include entering up seemingly endless pages of additions, alterations and corrections, or, indeed, after he spent a considerable time amending one aspect of the format, being asked to change it back again! All this he has done uncomplainingly and with great good humour. For this, and for his enthusiasm about the book, I am deeply grateful.

Philip Bye, Senior Archivist (Public Services) at East Sussex Record Office, is another who has been consistently encouraging and supportive. He transformed my originally very clumsy transcription of the letters into the form in which they appear here and has since been involved in the project in many ways, most recently preparing potential illustrations. My warm and indebted thanks.

My thanks are due to many others:

To the Rector and Churchwardens of St Thomas's Church, Winchelsea; to the Mayor and Jurats of Winchelsea Corporation; and to Elizabeth Hughes, County Archivist, on behalf of East Sussex County Council, for permission to publish transcriptions of documents from their archives.

To Andrew Foster, Literary Director of the Sussex Record Society, for his supportive interest in my work and particularly for his wise and extremely helpful guidance during the preparation of my introduction.

To Christopher Whittick, Senior Archivist (Document Services) at East Sussex Record Office who has used his unrivalled knowledge of, and enthusiasm for, Sussex historical archives actively to support the publication of so many books about the county. In this case he undertook research on my behalf about lawyers who feature in the book. Where Christopher's work is referred to in the notes, it is acknowledged with his initials.

To Roger Davey, Melvyn Pett and Brian Short, who kindly agreed to read versions of my introduction as it developed, for their perceptive and helpful comments.

To Peter Wilkinson who has also commented most helpfully on the introduction, has taken responsibility for the dust-jacket and has offered much other invaluable help and advice during the later stages of the project.

To staff and former staff of the Search Room at East Sussex Record Office, particularly Jennifer Nash, Andrew Lusted, Izabella Bicsak-Snitter and Andrew Boulton, for their patient and unfailingly helpful response to my many inquiries.

To Hugh Davie, Melvyn Pett, Brian Short, Kim Leslie, David Simkin, Phyllis Nordstrom, Elizabeth Hughes and The Francis Frith Collection for invaluable help in providing illustrations and giving permission for their use.

To Revd Canon Howard Cocks, recently retired Rector of Winchelsea, for his interest and encouragement.

To Esme Evans, Honorary Librarian, Sussex Archaeological Society, for her advice and support.

To Andrew Bennett, Brighton and Hove Archivist at East Sussex Record Office, for his interest. He and I have discussed the project on a number of occasions.

To the members of the Sussex Record Society Council who so readily accepted my proposal that this book might be published within their annual series, and who have been consistently supportive since.

And finally, of course, to my family. To Jeremy, Nick and Adam for help in particular ways and most importantly, with my love, to Bridget for her tolerance during the twenty years I have spent researching and recording Winchelsea's history. I have promised her that this is my last book; now she has it in writing!

Malcolm Pratt
December 2012

Introduction

Winchelsea provides a wonderful opportunity to examine the lives of individual paupers of the early nineteenth century. It does so because not only do we have available unusually full records for its parish, for the local judiciary and for its Poor Law Union, but also a substantial collection of letters written by or for its poor. From these prolific sources, all held at East Sussex Record Office (ESRO), it has been possible to extract details about the lives of ninety-eight paupers and much information about Winchelsea's administration of the Poor Law. Perhaps the most remarkable and rewarding outcome is that the hopes, fears, insecurity and plight of individual poor persons (the paupers) emerge, frequently expressed in their own words. We find, for example, a woman desperately seeking help for her smallpox-ridden family; a man suggesting that if he were to be provided with a cow he could eke out a meagre living for his family; a woman urgently requesting that her much younger brother who had never been on the outside of a coach should be looked after by the coachman; a prison inmate pleading for clemency because of his medical distress; and, perhaps the most poignant of all, letters from a man under sentence of death in London's Newgate prison entreating the authorities of his parish to care for his wife and children should his sentence be carried out.[1] The book contains not only these and many other revealing insights into the lives of Winchelsea's poor but also illustrates the severe demands made upon those responsible for making provision for them.

It becomes immediately clear from the documents reproduced that Winchelsea, a port of considerable national importance in medieval times and a quiet, well-preserved small town in the twenty-first century, was, during the late eighteenth and early nineteenth centuries a place which had, in common with many other local parishes, to endure and ameliorate much poverty. Although the available statistics permit only a very general estimation, it seems that at some time between 1790 and 1841 almost a third of Winchelsea's population fell in need of some kind of relief.

The Sources

The project which led to the publication of this volume originated with the discovery within the archives of St Thomas's Church, Winchelsea of a collection of more than three hundred and fifty documents written by and about the town's poor and about provision made for their support.[2] A considerable majority of these documents are letters written to the Winchelsea overseers by or on behalf of paupers who had their settlement in Winchelsea but were living elsewhere. This sequence of documents which will be referred to collectively from now on as 'the letters' even though they are not, strictly speaking, all 'letters', was first published, in chronological order with an index enabling researchers to find those about any individual, on the Sussex Record Society website (www.sussexrecordsociety.org)

in 2008. The late Dr Roy Hunnisett, then serving as one of the Society's literary directors, suggested that there must be plenty of associated material which would allow the project to be expanded for publication as one of the Society's annual volumes. His suggestion has proved correct and to him this, the resulting volume, is dedicated. All that material associated with the people and topics mentioned in the letters has been noted and extracted from the following principal sources:

(a) The minute books of the Winchelsea parish vestry, 1754-1831.[3]
These were originally public meetings although usually only attended by leading residents involved in parish affairs. Later an elected select vestry was appointed to undertake all the required responsibilities for the management of the poor and the poor rate on the parish's behalf. Within the period 1790 to 1841 these books provide a wealth of information about such subjects as: the annual elections of churchwardens and overseers of the poor; authorisation of poor rate demands on Winchelsea's residents and landowners; confirmation of the accuracy of churchwardens' and overseers' accounts; agreement to the removal of paupers from the parish; resolutions about the management of the poor and allowances for paupers according to need; agreements with doctors to treat the poor; the management and maintenance of the town workhouse; and the placing of pauper children to work in local houses and businesses.

(b) The account books of the Winchelsea overseers, 1794-1835.[4]
These make it possible to trace all payments made, either on a regular or casual basis and whether in cash or kind to Winchelsea's poor. The books also give full details of every occasion when a poor rate was demanded to finance such payments including the amount collected from each of the town's owners or occupiers, businesses and land. Examples are published as Appendix D.

(c) The Court Books of Winchelsea Corporation, 1769-1881.[5]
The mayor and jurats of Winchelsea served as ex-officio justices of the peace and held their courts and quarter sessions in the upper room of the present Court Hall. Their records provide details of individuals who were examined as to their settlement, appeared before the court to give evidence or make a complaint, or were tried for a criminal offence.[6]

(d) The Hundred and Assembly Books of Winchelsea Corporation, 1769-1882.[7]
The particular value of these volumes is that they make it possible to trace the appointment of all town officials such as the mayor, deputy mayor, jurats, town clerk, town sergeant, constables and gaoler. In various ways the holders of these offices were responsible for the poor and much information drawn from them has been used in Appendix A.

(e) Minute and Workhouse Record Books of the Rye Poor Law Union, 1835-1841.[8] Here are recorded many matters affecting Winchelsea after the formation of the Rye Poor Law Union following the Poor Law Amendment Act of 1834. The Union's area included many of the parishes of East Sussex (see **972**), nevertheless, even if only occasionally, the affairs of individual Winchelsea paupers who feature in this study can be found.[9]

The dates of the transfer of the parish records of St Thomas's Church, Winchelsea to ESRO, 1959 and 1960, suggest that those used here were found by Rev[d] Rex M Ware in the rambling and partly unused rectory (now known as The Old Rectory in Rectory Lane) into which he moved on his induction as Rector of Winchelsea in 1959. Certainly we know that he transferred many parish registers for, on the flyleaf of the baptismal register 1813-1833,[10] above a list of parish registers written by his predecessor, Rev[d] Drake Hollingberry, Mr Ware has added, 'Deposited with Diocesan Record Office, Lewes 26 June 1960'. It is extremely fortunate that the overseers' accounts, the vestry minutes and the letters have survived, no doubt set aside and neglected for many years. Many parishes have no similar surviving records, probably because they were destroyed through lack of interest and space.

The Period (1790-1841)
This period has been chosen because it permits the inclusion of valuable material which explains the operation of the Poor Law in Winchelsea. A few documents which pre-date 1790 but serve the same purpose have also been used. The end-date of 1841 marks the last of the letters and allows valuable information to be extracted from the first detailed census for Winchelsea. It should be emphasised, however, that the bulk of the letters are dated between 1823 and 1828, the time when Charles Arnett was in office as assistant overseer. See below.

The Geographical Area
The area for which such a prolific archive survives is small but unusually complex. The Ancient Town of Winchelsea stood, as it does today, on the Hill of Iham where it was sited in the late thirteenth century under the personal direction of King Edward I. That monarch's new bastide town was built to replace Old Winchelsea which had stood on a shingle bank in what is now Rye Bay and had been destroyed by the elements. Winchelsea's importance as a port demanded that the Ancient Town should also include a waterfront and inner harbour on the River Brede at the foot of the hill.

The Parish of St Thomas the Apostle covered the same area as the Ancient Town but with a large detached section east of the River Rother added. It is possible that this unusually separated part of the parish had been part of Old Winchelsea whose church was also dedicated to St Thomas.

The Liberty of Winchelsea was the considerably larger area for which the town's mayor and jurats provided the judiciary, a responsibility originating in medieval times through Winchelsea's position as a head port of the Confederation of the Cinque Ports. The Liberty consisted of: both sections of the Parish of St Thomas; a large part of the parish of Icklesham; just a little of the parish of Pett; and all that part of the parish of Broomhill which lay within the county of Sussex. The remainder of Broomhill parish, including its church, lay within the neighbouring Cinque Port Liberty of New Romney in Kent and does not feature in this study. The continued existence in the early nineteenth century of Winchelsea's Cinque Port Liberty is important because the town's courts heard its cases, including any affecting paupers, and Winchelsea's mayor was its ex-officio coroner.

The population of Winchelsea's parish of St Thomas the Apostle was never large. In 1831 the recorded census figure was 772 (**857**). The same document states that this number is smaller than that for 1821. This is confirmed by the *Victoria County History* which gives the figures for 1801, 1811 and 1821 as 625, 652 and 817 respectively.[11] The town was garrisoned in 1801 and 1811 but the soldiers were not included in the census. In 1841, the year of Winchelsea's first detailed census which tells us so much, the population figure was 687. We also learn there of a considerable increase in the number of uninhabited houses, 23 compared with 5 in 1831, a trend which indicates that, for whatever reason, families were moving away. We are also told in 1841 that no one was in the gaol, that 24 men were employed in the coastguard service and that twelve men were living in barges or boats on rivers or canals within the parish. Both the 1831 and 1841 figures show the principal employment available to be in agriculture.[12]

The Structure

The book has three sections:

Part I provides, in alphabetical order, transcriptions of all the relevant documentary information available about each of the ninety-eight paupers who are named in the letters. These details are preceded by twenty-five documents (**2-26**) related to the appointment and service of Charles Arnett as assistant overseer.[13]

Part II gives transcribed information about each of the seven topics with which the letters deal apart from the affairs of individual paupers. This information is also extracted from the available records listed above. These topics concern: the Winchelsea workhouse; the administration of the parish; the revaluation of poor rate assessments; poor rate collection and related legal costs; parish tithes; emigration; and Winchelsea's inclusion within the Rye Poor Law Union, hereafter referred to as the Rye Union. This section has its own preface and additional introductory information about each of its sub-sections.

Five appendices are provided as follows:

Appendix A includes fifty mini-biographies of those who can be described as having been in responsible positions of one kind or another in the town and parish during this period.

Appendix B tells more about the poor and is divided into two lists. B1 names all those paupers who were assisted by Winchelsea during this period but who do not appear in Part I because they are not mentioned in the letters. B2 includes the names of the parishes other than Winchelsea with which Part I paupers were connected.

Appendix C records attempts to recruit within Winchelsea for both the navy and army during the Revolutionary and Napoleonic Wars with France. Here is available useful information about individuals because both parish officers and paupers often appear in these documents.

Appendix D reproduces in full two examples of the collection of poor rates in Winchelsea and thus indicates both the complexity of the work involved in preparing for and making such collections, and the extent of the demands made upon the ratepayers.

Appendix E contains transcriptions of two important supplementary documents: the extremely detailed job description of an assistant overseer of this period; and an article from *The Times* which refers to civil unrest in Winchelsea in the mid-1830s.

Further information on the thinking behind the inclusion of these appendices and the sources used to compile them appears with each.

The Overseers and the Law of Settlement

The overseers of the poor, in Winchelsea as elsewhere, were elected annually by the parish vestry. They were usually tradesmen, farmers or professional people. In those days of very local government there was a widespread feeling among such people that they should undertake a responsibility to assist in the administration of the parish. Except in the circumstances described below, they worked as a committee, conducting most of their business within parish vestry meetings. It was their duty: to ensure collection of the poor rate; to arrange the assessment of each property's contribution towards that rate; and to allocate the money collected to meet the various needs of the town's poor. These duties were demanding and unpaid, although occasionally overseers were rewarded for what they had done on behalf of their colleagues (**828**). The churchwardens worked with the overseers in implementing the decisions of the parish vestry and always signed the records of each meeting. The rector, or his curate, frequently took the chair at such meetings but was seldom otherwise involved.

The legislation which determined which paupers were the responsibility of the overseers of each parish was the Law of Settlement. In operation since 1662 this stipulated that paupers had a right to relief only in their own parishes. The qualifications by which a person acquired a settlement within a parish were many and varied. Those which are illustrated, directly or indirectly, within this volume were: the payment of taxes to the parish authorities; serving in an official office such as an overseer; serving an apprenticeship; employment as an unmarried person in domestic service for a full year; being born illegitimate (the terms bastard and bastardy were in constant use and therefore appear frequently in these pages); occupying as a tenant premises with an annual rateable value of £10 or more; marriage to a man whose settlement was in the parish; birth where the settlement of the parents was not known; and by occupying your own freehold premises however small.[14] Disputes about paupers' settlement caused an enormous amount of work and expense for the overseers. This included inquiries into the accuracy of settlement examinations which a pauper was required to make under oath when seeking relief, and legal action over the legitimacy of removal orders from parish to parish. Such removal orders involved compulsory escorted return to a person's 'home' parish. Illustrating the more dramatic examples included here we find Winchelsea accusing the neighbouring parish of Pett of smuggling a pregnant girl across the parish boundary so that her child would be Winchelsea's responsibility and the case of a woman who, despite former loyal service as Winchelsea's workhouse mistress, was, when she fell on hard times, removed to Hastings. By the time this disputed case was eventually considered by the County Quarter Sessions at Lewes she was already dead.[15]

The Poor and their Relief

Winchelsea's descent into poverty from its prosperous prominence in medieval times was accelerated in the sixteenth century by the dissolution of its monasteries and the closure of its three hospitals.

The Grey Friars (Franciscans) and the Black Friars (Dominicans), long established in the town, had been active in provision for the poor through the personal concerns of the monks and through funds received from benefactors and legacies. Their work was supplemented through direct bequests such as that of William Stonaker of Winchelsea who died in 1517 and left one penny to each of the poor people present on the day of his burial.[16] Similarly Peter Maister of Winchelsea in 1526 generously bequeathed, 'To every poor man and woman that will ask it at my burial and at [my] year's mind [i.e. the anniversary of his death] twopence and to every poor child one penny.[17] Another Winchelsea will, that of William Allen in 1541, leaves 'for the health of my soul at my burying to priests and clerks and to other poor people forty shillings in money and in bread and drink ten shillings'.[18] Two years later William Becher's will included, 'I do bequeath unto eight poor people eightpence of good money',[19] and in 1545 Henry Smith in his turn sought to alleviate poverty in the town by giving 'to every poor household two shillings at the discretion of my executors'.[20]

The hospitals (the term almshouses provides a better modern equivalent in describing their function) – in Winchelsea, those of St John, St Bartholomew and Holy Cross – also provided for the poor and were financed by donation and benefaction. They, however, had a more formal constitutional association with the town's civic authorities. The best example of this exists through the mayor's responsibility in connection with the Hospital of St John. He was required to visit it once a year and was authorised to remove 'any objectionable inmate'. In consultation with the jurats he most importantly controlled admissions. When vacancies occurred they were to admit any poor man or woman who had been, 'in good love and fame all their time'. Such inmates were cared for without any charge. The mayor and jurats were also responsible for appointing the master and mistress of both St John's and St Bartholomew's which they did as late as 1559 at which time these institutions had probably been combined on the St John's site.[21]

However, by the time of that last appointment, the situation in Winchelsea was already in serious decline. Things had become so bad that, when a group of Huguenot refugees established a Walloon church in Winchelsea in 1560, 'The town being poor and decaying, most of the refugees, shortly after landing there, proceeded inland to London, Canterbury or other places where settlements had already been formed'.[22]

The need to make better provision for the poor was becoming a growing national concern. Factors such as, in Winchelsea, the removal of the influence of the monasteries and hospitals eventually made it necessary for parliament, through legislation, to provide an alternative. In 1572 parishes were permitted to appoint, 'Collectors of assessments and overseers of the poor'.[23] The parish was the only unit of administration available throughout the country to implement such legislation and from that time it was the parish, through its officers the churchwardens and overseers, which had responsibility for its poor. Those responsible in Winchelsea's parish of St Thomas the Apostle soon became aware that, as money could be raised for this purpose through a compulsory rate, motivation for the kind of benevolent donations and bequests such as those mentioned above was largely removed. In levying a rate Winchelsea was not alone. Paul Slack observes that, 'In the forty years before 1660 poor rates became familiar. In the next forty years they became universal.'[24] Our ability to relate this general comment to Winchelsea is limited, but we do know that money for this purpose was being levied in the town during the period to which Slack refers because the earliest surviving record of a

Winchelsea poor rate is dated 1683.[25] The amount raised on that occasion from local householders and landowners was £8 5s 7d. Later in the same year a further £11 18s 2d was collected. While we should not assume that Winchelsea had made demands on its ratepayers earlier than 1683, the accounting layout and record in the town's earliest surviving ledger certainly suggests that this was an established practice rather than an innovation. For the year 1691 this same volume records that £31 12s 10d was collected and £34 14s 1d spent on the poor. Such discrepancies were to become the norm.

The requirement that the poor should be supported by regular compulsory rate demands was followed in 1723 by a further development implemented in Winchelsea. This was the result of Sir Edward Knatchbull's Act which confirmed parishes' right to provide workhouses. About six hundred workhouses had been established by 1750,[26] most, like Winchelsea's, very small and in cottages converted for the poor. Returns made in the mid-1830s stated that 'no work of any kind [is] done in the house or by any inmates (except occasional outdoor work on the roads)' and that, 'Until 1831 indoor paupers were maintained as a family in the house' (**761, 762**). No existing record enables us to date the opening of Winchelsea's workhouse, whose function as is indicated by the above statements is better described by the alternative title of poorhouse, beyond our knowing that it was in use by 1766 (**742**).

In the years leading up to the initial date of this volume, Winchelsea tried an alternative way of attempting to cope with rapidly growing demands for poor relief. In 1782 the churchwardens and overseers appointed Mr Abraham Kennett 'to take the poor', allowing him the fixed sum of £175 per annum from which, with a few exceptions, he was expected to meet the needs of the town's paupers (**803, 804**). Two years later Kennett was succeeded by George Mugliston who was given a slightly increased allowance of £194. His contract lasted until 1792 when responsibility was transferred back, possibly because of the problem of rising costs.

A principal cause of this was the weather. William Hague describes how, 'rain … fell heavily in August 1799 damaging the harvest and beginning a cycle of weather which would culminate in serious shortages of corn and record prices in the following two years'.[27] Further evidence of the impact of the weather on the plight of the poor over a longer period is provided by W E Minchinton. He reports, 'a scanty crop' in 1789 followed by a poor harvest in 1790 and several similarly bad years in the following decade. A 1791 increase in the level of the price of wheat which had to be reached before wheat could be imported (a new corn law) pleased the farmers but increased retail prices and thus the pressure on poor relief.[28] In 1795, an initiative by the justices of Speenhamland in Berkshire became widely adopted elsewhere. The general principle was that if the income of a family fell below an agreed minimum level, that income should be supplemented from the rates. However, not satisfied with such a generalisation, the Speenhamland justices proceeded to lay down specific qualifications among which were that 'when the 8lb

11oz loaf cost one shilling they reckoned that every man needed three shillings a week for himself and one shilling and sixpence for each of his family to survive; for every penny that the loaf rose above one shilling they reckoned that each man would need threepence more for himself and a penny more for each of his family.'[29] The motivation for this local legislation which was so widely copied seems to have been humanitarian, but also with the intention of preventing disorder by disaffected poor. One of its principal consequences was that farmers were encouraged to keep their wages low in the knowledge that the parish would supplement them.

The result of all this in Winchelsea was an explosion of costs which must have brought the parish close to bankruptcy. In the financial year from Easter 1801 the demands of the town's poor required that a total of £1229 was collected through the poor rate.[30] In addition to this enormous sum (which in 2012 equates to about £40,000), a further £600 was borrowed from local banks.[31] Clearly the situation was getting out of hand. In 1803 an attempt was made to regain control by placing the responsibility with a single person. Walter Fuller senior, a Winchelsea resident with considerable experience as an overseer, was therefore paid £15 a year 'to attend to the public accounts in a more accurate way than can be expected of the overseers' (**829**). Despite Fuller's efforts and those of his successors the amount of £1143 18s 0d (**831**) which was required in 1822 remained nearly as large. The parish vestry then resolved to appoint a full-time official as had been permitted by legislation dating from 1819. This person would be known as the assistant overseer and, in Winchelsea's case – but not usually elsewhere – would also serve as workhouse master (**2,3**). The successful candidate was Charles Arnett. For his career in the town and his important influence see (**1**) and below.

Charles Arnett was succeeded in 1828 by a local man, David Laurence, who undertook all the duties except that of workhouse master (**22**). Laurence's principal involvement as assistant overseer lasted only six years for the Poor Law Amendment Act of 1834 removed almost all the parish's responsibility for the poor and transferred it to the Rye Poor Law Union. The parishes which fell within the considerable area covered by the Rye Union are listed in (**972**). Under the 1834 Act Winchelsea elected one member to serve among the guardians of the Rye Union, had to make substantial contributions from its poor rate to the funds of that union, dealt only occasionally with the affairs of its own poor, while, a point which perhaps created the most resentment, income from the sale of the Winchelsea workhouse accrued to the Rye Union rather than to the town. The nature of the legislation also ensured that the Rye Union in its turn could not operate without constant reference to the supervisory national body, the Poor Law Commissioners. A sad effect of this change was to reduce the influence of local people who knew their parish and their poor. The actions and decisions of those who served Winchelsea as parish officers, corporation officers and justices of the peace and who through that service demonstrated how valuable their local knowledge was are fully documented in these pages and their lives briefly summarised in Appendix A.

Charles Arnett

It is Charles Arnett (**1-26**) whom we have to thank for the fact that we can know so much about Winchelsea's poor of two hundred years ago. He came to Winchelsea, in September 1823, aged 32, to serve as the town's first salaried assistant overseer and as master of the workhouse. His only previous experience was as an apprenticed clerk in Maidstone, the town of his birth, and as a schoolmaster in the small village of Iden near Rye. However inappropriate this experience may seem, particularly to his responsibility for collecting and administering the poor rate, he entered confidently into the job and within a few months was transforming the way in which records were kept of Winchelsea's dealings with its poor and its ratepayers. Clearly he had examined the existing methods and found them wanting. He therefore introduced two new ledgers and a new court book. Whereas previously the affairs of any pauper had had to be extracted from long lists within the general accounts, both the ledgers which Arnett initiated made immediately clear exactly how individuals were being supported. The first new ledger [32] has printed on the cover 'Weekly Pay List – Winchelsea Parish 1824'. As this title suggests it contained a detailed week by week record, beginning on 30 September 1824, of all those who were receiving regular relief. It is noticeable that when he started the book 46 paupers were being aided in this way; when he left the town that number had been reduced to 28. The second new ledger, [33] started six months later, treated the relief of individuals differently. Here, usually on a page per person basis, were listed all allowances whether they were weekly, monthly, occasional according to need (known as casual) and whether in cash or kind. These entries also frequently included the reason for casual payments; reasons such as 'out of work', 'sick', or 'funeral expenses of child'. The third of Arnett's new volumes [34] had on its cover the handwritten legend, 'Informations and Summary Proceedings before His Majesty's Justices of the Peace for the Ancient Town of Winchelsea'. It provided details, frequently in Arnett's hand and appended by his flourishing signature, of appearances before the magistrates and often of his own evidence about those with whom he was attempting to deal. The first of these appearances occurred on 26 June 1824 and the last on 29 February 1828, just over three weeks before Arnett resigned (**22**). The book was not used by his successor; the remaining pages are blank.

The above three volumes are vitally important in extracting information about individuals but it was another of Arnett's procedures which prompted the research published here. Charles Arnett retained his incoming correspondence and associated documents, [35] referred to above as the letters. Of these, thirteen must have been found on his arrival for they are dated before September 1823; two hundred and ninety-seven were received while he was there. Only another sixty-nine were added to the collection by his successors between 1828 and 1841. The retention of correspondence was not a commonly used administrative system at the time and without the letters the lives of those who feature here would remain obscure. It should perhaps be emphasised that there would have been very little such correspondence had Winchelsea not been so willing to support its paupers while they were living elsewhere, frequently on the grounds that it would be more expensive to keep them in the Winchelsea workhouse. Arnett did not, however, keep copies of letters he sent. He had no support staff and such a task would have made a difficult job even more time consuming. In fact only four occasions seem to have merited the keeping of a copy. However, the decisions of the parish vestry, conscientiously recorded in the three volumes noted above, provided the basis of his instructions and to those he could always refer.

It is unfortunate that Arnett left Winchelsea and later a similar post at Bexhill (**1**) amid controversy. There is no evidence among the Winchelsea records to suggest any impropriety on his part. He had admirably fulfilled the duties required of him by his employers and was prepared robustly to defend his record (**24**). We can only assume that personality clashes with some vestry members were involved and that as a result they sought his dismissal.

It is through the extensive family history researches of his great-great-great grandson, Philip Emerson of Cuckfield in West Sussex,[36] that it is possible to give a brief account here of Charles Arnett's career after he left Winchelsea and Bexhill. He moved first to Tenterden where he managed the Woolpack Inn in the High Street, at the same time setting up a carrier service between Tenterden and Maidstone. The carrier project failed and in 1833 Charles Arnett moved to Calais, returning later to fetch his family. His attempts to set up a school for the children of expatriate lace-makers was initially frustrated by the French authorities. He then worked as a book-keeper for a lace making company, set up briefly as a lace manufacturer himself, and finally achieved his ambition of running a school for English children living in France. There he is believed still to have been working at the time of his death in 1857. For a man who made such an impact during his five years as assistant overseer in Winchelsea – and through that work enabled us now to know so much about the Winchelsea people of his time – this was an intriguing and varied sequence of subsequent employment.

Life in Winchelsea between 1790 and 1841

We are provided with an insight into the town's circumstances by the researches of Sir Frederick Morton Eden. He reported that about one hundred families lived in Winchelsea in 1795 with an average of 5½ members per family. 'The inhabitants at present are entirely agricultural: a cambric manufactory once existed in the parish but it has been abandoned for several years.'[37] Eden went on to report that at that time labourers were paid 1s 6d a day for ordinary work, 2s a day in hay harvest and 2s 6d or more in corn harvest. 'Work, however, is generally performed by the piece'[38] i.e. by the task rather than by regular employment. There were fifty-five 'out-poor' receiving relief but not resident in the workhouse. Of these half were adults, chiefly old and infirm and half under fifteen years of age. The parish paid several house rents amounting altogether to about £30 a year and that 'until recently' the poor were 'farmed', i.e. made the responsibility of an individual, 'for about £200 a year'. He noted that the poor 'are mostly from the class of labourers' and that 'sickness, age, infirmities, numerous families and the high price of provisions are the usual causes that throw them on the parish'. Referring to the attitudes of the parish authorities he noted that certificates of residence elsewhere were seldom granted and that removals 'which do not occur often' were very expensive. Eden concluded by saying that there were no established charities in Winchelsea except 'the Poor's Rate'.[39] Whatever may have been his sources, Eden's conclusions are fully confirmed in these pages.

The above report also mentioned that there were 'some Methodists and a very few Baptists in the parish'. Methodism certainly had a considerable following in Winchelsea during our period. This had been nurtured and encouraged by the direct involvement of John Wesley. His personal presence on several occasions and his enthusiasm led to the construction in 1785 of the Chapel which survives in occasional use in Rectory Lane, a chapel in which he preached. Winchelsea's firm place in the history of Methodism has also been assured through Wesley's preaching of his last open-air sermon in German Street on 20 November 1790. A few of the town's poor joined the Methodist congregation; no doubt many more heard this sermon. The final entry in Wesley's diary is dated four days later.[40] Wesley died the following March; his influence in Winchelsea lived on and continues to do so.

Only three years after Wesley's last open air sermon the outbreak of the French Revolutionary and Napoleonic Wars caused Winchelsea to become a garrison town for the first time. The impact on the town and its people was considerable. Regiments stationed there between 1794 and 1813 included the Radnorshire, Worcestershire and East Kent Militias, the 14th and 19th Regiments of Foot and the Royal Regiment of Artillery.[41] The presence of the garrison between 1794 and 1814 brought about greatly increased use of both the font and the churchyard. The parish registers include the baptism of 185 children born to serving fathers during this period. Additionally, thirty-seven soldiers' marriages are recorded, mostly to local girls, and there were 118 burials of soldiers, their wives and children.[42] Many of the soldiers' deaths would have been of those returning wounded from the Peninsular campaigns but the squalid conditions in the barracks were almost certainly a potent additional cause for both soldiers and their families. Some evidence about those conditions appears in the records of Winchelsea's courts where it is clear that the presence of the garrison became a source of annoyance to the authorities and to Winchelsea people whose right it was, through the grand jury, to make presentments [complaints] at the sittings of Winchelsea quarter sessions. Opportunities seem to have been frequent. 'On 15 January 1805 the grand jury accused the barrack master general of failing to complete the building of the privy at "the new huts". The following year when the privy had been completed the barrack master was in trouble again for allowing sewage from it to run into the street. Later it was the commanding officer who incurred their wrath by allowing sentry boxes to stand "in the public high roads".'[43] In the first decade of the nineteenth century, as the war progressed, two enormous building projects were implemented because of the threat of invasion. Both affected Winchelsea and its people. The westernmost section of the Royal Military Canal begins right at the foot of Winchelsea's hill. Eight Martello Towers eventually stood along the shoreline between Rye Harbour and Pett Level at what is now Winchelsea Beach. The view towards the sea must have been of a single enormous building site. There is reasonable circumstantial evidence that these projects provided work for Winchelsea men including the poor. Between 1804 and 1809 demands on the poor rate were considerably reduced.[44]

During the 1820s and 1830s Winchelsea's parish of St Thomas the Apostle faced two major problems, both arising incidentally from the death of Rev[d] Drake Hollingberry who, on 5 January 1822, was buried in his churchyard at the age of 80 after many years devoted service to the parish.[45] The new rector was Rev[d] J W Dugdell, also rector of Preston in Kent. During his incumbency at Winchelsea he was an absentee who seldom visited the parish but instead appointed Rev[d] Thomas Richards, vicar of Icklesham, as his curate. Richards, a most conscientious and dedicated clergyman, had been considerably involved at Winchelsea through helping Hollingberry during the rector's declining years. Nevertheless he was quite unable to officiate at two Winchelsea services on a Sunday or, with two parishes, to give the time required at Winchelsea for other duties. Winchelsea resented what had happened and felt fully justified in expecting there to be a resident rector. Richard Stileman, the owner of The Friars and Winchelsea's leading resident at the time, led the resulting complaints but their correspondence showed Mr Dugdell to be resolutely unwilling to change the arrangements he had made. Stileman therefore convened a public vestry meeting on 13 January 1826 at which he reviewed his correspondence with the rector and particularly the point he had made that in a parish of 'about 800 souls' if there were only one Sunday service many parishioners would be unable 'to attend divine service on that sacred day'.[46] The meeting passed a formal resolution, 'That until the death of the late respected incumbent, the parish always enjoyed the advantage of having a resident clergyman which we consider essentially necessary to the welfare of the parish.'[47] Already informed by Stileman that further reference to Dugdell would be pointless, the meeting then decided to involve the Bishop of Chichester. Stileman was asked to write to the bishop and 'to impress upon him by the sense of this meeting our most anxious wish that he will take the earnest desire of the inhabitants of the parish … into his consideration and grant us such relief as the necessity and urgency of the case requires.'[48] A committee including Stileman, Thomas Dawes, Dr Adam Scott and David Laurence was established to support Stileman in this correspondence and to report progress to the vestry meeting when necessary. No progress resulted. There is no evidence of any follow-up at subsequent vestry meetings so we must assume that the bishop took the view either that Dugdell's arrangements were adequate or that they could not legally be challenged. Both Dugdell and his immediate successor, Rev[d] H S Mortimer, were absentees and it was only in the early 1830s when Rev[d] James John West became curate and later rector that a full time clergyman again served the parish.

Of great importance to the freemen of Winchelsea, although of considerably less importance to the townsfolk who had been so concerned about being unable to attend divine service on Sundays, was the loss in 1832 of the town's right to elect two members to parliament, a privilege dating from the time of Edward III. Winchelsea was what is known as a freeman borough with the very few enfranchised freemen voting under the direction of the borough's patron, at this time the Duke of Cleveland. Despite being in control of this and other rotten boroughs, the Duke was of liberal mind and instructed his sitting members to vote for the 1832 Reform Act and therefore for the loss of their own seats. On the very first page of the published Act the name of Winchelsea appears in the list of those boroughs which had previously had two seats and would in future have none.[49]

Having lost, with his own agreement, the right to nominate MPs for Winchelsea, the Duke of Cleveland felt that Winchelsea Corporation had lost all possible usefulness for him. He therefore instructed all those whose votes he had controlled, and over whom his influence continued, to have nothing to do with Corporation meetings or affairs. Had it proved impossible over time to raise the required quorum the Corporation would automatically have ceased to function. The duke failed, however, to make allowance for the determination of John Tilden who features in this volume extensively as a jurat and who eventually became mayor in 1835. A series of inquorate meetings caused Tilden great distress and, with the duke's influence declining, Tilden was eventually able to persuade enough of his former colleagues to attend a meeting on Tuesday 25 February 1834 at which a large number of new freemen were appointed.[50] The continuation of the mayoralty and of the legal jurisdiction of the mayor and jurats as the town's magistrates and of the mayor as coroner of the Liberty was thus assured.

In that same month, February 1834, Winchelsea Corporation was threatened by preparations for further legislation, the Municipal Corporations Act of 1835. Mr Daniel Maude, a commissioner investigating the surviving municipal corporations, visited Winchelsea to inquire into circumstances within the town and how it was being administered. In his report Maude made some scathing comments about the influence of the patron on Winchelsea while it had parliamentary election rights but that can hardly be seen as relevant for those rights were already lost. He gave an account of how the mayor was elected and the jurats appointed at the annual Easter Monday Hundred Court; approved of the appointment of the Corporation's officers, while qualifying this by saying that if they wanted to carry on they were automatically re-appointed; commented that Winchelsea had a strong prison and was of the opinion that the town's poor rate was well within acceptable limits.[51] This legislation, when enacted, abolished large numbers of the remaining unreformed medieval municipal corporations but of Winchelsea there was no mention.

Four years later, in 1838, an incident occurred which ensured that Winchelsea's place in the history of Methodism, described above, would be matched by its place in the history of smuggling. This was ensured by the death of the unfortunate Thomas Monk 'a poor fiddler' of Winchelsea who was said to be the last smuggler to be killed in an affray with the coastguard. This information was given to William Durrant Cooper, historian of Sussex smuggling as well as of Winchelsea, by Edwin Nathaniel Dawes, Winchelsea's town clerk at the time of the publication of Cooper's smuggling book.[52] We cannot be certain that Dawes was right, but we can be about Thomas Monk's fate. On 1 April 1838, near the mouth of the River Rother at a quarter to three in the morning a cargo of spirits was landed. As the kegs were being taken away excisemen mounted an attack and considerable fire was exchanged. The smugglers, perfectly capable of giving a good account of themselves, escaped but abandoned their boat at the water's edge. Henry Hyde, an officer of the Camber Coastguard Station went to pull it ashore and discovered something floating in the water nearby – the body of Thomas Monk.[53] The inquest into Monk's death was held the next day by the coroner, the Mayor of Winchelsea. The contemporary newspaper account makes us realise that when juries from a small area were gathered together with such promptitude it was quite possible that they included those with considerable knowledge of what happened. In this case one juror is reported as having interjected, 'He wasn't dead when I left him!'[54]

There is one other intriguing reference to smuggling in the area which merits mention here. When referring to the duties of the mayor as coroner, Mr Commissioner Maude, whose 1834 report about Winchelsea is referred to above, commented that 'the number of inquests is greater than might be expected.' He included among the reasons, 'Several instances have occurred of persons employed by the government in the blockade [customs and excise] service having destroyed themselves,' citing as possible reasons the poor quality of recruits, that continuation in the service was compulsory and that punishments were very severe.[55] Finding evidence to support this assertion, made almost one hundred and eighty years ago, has not been easy. No such inquest findings survive within Winchelsea's archives. However among the papers of Messrs Dawes & Co of Rye, the solicitors whose partners frequently served as Winchelsea's town clerk and thus attended inquests as legal advisers, there is some indication that Maude's claim was justified. In 1821 John Whayman, exciseman, shot himself near Camber Watch House. In February and September 1827 respectively Charles Carden shot himself 'in the privy near the Roundhouse' and Peter Player also shot himself. A number of other excisemen were drowned, with the inquest juries recording verdicts of accidental death but some could have been suicides.[56] Whatever may be the truth of that, we can assume that membership of the blockade service in those days was exceptionally hazardous.

The above events, while generally illustrating life in Winchelsea while it struggled to cope with the problem of poverty, also reflect directly or indirectly on the lives of the poor themselves. We know that some of the poor took the opportunity to join the Methodist congregation; we can safely assume that a good number were upset about the situation at the parish church; it is a near certainty that many of them benefited in some way from smuggling; and there is clear evidence that the able-bodied obtained employment through the building of the Martello Towers and the Military Canal. It must be admitted that the poor were unlikely to have been concerned about the Corporation's loss of the right to elect two members to the House of Commons, but John Tilden's subsequently successful attempt to save the Corporation is important to this study because it ensured that cases related to Winchelsea's poor would continue to be heard in the town and not elsewhere. That situation was threatened only a year later but was allowed to continue as a result of Mr Commissioner Maude's recommendation that Winchelsea's Corporation should not be abolished by the 1835 Municipal Corporation's Act. His conclusion that the town, including its poor, was being adequately managed must have brought some satisfaction to those responsible.

In Conclusion

It is hoped that this volume will provide the reader with the opportunity to assess the impact of poverty on a small community, a subject on which it offers valuable and detailed information. It also draws attention to an hitherto obscure official, Charles Arnett, and it is thanks to him that we are able, through letters written and evidence given in their own words, to obtain such an enlightening glimpse into how the poor felt about the whole system used in those days for their support when it was needed. We learn, for example, that many came to look upon the receipt of relief as a right rather than a privilege, while others sought help only in desperation and were truly grateful. We also learn that, while the administration of the Poor Law was in the hands of local officials and magistrates who – as this was such a small community – probably knew personally each individual who applied for help, that personal knowledge is likely to have ensured that help was given promptly and appropriately. This aspect of the matter is much clearer here than it would be in many communities because, with Winchelsea still enjoying and exercising the privileges of being a Cinque Port, all the magistrates were themselves residents, whereas elsewhere those sitting in judgement would have been appointed on a county-wide basis.

Can we therefore assume that Winchelsea coped well with the very considerable problems it faced? The evidence certainly seems to suggest that it did. The magistrates gave immediate support to those such as Arnett who were subjected to insult or violence because of the unpopularity of what they had to do. The poorhouse was most considerately managed with those who had to be there living as a family. The poor rate was reduced to a level which received Mr Commissioner Maude's approval without obvious distress resulting. The number of Winchelsea paupers needing help from the Rye Poor Law Union after 1834 was small but this may have resulted partly from the town's falling population.

Finally, of course, this is a study in isolation. Perhaps it might encourage others to carry out similar community studies which could provide comparisons for, in compiling this collection, the editor has become aware of how much more might be done through local research in furthering our understanding of the poor. Perhaps it might also suggest the need for more detailed study, both social and genealogical, into the lives of people, like those who feature only briefly in Appendix A who, conscientiously, usually uncomplainingly, and without monetary reward, put so much effort into dealing with the demands made on parishes by the circumstances of the time.

Editorial Method

It has been a matter of editorial policy from the beginning that all the documents in the collection on which this volume is based, the letters,[57] should be included and the remaining documents chosen on the basis of their relevance to the lives of the ninety-eight paupers and the seven principal topics mentioned in those documents.

In letters, in settlement and bastardy examinations, and in evidence given in court the spelling has been modernised, the punctuation amended for the purposes of clarity and the excessive use of capital letters which was universal in those days removed. Colloquial usages have not been edited. The most common of these is when correspondents seeking financial help insisted that they were 'very bad off'. It is hoped that when readers come across such colloquialisms of the time they will not consider them to be typographical errors.

Documents such as removal orders which were generally recorded on pre-printed forms remain substantially as in the original although unnecessary expansion has been reduced. For example, 'The Parish of St Thomas the Apostle in the Ancient Town and Port of Winchelsea in the County of Sussex' is reduced, where appropriate, simply to 'Winchelsea' or, more usually, just to the name of the parish. The constant repetition of the words 'the said' and 'the aforesaid' has, where the sense is perfectly clear without them, been left out. The meaning of the word 'premises', as used in these documents, is not likely to be immediately clear to the modern reader and therefore it has been replaced by [evidence].

Both surnames and forenames have been standardised throughout using the spelling most commonly appearing in the original documents. Alternative spellings have been recorded as part of the title for each person's section with the exception of that for Mary Clandenbold; her name, perhaps understandably, has at least fourteen different spellings used by confused clerks and letter writers. The surname of Thomas Milles is written thus in the originals of the published documents with absolute consistency so it has not been changed to the more likely modern Mills.

The italicised introductory paragraphs provided for each person in Part I are designed to draw attention to important points within the transcribed documents, to provide information not available within those documents and to give a general summary of the type of relief provided by the parish.

Where footnotes provide biographical information they usually appear after only one mention of the person concerned. Other references to the same person can, of course, be traced through the index.

No glossary has been provided because obscure words and phrases are explained as they appear, either in square brackets in the text or within footnotes. It is very seldom that terms likely to be unknown to the modern reader occur more than once. There is, however, one exception – the item of clothing then known as a round-frock. This is mentioned several times when clothing provision was being made by Winchelsea for its paupers. A round-frock was a Sussex labourer's protective smock worn over the upper body and hanging to below the waist.

It is extremely difficult to make meaningful comparisons between the monetary values of the period of this volume and the present. Only a single attempt has been made to do this. An examination of www.nationalarchives.gov.uk/currency suggested that a multiplier of 32.1 should be used to turn the values of 1800 into present ones. That has been used above to indicate that the large amount required in poor rate from the householders and landowners of Winchelsea in that year would equate to about £40,000 today. If there was inflation between 1790 and 1841 it certainly did not affect labourers' wages. Sir Frederick Morton Eden's researches about life in Winchelsea in 1795,[58] otherwise entirely confirmed by the contents of this volume, suggest that the average worker's wage at that time was 2s a day. In Appendix E2 we find *The Times* reporting forty years later that Winchelsea agricultural workers were striking because they had been refused an increase from 2s 3d to 2s 6d a day. It may be useful to use this figure of two shillings a day average pay to suggest the approximate value to recipients of money awarded in poor relief.[59] Throughout the book the notations of the time, for example 2s for two shillings, 4d for four pence and ¾d for three farthings are used without explanation. What might well need some explanation for younger readers is that before decimalisation there were twenty shillings in a pound, twelve pennies in a shilling and four farthings in a penny.

Some Winchelsea Technicalities

Those associated with Winchelsea as residents or otherwise are likely to notice that the town is consistently referred to here as an 'Ancient Town' whereas they will be used to the spelling 'Antient'. This change took place in the twentieth century. Over the centuries and during the period covered here the word ancient was correct with its archaic form, antient, appearing sometimes in documents, particularly in the early eighteenth century. The legal title of Winchelsea Corporation, granted by parliament in 1883, is 'The Mayor, Jurats and Commonalty of the Ancient Town of Winchelsea'. At some time in the twentieth century the use of the archaic form was noted and felt to be appropriate. It is now widely in use within the Confederation of the Cinque Ports but the Confederation's official title continues to refer to 'the two Ancient Towns'.

Another change likely to catch the Winchelsea reader's eye is that the parish church, within this book dedicated to St Thomas the Apostle, is now dedicated to St Thomas the Martyr of Canterbury. This change took place in the 1930s. The then rector, Rev[d] R A Cochrane, discovered that his church in pre-Reformation times had been dedicated to Becket and, apparently without local consultation, changed the dedication on the parish noticeboard. This produced protests, at a meeting held on 16 October 1931, from members of the Parochial Church Council (PCC).[60] Little documentary evidence follows except that, on 29 April 1932 Mr Cochrane told the PCC that he had found a reference to the presentation in 1310 of a rector to the living of St Thomas of Canterbury, Winchelsea. That a change was made at the time of the Reformation is borne out by mentions of the church in Winchelsea wills. Those before 1541 refer to the dedication as St Thomas the Martyr, meaning, and sometimes stating, Becket. Those after that date refer consistently to St Thomas the Apostle.[61] Clearly it would have been inopportune, in Henry VIII's time, to have one's church dedicated to a man who so consistently opposed his monarch. That Mr Cochrane had been successful in proposing that the dedication be changed back is clear from a new edition of the church guide published in 1937 which is entitled 'The Church of St Thomas the Martyr of Canterbury'.[62]

Notes – All references are ESRO unless otherwise stated

1   These brief examples relate to the cases of Elizabeth Lowes (**370-375**), John Simmons (**502-504**), Sarah Cole (**151-154**), Samuel Easton (**202-222**) and John Eagles (**165-191**)

2   PAR 511/35/1/1-371

3   PAR 511/12/1-3

4   AMS 2329 & PAR 511/31/1/11-16

5   AMS 2330, WIN 61 ff.73-138, 61D & 237A

6   Winchelsea Corporation, whose legal title is The Mayor, Jurats and Commonalty of the Ancient Town of Winchelsea, remains in existence, as a charity, in the twenty-first century. The Hundred and Assembly and Court books referred to are part of its major archive, dating from the fifteenth century to the present day, held at East Sussex Record Office.

7   WIN 61 ff.139r-166r, WIN 61AA & 61B

8   G 8/1a/1-3, G 8/19/2 & 4

9   Further information about all these minute, court and account books can be found in the list of primary sources (pp.xxxiii-xxxiv)

10   PAR 511/1/2/1

11   VCH ii p.228

12   For a detailed analysis of the 1841 figures for the town and the Strand, not the whole parish, see Malcolm Pratt *Winchelsea – A Port of Stranded Pride* (1998) pp.263-264

13   For further information about Arnett see (**1**) and pp.xx-xxi.

14   In preparing this necessarily incomplete and simplified list the editor has used particularly J L and Barbara Hammond, *The Village Labourer 1760-1832,* paperback edition 1987 reprinted 1995 pp.113-114

15   The cases referred to here are those of Lucy Barnes (**50-61**) and Mercy Eastman (**192-195**)

16   Walter H Godfrey FSA Ed *Sussex Wills Volume 4 Racton to Yapton* SRS Volume 45 (1941) p.365

17   ibid p.366

18   ibid

19   ibid

20   ibid p.368

21   David and Barbara Martin, *New Winchelsea, Sussex – A Medieval Port Town* (2004) p.90. Malcolm Pratt, *Winchelsea – The Tale of a Medieval Town* (2005) pp.48-49

22   Samuel Smiles, *The Huguenots, their Settlements, Churches and Industries in England and Wales* (1905) p.118

23   Paul Slack *The English Poor Law 1531 to 1872* (1990) p.60

24   ibid p.26

25   PAR 511/9/1/1

26   Simon Fowler, *Workhouse: The People, the Places, the Life Behind Doors,* Paperback Edition (2008) p.46

27   William Hague, *Pitt the Younger* (2004) p.447

28   W E Minchinton, 'Agricultural returns and the Government during the Napoleonic Wars', *Agricultural History Review No 1* (1953) pp. 29-43. The editor is grateful to Melvyn Pett for drawing his attention to this article.

29   J Steven Watson, *Oxford History of England – The Reign of George III 1760-1815*

(1960) pp. 527-528

30   AMS 2329

31   ibid

32   PAR 511/31/1/14

33   PAR 511/31/1/15

34   WIN 237A

35   PAR 511/35/1/1-371

36   Philip Emerson, *Charles Arnett 1791-1857 His Ancestors and Descendants* (unpub 2012)

37   Sir Frederick Morton Eden, *The State of the Poor, or, An History of the Labouring Classes in England, from the Conquest to the Present Period: Together with Parochial Reports* (1797). The editor is grateful to Melvyn Pett for drawing his attention to this work and for providing a print-out of the Winchelsea section from http://books.google.co.uk.

38   ibid

39   ibid

40   Roy Hattersley, *A Brand from the Burning – The Life of John Wesley* (2002) p.394

41   The names of these units appear in the parish registers

42   PAR 511/1/1/4

43   WIN 203, 204, 207; Pratt (1998) p.26

44   AMS 2329

45   PAR 511/1/5/1

46   PAR 511/12/2 13 Jan 1826

47   ibid

48   ibid

49   2W IV Cap 45 Clause 1

50   WIN 61B f.50

51   WIN 616/3

52   William Cooper, *Smuggling in Sussex* (1858) p.41

53   Pratt 1998 pp. 39-40

54   *Sussex Express* 7 April 1838

55   WIN 616/3

56   DAP Box 70/1

57   PAR 511/35/1/1-371

58   Morton Eden op cit

59   Wages were, of course, much lower when employees were enjoying the benefits of living in - see, for example, (**135**).

60   PAR 511/14/1/1

61   Godfrey Ed op cit pp.358-376

62   PAR 511/7/3/24

Abbreviations used in the text, references and footnotes

a r p	acres, rods, perches
b.	born
d	pence
d.	died
E	Easter
EHR	*English Historical Review*
ESRO	East Sussex Record Office
Exc^d	excused
f	folio
ff	folios
HMC	His Majesty's Commissioners
inst	the present month
jnr	junior
lb	pound
n	note
occ^d	occupied
ODNB	*Oxford Dictionary of National Biography*
OED	*Oxford English Dictionary*
OH	Old Harbour (now Camber)
oz	ounce
p	page
pp	pages
pt	part
QE	quarter ending
s	shillings
snr	senior
SRS	Sussex Record Society
TNA	The National Archives
ult	the previous month
VCH	*Victoria County History*

Primary sources (all references are ESRO)

Records of the Parish of St Thomas the Apostle, Winchelsea:

PAR 511/12/1 Minute book of the Winchelsea Public Vestry Jun 1954 – Nov 1820. ff.245

PAR 511/12/2 Winchelsea Vestry Minute Book Jun 1820 – Mar 1853. ff.233 (only 1-42 numbered) Contains records of both public and select vestries up to May 1825 and public vestries thereafter.

PAR 511/12/3 Minute Book of the Winchelsea Select Vestry May 1825 – Mar 1831. ff.76 (not numbered)

AMS 2329 Overseers' Accounts Easter 1794 – Easter 1811. ff.350 (not numbered)

PAR 511/31/1/11 Overseers' Accounts May 1811 – Sep 1820. ff.338 (not numbered)

PAR 511/31/1/12 Overseers' Accounts Nov 1820 – Jun 1824. ff.320

In this volume entries are made on a page per person basis.

PAR 511/31/1/13 Overseers' Accounts Sep 1820 – Mar 1831. ff.465 (not numbered)

Immediately follows PAR 511/31/1/11.

PAR 511/31/1/14 Weekly Pay List – Winchelsea Parish 1824. Sep 1824 – Aug 1828 ff.25.

Weekly entries of all payments made to individuals.

PAR 511/31/1/15 Overseers' Accounts Mar 1825 – Sep 1834. ff.54

In this volume entries are made on a page per person basis.

PAR 511/31/1/16 Overseers' Accounts Apr 1831 – Jan 1858. ff.350

Immediately follows PAR 511/31/1/13. Includes detailed records up to September 1835 at which time Rye Poor Law Union assumed general responsibility for the poor. Thereafter the volume contains mostly totals of money raised through poor rate collections in Winchelsea and the amounts from those sums which were paid to the Rye Union treasurer. There are some details of expenses incurred in Winchelsea which were not the responsibility of the Union.

With the exception of AMS 2330, the following parish records are in document rather than volume form. The bracketed numbers indicate how many from each sequence have been transcribed into this book because they are about one of the paupers featured in Part I. Others are referred to in footnotes.

PAR 511/32/1/51-56 Settlement certificates, May 1785 – Aug 1822 (1)

PAR 511/32/2/71-106 Removal orders from Winchelsea Dec 1820 – May 1842 (5)

PAR 511/32/3/16-85 Removal orders to Winchelsea Aug 1801 – May 1847 (33)

PAR 511/32/4/38-205 Settlement examinations, May 1772 – Aug 1841 (10)

AMS 2330 Settlement examinations, Jul 1822 – Feb 1835 (19)

PAR 511/34/1/21-73 Bastardy examinations, Nov 1776 – Oct 1822 (9)

PAR 511/34/2/23-34 Warrants to arrest putative and absconding fathers, Nov 1801 – Feb 1828 (5)

PAR 511/34/3/3-19 Bastardy bonds, May 1778 – Dec 1825 (2)

PAR 511/34/4/1-28 Bastardy orders, Dec 1810 – Feb 1828 (12)

PAR 511/35/1/1-371 The letters (all transcribed into Part I or Part II)

Records of the Winchelsea Corporation and its Courts:

WIN 61 General Court Book Apr 1769 – Mar 1823 ff.166 subdivided as follows:
Court of Record between Apr 1769 – Mar 1823 ff. 2-44r (mostly adjournments)
General Quarter Sessions of the Peace Apr 1769 – Feb 1823 ff. 73-138
Hundreds and Assemblies Mar 1769 – Apr 1792 ff. 139r-166r
Note: At the Court of Hundred the mayor and other officers of the Corporation are appointed. An
Assembly is for the appointment of freemen and some administrative matters – see also below.
WIN 61AA Hundred and Assembly Book 23 Jun 1792 – 20 Feb 1823 ff.207 (not
numbered)
In the reverse: Court of Record Oct 1792 – Dec 1810.
WIN 61B Hundred and Assembly Book Apr 1823 – Jun 1882 ff.188 (immediately
follows 61AA above)
WIN 61D General Quarter Sessions of the Peace Apr 1823 = Jul 1881 ff.420
The earlier sections providing information relevant to this study include:
(a) Lists of the names of empanelled grand juries
(b) Test Act certificates of magistrates and others
(c) Rate demands on the parishes within the Liberty
(d) Criminal cases
(e) General administrative matters brought before the court
WIN 237A Notes of appearances before the Winchelsea Justices: Jun 1824 – 29
Feb 1828 ff.69 (not numbered) see p.xx.

Records of the Guardians of the Rye Poor Law Union

G 8/1a/1 Minute Book Jul 1835 – Jun 1837 ff.406
G 8/1a/2 Minute Book Jun 1837 – Aug 1839 ff.425
G 8/1a/3 Minute Book Sep 1839 – Mar 1841 ff.399
G 8/19/2 Indoor Relief List Rye Union Workhouse Mar 1837 – Sep 1841 ff.263
G 8/19/4 ff.276 Indoor Relief List – Brede Union Workhouse Dec 1836 – Mar 1841

Further correspondence between the Guardians of the Rye Union and the Poor Law
Commissioners which is partly relevant to the period covered by this volume but
is not included here is preserved at The National Archives (TNA) in the sequence
TNA: MH12/13076-13097. Full details about these documents can be found on
The National Archives website.

Secondary Sources – Select Bibliography

Books consulted during the preparation of this volume:

Baines, J Manwaring *Historic Hastings – A Tapestry of Life* Amended and revised edition (1986)

Baugh D A 'The Cost of Poor Relief in South-East England 1790-1834', *English Historical Review No 1* (1975)

Bew, John *Castlereagh: Enlightenment, War and Tyranny.* (2011)

Black, J and McGaild D *Nineteenth Century Britain* (1903)

Briggs, Asa *The Age of Improvement 1783-1867* Second Impression (1978)

Briggs, Asa *A Social History of England* New Edition (1994)

Cooper, William Durrant *Winchelsea – One of the Ancient Towns added to the Cinque Ports* (1850)

Cooper, William Durrant *Smuggling in Sussex* (1858)

Crook, Diana *Defying the Demon – Smallpox in Sussex* (2006)

Crowther, M A *The Workhouse System 1834-1929: The History of an English Social Institution* (1983)

Cunningham, Timothy [attributed to] *New Treatise on the Laws Concerning Tithes* by A Gentleman of the Middle Temple (1765)

Emerson, Philip *Charles Arnett 1791-1857 His Ancestors and Descendants* (unpub 2012)

Evans, Eric J *The Contentious Tithe – The Tithe Problem and English Agriculture 1750-1850* (1976)

Evans, Eric J *The Forging of the Modern State – Early Industrial Britain 1783-1870* Second Edition (1996)

Fisher, D R [Ed] *The History of Parliament – The House of Commons 1820-1832 Volume 7* (2009)

Fowler, Simon *Workhouse – The People, the Places, the Life Behind Doors* Paperback edition (2008)

Fraser, Rebecca *A People's History of Britain* (2003)

Godfrey, Walter H [Ed] *Sussex Wills Volume 4 Racton to Yapton.* SRS Volume 45 (1941)

Hague, William *William Pitt the Younger* (2004)

Hammond, J L and Barbara *The Village Labourer 1760-1832 A Study of the Government of England before the Reform Bill* Paperback Edition (1987) reprinted (1995)

Hattersley, Roy *A Brand from the Burning – The Life of John Wesley* (2002)

Higgs, Michelle *Life in the Victorian and Edwardian Workhouse* (2007)

Hilton, Boyd, *A Mad, Bad and Dangerous People – England 1783-1846* The New Oxford History of England (2006)

H M Government [by authority of] *Report from His Majesty's Commissioners* [HMC] *for inquiring into the administration and practical operation of The Poor Laws.* (1834)

Hobsbawm, E J and Rudé, George *Captain Swing* (1969)

Holloway, William *History and Antiquities of the Ancient Town and Port of Rye* (1847)

Hunnisett, Roy *East Sussex Coroners' Records 1688-1838* SRS Volume 89 (2005)

Hurd, Douglas *Robert Peel* (2007)

Kain, Roger J P & Prince, Hugh C *The Tithe Surveys of England and Wales* (1985)

Llewellyn, Nigel [Ed] *East Sussex Church Monuments 1530-1830* SRS Volume 93 (2011)

Longmate, Norman *Island Fortress – The Defence of Great Britain 1603-1945* Pimlico Edition (2001)

Leslie, Kim and Short, Brian [Ed] *An Historical Atlas of Sussex* (1999)

Marshall, J D *The Old Poor Law 1795-1834* Second Edition (1985)

Martin, David & Barbara *New Winchelsea, Sussex – A Medieval Port Town* (2004)

Matthews, Mike *Captain Swing in Sussex and Kent – Rural rebellion in 1830* (2006)

Minchinton, W E, 'Agricultural Returns and the Government during the Napoleonic War', *Agricultural History Review No 1* (1953)

Morton Eden, Sir Frederick, *The State of the Poor, or An History of the Labouring Classes in England, from the Conquest to the Present Period: Together with Parochial Reports* (1797)

Pearce, Edward *Reform! The Fight for the 1832 Reform Act* (2003)

Philp, Roy *The Coast Blockade – The Royal Navy's War on Smuggling in Kent and Sussex 1817-31* (1999)

Pilbeam, Norma & Nelson, Ian *Mid Sussex Poor Law Records 1601-1835* SRS Volume 83 (2001)

Plumb, J H *England in the Eighteenth Century 1714-1815* (1950)

Poynter, J R *Society and Pauperism – English Ideas on Poor Law Relief, 1795-1834* (1969)

Pratt, Malcolm *Winchelsea – A Port of Stranded Pride* (1998)

Pratt, Malcolm *Winchelsea – The Tale of a Medieval Town* (2005)

Salzman, L F [Ed] *The Victoria History of the Counties of England: Sussex – Volume IX The Rape of Hastings* (1937)

Schama, Simon *A History of Britain Volume III The Facts of Empire 1776-2000* (2002)

Slack, P *The English Poor Law 1531-1782* (1990)

Smiles, Samuel *The Huguenots, their settlements, churches and industries in England and Wales* (1905)

Tate, W E *The Parish Chest – A study of the Records of Parochial Administration in England.* 3rd edition (1969)

Watson, J Steven *The Reign of George III 1760-1815* The Oxford History of England (1960)

Waugh, Mary *Smuggling in Kent and Sussex 1700-1840* (1985)

Part I People

Charles Arnett, assistant overseer.

1 *Charles Arnett was Winchelsea's first professional assistant overseer, appointed following the public vestry's determination that such an official was badly needed (***2***). Considering that he and his wife were expected also to serve as master and mistress of the workhouse, the terms offered (***3***) were ungenerous. However, the salary was later increased to £40 per annum (***11***) and this he supplemented by earning another £6 as vestry clerk.[1] Although the appointment seemed to have been made permanent when the town clerk was paid three shillings for issuing a warrant of confirmation,[2] Arnett continued to be re-appointed by the parish vestry every six months.[3] When he and his wife Mary came to Winchelsea they were allowed to have James Charles, Arnett's only surviving child of a previous marriage, with them in the workhouse but had to pay for the privilege (***4***). No mention is made of their further family except in the parish registers which reveal that a daughter, Mary Ann, was born just before their arrival but died at the age of two and was buried at St Thomas's.[4] A second son, William Henry, was baptised five months after his sister's death.[5]*

*On his appointment Charles Arnett set about reorganising the parish's accounting systems,[6] finding ways of reducing payments in weekly poor relief, tightening up on workhouse admissions and pressing for removals from the parish. His initiatives were generally successful which pleased his employers but often created resentment among those paupers affected, an outcome illustrated by the number of recorded abuses and assaults against him (***6-10, 13-16***). It has not been possible to ascertain what went so badly wrong as to provoke his dismissal (***19***). It can hardly have been through prior knowledge that Arnett was about to take a much better paid equivalent position in Bexhill because the general meeting of the inhabitants of Bexhill which proposed such an appointment was not held until three months later.[7] While considerable acrimony was directed against Arnett before he left for Bexhill and his accounts, despite having earlier been formally approved (***20, 22***), were challenged (***23***), two leading Winchelsea residents, Henry Powell and John Edward Wright, continued to support him and provided substantial sureties for his Bexhill appointment.[8] Arnett's robust and spirited defence of his role in Winchelsea (***24***), quite apart from the detail it provides about how the assistant overseer's accounts were examined and checked, makes convincing reading. His claim that during his time poor law rate demands on the parish ratepayers had been more than halved can be substantiated from the records.[9] His complaint that his wife had never received her promised leaving present adds an authenticating touch!*

Whatever personal animosity or other inappropriate behaviour led to his leaving Winchelsea, the documentary evidence leaves him untainted. However, doubts about his conduct do begin to surface when consideration is given to what happened at Bexhill. Within two years he had left precipitately and on 31 January 1831 a general meeting of residents of that town held at the Bell Inn resolved that a letter be sent to Arnett setting out the balances due from him to the parish and requiring his attendance at a meeting to settle these accounts otherwise legal proceedings would be taken to recover the money.[10] Against these claims, as at Winchelsea, Arnett counter-claimed. Bexhill's final submission was somewhat lame. Arnett's successor was to ask Mr [Thomas] Bellingham – presumably the parish's legal adviser – to write to Arnett expressing astonishment at his not fulfilling his engagement and desiring him 'to do without loss of time'.[11] Scottish law would no doubt declare any suggestion that Charles Arnett was guilty of misdemeanour as, on the evidence of these documents, 'not proven'.

Note: In order to provide the fullest possible documentary information about those included in this study, and to avoid unnecessary cross-referencing, documents relating to assaults and abuses against Charles Arnett as assistant overseer have been placed both here and in the sections about the perpetrators.

2 21 Aug 1823 *Minute of a meeting of the Winchelsea public vestry*:
Resolved unanimously that it is expedient to appoint an assistant overseer to reside in the poorhouse if a competent person should be found and elected by a vestry and that public notice shall be given in the neighbourhood for such persons as shall wish to apply to fill this office to attend at the vestry room on Thursday the 4th day of September at 11 o'clock forenoon and any person so elected will be required to procure security for the due performance of such office.   [PAR 511/12/2]
Note: For applicants other than Arnett see (**396, 757, 758**).

3 4 Sep 1823 *Minute of a meeting of the Winchelsea [public] vestry*:
Resolved at a vestry held this day agreeable to a public notice duly given for the purpose of electing an assistant overseer and master of the workhouse at Winchelsea that Charles Arnett be elected to fill this joint office from the twenty-ninth of September next ensuing to the twenty-fifth of March 1824 at the salary of fifteen pounds; that the said Charles Arnett give security in a bond of one hundred pounds and that the bonds of William Woollett and William Hunter, both of Rye, in the sum of fifty pounds each be received as security for the due performance of the office by Charles Arnett. [Further resolved] that the wife of Charles Arnett be appointed matron of the workhouse.   [PAR 511/12/2]
Note: A draft of this bond, drawn up by Henry Butler, town clerk, reveals that before coming to Winchelsea Charles Arnett was a schoolmaster in Iden.[12]

4 18 Sep 1823 *Minute of a meeting of the Winchelsea [public] vestry*:
Resolved that the bond, a draft of which has been now read, is approved of and that the same be executed prior to the twenty-ninth of September inst and laid before the vestry to be holden on the twenty-ninth day of September at six o'clock. [Further] resolved that Charles Arnett be allowed to keep his son in the [work] house on paying two shillings and sixpence a week to the parish for his board.
[PAR 511/12/2]

5 29 Sep 1823 *Minute of a meeting of the Winchelsea [public] vestry*:
Resolved that Charles Arnett be accepted as assistant overseer though the bond has not been executed by William Hunter, Mr [Richard] Stileman undertaking to be security in case William Hunter does not sign the bond.   [PAR 511/12/2]

6 24 May 1824 *Order made to the constables of the Ancient Town of Winchelsea, Sussex, by Henry Powell, justice of the peace for Winchelsea*:
Whereas Charles Arnett of Winchelsea hath this day made information and complaint upon oath before me that Richard Edwards, late of Winchelsea, did on

the 22nd instant unlawfully threaten and [?assault] him whereby he has on oath declared that he goes in danger of his life or that some bodily harm will be done or caused to be done to him. These are therefore to command you in His Majesty's name forthwith to apprehend and bring before me, or some other justice of the peace for Winchelsea, the body of Richard Edwards to answer unto the said complaint and to be further dealt with according to law. Herein fail not, as you will answer the contrary at your peril.   [WIN 221]

7 12 Oct 1824 *Minute of the Winchelsea select vestry*:
[Resolved] that a warrant be taken out against William Morris for his gross misbehaviour to the assistant overseer [Charles Arnett].   [PAR 511/12/2]

8 12 Oct 1824 *Information given before Henry Powell, justice of the peace for Winchelsea, by Charles Arnett of Winchelsea, assistant overseer*:
who on oath charges William Morris with abusing [him] on Sunday the third day of October instant in the due execution of his office as such assistant overseer at the parish of St Thomas the Apostle, Winchelsea.
[*appended note*] [same day] Defendant entered into his own recognisance in £40 to keep the peace towards Mr Arnett and all other persons for 12 months from this date before me. [*signature of*] H[enry] Powell.   [WIN 237A]

9 19 Mar 1825 *Letter from Weeden Dawes, [Rye] to Charles Arnett [Winchelsea assistant overseer]*:
I am sorry to hear of your loss. I thank you for the letter [received] some little time since. I hope you can put your hand on the receipt when it is wanted. Pray tell me on what day it was that [Isaac] Hearnden spit in your face etc. You have not mentioned the day in your statement. PS you must prepare yourself to be at Horsham the 23rd March. I shall be at Winchelsea tomorrow and if you can see me I shall be at my late brother's till 5 or 6.   [PAR 511/35/1/161]
Notes: 1. 21 Mar 1825 *Expenses claimed by Charles Arnett, assistant overseer, for taking out an indictment against Isaac Hearnden for an assault*: coach hire to Horsham: £1 7s 0d; coach hire to Rye: £1 7s 0d; 6 days board at 10s 6d: £3 3s 0d; bed at Horsham: £1 1s 0d; indictment: £1 11s 6d; affidavit: 1s; officers' fees: 2s; certificate: 8s; bench warrant: 5s; judge's butler's fee: 1s; copy indictment: 13s 6d; [Total] £10.¹³
2. Nothing has been discovered to indicate the nature of Arnett's loss.

10 23 Mar 1825 *Warrant issued by the Rt Hon Sir William Alexander, judge of the Sessions of Oyer and Terminer and general gaol delivery held at Horsham*:
To William Woodroffe, my tipstaff, and all chief constables, headboroughs, tything men, and others whom it may concern. Whereas it appears by the certificate of Thomas George Knapp Esq, clerk of assize on the home circuit, that … Isaac Hearnden late of the parish of St Thomas the Apostle, Winchelsea, Sussex, labourer, was and now stands indicted for an assault on Charles Arnett to which indictment he hath not appeared or pleaded; these are therefore to will and require you and every of you upon sight hereof to apprehend and take the said Isaac Hearnden if he

shall be found in your bailiwick and him safely keep and bring before me if taken during the present assize otherwise before some one of His Majesty's justices of the peace near to where he shall be so taken to the end that he may answer the said indictment and be further dealt with according to law.   [PAR 511/29/2]
Notes: 1. Headboroughs and tything men were officers of hundred courts.
2. Sessions of Oyer and Terminer, from the French 'to hear and determine', were held as a result of a commission issued to judges directing them to hold courts for the trial of offences.
3. Sir William Alexander was a distinguished lawyer admitted to Middle Temple 1771, called to the bar 1782, created Serjeant at Law 1824, chief baron of the Exchequer 1824-1831, knighted 1824.[14]
4. Thomas George Knapp in 1815 succeeded his brother as Deputy Clerk of Arraigns of the Home Circuit. He was called to the bar in 1829.[15]
5. For further notes about this case and those involved see (**329**).

11 31 Mar 1825 *Minute of the Winchelsea public vestry*:
Resolved that the account of the assistant overseer [as] submitted to this public vestry, having been previously examined and allowed by the select vestry and the same having been examined by this vestry, [is] approved and allowed and confirmed; the accounts containing receipts and payments from 25th September 1824 to 25th December 1824, payments amounting to £224 19s 6d and the receipts £139 14s 1¼d, leaving a balance against the parish of £85 5s 4¾d. [Further] resolved that Charles Arnett be re-elected as assistant overseer for the ensuing half year ending Michaelmas at a salary of £20.   [PAR 511/12/2]

12 8 Oct 1825 *Minute of the Winchelsea select vestry*:
Resolved that Mr [Charles] Arnett is instructed to make broth and [that it] be distributed to the sick according to the order of the parish surgeon.
                                                                                            [PAR 511/12/3]

13 26 Nov 1825 *Appearance before Henry Powell and John Tilden, justices of the peace for Winchelsea, of Charles Arnett, gentleman [and assistant overseer]*:
who on oath charges David Tree, Edward Whiteman, William Foster, Thomas Fisher [and] George Hearnden with a breach of the peace and that he verily believes he goes in danger of his life and that they or some one of them [will] do unto him some grievous bodily harm.   [WIN 237A]
Note: Henry Pearch Butler, town clerk, in an account dated the same day, charged the parish fifteen shillings for issuing a summons 'against David Tree and four others'.[16]

14 26 Nov 1825 *Information given before Henry Powell and John Tilden, justices of the peace for Winchelsea, by Charles Arnett, gentleman*:
who on oath charges William Martin with unlawfully assaulting [him] on the 14th day of November instant at Winchelsea.   [WIN 237A]

Note: In this case the town clerk charged three shillings for 'information and warrant against William Martin' and a further three shillings for 'taking depositions against him'.[17]

15 26 Nov 1825 *Recognisances taken and acknowledged before Henry Powell and John Tilden, justices of the peace for Winchelsea*:

by William Martin of Winchelsea, shoemaker – 50s [and] Richard Osborne of Winchelsea, victualler – 40s [requiring] William Martin to appear [at the next quarter sessions to be held at Lewes] and in the meantime to keep the peace towards all His Majesty's liege subjects and particularly towards Charles Arnett.

[WIN 237A]

Note: On 12 January 1826 Charles Arnett submitted an expenses claim totalling £4 19s 3d for a three day attendance at Lewes to prosecute Martin, the items including 'horse and gig, turnpike'.[18]

16 29 Nov 1825 *Deposition taken on oath [magistrate(s) not named] of Charles Arnett, assistant overseer of the poor, Winchelsea*:

About one o'clock in the day of Monday the 14th I was going home. Just before I got to the gatehouse [Strand Gate] David Tree came down from the steps at the Watchhouse and insisted on knowing in what way I walked as I did. I looked at him for a short time and he replied he should suppose he should get his head broke through me. He said that on the night before a boulder had been thrown at him as he was going up the hill [and] that he called out to them, 'Halloa' and the parties who threw thought it was Arnett. He then called me a hypocrite and said I deserved to have my arse kicked. After some more words he said that if he [had] not a bad leg he would kick my arse. I was about to proceed home when several came down the steps and on my saying there were such a ?clan of them that I did not know what they meant, one person amongst them said, 'If you repeat that again I'm damned if I don't give it you.' I said to them all it was not for me to pick my words to oblige them. The same person then said he would give it me. He pulled off his coat and hat and put himself in a posture but was prevented from attacking me by George Hearnden. Afterwards several of them abused him very much with words. I then went away. I am certain that the five defendants were all there around me in one company. They came down from the Watchhouse into the main road. I was after that again abused by David Tree at the bottom of the hill. I have every reason to believe from their assembling together and the boulders being thrown that I go in danger of my [life] or that some bodily harm will be done me. I have since received information that a plan had been laid to attack me on that day. [*signature of*] C[harles] Arnett. [WIN 237]

Notes: 1. The names included in the preamble to this document of others due to give evidence on oath are those of David Tree, Edward Whiteman, William Foster, Thomas Fisher and George Hearnden.

2. The Watchhouse, as its name suggests, was, for at least part of this period, an excise observation post. It is now known as The Lookout, a public shelter and viewpoint from Winchelsea towards the sea.

17 13 Jan 1826 *Report submitted to the Winchelsea public vestry dated 3 Jan 1826, prepared by Thomas Dawes and David Laurence about the financial position of the parish when Charles Arnett was appointed assistant overseer*:
We, the undersigned Thomas Dawes and David Laurence, in pursuance of the resolution of a general vestry held the 7th day of April 1825 whereby it was referred to us to ascertain 'whether or not the parish was in debt at the time Mr [Charles] Arnett took the parish accounts at Michaelmas 1823 and to what amount', having referred to the settlement of accounts of the overseers ending at Michaelmas 1823 find that the balance then in their hands amounted to the sum of £187 4s 4½d, and we further find that the several debts and sums specified in the schedule hereunder written [*the schedule does not appear in the vestry minute book*] amounting to the sum of £456 15s 4¼d was due and owing by the parish at Michaelmas 1823 including rates craved; and therefore we find that at Michaelmas 1823 when Mr Arnett took the parish accounts the parish was in debt the sum of £456 15s 4¼d and that the overseer had in hand only the sum of £187 4s 4½d applicable to the payment of that debt, and we find from the [assistant] overseer that he received from the late Mr [Edwin] Dawes a sum of twelve pounds being for rates omitted to be charged to him. Also we further state that a receipt has been produced to us showing a payment of £36 18s 0d made on the 19th day of January 1824 of a gaol rate made at the adjourned sessions of the Corporation held on the 25th day of November 1823 and from a return made to us by Mr [Walter] Fuller, the treasurer, it appears to us that although the assessment was made by the Corporation in November 1823 the sum of £34 5s 1d, part of that assessment, accrued previous to Michaelmas 1823 but inasmuch that the assessment was not made until November 1823 the undersigned David Laurence does not think the sum of £34 5s 1d ought to be considered as a debt from the parish at Michaelmas 1823, but the undersigned Thomas Dawes considers that sum as a debt incurred and therefore due from the parish at Michaelmas 1823. [PAR 511/12/2]

18 12 Jul 1826 *Inquiries for legal advice made by Charles Arnett, assistant overseer, to John Fisher, solicitor of Rye*:
[1] Will paying the rental of £10 a year (the parish allowing a gallon of flour monthly) gain a settlement? 'Mr Fisher says it will.'
[2] Have I (the assistant overseer) a right to give a copy of any resolution passed by the vestry to any overseer of an adjoining parish without the consent of the vestry. 'Mr Fisher [says] I can have no right'. [PAR 511/35/2/7]

19 2 Nov 1827 *Minute of the Winchelsea select vestry*:
Resolved that Charles Arnett [*who attended the meeting*] be from this day removed from the situation of vestry clerk for what appears to the vestry to be highly improper conduct and that Mr. [John] Winstone be appointed in his stead and also for the same improper conduct that Mr. Arnett be suspended from this day forward from the collection of the parish rates and that Mr. [George] Hill and Mr. John Fuller the overseers do henceforward collect the said rates and be held responsible

to the parish. That Charles Arnett is hereby required to get his accounts in order and present them to the vestry to be holden on Wednesday next the 7th instant for the purpose of being settled and handed over to the overseers. [Further] resolved that a general vestry be held on Thursday the 15th instant for the purpose of requesting the magistrates to withhold their sanction from the appointment of the assistant overseer whose conduct in the opinion of this vestry has disqualified him from that office.   [PAR 511/12/3]

20 29 Nov 1827 *Minute of Winchelsea select vestry [Charles Arnett present]*:
Resolved that the assistant overseer's accounts were examined and passed to November 15th and a balance of £3 4s 4¼d in favour of the assistant overseer.
[PAR 511/12/3]

21 15 Mar 1828 *Minute of the Winchelsea select vestry*:
Resolved that a public vestry should be holden on Thursday 27th inst at 11 o'clock in the forenoon for the purpose of determining whether an assistant overseer will be necessary for conducting the parish business in future and if considered necessary at what salary, for what period and under what regulations he shall be appointed to that office.   [PAR 511/12/3]

22 27 Mar 1828 *Minute of a meeting of the Winchelsea public vestry*:
Resolved that the accounts of the assistant overseer for the last six months [were] passed and a balance of £1 8s 11¼d due to the assistant overseer. [Further] resolved that Mr C[harles] Arnett having resigned the office of assistant overseer, Mr D[avid] Laurence be appointed to that office for the six months ensuing, to perform all the services of his predecessor, except residing in the [work]house, at a salary of ten pounds.   [PAR 511/12/2]
Note: Revd J W Dugdell, absentee rector of Winchelsea at the time, visited the town and took the chair at this meeting.

23 15 Jan 1829 *Minute of the Winchelsea select vestry*:
Resolved that the assistant overseer [David Laurence] do apply to Mr William Bray to settle the account of Mr Arnett's errors he having been deputed to do the same.   [PAR 511/12/3]

24 19 Feb 1829 *Letter from Charles Arnett, assistant overseer, Bexhill, to the chairman of the public vestry, Winchelsea*:
Sir, Allow me to address you upon a subject [about] which the select vestry desired your assistant overseer to write to me. I am sorry I cannot attend the public vestry, it being upon a Friday [which] was known to your assistant overseer and several of the select vestry to be my pay day here. I do not wish to be considered harsh in my opinion but I cannot help thinking it was called upon that day because I should not attend. Those gentlemen who attended the select vestry on Thursday the 1st day of January last will be candid enough to say I attended also on that day and

was ready to meet the select vestry as to the accounts but there was not sufficient to make a vestry [so] that I could not help. I now beg to state I am informed by the assistant overseer [that] there appears to be some mistakes arisen in the accounts amounting to £8 2s 6d on the one side and £1 11s 0d on the other (errors excepted) which leaves a balance of £6 11s 6d. Now, sir, if those errors exist I would ask this public vestry by whom were those accounts examined? First by the select vestry! Secondly by the public vestry! and in that vestry scrutinised even to a farthing and in the third place allowed by the magistrates!!! Now, sir, look at the situation I was placed in; the vestries by their errors actually caused me to go before the magistrates and make oath to their correctness, they plunge me into sin and then threaten to make me pay for their (not my own) errors. If there has been a few trifling errors discovered by honest and conscientious men, they as gentlemen will say the parties who passed them were wrong and much to blame, as always when the accounts were passed the figures were put in pencil mark until cash up and declared by the vestry and whom I can say in several instances did not remove their eyes from the pencil marks until they were covered with ink and there are several gentlemen who can vouch to that effect. I disdain the party who proposed that inquisition because after such investigation and passing of accounts no gentleman would have made such a dishonourable proposition but I am sorry to say there appears to be several that would persecute me if it laid within their power; but I expect again there is no gentleman that would have made such a proposition unless a public vestry had been called and a general investigation agreed upon. That would be open and candid and not got up in holes and corners as this case was, indeed, so private was their work that one of the overseers did not know of it and tho the parish books was taken to the house of the parties, whoever they may be, the one overseer was kept entirely in the dark. Now, sir, was this a partial or impartial investigation? Certainly not an impartial one. I now, sir, put to you whether you consider I have been fairly done by, but stop, sir, I do not know whom I am addressing myself to, perhaps an avowed enemy! but there, if the parish of St Thomas the Apostle have placed you in the chair of this public vestry I have a right to think you will act with candour and justice. You will therefore be pleased to consider whether I have been fairly done by or not. I have a balance in the assistant overseer's hands of £1 1s 1½d ever since I left which is yet unpaid and it must still be in the recollection of most of the gentlemen who attended on the day that your now assistant overseer was appointed to that office it was stated that Mrs Arnett having attended to the cleanliness and comfort of the poor in the workhouse the last four years and a half was deserving a present from the hands of the parish and several gentlemen said so and they with the chairman said, as several had retired, it was promised to be done at the next meeting of the select vestry as particularly its being the last time of their meeting which promise I understand has been put off from time to time until they desired the assistant overseer not to mention it again so to yours and the vestry's honour I leave it. I now wish to call your attention to [the] time I was servant to the parish. I was placed in the situation when the rates were 24s in the pound [per annum] and when I left they were only 10s, that I think speaks sufficiently my assiduity and attention to all your interests but at the end of my servitude a spirit of opposition had seated itself in the place and nothing but a riddance of me would satisfy some part of the parishioners and others to reconcile them gave way, that aim accomplished what more do you want? Do you want to ruin me (knowing the pocket of the parish was deeper than mine), to bring me to beggary and a pauper to your parish? God forbid! Indeed I would pay or settle anything that is right but I cannot consent to this (and I am sure the gentlemen of the parish do not wish it) unless you go through a general investigation of the accounts of all former overseers who are alive but do not make me the ?pointed object. Do not verify the old adage, 'One man may steal a house but another dares not look over the hedge'. I shall conclude, sir, by saying my accounts were all passed in a public and regular manner and the blame (if any) is to them who agreed to them and if they were wrong you know I had no contract after the vestries pronounced they were right, signed etc. If they were right as they ought to have been the parish would have no more to do with me than they have now, that is to pay me over my balance and if they do not please to make Mrs A her present why I cannot help it.

[PAR 511/13/8]

25 20 Feb 1829 *Letter from William Woodhams, Udimore to the chairman of the public vestry, Winchelsea*:
…[I understand] by Mr [William] Bray that you are going to take proceedings against Mr [Charles] Arnett, late [assistant] overseer, for a few small errors in his accounts which were overlooked by the select and public vestries and passed by the chairman and magistrates. Surely there cannot be any grounds for taking any proceedings against him. I am sorry that my health is such that it is out of my power to attend the vestry.   [PAR 511/35/1/322]

26 20 Feb 1829 *Minute of a meeting of the Winchelsea public vestry*:
Resolved that the chairman do write to Mr [Charles] Arnett, the late assistant overseer, to liquidate the balance of certain errors standing against him as assistant overseer and informing him that legal proceedings would otherwise be resorted to.   [PAR 511/12/2]
Notes: 1. No record has been found to indicate that any such action was ever taken.
2. Arnett's letter (**24**), which is dated the previous day, may not, of course, have reached Winchelsea by the time this minute was written.

1 PAR 511/31/1/13 QE Sep 1825   2 PAR 511/31/2/129   3 e.g. PAR 511/12/2 18 Oct 1826   4 PAR 511/1/5/1   5 PAR 511/1/2/1   6 see PAR 511/31/1/14-15   7 DR/B34/2 7 Feb 1828   8 DR/B34/2 13 Mar 1828   9 PAR 511/31/1/13 1823-1824, 1827-1828   10 DR/B34/2 31 Jan 1831   11 DR/B34/2 9 Apr 1832   12 WIN 2229   13 PAR 511/31/2/129   14 Middle Temple admission register 1 (1949) p.372; The order of serjeants at law (Selden Society 1984) pp.229, 496 (CW)   15 New Monthly Magazine 4.454 (CW)   16 PAR 511/31/2/129   17 ibid   18 ibid

Joseph Bailey (Bayley)

27 *If the presumed date of* (**28**) *is correct (it appears within a block of letters dated 1824), Joseph Bailey and family must have gone back to Rye before they were formally removed in 1828* (**29**). *After returning to Winchelsea, Bailey frequently received casual relief of amounts varying from 2s 6d to 19s.*[1] *By 1836 and by then receiving a weekly allowance of 1s 6d,*[2] *Bailey is listed among Winchelsea's 'partially infirm poor'.*[3] *On 24 Jun 1841 he received from the guardians of the Rye Union the sum of £1 8s 3¾d in casual out-relief. The reason that this was required is given as 'age'.*[4] *Nevertheless, a Joseph Bailey served on the quarter sessions grand jury in 1840*[5] *but this could have been Joseph junior who was nineteen at the time. Of the two girls little is revealed. The Mary Bailey included below* (**35-39**) *was too old to be one of them. A Mary Bailey of the correct age was buried in Winchelsea in 1864.*[6] *The sole mention of Jane is that on 17 Dec 1830 she received an allowance of £1 5s 0d for clothes.*[7]

28 [c.1824] *Letter from J[ohn] H[addock] Lardner, [Rye] to D[avid] Laurence, Winchelsea*:
Mr [Joseph] Mills [assistant overseer, Rye] will leave you this afternoon Joseph Bailey and his three children chargeable to Winchelsea ...... [PAR 511/35/1/124]

29 24 Apr 1828 *Removal order made by Nathaniel Porter and R W Butler, justices of the peace for Rye, to the churchwardens and overseers of the poor of that part of the parish of Rye which lies within the liberty of the Ancient Town of Rye*:
Whereas complaint hath been made to us that Joseph Bailey and his three children namely Mary aged about 10 years, Jane aged about 8 years and Joseph aged about 7 years lately intruded and came into the said part of the parish of Rye and are become chargeable to the same, we upon examination of the [evidence] upon oath do adjudge the same to be true and do also adjudge the place of last legal settlement of Joseph Bailey and his three children to be Winchelsea. These are therefore, in His Majesty's name, to require you to remove and convey them to Winchelsea and them deliver, together with this our order or a true copy thereof, to the churchwardens and overseers of the poor who are hereby required to receive and provide for them according to law.   [PAR 511/32/3/56]

30 7 Apr 1831 *Minute of the Winchelsea parish vestry*:
[*following a decision to 'break up the establishment of the poorhouse' – see also* (**752**)] [Resolved] that Joseph Bailey be allowed 5s per week for himself and son and to live with [Thomas] Chester [in a room in the poorhouse]. [PAR 511/12/2]
Notes: 1. A workhouse stocktaking dated 11 April 1831 shows Chester and Bailey occupying room 5.[8]
2. The allowance of five shillings was paid between March 1831 and September 1833, then reduced to 2s 6d and finally to 1s 6d.[9]

1 PAR 511/31/1/13; PAR 511/12/3   2 PAR 51/12/2 27 Mar 1835   3 PAR 511/37/7/29   4 PAR 511/38/4/3   5 WIN 61D f.154   6 PAR 511/1/5/1   7 PAR 511/12/3   8 AMS 2331   9 PAR 511/31/1/16

Lucy Bailey (Bayley)

31 *Lucy Bailey was a daughter of Stephen of Lydd. She is shown in one family listing (**43**)* *as being aged 12 in 1821 but she does not appear in the 1826 listing (**40**) because she* *was already in service (**32-34**). No record has been found of clothing allowances made in* *response to these letters which suggests that the endorsed assertion about her settlement* *(**34**) was correct despite the evidence in (**33**), probably because she had been continuously* *in service elsewhere.*

32 26 Jan 1824 *Letter from Mrs [Elizabeth] Bailey, Lydd [Kent] to [the overseers* *of Winchelsea]*:
I am sorry to trouble you with [a] letter. [Please] have the goodness to give one of my girls a little clothes as she is out at service. She is so bare of clothes and it is out of our power to buy any. And be so good as to send her a pair of shoes. What she is most in need of is too a flannel petticoat, a frock and a woollen apron. We hope you will be so good as to send it for it is out of [our] power to buy any for my husband doth have such a bad state of health there is not a week for what we have medicine to pay for beside losing his work and we are much obliged to you for sending the rent. [PAR 511/35/1/54]
Note: On 20 November 1823 the Winchelsea public vestry had resolved that Stephen Bailey's rent be paid up to a maximum of £6.[1] – see also (**43**).

33 24 Oct 1824 *Letter from Mrs [John] Laurence, Rye to the overseers of* *Winchelsea*:
[I] am taking the liberty of writing a few lines to the gentlemen of the parish of Winchelsea respecting a servant girl by the name of [Lucy] Bailey. I suppose her friends [who] live at Lydd and are very steady honest people but very poor, have taking the girl on trial but being so very bare of clothes many would not like to have her. Do not think of giving her more than a shilling a week at present. I am certain she is not carried away with pride of dress as too many of them are at this age.
[*Annotated*] Age 17, 15s ½ year winter, 26s ½ year summer, Mrs Brignall, Broomhill; 1 pair stockings, changes, petticoat, apron, 1 gown, 1 shawl.
[PAR 511/35/1/123]

34 4 Nov 1824 *Letter from John Laurence, Rye to the gentlemen of the committee* *of Winchelsea*:
The bearer of this [Lucy Bailey] is a daughter of Stephen Bailey now liv[ing] at Lydd. The girl bears a good character. She has been with Mr Laurence 5 weeks. She has had no opportunity to improve herself much in service. The girl seems willing to learn and wishes to continue in place. Mr Laurence expected Mr [Charles] Arnett to have call[ed] upon him at Rye as he wrote letter and suit by the girl [a] little time since – business prevented him. If she does not have a proper supply for her use Mr L[aurence] cannot think of keeping her as she is very bare indeed of any necessary

thing for her use. As she is deserving and I have no doubt it will be the last time she will trouble you I hope your good nature will assist her. Being inform[ed] today at ten o'clock is the day the committee meets I have sent the girl over this morning. [*Endorsed*] Mr Laurence, Rye, for clothes a/c Lucy Bailey who does not belong here.   [PAR 511/35/1/128]

1 PAR 511/12/2

Mary Bailey

35 *Age discrepancy makes it clear that this is not the Mary Bailey who was the daughter of Joseph (**27-30**). This Mary Bailey, after her service with Stephen Southerden in Stone-in-Oxney (**36-39**) was sent by Winchelsea parish as a servant, first to the household of a Mrs Bennett[1] and then to Walter Fuller junior and his wife who received an allowance of ninepence per week towards her keep.[2] While she was with the Fullers the parish met Mary's clothing bills as it had done when she was with the Southerdens. For example, Mrs Fuller is recorded as receiving £1 5s 0d for that reason in the autumn of 1830.[3]*

36 26 May 1824 *Letter from S[tephen] Southerden, Stone [-in-Oxney, Kent] to the [vestry] committee of Winchelsea*:
This is to inform you that Mary Bailey wants some clothes which is two gowns, one for every day and one for Sunday (one: 4s 9d), two pairs of stockings (one: 1s 4d), one pair of shoes (6s 6d), under petticoat (2s 6d), ?skusling apron (9d) and two changes (one: 2s 4d) likewise two aprons (one: 1s). If you don't think of finding her clothes we must send her home.   [PAR 511/35/1/86]
Note: The bracketed notes showing that where two have been asked for one would be supplied and the cost of each item were added by the Winchelsea overseers.

37 4 Jul 1824 *Letter from Stephen Southerden, Stone[-in-Oxney, Kent] to [Charles] Arnett, Winchelsea [assistant[overseer*:
This is to inform you that I have sent the bills of Mary Bailey['s] things (**(38)** & **(39)** below). We were forced to have her old shoes soled because there was not enough to have new ones.   [PAR 511/35/1/93]

38 2 Jul 1824 *Bill from John Dengate to Winchelsea parish for Mary Bailey at Stephen Southerden's*:
A pair of ½ boots soled and heeled – two pieces: 2s 8d.   [PAR 511/35/1/94]

39 2 Jul 1824 *Bill from Thomas Thorpe to S[tephen] Southerden (for M[ary] Bailey)*:
For 2 pairs hose, 6 yards blue print, 5 yards cotton print, 2 yards flannel, 1 yard print, tape and cotton, 1 handkerchief, 1 yard print: 18s 4½d. [PAR 511/35/1/95]

1 PAR 511/31/1/13 QE 25 Dec 1829   2 ibid Jun 1830-Mar 1831   3 ibid QE 25 Dec 1830

Richard Bailey (Bayley)

40 *There is little mention in the Winchelsea parish records of Richard Bailey, son of Stephen* (**43-49**) *but his mental condition is clearly indicated in the style of the day in the listing of Stephen's family. For 1826 this reads: Stephen Bailey 58, wife [Elizabeth] 50 and three children, William 20, Richard 10 idiot, John 6.[1] The letters below show that in 1840 Richard was being maintained at Winchelsea's expense at the home for 'pauper lunatics' maintained by Benjamin and Jane Rix at West Malling, Kent. In 1833 expenses of £4 11s 6d had been paid by Winchelsea for taking him there and his father was later allowed ten shillings towards the cost of visiting him.[2] In 1834 the Winchelsea overseers were paying Mr and Mrs Rix twelve shillings a week.[3] The guardians of the Rye Union continued to pay for Richard Bailey's care. In 1841 their records note the payment of £7 17s 0d in out-relief for Richard Bailey with the note, 'cause of requiring relief out of the workhouse – insane'.[4] See also Thomas Bennett* (**62**).

41 1 May 1840 *Letter from Benjamin Rix, West Malling, [Kent] to the overseers of Winchelsea*:
Enclosed I send you the receipt for the sum of £7 16s 0d which I have received at the Maidstone Bank and due to me by Winchelsea parish in account of Richard Bailey, a pauper lunatic, for which I am much obliged.   [PAR 511/35/1/361]

42 14 Aug 1840 *From [illegible] for Jane Rix, West Malling, [Kent] to the overseers of Winchelsea parish.*
Enclosed I send you the receipt for £7 16s 0d amount that I have received from Messrs Corrall & Co, Maidstone and due to me by Winchelsea parish for the care and maintenance of Richard Bailey, a pauper lunatic, up to June 25th 1840 and for which I am much obliged.   [PAR 511/38/6/1]

1 PAR 511/31/1/15 f.5   2 PAR 511/31/1/16 QE Sep 1833; QE Mar 1835   3 PAR 511/31/1/15 f.48
4 PAR 511/38/4/3

Stephen Bailey (Bayley)

43 *Recorded payments to Stephen Bailey and his family, a pauper with a Winchelsea settlement already by then living in Lydd, Kent, commence in 1801.[1] These were paid on a casual basis according to need. The family's annual rent of £8 8s 0d was paid by Winchelsea in 1810.[2] Later this sum was reduced to £7.[3] In 1821 family members are listed as Stephen and wife [Elizabeth] (no ages given), William 18, Mary 14, Lucy 12 (**31-34**), Richard 9 (**40-42**) and John 6.[4] By 1824 regular poor relief was being paid at 1s 3d per week, usually as a lump sum after some weeks.[5] By 1826 this arrangement had been changed to casual payments according to need, for example, 'Stephen Bailey out of work ten shillings'.[6] In 1828 he was allowed five shillings, 'his wife [Elizabeth] being sick'.[7] Immediately after the family were removed from Lydd to Winchelsea (**49**) they received £2 11s 6d.[8] Thereafter payments continued on a weekly basis until September 1833 and often on a casual basis as well.[9] By 1836 Stephen Bailey was listed among Winchelsea's 'partially infirm poor'.[10] He was admitted to Rye workhouse in 1841.[11] The only later record of him shows that between 1847 and 1849 he was being excused the payment of the poor rate[12] so he can by* *then no longer have been a workhouse inmate. No evidence has been found to clarify the discrepancies between the children's ages in* (**40**) *and* (**43**). *It probably just illustrates the unreliability of age recording in those days.*

44 6 Apr 1817 *Letter from Elizabeth Bailey, Lydd to [the overseers of Winchelsea]*:
I trouble you with these lines to inform you we never received the flour Mr [William] Sargent [junior] promised my husband when he went for relief. He would not have come to trouble the gentlemen if we had not been in distress. I think there must be some mistake as we never received it. My children are very bad for changes and shoes. We thought if the gentlemen would be so kind as to help us with a grist [a supply of ground corn] we would endeavour to make shift so I hope you will have the goodness to perform your promise. [PAR 511/31/2/122]

45 27 Jan 1825 *Letter from William Longley, Lydd, [Kent] to the overseers of Winchelsea:*
I have a person by the name of [Stephen] Bailey who works for me and belongs to Winchelsea. He has wished me to write to the overseers to get his house rent paid as it is impossible for him to pay it without the assistance of [his] parish. The unfortunate man has a family of three children one of whom is affected with insanity and no doubt a great burden to the father. Bailey is a very honest, sober, industrious man and has worked for me 3 years but if the parish of Winchelsea does not assist him I must be under the necessity of discharging him and he must come home to the parish as all the rest of our parishioners employ their own people. PS A line from you after the next vestry will oblige. [PAR 511/35/1/155]

46 3 Nov 1830 *Letter from W J Green, Lydd, [Kent], assistant overseer, to the overseers of Winchelsea*:
I write to you on behalf of Stephen Bailey, a parishioner of yours, he having most of his family very ill with the smallpox, stands in need of some assistance from you and a doctor to attend them. I will relieve them on your account and speak to a doctor if you give the order. [PAR 511/35/1/340]
Note: On 12 November 1830 Stephen Bailey was allowed by the parish vestry £1 10s 0d in cash as a casual relief with a further £1 on 10 December.[13]

47 18 Nov 1830 *Letter from F. Plomley, Lydd, [Kent, surgeon] to Mr [Richard John] Collin[g]s, [surgeon], Winchelsea*:
Master Bailey with smallpox is improving but the boy is much worse from the extending of the sore in the left leg, it has increased to the size of a small plate. I have allowed them 3 pounds of meat daily which will be continued till further ?authorisation from you. I should have written yesterday but unfortunately was prevented. [PAR 511/35/1/344]
[*Enclosed*] *Certificate by F Plomley, surgeon dated 20 Oct 1830*: I hereby certify that John Bailey, son of Stephen Bailey, has been extremely ill since June last so as to be incapable of leaving his bed. The whole family appear to be in the greatest possible distress and had it not been for the kindness of friends in Lydd the boy must have sunk. [PAR 511/35/1/345]

48 [Nov 1830] *Letter from F Plomley, Lydd, [Kent, surgeon] to [William] Sargent, Winchelsea, overseer*:
Master Bailey's boy [John] improves but very slowly and from the state of his general health at present there is no appearance of any improvement at any date for some time. He continues a daily allowance of animal food etc and occasionally medicine as by order of Mr Collin[g]s. The man with smallpox is well. It is possible I shall see you shortly. If not perhaps you will drop a line.   [PAR 511/35/1/346]

49 25 Oct 1831 *Removal order made by David Deane and John Maxsted, justices of the peace for Lydd, Kent, to the churchwardens and overseers of the poor for the parish of Lydd in the town of Lydd in the county of Kent*:
Upon complaint of the churchwardens and overseers of the poor of the parish of Lydd that Stephen Bayley, labourer, and his three children namely William aged 26 years, Richard aged 19 years and John aged 15 years or thereabouts (who now reside with the said Stephen Bailey) have come to inhabit in Lydd not having gained a last legal settlement there and that they are actually chargeable there, we upon due proof thereof as well upon the examination of Stephen Bailey and likewise upon due examination of the [evidence] do adjudge this to be true and also adjudge the last place of legal settlement of Stephen Bailey and his three sons to be Winchelsea. We do therefore require you to convey them to Winchelsea and them deliver to the churchwardens and overseers of the poor there and we do hereby require you, the churchwardens and overseers of Winchelsea to receive and provide for them as inhabitants of your parish.   [PAR 511/32/3/63]

1 AMS 2329   2 ibid QE 29 Sep 1810   3 PAR 511/31/1/11 QE 25 Dec 1817   4 PAR 511/31/1/12 f.50
5 PAR 511/31/1/14   6 PAR 511/31/1/13 QE 25 Dec 1826   7 PAR 511/12/3 22 Aug 1828   8 PAR
511/12/2 11 Nov 1831   9 ibid 1831-1835; PAR 511/31/1/16   10 PAR 511/37/7/29   11 G 8/19/2   12
PAR 511/12/2   13 PAR 511/31/1/15 f.5

Lucy Barnes (formerly Stonestreet)

50 *These documents include details of a complaint, not eventually sustained, in which Winchelsea charged Pett with smuggling Lucy Stonestreet over the parish boundary so that her illegitimate child (b.1813)* (**55**) *should be born in and chargeable to Winchelsea. The considerable legal expense involved is also clear. By 1816 Lucy had married Thomas Barnes, a Hastings milkman. Her husband accepted responsibility for the child and from September of that year received 2s 6d per week for the maintenance of the boy.[1] This amount was later reduced, by stages, to 1s per week.[2] The child's father, William French, was not a regular payer. At Lady Day 1822 his debt of £26 is recorded as 'paid by imprisonment'.[3] French later paid much more regularly,[4] sometimes by agreed stages.[5] As the note to* (**61**) *suggests, payments were resumed after French's re-arrest. The boy was given his father's first name and his mother's surname – for William Stonestreet at the age of 14 and beyond see* (**538-542**).

51 17 Oct 1815 *[Edited] account submitted to the parish officers of Winchelsea by Dawes & Co., solicitors of Rye*:
Very long attendance on the magistrates and Mr [John] Tompsett of Hastings on his application for an order from the magistrates to pay the parish of St Clement's for the maintenance of Mrs Barnes's (then Stonestreet) bastard child born in Winchelsea: 13s 4d; drawing very special examination of Mrs Barnes touching the birth of the child and the manner of her being brought into the parish [of Winchelsea] etc: £1 5s 0d.   [PAR 511/31/2/122]
Note: John Tompsett was town clerk of Hastings 1812-1829.

52 22 Oct 1815 *Minute of the Winchelsea public vestry*:
At a meeting of parishioners held this day at the vestry it was agreed that instructions should be given to Mr [Weeden] Dawes to institute proceedings against the parish of Pett or such persons in the same parish as he shall deem expedient in consequence of having moved [Lucy] Stonestreet, being at that time in a state of labour, into the parish of Winchelsea thereby subjecting the parish of Winchelsea to the charge of maintaining the child of which she was delivered.   [PAR 511/12/1 f.202]

53 4 Jan 1816*[Edited] account submitted to the parish officers of Winchelsea by Dawes & Co., solicitors of Rye*:
Long attendance conferring with Mr [William Lucas] Shadwell respecting the conduct of the Pett parish officers in sending Mrs Barnes into the parish [of Winchelsea] to lay in and attending Mr [John Edward] Wright and Mr [Richard] Stileman in consequence when I [John Fisher] was directed to furnish Mr Shadwell with a copy of the examination of the woman that he might make the necessary inquiry into the matter: 13s 4d. 9 Jan 1816 Attending Mr [William] Thorpe advising on the case of Mrs Barnes and as to her examination which they contended was false in many particulars. Attending Mr Thorpe and Mr [Richard] Stileman examining the statement sent by Mr Shadwell as contradicting Mrs Barnes when it was agreed the matter should stand over and upon receipt of further information from them we were to meet again and see where the conspiracy lay: 13s 4d.

[PAR 511/31/2/122]
Notes: 1. William Lucas Shadwell of Fairlight Hall was a wealthy landowner and a county magistrate.
2. William Thorpe was a Hastings magistrate and coroner for the Rape of Hastings between 1810 and 1819.[6] Described as 'of Fairlight, bachelor', he was married to Maria Fuller of Winchelsea at St Thomas's on 14 April 1835[7] by licence issued the previous day.[8] see also **(375, 937)**

54 30 Dec 1816 *Minute of the Winchelsea public vestry*:
At a vestry held this day by adjournment it is agreed that Mr [Weeden] Dawes should be directed to stop all further proceedings against the parish officers of Pett as agreed upon by a vestry held on the 22nd of October 1815 for moving Lucy Barnes [formerly Stonestreet], being then in a state of labour, into Winchelsea

parish thereby subjecting Winchelsea to the expense of maintaining a bastard child of which she was there delivered, as it does not at present appear that she was moved into [Winchelsea] parish by the consent or knowledge of the parish officers of Pett.   [PAR 511/12/1 f.213]

55 14 Jan 1817 *Bastardy order of George Tilden and Charles Terry, justices of the peace for Winchelsea, concerning the child of Lucy Barnes, then Lucy Stonestreet, singlewoman*:
Whereas it hath been duly made appear unto us as well upon the complaint of the churchwardens and overseers of the poor of Winchelsea as upon the oath of Lucy Barnes that she was delivered of a male bastard child at the house of [*blank*] Fairhall in Winchelsea on the 6th day of May 1813 and that the child is now chargeable to Winchelsea and likely so to continue; and further that William French of the parish of Guestling, Sussex, did beget the child on the body of her, Lucy Barnes, and whereas William French hath not shown any sufficient cause why he shall not be the reputed father of the child. We therefore upon examination of the cause and circumstances of the [evidence] as well upon the oath of Lucy Barnes as otherwise do adjudge William French to be the reputed father of the child, and thereupon we do order, for the better relief of the parish of St Thomas the Apostle, Winchelsea as for the sustentation and relief of the child that William French shall and do forthwith, upon notice of this our order, pay or cause to be paid to the churchwardens or overseers of the poor of Winchelsea or to some or one of them the sum of eight pounds two shillings and sixpence for and towards the maintenance of the child to the 11th day of this inst January. And we do also hereby further order that William French shall likewise pay the sum of two shillings and sixpence weekly and every week from the said day of January inst for and towards the keeping, sustentation and maintenance of the child for and during so long time as the child shall be chargeable to Winchelsea. And we do further order that Lucy Barnes shall pay the sum of one shilling weekly in case she shall not take care of the child herself.   [PAR 511/34/4/6]

56 15 Jan 1819 et seq *[Edited] account submitted to the parish officers of Winchelsea by Dawes & Co. [of Rye, parish solicitors]*:
Writing to Mr [William] French of Guestling for payment of debt owing to the parish for Lucy Barnes's child: 5s; attending William French when he proposed to pay £5 at Xmas, £5 at Lady Day and the remainder at Midsummer Day: 3s 6d. 19 Oct 1819 Attending the magistrates on the summons against French who also attended and a warrant of commitment awarded for not obeying an order of bastardy: 6s 8d. 23 Oct [1819] Writing special commitment of William French: 5s. 14 Feb 1820 Journey to Winchelsea, French having been taken and making out commitment: £1. 31 Jul 1820 Writing to French to inform him he would be committed if he did not immediately pay up his arrears of maintenance of Lucy Barnes's child. Writing to Mr [Edward] Jeakens [overseer] afterwards to [explain]

what we had done and [asking him] to demand the money due if French should come and not pay the money: 10s. 4 Aug [1820] Special commitment of William French for not obeying order of affiliation: 5s.   [PAR 511/31/2/131]

57 7 Feb 1822 et seq. *[Edited] account submitted to the parish officers of Winchelsea by Dawes, Lardner and Fisher [of Rye, parish solicitors]*:
Preparing a special warrant to apprehend William French for non-payment of arrears of maintenance of his bastard child – warrant and commitment: 10s; the like for Sheather: 10s. 13 Feb 1822 Attending Mr [Edward] Jeakens instructing him as to getting warrants executed on French and Sheather and writing endorsements on warrants for apprehending Sheather to be executed in the county: 8s 8d.
[PAR 511/31/2/135]
Notes: 1. For William Sheather see (**498-501**).
2. In view of French's failure to pay the select vestry resolved on 26 July 1821 to allow two shillings a week 'from midsummer last for the keeping of French's child'.[9]

58 26 Nov 1824 *Information and summary proceedings before Henry Powell, justice of the peace for Winchelsea*:
Charles Arnett, assistant overseer of the parish of St Thomas the Apostle, Winchelsea, on oath saith that by virtue of an order under the hands and seals of two of His Majesty's justices of the peace for Winchelsea William French was adjudged to be the father of a bastard child then lately born of the body of Lucy Barnes (then Lucy Stonestreet, singlewoman) at the house of [*blank*] Fairhall in Winchelsea; and that it was ordered that William French should pay to the churchwardens and overseers of the poor of Winchelsea the sum of two shillings and sixpence weekly for the maintenance of the child; and this deponent further saith that there is now due and owing the sum of four pounds from William French [and] that he, Charles Arnett, has applied to William French for payment thereof who has refused the same.
[*Appended note*] Settled.   [WIN 237A]

59 4 Dec 1824 *Letter from William French, Rye to Mr [George] Harrod, [overseer], Winchelsea*:
Mr Harrod I have sent your parish £2 more in part of what I agreed to pay them and will pay the remainder at Christmas. I shall be much obliged to you to pay it to Mr [Charles] Arnett.   [PAR 511/35/1/141]

60 13 Dec 1824 *Letter from William French to the overseers of Winchelsea*:
I hereby give notice and order you not to pay any more money to Barnes or his wife on my account for her child belonging to your parish. NB And likewise to send me a receipt for the money I have paid you.   [PAR 511/35/1/145]
Note: French had paid £2 on 4 December and another £2 on 8 December. The latter entry is marked 'W French to 1 July 1824'. The above demand that no further payment should be made on his behalf was clearly not acceptable to the Winchelsea overseers for French continued to make payments of at least part of the required amounts.[10]

61 25 May 1825 *Information and charge made before Henry Powell, justice of the peace for Winchelsea*:

Charles Arnett, assistant overseer of the poor of the parish of St Thomas the Apostle, Winchelsea, on oath charges William French with unlawfully neglecting to maintain a male bastard child which has been duly affiliated to him and which is now chargeable to the said parish; and this examinant further saith that the sum of six shillings is now due from William French for the maintenance of the child which he has neglected to pay although the same had been demanded of him.

[*Appended note*] Warrant granted on date. [Thomas Sylvester] Keene attended but did not take defendant. 28th: Defendant taken and brought here by Mailey and settled.   [WIN 237A]

1 PAR 511/31/1/11   2 PAR 511/31/1/12 f.187   3 PAR 511/31/1/13   4 ibid QE 25 Sep 1824 et seq   5 PAR 511/12/2 27 Aug 1824   6 Hunnisett p.xxi   7 PAR 511/1/3/1   8 PAR 511/2/2/13   9 PAR 511/12/2 f.16   10 PAR 511/31/1/13

Thomas Bennett alias Selden

62 *As these documents show, Thomas Bennett's increasingly anti-social behaviour, fuelled by his mental condition, became a problem for the Winchelsea authorities. Thomas Bennett was born in 1801, the illegitimate son of Ann Selden and Thomas Bennett senior (**63**). He worked, as a pauper boy, mostly on George Bray's farm at Guestling between 1813 and 1817 during which time Bray paid five shillings a week to the parish for Bennett's services.[1] When discharged by Bray the first time, Bennett was paid three shillings weekly from the poor rate[2] until re-employed (**64**). On 22 Oct 1824 he was ordered to be taken before the magistrates for misconduct and discharged from the workhouse, on which the parish allowed him fourpence a day in addition to his wages.[3] In April 1827 he was working on the parish highways but at only sixpence a day, half the usual rate.[4] He also received casual payments for breaking stones.[5] From 1827 until 1829, as his mental condition deteriorated, the parish paid a Mrs Pitt one shilling a week to look after him.[6] That responsibility later passed to John Cogger and his wife Ellis who were paid three shillings weekly.[7] On 10 Nov 1831, following the death of John Cogger earlier in the year,[8] the parish vestry resolved that Bennett 'should be sent to Mr Perivell at 13s per week'.[9] There is no other record of this arrangement but in early 1832 the overseers paid £5 'to hire a horse and cart for Thomas Bennett'.[10] This was to take him to West Malling in Kent where he was admitted to a home for 'pauper lunatics' run by Benjamin and Jane Rix. There he was visited later in the same year by Stephen Laurence who presumably reported back to the overseers.[11] The Rixes were paid 13s a week for Bennett's keep until October 1835 when the overseers' detailed records cease.[12]*

63 13 Nov 1801 *Voluntary examination of Ann Selden made before Thomas Marten, deputy mayor and justice of the peace for Winchelsea*:

This examinant on her oath doth declare that she is with child and the child is likely to be born a bastard and to be chargeable to the parish of Winchelsea. And Ann Selden doth charge Thomas Bennett, labourer, with having gotten the child on her body with which she is now pregnant and that he is the father thereof. [*mark of*] Ann Selden.   [PAR 511/34/1/56]

64 24 Feb 1820 *Minute of the Winchelsea public vestry*:
It is agreed for Mr George Bray to employ Thomas Bennett from Lady Day 1820 to Lady Day 1821 at 6s 6d per week – in case of sickness it is understood his wages are discontinued.   [PAR 511/12/1 f.236]

65 10 Dec 1824 *Declaration made before Richard Stileman, county magistrate*:
George Bray of the parish of Winchelsea, farmer, maketh oath and saith that Thomas Bennett, servant in husbandry to him, George Bray, at Guestling in Sussex, hath in his service been guilty of divers misdemeanours and misbehaviour towards him and particularly that during the last week he abused George Bray's horses and that on Monday the sixth instant Bennett refused and neglected to go to work as ordered by his master.   [AMS 6192/1 f.144]

66 12 Jan [1825] *Appearance before Henry Powell, justice of the peace for Winchelsea, of Charles Arnett, assistant overseer*:
who charges Thomas Bennett with unlawfully breaking several squares of glass in the poorhouse, the property of the churchwardens and overseers of Winchelsea. [*Appended note*]: Defendant committed to the Battle House of Correction for 28 days and once privately whipped.   [WIN 237A]

67 25 Jul 1825 *Appearance before Henry Powell and John Tilden, justices of the peace for Winchelsea, of Charles Arnett, assistant overseer*:
who on oath charges Thomas Bennett, a rogue and vagabond, [with] not maintaining himself in whole or in part and that [he] is now and has been for some time chargeable to Winchelsea. Sentence: Committed same day to Lewes House of Correction for two months.   [WIN 237A]

68 26 Jul 1825 *Bill for expenses submitted by Samuel Easton, constable*:
To conveying Thomas Bennett and Thomas Turner from Winchelsea to the House of Correction at Lewes, committed by Henry Powell Esq and John Tilden Esq, 40 miles distant at 1s 6d per mile: £3; to subsistence of prisoners while in custody, Bennett 1 day and 1 night, Turner 1 day and 2 nights: 3s 9d; lodging for prisoners 3 nights: 2s 3d; assistants to constables 3 days and 2 nights at 2s 6d each: 12s 6d; subsistence for the constable and assistant 3 days and 2 nights at 2s 6d each per day and 2s 9d per night each: £1 5s 0d; horse hire 3 days at 10s per day: £1 10s 0d; [total] £6 13s 6d.
[*Endorsed*] Allowed on the oath of Samuel Easton [by] H[enry] Powell [and] J[ohn] Tilden.   [WIN 754]
Note: Thomas Turner, who does not otherwise appear in this volume, had been charged with being a vagrant who had begged at homes in Winchelsea and, on being found guilty, had been sentenced to two months' detention at the House of Correction, Lewes.[13]

69 21 Feb 1826 *Appearance before Henry Powell and John Tilden, justices of the peace for Winchelsea, of Charles Arnett, assistant overseer:*
who on oath charges Thomas Bennett with unlawfully exposing his person indecently on the 8th instant at Winchelsea contrary to the statute and further that William Morris and Rowland Price are material and necessary witnesses against Bennett. [WIN 237A]
Note: Bennett had earlier been committed to 'Battle gaol'.[14]

70 5 Oct 1826 *Appearance before Henry Powell, justice of the peace for Winchelsea, of Job Watt, labourer of Winchelsea:*
who on oath charges Thomas Selden alias Bennett with assaulting him in his own house on Wednesday the 4th day of October 1826 in Winchelsea. [*mark of*] Job Watt.
[*Appended note*] Discharged as Job Watt would not appear against him.
[WIN 237A]

71 28 Nov 1826 *At a hearing conducted by Joseph Hennah and John Tilden, justices of the peace for Winchelsea:*
Thomas Bennett alias Selden was charged with committing an act of vagrancy against the statute; also charged with committing an act of indecency viz. exposing his person in the public streets. Ordered that a certificate from Dr Adamson be obtained to ascertain if Bennett was capable to work. [*Appended note*] Certificate obtained November 30th which says 'he is capable to work'. [WIN 237A]

72 24 Jan 1827 *Appearance before Henry Powell, justice of the peace for Winchelsea, of Charles Arnett, assistant overseer:*
who on oath charges Thomas Selden alias Bennett with a breach of the peace and that he, [Charles Arnett], verily believes he goes in danger of his life and that [Selden] will do him some grievous bodily harm. Thomas Selden alias Bennett was adjudged to find two sureties of £10 each and himself in £20 to keep the peace for the space of one year and having no bail to offer he was committed to this [Winchelsea] gaol. [*Appended note*] Discharged by H. Powell Esq April 12th 1827. [WIN 237A]

73 19 Jun 1827 *Evidence given before Henry Powell, justice of the peace for Winchelsea, by Charles Arnett, assistant overseer and Charles Hill, constable:*
that Thomas Selden alias Bennett is an incorrigible rogue for having on Sunday the 18th instant wilfully openly and lewdly exposed his person in the public streets and highway in Winchelsea and [he was] committed to the gaol of Winchelsea until the next general quarter sessions. [WIN 237A]

74 10 Jul 1827 *General quarter sessions of the peace held at the Guildhall, Winchelsea, before John Tilden, deputy mayor, Henry Powell, Joseph Hennah and Fielding Browne, jurats and justices*:

At this sessions Henry Powell Esq delivered in a conviction made by him against Thomas Bennett otherwise Thomas Selden late of the parish of St Thomas the Apostle, Winchelsea, labourer, who was on the 19th day of June now last past duly convicted before [me] of being an incorrigible rogue and vagabond within the intent and meaning of the statute made in the fifth year of the reign of His Majesty King George IV instituted 'An Act for the punishment of idle and disorderly persons and rogues and vagabonds in the part of Great Britain called England'; that is to say for that Thomas Bennett otherwise Thomas Selden did on the 18th day of June 1827 at Winchelsea and within the jurisdiction of Henry Powell, justice of the peace, unlawfully, openly, lewdly and obscenely expose his person in the public streets and highways there, for which offence Bennett was ordered to be committed to the [Winchelsea] common gaol there to remain until the general quarter sessions of the peace to have been holden this day. Now upon reading the record of the conviction and upon due examination of the witnesses on oath of the facts therein contained, it is ordered that the conviction be confirmed and upon the records of the two former convictions of Bennett being produced and duly verified upon oath, that Bennett is adjudged to be an incorrigible rogue and vagabond within the true intent and meaning of the statute. And it is ordered and adjudged that Bennett be forthwith stripped by the middle upwards and affixed to a cart's tail and that he do receive six stripes on his naked back at each place the crier makes his proclamation within this ancient town and that he be imprisoned afterwards in the house of correction at Lewes for the space of six weeks now next ensuing, there to be kept to hard labour. Ordered that the corporal punishment be inflicted tomorrow at twelve o'clock and that the constables be ordered to attend.   [WIN 61D ff.57-58]

75 29 Jun 1829 *Lunacy Certificate*:

This is to certify that it is my opinion that Thomas Bennett is decidedly of unsound mind and unfit to be at large. [*signed*] Richard John Collings [surgeon], Winchelsea.   [PAR 511/37/7/13]

76 30 Jun 1829 *Order to the constables, churchwardens and overseers of the poor of Winchelsea.*

Whereas it hath been proved before us, John Tilden and Joseph Hennah, justices of the peace for Winchelsea, upon the oath of Joseph Bigg and David Laurence, both of Winchelsea, that Thomas Bennett is by lunacy so far disordered in his senses that he is dangerous to be permitted to go abroad, these are therefore to authorise and require you and every [one] of you to cause Thomas Bennett to be apprehended and committed to safe custody so long as such lunacy or disorder shall continue or until he shall be discharged by the order of two of His Majesty's justices of the peace.   [PAR 511/37/7/14]

1 PAR 511/31/1/11   2 ibid QE 25 Sep 1817   3 PAR 511/12/2   4 PAR 511/40/1/2   5 PAR 511/31/1/13 QE 25 Jun 1827   6 ibid QE 25 Sep 1827 et seq   7 ibid QE 25 Sep 1829   8 PAR 511/1/5/1 9 PAR 511/12/2   10 PAR 511/31/1/16 QE Mar 1832   11 ibid QE Dec 1832   12 ibid QE Oct 1835   13 WIN 237A 25 July 1825   14 PAR 511/31/2/129 12 Jan 1826

Walter Blackhall (Blackall)

77 *Walter Blackhall, son of William (**80-90**) and Elizabeth was born in 1813.[1] In 1825 he is recorded as being an inmate of the Winchelsea workhouse.[2] Two years later he went into service with Dr Adam Scott of Winchelsea[3] and in 1830 he was allowed casual relief of three shillings plus clothes and his expenses 'to go to Dr Scott at Sydenham'.[4] By 1840 he was back in Winchelsea and being paid two shillings a day for occasional work on the highways.[5] The 1841 census shows him living at 'Money Cellar House' [North Street] with Sarah 20, William 2 and Elizabeth 6 months.*

78 19 Nov 1830 *Endorsed upon a letter from Mrs Hannah Francis, Brighton, to Joseph Bigg, Winchelsea, grocer, are notes concerning payments made to paupers and requests received*:
[inter alia] Walter Blackhall X   [PAR 511/35/1/341]
Note: Despite Walter Blackhall's name being marked with a cross suggesting that any application from him should not be granted, casual relief of six shillings was paid to him on 3 December 1830.[6]

79 2 Nov 1840 *Submission by the guardians of the Rye Union to the Poor Law Commissioners giving reasons for providing outdoor relief*:
To Walter Blackhall aged 23 belonging to Winchelsea parish having a wife and one child two years old to maintain: that he has been out of employ during the three last weeks, that he has no permanent master and when in employ does not obtain as an agricultural labour[er] more that 2s per day. Allowed 2 gallons flour.
[G 8/1a/3 f.285]

1 PAR 511/1/2/1   2 PAR 511/31/1/15 f.2   3 PAR 511/12/3 12 Oct 1827   4 ibid 17 Dec 1830   5 PAR 511/40/1/9   6 PAR 511/12/3

William Blackhall (Blackall)

80 *William Blackhall senior married Elizabeth Haisell at St Thomas's on 22 August 1810[1] after the death of his first wife Isabella – see (**87**). Before their marriage Elizabeth bore him several children, one of whom was Amy, the subject of (**82-84**) who was baptised on 29 December 1802 and listed in the parish register as 'baseborn daughter of Elizabeth Haisell'.[2] A listing of William senior's family is given in (**87**) although it does not include Amy who was already in service with Thomas Veness, a Winchelsea butcher who received 1s 6d per week from the parish towards her keep.[3] William junior, baptised 19 Feb 1807,[4] who features in (**85**) was also born before his parents' marriage. An earlier William, who is the subject of (**81**) had died only five days after his baptism.[5] Another child, Harriett, went into service with Thomas Hoad junior (**340-343**).[6] Of the younger family members,*

*George is recorded as wishing to emigrate in 1841 (**968-970**). William senior and his family received regular weekly relief of amounts varying between two shillings and six shillings between 1814 and 1832,[7] together with casual relief according to need, particularly cash and flour.[8] Payments were reduced in 1822 because of some of the children 'going into servitude'.[9] The family lived in Barrack Square in a property rented by the parish from Walter Fuller.[10] The reasons for their attempted eviction (**88-90**) are not clear. By 1836 William senior is listed as among Winchelsea's 'partially infirm poor'[11] and in 1841, when he received help from the Rye Union guardians, the reason is given as 'age'.[12] The census of the same year shows him aged 72 and living in The Strand with George, 20; both are recorded as agricultural labourers.*

81 5 Nov 1801 *Order made by George Stace, justice of the peace for Winchelsea, to the constables of Winchelsea*:
Whereas Elizabeth Haisell, singlewoman, hath by her voluntary examination, taken in writing upon oath before me this present day declared herself to be with child and that the child is likely to be born a bastard and to be chargeable to the parish of St Thomas the Apostle, Winchelsea, and that Elizabeth Haisell in her examination charged William Blackhall of Winchelsea, servant, with having begotten the child on her body of which she is now pregnant and whereas Thomas Marten, junior, one of the overseers of the poor of Winchelsea in order to indemnify the parish hath applied to me to issue my warrant for the apprehending of the said William Blackhall; I therefore command you immediately to apprehend William Blackhall and to bring him before me or some other of His Majesty's justices of the peace for Winchelsea to find security to indemnify Winchelsea or else to find surety for his appearance at the next quarter sessions of the peace to be holden in or for Winchelsea and abide [by] and perform such order or orders as shall be made in pursuance of an act passed in the 18th year of the reign of Her late Majesty Queen Elizabeth [1575/6] concerning bastards born out of lawful matrimony.

[PAR 511/34/2/23]

82 12 Jan 1803 *Examination taken on oath before Thomas Marten, justice of the peace for Winchelsea, of Elizabeth Haisell of Winchelsea, singlewoman*:
who doth declare that on Monday the 18th day of October now last past at Thomas Haisell's in Winchelsea she was delivered of a female bastard child and that the child is likely to become chargeable to the parish of St Thomas the Apostle, Winchelsea and that William Blackhall, servant, of Winchelsea did get her with child of the said bastard child. [*signature of*] Elizabeth Haisell.[PAR 511/34/1/59]

83 13 Jan 1803 *Order made by Thomas Marten, deputy mayor, and George Stace, justices of the peace for Winchelsea*:
Whereas it hath been duly made to appear unto us upon the complaint of the churchwardens and overseers of the poor of the parish of St Thomas the Apostle, Winchelsea and upon the oath of Elizabeth Haisell that she was delivered of a female bastard child at Winchelsea on the 18th day of October last and that the said bastard child is now become chargeable to Winchelsea and likely so to continue and

further that William Blackhall of Winchelsea, labourer, did beget the child upon the body of Elizabeth Haisell and whereas William Blackhall hath not shown any sufficient cause why he shall not be the reputed father of the child; we, therefore, upon examination of the [evidence] adjudge William Blackhall to be the reputed father; and we do order that William Blackhall shall pay or cause to be paid to the churchwardens and overseers of the poor of Winchelsea the sum of two shillings and sixpence weekly and every week from this present time for and towards the keeping, sustentation and maintenance of the child for and during so long time as the child shall be chargeable to the parish; and we do further order that Elizabeth Haisell shall pay to the churchwardens and overseers of the poor of Winchelsea the sum of sixpence weekly in case she shall not nurse and take care of the child herself. [*mark of*] William Blackhall [*signature of*] Elizabeth Haisell.

[PAR 511/34/1/60]

Note: No explanation has been found as to why, the day after being correctly described as a servant, Blackhall should be described here as a labourer. Probably, as so many of Winchelsea's poor were labourers, the clerk used the word absent-mindedly out of habit.

84 13 Jan 1803 *Letter from Thomas Marten, deputy mayor, and George Stace, justices of the peace for Winchelsea, to [John] Woollett, [town clerk of Winchelsea], Rye, Sussex*:
At a meeting this day it was agreed that William Blackhall shall pay 2s 6d per week and Elizabeth Haisell 6d towards the maintenance of a female bastard child named Amy. [PAR 511/34/1/58]

85 10 Jan 1824 *Letter from [Dr] Adam Scott, Winchelsea, to the vestry, Winchelsea*:
Having come to the resolution of relinquishing any claim I have on the services of William Blackhall up to the expiry of the time for which Thomas Fisher was engaged to me I owe it to myself to state that I have felt compelled to this in consequence of the refusal of the overseers to provide the boy with such necessaries as are indispensable for his comfort or the respectability of the person in whose service he is placed. It was with reluctance I have taken this step but finding from the assistant overseer after repeated applications that he did not feel warranted in giving even a pair of shoes though the lad was literally bare-footed and seeing that his spirit was broken and of course his attention to his business lessened, I have not hesitated to engage another. As I trust the parish have good reason for this line of conduct they have followed so I hope that which I have adopted will set matters to rights, it being far from my wish to interfere with their interests.

[PAR 511/35/1/46]

Note: This document refers to William Blackhall junior who was later returned to Dr Scott's service by the parish and encouraged to resume this employment by being allowed sixpence a week while there.[13] He was succeeded by his brother Walter – see (**77**).

86 29 Jun 1824 *Information given before Henry Powell, justice of the peace for Winchelsea by Charles Arnett, assistant overseer*:
[who] on oath saith that William Blackhall, a pauper of St Thomas's, Winchelsea did this day refuse to be examined as to his place of last legal settlement.
[*Appended note*] (same day) Blackhall examined and his further examination postponed sine die. [*signed*] Henry Butler [town clerk]   [WIN 237A]

87 30 Jun 1824 *Examination taken before Henry Powell and Joseph Hennah, justices of the peace for Winchelsea, of William Blackhall*:
who upon his oath saith [I] was born in the parish of Grays near Henley-on-Thames in the county of Oxford. I am now of the age of 50 years and upwards. My father was at that time resident there and was a certificate man from St Mary's in the town of Reading, Berkshire. My father received relief from that parish. At the age of 14 or thereabouts I went of my own accord and hired myself for twelve months to Mr Samuel Bitmead, a farmer of that parish, at the wages of three guineas per annum. I served the whole year and slept in the house during that time. I received my wages for that year. I then agreed with him as a weekly servant and served him upwards of twelve months. After I left Mr Bitmead I went and worked with my father till I enlisted into the Cinque Ports Fencibles at that place under the command of Lord Oxberry and was sworn in at Reading about the year 1793. I continued in that regiment nearly six years and was then discharged at Bath. At the time I was in the regiment I was servant to Captain Luxford who belonged thereto. I then came with him to Winchelsea and agreed to live with him at a guinea a week wages and board and lodging in the house, either party to be at liberty to leave each other at a month's notice or wages and continued in his service for twelve months or upwards. I then hired myself to Mr. George Harrod of Winchelsea, innkeeper, as ostler at the wages of three shillings per week, board and lodging included, with an understanding that a month's warning was to be given either way if we wished to separate. I remained under that hiring five years. I was married by a magistrate about the years 1797 or 1798 to Isabella [*blank*] at Jedborough in Scotland. I was in the army at that time. In the year [1810] I was married to Elizabeth Haisell of Winchelsea at the parish church and have now seven children viz: William aged 15 or thereabouts, Ann aged 14 or thereabouts, Harriet aged 13 or thereabouts, Walter aged 12 or thereabouts, Richard aged 6 or thereabouts, George aged 3 or thereabouts, John about six months. After the expiration of 5 years I made a fresh agreement with Mr Harrod and agreed with him to board and lodge myself at 10s a week. I am a weekly servant to Mr Harrod and if we wish to part each party to give a month's notice. I have remained in Mr Harrod's service upwards of 22 years.
[*mark of*] William Blackhall.   [AMS 2330 f 31]
Notes: 1. William Blackhall, widower, and Elizabeth Haisell, spinster, were married at St Thomas's on 22 August 1810.[14]
2. Fencibles were soldiers liable only for defensive service at home.

88 24 Feb 1825 *Notice issued by Charles Arnett, assistant overseer, on behalf of the churchwardens and overseers of Winchelsea to [inter alia] William Blackhall*: We hereby give you warning of quitting all that house and premises now in your occupation on or before this day month of which be pleased to take notice.

[PAR 511/37/3/14]

Note: The overseers' records show that at this time they were paying £1 5s 0d per quarter for William Blackhall's rent.[15]

89 14 Mar 1826 *Information given before Henry Powell and John Tilden, justices of the peace for Winchelsea*: Charles Arnett of the parish of St Thomas the Apostle, Winchelsea, assistant overseer, charges William Blackhall the elder, labourer, and Jane Foster, widow, both of Winchelsea, with unlawfully keeping possession of certain premises in the Barrack Square, Winchelsea after due notice given by the churchwardens and overseers of the poor of Winchelsea or the major part of them contrary to the statute in that case made and provided. [WIN 237A]

90 14 Mar 1827 *Information given before John Tilden, justice of the peace for Winchelsea:* Charles Arnett of the parish of St Thomas the Apostle, Winchelsea, assistant overseer, charges William Blackhall the elder with unlawfully retaining possession of a house and premises after due notice being given by the churchwardens and overseers of the poor or a majority of them. [WIN 237A]

1 PAR 511/1/1/4   2 ibid   3 PAR 511/31/1/13 QE 29 Sep 1824 et seq   4 PAR 511/1/1/4   5 ibid 21 Nov 1801   6 PAR 511/12/3 4 May 1827   7/8 PAR 511/31/1/11 E1814 et seq; PAR 511/31/1/13 25 Mar 1821 et seq; PAR 511/12/3 17 Feb 1826 et seq   9 PAR 511/12/2 f.28 27 Jun 1822   10 PAR 511/31/2/134   11 PAR 511/37/7/29   12 PAR 511/38/4/3   13 PAR 511/12/2 8 Jul 1824   14 PAR 511/1/1/4   15 PAR 511/31/1/15 f.5

Josiah Boots

91 *Josiah Boots was a carpenter and a highly respected member of the Winchelsea community. He served as a town constable between 1796 and 1811[1] and as sergeant-at-mace [mayor's sergeant] between 1799 and 1812[2] in which year he was replaced by Thomas Sylvester Keene. He is recorded serving as foreman of Winchelsea's grand jury in 1797.[3] In 1807 his standing was sufficient for him to be granted a five hundred-year lease at four shillings per annum on a piece of ground which, according to the measurements given, appears to have stretched 97 feet westward of the present entrance to the top of the footpath now known as Spring Steps.[4] By 1824 Boots had become very ill and from June of that year he began receiving poor rate relief.[5] Despite the doubts expressed in (**92**) this continued until his death. He died at the age of 66 and was buried only six days after the date of (**93**).[6] At the time of his death he had only been married eight years and left a widow and three young children, Josiah junior 6, Eliza 4 and Jesse Ann 2.[7] They were generously supported by the parish even after they moved to Brighton in December 1825.[8] Throughout most of that time Mrs Boots received one shilling and sixpence per week for each child.*

92 12 Oct 1824 *Minute of the Winchelsea select vestry*:
Resolved that this vestry decline acting in the case of Josiah Boots until something
more satisfactory is laid before them.   [PAR 511/12/2]

93 3 Dec 1824 *Letter from William Chatterton, Winchelsea to Richard Stileman,
chairman of the committee, Winchelsea*:
Since I saw you I waited on Mrs Boots who informs me she paid a great part of the
money which you were kind enough to let her have as follows: to William Lennard
£1 6s 5d; to Mrs Winter £1 5s 8½d; to Mrs Bennett £2 6s 2d; to church tax 5s 6d;
[total] £5 3s 3½d. These bills were for articles she stood in need of and the persons
who had supplied her with the necessaries wanted the money much. As such she
thought it her bounden duty to pay. Mrs B[oots] would have waited upon you but
thinks Mr B[oots] is sinking very fast. You'll excuse my writing this not knowing
when I waited on you this morning what she had received or paid. [*Endorsed*]
From William Chatterton relating to Josiah Boots' interest in the house he lives
in.   [PAR 511/35/1/140]
Note: A poor rate assessment dated 11 March 1824 shows Josiah Boots as occupying a
house and shop with an annual rental value of £5 10s 0d.[9] This suggests quite a substantial
property.

1 WIN 96 et seq; WIN 61AA 2 ibid 3 WIN 61 f.101r 4 WIN 116; WIN 118 5 PAR 511/31/1/13
QE 29 Sep 1824 6 PAR 511/1/5/1 7 PAR 511/31/1/15 f.4 8 PAR 511/31/1/13 1825-1831, PAR
511/31/1/15 f.49 9 PAR 511/31/1/13

Robert Broadfoot

94 *Robert Broadfoot, aged 12 in 1822, and his sister Sarah who was two years older
were the children of Mary Broadfoot, widow of a Winchelsea labourer.[1] In 1824 Robert, a
Winchelsea workhouse boy for much of his young life, was put out to service with Walter
Fuller, Fuller being required to pay the parish two shillings and sixpence per week for
Robert's labour.[2] In August of that year the overseers decided that Robert should 'go out
of the house on Monday' and should receive in relief only the two shillings and sixpence
which his master was paying.[3] In the following years Robert was twice taken back into the
workhouse.[4] He was later fairly regularly provided with clothing, for example two shirts
and two pairs of stockings in 1827.[5] It may be that the terms offered to Robert's mother
on leaving the workhouse in 1820* (**95**) *were not implemented for she is again recorded
as leaving in March 1821 when it was decided that she should receive three shillings
and sixpence a week 'and one pair of shoes for herself and boy'.[6] Mrs Broadfoot worked
occasionally as a nurse in the parish but was frequently ill herself. She received regular
poor law relief, usually weekly but sometimes on a casual basis, until 1831.[7] In 1823 Sarah
Broadfoot was given a position with Andrew Woodhams, the parish agreeing to provide
clothing and one shilling a week if Mr Woodhams arranged for her washing and mending.[8]
However, she was taken back into the workhouse in June 1824.[9] The 1841 census shows
Mary Broadfoot living in Cleveland Street [Friars Road] as a servant of Jane Stephens,
aged 80, a lady of independent means.*

95 15 Jun 1820 *Minute of the Winchelsea select vestry*:
Resolved that Widow Broadfoot have one change, one frock and undercoat for Sarah, also one pair hose and one change and pair trousers for son Robert and to take herself and her children from the house and to be allowed 2s per week with her son.   [PAR 511/12/2 f.1]

96 5 Dec 1827 *Letter from Edward K Nares, Newchurch, [Kent] to C[harles] Arnett, Winchelsea, vestry clerk*:
I am sorry your letter has remained so long unnoticed owing to my having been from home. My agreement with Robert Broadfoot is to feed him and find him his outer clothes, that is his coat, waistcoat and trousers.   [PAR 511/35/1/306]

1 PAR 511/31/1/12 f.149   2 PAR 511/12/2 4 Mar 1824   3 ibid 27 Aug 1824   4 ibid 4 Feb 1825; PAR 511/12/3 16 Mar 1826   5 PAR 511/12/3 2 Nov 1827   6 PAR 511/12/2 f.9   7 PAR 511/31/1/13 1821-1830; PAR 511/12/3 1826-1831; PAR 511/12/2 1831-1832   8 PAR 511/12/2 f.41 3 Apr 1823 9 PAR 511/12/2 24 Jun 1824

Isaiah Burwash

97 *The only further record of Isaiah Burwash's apparent employment at Camber Castle (**98**) is that James Wilson was paid one shilling and sixpence a week for 'keeping I Burwash' for the year ending 11 Jan 1825.[1] He had earlier been in the service, on the same terms, of Thomas Fuller, a local farmer and substantial landowner.[2] Burwash was often provided with clothing, for example, a greatcoat costing nineteen shillings[3] and, resolved by the parish only a week before the date of (**98**), '1 hat, 1 pair stockings, 1 change and 1 round frock'.[4] He also had his hair cut by the Winchelsea barber, George Haisell, at a charge to the parish of one shilling a quarter.[5]*

98 21 Aug 1824 *Letter from James Wilson, Winchelsea Castle, to [Charles] Arnett, Winchelsea*:
I should be obliged to you to lay before a vestry for Isaiah Burwash – a hat, 1 round frock, 2 shirts, 2 pairs stockings, 1 jacket.   [PAR 511/35/1/106]
Note: Winchelsea Castle was the former name for Camber Castle.

1 PAR 511/31/1/13 QE 25 Mar 1825   2 AMS 2329 E1806-E1807   3 PAR 511/31/1/13 25 Sep 1823-28 Feb 1824   4 PAR 511/12/2 13 Aug 1824   5 PAR 511/31/2/162

Frances Butler

99 *The child who is the principal subject of these documents was baptised in Winchelsea on 20 December 1818 and named Edward Sisley Butler.[1] The request to the Winchelsea overseers 'to see to my little boy' (**102**) indicates that at that time at least he was in the Winchelsea workhouse. Between September 1819 and early 1824 Frances Butler received two shillings and sixpence a week from the Winchelsea overseers plus occasional additional casual support.[2] There is no record of Sherington Sisley being required to pay towards the child's keep. All records of payments by Winchelsea to Frances Butler end on 19 February*

1824[3] which explains the anxiety expressed in (**104**). *No reason has been found why the overseers of Brighton had assumed responsibility for her payments by June 1824* (**105**). *Edward Sisley Butler died in March 1829 aged 10 and was buried in Winchelsea.[4]*

100 5 Jan 1819 *Voluntary examination taken before George Stace, justice of the peace for Winchelsea, of Frances Butler of Winchelsea, singlewoman*:
who on oath saith that on the 11th day of December last past at the house of Thomas Cornwall in Winchelsea she was delivered of a male bastard child and that the child is likely to become chargeable to the parish of St Thomas the Apostle, Winchelsea and that Sherington Sisley late of Hastings, Sussex, shopkeeper, did get her with child of the said bastard child.　　　　　　　　　　　[PAR 511/34/1/22]

101 13 Aug 1822 *Letter from Frances Butler, Battle to Messrs [Robert] Alce and [George] Hill, Winchelsea, overseers*:
I should be obliged to you if you would pay to Mr Cramp the sum of one pound that is due to me of the child's money as I owe it to him. By so doing you will greatly oblige.　　　　　　　　　　　　　　　　　　　　[PAR 511/35/1/12]

102 25 Oct 1823 *Letter from Frances Butler, Battle, to [George] Hill, Winchelsea*:
Please to pay to the bearer the money that is due to me and I should think it a great favour if you would have the goodness to see to my little boy [Edward] as I understand there are fresh people in the [work]house and as he is very unhealthy he is likely to have a good many hardships and if he stands in need of anything of clothing more than the parish allows if you would have the goodness to grant it I will pay you or you will stop it out of the child's pay. By so doing you will greatly oblige.　　　　　　　　　　　　　　　　　　　[PAR 511/35/1/30]

103 12 Feb 1824 *Letter from Frances Butler, Battle to [the overseers of Winchelsea]*:
I should be much obliged to you if you would send by the bearer all the money that I have due as I am very much in want of it.　　　　　[PAR 511/35/1/60]

104 25 Apr 1824 *Letter from Frances Butler, Battle to [the overseers of Winchelsea]*:
I am sorry to have occasion to trouble you but not knowing who is overseer I have taken this liberty to ascertain the reason I do not receive my money for the child as I have sent repeatedly by Cogger and once I hired a man and sent and then I was promised that I should receive it the next week and never have we received one farthing since and I am so distressed for it that I must leave my place in consequence of it if I do not have some soon. If the money is paid now to Brighton I see no reason why I should not receive it and if it is not please send me word and it soon shall. Sir, if you will put this in force I shall be extremely obliged and send an answer by Cogger on Friday.　　　　　　　[PAR 511/35/1/78]

105 30 Jun 1824 *Letter from G Chassereau, Brighton, assistant overseer, to the overseers of Winchelsea*:

I am desired to inform you that the overseers of this parish have paid the sum of £4 2s 6d to Willis and Company on account of Rye Bank for the overseers of Winchelsea and which they would have paid before but they expected to have had an opportunity of sending to you by a friend. The above sum has been demanded of them as having been advanced to F[rances] Butler.   [PAR 511/35/1/92]

1 PAR 511/1/2/1 2 PAR 511/31/1/11 1819-1820; PAR 511/31/1/13 1820-1824; PAR 511/37/7/18-20
1 Jan 1824-19 Feb 1824 3 PAR 511/37/7/20-23 4 PAR 511/1/5/1

John Chester

106 *John Chester was removed from Beckley to Winchelsea in 1822. Winchelsea's unsuccessful attempts to show that this should not have happened and that he had established a settlement in Beckley are illustrated in (107). In late 1823 he received several casual payments of 1s 6d and in November of that year he is recorded as 'being in the [Winchelsea work]house'.[1] Chester took up the duties of parish beadle in 1824 (108) but was removed on 19 May 1826 following Henry Powell's letter (110). Henry Tilden was appointed in his place and as an encouragement Tilden was allowed 'sixpence a week to find him in small beer'.[2] There is no evidence that Chester had ever received such an allowance. However, for most of the time he served as beadle he did receive weekly poor law relief of four shillings.[3] Between December 1837 and September 1839 Chester was an inmate of the Rye workhouse.[4]*

107 8 Jul 1822 *[Edited] account of Messrs Dawes & Co to the parish officers of Winchelsea*:

Attending Mr [John] Woods advising on the removal of John Chester from Beckley when it appeared necessary to make inquiries as to his service with the Rev[d] Mr [Henry] Hodges and recommending as he was about to enter and respite the appeal which it was agreed should be done: 6s 8d. Writing to Mr Barton for a copy of Chester's examination: 3s 6d. 10 Jul 1822 Long attendance on Mr Woods and Master Chester, examining the latter touching his settlement and making minutes thereof and afterwards also examining Mr Apps thereon: 13s 4d. 30 Jul 1822 Writing long letter to Rev[d] Mr Hodges making inquiries as to Chester's hiring and service with him and requesting an answer: 5s. 8 Oct 1822 Writing to Mr Woods in consequence of a letter received from Mr Hodges in answer to ours of the 30th [July] on the subject of Chester's settlement on the propriety of abandoning which they afterwards determined to do: 3s 6d.   [PAR 511/31/2/137]

Notes: 1. Unusually, John Chester's examination has not survived within the parish records.
2. Rev[d] Henry Hodges was Rector of Beckley from 1804-1827.[5]

108 8 Jul 1824 *Minute of the Winchelsea select vestry*:
[Resolved] that, John Sinden having deserted his office of beadle, John Chester be appointed to act pro tempo.　　　　　　　　　　　　　　　　　[PAR 511/12/2]

109 21 Apr 1826 *Minute of the Winchelsea select vestry*:
Resolved that John Chester be taken into the house and that his attention be entirely confined to the duties of beadle.　　　　　　　　　　　　[PAR 511/12/3]
Note: On 4 May 1826 weekly payments to John Chester ceased. Not until 18 April 1828 was he allowed further relief and then on a casual basis.[6]

110 2 May 1826 *Letter from Henry Powell, [Winchelsea] to the chairman of the select vestry, Winchelsea*:
I beg to inform you that the beadle of this parish [John Chester] neglects his duty so far that travellers are repeatedly knocking on my door which makes it very troublous to me and I assure you he seems to be so often employed elsewhere that those travelling have the range of the town. I shall feel obliged if you will remedy it.　　　　　　　　　　　　　　　　　　　　[PAR 511/35/1/221]

1 PAR 511/31/1/12 f.55　2 PAR 511/12/3 19 May 1826　3 PAR 511/31/1/15 f.9　4 G 8/19/2　5 PAR 237/2/1/1　6 PAR 511/31/1/15 f.9

Mary Clandenbold (many spellings of the name)

111 *Mary Clandenbold's surname is spelt many different ways within the available Winchelsea records. Clandenbold has been selected as the preferred editorial spelling because it is used in a considerable majority of the letters she, and others on her behalf, wrote to the Winchelsea overseers (**115-131**). The Winchelsea parish registers provide the name of Mary Clandenbold's husband and show that the couple had a daughter named for her mother who died in infancy for Mary 'daughter of John and Mary Clandenbold' was baptised at St Thomas's Church on 22 February 1784 and buried there the following November.[1] While the child was alive Mary Clandenbold's clothes were included in 'A true and perfect list of the wearing apparel belonging to the poor of the parish'. She is said to have owned two check frocks, two shirts, two caps, a yellow skirt, two coats [and] one old pair of shoes [total value] 5s 9d.[2] The description in (**114**) of Mary Clandenbold as wife or widow indicates that her husband John's whereabouts were then unknown. The overseers' books covering the period of the letters from Mrs Clandenbold and those acting for her[3] show regular payments of three shillings a week between January 1824 and 11 October 1827 when a final payment of nine shillings was made.[4] Her pleas in the letters that money should be sent to her suggest that regularity of ledger entry did not match regularity of despatch. Delays may also have been caused by the frequent requirement that she should send proof of her continued Canterbury residence and her address (**119, 121, 125, 131**). The ending of the regular weekly payments in October 1827 is likely to have been because she was admitted to the Winchelsea workhouse. She was certainly there when it was closed as a workhouse for she was one of those occupants offered accommodation in the building after that closure (**132-133**). In December 1835, when her age was given as 78, she was admitted by the guardians of the Rye Union to the Rye workhouse.[5] In the following year she was listed among Winchelsea's 'totally disabled poor'.[6]*

112 28 Feb 1801 *Examinations, taken before Thomas Marten, deputy mayor and justice of the peace for Winchelsea, of Simon Graddon of Winchelsea, an officer of the excise, Mary his wife and Mary Colegate of Winchelsea, spinster*:
And first Mary Graddon, on her oath saith that she hath at different times lost several tea cloths, towels and other things, the property of Simon Graddon her husband, out of the house wherein she and her husband now [reside] in Winchelsea and which she hath suspected to have been feloniously stolen thereout by some person or persons and, having cause to suspect Mary Clandenbold of Winchelsea, she communicated her suspicions to her husband on Thursday the 26th of this instant, February, and all these examinants, Mary Graddon, Simon Graddon and Mary Colegate, on their oaths severally say that on yesterday, the 27th day of February, they did together go and search the room wherein Mary Clandenbold doth now lodge in Winchelsea and that they did find therein and in a chest in the room pieces of sheeting made into four tea cloths, one small piece of diaper cloth and several pieces of rags which these examinants severally say are the property of Simon Graddon and ... that they do suspect and verily believe that the same were feloniously stolen by Mary Clandenbold and that she is guilty of the offence. [*signatures of*] Mary Graddon and Mary Colegate.   [WIN 275]
Note: diaper cloth = a linen or cotton fabric with a small diamond pattern.

113 28 Feb 1801 *Examination of Mary Clandenbold, taken before Thomas Marten, deputy mayor and justice of the peace for Winchelsea*:
Mary Clandenbold [is] charged before me by Simon Graddon of Winchelsea, excise officer, with the felonious stealing out of his house of several items, the following goods, that is to say four pieces of sheeting made into tea cloths, one small piece of diaper and several pieces of rags of the value of eightpence. She, Mary Clandenbold, upon her examination now taken before me confesseth that she hath at several times feloniously stolen from and out of the house of Simon Graddon the several goods above particularly mentioned. [*signature of*] Mary Clandenbold.   [WIN 275]

114 14 Apr 1801 *General quarter sessions of the peace held at the Guildhall, Winchelsea before Thomas Marten Esq deputy mayor, George Stace and Richard Lamb, jurats and justices of the peace for Winchelsea*:
At this sessions a bill of indictment was preferred against Mary Clandenbold the wife of John Clandenbold late of the Ancient Town of Winchelsea in the county of Sussex, labourer, otherwise Mary Clandenbold, widow, for stealing four pieces of linen cloth commonly called sheeting, one small piece of other linen cloth commonly called diaper cloth and several pieces of linen rags of the value of 8d of the goods and chattels of Simon Graddon. The [grand] jury upon their oaths did say that the said bill was a true bill against Mary Clarenbold whereupon she was arraigned for the petty larceny and thereto pleaded guilty and it was considered and by this court adjudged, ordered and pronounced that she be immediately stripped from the waist upwards and do receive twelve stripes from a cat of 9 tails on her

bare back at the foot of the steps leading up to the Guildhall of Winchelsea and then be discharged paying her fees. [WIN 61 f.108r]

Notes: 1. Winchelsea Court Hall was also known as the Guildhall.

2. Mary Clandenbold's gaol fees were entered as an expense of £1 3s 10½ in the Winchelsea Corporation chamberlain's account for Easter 1800 to Easter 1801.[7] The above sentence suggests that she was expected to pay this amount but there is no evidence that she did so.

115 23 Sep 1823 *Letter from Francis Thomas White, Canterbury, [Kent] to [John] Woods, Winchelsea, grocer [and overseer]*:

I send these few lines to you for your kindness as to send me Mrs [Mary] Clandenbold's quarter's money which is due [for] which I should be very much obliged to you. [PAR 511/35/1/24]

116 22 Oct 1823 *Letter from [Francis] Thomas White, Canterbury, [Kent] to [John] Woods, Winchelsea*:

I write these few lines to you in asking you to be so kind as to send me Mrs [Mary] Clandenbold's quarter's money which is due for I am very much in want of it for I sent a letter on 11 October and have not had any answer. Directions: Thomas White near the Little Rose, Borough, Canterbury. [PAR 511/35/1/29]

117 2 Nov 1823 *Letter from Mary Clandenbold, Canterbury, [Kent], to Mr [Abraham] Kennett, Winchelsea, overseer*:

I have received your letter on Thursday last with my money in it and I am very much obliged to you for it. [PAR 511/35/1/36]

118 14 Jan 1824 *Letter from [Mary] Clandenbold, Canterbury, [Kent] to [Charles] Arnett, Winchelsea, overseer*:

I have taken this opportunity of sending these few lines to you if it is your pleasure to send me my quarter's money which is due for I should be very much obliged to you for I am very much in want of it. Please to send as soon as you can and please to send it the same way as you did before. Directions: For [Francis] Thomas White, near the Little Rose, Borough, Canterbury. [PAR 511/35/1/49]

119 22 Jan 1824 *Letter from [Francis] T[homas] White [on behalf of Mary Clandenbold], Canterbury to [Charles] Arnett, Winchelsea, overseer*:

I received your letter and here is [Mrs Clandenbold's] certificate signed. I should be much obliged to you to send [the money] as soon as you can and if you have not sent Mrs Taunton's please to send them both together.

[*Enclosed*] This is to certify that Mary Clandenbold is now living in the Borough of Northgate. [*signed*] John Goulden, guardian, Mark Burrows, overseer.

[PAR 511/35/1/52]

120 10 Oct 1824 *Letter from Mary Clandenbold, Canterbury, [Kent] to [Charles] Arnett, Winchelsea, [assistant] overseer*:
I write to you for my quarter's pay which is due. If you will be so kind as to send it I should be very much obliged to you for it and, sir, I should be very much obliged too if you would send me some clothes for I am very much in want of some pairs of shoes and stockings and ?gown and petticoat. I should be very much obliged to you for them.   [PAR 511/35/1/118]

121 2 Jan 1825 *Letter from Mary Clandenbold to [the overseers of Winchelsea]*:
I write to you for my quarter's [pay] is due and here is a certificate from the churchwardens and overseers of the parish. Please to send it by the return of post and please to send it the same way as before.
[Enclosure] 31 Dec 1824 *Certificate issued and signed by James Ridout and J J Williamson [churchwardens]*:
This is to certify that Mary Clandenbold is now living and residing in the Borough of Staplegate in the parish of St Alphage in the City of Canterbury.
[PAR 511/37/7/6]

122 18 Jan 1825 *Letter from Mrs [Mary] Clandenbold, Canterbury, [Kent] to [Charles] Arnett, Winchelsea, [assistant] overseer*:
I should be very much obliged to you to send me my quarter's pay which is due for I am very much in want of it and I have sent a letter and received no answer which I think very strange that you have not sent it.   [PAR 511/35/1/152]

123 29 Jan 1825 *Letter from Mary Clandenbold, Canterbury, [Kent] to [Charles] Arnett, Winchelsea, [assistant] overseer*:
I think it very strange that you have not sent me my quarter's money which was due 7th January and I have sent two letters and have received no answer so I should be very much obliged to you to send it by the return of post and the same way as you sent it before for I am very much in want of it.   [PAR 511/35/1/156]

124 12 Jul 1825 *Letter from Mrs [Mary] Clandenbold, Canterbury, [Kent] to [Charles] Arnett, Winchelsea, [assistant] overseer*:
I write to you for my quarter's pay which is due the 7th and I thank you to send it as soon as you can.   [PAR 511/35/1/182]

125 11 Jul 1826 *Letter from Mary Clandenbold, Canterbury, [Kent] to [Charles] Arnett, Winchelsea, [assistant] overseer:*
I have sent my certificates by your desire and I [would] be much obliged to you to send it as the quarter is due.
[Endorsed] This is to certify that Mary Clandenbold is now living in the Borough of Staplegate. *[signed]* James Ridout and J J Williamson, churchwardens [of St Alphage].   [PAR 511/35/1/235]

126 21 Aug 1826 *Letter from Mary Clandenbold, Canterbury, [Kent] to [Charles] Arnett, Winchelsea, [assistant] overseer*:
I have sent you answer to [your] letter and have not received no money which I think so strange because I am so much in want of the money for I can't live without it so I should be glad if you would send it as soon as possible for I can't do without it and if not I must come home for things are severe.   [PAR 511/35/1/238]

127 4 Sep 1826 *Letter from Mary Clandenbold, Canterbury, [Kent] to [Charles] Arnett, Winchelsea, [assistant] overseer*:
I once more write to you to know the reason that you have not sent the answer to my letter to let me know what I am to do which I think so strange you have not sent my money for I do not know what to do without it. Therefore I hope you will send me word what I have to do. Sir, I am very sorry to trouble you so much.
                                                          [PAR 511/35/1/239]

128 4 Oct 1826 *Letter from Mary Clandenbold, Canterbury, [Kent] to [Charles] Arnett, Winchelsea, [assistant] overseer*:
I hope you excuse my writing for I have sent three letters and have received no answer which I think so strange and I am so much in want of money or I should not have troubled you if I did not want it. I hope you won't delay no time in sending of it for I am quite distressed for it and please to send it by the Ashford conveyance for I think it is safest.   [PAR 511/35/1/241]

129 5 Oct 1826 *Letter from Mary Clandenbold, Canterbury, [Kent] to [Charles] Arnett, Winchelsea, [assistant] overseer*:
I write to inform you that I received the £2 2s, the money that was lost, my last quarter's pay, and I am informed that the money was lost from Dover to Canterbury for I did not receive it till this morning so I thought that I would write to inform you that I have got it and Mrs [Elizabeth] Taunton wished me to mention she would be obliged to you to send on money with [mine].   [PAR 511/35/1/242]
Note: Mary Clandenbold's quarterly allowance at this time is entered in the overseers' accounts as 13 weeks at 3s = £1 19s 0d.[8] It would seem from the above that she had been paid for fourteen weeks but such a payment is not included in the records.

130 19 Jul 1827 *Letter from Mary Clandenbold, Canterbury, [Kent] to [Charles] Arnett, Winchelsea, [assistant] overseer*:
I should be much obliged to you if you be so kind [as] to send my quarter's money. It has been due nearly a fortnight and I am very much in want of it. [I] hope you will not fail sending it directly. Please to direct as usual.   [PAR 511/35/1/290]

131 26 Sep 1827 *Letter from Mary Clandenbold, Canterbury, [Kent] to [Charles] Arnett, Winchelsea, [assistant] overseer*:
I have sent my certificate as you wish me to do and I should be very glad if you would be so kind as to send my quarter's pay which is due.

[*Endorsed*] This is to certify that Mary Clandenbold is now living in the Borough of Staplegate in this city. James Ridout and J J Williamson, churchwardens of St Alphage.   [PAR 511/35/1/299]

132 7 Apr 1831 *Minute of the Winchelsea parish vestry* [*following a decision to 'break up the establishment of the poorhouse'*]:
[Resolved] that Mrs Clandenbold be allowed 4s per week and the use of one room in the house.   [PAR 511/12/2]
Note: The allowance of four shillings was paid regularly until October 1835 when the relevant records cease.[9]

133 11 Apr 1831 *Inventory of the Winchelsea workhouse includes*:
Bedroom No. 4 [Occupied by] Old dame [Mary Clandenbold] 1 bed and bolster and 1 pillow, 1 pair sheets, 1 pair blankets, 1 chamber pot, 1 table, 1 chair and 1 rug.   [AMS 2331]

1 PAR 511/1/1/2   2 PAR 511/37/4/3   3 PAR 511/31/1/12 f.300; PAR 511/31/1/13; PAR 511/31/1/14   4 PAR 511/31/1/14   5 G 8/1a/1 f.65   6 PAR 511/37/7/29   7 WIN 618 E1800-E1801   8 PAR 511/31/1/13   9 PAR 511/31/1/16

Cornelius Clarke (Clark)

134 *Cornelius Clarke was baptised in Winchelsea on 18 September 1803.[1] On his marriage he went to live in Icklesham. Following his removal back to Winchelsea (**136**) his family grew rapidly. By 1834 five children were listed.[2] In the 1841 census he is recorded as an agricultural labourer (**137**) living in The Strand with his wife, Sarah aged 40, and their children Isaac 14, Jane 11, Sarah 10, Mary 7, James 5 and Hannah 2. At that time Harriett (**136**), who died in 1846 at the age of 22,[3] would have been 16 and can be presumed to have gone into service. The 1842 Tithe Map suggests that their home could well have been the property now known as The Old Malt House.[4] From early 1827 until June 1835 Cornelius Clarke was granted poor relief of amounts varying from £2 to three shillings on a casual basis according to need.[5] Between March 1831 and October 1835 these casual payments were supplemented by a weekly allowance varying between 1s 6d and 3s.[6] He was occasionally employed on the parish highways, for example between November 1830 and May 1831.[7] In 1836 he was listed among Winchelsea's able-bodied poor.[8] On 24 January 1841 his entry in the records of the guardians of the Rye Union reads, 'Amount of relief out of the workhouse: 6s 6d. Cause of requiring relief – illness.[9] After that, the only evidence found shows that, between 1847 and 1849, as a Winchelsea pauper, he was excused paying the poor rate.[10]*

135 24 Jan 1827 *Settlement examination, taken on oath at Hastings, Sussex, before Musgrove Brisco and W Lucas Shadwell, justices of the peace for the county of Sussex, of Cornelius Clarke now residing in the parish of Icklesham*:
who upon his oath saith that he was born in the parish of St Thomas the Apostle, Winchelsea where his parents were inhabitants legally settled as he has been informed and believes; that when he was about 19 years old he went to Mr [Henry]

Farncomb of Icklesham a week after new Michaelmas Day and agreed to serve him at one shilling a week and he served under that agreement until new Lady Day following; that he then agreed to serve him as carter at three shillings a week and served under that agreement until the new Michaelmas Day following, and then agreed to serve him at 2s 6d a week and served until the latter end of April following; that he then married and had served Mr Farncomb nearly four years under weekly agreement, sometimes as a carter and sometimes as a labourer during which time his wages were altered and Mr Farncomb paid him according to the wages other labourers were receiving in the parish; that he has a wife named Sarah and one child named Harriett aged about two years who with himself are now actually chargeable to the parish of Icklesham. [*mark of*] Cornelius Clarke.

[PAR 511/32/4/200]

136 24 Jan 1827 *Removal order made by Musgrove Brisco and W Lucas Shadwell, justices of the peace for the county of Sussex, to the churchwardens and overseers of the poor for the parish of Icklesham, Sussex*:

Whereas complaint hath been made unto us that Cornelius Clarke, his wife named Sarah and their one child named Harriett aged about two years lately intruded and came into the parish of Icklesham and are actually become chargeable to the same, we upon due proof thereof as well as upon the examination of Cornelius Clarke do adjudge the same to be true and also adjudge the place of their last legal settlement to be Winchelsea. These are therefore in His Majesty's name to require you to remove and convey them to Winchelsea and them deliver, together with this our order or a true copy thereof, to the churchwardens and overseers of the poor there who are hereby required to receive them and provide for them according to law.

[PAR 511/32/3/52]

Note: On arrival in Winchelsea Clarke was allowed a payment of five shillings. The entry is marked, 'Cash – brought from Icklesham'.[11]

137 6 Feb 1830 *Letter from G Packham, Camber Farm, to [David] Laurence, Winchelsea, [assistant overseer]*:

This is to say Master [Cornelius] Clarke is quite distressed for want of fireing. Mrs Clarke is now just confined and I believe them to stand in need of your assistance. [PAR 511/35/1/326]

138 13 Oct 1830 *Minute of the Winchelsea select vestry*:

Resolved that Cornelius Clarke [be provided with] ½ gall flour per week and that he be allowed 8s as a casual relief he being sick. [PAR 511/12/3]

1 PAR 511/1/1/4 2 PAR 511/31/1/15 f.53 3 PAR 511/1/5/1 4 TD/E 90/1/2 5 PAR 511/31/1/13 QE 25 Mar 1827-QE 25 Mar 1831; PAR 511/12/3 12 Feb 1830-31 Mar 1831; PAR 511/12/2 3 Jun 1831-3 Jun 1835 6 PAR 511/31/1/16 7 PAR 511/40/1/7 8 PAR 511/37/7/29 9 PAR 511/38/4/3 10 PAR 511/12/2 11 PAR 511/31/1/15 f.25

Sussex)   The Examination of Cornelius Clark now residing
to wit)   in the Parish of Icklesham in the said County, touching
the place of his last legal settlement, taken on Oath this
24th day of January 1807, before us two of his Majesty's
Justices of the Peace, acting in and for the said County
who saith That he was born in the Parish of St Thos the Apostle in
the ancient Town of Winchelsea where his parents were Inhabitants
legally settled as he has been informed and believes —

That when he was about 19 years old he went to Mr
Fancomb of Icklesham a week after new Michaelmas day
and agreed to serve him at 1/. a week and he served under that
agreement untill new Lady day following. —

That he then agreed to serve him as Carter at 3/.
a week and served under that agreement untill new Michaelmas
day following and then agreed to serve him at 2.6 a week, and
served untill the latter end of April following. —

That he then married and has served Mr Fancomb
nearly four years under weekly agreement, sometimes as a
Carter and sometimes a Labourer, during which time his wages
were altered, and Mr Fancomb paid him according to the wages
other labourers were receiving in the Parish. —

That he has a wife named Sarah and one Child
named Harriott aged about two years who with himself, are
now actually chargeable to the Parish of Icklesham aforesaid —

Sworn at Hastings the
day and year first above)
written   Before us)
Signed   Musgrove Brisco
         Wilson Shadwell

                                    The mark of
                                         X
                                    Cornelius Clark

E.S.R.O.
PAR. 511/32/4/200

The settlement examination of Cornelius Clarke

PAR 511/32/4/200 transcribed as (135)
reproduced by arrangement with the County Archivist

Thomas Clarke (Clark)

139 *Despite their common circumstance as Winchelsea paupers who were sometime residents of Icklesham and the usual spelling of their surname with the final e, no evidence has been found of any family relationship between Cornelius* (**134-138**) *and Thomas Clarke. Following his first removal to Winchelsea* (**140**), *Thomas moved back to Icklesham in 1821 with his wife Mary and their children[1] to work for Mr H[enry] Farncomb and by 1822 the Winchelsea overseers were paying Mr Farncomb the rent for Clarke's home.[2] Between April 1822 and June 1825 the family received weekly relief of two shillings, later increased to three shillings.[3] They were also helped with grants of coal[4] and of clothes for the children.[5] However, these allowances stopped when Clarke agreed to stay with Mr Farncomb and turned down a job which would have relieved Winchelsea of much of this expense* (**142**). *By 1826, following the removal of his wife and children to Winchelsea* (**143**) *Thomas was out of work and was admitted to the Winchelsea workhouse.[6] Whatever home he acquired in November of that year was furnished from the workhouse* (**144**). *He received a weekly allowance of 4s 6d between March 1831 and March 1835 when it was reduced to 2s.[7] Of Thomas and Mary's children* (**143**), *Zebulon is referred to in a bill of Edwin Nathaniel Dawes as a prisoner at Lewes quarter sessions accused of misdemeanour, apparently at the age of only 13.[8] He was charged, with William and Charles Barden of Icklesham, with riotous assembly and disturbance of the peace and assaulting Richard Goble. They pleaded guilty. Zebulon was sentenced to three months hard labour at Lewes House of Correction and the Bardens to one month each.[9] Harriett was admitted to Brede workhouse in September 1838, had a child there in December and both left in February 1839.[10] Sarah and her infant son, William Henry, appear on the indoor relief list of Rye workhouse in 1841.[11]*

140 11 Feb 1817 *Removal order made by G Webster and E J Curteis, justices of the peace for the county of Sussex, to the churchwardens and overseers of the poor of the parish of Icklesham*:
Whereas complaint hath been made to us that Thomas Clarke and Mary his wife lately intruded and came into the parish of Icklesham and are actually become chargeable to the same, we upon due proof thereof and the examination of Thomas Clarke do adjudge the same to be true and we also adjudge the place of legal settlement of Thomas Clarke to be the parish of Winchelsea. These are therefore in His Majesty's name to require you on sight hereof to remove and convey [them] from out of your parish of Icklesham to the parish of Winchelsea and them deliver unto the churchwardens and overseers there, or to some or one of them, together with this our order, or a true copy thereof, who are hereby required to receive and provide for them according to law. [PAR 511/32/3/31]

141 10 Nov 1824 *Letter from H[enry] Farncomb, Icklesham to the master of Winchelsea workhouse*:
Thomas Clarke of your parish is out of fireing as he cannot purchase wood or coal for himself. I think the parish should allow him some even if he be stinted in his

pay which I understand he has weekly. If he is allowed as your other parishioners are he must not complain but the fireing should be the first object as he does not provide for himself. [PAR 511/35/1/133]

142 29 Mar 1825 *Minute of the Winchelsea select vestry*:
Resolved that Thomas Clarke's pay be discontinued in consequence of his making a fresh agreement with Mr Farncomb when a place was offered him by Mr [Samuel] Southerden to the amount of 17s or 18s a week. [PAR 511/12/2]
Note: This resolution was immediately implemented and his allowance of three shillings a week withdrawn. No payments were made to Thomas Clarke between 31 March 1825 and 30 October 1826 when he received a casual payment of 2s 6d. Fairly regular casual payments then resumed.[12]

143 25 Oct 1825 *Removal order made by P ?Hedingfield and E J Curteis, justices of the peace for the county of Sussex to the churchwardens and overseers of the poor of the parish of Icklesham*:
Whereas complaint hath been made to us that Mary Clarke, the wife of Thomas Clarke late of Icklesham, labourer, and her four children viz. Sarah aged about 8 years, Harriett aged about 6 years, James aged about 4 years and Zebulon aged about 2 years lately intruded and came into the parish of Icklesham and are actually become chargeable to the same, we upon due proof thereof and also upon the examination of Mary Clarke adjudge this to be true and also adjudge their place of last legal settlement to be Winchelsea. These are therefore to require you upon sight hereof to remove and convey them to Winchelsea and them deliver, together with this our order or a true copy thereof, to the churchwardens and overseers of the poor there who are hereby required to receive and provide for them according to law. [PAR 511/32/3/48]

144 28 Nov 1826 *Entry in the inventory book of the Winchelsea workhouse*:
List of the goods had from the house for Thomas Clarke: 3 bedsteads, 2 sackings and 20 yards of cord, 2 bed ticks [under pillowcases] 2 bolsters, 2 pairs of sheets, 2 pairs of blankets, 2 rugs, 1 box, 2 tables, 4 chairs, 1 child's chair, 1 iron pot, 1 stool, 1 pail, 1 keeler [a vessel for cooling liquids], 1 cradle, 4 brown plates, 4 spoons, 3 knives and forks, 1 tea pot, 2 cups and saucers. [AMS 2331]

1 PAR 511/31/12 f.114 2 PAR 511/31/1/13 29 Sep 1822-25 Mar 1823 3 ibid Apr 1822-Jun 1825 4 e.g. PAR 511/12/2 f.19 5 ibid f.37 6 PAR 511/12/3 10 Nov 1826 7 PAR 511/31/1/16 8 WIN 763 9 QO/EW/54 10 G 8/19/4 11 G 8/19/2 12 PAR 511/31/1/15 f.7

Joseph Cogger

145 *The subject of* (**146**) *is Joseph Cogger, buried in Winchelsea at the age of 78 six days before the letter was written.[1] It has not been possible positively to identify the sons who unsuccessfully sought help because two Joseph Coggers were married in Winchelsea, one in 1781 and the other in 1791, and both wives were called Mary.[2] The most likely to be one* *of the sons is John Cogger, baptised 9 September 1792,[3] who was in receipt of Winchelsea poor relief for many years. He and his wife were, two years after this letter, engaged by the parish to look after Thomas Bennett (62). For N Cogger's father see (337, 339)*

146 20 Apr 1827 *Letter from N Cogger, Rye to [Charles] Arnett, workhouse, Winchelsea*:
My father, Mr [Captain] Cogger, having sailed this morning for Boulogne, I beg to say his nephew applied to him a few days since to defray the funeral expenses of his late father which he declined having anything to do with as the family have already at different times been assisted by him and he has many of his own who, of course, have greater claim to his property. You will oblige us by letting the sons know this. [PAR 511/35/1/275]

1 PAR 511/1/5/1   2 PAR 511/1/1/2; PAR 511/1/1/4   3 PAR 511/1/1/4

Thomas Cogger

147 *Thomas Cogger was a pauper who had a Winchelsea settlement but lived in Rye until February 1828 when he and his family were removed to Winchelsea (150). The Winchelsea overseers responded to the request in (148) and casual payments are recorded to him beginning in February 1827 when he was 'out of work through frost' and ending in February 1832. Amounts vary between 7s and 10s.[1] From April 1829 his income was supplemented by employment on the parish highways for which he was paid two shillings a day.[2] His son, Thomas junior, then aged 11 was, in 1835, supplied with '1 pair ½ boots, [1] round frock, trousers and a pair of stockings, 1 shirt.[3] In June 1841 Thomas senior received relief from the guardians of the Rye Union. This entry reads, 'Amount of relief out of the workhouse £1 0s 3d. Cause of requiring relief – illness'.[4]*

148 21 Feb 1827 *Letter from J Vidler, Rye to [Charles] Arnett, [Winchelsea assistant overseer]*:
The bearer, Thomas Cogger, a native of your town and belonging to your parish is now out of employ on account of the frost and has been so mainly since Xmas. If you assist him for a fortnight or until the frost breaks I think he will be able to do except paying the poor rates viz 6 books in the year at 2s 3d each. He has a wife and two children. [PAR 511/35/1/259]

149 29 Mar 1827 *Letter from Joseph Mills [assistant overseer], Rye, to [Charles] Arnett, Winchelsea, [assistant overseer]*:
The rates to this parish are as under [*inter alia*]: Cogger, Thomas 6 rates from March 1826 to March 1827 at 2s 3d: 13s 6d. [PAR 511/35/1/269]

150 16 Feb 1828 *Removal order made by Nathaniel Porter and William Watson, justices of the peace for Rye, to the churchwardens and overseers of the poor of that part of the parish of Rye which lies within the Liberty of the Ancient Town of Rye, Sussex*:
Whereas complaint hath been made unto us that Thomas Cogger and Mary his

wife and their three children namely Thomas aged four years and upwards, George aged two years and upwards and Charles aged about four months lately intruded into the said part of the parish of Rye and are become chargeable there, we upon examination of the [evidence] upon oath and other circumstances do adjudge the same to be true and also adjudge the last place of legal settlement of Thomas Cogger, his wife and children to be Winchelsea, Sussex. These are therefore in His Majesty's name to require you to remove and convey them to Winchelsea and them deliver, together with this our order or a true copy thereof, to the churchwardens and overseers of the poor there who are hereby required to receive and provide for them according to law.   [PAR 511/32/3/55]
Note: On 21 February 1828 Cogger was allowed by Winchelsea a casual payment of five shillings. The entry is marked, 'Brought by order from Rye'.[5]

1 PAR 511/31/1/15 f.25; PAR 511/31/1/13; PAR 511/12/2 3 Feb 1832   2 PAR 511/40/1/4   3 PAR 511/12/2 8 Apr 1835   4 PAR 511/38/4/3   5 PAR 511/31/1/15 f.25

Sarah Cole née Keene

151 *Sarah Cole was the daughter of Thomas Sylvester Keene. Her father served Winchelsea with distinction as a town constable between 1809 and 1827 and as sergeant-at-mace between 1822 and the same date.[1] He was also Winchelsea's gaoler, during which service he complained that so many smugglers were being placed in the town prison that he deserved an increase in pay.[2] Keene died in February 1828 aged 55[3] which led to the situation described in (**152-154**). His wife had pre-deceased him.[4] The boy who is the subject of his older sister's concern and entreaties was Thomas Sylvester Keene junior who, despite the tone of his sister's entreaties on his behalf (**152**), was 16 at the time.[5] It would seem from (**152**) that William Cole had helped his wife's family before and from (**153**) that the parish overseers responded, if not very generously. It is not known whether Thomas junior eventually joined his sister and brother-in-law in the way proposed.*

152 6 May 1828 *Letter from Sarah Cole, 18 Heddon Street, Regent Street to David Laurence, Winchelsea, [assistant overseer]*:
We received your letter yesterday dated 1 May which my husband wishes me to answer as he is obliged to be from home today. Respecting my brother it was our intention from the first that he should come to town unless he would have been better provided for in the country with a trade. The poor boy has no one to look to but us to keep him from the parish. I trust we shall be able to do that if he is a good boy although it is a great undertaking for us to bring him up. Cole is willing to take him and learn him his trade after he has been with us a short time. He must be bound for seven years. The laws of the trade will not allow Cole or any other man to take a boy under and you are aware that will be attended with an expense to get him bound. We hope the gentlemen will take it into consideration and give the boy a suit of black clothes for Sundays as what he has got will only be fit for every day. We should wish him to appear decent. I know he is very bare and will want a great deal before he is able to earn anything. That we must expect. Cole will do his best

for him as he has for Betty and Henry. We will appoint for him to come on Monday the 19th of May and Cole will be at the ?Boltinton to meet him when the Rye coach comes in. I hope some friend will speak to the coachman as he was never on the outside of a coach in his life. May I further trouble you to speak about my brother bringing a picture belonging to me, the likeness of my grandmother as it will be a good opportunity for it to come safe. Every letter we have written in the country to Mr [George] Hill and [Charles] Arnett we have warned about my brother but [we] get no answer from anyone. I am quite aware my aunt can't keep him. We shall expect my brother the day I have named if the gentlemen will do the little I have asked for him. If not we shall be glad of [an] answer as we live some distance from the coach office.   [PAR 511/35/1/312]

Note: Betty [Elizabeth] and Henry were Thomas Sylvester Keene junior's older sister and brother.[6]

153 16 May 1828 *Minute of the Winchelsea select vestry*:
Resolved that Thomas Keene be offered £2 to pay his expenses to London and find him in necessary clothing provided his brother-in-law William Cole should agree to take charge of and maintain him in future.   [PAR 511/12/3]

154 18 May 1828 *Letter from Sarah Cole, [18 Heddon Street, Regent Street] to David Laurence, Winchelsea, [assistant overseer]*:
We received your letter today. My husband desires me to say he shall decline taking my brother unless the parish will give him a new suit of black as we are certain he cannot have any new that we won't see him put on of a Sunday here. The father's clothes all belong to my brother John and what Tom has got I know is very little worth bringing to town. He will want a great many other things as well as what we have asked for. He will indeed be an expense directly he comes and Cole thinks it's as little as the parish can do for him as he will entirely be off their hands after he is bound which he must be and that will cost us £3 or £4. As to his part of the furniture [it] is not much to be kept in remembrance of his poor father. I should think the gentlemen won't take that. If the parish consent to give my brother the clothes we have asked for and pay his fare to town, we will meet him any time they please to name but if not Cole will decline it altogether. He can have an apprentice if he wants one at any time with £20 or £30 a year [but] out of respect to my father he has offered to take my brother and do the boy good.   [PAR 511/35/1/314]

1 WIN 61AA; WIN 61B   2 WIN 61AA 8 Apr 1822   3 PAR 511/1/5/1 17 Feb 1828   4 ibid 22 Jun 1816   5 PAR 511/1/1/4   6 ibid

William Coleman

155 *Following his removal with his family from Udimore to Winchelsea* (**156**), *William Coleman was supported by the Winchelsea overseers with grants of clothes and coal rather than cash.[1] It would seem that Samuel Southerden's threat to end Coleman's employment* (**157**) *was carried out for entries showing payments to him when living at Camber (O.H. for*

Old Harbour) end on 12 May 1825.² The Colemans returned to Udimore where they were regularly supported by Winchelsea.³ In 1825 the family listing read, 'William Coleman, Udimore, wife and three children 6, 4 [and] 2'.⁴ The family's cash payments were often for unusual amounts, not found elsewhere in the Winchelsea poor law records, for example 1s 7¾d per week.⁵ In 1827 the Winchelsea overseers reimbursed Udimore 'for burying William Coleman's child'.⁶ This was Charlotte aged 6 months who was buried at Udimore on 12 November 1827.⁷ In 1829 William Coleman fell fatally ill and Winchelsea paid a Mrs Edmunds five shillings to nurse him.⁸ He was buried at Udimore on 17 July 1829 aged 35.⁹ On 23 Jul 1829 the select vestry resolved that, 'Mrs [Elizabeth] Coleman, the widow of William Coleman, be allowed six shillings a week with her four children'.¹⁰ This continued until 14 Jan 1835 when it was decided 'that Mrs Coleman's pay be taken off'.¹¹ No reason for this is given in the vestry minute.

156 27 Feb 1821 *Removal order made by Richard Stileman and John Bishop, justices of the peace for the county of Sussex to the churchwardens and overseers of the poor of the parish of Udimore, Sussex:*
Whereas complaint hath been made to us that William Coleman, his wife Elizabeth and child Ann aged about 2 years lately intruded and came into the parish of Udimore and are actually become chargeable to the same, we upon due proof thereof as well upon the examination of William Coleman do adjudge the same to be true and we do also adjudge [their] place of last legal settlement to be Winchelsea. These are therefore in His Majesty's name to require you on sight hereof to convey William Coleman, his wife and child, out of your parish of Udimore to Winchelsea and them deliver, together with this order or a true copy thereof, unto the churchwardens and overseers of the poor there who are hereby required to receive and provide for them according to law. [PAR 511/32/3/36]

157 19 Jun 1824 *Letter from S[amuel] Southerden, Camber to the overseers of Winchelsea:*
William Coleman owes me about £4 4s 0d with rent included. He gets further in my debt every week. I do not mean to trust him with any more goods and his rent must be paid at Michaelmas next or I shall not want him any longer. [PAR 511/35/1/90]

1 PAR 511/12/2 21 Mar 1822-20 Nov 1823 2 PAR 511/31/1/14 f.3 3 PAR 511/31/1/13 1824-1829
4 PAR 511/31/1/15 f.8 5 PAR 511/31/1/13 Dec 1826-Nov 1827 6 ibid QE 16 Nov 1827 7 PAR
497/1/5/1 8 PAR 511/31/1/13 QE 25 Sep 1829 9 PAR 497/1/5/1 10 PAR 511/12/3 11 PAR
511/12/2

James Crowhurst

158 *James Crowhurst qualified as having a Winchelsea settlement through his time as servant in the town* (**159**). *The Winchelsea overseers had commenced payments in his support on 25 October 1799¹ and this continued, on an occasional casual basis, until February 1803.² Apart from one payment of £1 10s 0d in 1819/20³ he made no demands on the parish until he fell ill in 1827* (**160**) *when he received the sum of £1.⁴ Casual payments*

continued until 12 March 1830 when the select vestry resolved 'that James Crowhurst be allowed three shillings a week while sick'.[5] This weekly payment continued beyond the date of (**161**) *until as late as March 1835, only then being reduced to two shillings.[6] In 1836 he was listed among Winchelsea's 'partially infirm poor'.[7] In 1841 he was allowed £2 8s 11 5/8d (sic) by the guardians of the Rye Union who recorded the cause of requiring relief as 'age'.[8] The Winchelsea records contain no details about James Crowhurst's family but he is occasionally referred to as James Crowhurst senior. It must therefore be his son, James Crowhurst junior who was buried in Winchelsea aged 82 in 1870.[9]*

159 14 Jan 1800 *Settlement examination, taken before Thomas Marten and Richard Lamb, justices of the peace for Winchelsea of James Crowhurst:*
who upon his oath saith that he was born at Wartling, Sussex as he hath frequently heard and verily believes, that about sixteen or seventeen years ago he, being single and unmarried, hired himself to Thomas Parker, then of Winchelsea, innkeeper, to serve him as servant from Lady Day till the Lady Day following at the wages of six guineas or thereabouts; that he only performed such year's service in Winchelsea and received his full wages for the same and he continued two or three 3 months longer in the service of Thomas Parker in Winchelsea; that about thirteen years ago he was legally married at Rye to Judith Guy, singlewoman, by whom he has six children all resident in Rye and he, on his oath, saith he hath not to his knowledge done any act to gain a subsequent settlement; that ever since the 6th day of June 1797 he has been rated and [has] paid the parochial rate of and for the town of Rye. [*signature of*] James Crowhurst. [PAR 511/32/4/133]
Notes: 1. James Crowhurst, 'son of Ann', was baptised at Wartling on 17 April 1763.[10]
2. James Crowhurst and Judith Guy were married at St Mary's, Rye on 15 October 1786. Both are described as 'of this parish' and both signed the register with a cross as their mark.[11]

160 2 Mar 1827 *Letter from ?T H Wilson, surgeon, Rye, to the overseers of Winchelsea:*
James Crowhurst of this town is very unwell and unable to work – he requires good nourishment such as mutton broth etc etc [PAR 511 35/1/261]

161 31 Jan 1831 *Letter from James Crowhurst, Rye to [David] Laurence, Winchelsea, [assistant] overseer:*
Having been informed by Mr [William] Chatterton you wished to know how I was getting on I beg to say that although my hand is well I have lost the use of two fingers and I am in such a state with my former complaint that I am quite disabled from doing any work. This Mr Moore and Mr Jones [have] seen last Friday. I can assure you [that] was it not for my children assisting me I could not live.
[PAR 511/35/1/357]

1 AMS 2329 2 ibid 3 PAR 511/31/1/11 25 Sep 1819-15 Mar 1820 4 PAR 511/31/1/13 QE 25 Mar 1827 5 PAR 511/12/3 6 PAR 511/12/2; PAR 511/31/1/16 7 PAR 511/37/7/29 8 PAR 511/38/4/3 9 PAR 511/1/5/1 10 PAR 503/1/1/2 11 PAR 467/1/1/7

William Cutbeard

162 *Beyond the information included in* (**163-164**) *the Winchelsea records reveal only that, on 17 November 1823, a casual payment of five shillings was made to 'William Cutbeard, coachman, Crown Street, St Giles's.[1]*

163 1 Nov 1823 *Letter from W[illiam] Denne, London to [the overseers, Winchelsea]*:
A man by the name of Cutbeard lived in our service as coachman some years ago – he has lately had a bad accident and is in consequence thrown out of employ at present and was obliged to apply to the parish of St Giles for relief. As he belongs to Winchelsea (from service with my father) St Giles parish intend to put Winchelsea parish to the expense of passing him there. But the man wishes Winchelsea parish to be informed that he will be willing to save them this expense as he knows he shall be able to support his family again as soon as he gets well enough to work which will be in about a fortnight or three weeks. He wishes therefore to know whether the parish of Winchelsea will assist him for that time with a trifle. Otherwise he must submit to be sent home to Winchelsea as he has not a shilling at present to support himself and family.   [PAR 511/35/1/35]
Note: William Cutbush [sic], servant to Richard Denne, was included in an 1813 list of those liable for militia service.[2]

164 20 Nov 1823 *Copy of W[illiam] Cutbeard's affidavit sworn before Thomas Conant at [the] Public Office Gr[eater] Marlborough [Street]*:
This deponent maketh oath and saith that he was born in the parish of New Romney and is the legitimate son of William and Mary Cutbeard who he has always been informed and believes were legally settled in the above parish and that [he] has done no act since that period to gain a settlement either at Winchelsea or any other parish having at the time he lived as a hired servant at Winchelsea a child of seven years old, unemancipated at the time of the said hiring. [*signature of*] W Cutbeard.   [PAR 511/32/4/196]

1 PAR 511/31/1/12 f.99   2 WIN 1732

John Eagles

165 *The following documents recount in considerable detail John Eagles' decline from the time he was an elected Winchelsea overseer trusted with the care of the town's paupers* (**166, 170**) *to his execution at Newgate* (**189**). *Eagles was first appointed as an overseer on 14 April 1814[1] and, despite his legal involvement with the magistrates because of the birth of his illegitimate child* (**167-168**), *was reappointed as late as 1 April 1819.[2] He married his first wife, the widow Elizabeth Jenkins at Winchelsea on 15 September 1812.[3] Jane Jenkins, the mother of his child* (**167-168**) *was one of the witnesses at the wedding and is therefore presumed to be a relation, probably his sister-in-law. By the time of the birth of John, her son by Eagles, Jane Jenkins already had an illegitimate daughter by John*

Aylmer. That child, Harriett, was born at Burwash.[4] Eagles was a Winchelsea butcher who regularly submitted bills to the parish for the supply of meat for the workhouse.[5] His house and shop had an annual rateable value of £8 which suggests a substantial property and he also paid, as tenant, poor rate on the £3 rateable value of the churchyard which he used for grazing.[6] Joash Jones who was accused of attacking Eagles (171-172) was another Winchelsea butcher who also regularly supplied the parish and was, after Eagles left the town, to take over the tenancy of the churchyard.[7] Following his three months' sentence of imprisonment in the Winchelsea gaol for defaulting on the payments for Jane Jenkins' child (180) Eagles was released a month early on 17 October 1822[8] and later that month their boy, John Jenkins, was admitted to the workhouse.[9] After Eagles' execution for theft in May 1827, (see note (189)), his second wife, Frances, was permitted by the Winchelsea overseers to return to Milton, near Sittingbourne in Kent[10] and, while living there, she was paid three shillings a week in poor relief until October 1835.[11] By 1836 she was back in Winchelsea and is listed as Widow Eagles among Winchelsea's able-bodied poor.[12] The 1841 census shows that John Jenkins aged 24 was following his late father's trade as a butcher and was living in Mill Road with his mother, then aged 55, his half-sister, Harriett Aylmer aged 30 and Henry Aylmer aged 7, presumably Harriett's son for on 9 April 1832 she had been removed from Winchelsea to Burwash as 'singlewoman, pregnant'.[13]

Note: The only evidence of John Eagles' age available in the Winchelsea records is that a militia return of 1809, prepared by the town constables, shows him as being aged 27 and exempt from military service as 'a cripple'.[14] There is no explanation of the term cripple or other evidence of it. It is not possible to reconcile his being 27 in 1809 with his recorded age of 35 at the time of his execution in May 1827.[15] All the available evidence suggests that the former is correct in which case he would have been 45 and not 35 at the time of his death.

166 6 Feb 1815 *Minute of the Winchelsea parish vestry*:
At [this] vestry it is agreed that Mr J[ohn] Eagles do agree to take William Selden from Lady Day 1815 to Lady Day 1816 to keep and clothe at 3s per week, the parish to find him in proper clothing for his service and that Mr J Eagles to have him at the end of service as well clothed as he found him.   [PAR 511/12/1 f.193]

167 16 Aug 1815 *Voluntary examination taken on oath before George Stace, justice of the peace for Winchelsea, of Jane Jenkins of Winchelsea, singlewoman*:
who saith that on the 22nd day of July now last past, at the house of Mary Jenkins in Winchelsea, she was delivered of a male bastard child and that the child is likely to become chargeable to the parish of St Thomas the Apostle, Winchelsea and that John Eagles of Winchelsea, butcher, did get her with child of the said bastard child. [*signature of*] Jane Jenkins.   [PAR 511/34/1/44]

168 5 Sep 1815 *Bastardy order made by George Stace the elder and Charles Terry, justices of the peace for Winchelsea, concerning the child of Jane Jenkins*:
Whereas it hath been duly made to appear unto us as well upon the complaint of the churchwardens and overseers of the poor of Winchelsea as upon oath of Jane Jenkins, singlewoman, that she was delivered of a male bastard child at the house of Mary Jenkins in Winchelsea on the 22nd day of July now last past and that the

child is now chargeable to Winchelsea and likely so to continue; and further that John Eagles of Winchelsea, butcher, did beget the child on the body of her, Jane Jenkins; and whereas John Eagles hath not shown any sufficient cause why he shall not be the reputed father of the child, we therefore, upon examination of the cause and circumstances of the [evidence] as well upon the oath if Jane Jenkins as otherwise do hereby adjudge him to be the reputed father of the child; and thereupon we do order as well for the better relief of the parish of St Thomas the Apostle, Winchelsea as for the sustentation and relief of the child that John Eagles shall, and do forthwith, upon notice of this our order pay or cause to be paid to the churchwardens and overseers of the poor of the parish or to some one of them the sum of four pounds eleven shillings for and towards the lying-in of Jane Jenkins and the maintenance of the child to the time of the making of this our order; and we do hereby further order that John Eagles shall likewise pay the sum of three shillings and sixpence weekly and every week from this present time for and towards the keeping, sustentation and maintenance of the child for and during so long time as the child shall be chargeable to Winchelsea; and we do further order that Jane Jenkins shall also [similarly] pay the sum of one shilling weekly for so long as the child shall be chargeable to Winchelsea in case she shall not nurse and take care of the child herself.

[*Endorsed*] 5 Sep 1815 Delivered a copy of this order to the within named John Eagles. [*signed*] David Laurence [*overseer*]. [PAR 511/34/4/4]

169 18 Dec 1815 *Minute of the Winchelsea parish vestry*:
It is agreed that Mr John Eagles shall not be paid the 3s per week for William Selden in consequence of his not having fulfilled his agreement.
[PAR 511/12/1 f.204]

170 24 Feb 1820 *Minute of the Winchelsea parish vestry*:
It is agreed for Mr John Eagles to employ Stephen Whiteman from Lady Day 1820 to Lady Day 1821 at 3s per week. [PAR 511/12/1 f.237]

171 17 Oct 1820 *Warrant issued by George Stace, deputy mayor and justice of the peace for Winchelsea, to the constables of Winchelsea*:
Forasmuch as John Eagles of Winchelsea, butcher, hath this day made information and complaint upon oath before me that Joash Jones of Winchelsea, butcher, did on Monday the ninth day of this instant, October, shick [insult] and assault John Eagles; these are therefore to command you in His Majesty's name forthwith to apprehend and bring before me or some other justice of the peace for Winchelsea the body of Joash Jones to answer unto the said complaint and to be further dealt withal according to law. Hereof fail you not. [PAR 511/29/1]
Note: The cause of the dispute between Eagles and Jones is not known.

172 17 Oct 1820 *Recognisance taken and acknowledged before George Stace, justice of the peace for Winchelsea*:

[Wherein the magistrate states that] Joash Jones of Winchelsea, butcher, Edward Jeakens of Winchelsea, tanner and Joseph Hoad of Winchelsea, shopkeeper, personally came before me and acknowledged themselves to be indebted to our sovereign lord the king, Joash Jones in the sum of fifty pounds, Edward Jeakens in the sum of £25 and Joseph Hoad in the sum of £25 of lawful money of Great Britain to be levied on their respective goods and chattels, lands and tenements for the use of our lord the king, his heirs and successors, if Joash Jones shall make default in the condition hereunder written.

The condition of this recognisance is that if the above bounden Joash Jones do and shall personally appear at the next general quarter sessions of the peace to be holden in and for the Ancient Town of Winchelsea to answer for assaulting, beating and ill-treating John Eagles of Winchelsea, butcher, and in the same time keep the peace and be of good behaviour towards our lord the king and all his liege people and especially towards John Eagles then this recognisance to be void otherwise of force.   [WIN 253]

173 5 Apr 1821 *Minute of the Winchelsea select vestry*:

Resolved that Mr [George] Harrod agrees to take Stephen Whiteman from Mr Eagles, the parish to allow him one shilling a week and clothe him.

[PAR 511/12/2 f.11]

174 12 Aug 1822 *Order made by Henry Powell, justice of the peace for Winchelsea, to all and every of the constables of Winchelsea*:

Whereas John Woods, one of the overseers of the poor of Winchelsea, hath this day made information and complaint upon oath before me that John Eagles, butcher, of Winchelsea hath been duly adjudged and declared to be the reputed father of a male bastard child born of the body of Jane Jenkins of Winchelsea, singlewoman, and hath neglected or refused to pay or cause to be paid the sum of £12 12s 0d due and owing from him to the overseers of the poor of Winchelsea for the maintenance of the child; and whereas John Woods, as overseer, hath applied to me for my summons against John Eagles to show cause why he should not pay the said sum of money or be committed in default thereof; these are therefore to command you in His Majesty's name forthwith to summon John Eagles to appear before me or such other of His Majesty's justices of the peace for Winchelsea as shall be present at the Guildhall, Winchelsea on Tuesday the 20th day of August instant at noon then and there to answer the said complaint and information of John Woods who is likewise directed to be present to make good the same. Herein fail not.

[PAR 511/34/2/33]

175 22 Aug 1822 *Letter from John Woods [overseer], Winchelsea to Henry P Butler, [Winchelsea town clerk] solicitor, Rye*:
I have found the order of filiation and will therefore thank you to send me over two summons for Mr John Eagles to appear at the Guildhall on Tuesday and I will have one served on him and keep the copy. You may as well let Mr [Henry] Powell sign the summons as he signed the other two. [WIN 2214]

176 22 Aug 1822 *Letter from John Woods [overseer], Winchelsea to [Winchelsea town clerk] Henry P Butler, solicitor, Rye*:
I have seen Mr [Henry] Powell who requests me to say he wishes you to prepare a blank warrant for you to bring with you on Tuesday as he has no doubt of its being wanted. I have sent the order of filiation which you will also return to me on Tuesday and let me have the summons tomorrow. [WIN 2213]

177 22 Aug 1822 *Letter from H P Butler [Winchelsea town clerk, solicitor], Rye to John Woods [overseer], Winchelsea*:
I am glad you have found the order of filiation against John Eagles and if you will send it over to me by tomorrow morning's post I will send you by the evening post a summons and copy for Eagles to appear on Tuesday next. [WIN 2214]

178 23 Aug 1822 *Letter from H P Butler [Winchelsea town clerk, solicitor], Rye to John Woods, grocer [overseer], Winchelsea*:
'The King against Eagles'. I have read your letter dated 22nd instant enclosing the order of filiation dated 5 Sept 1815 made on this defendant respecting the male bastard child born of the body of Jane Jenkins, singlewoman, and send you enclosed a warrant to apprehend John Eagles, the reputed father for disobeying that order of filiation and maintenance which, as I could not venture to make out a warrant against him on the 12th instant by reason that I had not the order of filiation then before me and therefore I made a summons out against him in lieu of a warrant. Any one of the constables to whom you may give this warrant may apprehend him early on Tuesday morning (which I think is the 27th instant) and bring him to the Guildhall at Winchelsea by eleven o'clock that forenoon where I shall attend with a commitment (and the other papers you speak of) ready to send him to gaol, if necessary. Pray take this warrant along to Mr [Henry] Powell for his perusal and signature and shew him this letter which will explain to him the reason I have made out a warrant against the defendant rather than another summons, and get him to sign it and deliver it to one of the constables and tell him to have Eagles at the Court Hall by a quarter before eleven o'clock next Tuesday morning and please to attend there yourself with Mr David Laurence as you will both be wanted as evidence against him. [WIN 2213]

179 24 Aug 1822 *Warrant issued to the constables of Winchelsea by Henry Powell, justice of the peace for Winchelsea*:
Whereas it hath been duly made appear unto me upon the oath of John Woods, one of the present overseers of the poor of the Ancient Town of Winchelsea, that by an order under the hands and seals of George Stace and Charles Terry, two of His Majesty's justices of the peace for Winchelsea, (one whereof at the time of making the said order was of the quorum) and both residing next unto the limits of the parish church of Winchelsea bearing date the fifth day of September which was in the year of our lord one thousand eight hundred and fifteen, John Eagles of Winchelsea, butcher, was adjudged by [those] justices, to be the reputed father of a male bastard child born of the body of Jane Jenkins, singlewoman, in the parish of St Thomas the Apostle, Winchelsea, on the twenty-second day of July, 1815 [*the document here recites in full the terms of the order against Eagles* (**168**)] and whereas John Eagles had due notice of the order, a true copy thereof in writing having been personally delivered to him by David Laurence, then one of the overseers of the poor of Winchelsea, on the fifth day of September 1815, and that no appeal had been made to the court of quarter sessions against the order and whereas upon the oath of John Woods it manifestly appears to me that the sum of twelve pounds twelve shillings now remaining justly due, owing and unpaid from John Eagles under and by notice of the order which he hath neglected and refused to pay and still doth neglect and refuse to pay although payment of twelve pounds twelve shillings hath been and is now duly demanded from him by John Woods. Now these are therefore to command you, the [Winchelsea] constables and every one of you in His Majesty's name to apprehend John Eagles and bring him before me or some other of His Majesty's justices of the peace for Winchelsea as shall be sitting at the Guildhall, Winchelsea on Tuesday next the twenty-seventh day of this instant month of August by eleven o'clock in the forenoon then and there to answer such complaint and to be further dealt with according to law. Herein fail you not at your peril.   [WIN 2216]

180 27 Aug 1822 *Appearance at the Winchelsea Petty Sessions of John Eagles before George Stace, deputy mayor and jurat and Henry Powell, jurat, justices of the peace for Winchelsea*:
[*Recites the legal history of the offence exactly as* (**168 & 179**) *above*] And the said John Eagles being now called upon by us, the justices, to show cause why the sum of twelve pounds and nineteen shillings is so due and unpaid by him, [he] doth not show to us any reasonable or sufficient cause for [the offence] and doth now neglect and refuse to pay the said sum of money or any part thereof to John Woods, one of the overseers of the poor for Winchelsea. Therefore, we, the justices, do adjudge John Eagles guilty of the offence and that for this offence he be committed, and he is accordingly by us hereby committed to the house of correction of and for the town of Winchelsea there to be kept to hard labour for the space of three months unless he shall, before the expiration of the three months pay or cause to be paid

to one of the overseers of the poor of Winchelsea the sum of twelve pounds and nineteen shillings [now] due and unpaid. And we do charge and hereby command you, the constables, and every of you, forthwith to take and convey John Eagles to the house of correction for Winchelsea and there deliver him to the keeper together with this precept. And we do hereby also command you, the keeper of the house of correction, to receive John Eagles into your custody and him there safely to keep to hard labour for the space of three months unless he shall before the expiration of the three months pay [the aforesaid sum].   [WIN 2217B]

Note: On this document the amount earlier quoted as twelve pounds twelve shillings has been deleted and twelve pounds nineteen shillings substituted without explanation.

181 2 Mar 1827 *Letter from John Eagles, Newgate [prison, London] to the overseers of Winchelsea*:

I am sorry to inform you of my unfortunate case. I am confined in Newgate under sentence of death and the expense of my trial has reduced me to go to the parish for relief and the parish I dwelt in last was St Saviour's parish, Southwark, [London]. They have relieved my wife by whom there is two children. One is two years old and the other 4 months. The parish of St Saviour's sent the officers this day and I have gained no other settlement, not living twelve months at one place since I left Winchelsea. I have paid no taxes since I left Winchelsea. My wife's brother has offered to have my wife and two children for 5s per week if you gentlemen think it proper to pay it as it [is] out of her power to do anything with a child of 4 months and in a bad state of health. Please to send answer by return of post as this parish will be forced to bring the family home [at the] beginning of the next week. If you gentlemen think it proper [to] allow that sum it will save her friend and the parish great expense. My wife's brother lives at Minster, Isle of Sheppey, Kent. Please to direct to governors of St Saviour's parish, Southwark, London.

[PAR 511/35/1/260]

182 12 Mar 1827 *Settlement examination of John Eagles, a prisoner in Newgate, touching his legal place of settlement*:

This examinant saith that he occupied a house and garden in Winchelsea for about ten years at the annual rental of twelve pounds ten shillings; that [he] quitted Winchelsea in the month of March 1823 and went to reside at Sheerness where he was hired by and served George Macket as a journeyman butcher at the weekly wages of one pound living in the house of George Macket and that he continued in such service for eleven months; that at the expiration of [that time he] quitted the service of George Macket and took a shop in Sheerness which he occupied for six weeks at the weekly rent of 4s 6d, that during that time [he] was married at Minster in the Isle of Sheppey to Frances Hobbs; that early in 1824 [he] came to London and took a furnished lodging at 5s per week in Pitt's Place in the parish of St Saviour's, Southwark which he occupied for twelve months; that he then quitted Pitt's Place and went to reside at Bear Court, Bear Lane in the parish of St. Saviour's in a furnished lodging for which he paid five shillings per week and

occupied for about five months; that [he] then went to reside in a furnished lodging at No. 5 Great Guildford Street in the parish of St Saviour's for which he paid five shillings per week and occupied it about six months; that he then quitted such lodging and took a shop at No. 4 Great Guildford Street at the rent of nineteen guineas a year which he occupied and paid rent for from the 10th of July 182[5] to the 18th of December following; that he did not pay any taxes for the shop nor were any ever demanded of him; that [he] then went to live in a furnished lodging in Keppel Street in St Saviour's Parish for which he paid three shillings per week where his wife and two children now live. [*signature of*] John Eagles. Witness: Atwood Smith.   [PAR 511/32/4/201]
Note: John Eagles' first wife, Elizabeth, died in 1822 and was buried at St Thomas's on 4 October.[16]

183 16 Mar [1827] *Letter from [John] Fisher, [solicitor of] Rye to [Charles] Arnett, [Winchelsea]:*
[I] forward [herewith] the examination of Eagles which [I] considered [it] right to procure and therefore instructed a Mr [Atwood] Smith of London, an attorney versed in parish matters, to take it. It will be seen the settlement is in Winchelsea but the family had better not be received without an order.
[*Endorsed*] Mr Horton, Milton, pays to Mrs Eagles 3s per week to be remitted quarterly.   [PAR 511/35/1/6]

184 23 Mar 1827 *Removal order made by [illegible] and John Davies, justices of the peace for the county of Surrey to the churchwardens and overseers of the poor of the parish of St Saviour, Southwark:*
Whereas complaint hath been made to us that Frances Eagles with her two children namely Frances aged two years and Jane aged five months lately intruded and came into the parish of St Saviour, Southwark and are become chargeable to the same, we upon examination of the [evidence] upon oath and other circumstances do adjudge the same to be true and also adjudge the place of last legal settlement of Frances Eagles and her children to be Winchelsea, Sussex. These are therefore in His Majesty's name to require you on sight hereof to remove and convey them to Winchelsea and them deliver, together with this our order or a true copy thereof, to the churchwardens and overseers there who are hereby required to receive and provide for them according to law.   [PAR 511/32/3/53]

185 26 Mar 1827 *Letter from John Eagles, Newgate [prison, London] to the overseers of Winchelsea:*
I have taken the liberty of writing to you to inform you that there has been a gentleman sent by someone from Mr [Weeden] Dawes of Rye concerning of my parish and I informed him where I had resided since I left Winchelsea. He said I belonged to Winchelsea parish in his opinion. My wife saw the parish officer[s] of St Saviour's last night. They informed her that I had better write to you to know if [you] would allow her the weekly pay and for her to stop in town or for them to

send her home [at the] beginning of next week. I should be very much obliged to you if you would let her receive her pay in London. If she is forced to come home I shall have no one to wash and do for me as I have no friends in London to do it. I expect that it will be a month before I shall know if I die or be transported for life. If the latter I shall hope with the assistance of friends to take my wife and family with me. I should be very much obliged to you to send answer by return of post. Direct it, if you please, to J Eagles, Newgate. I make no doubt that the governor of St Saviour's parish would pay the sum of 5s a week to my wife by your order. I should be very much obliged to you to send me answer by return of post as my money is entirely gone and [I] am drove very short and my friends have been at a very great expense.   [PAR 511/35/1/267]

186 29 Mar 1827 *Minute of the Winchelsea public vestry*:
Resolved that the wife of John Eagles be allowed £3 to go to her husband in his present peculiar circumstances.   [PAR 511/12/2]

187 18 Apr 1827 *Letter from John Eagles, Newgate cells, [London] to [Charles] Arnett, Winchelsea, parish officer*:
This is to acquaint you my wife is come to London and is very ill and I think is likely to remain so. She wished me to write to you as she said she was to write to you about this time for you to let me know concerning where she and the children belong. I am afraid my wife is going in a decline by what the doctor says and thinks it will be better for her to go to Mr Gooding's, her brother's, at Sheerness [Kent] if you will allow her 6s per week for herself and two children. I am afraid she will never be able to do anything [to] help herself without a great alteration in her. The parish officer at Sheerness will most likely pay her the money by your order as I think the sooner she goes there the better as her sister will do what lies in her power for her as there is no one belonging to me that can do for her. Please to send me answer by return of post. Direct to me at Newgate Gaol, London. I hope you answer by return of post as I expect the report every hour so that I shall know my fate. If, please God, my life is spared I think I have hopes that I should go to Botany Bay and my wife's health gets better, with my friends' help I will get her over to me as that is a good country and healthy. I hope you will do the best you can for my wife and children. I hope you will send answer by return of post.
                                          [PAR 511/35/1/274]

188 22 May 1827 *Letter from W S Tonge, Sittingbourne, [Kent] to [Charles] Arnett, Winchelsea, [assistant overseer]*:
Feeling great interest for the family of poor [John] Eagles, now under sentence of death at Newgate, who I understand have been removed from St Saviour's [Southwark, Surrey] to the parish to which you belong, induces me to write to you on their distress[ed] situation for independent of the constant expectation of hearing that her husband is left for execution she has poverty to contend with and

was it not for her friends (who cannot do it any longer), she must have starved. This I hope will be sufficient to induce you to send her some relief but I could urge you on the score of the poor man whose mind is racked with the idea of leaving his beloved wife and children unprovided for. Could he hear you have made an arrangement with his wife it would calm his mind in a great degree and I hope enable him to strive more and more to make his peace with his God. Hoping I shall stand excused in interfering by the motive. [PAR 511/35/1/281]

189 29 May 1827 *Copy letter from C[harles] Arnett, Winchelsea, assistant overseer, to W S Tonge, Sittingbourne, [Kent]*:
I received yours of the 22nd instant but knowing the result of the recorders' report as it affected John Eagles refrained from answering until the sentence was put into execution. Indeed, I was ordered by the [select] vestry not to answer any letter that was asking anything like weekly pay, for it was expressly understood that £3 given her (**186**) was for her (Mrs Eagles) to go to her husband directly agreeable to their joint wish and to pay her expenses home [and] that nothing further could be done until she returned here. The parish still hold that opinion and as they want such a woman in the [poor]house it would be less expensive to keep her and [her] children there than it would to allow the 6s a week as cash asked – or indeed any sum. Your communicating the above to Mrs Eagles will oblige. [PAR 511/35/1/283]
Note: It was a one pound note which cost Eagles his life. After the various jobs described in (**182**) he worked for the Post Office at their sorting office in the parish of St. Mary Woolnoth in London. On 1 May 1826 three letters addressed to A.W. Roberts Esq, M.P. passed through that office for delivery; two contained money, only one of them was delivered. The bulk of the money was in promissory notes but the amount was made up with cash. That afternoon Eagles paid a debt of two shillings and sevenpence halfpenny and purchased twopence worth of gin from William Evans, landlord of the Queen's Arms, Great Guildford Street, Southwark. Evans wrote Eagles' name on the back of the note he paid with before passing it to the brewery's clerk. The note's number had been recorded before despatch to Mr. Roberts. The detailed account of the evidence given at Eagles' Old Bailey trial before Mr Justice Gaselee is followed by the stark legend 'GUILTY–DEATH'.[17] This was a time when the number of capital crimes was being reduced and many death sentences were being commuted to life imprisonment or transportation. That Eagles hanged is likely to have been because the judge, jury and authorities thought he had stolen a great deal more than the note which actually incriminated him.

190 24 Jun 1827 *Letter from Joseph Gooding, Halfway House, Minster in Sheppey, [Kent] to [Charles] Arnett, poorhouse, Winchelsea*:
I have taken the liberty of writing respecting the case of Mrs Eagles, to know what is to become of her. You told me when at my house that you would do all that [lay] in your power for her. I can assure you that she is very bad off and has not a shilling in the world to help herself with and I hope that the overseers will be so kind as to allow her a trifle for the two children a week and if they do not think proper so to do the two babes must come home to the house and [the] woman must go into service. I think it a very hard case for the parish not to allow her the small sum of 4s per week for the two children for if they have to come home it will be more expense to

you. If I had it in my power she should not be a trouble to you or anyone else but I have nothing only what I work hard for. I hope, sir, that you will be so kind as to answer this letter and by so doing you will oblige.   [PAR 511/35/1/284]

191 13 Aug 1827 *Removal order made by John ?Good and G Goschen, justices of the peace for the county of Kent to the churchwardens and overseers of the parish of Milton near Sittingbourne, Kent*:

Whereas complaint hath been made unto us that Frances Eagles, widow, and her two children, Frances aged two years and a quarter and Jane aged eleven months, lately intruded into the parish of Milton not having gained a legal settlement there nor produced any certificate owning them to be settled elsewhere and are actually become chargeable to the same, we upon examination of the [evidence] upon oath and other circumstances do adjudge the same to be true. We also adjudge that the place of last legal settlement of Frances Eagles and her children was Winchelsea, Sussex and also that no sufficient security has been given to discharge the parish of Milton. These are therefore in His Majesty's name to require you on sight hereof to remove and convey them to Winchelsea and them deliver, together with this our order or a true copy thereof, to the churchwardens and overseers of the poor there who are hereby required to receive and provide for them according to law. [*Endorsed*] Received 16 August 1827 the within-named paupers. C. Arnett

[PAR 511/32/3/54]

1 PAR 511/12/1 f.188   2 ibid f.228   3 PAR 511/1/1/4; PAR 511/1/1/6   4 AMS 2330 f.119   5 e.g. PAR 511/31/1/11 E1813-E1814; PAR 511/31/1/120   6 PAR 511/31/1/11 30 Jul 1815 etc   7 PAR 511/31/1/13 11 Mar 1824   8 PAR 511/12/2 f.33   9 ibid   10 PAR 511/12/3 24 Aug 1827   11 PAR 511/31/1/15 f.28; PAR 511/31/1/13; PAR 511/31/1/16   12 PAR 511/37/7/29   13 PAR 511/32/2/91   14 WIN 2359/3/1   15 Old Bailey Sessions Papers 1826-1827 p.207   16 PAR 511//1/5/1   17 Old Bailey Sessions Papers 1826-1827 pp.205-207

Mercy Eastman

192 *This case illustrates that even loyal service as mistress of the workhouse did not establish a settlement in Winchelsea or the right to poor law relief in old age. Mercy Eastman was paid her agreed seven guineas for the year to Lady Day 1810[1]* (**193**). *This was later reduced to six guineas.[2] No record has been found of either the £4 per annum stated in her settlement examination* (**194**) *or later wage payments. She first received casual payments of poor relief in the months before she was removed to Hastings.[3] She was buried in Winchelsea on 8 April 1827 when her age was given in the register as 72.[4]*

193 20 Aug 1809 *Minute of an adjourned meeting of the Winchelsea parish vestry*:
An agreement was entered into between Mrs [Mercy] Eastman and this parish that she should superintend the poorhouse from this time to Lady Day 1810 for the sum of seven guineas giving a month's notice if intending to quit it at that period.

[PAR 511/12/1 f.165]

194 8 Apr 1825 *Settlement examination taken before Henry Powell and John Tilden, justices of the peace for Winchelsea, of Mercy Eastman:*
who upon her oath saith that [I] was born in the parish of All Saints in the town and port of Hastings; my father and mother were legally settled at Battle, Sussex. The last place I lived as a yearly hired servant was with Miss Sally Crouch in the parish of St Clement in Hastings. I lived with her better than three years at one living at the wages of three pounds. I was about thirty years of age at that time. I then went home and lived with my father and mother in the parish of All Saints and there followed my business as a mantua [a loose gown] maker for about seven years. I was married to William Eastman, a hairdresser residing in the parish of St Clement, Hastings about thirty years ago at the church of [that] parish by whom I had one son named William [now] aged about thirty years or upwards and who I believe is now residing in Peru who has been absent from me nearly seven years. My husband lived at Sheerness for three years and there rented a room at three shillings and sixpence per week. I never knew anything of my husband's settlement nor did I ever hear him say where he belonged further [than] that he was apprentice in London. About twenty-seven or twenty-eight years ago he left me and went to London where he wished me to follow which I declined. I had two letters from him and in less than six months after he left I heard he was dead and have never heard anything of him since. I then left Sheerness and came to Winchelsea and brought my son William, between four and five years old, with me and worked at my business between four and five years. I was then put in as mistress of the workhouse at Winchelsea with a salary of £4 per annum including my son's board and lodging as well as my own. I remained a mistress of the workhouse upwards of seven years; my son remained 4 years and upwards with me in the workhouse and when he left my wages were advanced to twelve guineas per annum. My son was never bound apprentice nor did he ever do any act to gain a legal settlement to the best of my knowledge. After I left the workhouse I carried on my business in Winchelsea and have never done any act to gain a legal settlement and am now actually chargeable to the parish of St Thomas the Apostle, Winchelsea. [*signature of*] Mercy Eastman. [AMS 2330 ff.45-46]
Notes: 1. William Eastman 'of this parish, bachelor', married Mercy Crouch 'of the parish of All Saints, widow' at St Clement's Church, Hastings on 3 December 1792.[5] As her surname name is the same of that of her former employer (see above), it may be that she had been working for a relation. There is nothing in her settlement examination about her being already a widow when she entered into this marriage.
2. On the same date, 8 April 1825, Henry Pearch Butler, solicitor, town clerk of Winchelsea, charged the parish six shillings and eightpence for taking Mercy Eastman's settlement examination and seven shillings for preparing her removal order.[6]

195 26 Apr 1827 *Order made at the general quarter sessions of the peace at Lewes:*
It is ordered by this court that the order or warrant of Henry Powell and John Tilden, two of His Majesty's justices of the peace for [Winchelsea], for the removal of Mercy Eastman aged seventy years and upwards from the parish of St Thomas the

Apostle, Winchelsea to the parish of St Clement in the town and port of Hastings, is by this court recorded and confirmed, the inhabitants of St Clement's, Hastings not appealing from the said order at the present sessions and proof being made upon oath of the due service of the order.   [PAR 511/35/3/17]

Note*s*: 1. The overseers of St Clement's, Hastings had given notice of their intention to appeal against Winchelsea's removal order at the Lewes Easter Sessions on 14 April 1825. On that occasion consideration was referred to 'the next general quarter sessions'.[7]
2. The date on this document is quite clear. The reason that the matter proceeded in court on that date is, however, unclear because Mercy Eastman had died and was buried at St Thomas's, Winchelsea eighteen days previously – see (**192**).

1 AMS 2329 E1809-E1810   2 ibid Jul 1810-Sep 1810   3 PAR 511/31/1/13 QE 25 Jun 1825   4 PAR 511/1/5/15   5 PAR 367/1/1/8   6 PAR 511/31/2/149   7 QO/EW/47

Ann Easton

196 *Ann Easton was baptised in Winchelsea on 9 October 1805.[1] She was the illegitimate daughter of Ann Tapp née Easton and James Brasselay, described as footman to George Shifnor Esq[2] and later as a labourer of Hamsey in Sussex.[3] Despite two settlement examinations (**197**) and a request for a legal opinion (**197**) Winchelsea was unable to sustain any objection to the settlement obtained as a result of Ann Easton's birth in the town. The parish authorities were, however, able to establish that John White was Ann's child's father (**200-201**). Regular payments of two shillings a week were made to Ann Easton between March and December 1828[4] but no evidence has been found that this money was coming from John White. Ann and John's daughter, Mary Jane, was baptised in Winchelsea on 24 February 1828.[5]*

197 22 Nov 1827 *Settlement examinations of Ann Tapp and Ann Easton taken on oath before John Cossum and D Gill, justices of the peace for the town and port of Hastings*:
First Ann Tapp for herself saith that on the 20th day of September 1805 she was delivered of Ann Easton (who is a bastard and was born out of lawful wedlock) in the parish of St Thomas the Apostle, Winchelsea where this examinant belonged. That she, Ann Easton, has never done any act whereby to gain a settlement to the best of this examinant's belief and that she is now living in the parish of the Holy Trinity, Hastings.
[*mark of*] Ann Tapp.
And secondly Ann Easton for herself saith that when she was about 15 years of age she hired herself to Mrs Piddlesden of New Romney as nursemaid at the wages of 1s per week under which agreement she served for six months and then agreed for another six months at the wages of £2 which time she also served and received her wages. That she then agreed with her mistress to serve for another six months at the wages of £2 10s which time she also served and received her wages and then left. That since that time she has lived in several families but never stopped in any of them more than ten months nor has she ever since done any act to gain a

settlement. That she is now with child which child is likely to be born a bastard and to be chargeable to the parish of Holy Trinity, Hastings, otherwise dissolved Priory. [*On the reverse of this document*] 21 Dec 1827 *Settlement examination of Ann Easton taken on oath before John Tilden and Henry Powell, justices of the peace for Winchelsea:*

[In which she recites the details of the above examination with the following amendments] [1]After the first agreement to work for Mrs Piddlesden as a nursemaid at one shilling per week it was with the understanding that Mrs Piddlesden or herself was to give one month's notice to leave the service. [2] After service with Mrs Piddlesden she then went and lived in the service of Dr Wellesley at the wages of £10 and lived there about 10 months and that she has not done any act or deed whereby to gain a settlement since she left Dr Wellesley's service.

[*Appended to these examinations*] [No date] *Legal opinion sought by Messrs Dawes, Lardner, Fisher and Pomfret, solicitors, Rye, Sussex:*

For the satisfaction of the parish of Winchelsea the opinion of Mr [George Clough] Marshall is requested whether or not Winchelsea can with any chance of success appeal at the next Lewes sessions against an order of removal made from Hastings upon the grounds of a general hiring with Mrs Piddlesden at New Romney.

[*Opinion*] If upon appeal Winchelsea should be compelled to call the pauper as their witness then I think that they would have no chance but if they can get the benefit of her cross-examination then that they have a chance though a slight one. In fact Winchelsea must rely not on their own strength but on the weakness of their adversary. The two accounts given by the girl are directly in the teeth of each other. As to the first it is clear that no settlement was formed in New Romney. And as to the second, considered without reference to the first, I infer from the terms if not that the parties <u>actually</u> agreed for a month's notice but that the girl agreed she was to receive or give such notice before dismissal which of course would not convert the hiring at a shilling a week into an implied yearly hiring. Supposing the girl's second account to be the correct one there is, one concurs, circumstance which may afford some hope. Ann Easton agrees to serve and does so for six months certain at £2 and I suppose received her wages either during or at the end of that term. The contract is in the section <u>for a full year afterwards</u> without any new agreement and that will lead to the inference of a general hiring from the expiration of the six months before mentioned but upon this point the girl's evidence is not [?clear].   [PAR 511/35/2/8]

198 6 Dec 1827 *Letter from J[ohn] H[addock] Lardner, [Town Clerk of Winchelsea, Rye] to [the overseers of Winchelsea]:*
I will be at Winchelsea tomorrow, Friday at 11 o'clock if that hour will suit the magistrates. If I hear not to the contrary I shall take it for granted that it will.
[*Endorsed*] J H Lardner Esq about A[nn] Easton.   [PAR 511/35/1/307]

199 27 Feb 1828 *Examination taken before John Tilden and Henry Powell, justices of the peace for Winchelsea, of Ann Easton*:
who upon her oath saith that on the twenty-seventh day of January now last past in the parish of St Thomas the Apostle, Winchelsea she was delivered of a female bastard child and that the child is likely to become chargeable to Winchelsea and that John White, late servant to Robert Coningham Esq of Hanover House, Marine Parade, Brighton but now of Christchurch, Hampshire, as she verily believes, did get her with child of the said bastard child. [*signature of*] Ann Easton.

[AMS 2330 f.81]

200 27 Feb 1828 *Bastardy order made by John Tilden and Henry Powell, justices of the peace for Winchelsea*:
Whereas it hath been made duly appear unto us as well upon the complaint of the churchwardens and overseers of the poor of Winchelsea as upon oath of Ann Easton that she was delivered of a female bastard child at the house of Mary Broadfoot in Winchelsea on the 27th day of January and that the child is now chargeable to the parish of St Thomas the Apostle, Winchelsea and likely so to continue; and further that John White, late of Brighton, now of Christchurch, Hampshire, servant, did beget the child on the body of Ann Easton. We therefore, upon examination of the cause and circumstances of the [evidence] as well upon the oath of Ann Easton as otherwise, do adjudge John White to be the reputed father of the child; and thereupon we do order, as well for the better relief of the parish of St Thomas the Apostle, Winchelsea as for the sustenance and relief of the child that John White shall and do forthwith, upon notice of this our order, pay, or cause to be paid, to the churchwardens or overseers of the poor of Winchelsea or to some one of them the sum of [*blank*] for and towards the maintenance of the child to the time of the making of this our order; and we do also further order that John White shall likewise pay the sum of two shillings weekly and every week from this present time towards the keeping, sustentation and maintenance of the child for and during so long time as the child shall be chargeable to the parish; and further order that Ann Easton shall also pay the sum of one shilling weekly in case she shall not nurse or take care of the child herself. [PAR 511/34/4/28]

201 29 Feb 1828 *Order made by Henry Powell and John Tilden, justices of the peace for Winchelsea, to the constables of Winchelsea*:
Whereas Ann Easton of Winchelsea, singlewoman, hath by her examination taken in writing before us declared that on the 22nd day of Jan now last past she was, in Winchelsea, delivered of a female bastard child and that the child is likely to become chargeable to the parish of St Thomas the Apostle, Winchelsea, and hath charged John White, late servant to Robert Coningham Esq. of Hanover House, Marine Parade, Brighton, Sussex and now of the parish of Christchurch, Hampshire, with having gotten her with child of the said bastard child; and whereas Charles Arnett, assistant overseer of the poor of Winchelsea, in order to indemnify the parish in

the [evidence] hath applied to us to issue our warrant for the apprehension of John White. These are therefore to command you in His Majesty's name forthwith to apprehend and bring before us the said John White to find security to indemnify the parish or else to find sufficient surety for his appearance at the next quarter sessions of the peace to be holden for Winchelsea, then and there to abide [by] and perform such order or orders as shall be made in pursuance of the statutes in that case made and provided.   [PAR 511/34/2/34]

1 PAR 511/1/1/4 2 PAR 511/31/1/64 3 WIN 61 ff.114-114r 4 PAR 511/31/1/14; PAR 511/31/1/13
5 PAR 511/1/2/1

Samuel Easton

202 *Samuel Easton of Winchelsea had a varied career on both sides of the law. He was appointed a Winchelsea parish constable in 1825[1] carrying out duties which included making arrests, serving warrants and escorting convicted prisoners, for example, to Lewes House of Correction* (**208**). *In the following year he abandoned his family, was arrested in London and returned to Winchelsea after himself serving his sentence at Lewes* (**210-216**). *On his release he applied for financial support to permit him emigrate with his family to the USA, thus provoking a legal debate over whether an annuity left to his wife, Mary, by her late father was eligible as security for any loan* (**217-224**). *Whether Samuel and Mary Easton were eventually successful in emigrating seems unlikely for their two youngest children, William and Edward were admitted to the Northiam workhouse in July 1836[2] and the same annuity from their grandfather was used to support them.[3]*
Samuel Easton, born 1793, son of Thomas and Sarah,[4] was a shoemaker, frequently referred to synonymously as a cordwainer. He often worked for the parish and on several occasions was supplied with leather or money by the overseers to allow him to carry out that work, e.g. (**206-207**). *Payments of his bills for shoemaking and repairs are frequently recorded in the overseers' accounts.[5] However, this income was insufficient to meet the needs of his large family for he and his wife, Mary, had eight children. The same accounts provide details of the weekly and casual payments, together with allowances of flour and coal which they received.[6] During the time that Samuel deserted his family the overseers agreed that poor law relief should be paid direct to Mrs Easton.[7] For a time Samuel supplemented his income by taking occasional work on the parish highways when it was available.[8] The parish registers of St Thomas's contain a most unusual entry related to this family. Three of Samuel and Mary's children, Thomas, George and John, were baptised on the same day, 5 August 1821. Each entry has the added note, 'born according to declaration of father' followed by dates showing that Thomas was claimed by his father to be 8 at the time of his baptism, George 6 and John 2. The other children were baptised soon after birth as was usual.[9] The 1841 census lists Samuel and Mary's son Thomas, 29, as following his father's trade of shoemaker and living in Mill Road with his wife, Ann, and their family. This seems to represent an improvement in their fortunes for Thomas had earlier been on poor relief.[10]*

and in 1836 he was, like his father before him, charged with deserting his family.[11] He and his wife Ann were later both inmates of Brede workhouse.[12] The 1841 census also shows that Thomas's brother Neriah, 15, was a butcher's apprentice living in Castle Street and that their grandparents, Thomas senior, listed as an agricultural labourer aged 85 and his wife Sarah, 79, were living in North Street.

Another Samuel Easton, a wheelwright who appears in the militia roll of 1803 reproduced in appendix C3, as eligible for service was born in 1777, the illegitimate son of Samuel Easton, wheelwright, and Elizabeth Stevens.[13] Like Thomas junior he was following his father's trade. No evidence has been found that any documents in the following sequence could apply to him or that he was of the same immediate family.

203 1 Feb 1819 *[Edited] account submitted to the parish officers of Winchelsea by Dawes & Co [of Rye, parish solicitors]*:

Attending Mr [Edward] Jeakens and Samuel Easton, examining the latter touching his settlement and considering the case when it appeared his settlement was in Winchelsea and reducing same to writing and appointing to meet the magistrates at Winchelsea to have the pauper sworn: 13s 4d; it being considered necessary to have the particulars of Easton's renting the tenement in Winchelsea of his father to see if the story was correct, writing to his father by desire of the parish officers to beg of him to send us the particulars of their agreement etc etc: 5s.

[PAR 511/31/2/131]

204 15 Feb 1821 *Minute of the Winchelsea select vestry*:

Resolved that Samuel Easton receive ten shillings and two bushels of coals as casual relief. [PAR 511/12/2 f.8]

205 9 Jan 1821 *[Edited] account submitted to the parish officers by Messrs Dawes, Lardner and Fisher of Rye*:

Attending parish officers and examining Samuel Easton respecting the property of his father-in-law Welch [Walsh] and taking down minutes to enable us to make inquiry relevant thereto: 6s 8d. [PAR 511/31/2/135]

206 16 Jan 1823 *Letter from John Woods [Winchelsea overseer of the poor] to Mr John Foster of Rye*:

I will thank you to advance Samuel Easton leather to the value of £5 on the parish account. [PAR 511/31/2/138]

207 9 Sep 1823 *Letter from J[oseph] Bigg, Winchelsea, overseer, to John Foster, Rye*:

I will thank you to advance Samuel Easton leather to the amount of £5 on the parish account. [PAR 511/35/1/23]

208 26 Jul 1825 *Bill for expenses submitted by Samuel Easton, constable*:
To conveying Thomas Bennett and Thomas Turner from Winchelsea to the house
of correction at Lewes, committed by Henry Powell Esq. and John Tilden Esq. 40
miles distant at 1s 6d per mile: £3; to subsistence of prisoners while in custody,
Bennett 1 day and 1 night, Turner 1 day and 2 nights: 3s 9d; lodging for prisoners
3 nights: 2s 3d; assistants to constables 3 days and 2 nights at 2s 6d each: 12s 6d;
subsistence for the constable and assistant 3 days and 2 nights at 2s 6d each per
day and 2s 9d per night each: £1 5s 0d; horse hire 3 days at 10s per day: £1 10s 0d.
[total] £6 13s 6d.
[*Endorsed*] Allowed on the oath of Samuel Easton [by] H[enry] Powell [and]
J[ohn] Tilden.   [WIN 754]
See also (**68**) note.

209 2 Mar 1826 *Letter from John Edwards, Northiam to John Fuller, Winchelsea:*
I have been informed that Mrs Samuel Easton [Mary] is very dangerously ill and
in [a] most distressing situation – herself and children in a very pitiable state, I
mean actually in want. It is probable that the overseers of Winchelsea may suppose
that she does not require the assistance of a parish – thinking that her late father
had sufficiently provided for her. Had her husband been like herself, the amount
left by his will would certainly have been of great service to her but I can assure
you that she is in a much worse state than she would have been if the father had
not left her a shilling because it is no doubt supposed by her friends that she is
comfortably situated. Instead of this, sir, I can affirm to you that I have paid the
whole of the two last half-year's dividends by her consent to Mr Foster of Rye
for a debt contracted by her husband and the debt is not yet discharged. I have
written this to you knowing that you can rely on what I have said and to request the
favour of you to go to one or the other of the overseers to inform him of the state
of this poor distressed woman and children, or perhaps it would be better to go to
[Richard] Stileman Esq and state the case to him who I am sensible would give the
case immediate attention and this is what appears to me from the statement of Mrs
Bourner, her own sister, and my informants to be absolutely necessary. To comply
with my request would be an act of charity. I, as executor, cannot do anything safely
for, should she not survive, the cash advanced by me to her assistance would be
sacrificed for at her death the annuity ceases and her share immediately devolves
on the children, not to her husband. NB The medical gentlemen would be best to
consult before you go to the overseer, I can assure you I do verily believe the case
requires the most prompt attention.   [PAR 511/35/1/208]
Note: Following this appeal the overseers' accounts include three payments totalling £1 8s
0d made to Mrs Easton. The entries are marked 'loan'.[14]

210 14 Mar 1826 *Summary proceedings before Henry Powell and John Tilden, justices of the peace for Winchelsea at which Charles Arnett, assistant overseer:* on oath charges Samuel Easton, late of Winchelsea, shoemaker with unlawfully running away and leaving his wife and children whereby they are become chargeable to Winchelsea and [he has] thereby committed an act of vagrancy.
[*Appended note*] Warrant granted and Charles Arnett made special [constable].

[WIN237A]

Note: On 7 Mar 1826 Charles Arnett, assistant overseer charged the parish £7 13s 3d. for a 'Journey after S Easton 7 days, self, horse and gates'.[15]

211 3 May 1826 *Letter from Samuel Easton, Upton [in West Ham] Essex to Charles Arnett, Winchelsea [assistant overseer]:*
I would be very much obliged to you to lay this letter before the gentlemen of the first vestry which may be held at Winchelsea. Now, gentlemen, I do most humbly ask all your pardons for my late past conduct which I am ashamed to say is very bad. Now gentlemen I am got into a good situation which I get 24 shillings per week but not at my business shoemaking. Now I have told my master that I have a wife and family in the country and that my wife has got a small half-yearly income which will about pay our rent so he will let me a house and pay me my wages weekly which will be sufficient for my wife and family to live on. Now gentlemen if you will but forgive me it shall be for ever my study for the comfort and support of my unfortunate wife and children. Now gentlemen I have two things to propose to you if it meets with your approbations or any other measure that you think proper. Now first to sell off my house but to pay my poor aged father his rent which is seven pounds the tenth of this present month and I think there will be enough to pay you gentlemen what you have advanced my wife and children during my absence and to pay the expenses of my family up to town without selling our best bed. But this I must leave to you gentlemen to do as you think proper. I know gentlemen I ought to suffer the law but I do beg for mercy of you just this once for I will never trouble Winchelsea parish no more. I shall gain a settlement here in one year. I will endeavour to get my other business settled as soon as I can. My master is gone out for a walk. If he had not been out I would have sent my family one pound in this letter. I have only 6s in my pocket that I cannot send in this letter.

[PAR 511/35/1/223]

212 5 May 1826 *Minute of the Winchelsea select vestry:*
[Resolved] that instructions be given to the Bow Street officer holding a warrant for the apprehension of Samuel Easton that he put it into execution with all convenient dispatch.

[PAR 511/12/3]

213 8 May 1826 *Letter from Robert Duke, Public Office, Bow Street, [Middlesex] to C[harles] Arnett, Winchelsea, [assistant overseer]*:
I beg to inform you that I have succeeded in apprehending Samuel Easton. I have safely lodged him in the watch-house according to your desire. I had heard of him previous to receiving your letter but could not meet with him until Saturday when I found him at West Ham. He was perfectly aware of my being in search for him. I shall thank you to send for him as early as possible as delay will only increase the expenses at the watch-house. PS My charge for apprehension, coach hire and expenses is £2 5s 0d.   [PAR 511/35/1/226]

214 8 May 1826 *Letter from Samuel Easton, St Martin's Watch-house, London, to Charles Arnett, Winchelsea, [assistant] overseer*:
I have just received your letter brought by a friend to me here which is now 20 minutes past four so I have not time to say but little and, sir, you will know as the warrant is put into execution we cannot come to any terms now but happy should I have been had I received this letter from you before you sent to the gentlemen of Bow Street in answer to my last [in] which you lost no time I am certain. Now, Mr Arnett, I have no doubt you will receive this one and one from Bow Street in and at the same time tomorrow morning and I trust you will lose no time in getting me away from this unpleasant situation. I am ready to meet you gentlemen on any terms that you may think proper in [relation] to this unpleasant circumstance. But as the warrant is put into execution we cannot do anything at this unhappy moment. Now Mr Arnett when I come down I hope I shall find you as I have always done not to do me any harm. I mean no more than your duty requires. Then I shall be very much obliged to you from my very bleeding heart. Have the goodness to let my dear wife [Mary] know that I shall be down and you know best when.
                                                      [PAR 511/35/1/227]

215 10 May 1826 *Account submitted by Charles Hill [constable]*:
To going to London after Samuel Easton and bringing him to Winchelsea under warrant of Henry Powell Esq for having committed an act of vagrancy. Conveyance and expenses to Hastings to go by the mail: 7s 6d; coach hire and expenses to London: £1 16s 6d; paid expenses Samuel Easton at St Martin's watch-house as per bill: £1 6s 6d; constable's assistance, hackney coach hire and expense: 10s 6d; coach hire from London and expenses self: £1 5s 0d; coach hire from London and expenses Easton: £1 2s 6d; allowance 2 days and 1 night at 2s 6d: 7s 6d; loss of time 2 days and 1 night: 15s; assistant sitting up one night: 5s; [total] £7 16s 0d.
27 June 1826 This account certified correct after being verified on oath by the magistrates. [*signed*] Henry Powell   [PAR 511/31/2/148]

216 11 Jun 1826 *Letter from Samuel Easton, house of correction, Lewes to [Charles] Arnett, Winchelsea, [assistant] overseer*:

I am very sorry that I am under the painful and distressing circumstances of writing to the gentlemen of the parish praying that they will take it into their most serious consideration to mitigate my punishment as I am sorry to say that I have had a very bad complaint, a rupture, upon me from my infancy but for these last few years I have been much better with it. But now I am very sorry to say that through my close confinement and my low living and nothing but water to drink has brought me down so very weak and now that my rupture has returned upon me very bad that at times I am troubled to walk across my ward with my hand supporting my bowels from pressing down into my purse [scrotum]. Now gentlemen, it is not altogether what I do suffer here but what I shall for ever suffer hereafter in consequence of it. So I do most humbly beg, gentlemen, for lenity in this my most painful situation. This must all proceed from weakness because I am not sent to hard labour in consequence of my rupture. I would sooner be here six months without pain than I would one month in the misery that I am now in if that was possible. I must now gentlemen leave it to your wills and pleasure praying for feeling from you and if I find it you shall for ever see me a new man. And for ever it shall be my main study for the support of my family. [PAR 511/35/1/229]

217 12 Jul 1826 *Inquiry for legal advice made by Charles Arnett, assistant overseer, to John Fisher, solicitor of Rye*:

Can we as a parish make a claim on Samuel Easton's wife's annuity when she has assigned the right away to another? 'Mr Fisher [thinks] not but it will be best to give notice to Mr [Thomas] Edwards for the [vestry].' Desired him to do so.
[PAR 511/35/2/7]

218 10 Nov 1826 *Letter from Samuel Easton, Winchelsea to [Charles] Arnett, Winchelsea, [assistant] overseer*:

As I am short of work I beg of you to let me do your parish work. I will do it as cheap and as strong as you can get it done by anyone. [PAR 511/35/1/249]

219 20 Dec 1827 *Letter from Thomas Edwards, Newenden [Kent] to [Charles Arnett], Winchelsea, assistant overseer*:

Being from home at the arrival of yours of the 17th instant is a sufficient apology for not attending to its contents by the next post. In reply I beg to say that it would be both unsafe and imprudent to accede to the wishes of Samuel Easton, the sum arising to Mrs E[aston] under the will of her late father being given as an annuity. Consequently the payment of it depends solely on her life. She having, as you will perceive from the above, only a life interest in the same, and the amount, if advanced, with the large family they have, would, by their extreme poverty, be expended long before the period of its becoming due. Therefore what he considers as a favour would be rendered altogether to his own ?trust. I could not understand your signature. [PAR 511/35/1/308]

220 29 Dec 1827 *Letter from J[ohn] H[addock] Lardner, [town clerk of Winchelsea, Rye] to [the overseers of Winchelsea]*:
I think perhaps that if the overseers were to see the last examination of Easton that the order would be quashed for I do think that the general ?hearing appears very clear upon the examination at least. PS if the overseers refused then we must enter respite for madam will be too far gone for a trip to Lewes.   [PAR 511/35/1/309]

221 12 Feb 1829 *Minute of the Winchelsea select vestry*:
[Resolved] that a public vestry be called on Friday next to consider the application of Samuel Easton for the parish to advance him a sum of money to emigrate to America and other general purposes.   [PAR 511/12/3]

222 20 Feb 1829 *Minute of the Winchelsea public vestry*:
Resolved that the sum of £60 be advanced to Samuel Easton for the purpose of enabling him to emigrate to America with his wife and eight children, the parish being furnished with a power of attorney by Mrs [Mary] Easton for the receipt of her annuity of £15 a year for four years in repayment thereof; and also that the sum of £10 be further advanced for the purpose of providing his family with clothing. Further resolved that the overseer [David Laurence] should previous to making any advance obtain a legal opinion whether the above arrangement can be entertained by the parish and whether the majority of the vestry can make an advance of money in a case of the above description or whether the meeting should be unanimous. The individual has a sum of £50 in addition to the annuity above mentioned.
[PAR 511/12/2]

223 20 Feb 1829 *Letter from William Woodhams, Udimore to the chairman of the public vestry, Winchelsea*:
Mr [David] Laurence, the assistant overseer, was with me and mentioned to me yesterday the case of Samuel Easton applying to the parish of Winchelsea for the sum of £60 to enable him and his family to go to America. After considering the above case and finding that Samuel Easton [has] property [I] consider it an illegal thing for the parish to advance him any sum of money, he having the means himself by selling his annuity to save the sum wanted for the purpose. … I am sorry that my health is such that it is out of my power to attend the vestry. [PAR 511/35/1/322]

224 [c.21 Feb 1829] *Letter from J[ohn] H[addock] Lardner, [town clerk of Winchelsea], Rye to [David] Laurence, Winchelsea, [assistant overseer]*:
[Samuel] Easton and his wife may make an effectual assignment of their eighth of Harriett's share and (the trustees having notice of the assignment) the overseers may with perfect safety advance a sum not exceeding the value of that share on the security of it but in consequence of the restriction in the will against anticipation any assignment of the income of Mrs Easton's share would be ineffectual. It would

not be binding on her unless she confirmed each payment after it became due. This therefore is not such a security as the overseers can with propriety lend money upon. If, however, it be desirable that they should make the advance their best course would be to take a simple power of attorney from Mrs Easton to receive the income of her share. The overseers may retain it as they receive it until the debt be satisfied. She might obtain it from them notwithstanding the advance by them but not without a trust in equity which is a remedy which for so small a sum it is not probable would be adopted.   [PAR 511/35/1/323]

225 4 Sep 1837 *Minute of the guardians of the Rye Union*:
The clerk was directed to write to the parish officers of Winchelsea and request them to apply to a Mr [John] Edwards of Northiam for the payment to them of such monies as he is liable to pay to two children of the name of Easton belonging to and now chargeable to the parish of Winchelsea and now residing in the Brede workhouse, such monies when received to be applied for or towards payment of the expenses incurred by Winchelsea parish for the support of those children.
[G 8/1a/2 f.29]

226 26 Mar 1838 *Minute of the guardians of the Rye Union*:
The Governor of the Rye Workhouse produced the following account showing the amount of relief by way of loan allowed by order of the board at their meeting on the 5th instant to the following persons who lately left the Rye Workhouse not having sufficient clothing of their own. [inter alia] John Easton, Winchelsea: 7s 8d. Amount to be charged to the parish: 7s 8d.   [G 8/1a/2 ff.152-153]

227 2 Jul 1838 *Minute of the guardians of the Rye Union*:
A letter dated 27 June last from Mr John Edwards was read stating that the annuities payable under the will of the late John Walsh to the two children of Samuel Easton now in the Brede workhouse should now be regularly paid.   [G 8/1a/2 f.201]

1 WIN 61B   2 G 8/1a/1 f.204   3 G 8/1a/2 f.201   4 PAR 511/1/1/4   5 e.g. PAR 511/31/1/13 1821-1828   6 ibid   7 PAR 511/31/1/14 f.8; PAR 511/12/3 21 Apr 1826   8 PAR 511/40/1/3 1827-1828   9 PAR 511/1/2/1   10 PAR 511/12/3 Nov 1829 – May 1830   11 G 8/1a/1 f.222   12 G 8/19/4   13 PAR 511/34/3/3   14 PAR 511/31/1/15 f.24   15 PAR 511/31/2/129

Daniel Edwards

228 *It would appear from the parish records that Daniel Edwards was eighteen at the time of his apprenticeship* (**229**) *for a child of that name was baptised at St Thomas's on 26 August 1807.[1] Prior to his mother's receipt of the letter from Captain Stephens, Daniel had been receiving occasional casual relief. On 22 August 1822 the select vestry agreed to allow him a pair of half-boots.[2] The following January he was provided with a greatcoat[3] and later a jacket was bought for him.[4] Apart from this provision of clothing, during the summer of 1824 he was paid four shillings in cash.[5] Following his going to sea no further* *information about him has been discovered. Neither is there any record that the parish paid or contributed to the costs of his apprenticeship. Daniel's widowed mother – see* (**230**) *was in receipt of poor law relief between 1824 and 1826, usually a weekly payment of one shilling.[6] However, on 21 April 1826 the select vestry resolved, without explanation, 'that Widow Edwards' pay be discontinued'.[7] Thereafter she is recorded as receiving only a one-off casual payment of six shillings in 1833 when she was ill.[8]*

229 5 Mar 1825 *Letter from Captain Thomas Stephens, South Shields, [County Durham] to Mrs Edwards, [Winchelsea]:*
I have to inform you that I have bound your son Daniel for three years to Captain James Bains of South Shields, a very good man. He is to have £30 for the three years with the addition of 12s per annum for his washing and if he behaves I have no doubt but it will be the making of him. They are going to Rochester for the first voyage. Remember me to all my friends and relations about Winchelsea.

[PAR 511/35/1/158]

1 PAR 511/1/1/4   2 PAR 511/12/2 f.30   3 ibid f.36   4 PAR 511/31/1/13 Sep 1823-Feb 1824   5 ibid QE Sep 1824   6 PAR 511/31/1/13   7 PAR 511/12/3   8 PAR 511/12/2 29 Aug 1833

George Edwards

230 *An 1821 family listing shows George Edwards, labourer, of Winchelsea with his wife and two children, Daniel [age illegible] and Edward aged 6. In this entry the name George has been deleted and 'widow' substituted.[1] This suggests that that George and his wife were Daniel's parents, an assumption supported by the addressing in 1825 of* (**229**) *above to Mrs Edwards. It was another George Edwards to whom* (**231**) *applies and he is most unlikely to have been a member of the same immediate family as he was already receiving poor law relief in his own right; casual payments totalling 19s 6d, during the 1821/22 financial year.[2] Although his trade is not given, he also received a payment of ten shillings during that year 'for work at poorhouse'.[3] From that time until 1824 he was supported with frequent casual relief, for example between October 1823 and May 1824 he was being paid amounts between 1s and 2s 6d sometimes more often than weekly.[4] The dismissal recorded in* (**231**) *was very temporary for in 1826 and 1827 the records show that George Edwards was employed regularly by the surveyors of the highways at 1s 2d per day.[5]*

231 4 Feb 1826 *Letter from [Richard] Stileman, [The Friars, Winchelsea] to [Charles] Arnett, [Winchelsea, assistant overseer]:*
When you settle with the road men this evening you will tell them I shall not want any men next week excepting George Edwards and T[homas] Fisher and that after next week they must find other work. [PAR 511/35/1/205]

1 PAR 511/31/1/12 f.80   2 PAR 511/31/1/13   3 ibid   4 PAR 511/31/1/12 f.267(b)   5 PAR 511/40/1/2

South Shields March 5th 1825 —

Mrs Edwards —

*I have to inform you that I have bound
Your Son Daniel, for three Years.
to Captn James Bains of St Shields
a Very good Man, he is to have £30.
for the three Years With the addition of
12 Shillings Pr annum for his Washing
and if he behaves I have no doubt but
it will be the Making of him, they
are going to Rochester for the first
Voyage. remember My to all My friends
& relations about Winchelsea I remain
Your friend & Well wisher*

Thos Stephens —

E.S.R.O.
PAR. 511/35/1/248
158

Apprenticeship arrangements for Daniel Edwards

PAR 511/35/1/158 transcribed as (**229**)
reproduced by arrangement with the County Archivist

Richard Edwards

232 *Richard Edwards, labourer, of Winchelsea, married Hannah Tilman on 8 October 1821.[1] They had three children, Marianne b.1822, Richard James b.1824 and Maria Jane b.1826.[2] Sadly, as was common in those days, Richard junior died when only three weeks old.[3] The allegation that Richard senior had threatened to abandon his family (**233**) must have been pressed by Charles Arnett as a back-up to the charge of assault made the same day (**234**). However, with his wife currently pregnant and another child to be born less than two years later, Edwards does not seem to have had any such intention at that time. The constables responded immediately to Henry Powell's orders for Richard Edwards was tried the same day as they were made, found guilty and imprisoned.[4] He was released on 12 June – see (**235**). Richard did, however, later abandon his family so Arnett's suspicions might well have been justified. On 8 April 1830 the Winchelsea select vestry resolved 'that Marianne and Maria Edwards, the children of Richard Edwards who has absconded and left them be taken into the poorhouse'.[5]*
*Richard first appears as the recipient of poor law relief in 1816 when the parish vestry ordered that he was to be paid fifteen shillings.[6] In March 1824 he and his family were living in part of a house in Barrack Square, their part having a very low annual rental value of 7s 6d.[7] He was regularly supported by the parish until he left his family in 1830[8] and, even very soon after the children were admitted to the workhouse, received a casual payment of four shillings.[9] No further payments appear in the overseers' ledgers but Richard returned to Winchelsea for he is listed in 1836 as among Winchelsea's able-bodied poor.[10] No additional information has been found about the alleged assault by Hannah Beale on his wife (**236**).*

233 24 May 1824 *Order made to the constables of the Ancient Town of Winchelsea by Henry Powell, justice of the peace for Winchelsea*:
Whereas Charles Arnett of Winchelsea, assistant overseer, hath this day made information on oath before me that Richard Edwards, late of Winchelsea, did on the 22nd day of May instant unlawfully threaten to run away from the parish of Winchelsea leaving his wife and family chargeable thereto; these are therefore to command you in His Majesty's name forthwith to apprehend and bring before me or some other justice of the peace for Winchelsea the body of Richard Edwards to answer unto the said complaint and to be further dealt with according to law. Herein fail not as you will answer the contrary at your peril.   [WIN 220]

234 24 May 1824 *Order made to the constables of the Ancient Town of Winchelsea, Sussex, by Henry Powell, justice of the peace for Winchelsea*:
Whereas Charles Arnett of Winchelsea hath this day made information and complaint upon oath before me that Richard Edwards, late of Winchelsea, did on the 22nd instant unlawfully threaten and [?assault] him whereby he has on oath declared that he goes in danger of his life or that some bodily harm will be done or caused to be done to him; these are therefore to command you in His Majesty's name forthwith to apprehend and bring before me, or some other justice of the peace

for Winchelsea, the body of Richard Edwards to answer unto the said complaint and to be further dealt with according to law. Herein fail not, as you will answer the contrary at your peril. [WIN 221]

235 8 Jun 1824 *General quarter sessions of the peace held at the Guildhall, Winchelsea before Henry Powell, deputy mayor, George Stace and Joseph Hennah, jurats and justices of the peace*:
Ordered that Richard Edwards be discharged out of custody at the expiration of the calendar month for which he was committed as rogue and vagabond and that he enter into his own recognisance in the sum of forty pounds to keep the peace towards all His Majesty's liege subjects and particularly towards Charles Arnett, the assistant overseer, either for a limited period or for his appearance at the next general quarter sessions there to answer any charge that may be made against him. [WIN 61D f.18]

236 22 Jan 1825 *Information given before Henry Powell, justice of the peace for Winchelsea, by Hannah Edwards, the wife of Richard Edwards of Winchelsea*:
who, on oath, charges Hannah Beale with violently assaulting and beating her this day at Winchelsea. [*mark of*] Hannah Edwards
[*Appended note – same date*] Heard and discharged. [WIN 237A]

1 PAR 511/1/3/1   2 PAR 511/1/2/1   3 PAR 511/1/5/1   4 WIN 1228   5 PAR 511/12/3   6 PAR 511/31/1/11 25 Mar-4 Apr 1816   7 PAR 511/31/1/13   8 PAR 511/31/1/11 1816-1819; PAR 511/31/1/13 1820-1830 9 PAR 511/12/3 30 Apr 1830   10 PAR 511/37/7/29

Thomas Edwards

237 *It took four years for the Winchelsea overseers' persistent notices to landlord George Bray* (**238, 240-242**) *indicating that they would no longer be paying the rent of the families of Thomas Edwards and William Willard to be acted upon. The eventual outcome* (**244**) *reflects credit on Edwards and is something of a surprise for between 1815 and the time that he retained possession of his home by paying the rent himself he had been regularly the recipient of relief, both weekly and casual cash payments and the supply of clothing by the parish. Between December 1817 and March 1819 he received a weekly allowance of four shillings.[1] For three months in 1820/21 he received two gallons of flour per week, seventeen shillings for clothing for his children and his rent of £4 4s. 0d was paid to Mr Bray.[2] In December 1821 he was allowed three shillings weekly 'till he meets with employment'.[3] These allowances, and many similar examples were assisting in the support of a large family who, before the parish provided them with a home at Moneycellar House, had lived in far poorer accommodation in Barrack Square.[4]*
Thomas Edwards, labourer, and his wife Ann had seven children baptised at St Thomas's between 1806 and 1817.[5] Two sons, both named Francis, died young, one aged less than three weeks in 1805 and the other aged 5 in 1820.[6] Mrs Edwards died in 1827 at the age of 52 [7] when Jacob Holt as undertaker was paid a burial fee of ten shillings.[8] Shortly

before Ann Edwards' death the select vestry had resolved to allow Thomas Edwards 'nine shillings per week till the next vestry – himself and wife sick'.⁹ Of their children we know that Frederick received poor relief, in 1828 the select vestry allowing him three shillings 'or, if he will go to London for employ – ten shillings'.¹⁰ Hannah went into service with William Bray and Bray was paid one shilling a week for keeping her. The agreement stipulated that the parish would provide her clothing.¹¹ By 1841 Thomas was an inmate of Rye workhouse.¹² He was buried in Winchelsea in 1850.¹³

238 26 Sep 1822 *[Copy] notice of the churchwardens and overseers of the poor of Winchelsea to Mr George Bray [of Winchelsea]*:

We, the undersigned, being churchwardens and overseers of the poor of the parish of St Thomas the Apostle, Winchelsea, do hereby give you notice that Thomas Edwards and William Willard, paupers of the said parish, will quit possession of the messuages or tenements now in their occupation, and rented by the parish officers for the time being, at Lady-Day next or at the expiration of the year's tenancy if it should not end at Lady-Day and that we will deliver up the possession thereof to you at that time.   [PAR 511/37/3/20]

Notes: 1. No separate figures appear for the amount of Thomas Edwards' rent but between September 1822 and March 1823 the overseers paid George Bray the considerable sum of £10 18s 0d 'for [the rent of] Edwards, Willard and Perigo.¹⁴

2. For William Willard see (**693-703**)

239 8 Apr 1823 *General quarter sessions of the peace held at the Guildhall, Winchelsea before Henry Powell, deputy mayor, George Stace, Joseph Hennah and John Tilden, jurats and justices of the peace*:

At this sessions a bill of indictment was sent before the grand jury against Thomas Edwards late of the parish of St Thomas the Apostle, Winchelsea, labourer, for feloniously stealing on the twenty-fifth day of February [last] one shift of the value of two shillings of the goods and chattels of Mary Baker, and, the aforesaid grand jury having returned on their oaths by them respectively taken that the said bill of indictment was not a true bill and that no other indictment having been at the same sessions preferred against Thomas Edwards it is ordered that [he] be forthwith discharged out of the custody of the keeper of the common gaol of this ancient town into whose custody for the cause aforesaid he had been duly committed.

[WIN 61D ff.1-2]

240 15 Mar 1824 *Notice issued by the churchwardens and overseers of Winchelsea to George Bray, landlord*:

We hereby give you warning of quitting that part of the Moneycellar Houses now in the occupation of Thomas Edwards and that part lately occupied by William Willard on or before Michaelmas next of which be pleased to take notice.

[PAR 511/37/3/26]

241 [24] Sep 1825 *Copy notice of the churchwardens and overseers of the poor of Winchelsea to Mr George Bray, landlord*:
We hereby give you warning of quitting those two houses now in the occupation of Thomas Edwards and William Willard on or before Lady-Day next of which be pleased to take notice. [*Endorsed*] Copy of notice delivered to Mr George Bray, Sept 24 1825, by me [*mark of*] John Chester.   [PAR 511/37/3/31]

242 13 Feb 1826 *Copy notice of the churchwardens and overseers of the poor of Winchelsea to Mr George Bray, landlord*:
We hereby give you warning of quitting all that part of the Moneycellar House and premises now in the occupation of Thomas Edwards and William Willard on or before Michaelmas next of which be pleased to take notice.
[*Endorsed*] Delivered same day [*mark of*] John Chester [*initials of*] Charles Arnett.   [PAR 511/37/3/33]

243 11 Aug 1826 *Copy notice [of the Winchelsea overseers] to Thomas Edwards and William Willard:*
We hereby give you notice to quit that house and premises now in your occupation on or before this day month.
[*Appended note*] Served the 11th day of August 1826 by me, Henry Tilden.
                                                               [PAR 511/37/3/17]

244 16 Sep 1826 *Appearance of Charles Arnett, assistant overseer, before Henry Powell and John Tilden, justices of the peace for Winchelsea*:
[Information] against Thomas Edwards and William Willard for unlawfully retaining possession of the[ir] houses and premises after due notice from the churchwardens and overseers or a major part of them.
23 Sep 1826 [*At a further hearing before the same magistrates*] time given until Tuesday the 26th at 12 o'clock when they [were] to appear before the above two justices of the peace if they did not previously give up possession to the assistant overseer.
26 Sep 1826 [*At a further hearing*] the parties appeared again as they had not given up possession and a warrant granted against each to break open the house of each and forcibly to remove the goods.
[*Appended* note] Thomas Edwards hired the house he occupied of George Bray for the ensuing year. Willard's goods were removed by the constables.   [WIN 237A]

1 PAR 511/31/1/11   2 PAR 511/31/1/12 f.24   3 PAR 511/12/2 f.19   4 PAR 511/31/1/11 26 May 1811 5 PAR 511/1/1/4; PAR 511/2/1   6 PAR 511/1/1/4; PAR 511/1/5/1   7 PAR 511/1/5/1   8 PAR 511/31/1/13 Nov-Dec 1827 9 PAR 511/12/3 16 Nov 1827 10 ibid 31 Jan 1828 11 ibid 14 May 1830 12 G 8/19/2 13 PAR 511/1/5/1 14 PAR 511/31/1/13

William Edwards

245 *An order removing William Edwards, his wife Jane and their children Richard, 15 and Edwin 12 from Winchelsea to Snargate was confirmed by the Winchelsea quarter sessions on 13 July 1821.[1] The overseers' accounts for the year ending 25 March 1822 show that, presumably after Snargate had found accommodation for the family (246), Edwards received five shillings as a casual payment and twelve shillings for the journey to Snargate. The accounts also suggest that an overseer received five shillings for expenses incurred in accompanying them on the journey.[2]*

246 27 Apr 1821 *Letter from James Bourne, churchwarden, and George Hickman, overseer, Snargate [Kent] to the parish officers of Winchelsea*:
We will thank you to let Master Edwards and his family reside in the house where he was till we provide a place for him.   [PAR 511/35/1/11]

1 PAR 511/35/3/46   2 PAR 511/31/1/13

Benjamin Field

247 *Benjamin Field and his growing family had been supported by Winchelsea for ten years before the investigation to which (248) refers was carried out. The earliest record discovered is that in the autumn of 1816, Field was allowed five shillings by Winchelsea 'when out of employ'.[1] In 1825 the family was recorded by Winchelsea as consisting of husband, wife [Sarah] and five children, Benjamin junior 12, James 10, Sarah 6, Harriett 4, and John 2.[2] By 1829 two more children were added, Henry then 4 and Robert 2.[3] The family were receiving weekly relief from Winchelsea before the Winchelsea authorities challenged Benjamin's settlement.[4] After John Fisher's assertion that Field had not gained a settlement in Rye (248), Winchelsea assumed responsibility for paying the poor rates on his home there, for example (249), but other payments were on a casual basis, occasionally as high as £1 5s 0d [5] but more usually ten shillings or five shillings.[6] From March 1831 he did receive a regular allowance, initially as much as 4s 6d a week, but later reduced.[7] In 1833 Winchelsea paid 7s 6d towards the expenses of the burial at Rye of Benjamin and Sarah's 8 month old daughter Elizabeth.[8] However, all payments, both weekly and casual, from Winchelsea were stopped by the public vestry on 25 Jun 1835 when it was resolved, without explanation, 'that Benjamin Field's pay be taken off'.[9] In 1836 he was listed among Winchelsea's able-bodied poor.[10]*

248 13 Jun 1826 *Letter from John Fisher [solicitor], Rye, to [the overseers of Winchelsea]*:
Master [Benjamin] Field has been with me on the subject of his settlement in Rye in consequence of your referring him to me. I have questioned him upon it and he tells me a very different story from what I understood he told you. He says he hired the house in Rye by the quarter and not by the year. If this be the fact he has not gained a settlement. If he had been rated and paid taxes in respect of the house he might have gained a settlement by that means, the tenement being of the value of £10 per annum but he states he has never paid any taxes.   [PAR 511/35/1/230]

249 29 Mar 1827 *Letter from Joseph Mills, [assistant overseer], Rye, to [Charles] Arnett, Winchelsea, [assistant overseer]*:

The rates to this parish are as under: [*inter alia*] Field, Benjamin 6 rates from March 1826 to March 1827 at 4s 6d, £1 7s 0d.   [PAR 511/35/1/269]

Note: On 25 June 1827 Winchelsea paid, on Benjamin Field's behalf, the sum of £1 13s 0d. The entry is marked, 'Rates to Rye Parish'.[11] Winchelsea continued paying Benjamin Field's Rye poor rate until 1829.[12]

1 PAR 511/31/1/11 QE Dec 1816   2 PAR 511/31/1/15 f.12   3 ibid   4 PAR 511/31/1/13 Sep 1824-Sep 1826 5 ibid QE Mar 1831 6 PAR 511/12/3 29 Jan 1829-7 Jan 1831; PAR 511/31/1/13 QE Mar 1829-QE Dec 1830   7 PAR 511/31/1/16   8 PAR 511/31/1/16; PAR 467/1/5/1   9 PAR 511/12/2   10 PAR 511/37/7/29   11 PAR 511/31/1/15 f.12   12 PAR 511/31/1/13

Stephen Field

250 *No evidence has been found to explain why Stephen Field senior was on bail (**251**) or to permit elaboration of the charge that Stephen junior was responsible for allowing a driverless horse-drawn cart on Winchelsea's roads (**253**). It is, however, clear that the parish made an immediate and positive response to Stephen Field senior's appeal to be provided with work (**254**) for between 27 November 1830 and 12 May 1831 he was employed regularly by the surveyors of the highways at 1s 10d per day.[1]*

*In 1825 this family was recorded as consisting of Stephen senior aged 42 and his wife, Judith, 40, with Stephen junior aged 20, Elizabeth 17, William 14, Ann 9, James 5 and John 1½.[2] Stephen senior was an agricultural labourer of whom one entry in the overseers' accounts shows that he was paid two shillings for supplying the parish with 200 cabbage plants.[3] The Fields were constantly supported by the parish from 1805 (the year of Stephen junior's birth) until as late as 1849 when both Stephens were being excused payment of the poor rates.[4] Little else is known of the children apart from the birth of Ann's child (**255**) and that, in 1833, without a reason given, either Elizabeth or Ann (the record reads 'Stephen Field daughter') had received an allowance of four shillings for just five weeks.[5] However, some of Stephen's family feature in the 1841 census when Stephen senior and Judith were living at The Ferry with Ann 20, James, recorded as also being aged 20 and an agricultural labourer like his father, and Hannah 13. Living with them was James junior aged 1, presumed to be Ann's illegitimate son. Stephen junior aged 35 was living in Cook Street [Barrack Square] with his wife Jane and a young family.*

251 15 Dec 1818 *Minute of the Winchelsea public vestry*:

It is agreed to indemnify Richard Denne Esq and Mr Edward Jeakens from the expense [of] attending the bail of Stephen Field, a pauper of this parish.

[PAR 511/12/1 f.226]

252 15 Jun 1820 *Minute of the Winchelsea select vestry*:

Resolved that Stephen Field have one ?sheetings round frock and one change for son Stephen, and frock, change and one pair hose for daughter and one gallon flour per week.   [PAR 511/12/1 f.1]

253 17 Oct 1826 *Appearance before Henry Powell, justice of the peace for Winchelsea, of Charles Hill [constable]*:

[who on his oath saith] that Stephen Field the younger of Winchelsea did on Saturday last the 14th instant allow his team to pass along the highway within the parish of St Thomas the Apostle, Winchelsea, without any driver or person (either on foot or on horseback) to the damage of His Majesty's liege subjects and contrary to the statute of 13 Geo III which hath imposed a forfeiture of ten shillings for the offence.

[*sentence*] Convicted at sessions same day in the penalty of 5s and 3s costs. Paid by David Tree [owner of the cart].   [WIN 237A]

254 19 Nov 1830 *Endorsed upon a letter from Mrs Hannah Francis, Brighton, to Joseph Bigg, Winchelsea, grocer, are notes concerning payments made to paupers and requests received*:

[*inter alia*] Stephen Field [seeks] work.   [PAR 511/35/1/341]
Note: Stephen Field was employed on the parish highways between 8 Jan and 12 Feb 1831 at 1s 10d per day.[6]

255 9 Mar 1840 *Minute of the guardians of the Rye Union*:
Ordered that the clerk take the necessary steps to obtain an order of maintenance on the putative father of the illegitimate child of Ann Field belonging to the parish of Winchelsea who had become chargeable to that parish.   [G 8/1a/3 f.126]

1 PAR 511/40/1/8   2 PAR 511/31/1/15 f.10   3 PAR 511/31/1/11 QE Mar 1817   4 PAR 511/12/2   5 PAR 511/31/1/16 QE Jun 1833   6 PAR 511/40/1/6

Thomas Fisher

256 *Thomas Fisher was one of his widowed mother's five children, the others being Caroline (aged 14 in 1825), Eleanor, 9, George, 7 and Walter 3.[1] On 17 December 1824 the parish vestry resolved that Thomas's four siblings should be taken into the poorhouse and their mother's pay was discontinued.[2] However, this situation lasted only until 4 February 1825 when the children were discharged and their mother was allowed nine shillings a week.[3] This was reduced to 6s 9d in 1826 and further reduced to three shillings in 1829,[4] presumably because the girls went into service. Mrs Fisher had an occasional income from undertaking nursing work in the parish such as eight shillings for 'nursing and weaning Mrs Willard's infant while [Mrs Willard] lay ill of a fever.[5] Before getting himself and his mother into trouble by leaving the ship to which the parish had sent him and failing to return the clothing with which he had been provided* (**257-258**), *Thomas Fisher had worked as a servant in the household of Dr Adam Scott of Winchelsea but had left that employment by January 1824* (**85**). *However, after losing his job on the parish highways* (**259**) *he changed his mind about going to sea and accepted an apprenticeship with Mr B Breeds of a local seafaring family. The parish, despite the earlier incident, allowed him fifty shillings 'to find him in clothes' suitable for that work*[6] *and paid £4 towards the cost of the apprenticeship.[7] On 1 April 1826 Fisher also received from Charles Arnett a payment of 2s 6d 'on going to sea'.[8]*

257 10 Jun 1825 *Minute of the Winchelsea select vestry*:
Resolved that Mrs Fisher's pay be suspended for one week for encouraging her son Thomas (at home) after he had left his employment on board a vessel [after] being fitted out by the parish. [PAR 511/12/3]

258 14 Jun 1825 *Appearance before Henry Powell, justice of the peace for Winchelsea, of Charles Arnett, assistant overseer*:
who on oath charges Thomas Fisher with unlawfully by means of certain false pretences obtaining from [him] a quantity of wearing apparel the property of the parish officers and inhabitants of St Thomas the Apostle.
[*Town clerk's appended note*] Discharged on date. [WIN 237A]
Notes: 1 Samuel Easton was paid 2s 6d as a town constable for apprehending Thomas Fisher to answer this charge.[9]
2. Thomas Fisher was among those who threatened the assistant overseer, Charles Arnett, on 29 November 1825 (**16**).

259 4 Feb 1826 *Letter from [Richard] Stileman, [The Friars, Winchelsea] to [Charles] Arnett, [Winchelsea, assistant overseer]*:
When you settle with the road men this evening you will tell them I shall not want any men next week excepting George Edwards and T[homas] Fisher and that after next week they must find other work. [PAR 511/35/1/205]

1 PAR 511/31/1/15 f.10   2 PAR 511/12/2   3 ibid   4 PAR 511/31/1/13   5 ibid QE Dec 1824   6 PAR 511/12/3 16 Mar 1826   7 PAR 511/31/1/13 QE Jun 1826   8 PAR 511/31/2/148   9 PAR 511/31/2/142

William Fisher

260 *It would seem that the William Fisher to whom the following documents refer, was Thomas's (**256-259**) older brother. A family listing dated 1821 shows William senior and his wife with William 17, Thomas 15, Caroline 11, Eleanor 6 and George 4.[1] William senior died in 1823 at the age of 45[2] when Jacob Holt, undertaker, was reimbursed ten shillings by the parish for payments he had made to the minister and the clerk after the burial.[3] If William junior went on his trial voyage (**263**) it was with the same company as his brother (**256**). In any case, he did not stay at sea long for in 1827 he was taken into the Winchelsea workhouse.[4] The following year, in accordance with the parish policy of encouraging paupers to seek work elsewhere, the select vestry resolved, 'that W Fisher be allowed three shillings or, if he will go to London for employ, ten shillings.[5] William may well have accepted the ten shillings and found work in London for from that time he disappears from the parish records.*

261 30 Mar 1818 *Minute of the Winchelsea public vestry*:
William Fisher is put out to Mr F Meads of Hastings at 2s per week, the parish to clothe him. [PAR 511/12/1 f.224]
Note: This arrangement was renewed on 1 April 1819.[6]

262 15 Feb 1821 *Minute of the Winchelsea public vestry*:
Resolved that Mr Walter Fuller [farmer] give 3s 6d per week for the labour of William Fisher (provided he learn to milk) from Lady Day 1821 to Lady Day 1822.   [PAR 511/12/2]

263 19 Mar 1824 *Letter from Thomas Breeds and Company, Hastings to the overseers of Winchelsea*:
Thomas Breeds and Co wish to know if the overseers of Winchelsea will allow the bearer, William Fisher, a jacket as he seems desirous of going to sea. He had better go one voyage on liking and when he is bound we shall require about eight pounds to clothe him. If the parish will undertake to allow him sums we shall have no objection in taking. We have desired him not to leave without a note from the overseers.   [PAR 511/35/1/69]

1 PAR 511/31/1/12 f.82   2 PAR 511/1/5/1   3 PAR 511/31/2/138   4 PAR 511/12/3 11 Apr 1827   5 ibid 31 Jan 1828   6 PAR 511/12/1 f.229

[--] Foster

264 *The only evidence discovered in the parish records which could apply to this letter is in the overseers' accounts for the period Easter 1805 to Easter 1806 and reads: 'Relieved Mrs Foster for lying-in and one month after: £2 7s 0d.'[1]*

265 13 Mar 1805 *Letter from W[eeden] Dawes, Rye to Thomas Marten, Winchelsea*:
Enclosed you receive the order for the payment of 2s weekly to Foster's wife for your signature. Your signature is sufficient. We have stated the allowance to commence 13 February a month back. The certificate of the Colonel must remain pinned to the order.
PS You will be pleased to swear Mrs Foster as to the truth of her being unable to maintain herself and of her husband being serving with the militia as stated in the order.   [PAR 511/35/1/2]

1 AMS 2329

Thomas Foster

266 *At least three Thomas Fosters feature in the Winchelsea parish records of this time. One had apparently abandoned his family and gone to America by September 1829[1] leaving a young family including Thomas junior then aged 10.[2] A third made the apologetic pleas in (**267-269**). Entries in the overseers' accounts show Thomas Foster being allowed ten shillings on 7 January 1831.[3] This could have been in response to the appeal in (**268**).*

Similarly, a resolution passed by the select vestry on 31 March 1831, 'that the following advance by the assistant overseer since the previous meeting be confirmed: Thomas Foster 8s 6d'⁴ is likely to represent a response to (**269**).

267 24 Mar 1830 *Letter from Thomas Foster, Tovil, near Maidstone, [Kent] to [David] Laurence, Winchelsea, [assistant overseer]*:
I am truly sorry that we are so troublesome to you – Mrs Foster tells me she has wrote to you and wishes the gentlemen would take it into consideration and send us a little money. As I do assure you, sir, we are very much in want of 30s by Saturday without fail to pay some rent with or I do not know what will be the consequence. I have been to London for a situation that I have heard of and I hope and trust I shall be successful but I shall not be able to have it for a fortnight's time at least. The situation I expected to have had by the 25ᵗʰ of this month, the other I do prefer by a great deal as the salary is twice as much. We hope this will be the last time that we have to send to you any more unless illness should take place. Therefore we hope you will not disappoint us by sending the 30s by post on Friday evening. In doing so we shall feel ourselves much indebted to you for our necessity makes us send to you.   [PAR 511/35/1/327]

268 [Jan 1831] *Letter from Thomas Foster, East Farleigh, [Kent] to [David] Laurence, Winchelsea, [assistant] overseer*:
I am sorry to say that we are obliged to trouble you again for more relief. I have been to Mr Tapsfield, overseer of East Farleigh, for him to bring us down to you but he wishes to hear from you first. Therefore please will you write to him by return of post that we may know what to do as we have not got one shilling to help ourselves with and he will not pay us anything till he hears from you. Please direct to him: Mr Thomas Tapsfield, overseer, East Farleigh, near Maidstone. Please send word whether he is to come with us or if you will fetch us – and I hope you will enclose a little money or give him an order to let us have a little. I hope you will not write to me for I have not got a halfpenny to pay the letter.   [PAR 511/35/1/355]

269 31 Jan 1831 *Letter from Thomas Foster, Tovil, [Maidstone, Kent] to [David] Laurence, Winchelsea, [assistant] overseer*:
I received your letter this morning and I do assure you if you will enclose me a sovereign it will be very acceptable and I hope after two months more we shall be able to get on without coming down to Winchelsea. Pray return me the money by return of post if you possibly can. In so doing you will oblige. Please to direct to Tovil near Maidstone.   [PAR 511/35/1/356]

1 AMS 2330 f.99   2 ibid   3 PAR 511/12/3   4 ibid

William Foster

270 *No evidence has been found in the parish records directly attributable to the case of the William Foster arrested in Liverpool and imprisoned at Lewes (**271-272**). However, a William Foster was among those named as threatening the assistant overseer, Charles Arnett, on 29 November 1825 (**16**).*

271 12 Apr 1826 *Summary proceedings before Henry Powell, justice of the peace for Winchelsea, at which Charles Arnett, assistant overseer:*
on his oath charges William Foster, late of Winchelsea, shoemaker, with having run away and left his wife and one child chargeable to Winchelsea and thereby committed an act of vagrancy.
[*Appended notes*] Warrant granted this day by the same magistrate. William Foster was taken at Liverpool on the 15th instant by Charles Hill, constable [of Winchelsea] after great perseverance and committed to the house of correction at Lewes for the space of three months and there kept to hard labour.   [WIN 237A]
Note: Sarah, daughter of William (cordwainer) and Louisa Jane Foster, was baptised at St Thomas's on 29 January 1826.[1]

272 21 Apr 1826 *Letter from D[avid] Stonham, Rye to [Charles] Arnett, Winchelsea, [assistant] overseer:*
I have heard you are in possession of William Foster's money. If so £1 16s 0d belongs to me for bedding I supplied his family with and which they now have in use. He was to have paid me on the evening himself and James Clark came over to Rye to receive their money but the bank being shut they could not change their cheques. I was therefore ignorant of their proceedings until Foster was gone. When I heard of his absence I complained to Master Clark of ill usage and he promised me if Foster returned he [would] get the money and send it to me. Yesterday I heard Foster was sent away to Lewes and that his money was left in your house. These are the particulars of my situation and being a just demand on Foster for family necessaries I trust you will see it right to send me the amount and I will give you a discharge for the same.   [PAR 511/35/1/219]

1 PAR 511/1/2/1

Hannah Francis

273 *David Francis, variously described as 'clerk in the ordnance', 'Staff Corps', 'barrack sergeant' and 'barrack master', was stationed in Winchelsea when it was a garrison town during the Napoleonic wars and was married at St Thomas's to Hannah Knight on 6 December 1812.[1] Their eldest son, David junior, was baptised in Rye on 12 January 1816 (**305**). Their three other children were baptised in Winchelsea, John in December 1816, Mary in 1818 and Ebenezer in 1819.[2] No further mention has been found of Ebenezer and he does not feature in the following documents. David Francis died in 1819 and was buried in Winchelsea.[3] His death provoked the inquiries (**274-276**) as to whether his* *residence during military service had established a settlement in the town and therefore whether Winchelsea was responsible for supporting his widow and children. On leaving the Winchelsea workhouse* (**277**) *the family moved to Brighton where William Elliott and later William Tully agreed to pay her allowance weekly on the guarantee that it would be refunded by the Winchelsea overseers. It is not possible to relate the regular overseers' account entries showing Mrs Francis's payments[4] with the letters indicating that receipt was late. Ledger entries did not indicate date of despatch. However, it is possible to confirm Mrs Francis's complaint* (**296**) *that her pay had been stopped[5] and that the previous December the parish vestry had resolved that her weekly pay of six shillings should be reduced to three shillings 'until next Lady Day'[6] – confirmed in* (**300**). *However, the decision to withhold her allowance was extremely temporary. Payments resumed at the new rate almost at once[7] and continued until March 1827.[8] Thereafter a single casual payment of £2 10s 0d[9] was insufficient to sustain the family with the result that Brighton insisted on their removal to Winchelsea* (**312**). *Clearly this was not immediately enforced – see* (**313-315**), *probably because Mrs Francis stopped seeking help from Brighton. No evidence has been found as to whether Winchelsea responded to the appeals in* (**313-315**) *or whether the family were ever returned there.*

274 24 Nov 1819 et seq *[Edited] account submitted to the parish officers of Winchelsea by Dawes & Co. [of Rye, parish solicitors]*:
24 Nov 1819 Journey to Winchelsea to attend the magistrates taking examination of Hannah Francis, widow of [David] Francis, on the supposition that grounds might arise for an order of removal: £1; 6 Dec 1819 Attending Mrs Francis and examining her as to the renting of the house by her husband and as to his being a soldier at the time. Horse hire etc [including other cases on the same day]: £1 11s 6d; 4 Mar 1820 Attending Mrs Francis and perusing agreement between M[ary] May and her husband as to renting house at Winchelsea and she stating her intention to be to bring her children from Battle and come herself in consequence of Mr [Edward] Jeakens having told her to do so. Desiring her not to do so but that she must apply to the Battle officers who would then remove her to the place they conceived she belonged to. Writing to the magistrates to advise them of the circumstance and to say she ought not to be received without an order: 11s 8d.
[PAR 511/31/2/131]

275 28 Apr 1820 et seq *[Edited] account submitted to the parish officers of Winchelsea by Messrs Dawes, Lardner and Fisher [of Rye, parish solicitors]*:
Attending Mr Bellew, examining him as to Mrs Francis's house whether hired by her husband [David] or by government and when he promised to refer [to] some books in his possession and let us see them: 6s; 2 May 1820 Attending Mr [Edward] Jeakens and Mrs Francis, also Mr Bellew, taking minutes of her settlement and afterwards long attendance on Mr Bellew perusing ordnance books and other papers and making extracts therefrom: 13s 4d; Paid Mr Bellew for his trouble then and before: 5s. [PAR 511/31/2/135]
Note: Mr Bellew is likely to have been an officer of the Board of Ordnance who would, as the document suggests, have access to information about the properties occupied by David Francis and his family.[10]

276 6 May 1820 *Copy of evidence and legal opinion of George Courthope regarding the settlement of David Francis in Winchelsea*:

David Francis, a barrack sergeant, about six years ago was married to Hannah Knight then living in Rye in Sussex. Francis was allowed, as a barrack sergeant, 2s 6d a day and 1s 6d a week for lodging. About a twelve-month after his marriage he hired a house in Rye by the quarter at £4 per quarter which he occupied about nine months. Francis afterwards hired another house in Rye which he gave 3s 10d a week for and hired it about six months. A short time before Lady Day 1816 he hired a house at Winchelsea in Sussex of Mary May of that place as from said Lady Day at £15 per annum. A day or two afterwards Mrs May came to Francis and said she would have £17 a year or he should not go into [the house] and Francis agreed to give it. Francis had the key of the house delivered to him and within a week afterwards went into it. A Mr Lewis, a barrack master who had the custody of the stores at Rye, having lately died, Mr Griffith, another barrack master stationed at Bexhill, at the request of Francis on the 29th of May 1816 applied to the [Ordnance] Board to permit him, Francis, to have the custody of the stores and to be allowed £20 a year for house rent which request was granted him and the board paid the rent for such house from the 1st of June 1816 up to the death of Francis which happened in November last, and the receipts from the said 1st of June 1816 all [seen] for rent received of the board. The widow of Francis quitted the house the 1st January last. The board notwithstanding paid the rent up to Lady Day last. Previously and up to the 1st of June 1816 Francis was allowed 1s 6d a week for lodging. Francis has left a widow and three children chargeable to Winchelsea. Francis was formerly in the wagon train and was regularly discharged from that service and had immediately the place of barrack sergeant given him. A barrack sergeant it is believed holds no commission.

Mr Courthope is requested to peruse the foregoing case and advise whether Francis gained a settlement in Winchelsea by renting the above tenements, he being during that time in the employ of the Ordnance Board and receiving an allowance from the board for lodgings.

[*Response*] I am of the opinion that David Francis acquired a settlement in Winchelsea by renting and residing on the above-mentioned tenement. [*Quoted as precedent*] '1 barn and Ald 270 The King v the Inhabitants of Brighthelmston'.

[*Endorsed*] 16 May 1820 Letter from John Fisher [solicitor, Rye] for partners and self to Mr [Edward] Jeakens, Winchelsea. Herewith you receive copy case upon the subject of Francis's settlement with Mr Courthope's opinion thereon.

[PAR 511/35/2/3]

277 18 May 1820 *Minute of the Winchelsea select vestry*:
It is agreed that the overseers shall allow Mrs Francis and her three children the sum of six shillings weekly on leaving the poorhouse.   [PAR 511/12/1 f.243]

278 13 Oct 1823 *Letter from William Elliott, Brighton to [Robert] Alce and [George] Hill, Winchelsea, overseers*:
I will thank you to remit me the amount as per bill paid to Mrs Francis and the bearer of Mr French's receipt will be your discharge.   [PAR 511/35/1/26]

279 21 Oct 1823 *Letter from William Elliott, 45 Albion Street, Brighton to the overseers, Winchelsea*:
I will thank you to remit me thirteen weeks pay at 6s (which I have advanced to Mrs Francis to the day) by the Hastings coach to be left at Mrs Bontin's, Richmond Arms Inn, Brighton where a receipt will be left for the £3 10s 0d. I sent a note by a friend that was at Battle market supposing you might be there it would save expense of carriage for the poor woman but I understand you was not there.
[PAR 511/35/1/28]
Note: The overseers' accounts from September 1823 to February 1824 include 'Weekly pay Widow Francis 26 weeks at 6s - £7 16s 0d'.[11]

280 14 Jan 1824 *Letter from William Tully, 80 Edward Street, Brighton to the overseers of Winchelsea*:
As Mr Elliott has declined business, I, William Tully, baker, 80 Edward Street have taken on me this last past 13 weeks ending 12 of January to pay Mrs Francis 6s per week which is her weekly allowance from your parish. I should be obliged to you [to] send the amount £3 18s 0d by the Hastings coach. In doing so you will much oblige. Please to direct: William Tully, Blue Coach Office, Brighton.
[PAR 511/35/1/50]

281 31 Jan 1824 *Letter from William Tully, 80 Edward Street, Brighton, baker, to the overseers of Winchelsea*:
I wrote to you several days ago concerning the money I have paid to Mrs Francis, a pauper of your parish, and have received no answer, therefore I suspect the letter miscarried. As Mr Elliott had declared himself the person that used to pay her I have taken it on me to [pay] her 6[s] per week which is her weekly allowance from your parish. I have paid it from the 22 October 1823 to January 22 1824. It amounts [to] £3 18s 0d. I should be obliged [if you would] remit the money by the return of the Hastings [coach] and then I will continue to pay the money weekly. NB Direct to Mr Tully to be left at the Blue Coach Office, Brighton.
[PAR 511/35/1/55]

282 9 Feb 1824 *Letter from William Tully, 80 Edward Street, Brighton to [the overseers of Winchelsea]*:
I have wrote twice to say that I had undertook to advance Mrs Francis 6s per week for this last three months up to the 22 January. I have received no answer from you. Therefore I should be obliged to you to send it by the return of the coach then I will continue to pay Mrs Francis as Mr Elliott the person who advanced it before has declined business. I hope you will not fail in sending. Direct to Tully, to be left at the Blue Coach Office, Brighton.   [PAR 511/35/1/57]

283 11 Feb 1824 *Letter from William Tully, 80 Edward Street, Brighton to C[harles] Arnett, Winchelsea, assistant overseer:*
You will see by the [enclosed letter from William Elliott] that my demands are correct from the twenty-second of October. I am sorry that I trouble you with so many letters but it was solely through the neglect of the people at the coach office as your answer came by the van in place of it coming by the coach and that stops at another office and they neglected to carry it to the place it was directed so it never came into my hands till this afternoon. You said that you sent a note by post that I never have received neither does it lay at this post office. I should have got Mr E[lliott] to have wrote before but I understood by him that you was aware that he had declined advancing the money to Mrs Francis. Please to direct to the Blue Coach Office. Send by the coach as that stays at that office. The van stops at another and they are very neglectful in delivering parcels.
[Endorsed: copy of letter from William Elliott, 45 Albion Street, Brighton] 10 Feb 1824 Having declined the bakery business I found it inconvenient to advance Mrs Francis her pay. [William] Tully has since paid her therefore I have no demand on you. [PAR 511/35/1/58]

284 2 Mar 1824 *Letter from William Tully, 80 Edward Street, Brighton to C[harles] Arnett, Winchelsea, assistant overseer:*
In answer to the first letter of yours that came into my hands [in] relation to the pay of Mrs Francis you wish[ed] me to get Mr [William] Elliott to write to you to certify that he had no more demands from your parish. Accordingly he wrote to that effect on the 10th of February. I have received no answer to it yet. Therefore I wish you to write to let me know if you have sent and by what conveyance as I may trace where it is lodged. NB The letter you sent to me by post has since been brought to me under a wrong direction. It was 80 East Street in place of 80 Edward Street. I return it back again as it was to the same purpose as the one I got after Mr Elliott wrote. [PAR 511/35/1/64]

285 3 Mar 1824 *Letter from William Tully, 80 Edward Street, Brighton to [Charles Arnett, Winchelsea, assistant overseer]:*
I have [to] acknowledge the receipt of 13 weeks pay of Mrs Francis up to 22 January. I hope [this] will come into your hands before you have answered the note I wrote to you yesterday. The parcel has this hour [been] brought into my hands. I happened [by chance] to meet the coachman. I [told] him about the parcel and he said it was at the coach office. He went with me and the book-keeper had got it in his possession. I understand it has laid there for several days and I have sent a number of times and they have always denied it. I continue to pay Mrs Francis and I hope we shall have a better understanding for the future. [PAR 511/35/1/66]

286 22 Apr 1824 *Letter from William Tully, 80 Edward Street, [Brighton] to [the overseers of Winchelsea]*:

I should be obliged to you to remit me 13 weeks pay of Mrs Francis by the Hastings coach. Direct to the Blue Coach Office, Brighton. In so doing you will much oblige. NB I have given orders at the coach office to prevent [a] mistake this time. Mrs Francis wishes me to mention to you about paying the carriages as she said you usually did.   [PAR 511/35/1/77]

Note: This payment appears in the overseers' accounts dated March to June 1824.[12]

287 25 Jul 1824 *Letter from William Tully, 80 Edward Street, Brighton to [the overseers of Winchelsea]*:

Mrs Francis has made several applications to the minister and he has neglected to sign her certificate and the last time he referred her to the overseers and they would not do it. But you may rest assured that her 3 children that she brought down here are all alive. But if this assertion is not satisfactory she shall be taken before a magistrate in order to certify that they are actually her own. 13 weeks pay was due on the 22nd. Please to send it by the Hastings coach to the Blue Coach Office, Brighton. In so doing you will much oblige.   [PAR 511/35/1/99]

288 10 Aug 1824 *Letter from Mrs H[annah] Francis, Brighton to [Charles] Arnett, Winchelsea, assistant overseer*:

Mr [William] Tully informs me today that he has not yet received the pay for my children and thinks perhaps his letter dated the 25th of July has not come to hand. If so he would be very much obliged to you to remit it as soon as convenient as he has payment to make up that he requires it. My children are all living and I have tried means to get a certificate in order to give you satisfaction according to your request. I went to the minister and he sent me to the overseer and he refused to grant me one. [He] said he had nothing at all to do with it. They are so prejudiced [against] people of another parish living in this place that they will do all in their power to keep them out so by this means they refuse to do anything for me. I would be very thankful [to] the gentlemen if they would have the goodness to give my boys a pair of shoes each as they are very bad off and rents are so high here that I am troubled to get along and shoes are so expensive that I cannot find them. I would not ask if I did not need them. I could get them made [here] with a note from your hand or if you would please allow that money that you may think proper. Direct as before to Mr William Tully, Blue Coach Office, Brighton, Sussex.

[PAR 511/35/1/102]

Note: This payment appears in the overseers' accounts for June to September 1824 as 'Widow Francis weekly pay 14 weeks at 6s - £4 4s 0d'.[13]

289 26 Aug 1824 *Letter from William Tully, 80 Edward Street, Brighton to [Charles] Arnett, Winchelsea, assistant overseer*:
Your letter dated the 5th of August has this day come to hand and I have advanced [Hannah Francis's] pay previous to this day which is a month from the time that you have sent up to, depending that you would continue her pay as usual, as she gave me a note from your hand when I first advanced it to say you would see it paid quarterly. Not only that but I have let her have £2 worth of goods forward depending that her pay would go on. I hope you will not let me be the first loser in advancing the money to the woman. The widow Mrs Francis desires me to say that her children are now more expensive to her than ever they have been before as neither of them are able to do anything for a living but as she has established a little school and met with encouragement she does not wish to leave it. She would try to do with five shillings per week from you with her 3 children and if you do not like to let her have that she says she must come home to you and wishes you to send a word in what way she is to come. It would be attended with a great expense for her to throw herself on this parish to bring her home. I wish you to send me the earliest opportunity by post in order that I may know how to proceed.

[PAR 511/35/1/107]

290 11 Oct 1824 *Letter from William Tully, 10 Gloster Street, Gloster Place, Brighton to [Charles] Arnett, Winchelsea, assistant overseer*:
I have removed my situation to [this] place dated from [*blank*]. I should be obliged to you to remit the 2 months pay up to 25th of September for the widow Francis by the Hastings coach to the Blue Coach Office, Brighton. NB The widow Francis wishes [to know] what pay she is to expect in future.   [PAR 511/35/1/119]
Note: It was at this time that Hannah Francis's allowance was reduced by Winchelsea from 6s to 3s per week.[14]

291 6 Nov 1824 *Letter from D[avid] Stonham, Rye to [the overseers of Winchelsea]*:
I received a letter dated 26th ultimo from Hannah Francis, widow of Francis once a deputy barrack master and I believe a parishioner of Winchelsea. Hannah Francis was once a servant in my family and a faithful one. I am therefore desirous of recommending her case to your notice believing it is your wish to give comforts to your poor in that way that shall be connected with economy. She is now at Brighton and is using every means to provide for her sustenance without becoming at all burdensome to her parish but finds her exertions inadequate to afford her the means of paying her rent and supporting her family. Her humble request is therefore that 'the gentlemen will be kind enough to allow her three shillings per week through the winter until Ladytide or if they prefer it the sending her two pounds will enable her to do what she otherwise cannot do, namely pay her way'. I believe, gentlemen, if you were to do this for her she would in the course of a short time be able to get out her boys where she is now which would be a valuable consideration no doubt for the parish and I am fully persuaded of this: that if it were at all possible for her to get on without your aid she would by no means apply. Your good attention to the

request of this poor woman as early as convenient will be esteemed a favour. PS Should you please to make me the channel of communication to the applicant I am at your service. [PAR 511/35/1/129]

292 19 Nov 1824 *Letter from D[avid] Stonham, Rye to [the overseers of Winchelsea]*:
The request of the widow [Hannah] Francis I took the liberty of communicating to you a short time since – I am persuaded this [is] of importance to her – to know whether or not the parish will grant her the temporary aid she has pleaded for under her present circumstances. Will you have the goodness to inform me whether you have replied to her request made to you through my letter or whether I am to be the channel of communication for sending to her the decision of your vestry. If so I shall hope soon to be favoured with the same. [PAR 511/35/1/136]

293 8 Dec 1824 *Letter from D[avid] Stonham, Rye to [the overseers of Winchelsea]*:
I shall feel much obliged if you will favour me with the decision of your committee on the petition of the widow [Hannah] Francis unless you have already transmitted the same to her at Brighton. I am certain she is in need of what she prayed for and is consequently anxious. [PAR 511/35/1/143]

294 18 Dec 1824 *Letter from H[annah] Francis, 18 Paradise Street, Brighton to [Charles] Arnett, Winchelsea, assistant overseer*:
Mr [William] Tully informs me that he has had no order from your hands to advance my pay and he was strictly charged to advance no more without an order. My brother said you was going to write the day he was at Winchelsea. Mr Tully thinks perhaps you will have the goodness to send the quarter's pay with the order. Sir, I should not have troubled you with a letter but I am truly very distressed for the pay. [PAR 511/35/1/146]
Note: On 3 December 1824 the select vestry had resolved 'That Widow Francis be allowed 3s per week until next Lady Day'.[15]

295 24 Mar 1825 *Letter from W[illiam] Tully, 10 Gloster Street [Brighton] to [Charles] Arnett, Winchelsea*:
I would be obliged to you to remit me Mrs [Hannah] Francis's pay up to Lady Day by the Hastings coach to the Blue Coach Office, Brighton. Please to send word as soon as you can to let me know what pay I am to advance in future as I shall not advance no more money without your orders.
[Endorsed with a letter from Hannah Francis] I should be very glad if the gentlemen would be so good as to put me on 1s per week more for a little while for I am some weeks behind in my rent and I owe Mr Tully some shillings for bread for being the winter time work has been very short and I have been ill with a pain in my side and have not been able to earn 2s per week for this 3 months nor [am I] hardly able to do for my family and things keep rising. If you will have the goodness to do this for me I should be very thankful. [PAR 511/35/1/162]
Note: No increase was made as a result of this appeal.

296 11 Apr 1825 *Letter from H[annah] Francis, 50 Hereford Street, Brighton to the overseers of Winchelsea*:

I having this day heard from Mr [William] Tully that my pay is stopped and it not being in my power to maintain my family without some allowance and I think it quite unreasonable for the gentlemen to suppose that I can so I must come home and I should be glad to know by what means I am to get there as soon as possible for I have nothing to live on. Please to send by the return of post if possible. If the parish will allow me 4s per week I will try and make shift and I am sure they can't keep us on that.   [PAR 511/35/1/164]

297 11 Apr 1825 *Letter from William Tully, 10 Gloster Street, [Brighton] to [the overseers of Winchelsea]*:

I wrote to you several days ago requesting the remittance of widow [Hannah] Francis's pay up to Lady Day and have not received it. I should be obliged to you to send as soon as convenient and let me know what pay I am to advance in the future. She is daily pestering me after it but I shall not advance any more without your orders.   [PAR 511/35/1/165]

298 22 Apr 1825 *Letter from [Mrs] H[annah] Francis, Brighton to the overseers of Winchelsea*:

The letter I sent you dated the 16th I thought perhaps not come to hand I not having no answer as yet and I can't live in this way so I would thank you to send me word as soon as possible whether the gentlemen have agreed to the offer I have made or whether I am to come home and by what means. My baker has advanced the pay from the 25th of March till he received your letter for he thought it would have gone on the same.   [PAR 511/35/1/168]

299 3 May 1825 *Letter from G Chassereau, Brighton, assistant overseer to the churchwardens and overseers of Winchelsea*:

A poor woman of the name of Hannah Francis applied to the magistrates acting in Brighton for relief stating as her reason for so doing that she was a widow with three young children (who she then produced) incapable of earning any part of their subsistence. And being a legal parishioner of Winchelsea was well known to the parish officers there, and with their knowledge and approbation and under a promise of a weekly allowance came to Brighton, since which her allowance has been reduced to 3s a week and finally discontinued. The magistrates, conceiving that some error must have taken place, have desired me to communicate the above to you and request to be informed whether it is your attention to afford the poor woman further relief, as it appears to be impossible for her and her family to exist without assistance. Should no answer be received from you before next Monday morning the family will then be removed by an order of the justices to your parish.   [PAR 511/35/1/169]

300 13 May 1825 *Minute of the Winchelsea select vestry*:
Resolved that in consequence of a letter received from the parish officers of Brighton relative to Mrs [Hannah] Francis it is agreed to allow her 3s per week from Lady Day last. [PAR 511/12/2]

301 24 Jun 1825 *Letter from William Tully, 10 Gloster Street, Gloster Place, Brighton to [Charles] Arnett, Winchelsea assistant overseer*:
From an order from the overseers I have advanced the pay to the widow [Hannah] Francis, 3s per week for 13 weeks up to 25th. I should be obliged to you to remit the money by the Hastings coach to the Blue Coach Office, Brighton. NB Please send as soon as convenient in order that I may know if there is any alteration in her pay. [PAR 511/35/1/179]

302 18 Apr 1826 *Letter from William Tully, 10 Gloster Street, Brighton to [Charles] Arnett, Winchelsea, assistant overseer*:
I should be obliged to you to remit Mrs [Hannah] Francis's quarterly pay up to the 25th March. [PAR 511/35/1/218]

303 11 Jul 1826 *Letter from William Tully, 10 Gloster Street, Brighton to [Charles] Arnett, Winchelsea, assistant overseer*:
I should be obliged to you to remit Mrs [Hannah] Francis's pay up to July. [PAR 511/35/1/234]

304 9 Aug 1826 *Letter from H[annah] Francis, Egremont Street, Brighton to [Charles] Arnett, Winchelsea, assistant overseer*:
I have this day received your letter dated July the 24 stating your request concerning my children which I will do in truth. David, the eldest, is 10 years of age, John 9 and Mary 8 and I have had for this last twelve months past 5s per week for assisting in a Free School five hours in the day and my children go with me and we are [*illegible*] able to do anything through the ?nature of trade in this place. There is hardly anything for men and much less for such a child as my David and as for John he has an abscess in his side for some months and has been under the advice of Mr Haddree, sergeant in this place which I have had free of expense or I must have been home before this for he said he must have half a pint of potion every day which you must think did not lay in my power to get so by making my case known a lady in this place give to me for him and had not my own friends rendered me their assistance I could not have gone on for I have 2s 6d to pay a week for rent and the allowance I have from the parish can supply us with bread and I only asked once for a pair of shoes for the boys and was denied and I do believe I have been as little trouble and had less assistance as any in the parish. I desire to be thankful for what I have already received but without this further assistance I cannot do and if this is [not] settled the children must come home. I have done my best for them and the parish and I do feel most discouraged and so I leave it with you to do what you

think is best. If you can keep and clothe them for one shilling per head it is more than I can do. David is a very delicate boy. If I had a trifle I might perhaps get him apprenticed out in this place but he is too little yet for he is very small [for] his age and what can a boy ten years of age do?

[*Endorsed*] 1822 Mr Woods' time David 11, John 9, Mary 5; 1824 the age sent [to] C[harles] Arnett David 13, John 11, Mary 7; 1826 she says David 10, John 9, Mary 8.   [PAR 511/35/1/237]

305 6 Nov 1826 *Letter from Hannah Francis to [Charles] Arnett, [assistant overseer of Winchelsea]*:
Mr. Tulley received a letter from the gentlemen dated October 15th and did not come to hand till the 4th November and specify that the pay for my children to be stopped and signifying that I have stated a false report of their age. I have herewith sent the certificates that there is no such thing and that David is not 11 years of age till the 3rd of next January and John 10 the 22 December next and Mary 9 in July next and they are not [receiving] one penny to aid their support. There is the Mrs ?G in place of your parish with three children and is receiving for them 16d per head. If the gentlemen will allow me the pay for six months longer, that is to May, I will endeavour to do without it for the summer. If not, sir, will you have the goodness to send me word I am to send the children by the van or what way for it is not in my power to defray the expense and the overseers of this parish refuse to take us so if the parish won't allow me for the winter I would be glad to know how we are to get home. Please to send as soon as possible.   [PAR 511/37/7/5]
[*Enclosures*]
6 Jun 1822 *Certificate issued and signed by Revᵈ John Myers, Vicar of Rye*:
David, son of David and Hannah Francis, tower sergeant, was baptised the twelfth day of January one thousand eight hundred and sixteen by John Myers, Vicar. Extracted [by me] from the parish register of Rye in the county of Sussex.
                                                                                   [PAR 511/37/7/5]
6 Jun 1822 *Certificate issued and signed by Revᵈ Thomas Richards, curate of Winchelsea*:
I hereby certify that John, son of David and Hannah Francis, was baptised in the parish of Winchelsea in the county of Sussex on the 27th day of December 1816 by the Revᵈ D Hollingbery [Rector]   [PAR 511/37/7/4]

306 22 Nov 1826 *Letter from [Mrs] H[annah] Francis, 20 Egremont Street, Brighton to Richard Stileman, The Friars, Winchelsea*:
I having not received no answer from you since the letter I wrote dated the 6 of this month with the certificates of the age of my children owing to some mistake which must have been made in Mr Woods' time. [I am anxious] to know if the gentlemen would put on the pay till the 1st of May and by what means I am to send the children home for I have not the wherewith[al] to do it and I must be under the necessity of applying to the magistrates if the gentlemen will neither allow me

for them nor say by what means they are to come home. I assure you, sir, I am in distress for the children as I said before are bringing in nothing. I have nothing but what I can get myself and what is a woman's earnings to maintain 3 children and pay rent and self. I don't know why it is that the gentlemen allow others and won't allow me such a trifle. I should not have sent again to have troubled you, sir, but having received no answer I knew not whether it came safe to hand. I do request [an] answer as soon as possible. Please direct to Mr [William] Tully as I am not home often and have no money to pay the postage.   [PAR 511/35/1/250]

307 12 Dec 1826 *Letter from [Mrs] Hannah Francis, Brighton to [Charles] Arnett at the poorhouse, Winchelsea*:
I am sorry to trouble you again but having sent 2 letters and received no answer respecting the age of my children on the time of Hoad's office on the mistake made then and request to know whether the gentlemen will allow the pay till the first of May as I have requested before. Mr Pennett has taken David on trial to shoemaking ever since 23 of November last and the boy likes the trade and the man seems to approve of him and I believe it will be a good thing for him and taking him [out] of your hands. Mr Pennett says he will soon allow me a trifle with him to aid his support and if you wish for any more information the gentleman will give it to you. I cannot support the three children by what I can get and I do not like to part with them now but I must be under the necessity of it if the gentlemen won't help me a little this winter as they are so young. It was a very great mistake of them [*illegible*] in your letter dated October 15th which no doubt you have seen before this. I don't wish to intrude on the parish for if possible I should rather do without any assistance from them. I hope you will please to answer this letter as soon as possible.   [PAR 511/35/1/252]
Note: The overseers' accounts include a payment of £1 10s to Hannah Francis dated 21 December 1826.[16]

308 20 Mar 1827 *Letter from [Mrs] H[annah Francis, 20 Egremont Street, Brighton to C[harles] Arnett at the poorhouse, Winchelsea*:
I would be very much obliged if you would be so good as to send my pay to me at Mrs Knight, Essex Street, number 19 because I am not at home [now]adays and they will not bring the letters twice. One quarter – 13 weeks at 3s per week £1 19s 0d.   [PAR 511/35/1/265]
Note: This payment was entered in the accounts on 22 March 1827.[17]

309 21 Apr 1827 *Letter from [Mrs] H[annah] Francis, to [Charles] Arnett at the poorhouse, Winchelsea*:
I send you these few lines first to say that my boy David has been at Mr Pennett, Crescent Street, ever since 23 of November last on trial to the shoemaking and his master is now willing to take him and will pay half the expenses of binding him if I will pay the other. [Mr Pennett will] allow him 2s per week after the first year, the time he has been to go into it, and advance [his pay by]1s per year for the whole

of his apprenticeship which will be 6s per week for the last year. It don't lay in my power to pay the part of the indentures which is 15s and the boy is very bare of clothes, one pair of shoes he has already had of his master and they remain yet unpaid for as I have quite as much as I can do to keep them. I wish to acquaint the gentlemen of this and [request] their aid which, if they will come forward to help me in this affair I will venture to keep him if I have my health [and] if they will give me 50s to pay the expense and clothe him up a little. An answer on the subject will be gratefully received. If the gentlemen doubt the truth of the above assertion they may have an answer from the said Mr Pennett by applying with a letter post paid [to] Crescent Street, number 4. [PAR 511/35/1/276]

310 22 Nov 1827 *Letter from [Mrs] Hannah Francis, Brighton to Charles Arnett, poorhouse, Winchelsea*:
It was not my wish to trouble you with this letter but having this day a bill for rent to the amount of £2 11s 0d from James Mills, house agent, and if not paid he will take my few things which I have. Part of this has been standing over since 29th of January to the amount of £1 13s 0d and I have not been able to pay it. This last summer I was under doctor's hands for nearly three weeks and could not attend to my own business and at the present I have only what I can get myself and having three children quite dependent on me, the oldest not yet 12 years of age. If the gentlemen would take it into consideration it is the first time I ever troubled for anything of this kind and I hope for the future I shall be enabled to pay it myself. If you doubt the truth of this I can and will send the bill from [Mr] Mills' own hand. The expense of postage has caused me not to [send] it now but if wished for I will. Please direct for H Francis to be left at Mrs Knight, Essex Street, number 17.
[PAR 511/35/1/305]

311 29 Dec 1827 *Letter from [Mrs] H[annah] Francis, 20 Egremont Street, Brighton to Charles Arnett at the poorhouse, Winchelsea*:
I having wrote to you ever since the 19 November last and one since and have had no answer I know not whether it has come to hand or not but I suppose it has. If so I would be glad to know the determination of the gentlemen for it is out of my power to settle the rent. If they will send me £2 in part the landlord will wait till I can pay the remainder. If they will not render me this little I must send the two youngest children home and this is very hard after managing so long as I have and there is a person would have taken John before this had he been old enough. It is no encouragement for me to get them off your hands at all. There is children in this place nearly as big as mine and their friends receiving 1s 6d per head a week and their parents can send them to school and pay £1 1s quarterly and mine have hardly any learning at all. I must leave this for the gentlemen to consider on but I hope at the same time they will consider it is a very dull time in Brighton at the present. Please to direct as follows: to be left at Mrs Knight's in Essex Street, number 17.
[PAR 511/35/1/310]

312 6 May 1830 *Removal order made by S T Milford and Thomas Fuller, justices of the peace for the county of Sussex, to the churchwardens and overseers of the poor of the parish of Brighthelmston, Sussex*:

Whereas complaint hath been made unto us that Hannah Francis, widow of David Francis and her two children by David Francis, born in lawful wedlock, viz. John aged about 13 years and Mary aged about 11 years, neither of whom has done any act to gain a settlement in their own right, lately intruded into and are now residing in Brighthelmston and are actually become chargeable to the same, we upon examination of the [evidence] upon oath do adjudge the same to be true and do further adjudge the place of last legal settlement of Hannah Francis and her two children to be Winchelsea, Sussex. These are therefore to require you to remove and convey them to Winchelsea and them deliver, together with this our order or a true copy thereof, to the churchwardens and overseers of the poor there who are hereby required to receive and provide for them according to law.

[PAR 511/32/3/58]

Note: On 14 May 1830 the select vestry approved a casual payment of £2 10s 0d to Mrs Francis.[18]

313 19 Oct 1830 *Letter from Mrs [Hannah] Francis, 47 Carlton Row, Brighton to Mr Bigg, Winchelsea, grocer*:

I am under the obligation of sending you these few lines to say my boy has got a place and has been there about six months but can't stop if he has not a great coat and pair of shoes which it don't lay in my power to get for him. I cannot get it for less than 3 or 4 and 20s. He is likely to [*illegible*] and it might be the means of his getting quit of my hands and the parish's too. If you will send me one pound I will do the best I can. If not I can't do it myself. Please to send as quick as possible.

[PAR 511/35/1/339]

314 4 Nov 1830 *Letter from [Mrs] H[annah] Francis, Brighton to [Joseph] Bigg, Winchelsea, grocer*:

Received no answer to the letter I sent. I am constrained to write the second time. The master says he can't be with him without shoes and if the gentlemen won't send him that trifle I must send him home. Be sure I should not trouble you no more this winter if this is granted, nor would I now if I could help it.

[PAR 511/35/1/341]

315 29 Nov 1830 *Letter from [Mrs] H[annah] Francis, 47 Carlton Row, Brighton to [Joseph] Bigg, Winchelsea*:

Having applied to you for a trifle of money for clothing for my boy now in place and received no answer. I once more say I would thank you to answer this that I may know how to proceed as it don't lay in my power to get him clothes that he needs.

[PAR 511/35/1/347]

1 PAR 511/1/1/4 & 6   2 PAR 511/1/2/1   3 PAR 511/1/5/1   4 PAR 511/31/1/12 ff.83, 118, 200, 245, 249   5 PAR 511/31/1/14 f.3   6 PAR 511/12/2 3 Dec 1824   7 PAR 511/31/1/13 QE Jun 1825   8 PAR 511/31/1/14 f.12   9 PAR 511/31/1/13 QE Jun 1830   10 (CW)   11 PAR 511/31/1/13   12 ibid   13 ibid   14 PAR 511/31/1/14   15 PAR 511/12/2   16 PAR 511/31/1/14   17 ibid   18 PAR 511/12/3

Thomas Fuller

316 *The Thomas Fuller removed with his family to Beckley (**317**) was the right age to have been going to sea in 1825 (**318**) but, unless for some reason he had been returned to Winchelsea, he would have been Beckley's responsibility. No other evidence about a Thomas Fuller of this age has been found in the Winchelsea parish records.*

317 14 Jan 1820 *Order made at the general quarter sessions of the peace for the county of Sussex held at Lewes*:
It is ordered by this court that the order or warrant of G[eorge] Tilden and G[eorge] Stace, two of His Majesty's justices of the peace for Winchelsea, for removing John Fuller, Sarah his wife and their two children namely Thomas aged eight years and upwards and John aged two years and upwards from the parish of St Thomas the Apostle, Winchelsea to the parish of Beckley in Sussex be, and is by this court, confirmed, the inhabitants of the parish of Beckley not appealing from the order at this present sessions and proof being made upon oath of the due service of the said order.   [PAR 511/35/3/33]

318 14 Jul 1825 *Letter from Captain William Hume, Sunderland, [County Durham] to [Charles] Arnett, Winchelsea, [assistant] overseer*:
I received your letter dated 10th and you wish to know the reason Thomas Fuller was not bound and the reason was that before the ship left Rye that his mother wished to see him before he was bound. I would have bound him when he went home but he was not agreeable as he thought he would not be able to stand the sea-sickness and he would have left at that time but I wished him to try again which he did and on the second voyage he was sea-sick the same and he said that if the ship was in port that he would never go to sea any more and that was the reason of him leaving the ship.   [PAR 511/35/1/183]

[--] Gilman

319 *The name Gilman has not been identified in the Winchelsea parish records of this period and the reason Winchelsea was seeking information about him is unknown.*

320 19 May 1815 *Letter from R Lepper, Chatham [Kent] to David Laurence, Winchelsea*:
I received yours of 14th and agreeable to your request have inquired into the family of Gilman but am fearful the information will not be of much service but

such as it is you're welcome to it. From what I am able to collect [he] has 5 small children. A sergeant's pay is from 15s to 17s 6d per week when on shore, at sea £20 per year. He lives in a house which rents, if I may judge from the others in the same row at £20 per year and keeps ladies of the ?inn but am not certain he's the occupier or only a lodger, but think he is tenant and hires apartments to others. I am sorry Mrs L[aurence] enjoys a bad state of health and hope she's better. Please to give my best respects to Mr and Mrs Laurence and family.   [PAR 511/35/1/3]

Sarah Haisell

321 *Despite the punitive charges proposed in* (**324**)*, and George Hayes Blake's apparent acceptance of them, the only payment or receipt noted which is related to this case is one of five shillings made in the first quarter of 1825 to 'Sarah Haisell – bastardy'.[1] It would seem that, following George Hayes Blake's eloquent letter,* (**323**) *the child was maintained in such a way that she did not remain chargeable to Winchelsea.*

322 16 Mar 1825 *Settlement examination taken before Henry Powell and John Tilden, justices of the peace for Winchelsea of Sarah Haisell aged nineteen years*: who upon her oath saith that she was born in the parish of St Thomas the Apostle, Winchelsea where her father and mother were legally settled as she has been informed and verily believes to be true; that she has never done any act to gain a legal settlement in any other parish or place to the best of her knowledge and belief; that on the 6th day of August last she was delivered at the dwelling house of her father, George Haisell, hairdresser of Winchelsea, of a female bastard child since baptised by the name of Eliza Hayes Haisell, and that George Hayes Blake, a lieutenant in His Majesty's navy and who formerly resided in Winchelsea is the father of the child and the child is now actually chargeable to Winchelsea. [*signature of*] Sarah Haisell.   [AMS 2330 ff.39-40]
Note: Sarah Haisell was baptised at St Thomas's on 27 July 1806.[2]

323 14 Aug 1825 *Letter from George H[ayes] Blake, 2 Barnards Inn, Holborn, [London] to the parish officers of Winchelsea*:
Having some days past addressed a letter to [Richard Curteis] Pomfret, solicitor, of Rye, on the subject of an illegitimate child sworn to me, as I conclude (for unless the child has been so sworn, the warrant, which in my opinion so vexatiously has been issued would be illegal) and not having received an answer I am desirous of directing my opinion and feeling to the fountain head. Any attempt to prove that the child, from human possibility cannot be mine, would in the first instance avail little against the girl's declaration and delicacy forbids me touching on the matter. Under these impressions, unalterable as they are, I shall only appeal to law and justice. Pray tell me, had I died before the child's birth would you have allowed it 5 shillings a week, so indispensably claimed from me, for a child which I deny to be mine. I believe I did all which common cases and common justice prescribe. I commissioned a gentleman of the legal profession to pay, yearly or half-yearly,

as Mr Pomfret might wish, a reasonable and just demand and never wishing or intending that the child should be a burden on your parish. You, gentlemen, not being forcibly touched with the imposition, issue a warrant in return. I have lived amongst you and may be perhaps known to you sufficiently I hope to convince you that, though there may be a difference of opinion as to legality or illegality of the claim you make on me, my word when once pledged to you would be held inviolate. May I beg you to withdraw the warrant and if I am not to be allowed the justice given to others in similar cases without further appeal, give me timely notice and I will appear before your bench of magistrates at Battle where I am confident of justice. Mr Ex-Sheriff Perkins, some few months since, in pursuance of the statute in such case before a London bench, was directed to pay 3s a week for the maintenance of the child. Mr [George] Haisell received £10 from me on my leaving Winchelsea which of course will be accounted for from the birth in conformity with your general donations in such matters.　　[PAR 511/35/1/188]

324 27 Sep 1825 *Bastardy order made by Henry Powell and John Tilden, justices of the peace for Winchelsea*:
Whereas it hath been duly made appear unto us as well upon complaint of the churchwardens and overseers of the poor of Winchelsea as upon the oath of Sarah Haisell that she was delivered of a female bastard child at the dwelling-house of her father in Winchelsea on the 6th day of August 1825 and that the child is now chargeable to the parish of St Thomas the Apostle, Winchelsea and likely so to continue, and further that George Hayes Blake, late of Winchelsea, did beget the child upon the body of Sarah Haisell. We therefore upon examination of the cause and circumstances of the [evidence] as well upon the oath of Sarah Haisell as otherwise do hereby adjudge George Hayes Blake to be the reputed father of the child; and thereupon we do order, as well for the better relief of the parish of St Thomas the Apostle, Winchelsea as for the sustenance and relief of the child that George Hayes Blake shall and do forthwith, upon notice of this our order, pay or cause to be paid to the churchwardens or overseers of the poor of Winchelsea, or some one of them, the sum of six pounds nineteen shillings and sixpence for and towards the maintenance of the child to the time of the making of this our order; and we do also hereby further order that George Hayes Blake shall likewise pay the sum of three shillings and sixpence weekly and every week from this present time for and towards the keeping, sustentation and maintenance of the child for and during so long time as the child shall be chargeable to Winchelsea; and further order that Sarah Haisell shall also pay the sum of one shilling weekly in case she shall not nurse and take care of the child herself; and we do also hereby further order that George Hayes Blake shall likewise pay the sum of £2 5s for the reasonable charges and expenses incidental to the birth of the child; and also the further sum of £8 15s 10d for the reasonable costs of obtaining our order for the filiation of the child; the said several sums of money being the reasonable charges and expenses incident to the birth of the child and the reasonable costs of apprehending and securing the said George Hayes Blake and of our order of filiation duly and respectively ascertained

on oath before us in pursuant of the statute such case made and provided.
[*endorsed*] Bastardy order upon George Hayes Blake, Lieutenant in the R[oyal]
N[avy] re Sarah Hayes Haisell, daughter of Sarah Haisell.   [PAR 511/34/4/14]

325 18 Oct 1825 *General quarter sessions of the peace held at the Guildhall before
Henry Powell, deputy mayor, George Stace and Joseph Hennah, jurats and justices*:
Ordered that a certain order of affiliation under the hands and seals of Henry Powell
and John Tilden Esquires and being dated the 27th day of September last on George
Hayes Blake Esq be confirmed with the consent of the said George Hayes Blake.
[WIN 61D ff.38-39]

1 PAR 511/31/1/13 QE Mar 1825   2 PAR 511/1/1/4

Isaac Hearnden

326 *Isaac Hearnden came with his family to Winchelsea in 1785 at the age of 12.[1] He
later established a grocery and haberdashery business in the town with which orders
were frequently placed for supplies for the workhouse. Many of his bills survive within the
overseers' accounts. For example, in early 1822 he charged the parish £11 9s 6½d for a
delivery which included soap, cheese, sugar, buttons, worsted, onions, seeds and starch.[2]
Despite the misdemeanour recorded in (**327**) Hearnden often did duty as a juror and in
September 1824 was sworn in as foreman of the Winchelsea grand jury.[3] It is therefore
something of a surprise to find that most of the documents reproduced below concern
insulting the county land commissioners (**328**), an assault on the assistant overseer
(**329-331, 333**), and slandering the deputy mayor (**333-335**). Despite having such a bad
record of behaviour towards officials, he continued to be used as a parish supplier,[4] and in
February 1834 he was one of the many new freemen of Winchelsea appointed to ensure that
Winchelsea Corporation could continue its local government and judicial responsibilities.[5]
The 1841 census shows him to have been living in Castle Street with Elizabeth, his wife,
and Thomas, a tailor who was the youngest of their three children.[6] Between February
1847 and September 1849 he was excused payment of the poor rates.[7] This suggests that
he had, through his business and official offices, established a Winchelsea settlement and
been reduced to pauperism. Isaac Hearnden died in 1855 at the then very good age of 82.[8]*

327 23 Apr 1811 *General quarter sessions of the peace held at the Guildhall,
Winchelsea before George Stace Esq deputy mayor, George Tilden and Charles
Terry jurats and justices of the peace for Winchelsea*:
It having been represented to the court by George Bray, the foreman of the grand
jury, that Isaac Hearnden, one of the jury, (who was called upon to perform his duty
as a juryman at the time the jury made their perambulation and view within the
town of Winchelsea on the 15th day of January then last) absented himself from his
duty having in his possession one of the weights belonging to the Corporation of
the town of Winchelsea in consequence of which the jury were unable to examine
and try some of the weights used within the Corporation which said Isaac Hearnden

was directed to be summoned to attend the next court of quarter sessions to be holden within the town to answer such neglect in his duty. [WIN 61 ff.121-121r]
Note: No record has been found of Hearnden appearing as required. The next three quarter sessions were adjourned without any cases being dealt with.[9]

328 20 Jul 1824 *Information and summary proceedings heard before Joseph Hennah, justice of the peace for Winchelsea*:
Henry Butler [town clerk] of Winchelsea on oath charges Isaac Hearnden with abusing Henry Powell Esq, George Stace Esq and John Tilden Esq, three of the county commissioners for the affairs of land and assessed taxes in and for Winchelsea in the due execution of their office and also with making use of divers profane oaths in the presence of the said commissioners on this present day.
[*Town clerk's appended note*] Defendant bailed on date. No fees paid.
[WIN 237A]

329 Jan 1825 et seq *Account of Messrs Dawes & Co [solicitors of Rye] to the Winchelsea overseers of the poor*:
On the prosecution of Hearnden for assaulting the overseer: Attending Mr Pollock with case: 3s 4d; fee to Mr Pollock and clerk: £2 4s 6d; attending him several times for same: 6s 8d; postage and booking same returned: 1s 8d; fair copy of the case for the opinion of Mr Bolland: 13s 4d; writing to agents to lay same before him: 5s; carriage to and from London: 3s 6d; attending Mr Bolland therewith and thereon: 3s 4d; fee to him and clerk: £2 4s 6d; attending him several times for same: 6s 8d; postage and booking: 1s 8d; attending upon Mr Knapp giving him instructions to prepare indictment: 6s 8d; several attendances for same when he informs us that he had not had time but would do so and give it to Mr [Weeden] Dawes at Horsham: [*amount missing*]. July 1825: Instructions for brief in this process: 6s 8d; drawing same 4 sheets: £1 6s 8d; fair copy for counsel: 13s 4d; paid Mr Bolland and clerk: £2 4s 6d; attending him: 6s 8d; paid for subpoena: 4s; copy and service on Mr Sanders: 5s; the prosecutor and witness not having attended at Lewes on the idea that Hearnden could traverse the indictment paid special messenger from Lewes to Winchelsea: £2 2s 0d; attending court – defendant convicted: £1; paid associate: £1 8s 0d; paid marshal: £1 4s 0d. October [1825] paid Mr [H P] Butler his charges for arresting Hearnden: £1 1s 0d.   [PAR 511/31/2/150]
Note: 1. William Bolland was called to the bar by Middle Temple in 1801. He practised at the Old Bailey with great success. Appointed Recorder of Reading 1817. Created a baron of the exchequer 1829.[10] Appeared for the prosecution in the trial of John Eagles – see (**189**).
2. Sir Frederick Pollock, first baronet, a barrister and later judge, was the son of a saddler. His mother was 'a lady of remarkable energy and forceful character' and he and his two brothers achieved great distinction. After an unsatisfactory early education he attended St Paul's School and Trinity College, Cambridge. His poverty would have led to his leaving Trinity without a degree but for the help of his tutor. Thanks to this help he graduated in 1806 and was elected a fellow of Trinity in the following year.[11]
3. The associate and the marshal were officers of the Chief Justice of the King's Bench. Dr

Ruth Paley, an expert on King's Bench, has confirmed to Christopher Whittick, who kindly inquired on the editor's behalf, that this case must have been heard there.[12]
4. For further notes about this case and those involved see (**10**).

330 19 Mar 1825 *Letter from Weeden Dawes, [Rye] to Charles Arnett [Winchelsea assistant overseer]*:
I am sorry to hear of your loss. I thank you for the letter [received] some little time since. I hope you can put your hand on the receipt when it is wanted. Pray tell me on what day it was that [Isaac] Hearnden [grocer] spit in your face etc. You have not mentioned the day in your statement. PS you must prepare yourself to be at Horsham the 23rd March. I shall be at Winchelsea tomorrow and if you can see me I shall be at my late brother's till 5 or 6.   [PAR 511/35/1/161]
Note: 21 Mar 1825 *Charles Arnett, assistant overseer, expenses involved in taking out an indictment against Isaac Hearnden for an assault*: coach hire to Horsham: £1 7s 0d; coach hire to Rye: £1 7s 0d; 6 days board at 10s 6d: £3 3s 0d; bed at Horsham: £1 1s 0d; indictment: £1 11s 6d; affidavit: 1s; officers' fees: 2s; certificate: 8s; bench warrant: 5s; judge's butler's fee: 1s; copy indictment: 13s 6d; [Total] £10.[13]

331 23 Mar 1825 *Warrant issued by the Rt Hon Sir William Alexander, judge of the sessions of oyer and terminer and general gaol delivery held at Horsham*:
To William Woodroffe, my tipstaff, and all chief constables, headboroughs, tything men, and others whom it may concern. Whereas it appears by the certificate of Thomas George Knapp Esq, clerk of assize on the home circuit that … Isaac Hearnden late of the parish of St Thomas the Apostle, Winchelsea, Sussex, labourer, was and now stands indicted for an assault on Charles Arnett to which indictment he hath not appeared or pleaded; these are therefore to will and require you and every of you upon sight hereof to apprehend and take the said Isaac Hearnden if he shall be found in your bailiwick and him safely keep and bring before me if taken during the present assize otherwise before some one of His Majesty's justices of the peace near to where he shall be so taken to the end that he may answer the said indictment and be further dealt with according to law.   [PAR 511/29/2]
Note: Headboroughs and tything men were officers of hundred courts.

332 21 Feb 1826 *Information given before Henry Powell, George Stace and John Tilden, justices of the peace for Winchelsea by Charles Arnett of Winchelsea, assistant overseer*:
who, on oath, charges Isaac Hearnden [inter alia] with unlawfully neglecting to pay one rate made for the relief of the poor of Winchelsea.   [WIN 237A]

333 18 May 1826 *Affidavit of Henry Powell and Charles Arnett, sworn before John Tilden, justice of the peace for Winchelsea*:
Henry Powell saith that he now is and hath been deputy mayor of the Ancient Town of Winchelsea and the liberties thereof for upwards of three years last past, and Charles Arnett saith that he now is and hath been assistant overseer of the poor

of the parish of St Thomas the Apostle, [Winchelsea], since the twenty-ninth day of September 1823 and Charles Arnett further saith that on the tenth day of January 1825 one Isaac Hearnden of Winchelsea, grocer, did violently assault [him] when in the execution of his office for which offence [Hearnden] was bound over to appear before the judges of assize at Lewes on the third day of August last and was fined one shilling and bound over to keep the peace for three years on his own recognizance for fifty pounds; and [Charles Arnett] further saith that he hath both before and since the twenty-eighth of March last heard Isaac Hearnden use very insulting language towards Henry Powell as a magistrate and also treat him with great derision and contempt. [WIN 287]

334 1 Jun 1826 *Affidavit of Henry Powell, sworn before John Tilden, justice of the peace for Winchelsea*:
Henry Powell of Winchelsea, one of His Majesty's justices of the peace in and for the Ancient Town and the liberties thereof saith that he attended a public vestry held in the parish church of Winchelsea on the twenty-eighth day of March last at which vestry Isaac Hearnden of Winchelsea, grocer, was also present and who, in [Henry Powell's] presence insulted him, by uttering the following words, 'Old Powell granted summonses against certain persons for the purpose of putting money into his own and Henry Butler's pockets (meaning as [Powell] believes the son of the town clerk) which money was paid out of the parish rates.' And [Henry Powell] further saith that the words so uttered by Isaac Hearnden are utterly false and untrue and that he never granted summonses or a summons against any person or persons for the intention or with the purpose of putting money into his pocket or into the pockets of Henry Butler or of any other person, or for the purpose or with the intention of benefiting him or Henry Butler in any way whatsoever and that he, never charged a fee upon any occasion as a magistrate; and he saith that the said words are a malicious defamation of [his] character. [WIN 288]
Note: Evidence exactly corroborating that of Henry Powell above was given on 4 May 1826 by Joseph Bigg of Winchelsea, grocer, and Adam Scott of Winchelsea, doctor of medicine.[14] Henry Butler, senior, was town clerk at that time.

335 n.d. [c.Jun 1826] *Note written by Isaac Hearnden seeking Henry Powell's pardon*:
Whereas I, Isaac Hearnden of Winchelsea in the county of Sussex, grocer, did on the twenty-eighth day of March last at a public vestry held in the parish church of Winchelsea utter the following words, 'Old Powell granted summonses against certain persons for the purpose of putting money in his own and Henry Butler's pockets (meaning the town clerk's son) which money was paid out of the Winchelsea rates.' For which offence the said Henry Powell has proceeded against me in the magistrates' court of [?] but upon my asking this public pardon and paying the expenses already incurred, he has kindly agreed to withdraw any further proceedings; I therefore ask his pardon accordingly and do thank him for the lenity

he has shown to me, as I believe the charge uttered by me against him was utterly false and untrue. [WIN 289]

1 PAR 511/32/1/51 2 PAR 511/31/2/132 3 WIN 61D f.10 4 PAR 511/31/1/13 1828-1831 5 WIN 61B 6 PAR 511/1/1/4 25 Sep 1806 7 PAR 511/12/2 8 PAR 511/1/5/1 9 WIN 61 10 ODNB (CW) 11 The Times, 24 Aug 1870; ODNB; (CW) 12 (CW) 13 PAR 511/31/2/129 14 WIN 285, 286

Joseph Hoad

336 *The family 'by the name of Hoad' resident in Boulogne* (**337**) *was that of Joseph Hoad junior. His father, Joseph senior, who was born in Rye[1] became a long serving and respected Winchelsea Corporation officer who served as a town constable between 1808 and 1829[2] and as town or common sergeant from 1814 to 1824.[3] For the latter office he received a regular salary of £3 1s 8d per annum plus expenses.[4] Joseph Hoad junior, however, had no such income and first received poor relief on 2 November 1820 when he was allowed five shillings a week.[5] This weekly benefit was soon stopped but later that month he received a casual payment of ten shillings.[6] In February 1821 the parish vestry, no doubt wishing to avoid having an extra pauper receiving regular relief supported his desire to leave Winchelsea and allowed him 'the sum of four pounds to defray expenses of going to France, himself, wife and family'.[7] After the appeal on his behalf and Winchelsea's response* (**337-339**) *only one further payment to Joseph Hoad junior of three shillings, made in November 1830, appears in the select vestry minutes and the overseers' accounts.[8] This suggests that the considerable support of his friends and the limited support of his parish led to Hoad's bakery business in Boulogne being successful.*

337 2 Feb 1829 *Letter from John Larking JP for Kent, Boulogne, [France] to the overseers of Winchelsea [delivered] by Captain Cogger of the Rye packet*:
There is a family here by the name of Hoad, consisting of the husband, Joseph, his wife and five small children whom I find upon examination to belong to your parish. They have been a long time out of employment and supported by the charity of the Rev[d] Mr Symonds of the English Chapel of this place who has applied to me for my aid and assistance together with other families of this place who are willing to assist the poor man by setting him up in a small bakery by which he has a fair prospect of gaining a moderate livelihood, provided the sum of £20 can be raised to set him going – we have collected more than half that sum and if you think proper to send £6 or £7 we shall be able to get the rest and by this means prevent the necessity of sending this large family to their parish, as must otherwise be done. Captain Cogger of the Rye packet, to whom I have spoken on the subject, will take charge of what money you think it proper to send and Mr Symonds and myself will take care to dispose of it for the benefit of Hoad and his family. I think you will allow this mode of proceeding to be for the interest of the parish as well as for that of the poor family who require your support. I would have written to Mr Denne with whom I am acquainted but Cogger tells me he is not at present at Winchelsea. [PAR 511/35/1/321]

338 20 Feb 1829 *Minute of the Winchelsea public vestry*:

Resolved that a sum not exceeding £5 be advanced to Joseph Hoad junior at Boulogne if upon inquiry the statement made of John Larking Esq be found to be correct. [PAR 511/12/2]

339 28 Mar 1829 *Letter from John Larking [JP], Boulogne sur Mer, [France] to William Chatterton, Winchelsea, overseer, [delivered] by Captain Cogger of the Rye packet*:

Captain Cogger having informed me that you are ready to relieve the family of [Joseph] Hoad (now residing here) to the amount of £5 I have got him to draw on you for that sum which Cogger will bring over with him – this sum will serve to help him on for the present but not for the full extent of his wants for the payment of sundry articles required to set him fully going in his bakery, in which pursuit he and his wife are very industrious and worthy of support – we are making all the friends we can for them as customers and I have no doubt that they will get a living without again troubling your parish beyond the sum of £5 some time hence, for which, in case of need, we will apply to you for the last time. We keep a watchful eye over him so that whatever he gets or makes in his business will be carefully and properly applied. [PAR 511/35/1/324]

1 PAR 511/32/4/38 2 WIN 61AA; WIN 61B 3 WIN 618 4 ibid 5 PAR 511/12/2 f.4 6 ibid f.5 7 ibid f.78 PAR 511/12/3; PAR 511/31/1/13 QE Dec 1830

Thomas Hoad

340 *The following documents are about father and son. The Thomas Hoad to whom (**341-342**) refer was the son. Both suffered from seriously poor health and both were a drain on the parish poor rate over many years. Thomas Hoad junior's children's names are not given in the overseers' records[1] but from the parish registers it is possible to establish that the children were Thomas b. 1820, George b. 1822, William b. 1823 and Mercy b.1825.[2] Their father was a labourer who, even after his serious illness, occasionally earned one shilling a week for working on the roads.[3] His income was also supplemented by allowances of one shilling a week for taking Caroline Fisher, daughter of William (**260**), into his family's service. From this sum he was supposed to 'find her in necessary clothing'.[4] The similar arrangement made when Harriett Blackhall, daughter of William (**80**), joined Thomas junior's household was more generous for the parish paid the same one shilling a week but also provided Harriett's clothing.[5] Between those two appointments tragedy struck the family when their youngest child Mercy died aged 2. As was necessary for a pauper child, the parish paid the funeral expenses, in this case five shillings for the coffin and 7s 6d for the minister's and clerk's fees.[6] Thomas junior did not long outlive his young daughter for he died in 1828 aged just 29 and was buried in Winchelsea.[7]*
*Thomas Hoad senior was a tailor. In 1825 he was aged 48, his wife, Elizabeth, was 37 and their seven children were Elizabeth junior, 18, who was in service, William 15 and Joseph 12 who were in the workhouse, Mary Ann 8, Edwin 6, Harriett 4 and Frederick 1 against whose name has been written 'dead'.[8] The reason given for refusing relief (**343**) is unusual and illustrates well the parish's caution. However it would seem that the select*

vestry relented for on 10 November 1826 it was resolved that Thomas senior be allowed '7s 6d a week till the next vestry'.⁹ Thereafter he received a weekly allowance of 2s reducing to 1s 6d between March 1831 and June 1834¹⁰ and frequent casual payments according to need. As examples, these include £1 when he was out of work,¹¹ '½ gallon of flour per week he having three children',¹² and 'fifteen shillings as a casual relief himself and wife both being sick'.¹³ Despite this and the illness referred to in (343) Thomas senior long outlived his son and died in 1856 aged 78.¹⁴

341 22 Oct 1824 *Minute of the Winchelsea select vestry*:
Resolved that Thomas Hoad junior in consequence of an opinion of Dr Scott and Dr Burgess be sent to an hospital and also that his family be taken into the [work] house [and] that they should receive casual relief until that time. [PAR 511/12/2]

342 28 Oct 1824 *Petition submitted to the president, treasurer and governors of St Bartholomew's Hospital [London]*:
The humble petition of Thomas Hoad of the parish of [Winchelsea] sheweth that your petitioner is afflicted with [*blank but document endorsed* Thomas Hoad – dropsy] and is likely to perish without the charitable assistance of this house. [He] therefore humbly prays to be admitted into the said hospital for care, and, as in duty bound, will ever pray. I promise to receive the petitioner when discharged from hospital and to bury him if he dies there.
[*Endorsed*] Mr [William] Croughton will be answerable for the above petition.
[*On the reverse*] Recommended by William Croughton. N.B. Admission on Thursdays only at 11 o'clock.
[*Further endorsed with*] An account dated 9 Dec [1824]. Payment for 42 days at 9d: £1 11s 6d and cash to take Hoad home: 7s. Total £1 18s 6d.
[PAR 511/35/4/10]
Notes: 1. William Croughton was a substantial local landowner – see appendix D2.
2. Dropsy is a form of oedema in which excess watery fluid collects in the body.

343 28 Oct 1826 *Letter from D[avid Stonham, Rye to Henry Powell, Winchelsea, deputy mayor*:
I beg your attention a moment to a fact relative to Thomas Hoad the elder of Winchelsea, now very ill and not being able to do anything for the support of his family, has applied for temporary relief which has been refused upon the grounds of his possessing a horse and cart. I am, however, able to satisfy those whom it may concern upon that head and beg to assure you, sir, that the horse and harness was bought by his sister in the month of February last and the cart in the month of May and paid for by her out of her earnings of her needle and sent to her brother Thomas for the sole purpose of enabling him to provide for his family so that he might not be under the necessity of appealing for relief. This, sir, is the fact – the property is not his and it is hoped that as his present appeal arises from the affliction of God whereby he is incapacitated for work the parish will through your advice grant him some temporary supplies.   [PAR 511/35/1/246]

Note: On the following day Hoad was allowed ten shillings casual relief. Casual payments of varying amounts continued until the end of February 1827.[15]

1 PAR 511/31/1/15 f.33 2 PAR 511/1/2/1 3 PAR 511/12/3 23 Dec 1825 4 ibid 21 Apr 1826 5 ibid 4 May 1827 6 PAR 511/31/2/150 7 PAR 511/1/5/1 8 PAR 511/31/1/15 f.13 9 PAR 511/12/3 10 PAR 511/31/1/16 11 PAR 511/31/1/13 QE Mar 1827 12 PAR 511/12/3 4 May 1827 13 ibid 25 Mar 1828 14 PAR 511/1/5/1 15 PAR 511/31/1/15 f.13

Burford Jeakens

344 *The parish registers show that the Burford Jeakens whose appeals to the Winchelsea overseers feature below was twenty-five at the time of his mother's death in 1829. His father had died three years earlier.[1] The siblings for whom he was assuming responsibility, Alfred and Sarah were, respectively, 13 and 10.[2] Burford's late father, Edward, had been a tanner and his son may have followed him but the records provide no information about the nature of his work or of Alfred's proposed apprenticeship. Burford's grandfather, another Edward, died in 1815.[3] Their home at Cook's Green and his other property remained in the name of Burford's grandmother (known in the records as Widow Jeakens senior) until 1825 (see appendix D2) when, without explanation, dues were recorded as being collected from her representatives. She first received weekly poor relief in June 1820.[4] Payments to her daughter-in-law, Burford's mother (Widow Jeakens junior), began when her husband died.[5] There is only one mention in the overseers' accounts of one-off cash sums such as those sought in (350-351) and (353-355). That is when, on 25th June 1830, the select vestry allowed £3 'for putting Alfred apprentice'.[6] Support of the children, later at 3s per week, continued until March 1833 when Alfred's payment ceased and Sarah was allocated 1s 6d per week. That allowance, too, ended in March 1834.[7] It is presumed that the Burford Jeakens, tanner aged 73, who is listed in appendix C2 was an uncle for whom this Burford was named. The carrier Cogger (349, 351) who was at best unreliable and at worst dishonest when taking money from Winchelsea to Battle has not been positively identified.*

345 26 Mar 1829 *Minute of the Winchelsea select vestry*:
Resolved that the assistant overseer write to Mr Burford Jeakens of Battle to propose to him to take charge of his brother and sister, Alfred and Sarah, now left orphans in consequence of the recent death of Widow Jeakens and to be allowed 6s a week by the parish for their maintenance.   [PAR 511/12/3]

346 28 May 1830 *Minute of the Winchelsea select vestry*:
Resolved that [the payment of] six shillings [per week] be continued to Burford Jeakens for the maintenance of his brother and sister to midsummer next.

[PAR 511/12/3]

347 [c. Jun 1830] *Letter from Burford Jeakens, Battle, to D[avid] Laurence, [Winchelsea] [assistant] overseer*:
I received yesterday a note from my sister who informs me that the vestry agree to allow with my family 6s per week but that the consideration of any sum they may allow with my brother is deferred as he cannot be apprenticed for some time. I am sorry for this delay because I am now at the expense of 6s per week for lodging, besides the additional expense of keeping two tables. We could live much cheaper

together and take lodging for 3s a week. I am sorry you was not at home to state this to the vestry. I have again spoken to Mr Noakes. He has kindly agreed to take Alfred as soon as I can arrange matters with you. I am very much obliged to the gentlemen for this additional allowance but I think they must see when they are so kind as to take it into their consideration that I cannot be expected, that I am unable to apprentice my brother without the sum advanced. Now if they are pleased to engage that this sum shall be continued for one year and will advance £10, I am willing to take the boy (not yet 13 years of age) off their hands for ever, and I really must positively say I hope they will excuse it for I think it best to be plain and not to equivocate that I cannot engage to do it for life. It is an expense, an encumbrance, which a young man will not easily take upon himself, the more I look at it the greater appears to be the difficulty; it blasts in a great measure my future prospects and breaks in upon my future plan of life. I hope, my dear sir, you will settle this business as soon as you can. Perhaps you will be so kind as to call a vestry tomorrow. You see at what expense I am now living, greater really than I can support and I must not you know get in debt. I would come to Winchelsea if I could but have lost so much time lately and have been so worried in my mind as well as body that I don't know how to it. Waiting your reply. Pray be quick and you will confer another obligation. [PAR 511/35/1/332]

348 [after 25 Jun 1830] *Letter from 'Mrs and B[urford] Jeakens', Battle, to D[avid] Laurence, Winchelsea, [assistant overseer]:*
I must agree to the arrangement proposed in your letter which I received this morning. You will therefore be so good as to send the £3 by Cogger on Monday and the 3s per week due from Ladytide to Midsummer and I will bind Alfred. I should be much obliged if you would send me an account of our affairs including my debt to you. Pray don't disappoint me on Monday for 'tis the pressing call I have for money is the principal inducement with me to agree to the arrangement.
[PAR 511/35/1/333]

349 27 Jul 1830 *Letter from Burford Jeakens, Battle, to David Laurence, Winchelsea, [assistant overseer]:*
I am fearful that you have made a remittance by Cogger and he has not delivered it. If this be the case I hope you will let me know by return of post. If you have not, surely you must think it quite time that I knew the determination of the parish for this month past. I ought to have taken something weekly for Alfred from Mr Noakes but I kept putting off binding him from week to week, expecting every day to receive an answer from you. All this time is lost. If I do not hear from you during this week I shall send the children to Winchelsea. Jane loses her place this week and must of course come home with the rest. I really am so horrified that I do wish to get rid altogether of my encumbrance. I am sure that if you knew only half the distress I am in you would not keep me in this suspense. [PAR 511/35/1/334]
Note: The overseers' accounts for June to September 1830 include 'Weekly pay Jeakens, Alfred and Sarah 13 weeks at 6s - £3 18s 0d.[8]

350 [?Aug 1830] *Letter from Burford Jeakens, Battle to [David] Laurence, [Winchelsea, assistant overseer]*:
If you would be so good as to send me £2 next Friday by Cogger I should be very much obliged to you. When I come to Winchelsea we will settle up. I hope you won't disappoint me next Friday for I am much in want [and] have refrained from asking as long as I possibly could do.   [PAR 511/35/1/335]

351 [?Aug 1830] *Letter from Burford Jeakens, Battle to [David] Laurence, [Winchelsea, assistant overseer]*:
I should feel greatly obliged if you would be so good as to send me £2 by Alfred on Thursday or by H Lambert on Monday next. It really is not safe to send by Cogger. A remittance from Rye to Mr Noakes of money Cogger has applied to his own use but a short time ago and Mr Noakes can't get it off him again.
[PAR 511/35/1/336]

352 [?Aug 1830] *Letter from Burford Jeakens, Battle to D[avid] Laurence, Winchelsea, [assistant overseer]*:
I am much surprised and disappointed that you have not sent me the determination of the vestry. I hope you will not fail in sending new word on Monday and you will truly oblige.   [PAR 511/35/1/337]

353 19 Jan 1831 *Letter from Burford Jeakens, Battle to D[avid] Laurence, Winchelsea, [assistant overseer]*:
I really am very much distressed for money. [I] wish you would be so good as to send me three pounds on Friday by Lambert. I have several little bills which must be paid this Christmas and people are continually calling for their money.
[PAR 511/35/1/351]
Note: The overseers' accounts for December 1830 to March 1831 include 'Weekly pay Jeakens, Alfred and Sarah 13 weeks at 3s - £1 19s 0d.'[9]

354 [?Jan 1831] *Letter from Burford Jeakens, Battle to D[avid] Laurence, Winchelsea, [assistant overseer]*:
I was prevented by the rain going to Winchelsea yesterday but I can now repeat what I said to you that if the parish persist in their present arrangement the children must come home. If they will allow £5 and continue to [provide] 8s a week 'till midsummer when the boy will have been with Mr Noakes a year, I will put him apprentice and am willing that from that time it shall go on as it now stands. It will cost about £2 for indentures. Jane did not leave me until more than a month after Ladytide and I have a doctor's bill of nearly £2 to pay for her and Alfred and was obliged to give Jane a pound when she left me to purchase a few things for her service. I think if the gentlemen take it into their serious consideration they will not consider this a common case and will agree to my proposal. If they do not the children certainly must come home to the workhouse.   [PAR 511/35/1/352]

355 [?Jan 1831] *Letter from Burford Jeakens, Battle to D[avid] Laurence, Winchelsea, [assistant overseer]*:

I should be very much obliged to you to send me £3. I am very sorry to trouble you so often but really cannot help it. I am now above £5 in debt in this place which ought to have been paid at Christmas. People come to me for money and I cannot pay them which really makes me quite miserable.   [PAR 511/35/1/353]

1 PAR 511/1/5/1   2 PAR 511/1/2/1   3 PAR 511/1/5/1   4 PAR 511/12/2 f.1   5 PAR 511/31/1/13 QE Mar 1825 6 PAR 511/31/1/15 f.27   7 PAR 511/31/1/16   8 PAR 511/31/1/13   9 ibid

George Jenkins

356 *On his enforced return from Lewisham to Winchelsea after his wife's death* (**357**) *George Jenkins was admitted to the Winchelsea workhouse but his stay was short as he left on 10 November 1826.[1] He seems then to have worked for an employer in the parish as the overseers' receipts for the first quarter of 1827 show, 'G Jenkins labour – seventeen shillings'.[2] Disbursements for the same quarter include the allocation of ten shillings to 'George Jenkins to go away with'.[3] This financed his return to Lewisham. There is no record that the parish responded to his request for £2 (*359*) or that he received further support from Winchelsea. A George Jenkins, possibly his father, is recorded in 1803 aged 32 as a butcher with a slaughterhouse. He regularly supplied meat to the parish.[4]*

357 11 Oct 1826 *Letter from Messrs Parker and Sons, Lewisham, [Kent], to the churchwardens and overseers of Winchelsea*:

We beg to inform you that orders of removal of your parishioners George Jenkins and his wife Elizabeth from this to your parish were this day signed by the magistrates and suspended on account of the wife's illness and that you will be charged with the expense of their maintenance etc during the suspension.

[PAR 511/35/1/243]

358 11 Oct 1826 *Removal order made by Matthew P Lucas and Joseph ?Jacken, justices of the peace for the county of Kent to the churchwardens and overseers of the poor for the parish of Lewisham, Kent*:

Whereas complaint hath been made to us that George Jenkins and Elizabeth his wife lately intruded and came into the parish of Lewisham and are actually become chargeable to the same, we upon due proof made thereof as well upon the examination of George Jenkins do adjudge the same to be true and do also adjudge [their] place of legal settlement to be the parish of St Thomas the Apostle, Winchelsea, Sussex. These are therefore in His Majesty's name to require you on sight hereof to remove and convey them to Winchelsea and them deliver together with this order or a true copy thereof unto the churchwardens and overseers of the poor there who are hereby required to receive and provide for them according to law.

[*Appended – same magistrates and date*] It appearing to us that the within named

Elizabeth, wife of George Jenkins, is unfit to be removed by reason of sickness and infirmity of body and that it would be dangerous for her to be removed, we therefore do hereby suspend the execution of the order until we are satisfied that it may be safely executed.

[*Further appended – same magistrates*] 21 Oct 1826 Whereas it duly appears unto us that the within named Elizabeth Jenkins (wife of George Jenkins) is dead and that the within order of removal as to the said George Jenkins may be executed without danger we therefore hereby grant our permission for the execution of the order and direct the churchwardens and overseers of the poor of the parish of St Thomas the Apostle, Winchelsea, to pay unto the churchwardens and overseers of the parish of Lewisham [the sum of] £3 16s 6d being the amount of charges proved upon oath to have been incurred by the suspension of the order.

[PAR 511/32/3/50]

359 25 Jun 1827 *Letter from George Jenkins at Mrs Holmesbrook['s] near the bridge, Lewisham. Kent to [Charles] Arnett, Winchelsea, [assistant overseer]*:
I should be much obliged to you if you would be so good as to ask the gentlemen if they would let me have £2 to get some shirts with and stockings and shoes and some clothes for I am going to my place on Saturday next. I will pay them again in three months. Please to send me word whether you can or cannot by return of post. [PAR 511/35/1/285]

1 PAR 511/12/3   2 PAR 511/31/1/13   3 ibid   4 PAR 511/31/1/3; Appendices C2 D1

Lucy Kite, née Vennall, formerly Lucy May

360 *The bastardy order regarding Lucy Vennall's child made by the Winchelsea magistrates against James May (**361**) was followed by the couple's marriage (**362**). This first child was Jane and a second, James junior, was born in 1812.[1] James May senior, a shoemaker died in 1815 aged 35.[2] Two years later his widow married James Kite[3] and they moved to Scotland with her two children. Following her first husband's death the Winchelsea overseers had begun paying his widow an allowance for the maintenance of the children. Initially this was four shillings a week, reduced to two shillings on her re-marriage and eventually settled at three shillings.[4] In September 1824 these payments ceased but after Lucy Kite's representations (**364**) assistance resumed at 1s 6d per week but only briefly. James Kite clearly kept fully to his intention to send the children back to Winchelsea if the parish would not provide financial assistance (**364**) because on 23rd December 1825 the select vestry resolved that 'J May's two [children] be taken into the house until the return of the [step]father when he is to be [charged] with the expenses.[5] The parish records reveal nothing more of this case until Lucy Kite was removed from Rye to Winchelsea long after her second husband's death (**365**).*

361 18 Dec 1810 *Bastardy order of George Tilden and George Stace, justices of the peace for Winchelsea, concerning the child of Lucy Vennall*:
Whereas it hath been duly made to appear unto us as well upon the complaint of the

churchwardens and overseers of the poor of Winchelsea, as well as upon the oath of Lucy Vennall that she was delivered of a female bastard child in Winchelsea on the 22nd day of November 1810 and that the said child is now chargeable to Winchelsea and likely so to continue; and further that James May of Winchelsea, cordwainer, did beget the child upon the body of Lucy Vennall; and whereas the said James May hath not shown any sufficient cause why he shall not be the reputed father of the child but hath admitted to us that he is the father thereof. We therefore upon examination of the cause and circumstances of the [evidence] as well upon the oath of Lucy Vennall as otherwise do hereby adjudge him, James May, to be the reputed father of the child; and thereupon we do order as well for the better relief of the parish of St Thomas the Apostle, Winchelsea as for the sustentation and relief of the child that James May shall, and do forthwith, upon notice of this our order, pay or cause to be paid to the churchwardens or overseers of the poor of Winchelsea or to some one of them the sum of forty shillings for and towards the lying-in of Lucy Vennall and the maintenance of the child to the time of making this our order; and we do hereby also further order that James May shall likewise pay or cause to be paid the sum of two shillings and sixpence weekly and every week from this present time and towards the keeping, sustentation and maintenance of the child for and during so long time as the child shall be chargeable to the parish; and we do further order that Lucy Vennall shall [similarly] pay or cause to be paid one shilling and sixpence for the time being weekly and every week in case she shall not nurse and take care of the child herself.   [PAR 511/34/4/1]

Notes: 1. Lucy Vennall, 'singlewoman, pregnant' had been removed from Rye to Winchelsea by an order dated 9 Aug 1810.[6]

2. Jane May 'daughter of Lucy Vennall' was baptised at St Thomas's on 9 December 1810.[7]

362 20 Mar 1824 *Certificate issued and signed by William Robson, Methodist minister, Buckie [Banff, Scotland]*:

This is to certify that James and Jane May, son and daughter of Mrs Kite, formerly Mrs May, are alive and in a state of perfect health.   [PAR 511/37/7/7]

Notes: 1. This certificate is written on the back of the last part of a letter from Lucy Kite presumably to her parents. The text reads: 'I must think of concluding as my paper is nearly full. Give our kindest love to all my brothers and sisters, to my aunt and uncle Ruby and to all friends that are kind enough to ask after us and do not fail to write directly if anything happens. Kite and the children join me in kind love to you all from your ever dutiful son and daughter James and Lucy Kite.'

2. James Kite, Lucy's second husband, was baptised as an adult at Winchelsea on 15 June 1817 being then described as 'son of Susan Kite of St Mary's, Dover'.[8]

363 22 Jun 1824 *Certificate issued and signed by John Muir, minister at Auchmithie [Arbroath, Scotland]*:

It is hereby certified that Jane and James May, son and daughter of Lucy Kite and the late James May are both alive and in good health and residing at present in the parish of St Vijean's with their mother Lucy and their father-in-law [i.e. stepfather], James Kite.   [PAR 511/37/7/8]

364 7 Dec 1824 *Letter from Lucy Kite and her husband James Kite from the preventive boat Auchmithie, by Arbroath, North Britain to Richard Stileman, The Friars, Winchelsea*:

You will I hope pardon the liberty I take in troubling you with the parish business but finding the pay that was allowed for my children [has] been stopped for some time past induced me to trouble you which I should not have done but being in reduced circumstances ever since we left home we have continually been called to move from place to place which has been attended with considerable expense and we now find it impossible to travel with them any longer. My brother [Thomas] May would like to take the boy off the parish if there could be anything allowed to clothe him with which he informs me will not be granted. Sir, I hope you will consider my case and if there cannot be any more allowed for the girl you would be pleased to intercede for me in getting it a little longer for the boy or my husband is resolved to send them home and [we] would be humbly obliged to your honour if you could state any way that we could send them as we are at present between five and six hundred miles from home and have not money to pay their expenses. Sir, grant me the favour of a line from you.   [PAR 511/35/1/142]

365 19 Oct 1863 *Removal order made by A B Vidler and George H Edwards, justices of the peace for Rye, to the churchwardens and overseers of the parish of Rye*:

Whereas complaint hath been made unto us that Lucy Kite, widow, (whose second husband has been dead twenty-four years) has come to inhabit and is now inhabiting in that part of the parish of Rye which lies within the Borough of Rye, not having resided in the parish for the three years next before the application of this warrant and not having gained a legal settlement there, nor having produced any certificate acknowledging her to be settled elsewhere and that she is now actually chargeable to the parish of Rye and is now receiving relief therefrom and that the parish of St Thomas the Apostle, Winchelsea, is the place of her last legal settlement. We, the said justices, do upon proof thereof as well as by examination of witnesses upon oath and upon due consideration of the [evidence] do adjudge the same to be true. These are therefore, in Her Majesty's name, to require and order you or some one of you or some proper person or persons to be employed by you to remove and convey Lucy Kite at such time and in such manner as by law is provided and directed in that behalf, from and out of the parish of Rye to the parish of St Thomas the Apostle, Winchelsea, and her deliver, together with this our order or a duplicate or true copy thereof, unto the overseers of the poor there, or one of them, who are hereby required to receive and provide for her according to law.
                                                              [PAR 511/32/3/89]

1 PAR 511/1/1/4 2 PAR 511/1/5/1 3 PAR 511/1/3/1 4 PAR 511/31/1/11 Apr 1816-Mar 1820; PAR 511/31/1/13 Sep 1820-Sep 1824 5 PAR 511/12/3 6 PAR 511/32/3/21 7 PAR 511/1/2/1 8 PAR 511/1/2/1

Thomas Lancaster

366 *There were two Thomas Lancasters, father and son, both Winchelsea paupers living principally in Rye although the available records also note them in Rye Foreign, Peasmarsh and Iden. The settlement examination of Thomas Lancaster senior, taken before Thomas Marten (367) was preceded by a less informative version taken two days earlier with Thomas Lamb as the presiding magistrate.[1] It could be that this was superseded because Lamb was Lancaster's landlord. In 1822 Thomas senior was listed by the Winchelsea overseers as a labourer aged 50 of Peasmarsh, his wife, not named, was 49 and the children living at home at that time were George 17, Jane 12 and Elizabeth 8.[2] At the same time Thomas junior, also a labourer, was living with his family in Winchelsea. No ages are given for husband or wife. Their children were Caroline 4, Harriett 2 and Mary Ann 6 months.[3] If they were indeed in Winchelsea at that time, the removal order from Rye Foreign (368) had been carried out. However, by 1825 they were back in Rye.[4] Both families were regularly supported with weekly and casual payments and with allowances for clothing.[5] Their Rye poor rates were also paid by Winchelsea, the overseers' accounts containing, among other similar entries, 'Disbursements: overseers of Rye – poor rates for two Lancasters and [Nathaniel] Bragg £1 4s 9d'.[6] On 30 June 1826 the select vestry, 'Resolved that Thomas Lancaster senior be allowed £1 5s 0d to assist him to bury his wife'.[7] The following month Thomas junior was, 'allowed one guinea [to] find sheets etc the wife being pregnant and not having the advantage of doctor'.[8] It is not clear which Thomas Lancaster Rye wished Winchelsea to take without an order (369).*

367 15 Feb 1801 *Examination, taken on oath before Thomas Marten, justice of the peace for Winchelsea, of Thomas Lancaster*:
This examinant saith that he was born at Peasmarsh about the year 1770 and lived with his father John Lancaster about 14 years and then went to live with Mr Nicholas Woollett at Sittingbourne in Kent and lived with him one year and a week but had no wages but his master found him in clothes and gave him money occasionally and gave him half-a-crown at his coming away. He then came home to his father and worked with Mr Benjamin Wood by the week or day, he does not know which, and then came to live with Mr Burford Jeakens of Winchelsea at Lady Day and agreed with him at six pounds a year and then hired himself with him for another year at eight pounds and stayed his year and received his full wages. About 6 weeks before Lady Day 1799 he came to live in a house of Thomas Lamb Esq and lived there one year and paid his rent of three pounds five shillings to Mr Lamb's bailiff and continued to live there and has paid his rent to Michaelmas 1800. [*mark of*] Thomas Lancaster.   [PAR 511/32/4/136]
Note: Thomas Lancaster 'son of John and Rose' was baptised at Peasmarsh on 10 November 1771.[9]

368 31 Jan 1822 *Removal order made by Richard Stileman and John Bishop, justices of the peace for the county of Sussex to the churchwardens and overseers of the parish of Rye Foreign, Sussex*:
Whereas complaint hath been made to us that Thomas Lancaster, his wife Elizabeth

and their two children viz. Harriet aged about 3 years and a quarter and Caroline aged about 10 months lately intruded and came into the parish of Rye Foreign and are actually become chargeable to the same, we upon due proof thereof [and also] upon the examination of Thomas Lancaster do adjudge the same to be true and do also adjudge the last place of legal settlement of Thomas Lancaster, his wife and children to be the parish of St Thomas the Apostle in the Ancient Town of Winchelsea. These therefore require you on sight hereof to remove and convey them to Winchelsea and them deliver, together with this our order or a true copy thereof, to the churchwardens and overseers of the poor who are hereby required to receive and provide for them according to law.   [PAR 511/32/3/40]

369 3 Nov 1826 *Letter from Joseph Mills, Rye, assistant overseer, to [Charles] Arnett, Winchelsea, [assistant] overseer*:
Mr [Samuel] Selmes wished me to write to you to know the determination of your vestry respecting the rates due from your parishioners in this parish and if it would be agreeable for you to pay our parishioners and I pay yours in this parish and balance the account at the end of the year and if you will take Thomas Lancaster without an order.   [PAR 511/35/1/248]

1 PAR 511/32/4/135   2 PAR 511/31/1/12 f.73   3 ibid f.74   4 PAR 511/31/1/15 f.14   5 e.g. PAR 511/31/1/13 Feb 1824 to Jun 1827   6 ibid QE Dec 1825   7 PAR 511/12/3   8 ibid 4 Jul 1826   9 PAR 440/1/1/2

Elizabeth Lowes

370 *Elizabeth Lowes née Barden married Clifford Lowes at Winchelsea in 1818.[1] Her husband was born in Winchelsea but, when aged 11, had gone to live at Broomhill when his father was allowed to build a cottage on the beach there. The Winchelsea overseers sought counsel's opinion about this. Mr George Courthope was of the opinion that an attempt to remove Clifford Lowes and his family to Broomhill could not be supported.[2] As a result of the information received from naval surgeon Daniel Wilson (**371**) and the desperate pleas of Elizabeth on behalf of her smallpox-ridden family (**372-373**) the Winchelsea authorities resolved to make a payment of £2 2s 0d which is entered in the overseers' accounts as 'casual pay Lowes, Clifford - smallpox'.[3] The order removing Elizabeth Lowes, by then separated from her husband, from St Mary in the Castle, Hastings was deferred because of her illness (**375**). It was never implemented because she died. Winchelsea was subsequently charged the sum of £8 1s 0d for expenses incurred in maintaining her between the drawing up of the removal order and her death.[4]*

371 26 Jun 1827 *Letter from Daniel Wilson RN, assistant surgeon, Number 28 [Martello] Tower, [Rye Harbour] to the Rev [Thomas] Richards, Icklesham*:
I hope you will excuse the liberty I have taken of addressing you on a subject which I can assure you is of no small importance both as regards the individuals themselves and also the society around them. It is that of a family of four persons named Law or Lowe living near the *Enchantress*, two of whom, the mother and

daughter, are in a convalescent state from smallpox, but the husband of the daughter and a younger sister are now in the primary stage of the complaint. The husband, when in health, supplied the house with water and other necessaries from Rye and since his indisposition they have no way of getting such articles. And so by the desertion of their friends and neighbours from a dread of the disease they are likely to bring not a little disgrace on the parish to which they belong. I therefore hope your influence will cause an inquiry to be made after this suffering family.

[PAR 511/35/1/286]

Note: *HMS Enchantress* was the former French three-master *Recontre* which ran aground near the mouth of the River Rother and was converted for use as the local headquarters of the Royal Navy's Coast Blockade Service which sought to prevent smuggling along the coasts of Kent and Sussex between 1817 and 1831.[5]

372 16 Jul 1827 *Letter from Elizabeth Lowes, Rye Harbour, [Winchelsea] to [Charles] Arnett, Winchelsea, [assistant] overseer*:

I am under the necessity of making this application to you as we are in distress for the means of obtaining the necessaries of life. We have had no money since last Friday and have been under the necessity of borrowing a little money on account of the person who called at your house on Saturday last not obtaining anything for us, you not being at home. We fully expected you would have sent relief yesterday or this day as Mrs Arnett promised that she would send a boy with it but as no one has arrived I have come with this note myself as far as the white gate of the canal and hope you will have the goodness to step to that place as I should be glad to see you. I hope if it should not be convenient for you to come to the gate to see me you will not fail to send someone to meet me at the gate with the relief.

[PAR 511/35/1/288]

373 19 Jul 1827 *Letter from Elizabeth Lowes, Rye Harbour, [Winchelsea] to [Charles] Arnett, Winchelsea, [assistant] overseer*:

I have to acknowledge having received 5s this day by a boy sent by and from you, and I must take the liberty to say in answer that I am at a loss to know what you mean for I told you when I saw you last that I had been obliged to borrow a little money and I have been under the necessity of borrowing a little more since on account of not receiving any from you and I must pay it again with what you have sent me this day and then I shall have none to procure any of the necessities of life and which cannot be done without and I wish to know whether you intend to allow any regular relief merely so long as it is absolutely necessary or not. I expected from your word that the doctor would have been here and seen us and made his report to you as you said you would be ruled by his report and that what he said was necessary should be sent. I have taken the liberty of carrying this note myself as far as the white gate on the canal and should be glad to see you there if you can make it convenient. [PAR 511/35/1/289]

374 10 May 1837 *Examination, taken on oath before William Thorpe, justice of the peace for the borough of Hastings, of Elizabeth Lowes*:
who saith that in September 1818 she was married to Clifford Lowes, her present husband, from whom she has been separated about eight years and whose settlement then was and now is in the parish of St Thomas the Apostle, Winchelsea; that about sixteen years ago while residing with her husband in the parish of Icklesham [i.e. at Rye Harbour within the ecclesiastical parish of Icklesham but also within the Liberty of Winchelsea] relief was allowed by Winchelsea to her husband and herself during their illness; that she is now actually chargeable to the parish of St Mary in the Castle, Hastings. [*signature of*] Elizabeth Lowes

[*included within* PAR 511/32/3/79]

375 10 May 1837 *Removal order made by William Thorpe and Robert Montague Wilmot, justices of the peace for the borough of Hastings, Sussex, to the churchwardens and overseers of the poor of the parish of St Mary in the Castle, Hastings*:
Whereas complaint hath been made unto us that Elizabeth Lowes, wife of Clifford Lowes, lately intruded and came into the parish of St Mary in the Castle and is actually chargeable to the same, we upon due proof thereof as well as upon the examination of Elizabeth Lowes upon oath do adjudge the same to be true and do also adjudge her place of last legal settlement to be the parish of St Thomas the Apostle, Winchelsea, Sussex. These are therefore in His Majesty's name to require you on sight hereof to remove and convey Elizabeth Lowes to Winchelsea and her deliver, together with this order or a true copy thereof to the churchwardens and overseers of the poor who are hereby required to receive and provide for her according to law.
[*Endorsed*] Whereas it doth appear unto us that Elizabeth Lowes, the pauper within ordered to be removed, is at present unable to travel by reason of sickness and infirmity, we do therefore hereby suspend the execution of the order of removal until it shall be made appear unto us that the same may be executed without danger. [PAR 511/32/3/79]
Note: William Thorpe was serving as mayor of Hastings in 1837 but was removed from office for bankruptcy and replaced by Robert Ranking.[6]

1 PAR 511/1/3/1 2 PAR 511/35/2/5 3 PAR 511/31/1/13 QE Sep 1827 4 PAR 369/32/2/45 5 Philp (1999) p.43 6 Baines p.29

William Martin

376 *A confusingly large number of William Martins appear in the Winchelsea parish records for the period covered by this volume. William Martin I (**377-381**), resident in Icklesham but knowing his legal settlement to be in Winchelsea, approached Winchelsea for help in December 1815 but was told he 'must apply to the parish where he resides'.[1] When, as a result of that application, he was formally removed to Winchelsea with his wife Elizabeth (**377**) he was granted two shillings a week 'until further orders'.[2] This relief* *was paid until at least December 1817.[3] By then he had returned to Icklesham with his settlement certificate acknowledging Winchelsea's responsibility for him (380). Although William Martin II (383-389), perpetrator of one of several attacks on Charles Arnett, also worked for Samuel Putland of Icklesham he cannot be the same person as William Martin I because he and his wife Julia brought up their family in Winchelsea where their children were baptised between 1822 and 1828.[4] His extremely detailed and informative settlement examination (388) shows that, unlike William Martin I, his legal settlement was in Icklesham and he was removed there (389). William Martin III, a regular recipient of relief, lived at what is described as 'Old Harbour', that is the area now occupied by the village of Camber. There is just a possibility suggested by the way in which payments were made[5] that he is William Martin I who moved from Icklesham in 1819, but this cannot be definitely established. William Martin III may well have been a River Rother ferryman for he was once paid 2s 8d 'for carrying men over harbour to work on road'.[6] Yet another William Martin 'junior' began receiving relief in 1835.[7] The principal difficulty, however, in examining the relevant books has been that it has not been possible to establish whether one of these men or yet another William Martin was the father of Mary Chart's illegitimate child (382). We know that Mary Chart, widow, made a voluntary examination statement saying that on 30 August 1821 she was delivered of a female child and that William Martin, widower, was the father.[8] A Mary Martin aged 47, wife of William, was buried at Winchelsea on 4 October 1819.[9] If that was how this William Martin became a widower, it eliminates the William Martins whose wives are named above but still provides no definite answer. Whoever this William Martin was, the records show that he was far more assiduous in paying the required maintenance of two shillings weekly than any other father featured in this volume.[10]*

377 23 Jan 1816 *Removal order made by G Webster and E J Curteis, justices of the peace for the county of Sussex, to the churchwardens and overseers of the poor for the parish of Icklesham, Sussex:*

Whereas complaint hath been made to us that William Martin and Elizabeth his wife lately intruded and came into the parish of Icklesham and are actually become chargeable to the same, we upon due proof thereof as well as the examination of William Martin do adjudge the same to be true and also do adjudge the place of legal settlement of William Martin to be in the parish of Winchelsea. [We] therefore in His Majesty's name require you on sight hereof to remove and convey them to Winchelsea and them deliver, together with this our order or a true copy thereof, to the churchwardens and overseers of the poor there who are hereby required to receive and provide for them according to law.   [PAR 511/32/3/29]

378 7 Mar 1816 *Letter from Samuel Putland, Icklesham to the parish officers, Winchelsea:*

On Saturday last I received a note from David Laurence [overseer] respecting Martin and his wife returning into Icklesham parish with a note given from the gentlemen of Winchelsea to indemnify the parish of Icklesham from any expense in future by their returning. I laid the note before a vestry on Sunday and those that attended wish me to say [that] if the gentlemen of Winchelsea would pay the parish of Icklesham every expense which they were [caused] in consequence of his not [being] being taken without an order, they will then take a note. Otherwise do not think of letting them return without a certificate. [PAR 511/35/1/5]

379 29 Dec 1816 *Minute of the Winchelsea public vestry*:
Agreed that a certificate be granted to William Martin and his wife Elizabeth of being legally settled at Winchelsea, the certificate [below] is directed to the parish officers of Icklesham. [PAR 511/12/1 f.212]

380 29 Dec 1816 *Settlement certificate issued on behalf of the parish of St Thomas the Apostle, Winchelsea by Richard Stileman and Richard Maplesden, churchwardens and by Josiah Boots and George Harrod [overseers of the poor]. Witnessed by David Laurence and Jacob Holt*:
We, the churchwardens and overseers of the poor of the parish of Winchelsea in the county of Sussex do hereby certify [to] you, the churchwardens and overseers of the poor of the parish of Icklesham that William Martin, labourer, and Elizabeth his wife are inhabitants legally settled in our parish of Winchelsea; therefore if they shall think it convenient to sojourn in your parish of Icklesham for the convenience of their business and shall there become chargeable we do hereby promise to receive and provide for them as our poor according to the direction of the law.
[*Appended*] We, G[eorge] Tilden and C[harles] Terry, justices of the peace for Winchelsea, do allow of this certificate and do certify that David Laurence, one of the witnesses, did make oath before us that he saw the churchwardens and overseers whose names are thereunto set severally sign and seal the certificate and that the names of the two witnesses are of their own handwriting.
[PAR 401/32/1/52]

381 12 Aug 1822 *Settlement certificate addressed by the churchwardens (William Sargent and David Laurence) and overseers of the poor (John Woods and Henry Barham) of the parish of St Thomas the Apostle, Winchelsea to the churchwardens and overseers of the poor of the parish of Icklesham*:
Memorandum this 12th August 1822. We, the undersigned, do on behalf of the parish of St Thomas the Apostle in the Antient Town of Winchelsea engage that William Martin and his wife residing in the parish of Icklesham, but whose legal settlement is acknowledged to be in the parish of St Thomas the Apostle, Winchelsea and this is to indemnify the parish of Icklesham from any expense or trouble that may be incurred by the said pauper. [PAR 511/32/1/56]

382 15 Oct 1822 *Bastardy order made by Alexander Tulloch, the Revd Samuel Philip Sheppard and Joseph Hennah, justices of the peace for Winchelsea concerning the child of Mary Chart of Winchelsea, widow*:
Whereas it hath been duly made appear unto us as well upon complaint of the churchwardens and overseers of the poor of Winchelsea as upon the oath of Mary Chart that she was delivered of a female bastard child at Winchelsea on the 30th

day of August 1821 and that the child is now chargeable to Winchelsea and likely so to continue; and further that William Martin of Winchelsea did beget the child on the body of Mary Chart. We therefore, upon examination of the cause and circumstances of the [evidence] as well upon the oath of Mary Chart as otherwise do hereby adjudge him, William Martin, to be the father of the child; and thereupon we do order, as well for the better relief of the parish of St Thomas the Apostle, Winchelsea, as for the sustentation and relief of the child that William Martin shall, and do forthwith, upon notice of this our order pay, or cause to be paid, to the churchwardens and overseers of the poor of Winchelsea or to some or one of them the sum of [*blank*] for and towards the maintenance of the child to the time of the making of this order; and we do hereby further order that William Martin shall likewise pay the sum of two shillings weekly and every week from the present time for and towards the keeping, sustentation and maintenance of the child for and during as long time as the child shall be chargeable to Winchelsea; and further order that Mary Chart shall also pay the sum of sixpence weekly for so long as the child shall be chargeable to Winchelsea in case she shall not nurse and take care of the child herself.   [PAR 511/34/4/10]

Note: Caroline Chart, daughter of Mary, was baptised at Winchelsea on 7 September 1821.[11]

383 8 Jan 1825 *Information given before Henry Powell and John Tilden, justices of the peace for Winchelsea by Charles Arnett of Winchelsea, assistant overseer*:
that William Martin of Winchelsea hath neglected and refused to pay one rate assessment made [for the relief of the poor of the parish] although the same has been respectively demanded by this deponent.   [WIN 237A]

384 16 Feb 1825 *Information given before [?], justice of the peace for Winchelsea by Henry Butler [town clerk] of Winchelsea*:
who on oath charges William Martin with assaulting him that day at Winchelsea.
                                                                         [WIN 237A]

385 26 Nov 1825 *Information given before Henry Powell and John Tilden, justices of the peace for Winchelsea, by Charles Arnett, gentleman [and assistant overseer]*:
who on oath charges William Martin with unlawfully assaulting [him] on the 14th day of November instant at Winchelsea.   [WIN 237A]

Note: Henry Pearch Butler, the town clerk, charged the parish six shillings for providing information and a warrant against William Martin and for taking depositions against him.[12]

386 26 Nov 1825 *Recognisances taken and acknowledged before Henry Powell and John Tilden, justices of the peace for Winchelsea*:
by William Martin of Winchelsea, shoemaker – 50s [and] Richard Osborne of Winchelsea, victualler – 40s [requiring] William Martin to appear [at the next quarter sessions to be held at Lewes] and in the meantime to keep the peace towards all His Majesty's liege subjects and particularly towards Charles Arnett.
                                                                         [WIN 237A]

Notes: 1. On 12 January 1826 Charles Arnett submitted an expenses claim totalling £4 19s 3d for a three day attendance at Lewes to prosecute Martin, the items including 'horse and gig, turnpike'.[13]

2. On that same date William Martin had appeared at the Lewes Epiphany Sessions charged with assaulting Arnett. The charge as recorded included that at Winchelsea he 'did beat him [Arnett] so that his life was greatly despaired of and other wrongs etc.' Martin pleaded not guilty and, on being found guilty by the jury, was fined six pence,[14] probably less than half a day's wages.

387 21 Feb 1826 *Information given before Henry Powell, George Stace and John Tilden, justices of the peace for Winchelsea by Charles Arnett of Winchelsea, assistant overseer*:

that he verily believes that Thomas Martin of Wittersham in Kent, shoemaker, is a material and necessary witness to be examined as [to] the place of the last legal settlement of William Martin who now resides in the parish of St Thomas the Apostle, Winchelsea. [WIN 237A]

388 27 Feb 1826 *Examination taken before Henry Powell and John Tilden, Justices of the peace for Winchelsea, of William Martin aged twenty years or upwards*:

who upon his oath saith: I was born in the parish of St Thomas the Apostle, Winchelsea. My father was legally settled in the parish of Icklesham, Sussex, my mother received relief from the officers of that parish after my father's decease and resided at that time at Winchelsea. About fourteen years of age application was made to the parish officers of Icklesham to provide me with a situation which they did and I entered into the service of Mr Samuel Putland of Icklesham. I lived [with him] for a whole year which I served without any wages, the parish officers of Icklesham funding me in clothes and Mr Putland in board and lodging. I then worked in several other places for a few months at a time but never for one whole year. At about seventeen years of age I went to live with my uncle Thomas Martin of the parish of Wittersham, Kent, shoemaker, and lived with him two years under an expectation that the parish officers of Icklesham would give my uncle assurance to take me as an apprentice but at the expiration of that time they refused. A short time afterwards a piece of paper was brought to my uncle's cutting room. My uncle then called me out of the shop and said I was going to be bound. I signed my hand to the piece of paper as also did my uncle in the presence of one Thomas Hoskins, butcher at Wittersham but who is since dead. I do not recollect that there were any seals or whether it was written or printed; that when I signed the piece of paper I considered myself bound an apprentice to my uncle till I was twenty-one years of age. I served him six months and then ran away and went to Sevenoaks in Kent for a week and then returned to my uncle's, made a fresh agreement with him and he was to give me one shilling per week till I was of age. I served him under that agreement for three or four weeks and he paid me. About that time work fell off a great deal and my uncle then said, 'Well, you may go off and get work for two or three months and you may then come back if you like and if you can get a better seal of work you may as well stop.' I then went to Chart in Kent and worked there about three months, from thence to Chatham, ?Medwich and Seven Oaks, all in Kent and worked at these places altogether about 10 weeks, from thence I went to Croydon, Surrey and worked there a few days. I then worked in and about London about two years without the consent of my uncle and told him I was going to work with Mr Gould there to which he made no objection. I have never done any act to gain a legal settlement in any other parish or place to the best of my knowledge and belief. About 5 years ago last June I was married by banns at the parish church of Rye, Sussex to Julia Moon and have four children born in wedlock namely George aged 4 and upwards, Jane aged 3 and upwards, Lavinia aged about 16 months and a male child aged 3 weeks and upwards and I am now chargeable to the parish of St Thomas the Apostle, Winchelsea. [*signature of*] W[illiam] Martin

[AMS 2330 f.51]

Note: William Martin and Julia Moon were married at St Mary's, Rye on 25 June 1821.[15]

389 26 Apr 1827 *Order made at the general quarter sessions of the peace at Lewes*: It is ordered by this court that the order or warrant of Henry Powell and John Tilden, two of His Majesty's justices of the peace for [Winchelsea] for the removal of William Martin, Julia his wife and their children, namely George aged four years and upwards, Jane aged three years and upwards, Lavinia aged 16 months and upwards and a male infant child (not yet baptised) aged three weeks and upwards from the parish of St Thomas the Apostle, Winchelsea to the parish of Icklesham, Sussex be and it is by this court recorded and confirmed, the inhabitants of Icklesham not appealing from the order at this present sessions and proof being made upon oath of the due service of the order. [PAR 511/35/3/20]

Note: George, Jane and Lavinia Martin were all baptised at Winchelsea.[16] William and Julia's fourth child was Henry who was also baptised there on 18 June 1826[17] which fits exactly with the ages given above for his siblings. It must be assumed therefore that this case took a long time to reach court in Lewes with the wording unamended.

1 PAR 511/12/1 f.203   2 ibid f.206   3 PAR 511/31/1/11 QE Dec 1817   4 PAR 511/1/2/1   5 PAR 511/31/1/11 1819/20   6 PAR 511/31/1/13 Sep 1820-Mar 1821   7 PAR 511/12/2 14 Jan 1835   8 PAR 511/34/1/73   9 PAR 511/1/5/1   10 PAR 511/31/1/13 Sep 1822-Mar 1831   11 PAR 511/1/2/1   12 PAR 511/31/2/129   13 ibid   14 QO/EW/48   15 PAR 467/1/3/1   16 PAR 511/1/2/1   17 ibid

[--] Middleton

390 *No entry relating to this man has been found in the Winchelsea parish records.*

391 25 Dec 1830 *Letter from R Pilcher, Patrixbourne, [Kent] to David Laurence, Winchelsea, assistant overseer*:

I have received your letter respecting Middleton's application to you for relief etc. Under the peculiar circumstances of the present case I am desired by my brother parishioners to state that they agree to allow 7s 6d per week for himself and wife and child for 4 weeks and 20s for medicine and medical attendance but as the nature of that disease requires more caution in regard to food, which, I believe, ought to be light and cooling, rather than quantity of physic I shall be glad to find that half the sum that I have stated suffices for Middleton's case. An imposition we have lately witnessed in this quarter renders it necessary for a parish officer to be thus cautious when the person called in happens to be unknown to him. My readiness to save you the expense [of] attending an examination and removal will I trust be received in the same spirit as it is offered and should a few shillings extra expense be incurred you will as readily meet that in lieu of a still greater one added to a long journey at this season of the year.　　　　　[PAR 511/35/1/348]

Dive Milliner

392 *There were two Dive Milliners, father and son. It was the son who deserted his family* (**393-395**) *and the likeliest explanation of the contrasting nature of* (**396**) *is that it was the father who applied, unsuccessfully as it turned out, to become master of the Winchelsea workhouse. Milliner junior married Charlotte Bray at St Thomas's on 8 September 1819 and their son James was baptised there on 17 June 1821.[1] Winchelsea gave mother and son generous assistance to join her husband at Ramsgate* (**395**) *for an entry in the overseers' accounts reads, 'paid expenses to Ramsgate for D Milliner £5 10s 0d'[2]*

393 30 Jun 1821 *[Edited] account submitted to the overseers of Winchelsea by John Fisher on behalf of Dawes, Lardner and Fisher [solicitors of Rye]*:
Preparing Mr [Edward] Jeakens information of Dive Milliner having absconded leaving his wife and family chargeable: 2s 6d; also warrant to apprehend him: 2s 6d.　　　　　[PAR 511/31/2/135]

394 2 Jul 1821 *Order made by George Stace, justice of the peace for Winchelsea, to the constables of Winchelsea*:
Whereas Edward Jeakens, one of the overseers of the poor of Winchelsea, hath this day made information and complaint on oath before me that Dive Milliner, late of Winchelsea, farrier, hath run away and still absconds from Winchelsea leaving his wife and family chargeable thereto. These are therefore to command you in His Majesty's name forthwith to apprehend and bring before me or some other justices of the peace for Winchelsea the body of Dive Milliner to answer unto the said complaint and to be further dealt with according to law. Herein fail you not.
　　　　　[PAR 511/34/2/32]

395 5 July 1821 *[Edited] account submitted to the overseers of Winchelsea by John Fisher on behalf of Dawes, Lardner and Fisher [solicitors of Rye]*:
Attending Mr [George] Stace and afterwards attending the magistrates, Dive Milliner having been taken and examining him as to his settlement and reducing same to writing which appeared to be in Winchelsea and advising thereon when Milliner agreed to take his wife to Ramsgate where he then lived within a month

and that her father would keep his wife in the meantime so that she was to be no charge to the parish in the interim. Horse hire and expenses: 13s 4d.

[PAR 511/31/2/135]

396 [c.1] Sep 1823 *Letter from Samuel Finn, Lydd [Kent], Henry Terry and William Tunbridge, Romney [Kent] to the overseers of Winchelsea*:
We the undersigned know Mr Dive Milliner to be a sober, steady man and his wife an industrious woman and a good scholar and some years ago [he] was overseer of Old Romney and we believe with credit. [PAR 511/35/1/22]

1 PAR 511/1/3/1; PAR 511/1/2/1   2 PAR 511/31/1/13 1821/1822

William Morris

397 *William Morris was, like William Martin, a very common name within the Winchelsea records of this period. These documents concern three William Morrises, the father (**398-399**), his son, William junior, (**401-402, 404-407**) and an illegitimate son of William junior's wife (**400, 402-403**). Another William Morris, also receiving poor law relief but not featured in these documents, was, during the same period, living with his family at The Strand. One of his sons was another William.[1] They all received poor law relief in one form or another and the frequency of the same name makes it difficult to identify to which individual particular payments were made. However, it is clear that William Morris junior, like William Martin III (**376**), lived at the Old Harbour [Camber] where he received occasional payments of £1 2s 0d and a large one of £3 15s 2½d immediately prior to his settlement examination (**405**) and Winchelsea's eventually unsuccessful attempt to remove him to Guestling.[2] While he was at Guestling pending that parish's appeal (**407**) Winchelsea met the expenses which Guestling incurred. For example, on 2 July 1827, John Cloke, Guestling's assistant overseer submitted an account for £1 7s 6d 'To relief given to William Morris and family at different times'. Cloke has receipted the account as paid.[3] Of the children of this family, Mrs Morris's daughter Jane and her illegitimate half-brother were taken into the Winchelsea workhouse on 24 June 1824,[4] their stepfather later stating that he was unable to keep them (**402**). William Morris junior's brother Barnard – see (**398**) – was another of the family who received poor relief from Winchelsea, notably a payment of 9s 6d in 1831.[5] However, in 1833 his financial situation greatly improved when he was appointed beadle at a salary of 7s 3d a week.[6] He also served as a constable between 1834 and 1842 and as pound driver between 1835 and 1839.[7] The 1841 census provides a good deal of information about the family. William Morris junior, then aged 55, having returned from Guestling to Camber had become an innkeeper and was resident there with his wife Elizabeth and their children George 15, Eliza 15 and Mary 12. Elizabeth Morris's son William, an agricultural labourer, was also living at Camber, lodging in the home of Thomas Parsons, with his wife Eliza and their baby daughter Mary Ann 9 months. Barnard Morris, also described as an agricultural labourer, was living in Cook Street (Barrack Square) with his wife Sarah, Sarah junior aged 17 and yet another William, 14. It has not proved possible positively to identify the William Morris who was a 'material and necessary witness' in the indecent exposure case against Thomas Bennett (**69**).*

398 11 Aug 1801 *Removal order made to the churchwardens and overseers of the parish of Guestling by J. Fuller and Thomas Lamb, justices of the peace for the county of Sussex:*

Whereas complaint hath been made unto us that William Morris, Elizabeth his wife and their two children Mary aged about sixteen and Barnard aged about nine years lately intruded and came into the parish of Guestling and are actually become chargeable to the same, we upon due proof thereof as well upon the examination of William Morris do adjudge the place of legal settlement of William Morris, his wife and children to be in the parish of St Thomas the Apostle, Winchelsea. [We] therefore require you in His Majesty's name on sight hereof to remove and convey them to Winchelsea and them deliver, together with this order or a true copy thereof, to the churchwardens and overseers there who are hereby required to receive and provide for them according to law.   [PAR 511/32/3/16]

Notes: 1. On 21 July 1804 William Simmons of Pett, mariner, was required by a bastardy bond to pay the sum of £100 for the maintenance of a boy born to Mary Morris of Guestling.[8]
2. A settlement examination for Barnard Morris was taken by the Winchelsea justices on 18 Jun 1825 at which time he was serving in the army.[9]

399 6 Oct 1801 *Examination, taken on oath before Thomas Marten and George Stace, justices of the peace for Winchelsea, of William Morris:*

who saith he was born in the parish of Ore in Sussex where his father then lived and did duty as sexton for the parish of Fairlight. His father afterwards went and resided in Fairlight and was sexton of the parish until he died which was in 1781. [He] saith that while single and unmarried he hired himself to Mr Robert Alce of Winchelsea, miller deceased, to serve him for one year from Lady Day 1759 to Lady Day 1760, that he served the year and received his wages; that he bargained for another year, Lady Day 1760 – Lady Day 1761; that he served Mr Alce that year and received his wages; that between Lady Day 1761 and Lady Day 1762 he hired at different places but not under any yearly hiring; that at or before Lady Day 1762 he bargained with Mr [William] Marten, late of Winchelsea Esq deceased, to serve him for 1 year; that he entered the service of Mr Marten and served the year out and received his wages according to his hiring; that after leaving Mr Marten's service he went and lodged at his father's house in Fairlight and earned his living by making bricks as a journeyman at a certain sum of money per thousand; that during his residence with his father he occasionally did the duty of sexton for his father and [was] there for a whole year together before he was married as he best remembers; that during such time his father received all the salary, that on 5 Jan 1779 William Morris was married at Fairlight to Elizabeth Morris of the same parish, that on that day he and his wife went to live in Guestling and have lived in that parish ever since and never slept in Fairlight one night as he remembers; that at Easter 1781 his father died and he continued to do the duty of parish clerk and sexton till the summer following when he was appointed parish clerk and sexton and has ever since done the duty of sexton in the parish of Fairlight; [that] his wife and five children [are] living; that just before he was married he applied to the parish of Winchelsea for a certificate of his being a parishioner there; that he received such certificate just after he was married and he resided at Guestling some years with the certificate by him and then upon application delivered it to the parish of Guestling. He applied for the certificate because he was going to live at Guestling and to prevent any objection to the parish permitting him to reside there. [*signature of*] William Morris.   [PAR 511/32/4/138]

Notes: 1. No trace has been found of William Morris's baptism at either Ore or Fairlight.
2. William Morris senior 'Parish Clerk aged 84 years' was buried at Fairlight on 19 May 1781.[10]

400 20 Jun 1814 *Account of Messrs Woollett and Dawes*:
Attending Mr [George] Bray advising in consequence of Mrs Morris being with child and refusing to be sworn and who was the reputed father etc. [*amount missing*]
                                                                [PAR 511/31/2/120]

401 12 Oct 1824 *Minute of a meeting of the Winchelsea select vestry*:
[Resolved] that a warrant be taken out against William Morris for his gross misbehaviour to the assistant overseer [Charles Arnett].   [PAR 511/12/2]

Note: Following this 'gross misbehaviour', whatever form it may have taken, Charles Arnett, on 14 October and on his own initiative, stopped Morris's poor law relief payments. However, these were reinstated by the select vestry the following week.[11]

402 12 Oct 1824 *Appearance before Henry Powell, justice of the peace for Winchelsea by William Morris of Winchelsea, labourer*:
[who] upon his oath saith that he is unable to support Jane Elizabeth Morris aged nearly 14 years, the daughter of [his] wife by her former husband, Michael Morris, and also William Morris aged 9 years and upwards, an illegitimate child born of the body of [his] wife after the decease of her first husband.
[*Appended notes*] Charles Arnett, assistant overseer also appears [and] on oath charges William Morris with abusing [him] on Sunday the third day of October instant in the due execution of his office as such assistant overseer at the parish of St Thomas the Apostle, Winchelsea.
[same day] Defendant entered into his own recognisance in £40 to keep the peace towards Mr Arnett and all other persons for 12 months from this date before me, H[enry] Powell.   [WIN 237A]

Notes: 1. The family was subsequently further increased when Jane Elizabeth gave birth at her father's house at Camber to two illegitimate children by Lieutenant Francis Harris RN who was stationed at Camber Watchhouse. They were Frederick, born 1829 and Julia born 1832. Bastardy bonds, required Harris to pay to the parish £300 each for the maintenance of these children.[12]
2. Only one record has been found of a payment made directly to Jane Elizabeth. This was of five shillings on 15 October 1826.[13]

403 25 Feb 1825 *Letter from S[amuel] Southerden, Camber Farm, [Camber] to [Charles] Arnett, Winchelsea [assistant] overseer*:
Martin Packham has applied to you by my order for a boy. If William Morris is well clothed as agreed on then Morris may have immediate employ at 6d the day. I am informed by Martin Packham [that] the father of the boy will bound him and wash etc at the wages he will receive of me – the earlier you send the boy the better.   [PAR 511/35/1/157]

404 29 Aug 1825 *Information given before Henry Powell and Joseph Hennah, justices of the peace for Winchelsea, by Charles Arnett of Winchelsea, assistant overseer*:
that [inter alia] William Morris the younger now residing in Winchelsea hath neglected or refused to pay the several rates and assessments made for the relief of the poor of the parish.
[*Appended note*] To pay on Saturday next.   [WIN 237A]

405 3 Jun 1826 *Examination taken by Henry Powell and John Tilden, justices of the peace for Winchelsea, of William Morris aged about forty-five years*:
who upon his oath saith that he was born in the parish of Guestling where his father lived for upwards of 30 years; that for many years previous to his father's death he (the deponent's father) performed the office of parish clerk and sexton in the parish of Fairlight, that this deponent lived with his father until he was about seventeen years of age. He then enlisted in the Cinque Ports Fencibles and continued in the army about two years. In March 1810 he came home and lived as a day labourer with his father until the Michaelmas following. He then agreed to work with Joseph Easton of Fairlight for three years under an agreement in writing to receive for the first year nine shillings per week, the next year ten shillings per week and the last year twelve shillings per week; that he lived with Easton about 10 months. He then went to Sedlescombe as a carpenter and continued there nearly a year. He then returned to Joseph Easton's and continued with him about six weeks. He then went to sea and continued in His Majesty's service about eleven years. He then went on board the *Stag* cutter as a common seaman. Afterwards he married Elizabeth Morris and ever since has lived in the parish of Winchelsea as a day labourer. [*signature of*] William Morris.   [AMS 2330 f.55]
Note: William Morris 'son of William and Elizabeth' was baptised at Guestling on 11 December 1781.[14]

406 13 Apr 1827 *Letter from John Cloke, Guestling, assistant overseer to [Charles] Arnett, Winchelsea, assistant overseer*:
I should feel myself extremely obliged in your sending me by the bearer a copy of William Morris's examination as I applied to Mr [John Haddock] Lardner yesterday who told me he would write to you for you to send it tomorrow but as I wish to take it to Hastings tomorrow morning I shall esteem it a favour if you will send it today.
[*Endorsed reply by Arnett*] 13 Apr 1827 I beg to inform you [that] I have not seen

Mr Lardner for some time past. Tho' he called at the workhouse last night he did not say anything about Morris's examination. I shall see him on Monday next here and enquire of him if I am to do so as ordered of the select vestry as I do not think I have any right to furnish you with such document without the consent of that vestry. If they approve of it I can have no particular objection. The course we pursue is to take the pauper's examination [at] the first opportunity.

[PAR 511/35/1/272]

407 18 Apr 1827 *Notice issued to the churchwardens and overseers of the poor of Winchelsea by Martin and Son, solicitors, on behalf of the churchwardens and overseers of the poor of Guestling*:
As solicitors for and by the order and direction of the churchwardens and overseers of the poor of Guestling in Sussex, we do hereby give you notice that [they] do intend at the next general quarter sessions of the peace to be holden at Lewes in and for the county of Sussex to commence and prosecute an appeal against an order under the hands and seals of Henry Powell and John Tilden Esquires, two of His Majesty's justices of the peace acting in and for the town of Winchelsea for and concerning the removal of William Morris, his wife named Elizabeth and their three children named Mary Ann aged six years and upwards, George aged three years and upwards and Eliza aged one year and upwards from out of your parish of St Thomas the Apostle, Winchelsea to the parish of Guestling. [PAR 511/37/7/11]
Note: At the Lewes Easter Sessions on 26 April 1827 Guestling's appeal was heard. Counsel spoke for both sides and 'with the consent of all parties the order was quashed'.[15]

1 PAR 511/31/1/12 f.6   2 PAR 511/31/1/14 ff.8-9   3 PAR 511/31/2/151   4 PAR 511/12/2   5 PAR 511/12/3 18 Feb 1831   6 PAR 511/12/2 22 Mar 1833; PAR 511/31/1/16 Mar 1834-Oct 1835   7 WIN 61B   8 PAR 511/34/3/9 9 PAR 511/32/4/198   10 PAR 325/1/1/1   11 PAR 511/31/1/14 f.1   12 PAR 511/34/3/20 & 21   13 PAR 511/31/1/15 f.15   14 PAR 350/1/1/1   15 QO/EW/48

John Nash

408 *The letters below* (**410-415**) *provide an excellent example of a conscientious workman who won the support of his adopted parish struggling to raise a large family on the limited income available to him. John Nash, a Winchelsea shoemaker, married Mary Selman at St Thomas's on 16 April 1816.[1] He had a business in the town and between that date and March 1820 did regular work for the parish. His bills are recorded in the overseers' accounts.[2] A good example is one submitted on 16 October 1819 in which he charged seven shillings for a pair of shoes for Harriett Sinden, fifteen shillings for 'a pair of strong ½ boots' for John Perigo, threepence for a pair of laces for Ann Sinden, one shilling for mending a pair of Harriett Sinden's shoes and threepence for providing her also with laces.[3] The recipients of his work were Winchelsea paupers being assisted in kind. The first indication in the parish records that Nash had moved to Hawkhurst with his family is on 2 November 1821 when he was sent a casual payment of ten shillings.[4] The same month he was sent two pounds to purchase leather.[5] For thirteen years from that time the books record that he was allocated three shillings a week to assist in the bringing up of* *his rapidly growing family.⁶ The overseers' records confirm Nash's family listings (411, 412) and, indeed, add an unnamed infant in October 1830 and Caroline who was two in March 1831.⁷ Nevertheless there is no evidence until December 1830 that Winchelsea responded to his requests for additional sums such as those included in (410) and (411). (413) acknowledges receipt of an additional £1 10s which the select vestry had allowed him and this payment is confirmed in their minutes and accounts.⁸ Nash's regular relief was stopped in 1834 by the public vestry⁹ but they relented the following year and resolved 'that the vestry order of [23] June 1834 of J Nash pay being taken off be rescinded and that the pay be allowed to this day and after this day two shillings per week.'¹⁰ In 1836 John Nash was listed among Winchelsea's partially infirm poor.¹¹*

409 22 Dec 1819 *Apprenticeship bond notified by the overseers of the poor of Wittersham, Kent to the overseers of Winchelsea*:

We, Richard Knight and John Wood, overseers of the poor of the parish of Wittersham in the Isle of Oxney in the county of Kent do hereby give you, the overseers of the poor of the parish of St Thomas the Apostle, Winchelsea, Sussex, notice that pursuant to an order bearing the date 16th of December in the sixtieth year of the reign of His present Majesty [1819] given under the hands and seals of Robert Moneypenny and R W Forbes, justices of the peace for the county of Kent, whereby we are ordered and directed to bind one John Fuller, a poor male child of the age of seventeen years and upwards belonging to and having a settlement in Wittersham and whose parents are not able to support him, to be an apprentice to one John Nash, cordwainer, of Winchelsea and we do intend to bind such child apprentice to John Nash until John Fuller shall come to the age of twenty-one years and we do intend to apply on the 30th day of December in the present year to George Stace and Henry Powell, justices of the peace for Winchelsea, to allow the indenture of apprenticeship to bind John Fuller as aforesaid.   [PAR 511/33/33]

410 18 Dec 1823 *Letter from John Nash, Hawkhurst, [Kent] to Robert Alce, [overseer], Winchelsea*:

I am sorry I am under the necessity of applying again for some assistance towards paying my rent. I have applied twice before but I have had nothing granted. I owe a twelvemonth's rent at Michaelmas last which is £5 5s and I am certain I cannot pay any part of it this winter. My wife [Mary] was confined last hopping and was not able to earn anything towards the rent. Since that time I have had [such a] considerable deal of sickness in my family that I have been much troubled to provide for my family and have had nothing to spare for rent. I have all my fireing to buy at a very dear rate not being able to lay in any wood or coals last summer. My landlord certainly has shown me more lenity than I could expect but unless I can do something towards paying him this Christmas I expect he will put in a distress for it and if he does that I must be taken home with an order but I hope the gentlemen will assist me once more and if they will assist me this time with two pounds to take to my landlord this Christmas I will not apply for anything more all the winter. I hope the gentlemen will not think I wish to impose upon them. I do not. I am sincerely thankful for what they have done for me and would not apply for anything was I not in great distress. Sir, I hope to hear from you as soon as the business has been investigated.   [PAR 511/35/1/42]

411 3 Nov 1824 *Letter from John Nash, Hawkhurst, [Kent] to [Charles] Arnett, Winchelsea [assistant overseer]*:
I am very thankful to the gentlemen for what they have done for me without which I cannot possibly support my family and I hope they have not thought of taking any part of this off for I have no fireing for the winter only as I buy coals by the bushel which is buying them at a dear rate and we are all of us very bad off for clothes. The children have scarce sufficient to keep them warm. I do a little work on my own account when I can get goods to do it with but I work principally journey-work and wages are very low. I have worked very hard this summer and lived very hard but lifting long days makes me ill, causes pain in the stomach and I am often forced to give up work in consequence of it and last winter I could not get any journey-work and many weeks did not get as much as five shillings when I got a good deal behind with my own rent. Now I have been forced to pay it off or have my house and what little I have taken from me in doing which I am got behind with the miller. I owe Mr Tobitt, miller, about seven pounds. I also owe Mr Young, surgeon, a bill of about five pounds. An old bill of three pounds four shillings which I showed Mr [Edward] J[e]akens when I first applied for relief and about two pounds has been contracted since. I do not wish to impose on the parish. I hope they will give me some encouragement and no man is more willing than I am to do all I can to support my family. This is the true state of my family: I have four children all of which are now residing with me and their names and age are as follows: John – age 9 years and 1 month, Angelina – age 7 years and 6 months, Alfred – age 3 years and 5 months, Henshall – age 1 years and 2 months. The children at present are well except John. He is not well and is a very ailing boy. [*Witness*] Peter Pope, assistant overseer for Hawkhurst parish.
                                                            [PAR 511/35/1/127]
Note: Journey-work was work done on a casual basis for someone of the same trade.

412 11 Mar 1826 *Letter from John Nash, Hawkhurst, [Kent] to [Charles] Arnett, poorhouse, Winchelsea*:
The following are the names and ages of my children as requested: John – 10 years old last September; Angelina – 8 years old last April; Alfred 4 years last May; Henshall 2 years last August; William – 7 months the 25th [of] last month. John is an ailing boy and very weakly. I am thankful for what you do allow me and was I not really in distress I would not apply for anything more. Whatever more you may be pleased to grant me will be gratefully received.
[*Endorsed*] I believe the above statement to be correct and the man very sober and endeavours to get a living. P[eter] Pope, assistant overseer for Hawkhurst.
                                                            [PAR 511/35/1/209]

413 29 Dec 1830 *Letter from John Nash, Hawkhurst, [Kent] to David Laurence, Winchelsea, [assistant overseer]*:

Necessity again compels me to send these few lines to you. I thank the gentlemen for the £1 10s 0d which they gave me. I paid a quarter's rent with it but I am still no better off with respect to bread for my family and it is not in my power to get them what nature requires and my family is suffering with cold and hunger. I have not been able to lay in any fireing against the winter and my children are very bad off for clothes. I hope the gentlemen will add something more to my weekly allowance. I am certain I cannot support my family with less than 6s a week. I have tried to keep from the parish to the utmost of my power but I had rather my family go into the poorhouse or anywhere where they can have bread. If the gentlemen can think of anything I can do better for them at Winchelsea than where I am, I am willing to comply with anything they propose if I can only have what my family suffers for bread. I hope, sir, you will state my case to the vestry the next time they meet and send me a few lines to let me know what they would advise me to do. I should be greatly obliged to you. A gentleman present when I was at the vestry asked me if my eldest boy was an apprentice to me. I have thought perhaps it might be the wish of the gentlemen that he should be bound apprentice to which I have no objection if they will furnish me with the means to pay for the indenture with. I have no money to spare for that purpose.   [PAR 511/35/1/349]

Note: On 7 January 1831 John Nash was allowed an additional payment of £1, noted as 'Cash casual relief by vestry'.[12] See (**415**).

414 23 Jan 1831 *Letter from John Nash, Hawkhurst, [Kent] to David Laurence, Winchelsea, [assistant overseer]*:

I wrote to you about three weeks ago when I stated to you [truly] the state I and my family were in. I also told you what I did with the £1 10s 0d which I received of you when I was at Winchelsea – paid a quarter's rent. I have been expecting to receive an answer of you but as I have not heard I have taken the liberty to write to you again. I hope, sir, you will send me a few lines to let me know whether the gentlemen will assist me in any way or not as I cannot possibly live here any longer without they will do something here for me. I could do much better for my family if I had it in my power to do a little business for myself. I have no shoemaker nigh me by a mile and a half and there are several respectable families in the neighbourhood that have offered me their work if I liked to do it. I make no doubts but what I could get sufficient employ for myself but it is useless for me to receive orders as I have not goods to complete them. Now if the gentlemen would send me £5 0s 0d or lay me in goods to that amount I think with my present reliefs I could support my family. I dare say any leather cutter at Rye would give six months credit and I could do the utmost of my power to make my payment due in good time and perhaps the gentlemen would give me a little work for the parish. I would make them good strong men's half-boots for 13s a pair and the money I would leave towards paying what they are accountable for me to any persons. I hope the gentlemen will not think I want to take any advantage. I do assure you, sir, it is not my intent. If they will befriend me in this way I will be very punctual. Please to send me a few lines to let me know if they will do anything for me if I come down to Winchelsea and if I had better come, or whether they will not. If not, I must throw myself on Hawkhurst parish for it is not in my power to pay the expense of taking my family home. [PAR 511/35/1/354]

415 2 Mar 1831 *Letter from John Nash, Hawkhurst, [Kent] to David Laurence, Winchelsea, [assistant overseer]*:

I am sorry to trouble you with another but not receiving any letter from you I do not know how to proceed. I find I cannot possibly support my family by journey-work as almost everything [*document damaged*] provisions is getting dearer and another thing is I have a mile and a half to fetch and carry my work and can get but little at a time and always have to wait while they get it cut out for me so that a great part of my time is lost and having but very low wages for my work and so much trouble in getting it I cannot possibly live by what I earn. Since I wrote to you last I have been to several people and told them that I now intended doing a little for myself and solicited their custom. I have every reason to think I should find work. I have taken orders for ten pairs of half-boots and shoes and one pair of boots but now I am at a loss how to execute these orders having [*document damaged*] to go on with. Neither can I do anything with them unless the gentlemen will be pleased to grant me what I before applied for. Should they do this I will use every exertion to give them satisfaction. Respecting the money, should they be pleased to give me a little parish work I will make them shoes of any description as good and cheap as they can get them elsewhere. I expect your vestry will be on Friday next. I do not know how to set a day to come to Winchelsea. If you will be so good as to state what I have said and send me an answer I should be much obliged to you. I thank the gentlemen for the £1 I have received of Mr Bryant and hope they will send me a little to go on with or I must of necessity bring my family home to which I feel a great aversion as I never had my health in Winchelsea nor do I expect I ever should. [PAR 511/35/1/359]

Note: Regular payments to Nash of three shillings per week are recorded as having resumed during the quarter ending 25 March 1831.[13]

1 PAR 511/1/3/1   2 PAR 511/31/1/11   3 PAR 511/31/2/130   4 PAR 511/31/1/12 f.115   5 PAR 511/12/2 f.19   6 PAR 511/31/1/13; PAR 511/12/2   7 PAR 511/31/1/15 f.16   8 PAR 511/12/3 3 Dec 1830; PAR 511/31/1/15 f.16   9 PAR 511/12/2 23 Jun 1834   10 PAR 511/12/2 27 Mar 1835   11 PAR 511/37/7/29   12 PAR 511/12/3; PAR 511/31/1/13   13 PAR 511/31/1/15 f.16

Eliza Oyler (Oiller)

416 *Eliza Oyler, daughter of Thomas and Elizabeth Oyler (**435-438**), was one of many young women whose illegitimate children were a potential drain on the parish finances. These documents provide a good example of the steps taken to minimise the effects. Even before Eliza's voluntary examination (**417**) Thomas Sylvester Keene had been reimbursed*

*for 'executing a bastardy warrant against Samuel Dean at Hastings'.[1] Payments to her
began on 14 April 1825[2] by which time she had been taken into the workhouse, presumably
with her child.[3] It is not clear as to when she left. Regular weekly relief of 2s 6d was paid
between 2 June 1825 and 31 May 1827.[4] There is no direct evidence that this money was
being received from Samuel Dean but his name is written against most ledger entries. The
final entry – see (423) – is marked, in Charles Arnett's hand, 'child sent to London'.[5]*

417 27 Sep 1824 *Voluntary examination taken before Henry Powell and Joseph
Hennah, justices of the peace for Winchelsea of Eliza Oyler aged 18 years*:
who upon her oath saith [that] I am the daughter of Thomas Oyler and was born in
the parish of St. Thomas the Apostle, Winchelsea where my parents were legally
settled, that I resided with them in that parish until I was about fourteen years of
age and then left them. I have been living with several persons who have been
residing as visitors at Hastings as a weekly servant at weekly wages but never
remained in any one service more than three months at any one hiring and was at
liberty to leave such service at any time I pleased on giving a week's notice. I am
now pregnant and Samuel Dean, a journeyman shoemaker in the employ of Mr.
John Smith of Hastings is the father of the child or children likely to be born of my
body and likely to become chargeable to Winchelsea. [*signature of*] Eliza Oyler.
[AMS 2330 f.35]
Notes: 1. Eliza Oyler 'daughter of Thomas and Elizabeth' was baptised at St Thomas's on
23 May 1806.[6]
2. 27 Sep 1824 *Account of Henry Pearch Butler, town clerk*: The king against Samuel Dean.
To amount of costs allowed by the magistrates £2 10s 8d.[7]

418 19 Oct 1824 *General quarter sessions of the peace held at the Guildhall,
Winchelsea before Henry Powell, deputy mayor, George Stace, Joseph Hennah,
John Tilden jurats and justices of the peace for Winchelsea*:
Upon reading the affidavit of Charles Arnett and the certificate of Henry Powell
Esq it is ordered that the recognisance entered into by Samuel Dean and his surety
on the twenty-ninth day of September last be respited till the next quarter sessions
to be holden in January next.   [WIN 61D f.21]
Notes: 1. The recognisance was further respited on 11 January 1825.[8]
2 The order of affiliation made on Samuel Dean was confirmed at quarter sessions on 12
April 1825.[9]
3. Respited = deferred

419 30 Mar 1825 *Examination taken before Henry Powell and John Tilden, justices
of the peace for Winchelsea, of Eliza Oyler*:
who upon her oath saith [*settlement details as* (**417**) *above*] [that] on the twenty-
second day of February last I was delivered of a male bastard child at the house of
James Hoad in the Barrack Yard in Winchelsea to which parish the child is now
chargeable and that Samuel Dean of Hastings is father of the child. [*signature of*]
Eliza Oyler.   [AMS 2330 f.41]
Note: No entry appears in the Winchelsea parish register for the baptism of Eliza's child.[10]

420 12 Apr 1825 *Bastardy order made by Henry Powell and John Tilden, justices of the peace for Winchelsea, concerning the child of Eliza Oyler*:

Whereas it hath been duly made appear unto us as well upon the complaint of the churchwardens and overseers of the poor of Winchelsea as upon the oath of Eliza Oyler, singlewoman, that she was delivered of a male bastard child at the house of James Hoad in Winchelsea on the 22nd day of February last and that the child is now chargeable to Winchelsea and likely so to continue; and further that Samuel Dean of Hastings, Sussex, stonemason, did beget the child on the body of Eliza Oyler and whereas it hath been duly proved unto us upon oath that Samuel Dean hath been duly summoned to appear before us to the end we might examine into the cause and circumstances of the [evidence] but he hath neglected to appear according to such summons. We therefore, do hereby adjudge Samuel Dean to be the reputed father of the child; and thereupon we do order, as well for the better relief of the parish of St Thomas the Apostle, Winchelsea as for the sustentation and relief of the child, that Samuel Dean shall and do forthwith, upon notice of this our order, pay or cause to be paid to the churchwardens or overseers of the poor of Winchelsea or to some or one of them the sum of three pounds eight shillings and sixpence for and towards the maintenance of the child to the time of the making of this our order; and we do hereby also further order that Samuel Dean shall likewise pay the sum of two shillings weekly and every week from this present time for and towards the keeping, sustentation and maintenance of the child for and during so long time as the child shall be chargeable to the parish; and further order that Eliza Oyler shall also pay the sum of eightpence weekly in case she shall not nurse and take care of the child herself; and we do also hereby further order that Samuel Dean shall pay the sum of one pound and sixteen shillings for the reasonable charges and expenses incident to the birth of the child; and also the further sum of one pound fourteen shillings and sixpence for the reasonable costs of apprehending and securing the said Samuel Dean; and also the further sum of two pounds ten shillings and eightpence for the reasonable costs of obtaining our order for the filiation of the child; the said several sums of money being the reasonable charges and expenses incident to the birth of the child, of apprehending and securing Samuel Dean and of our order of filiation duly and respectively ascertained on oath before us in pursuance of the statute in such case made or provided.

[PAR 511/34/4/11]

Note: 1. No explanation has been found for the description of Samuel Dean as both a journeyman shoemaker (**417**) and as a stonemason (**420**).
2. Payments of 2s 6d weekly to Eliza Oyler began on 21 April 1825.[11]

421 24 Jan 1827 *Letter from Thomas Relfe for Mrs Collins, Hooe to the overseers of Winchelsea*:

I am requested by Mrs Collins of the parish of Hooe to inform you that she has got Eliza Oyler's child to keep and as she [Eliza Oyler] is gone to London Mrs Collins will thank you to send her the money that is due. If the money is not remitted the child must be sent home. It would be much more convenient if you would empower some person at Hastings to pay the money.　　　[PAR 511/35/1/257]

422 24 Mar 1827 *Letter from Thomas Relfe, Hooe to C[harles] Arnett, Winchelsea, [assistant] overseer*:
Mrs Collins will thank you to send the 2 months pay for Eliza Oyler's child.
　　　　　　　　　　　　　　　　　　　　　　　　[PAR 511/35/1/266]

423 9 May 1827 *Letter from Sarah Collins, Hooe, to the overseers of Winchelsea*:
I send this to inform you that I have heard from Eliza Oyler and she wishes me to send the boy I have of hers to her. If you will be so good as to advance two months pay to me besides the two months due, I will get him clothed up and take him to his mother in London and I think by what she writes to me the boy will be no more expense to you.　　　　　　　　　　　　　[PAR 511/35/1/278]

424 21 May 1827 *Letter from Mrs E Chapman, Hooe, to [Charles] Arnett, Winchelsea, [assistant] overseer*:
I make bold to trouble you with a line for I have heard from my sister saying that you had been there to inquire for me concerning my daughter [Eliza] to know if she was married. Sir, to the best of my knowledge she is. She sent me word she was and if you would be so kind as to advance something to clothe him up that he [her daughter's husband] would take the child and keep him and be no more expense to you. For my own part, sir, I return you with the gentlemen of Winchelsea a thousand thanks for your kindness to my daughter when she was in distress. I hope by the blessings of God that no more of my family will not be no more trouble.
　　　　　　　　　　　　　　　　　　　　　　　　[PAR 511/35/1/280]

425 29 May 1827 *Copy letter from [Charles] Arnett to Mrs [E] Chapman, [Hooe]*:
I received yours and beg to say if you can satisfy me that your daughter Eliza is actually married, by reference to the church and their address, I have no objection to accede to your wishes.　　　　　　　　　[PAR 511/35/1/283]
Note: A payment to Eliza Oyler of 25s was entered in the overseers' accounts on 31 May 1827.[12]

1 PAR 511/31/2/143　2 PAR 511/31/1/14　3 PAR 511/12/2　4 PAR 511/31/1/13 & 14　5 PAR 511/31/1/14 f.13　6 PAR 511/1/1/4　7 PAR 511/31/2/129　8 WIN 61D f.24　9 ibid f.29　10 PAR 511/1/2/1　11 PAR 511/31/1/14 f.3　12 PAR 511/31/1/14 f.13

Lucy Oyler (Oiller)

426 *Lucy Oyler (b.1809)[1], younger sister of Eliza, was a Winchelsea pauper sent out to work by the overseers. From 1821 she served in three different households[2] before, on 6 Mar 1823 Mrs Beaching's husband, Joseph, agreed that they would take Lucy if the parish paid them 1s 6d per week and provided her clothes.[3] In the following month and before*

this series of letters from Mrs Beaching begins, the parish had provided Lucy with 1 frock, 1 shawl, 1 undercoat, 1 pinafore, 2 nightcaps, 1 pair of ½ boots and 1 bonnet.[4] The note appended to (**430**) *is the only record of a direct response to Mrs Beaching's requests.*

427 20 Oct 1823 *Letter from P Beaching, Hastings to [the overseers, Winchelsea]*:
I should be very much obliged to you if you would give Lucy Oyler the underwear she is to have. Her boots mend only for I have paid 6s for her other boots mending. I should like to know how we are to go on before I go having further shop boots [which] are constantly wanting mending. If she was to have a good strong pair made for her it would be much better.   [PAR 511/35/1/27]

428 [Oct 1823] *Letter from Mrs [P] Beaching, Hastings to [John] Woods, Winchelsea, overseer*:
I beg to trouble with another line to say if it is not your goodwill to send my girl some shoes or order me to get her some and the other clothes that I sent for I will send her home for I can't send her out nowhere and that is the chief thing to go to gentlemen's houses, but she can't for she has not got a shoe to her foot. I wish I had sent before but I let it alone as long as I could before I sent. I have asked for as little as I can for she is very bad off for clothes to go clean as she ought for she is very bad off for frocks and laces.   [PAR 511/35/1/34]

429 19 Dec 1823 *Letter from Mrs [P] Beaching, Hastings to [Joseph] Bigg, Winchelsea, shopkeeper [and overseer]*:
I understand by the girl that you are overseer so I make bold to trouble you for a pair of half-boots for my girl. I would be much obliged to you for she has a great deal of running about and her poor feet are all out on the ground and the weather is very wet and cold. I am afraid she will get cold and be ill. If you please it will be best to have a pair made for her for the shop shoes have no strength for her as she is always about. Please to let me have them as soon as you can for she is very bad off.   [PAR 511/35/1/43]

430 27 Dec 1823 *Letter from [Mrs] P Beaching, Hastings to the overseers of Winchelsea*:
I should be very much obliged to you if you give Lucy Oyler a good strong pair of boots and to [provide] a good strong pair pattens then they will save her boots for she has a good deal of running about and she is no use to me without good strong shoes so I hope you gentlemen will let her have what I sent for as soon as you can for she is a good girl and [deserving] of it gentlemen if you can. Please you may send her money to pay for the last three-quarters of the year as she will take care of it and the money will be acceptable this Christmas.   [PAR 511/35/1/44]
Notes: 1. This request was granted by the provision of a pair of half-boots.[5]
2. Pattens were shoes or clogs with a raised sole or set on an iron ring for walking in mud etc.

431 23 Jan 1824 *Letter from Mrs [P] Beaching of Hastings to [Joseph] Bigg, Winchelsea, shopkeeper*:
I am sorry to trouble you with these lines but necessity obliges me as you have not sent my girl's shoes and clothes. I think I am used ill for you see there was no deception for you see how bad her shoes was. She had no shoes to her feet. I can't send her out to do my business which is very unpleasant to me. I hope you will send the things as soon as possible for she is very bad off indeed for clothes. I forgot to mention in my other note that she has not got a tuck to put on. I hope you will have the goodness to send her some for she cannot betide without tucks [pinafores]. [PAR 511/35/1/53]

432 19 Mar 1824 *Letter from [Mrs] P Beaching, Hastings to [Joseph] Bigg, Winchelsea, grocer [and overseer]*:
I thought I should have heard from you before now on Lucy Oyler's account as I sent word by Mrs Hadly the terms I should like to keep her for another year and have received no answer. I should be much obliged to you to send me word in [a] day or two to let me know whether I have to keep her or not that I may suit myself for. The terms that I should like to keep her for another year is to have for her clothes for her to be neat and decent in which is far more than what I have had for this last year. She would have had no stockings to her feet if I had not given her two which I think is very hard. When I sent for her boots I [said] she was in great need of stockings and pinafores and you sent them me. When I agreed to take her the gentlemen said I should have clothes made for her which I have not had. When she came to me she had no bonnet to appear decent in of Sunday and then I received one yard of black [*illegible*] and no [*illegible*] to trim it with which was not fit to appear decent in of Sunday. I then was obliged to go and buy her one for Sunday myself for I could not bear to see her go. I do not want no smart or fine clothes but neat as I wear no fine clothes myself. You gentlemen do not encourage the girl a bit to do her best. If the gentlemen like I should keep her another year I must have some clothes for her and six shillings to assist with her for the next year and when you please send her money for the last year please to send eight shillings and sixpence for her house-pinny mending which I have paid. Please to send an answer as soon as possible and if I do not hear from you she will come home Saturday.
[PAR 511/35/1/68]

433 29 Mar 1824 *Letter from [Mrs] P Beaching, Hastings to Charles Arnett, Winchelsea, assistant overseer*:
This is a list of clothes that Lucy Oyler is in true necessity of. She is in great want of 2 smocks one for Sunday and one for every day. She is in want of a bonnet, some pinafores and one pair of petticoats and some stockings, one pair of boots or shoes and some chemises and one pair of dark stays. Sir, I received the money quite safe that you sent by her and I should be much obliged to the gentlemen to send nine shillings and sixpence which I have paid for her boots being mending. I should be

much obliged to the gentlemen to let me know for she is to have them mending this year. She told me that you thought one shilling a week enough for this year which I will consent to take her for one shilling a week this year if the gentlemen will let her have the clothes that I have sent for as she is in great want of it.

[PAR 511/35/1/75]

434 3 Sep 1824 *Letter from P Beaching, Hastings to [Charles] Arnett, Winchelsea, assistant overseer*:

I have got a place for Lucy Oyler where she will have [a] little a week and her board without you allowing anything [per] week with her as I think my little girl will do for us without keeping anyone else. And I should be much obliged to the gentlemen if they would give her some clothes to go on with as she is so bare of anything. She will be much obliged to you for some calico to make her some changes, 1 pair of ?dark stays, 1 pair of stockings, 1 flannel petticoat, 1 upper petticoat, 2 frocks, 1 pair boots, 1 woollen apron, 3 pinafores, 1 bonnet. I should be much obliged to you gentlemen to give her these things as she is a good girl deserving of it. I hope you will take it into consideration and give it [to] her as I hope she will not trouble you again. [PAR 511/35/1/109]

Note: On 13 Aug 1824 the Winchelsea select vestry meeting had resolved not to provide clothes for Lucy Oyler 'for the present'.[6] However, the parish continued paying the Beachings, not the originally agreed 1s 6d but one shilling a week until 25 March 1825.[7]

1 PAR 511/1/1/4   2 PAR 511/12/2 ff.15, 25 & 35   3 ibid f.39   4 ibid f.41   5 PAR 511/12/2 1 Jan 1824   6 PAR 511/12/2   7 Par 511/31/1/13

Thomas Oyler (Oiller)

435 *Thomas Oyler and his wife Elizabeth, parents of Eliza and Lucy, had eight children baptised in Winchelsea between 1791 and 1814. Four of them died in infancy and one, Edward, is noted in the register as having drowned.[1] Thomas received regular poor law relief between 1799 and 1802.[2] On one occasion (**438**) this was felt to be too generous. However, after paying the parish £10 for a horse and cart,[3] he went into business as a carrier and between 1804 and 1819 submitted regular bills to the parish for his work on its behalf.[4] In an 1813 militia return he is described as a groom with the qualification 'lame'.[5] Thomas died in 1819.[6] His widow remarried and move to Hooe as Mrs Chapman (**424-425**). Between 1796 and 1815 (when the relevant records cease) they were both members of the Winchelsea Class of Methodists.[7]*

436 24 Oct 1799 *Minute of Winchelsea public vestry*:

At a public meeting held [this day] in consideration of the poor of the parish towards allowing them a part of their gristing [*ground corn*] owing to the dearth and scarcity of corn and the allowance to be given to the undermentioned persons: [*inter alia*] Thomas Oyler. [PAR 511/12/1 f.110]

Note: For this allowance see also (**811**)

437 17 Apr 1800 *Minute of Winchelsea public vestry*:
It is agreed that Thomas Oyler shall receive a weekly allowance of 5s.
[PAR 511/12/1 f.113]

438 4 May 1800 *Minute of Winchelsea public vestry*:
It is agreed that Thomas Oyler, being a pauper and receiving weekly pay, ought not
to occupy a house at a yearly rent of six pounds and that some other residence be
provided for him.   [PAR 511/12/1 f.115]
Note: It seems that action was taken as a result of the above resolution for in the Poor Rate
assessment dated 22 February 1801 the Oyler family are shown as occupying only part of
the house valued at £3 10s 0d per annum.[8]

1 PAR 511/1/1/4; PAR 511/1/2/1   2 AMS 2329   3 ibid Receipts E 1803-E 1804   4 AMS 2329; PAR
511/31/1/11   5 WIN 1734 49   6 PAR 511/1/5/1   7 NMA/4/1/1-2   8 AMS 2329 – see also appendix
D1

Joseph Parsons

439 *Joseph Parsons, when in Winchelsea, lived in Barrack Square in property on which he
regularly paid the poor rates.[1] His three settlement examinations reproduced below (**440**),
(**442**) and (**449**) show that his legal place of settlement was Stalbridge in Dorset and give
a clear account of his personal and family circumstances although they do not reveal that
three of his children, two from his first marriage and one from his second, died in infancy.[2]
Stalbridge accepted responsibility for Joseph and his family and in response to the request
in (**444**) Winchelsea, for a time, paid him one shilling a week on Stalbridge's account[3]
but by March 1825 Winchelsea expected Stalbridge to pay in advance[4] and Stalbridge
agreed (**448**). For some time the support of his home parish sustained the family, possibly
through the good offices of Mr Chaffey (**443**) who has not been identified. However, in
1829 Joseph died at the age of 57 and was buried in Winchelsea.[5] Winchelsea then spent
the considerable sum of £18 16s 0d removing his wife [Catherine] and their five children to
Stalbridge.[6] The records suggest that Joseph's oldest son by his first marriage, James, who
was 27 at the time of his father's death, remained in Winchelsea but no details are available
except that, as a pauper born in Winchelsea and presumably receiving poor relief, he was
excused payment of the poor rate.[7]*

440 11 Apr 1809 *Examination, taken before George Stace and Charles Terry,
justices of the peace for Winchelsea, of Joseph Parsons residing in the parish of St
Thomas the Apostle, Winchelsea*:
[who] on his oath saith he is about thirty-five years of age and was born in the
parish of Stalbridge, Dorset as he hath frequently heard and verily believes where
his father James Parsons since deceased was a parishioner legally settled as he
hath frequently heard and verily believes. This examinant about twelve years ago
last summer was legally married in the parish church of St Thomas the Apostle,
Winchelsea to Catharine Summers, singlewoman, by whom he has two children,
James aged about 7 years and Charles aged about 5 years, now resident with him
in Winchelsea. He further saith that he has not to his knowledge done any act

whatever to gain settlement other than the one he acquired in Stalbridge. [*signature of*] Joseph Parsons.   [PAR 511/32/4/167]
Note: Joseph Parsons and Catherine Summers were married at St Thomas's on 18 April 1796.[8]

441 21 Feb 1821 *Letter from Samuel Harris junior, Stalbridge [Dorset] to Joseph Parsons, Winchelsea*:
The select vestry have agreed to send you one pound more but they make it a rule never to send more than one pound at a time to anyone out of the town. Your mother is very well. She is very sorry to hear of your distress and illness.
[*Endorsed*] This is the last I ever heard from my parish. [*signed*] J Parsons
                                                                    [PAR 511/35/1/10]

442 8 Apr 1823 *Examination taken before Henry Powell and George Stace, justices of the peace for Winchelsea, of Joseph Parsons*:
who upon his oath saith that he is about fifty-one years of age and was born in the parish of Stalbridge in Dorset where he resided with his father and mother who were legally settled there till he was 20 years of age or thereabouts; that about 23 years ago he came to reside in Winchelsea and was married to Catherine Summers at the parish church there by whom he had one son named James [now] aged 20 years or thereabouts; that about 13 years ago his wife died and that about two years afterwards he married Jane Neeves at the parish church of Icklesham, Sussex; that he had never hired any house except in Winchelsea and never paid more than six pounds a year rent; that he had by his last wife four children now living namely Jane 9, George 6, Philip 4 and Simeon 1½; that about seven years ago he was relieved by the parish officers of Stalbridge who then acknowledged him as a parishioner and legally settled there and that he has never done any other act or deed to gain a legal settlement. [*signature of*] Joseph Parsons.
                                                                    [AMS 2330 f.19]
Notes: 1. Catherine Parsons 'wife of Joseph' was buried at Winchelsea on 26 May 1811.[9]
2. Joseph Parsons married Jane Neeves at Icklesham on 28 December 1812.[10]

443 4 May 1823 *Letter from Henry Taylor, Stalbridge [Dorset] to the overseers of Winchelsea*:
In answer to yours of the [*blank*] ultimo addressed to the minister of this parish respecting [Joseph] Parsons and family, one of your parishioners, wherein you state [that] you have frequently written to the officers of this parish but in no one instance [has] your letter been answered. I beg to say that I have never received any letter unless from Mr Chaffey who has been paid these last two or three years 2s a week for this family and in September last I informed him that this parish considered 1s per week for a man with a trade with only four children more than they allowed for any person in the same circumstances and they would not allow more. Enclosed is £2 for the use of this man and if he can do with 1s per week if you will advance it to him it shall be regularly paid to you but in the meantime

I should like to know if Mr Chaffey still continues to advance him money on the credit of this parish. Be so good as to acknowledge the receipt of this and any further observations you have to make on this business shall be attended to.
[*Endorsed*] Wrote some time about Michaelmas and 11 April 1824, 29 August 1824. [PAR 511/35/1/15]

444 1 May 1824 *Letter from George Moore, Stalbridge, Dorset, overseer to the overseers of Winchelsea*:
Having received your letter dated the 11ᵗʰ April stating the distress Joseph Parsons and his family was in, it was agreed by our vestry that I should remit to you £3 for him and his family which is enclosed and if you will pay him 1s per week in future I will remit you the money when demanded. [PAR 511/35/1/81]

445 11 Dec 1824 *Letter from George Moore, Stalbridge, [Dorset], overseer to the overseers of Winchelsea*:
I have received a letter from a pauper by the name of Joseph Parsons living at Winchelsea (belong[ing] to the parish of Stalbridge) saying he was in great distress and was in want of a one pound note. I should thank you if you would inquire into his family, what age the children are, and if you think they stand in need of further help. If you think it needful [I] should thank you to answer this by return of post.
[PAR 511/35/1/144]

446 19 Dec 1824 *List of the children of [Joseph Parsons to be sent to George Moore, Stalbridge, Dorset, overseer]*:
Jane Parsons 11½ years, George Parsons 8 years, Philip Parsons 5½ years, Joseph Parsons 8 months. [PAR 511/35/1/148]

447 28 Dec 1824 *Letter from George Moore, Stalbridge, [Dorset], overseer, to the overseers, Winchelsea*:
I received your letter of the 19ᵗʰ instant respecting the family of Joseph Parsons and find that the ages of his children and other circumstances [indicate] that they are in want of assistance at present. Enclosed I have sent him £1 which I should thank you to give him and am much obliged to you in making the inquiry into his circumstance. [*Endorsed*] 1 Jan 182[5] received the £2 note. [*signature of*] Joseph Parsons [PAR 511/35/1/150]

448 21 Apr 1825 *Letter from John Barrett, Stalbridge, [Dorset], overseer, to [Charles] Arnett, Winchelsea, assistant overseer*:
I received your account for money advanced by you for our parish to Joseph Parsons' family at Winchelsea. Enclosed is £3 which is 8s more than your demand which I should thank you to place on our account for the year ensuing if not too much trouble. I should thank you to send me an exact account of his family and earnings. [PAR 511/35/1/167]

449 16 Sep 1828 *Examination taken before John Tilden and Fielding Browne, justices of the peace for Winchelsea, of Joseph Parsons*:
who upon his oath saith that he was born at Stalbridge, Dorset at which place his father and mother belonged as he hath been informed and believes, from which parish he hath himself received relief; that he has never to the best of his belief gained a subsequent settlement to that at Stalbridge by hiring service or otherwise, that he has been twice married; that his second wife was Jane Neeves, that he was married to her by banns at Icklesham, by whom he has five children namely Jane aged about 15 years, George aged about 12 years, Philip aged about 9, Joseph aged about 4, Robert aged about 9 months and that himself, his wife and five children are now actually chargeable to the parish of St. Thomas the Apostle, Winchelsea. [*signature of*] Joseph Parsons. [AMS 2330 f.95]

1 e.g. PAR 511/31/1/11 16 Jan 1820 & 21 Sep 1820   2 PAR 511/1/1/4; PAR 511/1/5/1   3 PAR 511/31/1/13 QE Sep 1824 & QE Dec 1824   4 ibid QE Mar 1825   5 PAR 511/1/5/1   6 PAR 511/31/1/13 QE Jun 1829   7 PAR 511/12/2 Feb 1847-Sep 1849   8 PAR 511/1/1/4   9 ibid   10 PAR 401/1/1/3

Ann Ralph (Relf)

450 *Within a year before taking up a position as servant in the household of William and Elizabeth Tyrrell at Playden, Ann Ralph had been sent by the Winchelsea authorities to two other households, those of William and Joan Young[1] and of John and Mary Bennett.[2] In all three cases the householders were granted a weekly allowance. In the case of the Tyrrells the arrangement was that they would be paid two shillings a week which would include responsibility for doing her washing and mending but the parish would supply all necessary clothes.[3] Mrs Tyrrell's application (**451**) is a typical example of such arrangements. On 23 October 1823 the parish vestry considered this request which was not met in full but they resolved to provide Ann with 1 pair of ½ boots, 1 pin cloth, 1 shift, 1 undercoat, and 1 pair of stockings.[4] Despite the spelling of their names occasionally coinciding in the records, no family relationship has been discovered to link Ann Ralph with James and Mary Relfe (**452-471**). The usual spelling of her name, never used for James or Mary, suggests that she was not Mary's sister.*

451 5 Oct 1823 *Letter from Elizabeth Tyrrell, Playden to the overseers of Winchelsea*:
Ann Ralph, now in my service, is very short of a few articles of wearing apparel which I hope you will deem [it] proper to supply according to promise. 1 pair half boots, 1 frock, 2 pin cloths [pinafores], 1 shift, 1 under petticoat, 2 pair stockings. [PAR 511/35/1/25]

1 PAR 511/12/2 f.19   2 ibid f.29   3 ibid f.39   4 ibid

James Relfe (Relf)

452 *James Relfe's wife Ann died in 1821.[1] He received casual poor law relief in both cash and kind from the Winchelsea overseers between 11 January 1821[2] and September 1823.[3] At that time he can be presumed to have obtained employment with Thomas Gosley of Rye* (**456**). *On 24 September 1824 the select vestry resolved 'that James Relfe do take Elizabeth Relfe his daughter after this day fortnight',[4] meaning that after his release from prison* (**457-458**) *she was to live with and be maintained by him. Relfe was later imprisoned a second time for between 15 August 1829 and 12 November 1829 a weekly payment of 6s appears in the overseers' accounts marked 'Cash casual relief for the 4 children the man being sent to prison'.[5] However, no details of this second offence have been discovered. With the exception of Mary* (**461-471**) *it has not been possible to establish from the parish records the names of James Relfe's other children whom he was imprisoned in 1824 for neglecting. However, Richard and Jane are the two most likely. In 1826 Richard Relfe, a workhouse boy, was put out by the parish to work for Dr Adam Scott who was required to pay two shillings a week for his services.[6] Later Richard went to Joel Benfield who made no payment but agreed to board and lodge him if the parish provided his clothes and did his washing.[7] Jane first features in the overseers' accounts on 6 January 1832 when she was allowed a casual payment of eight shillings because she was ill.[8] Similar payments were made frequently until March 1834 when a Mrs Coomber agreed to take her and provide her clothes if the parish would pay 3s 6d per week.[9] This they did until October 1835 when the relevant surviving records cease.[10] Jane Relfe was admitted to Brede workhouse in February 1837 and remained there, with one brief break until January 1841.[11] Later that year she appears on the indoor relief list of Rye workhouse.[12]*

453 16 Jul 1824 *Minute of the Winchelsea select vestry*:
Resolved that [James] Relfe do pay 4s per week towards the maintenance of two of his children and that immediate application be made to him for that purpose.
[PAR 511/12/2]

454 19 Jul 1824 *Letter from James Relfe, Rye to [the overseers of Winchelsea]*:
I beg to acknowledge receipt of Mr [Charles] Arnett's letter of the 16th instant and would most gladly contribute the allowance you require towards the maintenance of my children if it was in my power, but from my labour I assure you I can scarcely make a living and being only a lodger it will be impossible for me to take them out of the [poor]house. I will use every effort in my power and as soon as I possibly can will contribute as much as I am able towards their support.
[PAR 511/35/1/98]

455 30 Jul 1824 *Minute of the Winchelsea select vestry*:
Resolved that a complaint be made to the magistrates against James Relfe for not doing [his] best to assist in the maintenance of [his] family.   [PAR 511/12/2]

456 22 Sep 1824 *Letter from Thomas Gosley, Lime Kiln near Rye to the gentlemen of the Corporation of Winchelsea*:
This serves to inform you that my men have not made more than twelve shillings

for this two years last past per week. Owing to the number of barges on the river and the beach being very difficult to get, many times occasions them to lay many days waiting to get at it. This gentlemen is a truth with my men you may rely on. [*Endorsed*] Thomas Gosley, Rye about the earnings of James Relfe.

[PAR 511/35/1/112]

457 3 Aug 1824 *Information given before Henry Powell, justice of the peace for Winchelsea, by Charles Arnett, assistant overseer*:
[who] on his oath charges James Relfe with unlawfully neglecting to maintain in whole or in part his family [he] having children born in lawful wedlock chargeable to the parish of St Thomas the Apostle, Winchelsea as he, this examinant, has been informed and verily believes to be true.
[*Appended notes*:]
[same day] [Charles Arnett] attended at Rye with [Thomas Sylvester] Keene, [Sergeant-at-Mace] after Relfe but did not succeed. 23 Aug [1824] Also attended with Keene but did not succeed. 27 Aug [1824] Relfe committed for one calendar month on the above information being duly verified before us: Henry Powell and Joseph Hennah, justices. [WIN 237A]

458 27 Aug 1824 – 23 Sep 1824 *Return of prisoners committed to Winchelsea gaol and receiving daily allowances at sixpence per day from Thomas Sylvester Keene, gaoler*:
James Relfe 28 days. 14 shillings. Discharged by order of the justices.

[WIN 1228]

459 21 Jul 1826 *Letter from William Judd, Rye to the parish officers of Winchelsea*:
I think it my duty to inform you [that] I must be under the necessity of selling James Relfe's furniture as he has upwards of four pounds arrears of rent. I should not have left it alone so long but I was in hopes work would have come on this summer but as work is scarce the man has not been able to earn more than 10s weekly. He has a wife and three children. It has been out of his power to pay me. If you will advance me three pounds I will not distress the family. If I do the family must come home. [PAR 511/35/1/236]

460 29 Mar 1827 *Letter from Joseph Mills, [assistant overseer], Rye, to [Charles] Arnett, Winchelsea, [assistant overseer]*:
The rates to this parish are as under: [inter alia] Relfe, James 6 rates from March 1826 to March 1827 at 3s 9d, £1 2s 6d. [PAR 511/35/1/269]
Note: No record has been found of Winchelsea paying either James Relfe's rent (**459**) or his Rye poor rates.

1 PAR 511/1/5/1   2 PAR 511/12/2 f.5   3 PAR 511/31/1/13 Mar-Sep 1823   4 PAR 511/12/2   5 PAR 511/31/1/15 f.36   6 PAR 511/12/3 16 Mar 1826   7 PAR 511/12/3 10 Oct 1828   8 PAR 511/12/2   9 ibid 27 Mar 1834   10 PAR 511/31/1/16   11 G 8/19/4   12 G 8/19/2

Mary Relfe (Relf)

461 *Mary Relfe, daughter of James, had been placed by Winchelsea with two previous households before she went into service with Thomas and Ann Smith under an arrangement whereby the Smiths would be paid one shilling a week to keep her and do her washing and mending while the parish provided her clothes.[1] After she left that house so precipitately and offered her services to Edward Brignall and his wife (462-463), the Winchelsea overseers agreed to regularise the position on the same terms.[2] The only indication that any response was made to the requests in (465-467) is that, on 8 July 1824, the select vestry resolved to allow Mary a pair of ½ boots.[3] However, a more generous provision was made the following November when she was to have '1 gown, 1 change, 1 undercoat, and 1 pair stockings'.[4] Mary Relfe's illegitimate child (471) was baptised Maria at St Thomas's on 30 July 1826[5] and buried there on 17 August.[6] The Winchelsea parish officers were charged 5s 6d for the coffin[7] but Edward Standen (471) paid the Winchelsea overseers the costs of Mary Relfe's lying-in.[8]*

462 24 Mar 1824 *Letter from Ann Smith, Iden to [the overseers of Winchelsea]*:
This is to let you know that Mary Relfe says she won't stop any longer than tomorrow night for she says that you have nothing to do with her and stop she won't for any of you for she will go to Bridewell first so I think the best way will be for you to come over tomorrow and put her to a house of correction for she will be of no use to me if she stops. I think she must have someone to [keep] her up to things for she is so contrary that there is no bearing the house with her and I do not wish to have her. I wish you to send word what is to be done if you cannot come over [and] whether I have to let her have her clothes or not. I think you will have a good deal of trouble with them if some correction is not given. Mrs Catt's girl stops again for I sent to her. Please send a line or two by the bearer. [PAR 511/35/1/70]
Notes: 1. During the quarter beginning on the following day, Winchelsea paid Mrs Smith £2 12s 0d in settlement of the amount owed up to the time of Mary's departure.[9]
2. Bridewell was a prison/reformatory.

463 24 Mar 1824 *Letter from Edward Brignall, Brookland [Kent] to [Charles] Arnett, Winchelsea, assistant overseer*:
I have had one of your girls come to offer to live with me – her name she says is Mary Relfe – if you like to give me one shilling a week with her I will take her. If you like to it please send me word in a few days as I shall want to engage with someone else if she don't come. She may come at the Lady Day.
[PAR 511/35/1/71]

464 27 Mar 1824 *Letter from E[dward] Brignall, Brookland, [Kent] to [Charles] Arnett, Winchelsea, assistant overseer*:
I received your letter but I can't think of taking her [Mary Relfe] in unless you give me the same as I mentioned in my other note as I can have that with a girl from another parish so that you must please yourself about giving of it. I should like to know as soon as you can give me word. [PAR 511/35/1/74]

465 27 Apr 1824 *Letter from E[dward] Brignall, Brookland, [Kent] to [Charles] Arnett, Winchelsea, assistant overseer*:
The girl we have is in want of some clothes, she wants two gowns, two petticoats, under and over, two chemises, two pairs of stockings, two aprons, a bonnet; I shall be needing one for her as she has none to go to church in; a pair of shoes.

[PAR 511/35/1/80]

466 17 May 1824 *Letter from E[dward] Brignall. Brookland, [Kent] to [Charles] Arnett, Winchelsea, [assistant overseer]*:
The girl [Mary Relfe] I have of your parish must have her clothes which we asked for, for she has not clothes to wear. If you did not think of giving her the clothes why did you put her out as she cannot go without. She just has not the clothes to wear as that was the agreement for her to have what clothes was necessary for her. Otherwise I shall send her back again if she is not to have clothes to wear.

[PAR 511/35/1/84]

467 3 Jun 1824 *Letter from E[dward] Brignall, Ivychurch, [Kent] to [Richard] Stileman, Winchelsea*:
The girl [Mary Relfe] I took of your parish the last Lady [Day] has not clothes to wear and I have wrote over to Mr [Charles] Arnett two or three times concerning some clothes for her and she has been over twice herself for it but they will not grant her any. I know [I have] not asked for any one thing for what the girl stands in need of. She has not a bonnet nor a pair of shoes to put on to go to church in nor any kind of other change. If the girl has not clothes allowed her I cannot think of keeping her so without clothes as they agreed when I took her to find her in clothes what she stood in need of.

[PAR 511/35/1/88]

468 20 Jan 1825 *Letter from Edward Brignall, Cheyne Court, [Brookland, Kent] to [Charles] Arnett, Winchelsea [assistant overseer]*:
The girl we had of your parish last [Mary Relfe] does not suit nor does not wish to stop. I think of her going away this afternoon. She thinks of going to her mother's I believe. If you will pay the money to the boy [bearing this letter] for the time she has been I should be much obliged to you.

[PAR 511/35/1/154]

469 12 Jul 1826 *Removal order made by William Lamb and William Watson, justices of the peace for Rye to the churchwardens and overseers of the poor for Rye*:
Whereas complaint hath been made to us that Mary Relfe, singlewoman, lately intruded and came into the parish of Rye and is actually become chargeable there, we do adjudge the same to be true and also adjudge the last place of legal settlement of Mary Relfe to be Winchelsea. These are therefore in His Majesty's name to require you on sight hereof to remove and convey her to Winchelsea and her deliver, together with this our order or a true copy thereof, to the churchwardens

and overseers of the poor there who are hereby required to receive and provide for her according to law.

[*Endorsed*] Woman with child received 14 July 1826.   [PAR 511/32/3/49]

470 12 Jul 1826 *Inquiry for legal advice made by Charles Arnett, assistant overseer, to John Fisher, solicitor of Rye:*
Mr Fisher says the order with Mary Relfe is superseded and another granted for Winchelsea.   [PAR 511/35/2/7]

471 31 Aug 1826 *Examination, taken before Henry Powell and John Tilden, justices of the peace for Winchelsea, of Mary Relfe:*
who upon her oath saith that I am the daughter of James Relfe who now lives at Rye, that I am of the age of twenty years and upwards, that I believe and have heard that I was born in the parish of Winchelsea where my father then lived, that on the twenty-fourth July last I was delivered of a female bastard child and that Edward Standen, a waiter of the London Trader Inn at Rye was the father of such child which is now dead. [*mark of*] Mary Relfe.   [AMS 2330 f.59]

1 PAR 511/12/2 f.39   2 PAR 511/31/1/13 QE Dec 1824   3 PAR 511/12/2   4 ibid 5 Nov 1824   5 PAR 511/1/2/1   6 PAR 511/1/5/1   7 PAR 511/31/2/144   8 PAR 511/31/1/13 QE Sep 1826   9 PAR 511/31/1/13

Richard Richardson

472 *Richard Richardson lived at 'Old Harbour' (Camber) where he worked for Samuel Southerden. He married Ann Giles Jones at St Thomas's, Winchelsea on 23 June 1797.[1] Their oldest son, Richard junior, was baptised the following October.[2] The parish registers record the baptism of nine more of their children, four of whom died in infancy.[3] A pauper bringing up such a family relied heavily on poor law relief, the first entry being recorded in 1801/1802 when he received a total of £3 2s 4d.[4] Frequent payments in kind also appear such as that on 17 December 1815 when the parish vestry resolved that he should be allowed '½ chaldron of coals and one gallon of flour per week'. The same resolution allowed him to reduce his family expenditure by sending one of his sons to the workhouse.[5] The name of the boy is not given. Cash payments to the family, six shillings a week between 1818 and 1821,[6] were then reduced to four shillings.[7] Following that cash reduction quite generous allowances were, however, made in kind, for example on 1 April 1824, following his dismissal by Samuel Southerden (**475**), the public vestry allowed, '¼ chaldron coals, 2 frocks, 2 pinafores, 2 changes for 2 children, 1 change for Mrs Richardson.'[8] On 12 October of the same year he was allowed an additional four shillings and four pounds of meat 'being very ill'.[9] The parish also continued to assist with his medical problem (**473-474**) by paying for another truss.[10] When Richard Stileman complained about Richardson to the select vestry (**476**) it is not clear which son was referred to. Neither is it clear why Richardson's weekly pay was stopped on 28 July 1826.[11] Despite this select vestry resolution, casual payments including one as large as £5 10s 0d[12] continued to be made.*

473 10 May [1819] *Account submitted to the parish of Winchelsea by [Samuel] Nye of Rye*:

To a portable rupture convenience for Richard Richardson agreeable to the order of Mr [Edward] Jeakens: £1 10s 0d. [PAR 511/31/2/131]

474 1821 *Receipted account submitted to the parish of Winchelsea by [Samuel] Nye of Rye*:

To a rupture truss suitable to the case of Richard Richardson: £1 1s 0d.

[PAR 511/31/2/132]

475 8 Nov 1823 *Letter from S[amuel] Southerden, Camber to the overseers, Winchelsea*:

Richard Richardson left my employ on Saturday last and he has not been to me since to inquire for work. If he should come to work again for me I shall not at any rate employ him longer than next Lady Day at which time I will thank you to find him another situation. If I find he is in the least slack in his work I shall turn him off before that time.

[*Appended note*] Richardson owes me £9 14s 3d for rent etc. I will therefore thank you to remit the money, namely the 4s a week allowed him by the parish to me as it has always been paid to me. I think he has earned the most money this last summer as a day labourer on my farm. [PAR 511/35/1/38]

Note: At this time Richardson's allowance of 4s a week was being paid regularly but the accounts do not show whether it went directly to Samuel Southerden as requested here.[13]

476 19 Nov 1824 *Letter from R[ichard] Stileman, The Friars, [Winchelsea] to the chairman of the select vestry, Winchelsea*:

I am sorry I cannot attend the select vestry this morning on account of the very damp weather. I understand Richardson intends again to apply to the overseers for relief for his boy. I can see no reason why he should be put on a different footing from others but I should not have troubled the vestry with my opinions if Richardson had not misrepresented what I said at the last meeting to his master. He stated to Mr [Samuel] Southerden that I and I believe others had said his wages were not enough and desired him to ask Mr Southerden for an increase. Gentlemen who were present must well remember that this was not the case but he was told by me that if his <u>boy</u> did not get a fair remuneration for his labour he might ask for more but not expect the parish to make up any differences. With regard to Mr Southerden's wages it would be presumption to interfere and indeed his wages are as high as any in the neighbourhood. [PAR 511/35/1/137]

1 PAR 511/1/1/4   2 ibid   3 ibid; PAR 51/1/2/1; PAR 511/1/5/1   4 AMS 2329   5 PAR 511/12/1 f.203   6 ibid f.222   7 PAR 511/31/1/13 E1821-E1822   8 PAR 511/12/2   9 ibid   10 ibid 4 Feb 1825   11 PAR 511/12/3   12 PAR 511/31/1/13 QE Jun 1829   13 PAR 511/31/1/13

Twosine Richardson

477 *Twosine was one of Richard and Ann Giles Richardson's sons. He was eighteen at the time of Samuel Southerden's letter (**478**).[1] There is no mention in the overseers' accounts of any payments made as a result of that letter but early the following year a payment of £2 was made to his brother Henry who was 14[2] and had bound himself to a five year apprenticeship at sea with the same Captain Bates.[3]*

478 23 Jun 1824 *Letter from S[amuel] Southerden, Camber to the overseers of Winchelsea*:
Twosine Richardson has got a situation (on liking) with Captain Bates to go to sea. If the weather be fine he will sail tomorrow. The boy has no clothes fit for a seafaring dress and I think it right to encourage anyone belonging to the parish to go to sea by assisting them.
[*Endorsed*] Mr G[eorge] Harrod will thank you and Mr [John] Maplesden to come down to C[harles] Arnett's.   [PAR 511/35/1/91]

1 PAR 511/1/1/4   2 ibid   3 PAR 511/31/1/13 QE Mar 1825

Joseph Ronalds

479 *No mention of Joseph Ronalds and his family has been found in the poor law records of Winchelsea other than (**480-484**) below. However, the settlement examinations of Ronalds and his wife and their removal to Hambledon with the threat, if Hambledon does not agree to keep the family together, that the children will be further removed back to St Clement's Hastings, tells their story more than adequately.*

480 29 Nov 1825 *Examination taken before George Stace and Henry Powell, justices of the peace for Winchelsea, of Joseph Ronalds aged 40 years and upwards*:
who upon his oath saith: I was born at Sutton Cotton in Hampshire where I believe my father was legally settled. My mother was relieved by that parish. I went at about nine or ten years of age to live with Mr Stickham of Sutton Cotton as under-carter of his second team and served him three quarters of a year at about thirty shillings wages. I then went to live with Mr Edney of the parish of Bullington, Hampshire and remained in his service twelve months at the wages of three pounds. I went afterwards to live with Mr Heasley at the Manor Farm in the parish of Micheldever in Hampshire and remained in his service twelve months at the wages of five pounds or five pounds ten shillings. I afterwards went to live with Mr German at Chidham in the parish of Hambledon, Hampshire and remained in his service twelve months as yearly hired servant and the wages of six guineas and a half, served him the whole of one year and took the whole of my wages. About thirteen years ago my examination was taken at Droxford, Hampshire and I went home to

Hambledon of my own accord and was relieved in the Hambledon workhouse. I never afterwards lived as a yearly servant in any place whatever but used to travel about the country and never paid more than two shillings and sixpence per week rent for any apartment I occupied which was in the parish of St Clement, Hastings, Sussex. I came from thence to the parish of St Thomas the Apostle, Winchelsea and resided there upwards of two years and a half at 2s a week rent and am now chargeable to Winchelsea. About three years ago last July I was married by banns to Elizabeth Voller at the parish church of St Mary in Romney Marsh, Kent and have never done any other acts or deeds to gain a legal settlement in any other parish or place whatever to the best of my knowledge and belief. [*Mark of*] Joseph Ronalds.   [AMS 2330 ff.47-48]

481 29 Nov 1825 *Examination taken before Henry Powell and George Stace, justices of the peace for Winchelsea, of Elizabeth Ronalds*:
who on her oath saith that I was born at Durley, Hants where my father and mother were legally settled as I believe. They received relief from that parish. I lived with Mr. Cousens in the parish of Bishop's Waltham, Hants as a yearly hired servant for one whole year at one hiring at the wages of £3. I also lived another year in like manner with Mr John Cousens in his parish of Exton, Hants for one whole year which I served at the wages of £4 10s. About twenty-two years ago I was married to John Voller at the parish church of Durley by banns. My maiden name was Elizabeth Warner. My husband was legally settled in the parish of Titchfield, Hants. He lived with me for several years and then absconded and I have never seen or heard from him in any way whatever. I was in the Titchfield workhouse and with my husband was acknowledged a parishioner of Titchfield. I have three children living by [Voller] all of whom were born in wedlock namely Abraham aged about 21 years, William 13 and Ann aged 12 years or thereabouts. Some years after my husband absconded I cohabited with Joseph Ronalds and had one male bastard child named Richard aged 5 years or upwards, born of my body in Mr Trill's huts in the parish of St Clement [&] All Saints, Hastings, Sussex, and have another male bastard child named Robert and aged three years and upwards born of my body in Mr Revell's huts in Hastings; and Joseph Ronalds who then cohabited with me is the father of these two bastard children. I was married to Joseph Ronalds in the month of July 1822 by banns at the parish church of St Mary's, Romney Marsh, Kent and am now, with Joseph Ronalds, chargeable to Winchelsea and have never done any acts or deeds to gain a legal settlement in any parish or place whatever to the best of my knowledge or belief. [*mark of*] Elizabeth Ronalds.
                                                                    [AMS 2330 f.49]

482 29 Nov 1825 *Removal order made by Henry Powell and George Stace, justices of the peace for Winchelsea, to the churchwardens and overseers of the poor of the parish of St Thomas the Apostle, Winchelsea*:

Whereas complaint hath been made unto us that Joseph Ronalds and Elizabeth his wife and their two illegitimate children, namely Richard aged 5 years and upwards and Robert aged 3 years and upwards, lately intruded and came into the parish of St Thomas the Apostle, Winchelsea and have become chargeable to the same, we upon examination of the [evidence] upon oath and other circumstances do adjudge the same to be true and also adjudge the place of last legal settlement of Joseph Ronalds and his wife to be Hambledon in the county of Hants and the settlement of the said two illegitimate children to be the parish of St Clement in the town and port of Hastings, Sussex. These are therefore to require you on sight hereof to remove and convey Joseph Ronalds, his wife and their children for [the time being] only to Hambledon and them to deliver, unto the churchwardens and overseers of the poor there, or to some or one of them, together with this our order or a true copy thereof, who are hereby required to receive and provide for them according to law. [*Appended - same date and justices*] Whereas it appears to us that Joseph Ronalds, the pauper within ordered to be removed is unable to travel by reason of sickness and infirmity, we therefore do suspend the execution of the order until it shall be made to appear to our satisfaction that it may be executed without danger to Joseph Ronalds. [PAR 511/32/2/79]

Notes: 1. The order had been carried out by 24 Jan 1826 – see (**484**)
2. Also on 29 Nov 1825 Abraham Voller aged 21 and his sister Ann, 12 – see (**481**) were removed to Titchfield, Hampshire.[1]
3. No evidence has been found that, after being removed to Hambledon under the above order, Richard and Robert Ronalds were then separated from their parents and further removed to St Clement's, Hastings.

483 11 Dec 1825 *Letter from William Friend, Hambledon, [Hampshire], vestry clerk, to Charles Arnett, Winchelsea, [assistant] overseer*:

In answer to your letter of the 9th instant the overseers of this parish request you will have the goodness to allow [Joseph] Ronalds what relief you think necessary during his illness. Should he require any assistance after his recovery it will be necessary for him to make application personally as none of the present overseers have any knowledge of him or his circumstances. Whenever you think proper to forward the account of what money you advance it shall be remitted. [PAR 511/35/1/202]

484 24 Jan 1826 *Letter from William Friend, Hambledon, [Hampshire], vestry clerk, to Charles Arnett, Winchelsea, assistant overseer*:

I have enclosed £4 2s 0d the amount expended by you on account of this parish of which I will thank you to acknowledge receipt by return of post. [*Endorsed*] 'Hambledon parish J Ronalds'. [PAR 511/35/1/204]

---

1 PAR 511/32/2/81

The Ancient Town of
WINCHELSEA,
in the County of
SUSSEX.
To wit.

TO the Churchwardens and Overseers of the Poor of the Parish of Saint Thomas the Apostle, in the Ancient Town of Winchelsea, in the County of Sussex, and to the Churchwardens and Overseers of the Poor of the Parish of *Hambledon* in the *County of Hants*

Whereas Complaint hath been made unto us, two of his Majesty's Justices of the Peace, acting in and for the Town of Winchelsea aforesaid (one whereof being of the Quorum), by the Churchwardens and Overseers of the Poor of the said Parish of Saint Thomas the Apostle, in Winchelsea, that *Joseph Ronalds and Elizabeth his Wife and their two illegitimate Children namely Richard aged five years and upwards and Robert aged three years and upwards*

lately intruded, and came into the said Parish of Saint Thomas the Apostle, and *have* become chargeable to the same: We, the said Justices, upon Examination of the Premises upon Oath, and other Circumstances, do adjudge the same to be true, and do also adjudge the Place of the last legal settlement of the said *Joseph Ronalds and Elizabeth his Wife* to be in the Parish of *Hambledon in the County of Hants - and the Settlement of the said two illegitimate Children to be in the parish of Saint Clement in the Town and port of Hastings in the County of Sussex* **These** are therefore in his Majesty's Name, to require you, the said Churchwardens and Overseers of the Poor of the said Parish of Saint Thomas the Apostle, on Sight hereof, to remove and convey the said *Joseph Ronalds and Elizabeth his Wife and their said two illegitimate Children for nurture only* from and out of your said Parish of Saint Thomas the Apostle, to the said Parish of *Hambledon in the said County of Hants*

and *them* to deliver unto the Churchwardens and Overseers of the Poor there, or to some or one of them, together with this our Order, or a true Copy hereof, who are hereby required to receive and provide for *them* according to Law. GIVEN under our Hands and Seals, this *twenty ninth* Day of *November* in the Year of our Lord One Thousand Eight Hundred and *twenty five*

The removal order of Joseph Ronalds and family

PAR 511/32/2/79 transcribed as part of (**482**)
reproduced by arrangement with the County Archivist

William Sands

485 *Two entries in the parish records illustrate the overseers' wish to encourage William Sands in his desire to go to sea. In the second quarter of 1825 he was paid five shillings 'to go to sea'[1] and a year later, more substantially, was allowed £3 on becoming 'bound to Mr Newton for three years.'[2] No other record has been found of his receiving poor law relief.*

486 2 May 1826 *Letter from Charles Poile, Rye to [Charles] Arnett, Winchelsea, [assistant overseer]:*
[Isaac] Newton at Sunderland [County Durham] has requested me to apply to you for a sum you promised the boys he has from your parish. I think when they went off you promised each of them £3 value for clothes. If you will send me the money in the course of [a] few days I shall be writing [to] Mr Newton then I will remit him their amount.   [PAR 511/35/1/222]

487 6 May 1826 *Letter from Isaac Newton, Sunderland, [County Durham] to [Charles] Arnett, Winchelsea, [assistant] overseer:*
I hereby certify that William Sands of the parish of Winchelsea was bound apprentice to me on the 27 June 1825 for three years to serve at sea, and is now on board my ship at London and it being his wish that you should pay his mother the £3 10s 0d allowance for clothes you hereby have my full concurrence to do so. I have the satisfaction to say he has hitherto conducted himself well and I trust will continue to do so. Should you have one or two more stout lads wishing to go to sea I can take them on board the same ship and on the same conditions provided they are sent down immediately. If you have a prospect of sending any please let me know immediately.   [PAR 511/35/1/225]

1 PAR 511/31/1/13 QE Jun 1825   2 ibid QE Jun 1826

Elizabeth Saunders (Sanders)

488 *Following the appeal contained in (**490**) the Winchelsea select vestry resolved that Elizabeth Saunders should receive casual relief of ten shillings.[1] Elizabeth and her family had lived in Winchelsea for many years. Her maiden name was Leonard and she married Thomas Saunders at St. Thomas's, Winchelsea on 13 April 1802.[2] They lived in 'a tenement in the Square' (Barrack Square) where, in support of their growing family, the parish was, by 1823, paying their rent of £6 per annum to the property's owner, Walter Fuller.[3] The parish registers record the baptism of their twelve children, three of whom died young. The youngest, Amelia, was born in April 1825 two months after the death of her father who was buried on 11 February.[4] Despite the fact that she was pregnant, the parish wasted no time in giving his widow notice to quit their Barrack Square home (**489**). This large family received poor law relief in cash and kind from 1815 when James Bray was paid £1 2s 0d by the parish for providing them with '½ chaldron of coals'[5] until 1833 when, on 29 August, a casual payment of £1 for clothes was made to Mrs Saunders.[6] The select vestry noted Mrs Saunders' move to Hastings after her husband's death – see (**492**) – when it resolved on 3*

April 1828 'that Mrs Thomas Saunders be allowed the relief she has had formerly upon her removing to Hastings'.[7] *The amount involved at that time was 6s 8d per week for herself and the younger children still with her. One of those children, Lavinia aged 6, died in 1830 and was buried in Winchelsea.*[8] *It must be assumed that the eventual withdrawal of this support led her to apply for relief to St Clement's, Hastings, thus provoking her settlement examination and her removal back to Winchelsea (491-492).*

489 24 Feb 1825 *Notice issued by Charles Arnett, assistant overseer on behalf of the churchwardens and overseers of Winchelsea to [inter alia] Widow T Saunders:* We hereby give you warning of quitting all that house and premises now in your occupation on or before this day month of which be pleased to take notice.

[PAR 511/37/3/14]

490 11 Jan 1831 *Letter from Elizabeth Saunders, Hastings to David Laurence, Winchelsea, [assistant] overseer:* I am sorry to be compelled to be troubling you. On this occasion I have been laid up with a bad hand from the effect of the prick of a pin for this fortnight past and have not been able to do anything since towards the maintenance of my family. You will therefore much oblige by sending me some assistance to Mr Woods as soon as you can do so – had it not been for this misfortune I should not have troubled you.   [PAR 511/35/1/350]

Note: In response to this request Winchelsea allowed Mrs Saunders a casual payment of five shillings on 21 January 1831 and of ten shillings on 4 February.[9]

491 20 May 1847 *Examinations taken on oath before Frederick Ticehurst, mayor, and Henry Smith, justices of the peace for the borough of Hastings, of Elizabeth Saunders, widow, and of Henry Coussins:* The said Elizabeth Saunders for herself saith: I am a widow aged about 64 years of age and am residing in Henbrey's Row on the late Barrack Ground in the parish of St Clement in the borough of Hastings at which place I have resided for twenty years and upwards. I was married to Thomas Saunders at Winchelsea church in Sussex about 43 years ago. He was legally settled in Winchelsea by birth and he never did any act to my knowledge to gain a settlement for himself. He resided at Winchelsea until his death in or about the year 1825 and he frequently received relief from Winchelsea for the support of myself and family as a parishioner thereof. About a year and a half after my husband's death I removed from Winchelsea to St Clement's, Hastings with five of my children at which parish I have resided from that time to the present and during the whole period of my residence in that parish I have received occasional relief from Winchelsea and for about two years and a half up to about last November I received the constant weekly relief of 2s 6d from Winchelsea while residing in St Clement's, Hastings and from about that time I have received the relief of 2s per week from St Clement's, Hastings to which parish I am now chargeable. I have never done any act to gain a settlement for myself.   [mark of] Elizabeth Saunders

The said Henry Coussins for himself saith: I reside in the parish of All Saints, Hastings and am the relieving officer for the parish of St Clement which is one of the parishes within the Hastings Union. I have relieved Elizabeth Saunders with the sum of 2s per week for the last nine weeks at the expense of the parish of St Clement where she is now residing and to which she is now chargeable. [*signed*] Henry Coussins   [*these examinations are attached to*] [PAR 511/32/3/85]

492 20 May 1847 *Removal order made by Frederick Ticehurst, mayor, and Henry Smith, justices of the peace for the borough of Hastings, to the churchwardens and overseers of the poor of the parish of St Clement, Hastings*:
Whereas complaint hath been made unto us that Elizabeth Saunders, widow, has come to inhabit in the parish of St Clement and is actually chargeable to the same, the said Elizabeth Saunders not having resided in the parish of St Clement for five years next before the said complaint and not having gained any legal settlement therein, we upon due proof thereof as well as upon the examinations of Elizabeth Saunders and Henry Coussins upon oath do adjudge the same to be true and also adjudge the place of last legal settlement of Elizabeth Saunders to be Winchelsea. These are therefore, in Her Majesty's name, at the time and in the manner prescribed by law to require you to remove and convey her to Winchelsea and her deliver, together with this our order or a true copy thereof, to the churchwardens and overseers of the poor there who are hereby required to receive and provide for her according to law.   [PAR 511/32/3/85]

1 PAR 511/12/3 4 Feb 1831   2 PAR 511/1/4/1   3 PAR 511/31/2/137   4 PAR 511/1/1/4; PAR 511/1/2/1; PAR 511/1/5/1   5 PAR 511/31/2/121   6 PAR 511/12/2   7 PAR 511/12/3   8 PAR 511/1/5/1 9 PAR 511/31/1/15 f.30; PAR 511/12/3

Mary Saunders (Sanders)

493 *Mary Saunders, born in 1811, was baptised at St Thomas's, Winchelsea with the Christian names Mary White and her surname spelt Sanders in the register.[1] She was one of Thomas and Elizabeth's many children (**488**). As the child of a pauper family she was put out to service in 1823, the relevant parish vestry minute reading, 'Resolved that Mr Henry Terry, Hastings, take Mary Saunders from 9 October to Lady Day 1824, the parish to pay 1s 6d per week and find her necessary clothing'.[2] (**494**) indicates that she did well, and (**495**) that she remained there a full year. It is highly likely that she returned home to help look after her younger siblings for at that time her father was seriously ill[3] (he died four months later)[4] and the parish was at the same time providing a nurse to look after her mother.[5]*

494 27 Mar 1824 *Letter from Henry Terry, Hastings to [Joseph] Bigg, Winchelsea, overseer*:
I intend sending Mary Saunders home next week as her father wish her to it. I should have liked to keep her the next half-year if agreeable. Please send the money when convenient.   [PAR 511/35/1/73]

495 21 Oct 1824 *Letter from E Terry, Hastings to [Charles] Arnett, Winchelsea [assistant] overseer*:

I have kept Mary Saunders twelve months according to agreement. She has been home better than a week. Therefore [I] will thank you to send the money. When you are in Hastings will thank you to call.   [PAR 511/35/1/121]

1 PAR 511/1/1/4   2 PAR 511/12/2 13 Oct 1823   3 PAR 511/31/1/13 QE Mar 1825   4 PAR 511/1/5/1
5 PAR 511/31/1/13 QE Mar 1825

William Selden

496 *Before his employment with Samuel Southerden (**497**), William Selden had worked first as a pauper boy for John Eagles (**166, 169**) and later for George Bray[1] and Thomas Hoadley who agreed to pay the parish 4s a week for Selden's work.[2] On 6 April 1820 the public vestry had agreed 'to give William Selden decent apparel and for him to provide otherwise for himself during the year'.[3] Samuel Southerden's request for him to be provided with a greatcoat (**497**) was allowed by the overseers and one pound allocated for the purchase.[4] Cordelia, daughter of William Selden and his wife Elizabeth, died when an infant and was buried at St Thomas's on 25 March 1834.[5] Sadly it is clear from the parish register baptism entry for their son, William junior, that Elizabeth Selden's situation became worse for it reads, '25 October 1835 Selden, William son of William (labourer) and Elizabeth (the father now dead)'.[6] William senior had been buried at St Thomas's on 29 March that year aged 33,[7] the inquest into his death having been held four days earlier. It records that he 'died in consequence of a cart having accidentally passed over him'. It was required at the time that any object involved in a death had to be given a valuation. In this case the cart was recorded as worth one shilling but the circumstances remain a mystery for the space where the name of the cart's owner should have appeared has been left blank.[8]*

497 21 Nov 1823 *Letter from S[amuel] Southerden, [farmer of] Camber to the overseers, Winchelsea*:

William Selden wished me to write to you to state that he is very much in want of a great coat as he goes about with my travelling team and is about the country very much in [the] winter part of the year frequently part of the nights as well as the days. If you will have the goodness to allow him one he will be extremely obliged to you. NB On the 20th instant I stated his receiving 1s 6d per day and 6d for all journeys exceeding ten miles. Travelling on the road is very expensive.
                                                                        [PAR 511/35/1/40]

1 PAR 511/31/1/11 QE Mar 1817   2 PAR 511/12/2 f.14   3 PAR 511/12/1 f.238   4 PAR 511/31/1/13
Sep 1823-Feb 1824   5 PAR 511/1/5/1   6 PAR 511/1/2/1   7 PAR 511/1/5/1   8 DAP Box 70/1

William Sheather

498 *William Sheather was, in 1815, accused of being the father of an illegitimate child born to Alice Whiteman (**499**). Entries in the overseers' accounts confirm that in 1825 the child was being looked after by Mrs [Ellis] Cogger, wife of John, (**500**) who was being paid 2s 6d per week.[1] During 1825 Sheather is recorded as paying £6 10s per quarter in maintenance but only £1 12s 6d in the December quarter after his letter (**501**).[2]*

499 17 Oct 1815 *Bastardy order of George Stace and George Tilden, justices of the peace for Winchelsea, concerning the child of Alice Whiteman, singlewoman*: Whereas it hath been duly made appear unto us as well upon the complaint of the churchwardens and overseers of the poor of Winchelsea as upon the oath of Alice Whiteman that she was delivered of a male bastard child at the Winchelsea workhouse on the 26th day of September 1815 and that the child is now chargeable to Winchelsea and likely so to continue; and further that William Sheather of the parish of Beckley, Sussex, did beget the child on the body of her, Alice Whiteman, and whereas William Sheather hath not shown any sufficient cause why he shall not be the reputed father of the child. We therefore upon examination of the cause and circumstances of the [evidence] as well upon the oath of Alice Whiteman as otherwise do adjudge William Sheather to be the reputed father of the child, and thereupon we do order, for the better relief of the parish of St Thomas the Apostle, Winchelsea as for the sustentation and relief of the child that William Sheather shall and do forthwith, upon notice of this our order, pay or cause to be paid to the churchwardens or overseers of the poor of Winchelsea or to some or one of them the sum of two pounds for and towards the lying-in of Alice Whiteman. And we do also hereby further order that William Sheather shall likewise pay the sum of two shillings and sixpence weekly and every week from this present time for and towards the keeping, sustentation and maintenance of the child for and during so long time as the child shall be chargeable to Winchelsea. And we do further order that Alice Whiteman shall pay the sum of one shilling weekly in case she shall not take care of the child herself. [Endorsed] Delivered a true copy of this order to the within named William Sheather. [signed] David Laurence   [PAR 511/34/4/5]
Note: On 7 February 1822 Messrs Dawes, Lardner and Fisher, solicitors of Rye, charged the parish ten shillings for preparing a special warrant for the arrest of William Sheather for non-payment of arrears of the maintenance required under this order.[3]

500 19 Jan 1825 *Letter from William Sheather, Brede to [the overseers of Winchelsea]*:
I have made arrangement with Mrs Cogger concerning the boy. This is to inform you that from 25 December 1825 I shall pay the money to her, Mrs Cogger, and I hope you will not give me any trouble concerning the last quarter's pay as I shall come and see you before long.
[*Endorsed*] W Sheather for bastardy.   [PAR 511/35/1/153]
Note: Between 25 March and 25 June 1825 the Winchelsea overseers received £6 10s 0d from Sheather.[4]

501 10 Oct 1825 *Letter from William Sheather, Brede to [Charles] Arnett, Winchelsea, [assistant overseer]*:
I am sorry [to] say that I have been so ill for this five weeks past that I have not been able to do the least thing but thank God I am now getting a little better and when I am able to come over I shall come and settle the account.
                                                          [PAR 511/35/1/198]

Notes: 1. Between 25 September and 25 December 1825 Sheather paid the Winchelsea overseers £1 12s 6d.[5]

2. In 1843 a William Sheather of Beckley, this William Sheather's place of residence in 1815 (**499**), was appointed assistant overseer of that parish.[6]

1 PAR 511/31/1/14   2 PAR 511/31/1/13   3 PAR 511/31/2/135   4 PAR 511/31/1/13   5 ibid   6 PAR 237/37/3/1

John Simmons

502 *Winchelsea paid Hythe's costs of £3 2s 0d resulting from the deferment of John Simmons' removal order (**503**). The overseers must have been persuaded that Simmons could, despite the order, manage where he and his family had lived before for they then gave him £2 10s 0d 'cash to go to Hythe' together with 2s 6d casual relief.[1] No further mention of his case has been found and it is extremely unlikely that Winchelsea would have provided the cow requested in (**504**).*

503 18 Mar 1825 *Removal order made by George Finnis, mayor, and Nathaniel Finnis, justice of the peace for the Cinque Port town of Hythe to the churchwardens and overseers of the parish of St Leonard, Hythe*:

Upon complaint unto us that John Simmons and Sarah his wife and their three children viz. William aged about 3 years, Mary Ann aged about 2 years and an infant not yet baptised have come to inhabit in the parish of St Leonard, Hythe without having gained a legal settlement there and are now chargeable to [that parish], we upon due proof thereof and also upon the examination of John Simmons do adjudge this to be true and likewise adjudge that the place of legal settlement of John Simmons, his wife and children is the parish of St Thomas the Apostle in the Ancient Town of Winchelsea in Sussex. We therefore require you to convey them from your parish of St Leonard to Winchelsea and them deliver, together with this order or a true copy thereof, to the churchwardens and overseers of the poor there [whom] we require to receive and provide for them as inhabitants of [their] parish.

[PAR 511/32/3/47]

Note: Endorsed on this order is a suspension by the magistrates on the grounds that Sarah Simmons is not fit to be moved because of her recent confinement. The suspension was lifted on 12 Apr 1825 and Winchelsea was charged £3 2s 0d for expenses incurred in the meantime.

504 1 Jul 1826 *Letter from John Simmons, [Hoxton, London] to the overseers of Winchelsea*:

I am very sorry to trouble you any more but necessity drives me to it. I was forced to leave Hythe for I could get nothing to do there so I [was] forced to sell my things off and my wife's father and my brother-in-law persuaded me to come to London to try which I did but I cannot get half work enough to keep my family. Therefore I am compelled to ask your charity, gentlemen, to help me. I have been thinking, gentlemen, if you will raise me a cow I think with the produce of the cow and what little I can earn I may endeavour to keep my family or otherwise I must trouble you to allow me 6 or 7 [shillings] a week but I must leave it to you, gentlemen, which you do but I have no doubt if you raise me a cow I may endeavour to maintain my family and if [not] we must come home to the [poor]house. We are at my wife's father's for I have nothing to invest in lodgings so something must be done very soon for I could not have lived so long as I have done were it not for my friends. I cannot intrude on good friends so long. I would gladly come home to the house if you like, gentlemen. If you will not do anything for me without [i.e. outside the parish] please let me know soon what I am to do. Direct to me: J Simmons at Mr Spain's, 12 Norris Street, Whitmore Road, Hoxton, London. [PAR 511/35/1/233] Note: A general provision for cows to be provided for the poor was included among the clauses in William Pitt's unsuccessful attempt at Poor Law reform in 1797. Despite support from philanthropists like the Earl of Winchilsea who championed allotment provision the proposal was greeted with derision and could never have been practicable.[2]

1 PAR 511/31/1/15 f.21   2 Poynter pp 71, 74

John Sinden

505 *Following his removal from Battle* (**511**) *and Winchelsea's inquiries into his legal settlement* (**506**), *John Sinden began receiving regular poor law relief such as that granted 'when sick' £4 12s 0d plus ten shillings 'for nursing'.[1] It seems the vestry members became annoyed by Sinden's constant applications because on 17 December 1815 they resolved, 'that Sinden do have £1 not to trouble the parish until 25 March next'.[2] After that date he and his family continued to be regularly supported in both cash and kind and by the payment of his rent.[3] It is something of a surprise that he and his wife, on 6 April 1820, were appointed governor and governess of the Winchelsea workhouse.[4] The following day the parish paid a bill of five shillings for a 'horse and cart moving John Sinden's furniture'.[5] Anyway, the position could not have lasted long for four months later Sinden was appointed parish beadle* (**507-510, 756**) *where his unsatisfactory conduct led to his background being further investigated* (**511**). *Later he did more to earn his own living by supplying the parish with potatoes[6] and working on the highways at 1s 8d per day.[7] However, he was still receiving relief in 1841 when the guardians of the Rye Union allowed him £1 8s 3¾d giving his advanced age as the reason.[8] The census of that year shows him living in Cleveland Street (Friars Road) in the household of Edmund Morris. His wife had pre-deceased him and he died aged 72 later that year.[9]*

506 18 Dec 1812 *Legal opinion of George Courthope, Temple, regarding the settlement in Winchelsea of John Sinden*:
I am of opinion that the settlement of the pauper and his family in Winchelsea entirely depends upon the annual value of the respective tenements in which he resided and that the first [document produced to me], taken by Mr Ashburnham, will in neither instance defeat the settlement if the court should be of opinion that either of the tenements were of the annual value of £10 during the pauper's residence upon them, and upon this question I think the opinion of two builders,

however experienced they may be, is not likely to prevail as to the value of the tenement hired of Eagles against the evidence of the rent agreed for and paid for that tenement. It is more than probable that the sessions would also consider the tenement hired of Tree to be of sufficient value to confer a settlement on the pauper, but as the question upon both the takings is a mere question of evidence it is impossible to say with absolute certainty what the opinion of the quarter sessions may be. At the same time I must add, as it is impossible for the most experienced valuers to ascertain with accuracy the precise value of property of this description, my own opinion is, that the rent agreed upon between the parties will be and ought to be considered as far outweighing the mere opinion of any valuers however respectable, where there is neither fraud imposition or want of knowledge in the parties to the contract. I cannot therefore hold out to the parish of Winchelsea any prospect of success upon appeal but in case they are determined to take the opinion of sessions, they must produce the pauper who will prove the principal part of the case; they must likewise produce persons of competent skill to show that neither of the tenements were of the value of £10 per annum and I should recommend them to have Mr Ashburnham in court that he may be examined in case it should be necessary in the course of the appeal.   [PAR 511/35/2/1]

Notes: 1. It is highly likely that the above Mr Ashburnham was Revd John Ashburnham, son of Sir William Ashburnham of Broomham, Guestling. The Battle Petty Sessions minute book – see (**511**) – shows that John Sinden's removal was from Guestling where the Revd John was rector at this time and thus involved in collecting evidence in support of the removal.[10]

2. George Courthope, of Bedford Square and Whiligh in Ticehurst, was frequently called on for opinions on settlement; his opinions and papers as arbitrator on a number of subjects are among the family archive at ESRO.[11]

507 10 Aug 1820 *Minute of the Winchelsea select vestry*:
Resolved that John Sinden be appointed parish beadle to clear the streets of vagrants [and] to be allowed a suitable dress for the occasion and a salary of three pounds per annum.
                    [PAR 511/12/2 f.2]

508 8 Jul 1824 *Minute of the Winchelsea select vestry*:
[Resolved] that, John Sinden having deserted his office of beadle, John Chester be appointed to act pro tempo.   [PAR 511/12/2]

509 30 Jul 1824 *Minute of the Winchelsea select vestry*:
Resolved that [a complaint be made to the magistrates] against John Sinden for not delivering up to the assistant overseer the clothes allowed by the parish as beadle.
                    [PAR 511/12/2]

510 2 Aug 1824 *Information and summary proceedings held before Henry Powell, justice of the peace for Winchelsea*:
Charles Arnett of Winchelsea, assistant overseer, on oath charges John Sinden with unlawfully detaining certain wearing apparel, the property of the churchwardens,

overseers and parishioners of the parish of St Thomas the Apostle, Winchelsea.
[*Town clerk's note*] 6 August 1824. Heard before Mr [John] Tilden and Mr [Henry] Powell and discharged.   [WIN 237A]
Note: On this date Thomas Sylvester Keene submitted to the churchwardens and overseers of Winchelsea a bill of one shilling for 'Serving a summons on John Sinden for detaining the beadle's clothes.[12]

511 11 Aug 1824 *Letter from Thomas Charles Bellingham, Battle to Richard Stileman, Winchelsea*:
John Sinden was examined at the Battle petty sessions on the 27th October 1812. Mr Millward, Mr Fuller and Mr Kemp were at the meeting and the examination is signed by the two latter. It is stated in the record book that orders were granted for returning him and his family to Winchelsea and they were probably put in force by the overseers for Guestling but as to this I of course can give no information. Mr Hawes might have been at the meeting although his name does not appear in the record.   [PAR 511/35/1/103]
Note: Thomas Charles Bellingham was a Battle solicitor who served as coroner for Hastings Rape between 1830 and 1838 when he died at the age of 41.[13]

512 24 Feb 1825 *Notice issued by Charles Arnett, assistant overseer on behalf of the churchwardens and overseers of Winchelsea to [inter alia] John Sinden*:
We hereby give you warning of quitting all that house and premises now in your occupation on or before this day month of which be pleased to take notice.
                                               [PAR 511/37/3/14]

1 PAR 511/31/1/11 E1814-E1815   2 PAR 511/12/1 f.203   3 PAR 511/31/1/11   4 PAR 511/12/1 f.238
5 PAR 511/31/2/131   6 e.g. PAR 511/31/1/13 QE Sep 1827   7 PAR 511/40/1/8   8 PAR 511/38/4/3
9 PAR 511/1/5/1   10 PBSA 1; (CW)   11 SAS/CO/4/222-224 (CW)   12 PAR 511/31/2/143   13 Hunnisett p.xxi

Stephen Sinden

513 *Stephen Sinden, son of John and his wife Jane, briefly master and mistress of the workhouse (**505**), first appears in the Winchelsea overseers' accounts in the autumn of 1823 when he was granted £2 5s 6d 'to go to sea'[1] and, on 18 November, £2 'for clothes to go to sea'.[2] No reason is given for the cancellation of his removal to Rye (**518**) but the overseers' inquiries about his service with Lewis Knight (**519-521**) would have been because his statement (**516**) suggests that a settlement might have been thus established. For Stephen Sinden's possible serious illness and admission to St Bartholomew's hospital see (**522**).*

514 20 Dec 1826 *Letter from D[avid]Stonham, Rye to [Charles] Arnett, superintendent of the parish of Winchelsea*:
At your request, for the information of the parish of Winchelsea, I beg to state that, as far as my memory serves me, Stephen Sinden was bound an apprentice

to the master of the *Brunswick* of Rye, William Gains, and continued a short time under his indenture which I believe was lodged with Mr Jarrett (who made them) on behalf of both parties. But upon a [disagreement] between the master and the apprentice, they agreed to part and the indenture was cancelled by mutual consent – this is all the knowledge I have of the matter, nor do I pledge myself to be perfectly correct herein but I believe it to have been in substance the same thing. [*Endorsed*] Pay the boy 3d.   [PAR 511/35/1/253]

515 21 Dec 1826 *Letter from D[avid] Stonham, Rye to [Charles] Arnett, [Winchelsea, assistant overseer]*:
The boy is returned without being paid. If I had supposed my answer to your questions was of no consequence I should have deferred it until your carrier came. I have paid the [*document damaged*] on your account.   [PAR 511/35/1/254]

516 29 Jan 1828 *Examination taken before John Tilden and Henry Powell, justices of the peace for Winchelsea, of Stephen Sinden aged about twenty-four years*:
who upon his oath saith he was born at Guestling, Sussex, and is the son of John and Jane Sinden. At the age of fourteen years he went to live with Mr Lloyd of the parish of St. Thomas the Apostle, Winchelsea, and lived with him two years. He then lived with Capt [John] Hollingberry of the same parish about two years. He then went to France and lived with Lord Nevill nearly twelve months. He then hired himself to Mr James Bellingham, surgeon in the parish of Rye in Sussex and lived with him nearly eighteen months at the wages of eight pounds per annum, then hired himself to Rev. Drake Hollingberry, Clerk, of Winchelsea at the wages of twelve pounds per annum and lived with him about nine months, then hired himself to Lewis Knight Esq, barrister-at-law, of Montague Square in the parish of Mary-le-Bow in the county of Middlesex at the wages of twelve pounds per annum and lived with him thirteen months, from thence he put himself apprentice to Mr David Stonham of the parish of Rye to serve him on board any of his vessels during the term of three years; he served till the 12th May 1824 being about six months; he then left his vessel at Chatham and gave himself up to the service of Mr Stonham on the 14th day of the same month. He was to receive £35 for his service during the three years. In the same month he went on board the *Speculation* schooner, Captain Catt, at the wages of thirty shillings per month and served with him about nine months, then left that vessel and a short time afterwards went on board the *Prometheus* schooner, Captain William Sinden, and served with him five months at the wages of 30s per month and had not since done any act or deed whereby he has gained a settlement. [*signed*] Stephen Sinden.   [AMS 2330 f.79]
Note: Stephen Sinden 'son of John and Jane' was baptised at Guestling on 24 May 1804.[3]

517 29 Jan 1828 *Removal order made by John Tilden and Henry Powell, justices of the peace for Winchelsea, to the churchwardens and overseers of the poor of the parish of St Thomas the Apostle, Winchelsea*:
Whereas complaint hath been made unto us that Stephen Sinden, aged about

24 years, lately intruded and came into the parish of St Thomas the Apostle, Winchelsea and is become chargeable to the same, we, upon examination of the [evidence] upon oath and other circumstances, do adjudge the same to be true and do also adjudge the last place of legal settlement of Stephen Sinden to be Rye, Sussex. These are therefore, in His Majesty's name, to require you to remove and convey him to Rye and there deliver him, together with this order or a true copy thereof, to the churchwardens and overseers of the poor who are hereby required to receive and provide for him according to law.   [PAR 511/32/2/83]

518 15 Apr 1828 *General quarter sessions of the peace held at the Guildhall, Winchelsea before Joseph Hennah, deputy mayor, Henry Powell, John Tilden and Fielding Browne, jurats and justices*:
Ordered that the order under the hands and seals of Henry Powell and John Tilden Esqs dated the 29th day of January 1828 made for the removal of Stephen Sinden from Winchelsea to Rye be quashed by mutual consent.   [WIN 61D f.66]

519 29 May 1828 *Letter from Mary Wood, London, to D[avid] Laurence, Winchelsea, [assistant overseer]*:
I received your letter concerning Stephen Sinden first coming to Mr Knight's service. I went to Mr Knight on 27 June and as far as I can recollect Stephen came about five months after me which is six years this June and I have not the least recollection when he left Mr Knight's service. Mary Winter was living with me at the same time therefore she may give you more intelligence than I can about it. Mr Laurence, as it is parish business they can better afford to pay the postage of this letter than I can so I will thank you to give [the £1] to my grandmother.
                                             [PAR 511/35/1/315]

520 3 Jun 1828 *Letter from L[ewis] Knight, Montague Square, [London] to David Laurence, Winchelsea, assistant overseer*:
I have not an accurate recollection of the particulars for which your letter of 1st instant asks but I will with pleasure give you such information as I can. I think that I engaged S[tephen] Sinden in the summer or autumn of the year 1821 in Winchelsea but that he did not actually enter my service until I had quitted that place. The hiring was that of a footman and in the manner usual in such cases, namely with an agreement for yearly wages and liveries but with nothing at all said about time, though I imagine that a tacit understanding always accompanies such engagements of indoor servants that the service may at any time be put an end to by a month's warning on either side. I think that he first entered my service in the autumn of 1821 at a house which I then occupied between Hastings and Fairlight. My family passed the winter of that year or part of it including Christmas at Hastings and he was then with us there. He came up with me to my present house in Montague Square in the spring of 1822 and continued there in my service until upon a month's warning given by himself he quitted it in the same year. My

impression is that he left me before the autumn of 1822 certainly and that he was not altogether in my service as much as a year. I cannot answer your questions with greater certainty or more particularly but perhaps Mr [John] Hollingberry or Mr [John] Shakespeare may be able to inform you further – he lived with the former gentleman before and I believe with the latter after quitting me.

[PAR 511/35/1/316]

521 17 Jul 1828 *Letter from John Kitchenham, London, to David Laurence, Winchelsea, [assistant overseer]*:
I arrived in town last night from the country and saw your letter which arrived on Monday. Therefore I hasten to inform you that I went to live with Mr Knight of Montague Square the first week in July 1822 and [Stephen] Sinden left only a day or two before I went there to live. This or any other information I can give you on the subject you are quite welcome to.   [PAR 511/35/1/319]

522 18 Jul 1828 *Letter from Edwin Beresford Dawes, 6 Featherstone Buildings, Holborn, [London] to David Laurence, Winchelsea, [assistant overseer]*:
In consequence of your application to my uncle I am directed by him to enclose the accompanying transfer which will enable the pauper to be admitted to Bartholomew's Hospital. You must fill up the blanks and state accurately what the nature of the disease is [and] how much he is paid by the churchwardens or overseers. If the case is such that Dr Scott can say that it ought to come under the consideration of the hospital there needs no further recommendation. He had better bring a certificate from Dr Scott with him. You will see by the back of the paper that £2 12s 6d must be brought by the pauper with him. If he leaves the hospital before the 70 days are expired what remains of the £2 12s 6d will be returned to him but if he continues longer 9d a day will have to be paid during his stay in the hospital. The day for his admission is the 25th of this month at 11 o'clock when he must be at the steward's office in the hospital. You will, of course, send the money with the man. My uncle is going to Ramsgate tomorrow morning and will not be in town for some time.   [PAR 511/35/1/320]
Note: Entries in the Winchelsea overseers' books suggest that Stephen Sinden was the subject of the above letter. The accounts for the quarter ending September 1828 which would, of course, include July payments, show him being paid £2 7s 0d 'expenses to and from London'.[4] The following quarter the overseers noted that he had at some time previously received £4 'expenses and entrance to hospital' and that William Lennard had been paid 2s 6d for taking him to Rye.[5] During the quarter ending June the following year he received £1 4s 0d 'expenses from London'.[6]

1 PAR 511/31/1/13 2 PAR 511/31/1/12 f.274 3 PAR 350/1/1/1 4 PAR 511/31/1/13 5 ibid 6 ibid

Ann Stevens

523 *Unlike the terms offered to George Martin* (**524**), *no record has been found of the arrangements under which Isaac Carpenter was employing Ann Stevens* (**525-527**) *but he seems to have taken her just after she had spent time in Winchelsea gaol where she was imprisoned from 29 July to 4 August 1824.[1] She was discharged by order of the justices but her crime is not recorded. She was again in trouble on 12 October that year when the public vestry resolved 'that Ann Stevens be taken and confined in the [work]house upon bread and water for some time'.[2] The overseers may therefore have been relieved to receive Dive Boorman's letter indicating that he wished to marry her* (**528**). *If that wedding actually happened it was not in Winchelsea and Ann was back there and in trouble again only four months later* (**529-530**) *In May 1837 she was admitted to Brede workhouse but left after only two weeks.[3]*

524 24 Feb 1820 *Minute of the Winchelsea public vestry:*
It is agreed for Mr George Martin to take Ann Stevens from Lady Day 1820 to Lady Day 1821, the parish to give him 2s per week, the parish to clothe, wash and mend for her.   [PAR 511/12/1 f.237]
Note: The parish paid George Martin £5 4s 0d in settlement of this commitment[4] and renewed the agreement for 1821-1822.[5] Before her first imprisonment – see (**523**) – she was also in service with Joseph Harman on similar terms.[6]

525 7 Aug 1824 *Letter from I[saac] Carpenter, Hastings to [Charles] Arnett, poorhouse, Winchelsea, assistant overseer:*
I write a few lines in answer to yours to say that if Ann Stevens is the same girl you mentioned to me when I was in Winchelsea I am almost afraid to have her as I am afraid she will not suit me. But if she thinks she shall like the place and will endeavour to stop I shall have no objection to trying her to Lady Day next.
                                                        [PAR 511/35/1/101]

526 24 Sep 1824 *Letter from I[saac] Carpenter, Hastings to [Charles] Arnett, poorhouse, Winchelsea, [assistant overseer]:*
I am sorry to send Ann Stevens home with the disorder that she has got but I cannot think of letting her remain with me till she is well of it as I have no other convenience for her to sleep than with the children and I think they are all in danger and Ann tells me she had it sometime before she came here which I was sorry to hear for if I had known I would not have taken her on any account. If she gets well of it I have no objection of taking her for the time agreed.   [PAR 511/35/1/114]

527 27 Sep 1824 *Information given before Henry Powell and Joseph Hennah, justices of the peace for Winchelsea by Charles Arnett, assistant overseer:*
[who] on oath charges Isaac Carpenter of Hastings, Sussex, shoemaker, with unlawfully discharging Ann Stevens, pauper of Winchelsea and a servant by contract to Isaac Carpenter, prior to the expiration of the term of the contract made

for the service of Ann Stevens.

[*Appended note*:] 30 Sep 1824 Defendant appeared and summons discharged. Mr Carpenter to take the girl back and pay expenses. [*signed*] H. P. Butler [town clerk]   [WIN 237A]

528 1 Mar 1826 *Letter from Dive Boorman, Winchelsea to [Charles] Arnett, Winchelsea, governor of the workhouse*:
I write this to inform you my real intention without flattery. I shall inform you in a free manner what I intend to do, that is, sir, I intend to make Ann Stevens my wife. If I can gain your approbation and the rest of the officers of the parish I should wish to have the banns called as soon as possible as I am in danger of being called away. Moreover I would wish to be called in another parish as I don't wish for anyone to know it. Therefore the banns can be called in a parish distant from this. However, I should wish to talk with you on the subject when you are at leisure.
[*Endorsed*] An application from Dive Boorman a parishioner of Woodchurch, Kent, and a private in His Majesty's Royal Staff Corps, to marry Ann Stevens.
[PAR 511/35/1/207]

529 11 Jul 1826 *Information given before Henry Powell and George Stace, justices of the peace for Winchelsea by Charles Arnett, assistant overseer*:
who on his oath saith that on 19 June last Ann Stevens, a pauper of Winchelsea, ran away from the workhouse of Winchelsea and took with her two gowns, one apron, two shifts and one flannel petticoat the property of the Winchelsea overseers.
[WIN 237A]

530 14 Jul 1826 *Information submitted to Henry Powell, justice of the peace for Winchelsea, by Charles Arnett, assistant overseer, in the case of Ann Stevens who is charged with being a rogue and vagabond*:
[Arnett] on his oath states that on Friday night last the 7th day of July last he and Charles Hill, constable, between the hours of 11 and 12 o'clock did find Ann Stevens in an outhouse commonly called the Watch House and that she would not give an account [of] how she maintained herself and she having no visible means thereof.
[*Appended notes*]: Charles Hill, constable, corroborated this evidence. Ann Stevens confessed the same to be true. She was then committed to the gaol at Winchelsea for the space of three calendar months [under] 5th GeoIV Cap 83 Sec 4.
[WIN 237A]

1 WIN 1228   2 PAR 511/12/2   3 G 8/19/4   4 PAR 511/31/1/13 Sep 1820-Mar 1821   5 PAR 511/12/2/f.11   6 ibid f.39

George Stevenson

531 *In the correspondence on which this volume is based George Stevenson features only in* (**532**) *seeking a casual payment of five shillings to help support his rapidly growing family. Nevertheless his time as a Winchelsea pauper is worth noting. He first appears in 1819 when the select vestry allowed him a casual payment of £1 2s 0d.[1] He was then found work on the highways with the proviso that the parish would allow him one shilling a week above his wages.[2] In January 1823 it was decreed that he must accept two shillings a week or go into the workhouse.[3] Two years later, by contrast, he is recorded as living in a house with an annual poor rate valuation of £2, an unusually high figure for someone on relief. As a pauper he was excused payment of the poor rate but he did pay for an additional garden in his possession.[4] The parish was again providing work in 1827, this time breaking stones.[5] In 1836 he was listed among Winchelsea's able-bodied poor[6] and his need for poor law relief features again in 1841 when the guardians of the Rye Union allowed him £1 16s 7½d, the reason given being 'illness'.[7] At that time he was shown by the census to be living in The Strand with his wife Fanny and their children John 14, Elizabeth 12, Esther 10, Joseph [8], Fanny junior 6 and Jane 4.*

532 19 Nov 1830 *Endorsed upon a letter from Mrs Hannah Francis, Brighton, to Joseph Bigg, Winchelsea, grocer, are notes concerning payments made to paupers and requests received*:
[inter alia] George Stevenson [requests] 5s.   [PAR 511/35/1/341]
Note: The list of requests endorsed on Mrs Francis's letter seems to have pre-dated the letter itself for on 12 November 1830 the select vestry 'Resolved that the following sum advanced by the assistant overseer since the previous meeting be confirmed: George Stevenson 5s.[8] The payment had been made by David Laurence on 6 November.[9]

1 PAR 511/31/1/11 QE Sep 1819 2 PAR 511/12/2 f.9 3 ibid f.37 4 PAR 511/31/1/13 16 Sep 1825 5 ibid QE Jun 1827 6 PAR 511/37/7/29 7 PAR 511/38/4/3 8 PAR 511/12/3 9 PAR 511/31/1/15 f.28

Susannah Stevenson

533 *Before their removal order* (**534**) *Susannah Stevenson and her husband James began receiving relief from Winchelsea in 1822, while living there.[1] They moved to Hastings the following year.[2] Payments to Susannah Stevenson as a widow continued until 1831, usually at 1s 6d per week.[3] No further mention has been found of her since the birth of her illegitimate child* (**536-537**). *However, the child, Elizabeth, was resident in the Northiam workhouse in 1836/7. She is included under Class 3 which lists 'Illegitimate children under 16 without their mother'.[4]*

534 30 Jun 1830 *Removal order made by W Crouch and D Gill, justices of the peace for the town and port of Hastings, to the churchwardens and overseers of the poor of the parish of St Clement, Hastings*:
Whereas complaint hath been made unto us that James Stevenson and Susannah his wife and their one child named Frederick aged 2 years and upwards lately intruded and came into the parish of St Clement and are become chargeable to

the same, we do adjudge the same to be true and also adjudge that the place of last legal settlement of James Stevenson his wife and child to be the parish of St Thomas the Apostle in the Ancient Town of Winchelsea. These are therefore in His Majesty's name to require you on sight hereof to remove and convey them to Winchelsea and them deliver, together with this our order or a true copy thereof, to the churchwardens and overseers of the poor who are hereby required to receive and provide for them according to law.

[Endorsed] (same date) Whereas it doth appear to us that James Stevenson, the pauper within ordered to be removed, is at present unable to travel by reason of sickness and infirmity, we do therefore hereby suspend the execution of the within order of removal until it shall be made appear unto us that the same may be safely executed without danger.

[Further endorsed] 5 Jul 1830 Whereas it is now made appear unto us [*same magistrates*] that the within order of removal may be executed without danger we do therefore hereby order the same to be forthwith put into execution accordingly; and whereas it is duly proved to us upon oath that James Stevenson, the pauper above mentioned, is dead and that the sum of £1 13s 6d hath been necessarily incurred by the suspension of the order, we do therefore order and direct the churchwardens and overseers of the poor of Winchelsea to which James Stevenson was ordered to be removed to pay the said sum of £1 13s 6d to Simon Bevill upon demand.

[Receipted] 7 Jul 1830 Received of the overseers of Winchelsea the sum of one pound 13 shillings and sixpence. S. Bevill, assistant overseer. [PAR 511/32/3/78]

535 13 Oct 1830 *Letter from John Woods to [David] Laurence, Winchelsea, [assistant overseer]*:
I have no objection to pay Mrs [Susannah] Stevenson when I receive your order to do so. [PAR 511/35/1/338]
Note: On the same date the select vestry resolved 'That Mrs Stevenson, widow of James Stevenson, be allowed 1s 6d per week with her child and 3s casual relief.[5]

536 14 Nov 1833 *Voluntary examination taken before Joseph Hennah, justice of the peace for Winchelsea, of Susannah Stevenson, widow of James Stevenson*:
who upon her oath saith that she is now with child and that the child is likely to be born a bastard and to be chargeable to the parish of St Thomas the Apostle, Winchelsea and that George Lamb, tide waiter third class of the Board of Customs, London, is the father of the child. [*mark of*] Susannah Stevenson
[AMS 2330 f.133]
Note: A tide waiter's responsibility was to check vessels on their arrival in port.

537 31 Dec 1833 *Examination taken before Joseph Hennah, Fielding Browne and William Lipscomb, justices of the peace for Winchelsea, of Susannah Stevenson*:
who upon her oath saith that she was delivered of a female bastard child at the house of James Hoad on the twenty-second day of this present month of December

which child is not yet baptised and that George Lamb, a tide waiter of the third class of the Board of Customs lately residing at No 2 St George's Court, White Street, Southwark, is the father of the child. [*mark of*] Susannah Stevenson

[AMS 2330 f.135]

Note: No entry appears in the Winchelsea parish register for the baptism of Susannah's child.[6]

1 PAR 511/31/1/13　2 PAR 511/31/1/12 f.239　3 PAR 511/31/1/13 QE Mar 1831　4 G 8/19/1　5 PAR 511/12/3　6 PAR 511/1/2/1

William Stonestreet

538 *For William Stonestreet's birth and early life see* (**50-59**). *In March 1827, after his removal from Hastings to Winchelsea* (**539**), *William was lodged by the parish with a Mr Almond.[1] Six months later he went into service with Dr Adam Scott. Dr Scott was initially paid two shillings a week to keep the boy,[2] but the arrangement was altered so that the doctor received no cash payment but provided board and lodging while the parish provided William with clothing and did his washing and mending.[3] This continued until March 1830* (**540**) *at which time William, on his own initiative, obtained a position with a Mr Gilbert of Hastings.[4] Thereafter he was allowed by Winchelsea money for clothes and occasionally cash as casual relief* (**542**). *By 1841 the census shows William back in Winchelsea and living in Mill Road with his wife Frances and their children Harriett 7, Lucy 5, William junior 3 and James 3 months.*

539 19 Jan 1827 *Removal order made by John Cossum and D Gill, justices of the peace for the Borough if Hastings to the churchwardens and overseers of the poor of the parish of Holy Trinity, otherwise Dissolved Priory, in the town and port of Hastings*:
Whereas complaint hath been made to us that William Stonestreet lately intruded and came into the parish of Holy Trinity, Hastings and is actually chargeable to the same, we upon due proof thereof and also upon the examination of Thomas Barnes do adjudge the same to be true and also adjudge the last place of legal settlement of William Stonestreet to be Winchelsea. These are therefore in His Majesty's name to require you upon sight hereof to remove and convey him to Winchelsea and him deliver, together with this our order or a true copy thereof, to the churchwardens and overseers of the poor there who are hereby required to receive and provide for him according to law.　　　　　　　　　　　　[PAR 511/32/3/51]

540 20 Feb 1829 *Minute of the Winchelsea public vestry*:
Resolved that Dr Scott do continue to keep William Stonestreet upon the same terms as before during the time Dr Scott may have occasion for him.

[PAR 511/12/2]

541 15 Nov 1830 *Letter from William Morris, Iden, to William Stonestreet at Joseph Amon's, Winchelsea*:

If you are not provided with a place and can come over to Iden on Wednesday morning, not later than 9 o'clock perhaps, I may be able to make an agreement with you. [PAR 511/35/1/342]

542 19 Nov 1830 *Endorsed upon a letter from Mrs Hannah Francis, Brighton, to Joseph Bigg, Winchelsea, grocer, are notes concerning payments made to paupers and requests received*:

[*inter alia*] William Stonestreet asks £1. [PAR 511/35/1/341]

Note: This request was granted by the parish officers.[5]

1 PAR 511/12/3 15 Mar 1827   2 ibid 12 Oct 1827   3 ibid 14 Mar 1828   4 ibid 11 Jun 1830   5 PAR 511/31/1/13 QE 25 Dec 1830

Solomon Suters

543 *Solomon Suters' father, Charles, was a Winchelsea carrier whose services were used for the removal of paupers. In 1819 he submitted to the parish a bill for fifteen shillings 'for the use of his tilted cart at different times removing families to different parishes'.[1] Solomon was baptised at St Thomas's on 12 December 1784, 'son of Charles and Ann'[2] and so was aged 22 when he was accused of assaulting George Dunn (**544-545**). No record has been found of any response to Solomon's plea from Crayford (**546**), The only recorded subsequent payments to him were of £1 when he was ill in 1831[3] and of a further £1 on 14 October in the same year.[4] His father had died in 1824[5] and his mother was admitted to the Winchelsea workhouse ten years later.[6] While there she received, as did other residents at the time, - see (**752**), an allowance, in her case of 2s 6d a week for her keep.[7]*

544 20 Aug 1806 *Recognizance made before Thomas Marten, deputy mayor, justice of the peace for Winchelsea*:

Solomon Suters of Winchelsea, labourer, acknowledges himself to be indebted to our sovereign lord the king in the sum of fifty pounds [as do] Charles Suters of Winchelsea, carrier, £25 and Joseph Hoad of Winchelsea, tailor, £25, upon condition that Solomon Suters do personally appear at the next general quarter sessions of the peace to be held for Winchelsea and there to answer such complaint as shall be preferred against him on His Majesty's behalf for unlawfully, notoriously and consciously assembling with certain other persons on the 17th day of August instant at and in Winchelsea with intent to disturb the peace of our lord the king and then and there making, exciting and causing to be made a great riot, disturbance or breach of the peace and then and there assaulting and ill-treating George Dunn, gentleman. [If he appears] and do[es] not depart the court without leave then this recognizance to be void or else to remain in full force.

[*Endorsed*] Appeared and discharged 7 Oct 1806. [WIN 244]

545 7 Oct 1806 *General quarter sessions of the peace held at the Guildhall, Winchelsea before Thomas Marten Esq deputy mayor, Richard Lamb and George Stace, jurats and justices of the peace for Winchelsea*:

At this sessions Solomon Suters appeared in pursuance of his recognizance to answer what should be alleged against him by Edmund Barford, gentleman, for assaulting and ill-treating him when, by consent of the prosecutor's agent, the recognizance was ordered to be discharged. Also Solomon Suters appeared in pursuance of his recognizance to answer in like manner as to assaulting George Dunn, gentleman, when, by consent of the prosecutor's agent, the recognizance was ordered to be discharged. [WIN 61 f.116]

546 28 Apr 1827 *Letter from W Burford, Crayford, [Kent] to the churchwardens or overseers of Winchelsea*:

The writer of the enclosed resides in our parish [and] is a sober and industrious man. I have inquired of his master and neighbours and am satisfied his statement is correct and that he has for some time suffered great privations. Your compliance with his request will prevent much trouble and inconvenience. I have no objection to your relief [being] properly applied and will inform you when he is enabled to attend to his labours.

[*Endorsed*] *Letter from Solomon Suters to W Burford*:

[Please will you] have the goodness to write to my parish as I am unable to provide for my wife and child as I have the ague and the fever twice in 24 hours and I have not been able to do any work for some time past. I have always had that that will support me in sickness till the present time but the box of my club was shut 26 of last December and will not be opened until 26 of next December and caused me to ask assistance of the parish until I am able to work and without some small aid I must be brought home. [PAR 511/35/1/277]

1 PAR 511/31/2/130   2 PAR 511/1/1/2   3 PAR 511/31/1/16 QE Sep 1831   4 PAR 511/12/2   5 PAR 511/1/5/1   6 PAR 511/12/2 2 Apr 1834   7 PAR 511/31/1/16 QE Dec 1834 et seq

Elizabeth Taunton

547 *A close examination of the following detailed sequence of documents perhaps reveals more about any one Winchelsea pauper of the early nineteenth century than any other case included in this volume. Elizabeth Taunton's settlement examinations (**553, 585**) tell of her somewhat disjointed and complicated private life. Her many letters to the Winchelsea overseers (**555, 557-565, 568-583**) are much more than simple requests for money; they include information about her personal circumstances and the reasons she is so desperate for money, her employment or lack of it, her health and that of her daughters and even on one occasion (**582**) that her home is threatened with demolition. The publication of (**549**) is particularly intended to draw attention to the extreme lengths to which the Winchelsea overseers were prepared to go, eventually unsuccessfully, to establish that Elizabeth Taunton was not their responsibility, including even the pursuit of her father round the country in an attempt to obtain evidence. He seems carefully to have avoided those seeking him. Of her character we learn much and, of specific events, that on one occasion when* *returned to Winchelsea she absconded from the workhouse leaving her children behind* (**568**).

It is only occasionally possible either to equate Elizabeth Taunton's many requests for her regular allowance and other casual payments with entries in the overseers' accounts, or to find any record of the delayed payments about which she regularly complained; as in other cases regularity of accounting does not necessarily indicate regularity of despatch or arrival. It is however clear that the six shillings per week agreed on 1 April 1819 (**551**) *was only paid until March 1820.[1] After her second removal from Canterbury to Winchelsea in 1824* (**567**), *the weekly allowance was established at four shillings and this remained in force until 1827 when it was reduced to two shillings – see* (**580**) *– at the time that Elizabeth junior had gone into service.[2] In early 1829, however, she did receive an additional casual payment of £1 12s 6d.[3] No reason for this has been discovered. In 1830 the former weekly figure of two shillings was further reduced to 1s 6d per week.[4] After 1831 Elizabeth Taunton received no weekly allowance. The ledger in which that allowance would have been entered is marked 'Widow Taunton not paid'.[5] She did, however, receive casual payments according to need, or the overseers' perception of her need. These included £1 5s 0d on 8 June 1832 when she was ill and on 29 August 1833, 'Allowance to Mrs Taunton and daughter for clothes - £1 and £1 12s 0d casual.'[6] The most unusual entry in this case occurs in September 1824, when, while in the Winchelsea workhouse, Elizabeth's daughters, Elizabeth and Harriett, were given sixpence each 'as an encouragement for their platting' [plaiting].[7]*

In 1836 Elizabeth Taunton was listed among Winchelsea's able-bodied poor.[8] In 1841, at the time that the surviving record ends, she was on the indoor relief list of Rye workhouse.[9]

548 4 Jun 1818 *Removal order made by M Pennington and J B Backhouse, justices of the peace for the parish of Walmer, Kent to the churchwardens and overseers of the poor of the parish of Walmer*:

Whereas complaint has been made to us that Elizabeth Taunton, the wife of James Taunton, lately intruded and came into the parish of Walmer and [has] become chargeable to the same, we upon due proof thereof as well upon the examination of Elizabeth Taunton do adjudge the same to be true and do also adjudge that [her] place of legal settlement is in the parish of St Thomas the Apostle, Winchelsea. [We] therefore order and require you to remove and convey her out of the parish of Walmer to Winchelsea and her deliver, together with this our order or a true copy thereof, to the churchwardens and overseers of the poor there who are hereby required to receive and provide for her according to law.   [PAR 511/32/3/33]

Note: At the general quarter sessions held at the Sessions House at St Augustine's near Canterbury on 14 Jul 1818 Winchelsea's appeal against the above order was entered and consideration postponed until the next quarter sessions.[10]

549 17 Jul 1818 et seq. *[Edited] account submitted to the parish officers of Winchelsea by Dawes & Co. [of Rye, parish solicitors]*:

17 Jul 1818 Journey to Winchelsea to take the examination of Elizabeth Taunton who had been removed from Walmer and attending pauper and magistrates and taking minutes there of very special [sic] and recommending that an appeal might be entered and respited: £1 13s 4d; on receipt of order of removal made for

removing Elizabeth Taunton from Walmer to Winchelsea writing motion paper to lodge and respite appeal from the order: 6s 8d; writing to the parish officers of Walmer to acquaint them of the intention of Winchelsea to lodge and respite: 5s; writing to Mr Starr of Canterbury with instructions to counsel and motion paper and to do the needful herein: 5s; writing long letter to agents to make inquiry where pauper's husband or father was to be found etc: 5s. 19 Aug 1818 Writing to Messrs May and Mercer [of Walmer] to procure copy of register of Taunton's marriage with names of witnesses: 5s; attending Mrs Taunton and questioning her as to proof of marriage when it was discovered that the witnesses of the marriage, Lowrey and wife, were living at Deal and that they kept their wedding at their house and lodged with them for a month after and that the other witness, Edward Freeman, was the clerk of the parish: 6s 8d. 21 Sep [1818] On receipt of letter from Mr Maule saying he had found the entry of the baptism of Taunton and that he would send us a copy, writing to him in answer: 6s 7d. 22 Sep [1818] Paid postage of [Mr Maule's] letter with the register: 2s 4d; writing to Messrs May and Mercer to get notice to prosecute served and to state to the parish officers that we had possessed ourselves of the evidence to show a settlement of the husband and the marriage and to prove that Walmer should consent to quash to save the parish expense and also to request an understanding to admit service of notice and to say we in turn would send them one to produce pauper: 5s. 23 Sep 1818 Attending Mr [Edward] Jeakens advising on this appeal and as to the manner, subpoenaing pauper's father etc: 6s 8d; paid postage of Mr Maule's letter as to affidavit: £1 1s 0d. 5 Oct 1818 On receipt of letter from Messrs May and Mercer informing us that Walmer intended to try the question, writing to Mr Jeakens thereon and to come to Rye: 5s; to pay[ing] Messrs May and Mercer for their trouble herein: 13s 4d. 10 Oct 1818 Writing to agents to retain Mr [Joseph] Berens: 5s; paid agents their attendance for that purpose: 6s 8d; paid Mr Berens retaining fee and clerk: £1 3s 6d. 12 Oct 1818 Journey to Woolwich to endeavour to find Old Taunton [James Peckham] where we had been instructed he was working as a journey[man] tailor when after a long search we found where he had been employed but that he had left Woolwich and journey next day to London where it was considered by Mr Mitchell, his last master, that he might be found and searching and inquiring for him at very many houses and at last it was learned at The Two Chairmen in Wardour Street by persons who know him that he was not in town and requesting of Mr Mitchell and also of the landlord of The [Two] Chairmen to learn if they could [say] where he was to be found and to write us thereof which they promised to do. From home 3 days: £9 9s 0d; paid coach hire and expenses: £4 19s 9d. 19 Oct 1818 Not being able to find Old Taunton writing to Messrs Samson & Leith to say so and to request them on the part of Walmer to consent to a further respite to save a journey to make an application to the court for that purpose: 5s; on receipt of their answer agreeing respite upon our engaging not to ask for maintenance beyond the present Michaelmas sessions in the event of the order being quashed. Writing to Mr Starr to request him to see Messrs Sampson & Leith to say we agreed to their proposal and for him to do the needful herein to save the expense of journey to Canterbury: 5s; paid Mr Starr for preparing motion paper to counsel to move the respite appeal and for fee paid to counsel etc and for his trouble herein: £2 13s 0d; paid court fees therein: 12s. 21 Oct 1818 It being imagined that old Taunton was likely to be found at Bath, writing long letter to Mr Maule with instructions to get subpoena served on him if he could be found: 5s. 18 Dec 1818 Proportion of journey to Hythe and Deal to collect evidence in appeals with Hythe and Walmer and first attending Mr Janaway, solicitor for Hythe, to endeavour to find out if they were going upon the value of the tenement at Hythe but who said he was not quite sure as to what point they were going upon but understood that the parish officers conceived he had gained a subsequent settlement in Winchelsea parish and where he promised to write us in time for their determination whether or not to prosecute this appeal and afterwards going to survey the tenement and examining the landlord as to the rent etc and found his story agreed with the pauper's and attending at Deal to procure evidence of the marriage of Taunton and wife and found that two of the witnesses were dead and the other was supposed to be in America and in consequence of going to Messrs Samson & Leith, solicitors for Walmer, to procure an admission of the certificate of the marriage as evidence on hearing of appeal and attending them thereon where they agreed to do so and obtaining their consent and undertaking in writing: £4 14s 6d; horsehire and expenses: £1 13s 0d. It being very doubtful if old Taunton would be found and having received a letter from Mr Maule saying old Taunton could not be found but mentioning that there was a gentleman named Atkins who was living on the spot where young Taunton was born consulting with parish officers as to stating a case for the opinion of counsel whether the evidence of Atkins supported by a copy of the register could be received to prove Taunton's birth settlement in Bath when it was determined that the opinion should be taken. Brief by way of case for the opinion of Mr Berens accordingly and writing to agents therewith: 13s 4d. 5 Jan 1819 Postage of Mr Berens' opinion advising not to try the appeal without old Taunton's evidence: 1s 2d. 15 Jan 1819 Close search having been made for old Taunton who it was clear kept out of the way purposely that he should not be served with the subpoena and considering the great expense likely to be incurred by obtaining further respite, attending the parish officers and requesting them to take the sense of the vestry as to the propriety of giving up the appeal which they determined to do: 6s. 22 Mar 1819 Writing to Mr Jeakens to know the determination of the parish as to Taunton's appeal: 5s. 24 Mar 1819 On receipt of letter from Mr Jeakens saying the parish would give up the appeal with Walmer, writing to Messrs Samson & Leith to that effect also to Mr Starr for his bill: 6s 8d; paid Mr Maule of Bath his bill for his trouble in endeavouring to look up old Taunton and other evidence etc: £3 9s 6d.   [PAR 511/31/2/131]

Notes: 1. A number of the dated entries above commence with the abbreviation Ats. This is 'a travers' and indicates an action in which the parish is being sued.
2. Joseph Berens was called to the bar in 1800, served as a Kent JP, appointed Recorder of Lydd in 1818 and of Romney Marsh in 1820.[11]
3. Mr Starr is highly likely to have been Thomas Starr, a Canterbury solicitor who in

1825, with Weeden Dawes of Rye, became co-mortgagee of the estate of George Augustus Lamb of Iden. Starr had earlier petitioned the House of Lords to change one of the judges to whom a petition concerning the Canterbury Guardians of the Poor had been referred.[12]

550 n.d. [c.1819] *[Winchelsea overseers'] copy of a certificate regarding the birth dates of Elizabeth Taunton senior's children*:
Elizabeth Taunton born at Walmer near Deal on the 14th October 1814. Harriett Chappell born in Jew's Row, Chelsea 26th December 1816.   [PAR 511/35/4/6]

551 1 Apr 1819 *Minute of Winchelsea public vestry*:
It is agreed to give Mrs Taunton 6s per week to provide for herself and two children.   [PAR 511/12/1 f.229]

552 1 Dec 1821 *[Edited] account submitted by Messrs Dawes, Lardner and Fisher [solicitors of Rye]*:
Attending the magistrates examining Mrs [Elizabeth] Taunton touching the settlement of her two bastard children and as to the relief afforded them and recommending the removal of the eldest child to Deal *[pencilled correction 'Walmer' in the margin]* the place of its birth and fixing for the woman to bring the child in a few days for that purpose: *[charge also including examination of Clifford Lowes at the same hearing]* 13s 4d. 10 Dec 1821 Employed some time in considering the removal of Mrs Taunton's eldest child and writing the mother's examination and also the child's etc etc: 13s 4d; preparing special order of removal to Deal and duplicate: 7s.   [PAR 511/31/2/135]

553 [-] Dec 1821 *Examination by two justices of the peace for Winchelsea* (no names given) *of Elizabeth Taunton, the wife of James Taunton, at present being in Winchelsea, concerning the place of legal settlement of her bastard daughter, [also named] Elizabeth Taunton*:
[Elizabeth Taunton, the elder,] on her oath saith that about twelve or thirteen years ago her husband James Taunton left her and that she hath never seen him since; that when her husband left her they were residing at Deal in Kent; that about four years after he left her she was delivered of Elizabeth at the house of John Weeling in the parish of Walmer, Kent and that [her daughter] was seven years of age on the *[blank]* day of *[blank]* last past and that Richard Purdith of Deal, mariner, is the father. This examinant further saith that she afterwards cohabited with one Thomas Chappell, formerly a sergeant in the 4th Regiment of Foot or King's Own who is a pensioner of Chelsea Hospital but, as she believes, now resides at High Wickham in Buckinghamshire, by whom she had a bastard child named Harriett Chappell who was born at a house in Jew's Row in Chelsea occupied by a person whose name she does not recollect; that she and her two bastard children are now actually chargeable to the parish of St Thomas the Apostle, Winchelsea and that her daughter Elizabeth Taunton hath never lived away from her, and the above named Elizabeth Taunton, the daughter, upon oath saith that she has never lived in any place of servitude. *[no signature]*   [PAR 511/32/4/190]

554 9 May 1822 *[Edited] account of Messrs Dawes & Co to the overseers of Winchelsea*:

Attending Mr [George] Stace advising as to Mrs Taunton's children having gained a settlement and writing to him thereon with copies of the order of removal of the mother from Walmer to Winchelsea to show that [the children] were not included in the order and consequently being illegitimate might be removed to the parish in which they were born: 10s 2d.   [PAR 511/31/2/137]

555 26 May 1823 *Letter from Elizabeth Taunton, Gallery Square, Northgate, Canterbury [Kent] to Robert Alce, Winchelsea, parish officer*:

I have taken the liberty of writing to you as you did not send to me according to promise as I should wish to know if the gentlemen have settled the business about my children – whether I am to bring them home or whether they will send me the money as usual. When I brought my children home before a gentleman told me never to bring them again without a right understanding and if the gentlemen have made up their mind to move the children, the youngest will not be seven years old until 22 December. Sir, it makes no difference to me where my children belong so I can but get money regular to maintain them. It is not in my power to wait from quarter to quarter as I am obliged to pay my rent weekly as I am so much behind with my rent. I owe six months rent now. Sir, please to answer this by return of post and let me know what I am to do with them as I am in great strait at present so I wait your answer. Please to treat for me.   [PAR 511/35/1/16]

Note: Payment to Mrs Taunton of £5 8s 0d, being 27 weeks pay at 4s, appears in the overseers' account for March to September 1823.[13]

556 5 Jul 1823 *[Edited] account submitted by Messrs Dawes & Co of Rye to the parish officers of Winchelsea*:

Attending Mr [Robert] Alce advising as to the removal of Mrs Taunton's child and recommending a removal and if the parish wish us we would confer with Mr [Henry] Butler, [town clerk], thereon; 6s 8d. 7 Jul 1823 On receipt of a message from the magistrates of Winchelsea attending them to confer as to making an order for removing Mrs Taunton's bastard child. Journey to Winchelsea accordingly and attending them and recommending as the younger child would be beyond the age of nurture at Christmas to continue the allowance until that time and not to receive the child without an order: £1 6s 0d.   [PAR 511/31/2/144]

557 12 Aug 1823 *Letter from Elizabeth Taunton, Canterbury [Kent] to Robert Alce, Winchelsea, parish officer*:

I take the liberty of writing to you to let you know that I have moved and if you would have the goodness to send my money to Mrs [Francis Thomas] White in the Borough and by so doing I shall get it safe as it was six weeks ago come next Monday that I was there.

Please to direct to Mrs White in the Borough, Canterbury.   [PAR 511/35/1/17]

558 26 Aug 1823 *Letter from Elizabeth Taunton, Canterbury, [Kent] to [Robert] Alce, Winchelsea, parish officer:*
Not having heard from you lately I take the liberty of troubling you in regard to my allowance. I understood you [to say] that when my six weeks allowance was expired you promised I should have two months allowance in advance, the six weeks have expired almost a fortnight. Therefore, sir, I humbly trust you will remit me the two months allowance immediately as I am in great want, therefore shall expect to hear from you in a post or two.
PS Please to direct for me at Mr [Francis Thomas] White's, Borough, Canterbury.
[PAR 511/35/1/19]
Note: At this time the overseers' accounts show only that Mrs Taunton is to receive 4s per week. There is no indication of how frequently this was to be paid.[14]

559 27 Oct 1823 *Letter from Elizabeth Taunton, Canterbury, [Kent] to [Joseph] Bigg [Winchelsea overseer]:*
I humbly hope you will excuse my troubling you again relative to the allowance granted me by the parish, sincerely hoping you will cause it to be remitted to me in the course of this week as I must pay my rent which is due on Saturday next and believe [me], sir, I am much distressed therefore hope and trust it will come to hand this week. Please to direct for me at [Francis Thomas] White's, Borough, Northgate, Canterbury.
[PAR 511/35/1/32]

560 16 Dec 1823 *Letter from Elizabeth Taunton, Canterbury, [Kent] to C[harles] Arnett, Winchelsea, assistant overseer:*
I humbly trust you will again excuse my troubling you relative to the allowance granted for me and family, trusting you will have the goodness to forward it so that I may receive it on the 24th of this month (though I am aware it is not due until the 27th). My reason for wishing it to be sent on the 24th is [that] I have little or no employment at this time of the year, therefore it of course will be of infinite service to me. On the arrival of it I will forward a receipt as required. Please direct to me at [Francis Thomas] White's, Borough, Northgate, Canterbury.
[PAR 511/35/1/41]

561 4 Jan 1824 *Letter from Elizabeth Taunton, Canterbury, [Kent], to [the overseers of Winchelsea]:*
I write to inform you that I have written two letters to Mr [Charles] Arnett, assistant overseer, relevant to the allowance which the gentlemen settled on my family and have no answer to either. Therefore, sir, I humbly hope you will cause my money to be sent me immediately as I am afraid of being turned out of my house being greatly in debt to my landlord. I have little or no employ. I have received the allowance up to the 27th December last. Therefore I trust you will excuse me by informing you I must be under the necessity of flinging myself and family on the parish I reside in if I don't hear from you in answer to this letter as soon as possible.

PS Direct for me at [Francis Thomas] White's, Borough, Northgate, Canterbury.

[PAR 511/35/1/45]

Note: A record for the week ending 1 January 1824 includes, without explanation, that Mrs Taunton and her two children received no payment.[15]

562 13 Jan 1824 *Letter from Elizabeth Taunton, Canterbury, [Kent] to [Charles] Arnett, assistant overseer, Winchelsea*:

I wrote to you on the 21st of last month requesting you would have the goodness to remit me my family's allowance. Not having received any answer I am again under the necessity of troubling you on the subject and humbly hope you will have the goodness to favour me with two pounds for believe me I have scarce any work at this time of year and am nearly the amount of two pounds due for rent. Therefore, sir, I hope and trust I shall receive the sum as soon as possible. PS It is or will be by the time you receive this a fortnight over the time my allowance became due. Direct for me at [Francis Thomas] White's, Borough, Northgate, Canterbury.

[PAR 511/35/1/48]

Note: A letter (**119**) dated 22 Jan 1824 from Francis Thomas White on behalf of Mary Clandenbold also asks that Mrs Taunton's money should be sent.

563 12 Feb 1824 *Letter from Elizabeth Taunton, at [Francis Thomas] White's, Borough, Northgate, Canterbury, [Kent] to [the overseers of Winchelsea]*:

I received your letter dated 9th instant and have to request you will have the goodness to lay my letter before the gentlemen humbly praying they will have the goodness to forward what is due to me which is six weeks last Saturday to enable me to pay my rent and support myself and my children on their way home to their parish – Winchelsea – without which it will be impossible to travel home and it is out of my power to keep them. If I apply to the parish where I reside for relief I must not live in it afterwards.   [PAR 511/35/1/59]

564 20 Feb 1824 *Letter from Elizabeth Taunton, Canterbury [Kent] to [the overseers of Winchelsea]*:

I received your letter and have to inform you that I and my children will be ready to proceed to Winchelsea on Tuesday next the 24th instant. I should be under very great obligation to you if you have the goodness to advance me a little money to pay my rent, for if that is not paid I shall be under the necessity of parting with what few trifles I have to discharge it.   [PAR 511/35/1/62]

565 25 Feb 1824 *Letter from E[lizabeth] Taunton, Canterbury, [Kent] to [the overseers of Winchelsea]*:

I received a letter this morning and [I am] very much surprised after your sending such a letter as you did promising to fetch me home which I put myself very much out of the way to get myself ready and being very much behind with my rent as I was in expectation of your sending me the money as before, so that I can expect nothing but to be turned out of house and home, so that I must be obliged to throw myself on the parish and the[y] must bring me home. I have applied to the president of Canterbury and he considers that I have been damned ill-used after your sending so many letters which cost me 2s 6d. And I was forced to pledge my things to get the money so that I am quite distressed so that you may expect me home in the next few days. I have been down so many times for the money and it cost me half of what I got to get it back again after your promising so fair to send the money so I am now determined to come home. [PAR 511/35/1/63]

566 3 Mar 1824 *Letter from John Nutt, [town clerk of] Canterbury, [Kent] to [the overseers of Winchelsea]*:
I am directed by the guardians of the poor of this city to inform you that they shall be compelled to remove home to your parish Elizabeth Taunton and family unless you continue to allow her a weekly sum towards their maintenance.
[PAR 511/35/1/65]

567 24 Apr 1824 *Removal order made by William Homersham and James Pierce, justices of the peace for the City of Canterbury to the churchwardens and overseers of the poor of the parish of St Mary, Northgate, Canterbury*:
Whereas complaint has been made to us that Elizabeth Taunton, wife of James Taunton, and her two children namely Elizabeth aged about 10 years and Harriett aged about 7 years lately intruded and came into the parish of St Mary, Northgate and are actually become chargeable to the same, we upon examination of the [evidence] upon oath adjudge this to be true and also adjudge that their place of last legal settlement to be the parish of St Thomas the Apostle in the Ancient Town of Winchelsea. We therefore hereby order you to remove and convey [them] to Winchelsea and them deliver, together with this our order or a true copy thereof, to the churchwardens and overseers of the poor of Winchelsea who are hereby required to receive and provide for them according to law. [PAR 511/32/3/44]
Note: Dawes & Co of Rye (solicitors acting for Winchelsea) informed the Canterbury magistrates of their intention to appeal against this order but as it had only been implemented on 28 Apr 1824 they could not be ready to do so at the Canterbury Easter sessions. They asked that the hearing should be respited to [postponed until] the next sessions.[16]

568 11 May 1824 *Letter from Elizabeth Taunton, Canterbury, [Kent] to [the overseers of Winchelsea*:
I write to inform you that the reason of my leaving as I did was I could not bear the confinement but I shall be ready when called on to attend the sessions or, if you should want me on any other occasion I shall always be ready to attend. I hope you have the goodness to take care of my two children and tell them that I have not forsaken them. [PAR 511/35/1/82]

569 5 May 1825 *Letter from Elizabeth Taunton, Canterbury [Kent] to [David] Laurence, Winchelsea*:
I take the liberty of writing to you. I should think it a great favour if you had got my business settled and if I had the four shillings as usual. I cannot maintain my

children. I must bring them home to the parish for I cannot maintain them with less. You [?talk] of my drawing my money weekly but it is of no use to me to think of drawing my money weekly until I hear from you. I would be greatly obliged to you if you would send the money by Mr Cadwell as you send my money by him once a month and that would be better to me than once a quarter so no more at present.   [PAR 511/35/1/170]

Note: Soon after the date of this letter regular payments of 4s a week were resumed.[17]

570 16 Oct 1825 *Letter from Elizabeth Taunton, Canterbury, [Kent] to [the overseers of Winchelsea]*:

I hope you will excuse the freedom I have taken in sending these few lines to you but I should not have sent to you so soon but I have been very ill for this month and am [in]capable of getting about and I should take it as a particular favour if you would send me a pound. Thank God my children are both got rid of the ague and are both well and hearty and I should be glad to know how Mrs Arnett is and little William Henry and I am sorry to say, sir, that my best friend I had in Canterbury is dead and I hope you won't fail sending to me for I am very much in want of money at present. When you write to me direct for Elizabeth Taunton to be left at [Francis Thomas] White's in the Borough, near Northgate, Canterbury. Please to send the same way as you send Mrs Clandenbold's.   [PAR 511/35/1/199]

Note: There is no record of any response to this letter but Mrs Taunton had been allowed a casual payment of 10s on 30 September 1825.[18]

571 11 Jan 1826 *Letter from Elizabeth Tomkin [recte Taunton], Canterbury, [Kent], to [Charles Arnett, assistant overseer, Winchelsea]*:

I have taken the liberty of writing to you. I received the £1 12s 0d which I am much obliged to you for it. I am sorry to say my Betsy has been ill ever since Christmas so that I have not been able to earn not one shilling since and I should be much obliged to you if you will make application to the gentlemen if they please to send me a little money for myself for I am quite destitute. I was obliged to leave my work on the account of my first girl being ill. If you will have the goodness to send me as soon as you can I should be very much obliged to you, sir. This is the first time that ever I asked the favour of the gentlemen for anything for myself. I would not now if I had not no one. I'll thank God little Harriett is quite well. My love to you all and I wish you a happy New Year. Please to send answer soon.

[*Endorsed*] 'E. Taunton'   [PAR 511/35/1/203]

Note: The £1 12s 0d had been allowed on 22 December.[19]

572 15 Feb 1826 *Letter from E[lizabeth] Taunton, Canterbury, [Kent] to [Charles] Arnett, Winchelsea, parish officer*:

Not hearing from you so long I have taken the liberty of writing to you about my children's money as I have not heard from you since the 21 of December. Sir, I should not have sent my last letter to you but my eldest daughter being very ill and the doctor's bill very expensive has left me now in distress. Sir, I hope you will

not think me troublesome by asking you to send my children's money as soon as possible as I am in much want. My respects [to Mrs] Arnett and family. Please to direct [to] Bailey's rents, Borough, near Northgate.   [PAR 511/35/1/206]
Note: Mrs Taunton is recorded as being paid 52s on 23 March 1826.[20]

573 11 Apr 1826 *Letter from Elizabeth Taunton, Canterbury, to [the overseers of Winchelsea]*:
I have taken the liberty of writing to you. I should take it as a particular favour if you will have the goodness to send me one pound. I have heard of a situation out of Canterbury which I think will suit me much better than stopping in Canterbury. I am at present in distress for want of a little money for to get my things for to go with. If you will have the goodness to send it as soon as possible I shall be obliged to you. You may send to me not till you hear from me again, not after this time.
                                                                    [PAR 511/35/1/217]

574 18 May 1826 *Letter from Mrs [Elizabeth] Taunton, Canterbury, [Kent] to [Charles] Arnett, Winchelsea, [assistant overseer]*:
I received your letter with the one pound in it which I return you many thanks for and I have been very much affected with my eyes which stopped me going to the situation I was going [to] and I am at present in distress. If you will have the goodness to send me one pound as soon as you can I should be very much obliged to you. I have the pleasure to tell you that the children are well. My respects to Mrs Arnett and family and accept it yourself.   [PAR 511/35/1/228]
Note: No reference to the payment acknowledged in this letter has been found in the overseers' accounts.

575 24 Jun 1826 *Letter from Elizabeth Taunton, Canterbury, [Kent] to [Charles] Arnett, Winchelsea, [assistant] overseer*:
I have been most anxiously waiting these three weeks expecting to receive my money from you as usual and have written two letters to you requesting that it might be sent to me as I am greatly distressed for want of it and not having had an answer from you I am obliged to trouble you again. My children have been ill for some time with typhus fever in consequence of which I have lost my work as the person where I worked was afraid of catching the fever. I am now completely reduced for want of money and I expect to be turned out of doors every day. I have put my landlord off from week to week expecting to receive money from you and he now tells me that he can't wait any longer so that unless I hear from you immediately I must with my children return to Winchelsea. I hope that you will not delay any longer but let me have my money immediately.   [PAR 511/35/1/231]

576 17 Sep 1826 *Letter from Elizabeth Taunton, Canterbury, [Kent] to [Charles] Arnett, Winchelsea, [assistant] overseer*:
I have taken the liberty of writing to you. I should be much obliged if you would have the goodness to send me my money what is due to me if you will have the

goodness. I should be very much obliged to you, sir. Please, sir, give my respects to Mrs Arnett and all the family and I hope they are in good health as it leaves us all at present. Sir, I should be much obliged to you if you will send it by Mr Cadwell as this is the safest way to send it. In so doing you will much oblige me. Please to direct to: Mrs Taunton in the Borough near North Gate, Mr Bailey's rents.

[PAR 511/35/1/240]

Note: For a further request of 5 Oct, forwarded by Mary Clandenbold, see (**129**).

577 30 Nov 1826 *Letter from Elizabeth Taunton, Canterbury [Kent] to [Charles] Arnett, Winchelsea, [assistant] overseer*:
I shall be much obliged to you to send the children's money as soon as you can for one of the children has been very ill and I have been at great expense for doctors so I shall be very much obliged to you to send it as soon as possible for I am in great want of it. I shall be very much obliged to you to send it by the caravan that comes to Hastings twice a week for they rather objected [to] it at the bank. My respects to Mrs Arnett and all the family. [PAR 511/35/1/251]

Note: Mrs Taunton is recorded as being paid £2 12s 0d on 21 December 1826.[21]

578 16 Apr 1827 *Letter from Elizabeth Taunton, Canterbury [Kent] to [Charles] Arnett, Winchelsea, parish officer*:
The reason I did not write before was [that] the lady that I was in expectation of taking Elizabeth [said] she was too young and not strong enough for the place but I have now got her a place for a few hours a day at Mrs Blackley's in Sun Street. Sir, [I] would be much obliged to you to send me what I have coming for to get her a few things and not to trouble the parish more than I can possibly help. Harriett is much better than she was when I was at Winchelsea. Sir, I delivered the message to Mr White and I believe they are considering about her [presumably Mary Clandenbold] coming home. Please to give my best respects to Mrs Arnett and all the family and I hope you will not neglect sending as soon as convenient for I want to get her a few necessary things. In so doing you will much oblige. Please to direct: Elizabeth Taunton, Mr Bailey's rents, Northgate. [PAR 511/35/1/273]

Note: The information that Elizabeth junior had gone into service caused Winchelsea to reduce Mrs Taunton's allowance from 4s to 2s per week.[22] See (**580**)

579 21 May 1827 *Letter from Mrs [Elizabeth] Taunton, Canterbury, [Kent] to [Charles] Arnett, Winchelsea, [assistant] overseer*:
I am sorry to be so troublesome in writing to you again having received no answer from you from the last letter I wrote for I am in want of the money very bad indeed. My daughter is in want of some very necessary things very much indeed and I am not able to get them until I receive my money from you and if you will have the goodness to send it immediately I should be very much obliged to you, sir, as I am in great distress for it. My respects to Mrs Arnett and family. Please to direct as usual. [PAR 511/35/1/279]

580 8 Aug 1827 *Letter from [Mrs] Elizabeth Taunton, Canterbury, [Kent] to [Charles] Arnett, Winchelsea, parish officer:*

I wrote according to promise concerning about my daughter's money being stopped as she was only in place one month. I should be much obliged to you if you will make application to the gentlemen for me to get my daughter's back money for me again as it is not in my power to maintain them both for 2s per week as my children have been a great expense to me through sickness and they are not healthy children at no time. If the gentlemen don't choose to let me have the money I must be obliged to send them home for I cannot maintain them. [I] do all that I can. I should be much obliged to you, sir, if you will send me an answer as soon as you can. If you please I will thank you. Please direct to me [at] Mr Bailey's rents, near Northgate.   [PAR 511/35/1/292]

Notes: 1. No evidence has been found of any response to this appeal – payments continued at 2s per week.[23]

2. The reduction of Elizabeth Taunton's weekly allowance from four shillings to two shillings is confirmed in the overseers' accounts as being effective from 7 June 1827.[24]

581 12 Nov 1827 *Letter from [Mrs] Elizabeth Taunton, Canterbury, [Kent] to [Charles] Arnett, Winchelsea, parish officer:*

I have taken the liberty of writing to you again to inform you that I have never received anything since I wrote before which is 6 weeks since and I am in great distress for the money. If you will be so obliging as to send it to me as soon as you can I would thank you kindly, sir. If I am not to have the money sent to me I would thank you if you please to send me an answer as soon as you can.

[PAR 511/35/1/304]

582 9 Apr 1830 *Letter from Mrs [Elizabeth] Taunton, Canterbury, [Kent] to [David] Laurence, Winchelsea, assistant overseer:*

I am sorry to trouble you but the house I now live in is going to be pulled down and I am obliged to leave and the landlord says if I don't pay my rent he will stop what trifles I have and if you will be so good as to send me what is due I should be much obliged. By doing so you will much oblige.   [PAR 511/35/1/329]

Note: On 12 March 1830 the select vestry had resolved that after 25 March Mrs Taunton's pay should be reduced from 2s to 1s 6d per week.[25]

583 24 Apr 1830 *Letter from Mrs [Elizabeth] Taunton, Canterbury, [Kent] to [David Laurence], Winchelsea, assistant overseer:*

I am sorry to trouble you the second time but I have been informed that a gentleman has been to Canterbury and made some inquiry after me but I never heard anything of it until he was gone and when I heard I went to Mr Doreham in Castle Street to inquire for him and they informed me that he was gone home and I am very much in trouble for my money for to pay my back rent and [for] the house I now live in I am obliged to pay every week so that I am in great distress and if you will be so good as to send to me my full money which is from 14 January I should be very much obliged to you, or I must apply to the parish now I live in for I am in a very poor state of health and very bad off. By so do[ing] you will relieve me in my distress. Please to direct for Mrs Taunton, Star Yard, Little ?Donston, Canterbury, Kent.   [PAR 511/35/1/331]

584 8 Feb 1841 *Letter from P[hilip] W[illiam] Duly, receiver of the guardians, Canterbury to the relieving officer, parish of Winchelsea, Sussex*:
Elizabeth Taunton, residing in the parish of St Mildred's in this city is chargeable to the guardians of the poor. She saith that she was removed with her two children from the parish of Walmer about 23 years since and I find by our records that she was removed from St Mary, Northgate to Winchelsea which order was not appealed against. The last removal is dated 24th April 1824 and she further saith that about seven years since she left Winchelsea and had been relieved for some time previous to her leaving. She is in great distress and when she can get work not able to do much. You will oblige by informing me by return whether your parish wish this city to be put to the expense of a second removal. [PS] The board of guardians [of Canterbury] will not allow out relief the woman being out of [their] union. If the parish of Winchelsea acknowledges her they may bring her home without an order to the parish officers of Winchelsea.   [PAR 511/38/6/1]
Note: The letter is marked 'Answered the 16th' and 'Acknowledged by W[inchelsea] parish'

585 2 Aug 1841 *Examinations of George Burch, one of the overseers of the poor of the parish of St Mary Bredman, Canterbury; of Philip William Duly, receiver to the court of guardians of the poor of Canterbury and of Elizabeth Taunton of the parish of St Mary Bredman, Canterbury, the wife of James Taunton, a tailor. These examinations taken on oath before William Masters Esq, Mayor, and John Brent Esq, justices of the peace for Canterbury*:
George Burch on his oath saith: I complain by direction of the guardians of the poor of the city of Canterbury that Elizabeth Taunton is chargeable to the parish of St Mary Bredman in order that she may be examined and removed to her last legal place of settlement and I am informed and believe that she is unable to travel and not fit to be removed by reason of sickness and I now apply for the order of removal to be suspended on account thereof.
Philip William Duly on his oath saith [that] Elizabeth Taunton applied to me on the 26th day of July now last past for relief for herself. I gave her an order to come into the workhouse of the city of Canterbury where she now is and continues chargeable to the parish of St Mary Bredman.
Elizabeth Taunton on her oath saith that I am nearly 60 years of age and was born at Winchelsea in Sussex as I have been informed and believe and at that time my father, James Peckham, was legally settled there; that about thirty years ago I was married to my husband James Taunton at Upper Deal in Kent; that my husband has deserted me for upwards of 20 years and I have not seen him since. I never knew or heard my husband say to what parish or place he belonged; that about the year 1818 I was with my two children removed from the parish of Walmer near

Deal to Winchelsea and continued to receive relief from there till about 1823; that the parish never appealed against the order; that in the year 1824 I with my two children became chargeable to the parish of St Mary Northgate in Canterbury and we were removed from that parish to Winchelsea by an order of two Canterbury justices. We were received by Winchelsea and they never appealed against the order. I received relief by Winchelsea from that time to within seven years last past. I have done no act to gain a subsequent settlement and am now chargeable to the parish of St [Mary Bredman].

Philip William Duly upon his oath further saith that I produce an examination for settlement of Elizabeth Taunton sworn before William Homersham and John James Pierce, justices of the peace for Canterbury on the 24th day of April 1824 wherein she states as follows: That she was born at Winchelsea in Sussex and at that time her father was legally settled there; that about fifteen or sixteen years ago she was married to her husband at Upper Deal; that her husband has deserted her and she never heard him say to what parish or place he belonged; that about six years ago she and her two children were removed from the parish of Walmer to Winchelsea and that she and her two children were received by Winchelsea and continued to receive relief till about six months ago; that the parish never appealed against the order; that she has two children namely Elizabeth aged about 10 years and Harriett aged about 7 years now residing with her in the parish of St Mary Northgate to which parish she and her children are actually become chargeable.

[*signatures of*] George Burch and P. W. Duly. [*mark of*] Elizabeth Taunton.

[*Appended*] The examinations took place at the Canterbury workhouse and the order of removal is suspended on account of Elizabeth Taunton's 'ill state of health'.   [PAR 511/32/4/205]

Notes: 1. James Peckham and Mary Bohanner were married at St Thomas's Winchelsea on 13 May 1779.[26]

2. Elizabeth Peckham 'daughter of James and Mary' was baptised at Winchelsea on 16 November 1783.[27]

586 2 Aug 1841 *Removal order made by William Masters, mayor, and John Brent, justices of the peace for the city and borough of Canterbury to the churchwardens and overseers of the poor of the parish of St Mary Bredman, Canterbury:*

Whereas complaint hath been made unto us that Elizabeth Taunton, wife of James Taunton, hath come to inhabit in the parish of St Mary Bredman, Canterbury not having gained a last legal settlement there and is actually become chargeable to the same, we upon examination of the [evidence] upon oath and other circumstances do adjudge the same to be true and do also adjudge her last place of legal settlement to be Winchelsea, Sussex. We therefore hereby order you to remove and convey Elizabeth Taunton to Winchelsea and her deliver, together with this our order or a true copy thereof, to the churchwardens and overseers of the poor there who are hereby required to receive and provide for her according to law.

[*Endorsed – same date and justices*] Whereas it appears to us that Elizabeth Taunton, the pauper within ordered to be removed, is at present unable to travel and not fit to be removed by reason of sickness and infirmity and that it would be dangerous for her to do so, we therefore hereby suspend the execution of the within order until we or any other two justices of the peace for Canterbury shall be satisfied that the same may be executed without danger to the said pauper.

[Further endorsed] 9 Sep 1841 Whereas it is now made appear unto us, William Masters and William Plummer, justices of the peace for the city and borough of Canterbury, that the within order of removal may be executed without danger [we] do therefore hereby order the same to be carried into execution accordingly and whereas it is duly proved to us upon oath that the sum of £4 1s 0d hath been incurred during the suspension of the order we therefore direct [payment of this amount by the churchwardens and overseers of the poor of Winchelsea].

[PAR 511/32/3/70]

587 4 Aug 1841 *Notification of removal order made by the guardians and overseers of the poor of the parish of St Mary Bredman, Canterbury to the overseers of the poor of the parish of St Thomas the Apostle, Winchelsea:*

We hereby give you notice that Elizabeth Taunton, lately residing at Jewry Lane in the parish of St Mary Bredman, Canterbury [and] now an inmate of the Canterbury workhouse has become chargeable to the parish of St Mary Bredman and that an order of the justices has been duly obtained for her removal to your parish of Winchelsea as her last place of legal settlement, which order has been suspended on account of [her] illness (a copy of which order and also a copy of the examination on which the same was made are herewith sent) and we hereby give you further notice that unless within twenty-one days from the date hereof you shall by writing under your hands agree to submit to such order and receipt, or unless you duly serve notice of appeal against the order, [she] will be removed to your parish of Winchelsea as soon after the said twenty-one days as the same may be executed without damage to Elizabeth Taunton in pursuance of the order.

[PAR 511/35/3/26]

588 13 Sep 1841 *Letter from Henry Edwards Paine, clerk to the guardians of the Rye Union, to [George] Blackman [overseer] Winchelsea:*

If either of the parish officers of Winchelsea were personally served with a notice of the suspended order of removal of Mrs [Elizabeth] Taunton together with a copy of the order and a copy of the examination within ten days after the order was suspended then I think under the Act GeoIII c101 the parish of Winchelsea are liable to pay the expense demanded to the Canterbury parish. If these acts were not done then I think neither cost of maintenance or otherwise relating to Mrs Taunton can be obtained. The Poor Law Commissioners have been asked their opinion upon the necessity of a personal notice of the order suspended and 'are of the opinion' that personal service is necessary although it is not necessary personally to serve the order of removal not suspended and having this opinion to which I suppose we must give way to there is no alternative but to pay and at all events it may be a saving to do so because the costs would be enforced under the Act of GeoIII not under the New Poor Law and being under £20 you (the parish officers) of Winchelsea could not appeal against them at the sessions but would be driven to the more expensive mode of defending an action at law.   [PAR 511/38/6/1]

589 Sep 1841 *Account submitted by the Winchelsea overseers to the guardians of the Rye Union*:
[includes inter alia] [September] 14: Conveyance of Mrs [Elizabeth] Taunton to Rye Union: 3s. [*Endorsed*] Settled: George Blackman.   [PAR 511/35/1/364]

590 12 Oct 1841 *Letter from P W Duly, Canterbury, [Kent], receiver to the guardians [of Canterbury], to the churchwardens and overseers of Winchelsea*:
I am directed by the guardians of the poor of this city to apply for £4 1s 0d for relief to [Mrs] Elizabeth Taunton under an order of removal suspended from the parish of St Mary Bredman. It ought to have been paid to the officer when the pauper was brought home to your parish. You will see the necessity of sending by return of post. My instructions are to apply to the magistrates to enforce payment if neglected after this note.   [PAR 511/35/1/368]

591 15 Oct 1841 *Letter from P W Duly, Canterbury, [Kent], receiver to the guardians, to Mr [H E] Paine, clerk to the guardians of Rye Union*:
I have to acknowledge the receipt of £4 1s 0d for relief to [Mrs] Elizabeth Taunton under order of removal. The poor woman applied here for relief sometime in 1840. [Your] parish was written to and the matter not attended to. Canterbury never puts any parish to a shilling expense for their paupers unnecessar[ily].
                                                                               [PAR 511/35/1/369]

1 PAR 511/31/1/11   2 PAR 511/31/1/13 1825-1827   3 PAR 511/31/1/13 QE Mar 1929   4 PAR 511/12/3 12 Mar 1830; PAR 511/31/1/15 f.21   5 PAR 511/31/1/16 QE Jun 1831   6 PAR 511/12/2 1832-1834   7 PAR 511/12/2   8 PAR 511/37/7/29   9 G 8/19/2   10 PAR 511/32/3/32   11 TNA HO 47/59/12 & 47/59/13; (CW)   12 PAB 243; Parliamentary Archives, Lords Journals HL/PO/JO/10/7/1017; (CW)   13 PAR 511/31/1/13   14 PAR 511/31/1/12 f.254   15 PAR 511/37/7/18   16 PAR 511/32/3/45   17 PAR 511/31/1/13 QE Sep 1925   18 PAR 511/12/3   19 PAR 511/31/1/14   20 ibid   21 ibid   22 PAR 511/31/1/13 QE Jan 1827   23 PAR 511/31/1/13 & 14   24 PAR 511/31/1/15 f.21   25 PAR 511/12/3   26 PAR 511/1/1/2   27 ibid

Elizabeth Tilden

592 *Elizabeth Tilden was, like Elizabeth Taunton above, a Winchelsea pauper who chose to live away from the town, in her case at Dover. Her published requests for help are, initially, uninformative (**594-596, 599**) although later we learn a good deal about her circumstances and particularly the illnesses of herself and her family, for example (**602-603**). What is particularly noticeable is the active support she receives from the authorities of her adopted town (**601, 605**), the doctors who treat the family (**604, 607**) and later from a concerned private citizen, John Belsey (**615**).*
*Following the removal order of 1811 (**593**) Mrs Tilden and her family were allowed to return*

to Dover and were granted generous relief, initially eight shillings a week but reduced to six shillings from May 1814.[1] This continued until March 1820[2] at which time the allowance was reduced to four shillings, an amount paid up to September 1824.[3] Thereafter, probably on the initiative of Charles Arnett who had been appointed assistant overseer, Mrs Tilden received no weekly allowance but was quite frequently granted casual payments. On 9 August 1825, in response to (**602**) *the select vestry resolved 'that Mrs Tilden, Dover, be allowed £1 as casual relief her daughter being very ill'.[4] Two years later an entry appears following the receipt of* (**610**) *which reads, 'Resolved that Mrs Tilden be allowed twenty shillings as a casual relief the son being sick'.[5] Similarly in June 1828 Winchelsea paid her £1 after receiving* (**611**).[6] *It would seem that these and other payments made were totally inadequate to prevent the situation described in John Belsey's letter* (**615**). *'Widow' Tilden had been listed among Winchelsea's able-bodied poor in 1836.[7]*

593 17 Jul 1811 *Removal order made by George Dell, mayor, and Robert Walker, justices of the peace for the town and port of Dover, Kent to the churchwardens and overseers of the parish of St James the Apostle, Dover*:

Whereas complaint hath been made to us that Elizabeth Tilden, widow, and her three children namely Henry aged nearly 5 years, Mary aged nearly 3 years and Jane aged about three months lately intruded and came into the parish of St James the Apostle, Dover and are actually become chargeable to the same [we] do adjudge the same to be true and do adjudge their place of legal settlement to be the parish of Winchelsea in Sussex. [We] therefore in His Majesty's name require you on sight hereof to remove them from out of your parish to the parish of Winchelsea and them deliver, together with this our order or a true copy thereof, to the churchwardens and overseers of the poor there who are required to receive them and provide for them according to law. [PAR 511/32/3/24]

594 26 Oct 1823 *Letter from Elizabeth Tilden, New Street, Dover, [Kent] to [the overseers, Winchelsea]*:

I entreat you will pardon my liberty. I will feel obliged by your kindness to forward or cause my relief to be sent as soon as convenient being much in want of it. [PAR 511/35/1/31]

595 31 Oct 1823 *Letter from Elizabeth Tilden, [New Street], Dover, [Kent] to [the overseers, Winchelsea]*:

In reference to your request I have to acknowledge yours of the 29th instant and the £3 for which I feel obliged. [PAR 511/35/1/33]

Note: The amount acknowledged is entered as a payment of 60s approved on 3 October.[8]

596 17 Jan 1824 *Letter from Elizabeth Tilden, New Street, Dover [Kent] to [Charles Arnett], Winchelsea, [assistant] overseer*:

I entreat your pardon for this liberty but beg you will be pleased to forward to me or cause to be sent my usual allowance as I am much in want of the same for which I will feel humbly obliged. [PAR 511/35/1/51]

597 2 Feb 1824 *Letter from John Baker, clerk to the guardians of St Mary, Dover to the overseers of Winchelsea*:
Mrs Tilden is very uneasy at not having received her money this quarter as usual and fears it may have miscarried. I will thank you to remit the same if it has hitherto escaped your memory which is the most likely case. An early answer will oblige.
[PAR 511/35/1/56]

598 9 Mar 1824 *Certificate issued by John Maule, minister, George Purdon and William Hubbard, churchwardens, of the parish of St Mary, Dover, Kent*:
This is to certify that Elizabeth Tilden and her two daughters, Mary and Jane, are living in the parish of St Mary, Dover.   [PAR 511/37/7/9]

599 27 Jul 1824 *Letter from Elizabeth Tilden, New Street, Dover, [Kent] to [the overseers of Winchelsea]*:
I beg you will pardon me for the liberty in writing but being much in want of my quarter's stipend, I humbly entreat your kindness to be pleased to send the same as soon as convenient which will much oblige.   [PAR 511/35/1/100]

600 20 Dec 1824 *Letter from Elizabeth Tilden, Dover, [Kent] to [Charles] Arnett, Winchelsea, overseer*:
I write to request you to send me a trifle as I am ill and not able to get a living at present for me and my family. I hope you will consider this. As you know I have not provided for and must be obliged to come down and have had a hard struggle to get on with my family, as you must know being ailing and do not wish to be troublesome to you but if you will be so kind as to send me a trifle I shall gratefully receive it.   [PAR 511/35/1/149]

601 16 Jul 1825 *Letter from John Baker, clerk to the guardians of St Mary, Dover, [Kent] to the overseers of Winchelsea*:
Mrs [Elizabeth] Tilden's youngest daughter is very ill I think who is going into a decline and the woman is very ill herself. She appears in great distress and stands in need of further relief. The girl has been ill some time and medicine is very expensive. If you will allow an extra weekly allowance I will advance the money for you if you wish it. An early answer will much oblige.   [PAR 511/35/1/184]

602 18 Jul 1825 *Letter from Elizabeth Tilden, New Street, Dover, [Kent] to the overseers of Winchelsea*:
I humbly beg pardon for the liberty in addressing you and am truly sorry to be under the necessity of stating the cause of the present application. I beg leave to say my daughter has been for some time past dangerously ill and not able to be removed from her bed in consequence of which a part of my allowance has obliged me to administer to her affliction which has reduced me to great distress. At present she has no command of arms or legs. I humbly entreat, gentlemen, you will be

pleased to take the same into consideration and forward me some relief. If required further reference can be received by applying to Dr Sankey, Snargate Street.

[PAR 511/35/1/185]

Note: For responses to this letter and (**610-611**) below see (**592**)

603 15 Aug 1825 *Letter from Elizabeth Tilden, Dover, [Kent] to [Charles] Arnett, Winchelsea, [assistant] overseer*:

I received your letter on the 13th and was very thankful for the money you sent me as I was in great distress and I was obliged to go [on] trust for a few things. Not being able to pay they refused to trust me more. When you sent the money I was obliged to put it all away. I did not have a shilling [for] nourishment. I did for my child till I laid myself up as I well knew I could not pay for a nurse but at last was obliged to have one. I could do without [no longer]. As we are both getting a little better if I could pay her and should be obliged if you would send me a trifle more. My son is 19, eldest daughter 16, the youngest almost 15. The girls are both very ailing but the boy is in place. [PAR 511/35/1/189]

Note: On 11 August 1825 the overseers entered in their books a payment of £1 to Elizabeth Tilden 'To cash (ill) by order of vestry'.[9]

604 15 Aug 1825 *Certificate issued and signed by W Robinson, surgeon, Dover dispensary*:

I hereby certify that Elizabeth Tilden and her daughter Jane [have] been confined to their beds through continued fevers and are at present in a state of convalescence requiring nourishment to gain their strength.

[*Appended in Charles Arnett's hand*] July 17 Said was to apply to Dr Sankey, Snargate Street [Dover]. [PAR 511/37/7/10]

605 18 Aug 1825 *Letter from John Baker, Dover, [Kent] to C[harles] Arnett, Winchelsea, assistant overseer*:

Re: Tilden. In your letter to me of 24th ultimo you promised the woman should hear from you after the meeting of the 29th. This I presume has slipped your memory and I now have to inform you both the woman and daughter keep their bed. When I wrote [to] you I thought the woman still received relief from you but I find this is not the case. Some charitable persons have got them to be attended by the surgeon of the Dover dispensary who are much surprised you do not attend to this case after being officially informed of it. St Mary's parish is very large and I never before had a doctor's certificate asked for in preference to an official application. I have done all I could to persuade these poor wretches to let me get them under a suspended order of removal but so great is their dread of a workhouse that I suppose until literally starved they will not consent and which would have been the case had it not been for the charitable persons before alluded to. I hope common humanity will induce you to attend to this case. [PAR 511/35/1/191]

606 12 Sep 1825 *Letter from Elizabeth Tilden, Dover, [Kent] to [Charles] Arnett, Winchelsea, [assistant] overseer*:
I now take the liberty to write to you again for a little assistance as I am not able to work much yet because I am still very weak and really do stand in need of it. It keeps me so bad off because I [have] been obliged to get a little trust when I was ill and I have had the woman come several times that was doing for me and the child when we was ill, but I have not been able to satisfy her yet. I should be obliged to you to send me an answer as soon as convenient.　　　　　　[PAR 511/35/1/194]

607 24 Sep 1825 *Letter from W Robinson, Dover [Kent], surgeon, to [Charles] Arnett, Winchelsea, [assistant] overseer*:
I hereby certify that Elizabeth Tilden was under my care from the 1st day of August to the 15th September with an affection of the chest. She is now labouring under extreme debility requiring nourishing diet to regain her former strength.
[*Endorsed letter from Mrs Tilden*] As you required me to have sent the ages of the children, my son is 19, my eldest girl is 16, the youngest fourteen. Both the girls are very ailing and not able for servitude. I have sent a letter with a certificate before, the 15th of August last, also with the children's ages.　[PAR 511/35/1/195]
Note: A casual payment of 10s was made on 29 September.[10]

608 26 Mar 1826 *Letter from Elizabeth Tilden, Dover, [Kent] to [Charles] Arnett, Winchelsea [assistant] overseer*:
I have taken the liberty of troubling you with a letter to ask you to allow me a small trifle a week as I am in a very ill state of health and have been all the winter. If not if you will be so good as to send me something to help pay my rent with as I owe half a year's rent and I am afraid of being turned out of doors if it is not paid. The winter has been very hard with me. Indeed I have been forced to part with everything that I could to support myself with and not been able to do anything. I have not been able to pay my rent and would not trouble you till I was quite forced to do it. Neither would I now if I had my health. PS May I beg you to answer this and direct [to] New Street as before.　　　　　　[PAR 511/35/1/210]

609 23 Oct 1826 *Letter from Elizabeth Tilden, New Street, Dover, [Kent] to the overseers of Winchelsea*:
I hope you will take it into consideration and allow me a trifle per week as the work is so dull that I cannot earn but little or send me a little money to help me out in my rent or I shall be troubled for it. I don't wish to be troublesome to you but if you don't send me some relief I must come home to my parish and wish you to send me an answer as soon as you can.　　　　　　[PAR 511/35/1/244]

610 11 Mar 1827 *Letter from Elizabeth Tilden, New Street, Dover, [Kent] to the overseers of Winchelsea*:
I take the liberty of writing to you as I am in present distress and hope you will

take it in[to] consideration as my son is laid up and not able to work. We have had a very hard winter too. I have had but very little work myself. I am not able to keep him myself. I am in but a poor state of health. Please to direct for: Widow Tilden, New Street.

[*Endorsed*] I hereby certify that Henry Tilden is a patient under my care labouring under a severe attack of rheumatism. W. Robinson, surgeon, 12 March 1827.

[PAR 511/35/1/263]

Notes: 1. On 15 March 1827 Elizabeth Tilden was allowed £1 'To cash – son ill'.[11]
2. Henry Tilden died in 1833 and was buried in Winchelsea.[12] The Winchelsea overseers paid 6s 6d for his laying out and to the bearers of his coffin.[13]

611 4 Jun 1828 *Letter from Elizabeth Tilden, New Street, Dover to the chief overseer of the poor of the parish of Winchelsea, Sussex:*
The humble petition of Elizabeth Tilden, a widow 18 years, showeth she is much reduced in all respects and that she is under the immediate necessity humbly to beseech the honourable gentlemen in the care of the poor of Winchelsea parish, her parish, to send her immediate relief. She is truly distraught in every sense and hope[s] her good character and the accompanying certificate will be her friend.
[*Endorsed*] [same date] I hereby certify that E. Tilden has been attended to by me for many weeks and is still so indisposed as to be altogether unable at present to follow her employ. I believe her statement above to be correct. Thomas Coleman, surgeon, Dover 4 Jun 1828.   [PAR 511/37/7/12]

612 13 Jun 1828 *Minute of the Winchelsea select vestry:*
Resolved that Elizabeth Tilden of Dover be allowed twenty shillings having been long unwell.   [PAR 511/12/3]

613 10 Oct 1828 *Minute of the Winchelsea select vestry:*
Resolved that Widow Elizabeth Tilden having applied for permanent relief be informed that no permanent relief can be granted but that she will be allowed to come home into the poorhouse.   [PAR 511/12/3]

614 29 Mar 1831 *Removal order made by George Dell and John Coleman, justices of the peace for the town and port of Dover, Kent, to the churchwardens and overseers of the poor of the parish of St Mary the Virgin, Dover:*
Whereas complaint hath been made to us that Elizabeth Tilden (widow) hath come to inhabit in the parish of St Mary the Virgin, Dover, not having gained any legal settlement there nor having produced any certificate acknowledging her to be settled elsewhere and is now actually chargeable to the same, we upon due proof thereof and also upon examination of Elizabeth Tilden do adjudge the same to be true and also adjudge her place of last legal settlement to be Winchelsea, Sussex. These are therefore to require you to remove and convey her to Winchelsea and her deliver, together with this our order or a true copy thereof, to the churchwardens

and overseers of the poor who are hereby required to receive and provide for her according to law.

Endorsed: [same date] Whereas it appears to us that Elizabeth Tilden is at present unable to travel by reason of sickness and infirmity of body, we, the same justices, do hereby suspend the execution of this order. You are hereby commanded to desist from conveying her out of your parish of St Mary the Virgin, Dover until you shall make it appear unto us that [she] hath recovered from her illness and may without danger be conveyed to Winchelsea. [PAR 511/32/3/59]

Note: This removal order was not enforced on her recovery because Winchelsea sent her £4.[14] She was also helped in 1834 when she received a weekly allowance of 1s 6d.[15]

615 26 Oct 1840 *Letter from John Belsey, 14 York Street, Dover to the guardians of the poor of Winchelsea*:

There is a person in Dover named Elizabeth Tilden, 56 years of age, who belongs to your parish and who is in a state of destitution. In fact she is so unwell, brought on by want of food, that the consequence will be something unpleasant unless she receives some assistance. My motive in writing to you is to inform you of such circumstance that she might receive a weekly allowance which you are in the habit of giving to persons in a similar situation in the shape of parochial assistance or to have her removed to the [work]house which will be attended with much greater expense. My motives are pure motives of humanity in stating this truly lamentable case and to recommend to your notice the above-mentioned unfortunate individual. An answer by return will oblige. [PAR 511/38/6/1]

616 2 Nov 1840 *Minute of the guardians of the Rye Union*:

Ordered that the clerk request the parish officers of Winchelsea to write to Mr Belsey of Dover and suggest to him the propriety of advising Elizabeth Tilden (belonging to Winchelsea parish and concerning whom Mr Belsey has written to the parish overseers of Winchelsea) to become chargeable to Dover, she being unwell and in necessitous circumstances as appears by his letter, in order that her case may be properly inquired into, but that the parish of Dover need not remove her, Mrs Tilden, as there appears no doubt of her settlement in Winchelsea and that on the circumstances of the case being received, that the guardians will then be prepared to come to some decision as to what relief can be allowed Mrs Tilden. [G 8/1a/3 f.284]

617 4 Nov 1840 *Letter from Henry Edwards Paine, clerk to the Rye Union to the parish officers of Winchelsea.*:

Enclosed I return you Mr Belsey's letter respecting Elizabeth Tilden and I am directed by the board to request that you will write to him and suggest to him the propriety of recommending Mrs Tilden to become chargeable to Dover that her circumstances may be officially enquired into and reported to you which (however correct Mr Belsey's statement concerning Mrs T[ilden] may be) is the proper and, in strictness, the only report which should be adhered to and as there appears no doubt that she belongs to Winchelsea it would be perhaps proper that you should request no order of removal to be made out but rather a statement of her present necessities which would save the parish of Dover the expense of removal and incur merely small temporary expense of relief. If Mrs Tilden shall appear likely to continue at Dover in necessitous circumstances that the board of guardians of this union will immediately on hearing the particulars of her case most probably come to some decision as to how relief may be afforded to her if possible without requiring her being brought within the union and at all events to save Dover parish the expense and trouble of her removal if by any means it is possible to do so.

[PAR 511/38/6/1]

1 PAR 511/31/1/11   2 ibid   3 PAR 511/31/1/14   4 PAR 511/12/3   5 ibid 15 Mar 1827   6 PAR 511/31/1/13 QE Jun 1828   7 PAR 511/37/7/29   8 PAR 511/31/1/12 f.257   9 PAR 511/31/1/15 f.20 10 PAR 511/31/1/14   11 PAR 511/31/1/15 f.20   12 PAR 511/1/5/1   13 PAR 511/31/1/16 QE Dec 1833   14 PAR 511/31/1/16 QE Jun 1831   15 PAR 511/31/1/16

Mary Tilden

618 *Mary Tilden was Elizabeth Tilden's elder daughter* (**593**). *At the time of her removal from Dover* (**619**) *she was 23. In August 1831 the Winchelsea public vestry resolved 'that Mary Tilden receive twelve shillings for three weeks and 18s 6d for clothing'.[1] She continued to receive four shillings a week although it was never a weekly allowance in the usual way, separate resolutions were passed monthly.[2] The first mention of her illegitimate child was on 14 December 1831 when the public vestry resolved, 'that Mary Tilden be allowed cloth [sic] for her child and a pair of shoes [costing] seven shillings, also that Mary Tilden be allowed four weeks at four shillings.[3] That allowance was paid for a good deal longer than the initially proposed four weeks, in fact until May 1833 when Mary and the child were returned to Dover with £1 2s 6d allocated for clothing and the expenses of the journey.[4] After the bastardy order* (**621**) *came into force Mary received only 1s 6d a week between December 1834 and October 1835.[5] There is no record of money being received from George Artlett as a result of that order. In 1835 Mary was listed as being among Winchelsea's able-bodied poor.[6]*

619 30 Jun 1831 *Removal order made by Henry Lulham and John Coleman, justices of the peace for the town and port of Dover, Kent, to the churchwardens and overseers of the poor of the parish of St Mary the Virgin, Dover:*
Whereas complaint hath been made unto us that Mary Tilden, singlewoman, hath come to inhabit in the town and port of Dover not having gained a legal settlement there, not having produced any certificate acknowledging her to be settled elsewhere and [is] now actually become chargeable to the same by reason of pregnancy, we upon due proof thereof as well as upon the examination of Mary Tilden do adjudge the same to be true and also adjudge her last place of legal settlement to be Winchelsea, Sussex. These are therefore to require you to remove and convey her to Winchelsea and her deliver, together with this our order or a

true copy thereof, to the churchwardens and overseers of the poor who are hereby required to receive and provide for her according to law.   [PAR 511/32/3/61]

620 19 Nov 1831 *Examination, taken before William Lipscomb, justice of the peace for Winchelsea, of Mary Tilden*:
who upon her oath saith that on about the twentieth day of October now last past she was delivered of a female bastard child and that the child is actually chargeable to Winchelsea and that George Artlett or Hartley of the parish of Deal, Kent, mariner, and who when last heard of was serving on board the *Old Peace,* a collier commanded by Capt[ain] Allen of Dover, did get her with child of the said bastard child. [*mark of*] Mary Tilden.   [AMS 2330 f.113]

621 24 Mar 1834 *Bastardy order made by Joseph Hennah and John Tilden, justices of the peace for Winchelsea*:
Whereas it hath been duly made appear unto us as well upon the complaint of the churchwardens and overseers of the poor of Winchelsea as upon oath of Mary Tilden that she was delivered of a female bastard child at Winchelsea on the twentieth day of October 1831 and that the child is now chargeable to Winchelsea and likely so to continue and further that George Artlett of Deal in Kent did beget the child on the body of Mary Tilden. We therefore upon examination of the cause and circumstances of the [evidence] as well upon the oath of Mary Tilden as otherwise do hereby adjudge George Artlett to be the reputed father of the child; and thereupon we do order as well for the better relief of the parish of St Thomas the Apostle, Winchelsea as for the sustenance and relief of the child that George Arlett shall and do forthwith, upon notice of this our order, pay or cause to be paid to the churchwardens or overseers of the poor of Winchelsea, or to some one of them, the sum of thirteen pounds seventeen shillings already expended for and towards the maintenance of the child; and we do also hereby further order that George Artlett shall likewise pay the sum of one shilling and sixpence weekly and every week from the present time for and towards the keeping, sustenance and maintenance of the child for and during so long time as the child shall be chargeable to Winchelsea; and further order that Mary Tilden shall also pay the sum of sixpence weekly so long as the child shall be chargeable in case she shall not nurse and take care of the child herself.   [PAR 511/34/4/18]

622 2 May 1839 *Letter from Mary Tilden, 5 Worthington's Lane, Dover, [Kent] to the parish officers of Winchelsea*:
Allow me to inform you that I am in the greatest distress in consequence of the want of employ part of last winter or I should not have troubled you and my daughter is eight years of age and of course I find it very difficult to maintain her. It is now four years since I received any parochial relief for her but at this moment I must claim your indulgence for a trifle to assist in supporting her. I am confident you will take my case into your kind consideration so as to enable me [to know] how to act

in respect [of] her future maintenance in Dover or by her being conveyed to her parish. An answer will oblige. PS The father of the child is at sea.

[PAR 511/35/1/360]

1 PAR 511/12/2   2 ibid   3 ibid   4 ibid; PAR 511/31/1/15   5 PAR 511/31/1/16   6 PAR 511/37/7/29

Philadelphia Tree

623 *Philadelphia Tree née Greigsby married Benjamin Tree junior at St Thomas's, Winchelsea on 18 December 1783.[1] Her husband was a stalwart of the Winchelsea community who, in succession to his father of the same name, served as a constable, as sergeant-at-mace and as water bailiff's sergeant between 1788 and 1798.[2] In the year that he last held these posts, Benjamin and Philadelphia, with others, were involved in a property dispute which is noted by the Winchelsea Court of Record and in the vestry minutes but without details.[3] The dispute was with Richard Barwell, a former Indian nabob of dubious repute, who at that time owned much property in Winchelsea and controlled Winchelsea Corporation as 'patron' of the town's two parliamentary seats. One account of the dispute concludes, 'Fine levied and acknowledged'.[4] If this was to be paid by the Trees and their co-defendants who had been found guilty it may well be that Benjamin was sacked rather than retiring. However, illness is just as likely a reason for he died the following year.[5] His widow was granted poor relief through weekly payments, initially of five shillings but soon increased to eight shillings.[6] Baptisms recorded in the parish registers indicate that her husband's death left her bringing up a family of five children aged between 4 and 14, hence the generosity of this allowance. By 1823, with the children grown up, Philadelphia Tree's poor relief payment had been reduced to three shillings a week and this was paid regularly until September 1827.[7] On the 7th of that month, having received Richard Stileman's letter (**624**) and in response to it, the select vestry 'Resolved that Widow Tree be allowed two shillings a week during her illness in addition to the three shillings already allowed'.[8] She did not receive this extra money for long as she died the following month at the age of 71.[9]*

624 7 Sep 1827 *Letter from Richard Stileman, [The Friars, Winchelsea] to the chairman of the select vestry, Winchelsea:*
I am afraid I shall not be enabled to attend the vestry this morning but having undertaken to state the situation of Mrs Philly [Philadelphia] Tree I shall be glad if the vestry will take her case into consideration as she appears to be in want of further assistance. Her daughter who came down to nurse her being herself taken ill and the poor old woman, being unable to get out of bed, she stands in great need of further assistance and from her kind and excellent character is well worthy [of] more than common attention.

[PAR 511/35/1/295]

1 PAR 511/1/1/2   2 WIN 61 f.161r; WIN 61AA   3 WIN 61 ff.33r-34; WIN 404   4 WIN 61 f.34   5 PAR 511/1/1/4   6 AMS 2329 E1801-E1802   7 PAR 511/31/1/13   8 PAR 511/12/3   9 PAR 511/1/5/1

Hannah Turk

625 *While awaiting the birth of her illegitimate baby, Hannah Turk stayed for five weeks at the home of James Hoad who was paid £1 5s 0d for his wife's looking after her.[1] The child (**627-628**), also Hannah, was baptised at St Thomas's on 7 January 1819[2] and buried there three weeks later.[3] Jacob Holt was paid 5s 6d as undertaker for the burial.[4] In view of the child's death the parish overseers took no action against David Tree and the mother features no further in their records.*

626 1 Oct 1818 *Letter from John Fisher [solicitor], Rye to Edward Jeakens, Winchelsea*:
Accompanying I send you the examination of Hannah Turk touching her settlement and in bastardy. Mr [Weeden] Dawes subscribes to the opinion I gave you, viz that a settlement was gained by the hiring and service with Mrs [Maria] Osborne. As the reputed father is a parishioner of Winchelsea there only remains to issue a warrant to apprehend him for the purpose of making an order of affiliation.

[PAR 511/35/1/9]

627 [1] Oct 1818 *Examination taken before* (no names given) *justices of the peace for Winchelsea of Hannah Turk at present residing at Winchelsea*:
who upon her oath saith that she is of the age of eighteen and upwards; that she was born in the parish of Playden as she has heard and believes to be true; that when she was about fifteen years old she went to live with Mr Mauger of Iden and stayed in his service about four months, then came to Rye and lived with Mrs Hunter about the same length of time, then hired herself to Mrs Moneypenny of Rye by the quarter and lived with her about eleven months when Mrs Moneypenny, not having occasion for her any longer, discharged her but provided her current quarter's wages; that in the month of May 1816 she went on a visit to Mrs Hoad of Winchelsea and at her request remained with her until the following August about which time Mrs Osborne of the Castle Public House in Winchelsea sent for her and asked if she would come and live with her which [she] agreed to do and it was agreed between them that [she] should come a little while on trial to see if she could do the work and if she could she was to continue; that nothing was then said about wages; that her mistress occasionally gave her clothes and when she had any money given to her by guests at the house she gave it to her mistress and her mistress used to put money to it and paid for clothes; that about a twelvemonth after she had been with Mrs Osborne she asked [her] if she would have any wages and [she] replied that she did not want wages if her mistress would continue finding her [in] clothes which her mistress agreed to do; that she continued living with Mrs Osborne without any other agreement until the 28th day of September last, her mistress finding her in clothes as she had before done; that on the said 28th day of September last her mistress discharged her; that she is now with child which child is likely to be born a bastard and become chargeable to the parish of St Thomas the Apostle, Winchelsea and that David Tree of Winchelsea, journeyman shoemaker,

is the father thereof.

[*no signature*] [*endorsed*] 'Settlement by a general hiring and service with Mrs Osborne'.   [PAR 511/32/4/183]

Notes 1. Hannah Turk 'daughter of Thomas and Elizabeth' was baptised at Playden on 7 November 1800.[5]

2. [she] in this document replaces the unusual use of 'pauper' in the original.

3. David Tree, the reputed father, was among those who abused Charles Arnett (**16**) and was the owner of the cart which Stephen Field the younger allowed to go unattended through Winchelsea (**253**).

628 30 Dec 1818 *Voluntary examination, taken on oath before George Stace, justice of the peace for Winchelsea, of Hannah Turk of Winchelsea, singlewoman:* who saith that she is with child and the said child is likely to be born a bastard and to become chargeable to the parish of St Thomas the Apostle, Winchelsea and that David Tree of Winchelsea, cordwainer did get her with child of the said bastard child and that he is the father thereof. [*mark of*] Hannah Turk [PAR 511/34/1/21]

1 PAR 511/31/1/11 Sep 1818-Mar 1819   2 PAR 511/1/2/1   3 PAR 511/1/5/1   4 PAR 511/31/2/119
5 PAR 445/1/1/2

Richard Unicume

629 *Between September 1823 and February 1824 the Winchelsea parish overseers went to considerable expense supporting Richard Unicume. They allowed him a casual payment of £2 10s 0d, paid Dr Adam Scott £1 8s 6d for attending his wife and a Mrs Pitt ten shillings for nursing her and paid £1 0s 4d 'for carrying Mrs [Jemima] Unicume home' to Cranbrook.[1] Whether she was taken back after her husband had abandoned her, or was suspected of intending to do so (**632**), is not clear. Whatever happened, they were back in Winchelsea by the end of the year (**633**).*

630 5 Jan 1824 *Examination taken before Henry Powell and George Stace, justices of the peace for Winchelsea, of Richard Unicume:*
who upon his oath saith that he is upwards of thirty-two 32 years of age and was born at Cranbrook, Kent where his parents were legally settled as he hath been informed and verily believes to be true; that he was married to Jemima Huggard, widow, about 12 months ago at the parish church of Rolvenden, Kent by banns; that he never lived as a yearly hired servant for the space of twelve months at one living; that whenever he hired any apartment the greatest rent he ever paid was one shilling and sixpence per week for a ready-furnished apartment in the parish of Rolvenden in the house of one Hoad, a labourer there, about three months ago; that he has never done any legal act to gain a legal settlement in any other parish or place whatsoever to the best of his knowledge and belief and that he is now chargeable to the parish of St. Thomas the Apostle, Winchelsea. [*signature of*] Richard Unicume.   [AMS 2330 f.27]

631 5 Jan 1824 *Removal order made by Henry Powell and George Stace, justices of the peace for Winchelsea, to the churchwardens and overseers of the poor of the parish of St Thomas the Apostle, Winchelsea*:
Whereas complaint hath been made unto us that Richard Unicume and Jemima his wife now pregnant lately intruded and came into the parish of St Thomas the Apostle, Winchelsea and have become chargeable to the same, we, upon examination of the [evidence] on oath and other circumstances, do adjudge the same to be true and also adjudge their last place of legal settlement to be the parish of Cranbrook in the county of Kent. These are therefore in His Majesty's name to require you, on sight hereof, to remove and convey Richard and Jemima Unicume to Cranbrook and them deliver, together with this our order or a true copy thereof, to the churchwardens and overseers of the poor there who are hereby required to receive and provide for them according to law.
[*Appended*] 6 Jan 1824 [*same justices*] Whereas it appears unto us that Jemima Unicume, the pauper within ordered to be removed is unable to travel by reason of sickness and infirmity, we therefore suspend the execution of the within order of removal until it shall be made appear to our satisfaction that it may be executed without danger to [her].
[*Further appended*] 20 Feb 1824 [*same justices*] Whereas it is now made appear unto us that the within order of removal may be executed without danger we do hereby order the same to be forthwith put into execution accordingly, and whereas it is duly proved to us upon oath that the charges incurred by the suspension amount to the sum of four pounds and ten shillings we therefore order you, the churchwardens and overseers of Cranbrook, to pay that sum on demand to Charles Arnett, one of the overseers of Winchelsea.   [PAR 511/32/2/77]
Note: A receipt within the overseers' accounts states, 'Received cash Cranbrook parish £4 10s 0d'.[2]

632 20 Feb 1824 *Statement on oath made before unnamed Winchelsea magistrate*:
Charles Arnett, assistant overseer [of Winchelsea] charges Richard Unicume on suspicion of being a rogue and vagabond by leaving or intending to leave his family chargeable to the parish of St Thomas the Apostle, Winchelsea, Sussex.
[WIN 2230]

633 18 Dec 1824 *Letter from C J Taylor, Cranbrook, [Kent] to [Charles] Arnett, Winchelsea, [assistant overseer]*:
You will much oblige me by paying the bearer Richard Unicume the sum of two shillings weekly for ten weeks and if he requires any assistance after that time he must make another application either personally or by letter. I will remit you the money [at] the first opportunity.   [PAR 511/35/1/147]
Note: In response to this letter Winchelsea paid Richard Unicume four shillings for the remaining two weeks of December.[3] However, when it was resolved to pay a further pound for the first ten weeks of 1825 the entry has been deleted and marked, 'to be charged to the overseers of [his] parish'.[4]

634 2 Nov 1826 *Letter from C J Taylor, Cranbrook, [Kent] to [Charles] Arnett, Winchelsea, [assistant overseer]*:
Having been out from home for two days on business is the cause of the delay in answering your letter. I have enclosed £1 for Unicume and if they are well enough to walk home by the time that is expended they had better come as he seems to me not to be able to do anything. Nor will he be for some time. Therefore [I] think we can keep him at home cheaper than at Winchelsea.   [PAR 511/35/1/247]

1 PAR 511/31/1/13   2 ibid Sep 1823-Mar 1824   3 ibid QE Dec 1824   4 ibid QE Mar 1825

Ann Vinall (Vinehall)

635 *Ann Vinall, 'baseborn daughter of Mary', was baptised in Winchelsea on 21 September 1801.[1] Her mother's bastardy examination (where her name is spelt Vinehall) is dated 11 November 1801 and charges Edward Waters of Rye, blacksmith with being father of her daughter born at Winchelsea workhouse on 15 September 1801.[2] Ann Vinall was still Winchelsea's responsibility between 1814 and 1816 when she was in service with Stephen Laurence (636). It seems to be the same person who features in (637-638) but it is not clear how she came to have a settlement in Brookland by 1823, probably through being in service in that village for some time. Anyway, Winchelsea continued to pay her 3s 6d per week on Brookland's behalf between August 1823 and April 1824 when payments ceased.[3] William Drury's allegation (638) that this had been reduced to two shillings is not confirmed by Winchelsea's records. The Winchelsea parish registers do, however, confirm that Ann Vinall married William Drury at St Thomas's on 8 February 1824 (638).[4]*

636 6 Feb 1815 *Minute of Winchelsea public vestry*:
Stephen Laurence does agree to take Ann Vinall [at] 2s per week, same terms as the last year.   [PAR 511/12/1 f.193]
Note: The previous year's terms are not recorded.

637 20 Aug 1823 *Letter from John Button, Brookland [Kent], overseer, to [John] Woods, Winchelsea, shopkeeper*:
Please have the goodness to pay Ann Vinall 3s 6d per week for her child beginning 23 August 1823 and I will repay you at Michaelmas on account of Brookland parish.   [PAR 511/35/1/18]

638 25 Mar 1824 *Letter from John Button, Brookland, [Kent], overseer, to [the overseers of Winchelsea]*:
Please to send by the bearer, William Drury, the account of money due to you from the parish of Brookland for Ann Vinall, as William Drury informs me they have had only 2s a week since February 8th 1824, the time they were married. Money paid into Rye bank up to 12th February 1824 = £4 11s 0d. What remains since I will pay you and after this time I can pay him myself.   [PAR 511/35/1/72]

1 PAR 511/1/1/4   2 PAR 511/34/1/16   3 PAR 511/31/1/13   4 PAR 511/1/3/1

Elizabeth Watson

639 *Both Elizabeth Watson's illegitimate children were baptised in Winchelsea, William Bourne Russell Watson on 2 July 1815 and Thomas Watson on 20 November 1822.[1] The following sequence of documents is concerned with Winchelsea's attempts to secure maintenance from the boys' respective fathers. Bourne Russell, following the order made against him (**644**), initially paid the Winchelsea overseers £2 10s 0d for Elizabeth Watson's lying-in and £4 11s 0d for twenty-six weeks maintenance at 3s 6d per week.[2] Between then and the charge brought against him for defaulting (**647**) Russell made occasional payments, the largest being £10.[3] Elizabeth Watson was paid her 3s 6d per week,[4] despite any shortfall in the amounts received from Russell, until 1822 when she returned to Iden (**648**). She was also paid from the time of Russell's arrest in Wapping (**647**), after his request to take the child into his own care was refused (**654**), and until he eventually took the child (**657**).[5] Payments from Thomas Bright as a result of his order (**655**) were much more regular and were paid to her by the overseers[6] until the time Bright's father wrote to say his son was likely to have difficulty paying (**658**). In fact Bright junior made further payments after the date of that letter, during which he made up the amount unpaid earlier.[7]*

640 3 Apr 1815 *Removal order made by E J Curteis and Thomas Lamb, justices of the peace for the county of Sussex to the churchwardens and overseers of the poor for the parish of Iden, Sussex:*
Whereas complaint has been made to us that Elizabeth Watson, singlewoman, lately intruded and came into the parish of Iden and is become chargeable to the same we adjudge the same to be true and also adjudge the place of the last legal settlement of Elizabeth Watson to be the parish of St Thomas the Apostle, Winchelsea. [We] therefore require you in His Majesty's name on sight hereof to remove and convey her to Winchelsea and her deliver, together with this our order or a true copy thereof, to the churchwardens and overseers of the poor there who are hereby required to receive and provide for her according to law.
[PAR 511/32/3/28]

641 6 Apr 1815 *Voluntary examination taken on oath before George Stace, justice of the peace for Winchelsea, of Elizabeth Watson of Winchelsea, singlewoman:*
who saith that she is with child and that the child is likely to be born a bastard and to become chargeable to the parish of St Thomas the Apostle, Winchelsea and that Bourne Russell of Rye, Sussex, mariner, did get her with child of the said bastard child and that he is the father thereof. [*signature of*] Elizabeth Watson.
[PAR 511/34/1/42]

642 6 Apr 1815 *Order made to all constables and other His Majesty's officers of the peace for Winchelsea by George Stace, justice of the peace for Winchelsea:*
Whereas Elizabeth Watson of Winchelsea, singlewoman, on her examination taken this day in writing and upon oath before me hath voluntarily declared that she is with child and that the child is likely to be born a bastard and to be chargeable to the parish of St Thomas the Apostle, Winchelsea, hath in [her] examination charged Bourne Russell of Rye, Sussex, mariner, with having begotten the child

on her body with which she is now pregnant and whereas David Laurence, one of the overseers of the poor of Winchelsea hath made application unto me for the immediate apprehending of Bourne Russell to answer to the [evidence] these are therefore in His Majesty's name to require you and every one of you to apprehend Bourne Russell and to bring him before me or some other of His Majesty's justices of the peace for Winchelsea that he may be proceeded against as the law directs.

[PAR 511/34/2/27]

643 4 Aug 1815 *Voluntary examination taken on oath before George Stace and George Tilden, justices of the peace for Winchelsea, of Elizabeth Watson of Winchelsea*:
who saith that on the 30th day of June now last past in the house of William Carman in Winchelsea she was delivered of a male bastard child and that the child is likely to become chargeable to the parish of St Thomas the Apostle, Winchelsea and that Bourne Russell of Rye, Sussex, mariner, did get her with child of the said bastard child. *[signature of]* Elizabeth Watson. [PAR 511/34/1/72]

644 4 Aug 1815 *Bastardy order made by George Stace the elder and George Tilden, justices of the peace for Winchelsea, concerning the child of Elizabeth Watson*:
Whereas it hath duly been made appear unto us that *[recites details in* (**642-643**)] ...... We therefore, upon examination of the causes and circumstance of the [evidence] as well upon the oath of Elizabeth Watson as otherwise do hereby adjudge Bourne Russell to be the reputed father of the child; and thereupon we do order as well for the better relief of the parish of St Thomas the Apostle, Winchelsea as for the sustentation and relief of the child that Bourne Russell shall and do forthwith, upon notice of this our order, pay or cause to be paid to the churchwardens or overseers of the poor of Winchelsea or to some one of them the sum of two pounds ten shillings for and towards the lying-in of Elizabeth Watson and the maintenance of the child to the time of making this our order; and we do hereby further order that Bourne Russell shall likewise pay or cause to be paid the sum of three shillings and sixpence weekly and every week from this present time for and towards the keeping, sustentation and maintenance of the child for and during so long time as the child shall be chargeable to Winchelsea; and we do further order that Elizabeth Watson shall also pay the sum of sixpence weekly so long as the child shall be chargeable to Winchelsea in case she shall not nurse and take care of the child herself. [PAR 511/34/4/3]

645 15 Jan 1819 *[Edited] account submitted to the parish officers of Winchelsea by Dawes & Co [of Rye, parish solicitors]*:
Attending Mr [Edward] Jeakens advising on the demand of this parish on Bourne Russell and afterwards attending Mr Crossley thereon when he promised me, [John Woollett], to write to Russell and recommend him to pay the money: 6s 8d.

[PAR 511/31/2/131]

646 11 Nov 1820 *[Edited] account submitted to the parish officers of Winchelsea by Dawes & Co. [of Rye, parish solicitors]*:
Attending Mr [Edward] Jeakens and taking instructions for proceeding against Bourne Russell: 6s; drawing out special information: 2s; warrant to apprehend: 1s.   [PAR 511/31/2/135]

647 16 Nov 1820 *Order made by George Stace, justice of the peace for Winchelsea, to the constables of the parish of Wapping in the county of Middlesex 'and others whom it may concern'*:
Whereas information and complaint upon oath hath been made before me that [*recites details in* (**642-644**)] ...... and that the child was living in and maintained by Winchelsea and that Bourne Russell had had due notice of the order and that the sum of money in the order had not been paid and that demand of payment thereof had been made upon Bourne Russell but that he had refused to pay the same whereby the sum of twenty-nine pounds and eleven shillings was then owing from Bourne Russell to the churchwardens and overseers of the poor of Winchelsea and therefore Edward Jeakens prayed of me, [George Stace], that Bourne Russell might be brought before me or some other of His Majesty's justices of the peace for Winchelsea to answer the [evidence] and make his defence therein. These are therefore to command you in His Majesty's name forthwith to apprehend and bring before me or some other justice of the peace for Winchelsea the body of Bourne Russell to answer unto the complaint and to be further dealt with according to law. Herein fail you not.
[*Endorsed*] 17 Nov 1820 Forasmuch as proof upon oath hath been made before me, Sir Robert Baker, Knight, one of His Majesty's justices of the peace for the county of Middlesex, that the name George Stace is of the hand of the justice of the peace within mentioned, I do hereby authorise Edward Jeakens who brings to me this warrant and all other persons to whom the warrant is directed to execute the same within the county of Middlesex.   [PAR 511/34/4/22]
Notes: 1. Following his arrest on this charge Bourne Russell paid the required sum of £20 11s 0d.[8]
2. Winchelsea parish was charged £8 19s 6d expenses by Edward Jeakens for himself and anyone who accompanied him 'going to London for Bourne Russell'.[9]

648 [Oct 1822] *Complaint made to Richard Stileman, sitting as a county magistrate*:
Samuel Skinner, one of the overseers of the parish of Iden, maketh oath and saith that Elizabeth Watson of the parish of Winchelsea hath returned and at present resides in the parish of Iden.   [AMS 6192/1 f.86]

649 22 Oct 1822 *Removal order made by E J Curteis and John Fuller, justices of the peace for the county of Sussex, to the churchwardens and overseers of the poor of the parish of Iden, Sussex:*
Whereas complaint hath been made to us that Elizabeth Watson, singlewoman, lately intruded and came into the parish of Iden and is actually become chargeable

to the same, we upon due proof thereof as well upon the examination of Elizabeth Watson do adjudge the same to be true and also adjudge that [her] place of last legal settlement was the parish of St Thomas the Apostle, Winchelsea. These are therefore in His Majesty's name to require you to remove and convey her to Winchelsea and her deliver, together with this our order or a true copy thereof, to the churchwardens and overseers of the poor there who are hereby required to receive and provide for her according to law. [PAR 511/32/3/41]

650 26 Nov 1822 *Examination, taken before Revd Samuel Philip Sheppard and Joseph Hennah justices of the peace for Winchelsea, of Elizabeth Watson*:
who upon her oath saith that on or about the 25th day of October last past in the parish and town of Winchelsea, Sussex at the house of Joseph Hoad the elder [she] was delivered of a male bastard child since baptised by the name of Thomas Watson and likely to become chargeable to Winchelsea; and this examinant further saith that Thomas Bright of the parish of Iden in Sussex, carpenter, is the truly and only father of the child of which she was delivered. (*signature of*) Elizabeth Watson. [AMS 2330 f.9]

651 4 Feb 1825 *Minute of Winchelsea select vestry*:
Resolved that it having appeared to this select vestry through the information of Mr [John] Woods that Elizabeth Watson can have no demand upon the parish for the pay of her child from June 1822 to July 1823 Mr Woods having demanded the child for the father and she proffering to keep it for twelve months and then Mr [Charles] Hill demanded the child which she refused to give up. [PAR 511/12/2]

652 17 May 1825 *Recognizances sought and preliminary hearing before Henry Powell and John Tilden, justices of the peace for Winchelsea*:
Thomas Bright the Younger, apprentice to William Ditch of Iden in Sussex, carpenter, an infant. On pain of imprisonment – 40s; William Ditch, the mainperson of the said apprentice – 20s; Thomas Bright the Elder of the parish of Tenterden, Kent, bailiff to Henry Godden Esq of Maidstone, Kent – 20s.
Winchelsea General quarter sessions holden 12th July 1825: Said Thomas Bright the Younger to answer the complaint of the parish officers of Winchelsea for unlawfully begetting Elizabeth Watson, singlewoman with child of a bastard child and likely to become chargeable to the parish of St Thomas the Apostle in the Ancient Town and then and there to abide such order as may be made.
Taken and acknowledged this 17th day of May 1825 before us [the above justices].
[*Unsigned note appended*] Executed warrant with [Samuel] Easton and defendant bailed as above. [WIN 237A]

653 6 Dec 1825 *Appearance before Henry Powell, justice of the peace for Winchelsea, of Charles Arnett, assistant overseer:*
who on oath charges Bourne Russell with unlawfully begetting Elizabeth Watson, singlewoman, with child and [Arnett] further saith that there appears by the books of account of the parish to be a considerable sum of money due from Bourne Russell for the maintenance of the bastard child. [WIN 237A]
Note: Following this appearance Bourne Russell paid the Winchelsea overseers £4 10s 6d.[10]

654 8 Dec 1825 *Letter from Bourne Russell of Rye to Charles Arnett [assistant overseer, Winchelsea]:*
I request you will not pay any further sum or sums of money on account of the parish for me to Elizabeth Watson for the child in her power belonging to me I having demanded the child of her in the month of July 1822 and she having refused to deliver him up to me. [PAR 511/34/3/19]

655 12 Jul 1826 *Bastardy order made by Henry Powell, George Stace, John Tilden and Joseph Hennah, justices of the peace for Winchelsea, regarding a child of Elizabeth Watson:*
Whereas it hath been duly made appear unto us that [*recites details in* (**650**) *and* (**652**)] …… We therefore do adjudge Thomas Bright to be the reputed father of the child; and thereupon we do order, as well for the better relief of the parish of St Thomas the Apostle, Winchelsea as for the sustentation and relief of the child, that Thomas Bright shall, and do forthwith upon notice of this our order, pay or cause to be paid to the churchwardens or overseers of the poor of Winchelsea or to some or one of them the sum of [*blank*] for and towards the maintenance of the child to the time of the making of this order; and we do hereby further order that Thomas Bright shall likewise pay the sum of two shillings and sixpence weekly and every week from this present time for and towards the keeping, sustentation and maintenance of the child for and during such time as the child shall be chargeable to Winchelsea; and further order that Elizabeth Watson shall also pay or cause to be paid the sum of eight pence weekly and every week so long as the child shall be chargeable to Winchelsea in case she shall not nurse or take care of the child herself. And we do hereby further order that Thomas Bright shall likewise pay the sum of [*blank*] for the reasonable charges and expenses incident to the birth of the child; and also the further sum of £2 6s 2d for the reasonable costs of apprehending and securing him [to appear before us], and also the further sum of 15s 6d for the reasonable cost of obtaining our order for the filiation of the child [these charges being] duly and respectively ascertained on oath before us in pursuance of the statute in such case made and provided. [PAR 511/34/4/13]
Note: Thomas Bright is recorded as paying the 2s 6d per week due at this time but no further amounts.[11]

656 16 Apr 1828 *Letter from Thomas Bright [senior], Tenterden, [Kent] to the overseers of Winchelsea*:
We have sent the pay for E[lizabeth] Watson's boy £1 12s 6d.[PAR 511/35/1/311]

657 1828 *Account of money paid by Bourne Russell for the maintenance of Elizabeth Watson's child*:
By the order of the magistrates made on or about the 3rd of August 1814 binding the overseers of the parish to pay me, Elizabeth Watson, for the support of my bastard child William Bourne Russell Watson [the sum of] 3s 6d per week [*there follows an account showing that between 1814 and 1828 Elizabeth Watson received a total of £54 1s 0d under this agreement. The document has a note added:*] On June 24th 1828 he was taken from me by his father.   [PAR 511/34/3/18]

658 14 Apr 1829 *Letter from Thomas Bright the elder, Tenterden, [Kent] to David Laurence, Winchelsea, assistant overseer*:
I received your letter and have wrote to my son to inform him the contents, though I am afraid he will not be able to meet it as I understand he has been out of employ for some time. He is allotted to pay 2s 6d per week. Young men our way if they are trade or farmers' sons do not pay more than 2s but I expect you will hear from him soon. I should like it settled by paying a certain sum down at once. I think if it is not settled that way he is likely to leave this country as he has no work.

[PAR 511/35/1/325]

Note: Despite this representation from his father, Thomas Bright junior's payments continued to be made until September 1830.[12]

1 PAR 511/1/2/1   2 PAR 511/31/1/11 1815-1816   3 ibid Mar-Sep 1819   4 ibid 1816-1820   5 PAR 511/31/1/13   6 ibid   7 ibid   8 ibid Sep 1820-Mar 1821   9 ibid   10 ibid QE Dec 1825   11 PAR 511/31/1/13 QE Sep 1826   12 PAR 511/31/1/13

James Weller

659 *Little appears in the Winchelsea records about James Weller apart from the documents published below. However, the 1841 census shows him aged 25, living at Camber with his wife Hannah aged 35, their children Frederick 3, Susanna 1 and Harriett 7 weeks. With them were living Sarah Foster 11 and Charlotte Foster 9. James Weller married Hannah Foster at St Thomas's, Winchelsea on 14 June 1837.[1] The difference of ten years in age between husband and wife would suggest that Sarah and Charlotte were Hannah's by an earlier relationship. This assumption is supported by Wittersham's contention (**662**) that the two eldest children listed in (**661**) did not have Wittersham settlements. The family were presumably removed to Wittersham as no further payments appear. However, James Weller junior (the census shows that his father James was also living at Camber in 1841) may have returned with some of his family for he was excused the payment of Winchelsea poor rates in 1848/1849.[2] Nothing exists in the Winchelsea accounts to show that Wittersham was paying them for him. Inquest papers dated 1880 exist for a James Weller who was 'accidentally killed in a cart.'[3] This may well be James Weller junior who would have been 64 at the time.*

660 15 May 1841 *Letter from William Longley, Camber, to the overseers of Winchelsea*:
The bearer, James Weller, belongs to Wittersham parish and on Friday last he made application to the Tenterden Board of Guardians for relief having five small children and his wife in a very dangerous state and has been so for a month. The board had no objection to grant him relief but he must just throw himself on Winchelsea parish. Now to save him a loss of a day's work I have sent him to you today, [Saturday], which I hope you will excuse seeing the motive I have in view.
[PAR 511/38/6/1]

661 18 May 1841 *Removal order made by John Beaumont and J[oseph] Hennah, justices of the peace for Winchelsea, to the churchwardens and overseers of the poor of the parish of St Thomas the Apostle, Winchelsea*:
Whereas complaint hath been made unto us that James Weller, his wife Hannah and five children namely Sarah aged 12 years, Charlotte aged 7 years, Frederick aged 3 years, Susannah aged 12 months and Harriett aged 1 month lately intruded and came into the parish of St Thomas the Apostle, Winchelsea and have become chargeable to the same; we do adjudge the same to be true and do also adjudge the place of last legal settlement of James Weller his wife and children to be the parish of Wittersham in the county of Kent. These are therefore in [Her] Majesty's name to require you to remove and convey them to Wittersham and there deliver them, together with this order or a true copy thereof, to the churchwardens and overseers of the poor who are hereby required to receive and provide for them according to law.
[*Appended – same justices.*] Dated the [*blank*] day of June 1841. Whereas it doth appear unto us that Hannah Weller, one of the paupers within ordered to be removed, is at present unable to travel by reason of sickness and infirmity, we do therefore hereby suspend the execution of the within order of removal until it shall be made appear unto us that [it] may be safely executed without danger.
[PAR 511/32/2/106]

662 28 May 1841 *Letter from Joseph Exall, clerk to the board of guardians of the Tenterden Union, to the churchwardens and overseers of the poor of Winchelsea*:
I am directed by the board of guardians on the part of the parish officers of Wittersham within [this] union to acknowledge that the legal settlement of James Weller whose examination before magistrates as to his settlement on the 18th instant is in the parish of Wittersham but that [of] the two eldest children named in the magistrates' adjudication viz. Sarah and Charlotte is not acknowledged to be in Wittersham. The board of guardians will direct that the maintenance of the said James Weller at the cost of your parish for 21 days will be paid and as they are informed that Weller's wife is unwell they will pay after that period what would be allowed under a suspension order.   [PAR 511/32/2/105]

663 10 Jul 1841 *Letter from Joseph Exall, clerk to the Tenterden Union, to the parish officers of Winchelsea*:
I shall be much obliged by your informing me of the expense you have been at in relieving the wife of James Weller. If I can be furnished with the same before next Friday I will lay it before the board of guardians that the amount may be discharged. [PAR 511/38/6/1]

664 10 Aug 1841 *Letter from Joseph Exall, Clerk of the Tenterden Union, to [George] Blackman, overseer, Winchelsea*:
I regret that the money for the relief of James Weller's wife [Hannah] is not paid as the board directed on the 16th of last month, the relieving officer to pay the same. I have written to him to pay the same as you direct immediately. [PAR 511/38/6/1]

665 11 Oct 1841 *Receipted bill from Messrs Lardner and Dawes, [Rye], solicitors to Winchelsea parish*:
Attending [on 18 May] to take the examination of James Weller: 6s 8d; taking same: 2s 6d; order of removal to Wittersham and duplicate: 4s; copy examination and order of removal: 6s 8d; notice to overseers: 2s. [*Endorsed*] Received for Lardner and Dawes by Henry Stocks 11 Oct 1841. [PAR 511/35/1/367]

1 PAR 511/1/3/1 2 PAR 511/12/2 3 WIN 601

Robert Wheeler

666 *The name Robert Wheeler has proved more difficult than any other within this volume to disentangle from the parish records. There was a Robert Wheeler of Winchelsea with a wife, Harriett, and a large family including another Robert. There were also a Robert Wheeler 'of Rye', a Robert Wheeler 'senior' and a Robert Wheeler 'junior', together with a vast number of entries simply in the name of Robert Wheeler. The best the editor has been able to achieve is to associate, wherever possible, one of the above with the documents published below without really knowing whether two of the Robert Wheelers are the same person.*
*The easiest to identify is Robert Wheeler of Winchelsea, a labourer. He and his wife were charged with threatening Edmund Morris and his wife Elizabeth (**671**), lived in a house owned by Thomas Easton where the rent was paid by the Winchelsea overseers (**672-673**) and his wife charged Thomas Hoadley with failing to pay for work she had done (**675**). This Robert Wheeler's age suggests that he may well also have been the Winchelsea pauper boy put out to work for Edwin Dawes (**667-668**). The family had seven children baptised in Winchelsea between 1819 and 1835[1] and two other children. Of these nine three died young and were buried at St Thomas's.[2] It is recorded that this Robert Wheeler, in the period January 1821 to December 1823, received frequent casual payments of between two shillings and 15s 6d and other allowances including 14s 6d for clothes on 7 January 1822 and fifteen shillings for boots on 26 September 1822. His rent of £4 10s was paid on 24 March 1823.[3] In 1825 a parish assessment shows that he was occupying a house and*

garden, presumably Thomas Easton's, valued at £1 rental per annum and, as a pauper, was excused paying the poor rate on the property.[4] At that time he was receiving a weekly payment of 1s 3½d.[5] It is quite likely that other unusual entries for the period were also paid to him such as 'Resolved that Robert Wheeler be allowed ten shillings per week while he is out of work through sickness, also a pint of porter a day'[6] and 'casual pay Robert Wheeler, child burnt, four shillings'.[7] What we know for certain is that at the time of the 1841 census he was listed as aged 50 living at the Strand with his wife Harriett 40, Robert 16, Thomas 12, Maria 7, James 5, and Jane 2. Jane died later the same year.[8]

The most likely of the above to be the same person are Robert Wheeler junior, a regular recipient of poor law relief from Winchelsea, and Robert Wheeler of Rye who, like Robert Wheeler of Winchelsea was, in February 1825, given notice to quit his home (674) and in 1827 reported to the Rye overseers that 'he is in distress being ill' (676). Robert Wheeler junior was listed in c.1836 as being among Winchelsea's able-bodied poor.[9] Regular weekly payments of varying amounts were made to both Robert Wheeler senior and junior between March 1831 and October 1835 at which time Robert Wheeler junior's allowance had been reduced to just 6d.[10] A casual payment of 8s 6d was, however, made to him for 'nurse and relief' when he was ill.[11]

In 1838 a most unusual request was received by the Rye guardians from Mr Thorpe, the governor of the Rye workhouse. He asked that 'Mrs Wheeler, widow of the late Robert Wheeler of Rye' be allowed to succeed Mrs Thorpe as 'a matron to assist in the management of the workhouse'. Mrs Thorpe had died. This was agreed subject to a probationary period of three months.[12] However, eventually the Rye guardians considered this arrangement inappropriate and indicated that 'the master and mistress of the workhouse should receive notice so that a man and his wife can be appointed'. The Poor Law Commissioners approved the decision but, with some tact, suggested it would be better if Mr Thorpe and Mrs Wheeler were allowed to resign. This they did.[13]

It has not been possible to ascertain which Robert Wheeler might be admitted to hospital in London (669) or, similarly, which R Wheeler (presumably Robert for no other Wheelers with that initial appear) was taken to and from hospital in 1841 (677).

667 18 Apr 1805 *Minute of the Winchelsea parish meeting*:
It is agreed that Mr [Edwin] Dawes is to have Robert Wheeler at 3s per week from Easter 1805 to Easter 1806   [PAR 511/12/1 f.144]
Note: During the same period Robert Wheeler received a casual payment of £1.[14]

668 14 Mar 1806 *Minute of the Winchelsea parish meeting*:
It is agreed that Mr [Edwin] Dawes is to have Robert Wheeler from Easter 1806 to Lady Day 1807 and to receive 1s per week on the same terms as above [i.e. that his master is to keep him and clothe him].   [PAR 511/12/1 f.148]

669 15 Oct 1818 *Minute of Winchelsea public vestry*:
It is agreed that in case Robert Wheeler is admitted into a hospital in London his expenses to and from London shall be allowed by the overseers and that the sum of twelve shillings shall be allowed weekly for the maintenance of his three children.   [PAR 511/12/1 ff.225-226]

Note: No record of the above proposed payments has been found in the overseers' accounts which suggests that Wheeler was not admitted. There is, however, in the 1819-1820 accounts an entry reading, 'Relieved Robert Wheeler, Rye, when lame £1 10s 6d'.[15]

670 10 Dec 1818 *Note addressed by George Bray, [overseer, Winchelsea] to Robert Wheeler 'at Mr Austin's, Rye':*
This is to inform you that you are to get one grist [grinding] of flour for your family and place it to the [Winchelsea] parish account.   [PAR 511/31/2/129]

671 21 Dec 1820 *Recognizance taken and acknowledged before George Stace, justice of the peace for Winchelsea:*
Be it remembered that Robert Wheeler of Winchelsea, labourer, personally came before me and acknowledged himself to be indebted to our sovereign lord the king in the sum of fifty pounds of lawful money of Great Britain to be levied on his goods and chattels, lands and tenements for the use of our lord the king, his heirs and successors, if default is made in the condition hereunder written:
The condition of this recognizance is such that if the above bounden Robert Wheeler and Harriett his wife do and from henceforth and until the twenty-first day of December 1821 keep the peace and be of good behaviour towards our lord the king and all his liege people and especially towards Edmund Morris of Winchelsea, labourer, and Elizabeth his wife, then this recognizance to be void otherwise of force.   [WIN 254]

672 11 May 1824 *Extract from letter from John Woods, Hastings to [Charles] Arnett, Winchelsea [assistant overseer]:*
In answer to your note I recollect the Sunday [Richard] Stileman and [Weeden] Dawes stopped to the vestry, but what was the business of the vestry I forget. Before we left Mr Easton made a demand of his rent and there was some difference of opinion about the parish paying Wheeler's rent but the result was that it was to be paid and that Easton was to put the house in tenantable repair and let the parish have it for £4 a year but his putting the house in repair was part of the condition and how far this has been complied with I must leave you and the parish to judge. Jacob Holt I well remember was present and we spoke of his doing this repair afterwards (possibly he may remember something of the affair). Easton's was not the business for which the vestry was called and was the last case heard and, as was often the case, the attendants being in haste, caused sometimes omissions of an entry in the vestry book. As to my having an order to record what the parties did not wait to sign I should think from the irregularity must be incorrect but I cannot positively say that no order was given to that effect when we next assembled [for a] select vestry.   [PAR 511/35/1/83]
Note: Between June and September 1824 a year's rent of £5 6s 0d for Wheeler was paid to 'E Austin'.[16]

673 10 Sep 1824 *Notice issued by the churchwardens and overseers of Winchelsea to Thomas Easton of Winchelsea, landlord*:
We hereby give you warning of quitting that house now in the occupation of Robert Wheeler on or before Lady Day next of which be pleased to take notice.

[PAR 511/37/3/29]

674 23 Feb 1825 *Notice issued by Charles Arnett, assistant overseer, on behalf of the churchwardens and overseers of Winchelsea to Robert Wheeler of Rye*:
We hereby give you notice to quit that house and premises now in your occupation on or before this day month of which be pleased to take notice.[PAR 511/37/3/13]

675 27 Feb 1826 *Information given before Henry Powell and John Tilden, justices of the peace for Winchelsea, by Harriett, the wife of Robert Wheeler, labourer*:
who, on oath, charges Thomas Hoadley with neglecting to pay the sum of forty shillings and upwards for work and labour done by this examinant. [*mark of*] Harriett Wheeler   [WIN 237A]

676 3 Apr 1827 *Letter from Joseph Mills, [assistant overseer] Rye to [Charles] Arnett, Winchelsea, [assistant] overseer*:
Robert Wheeler, a parishioner of your parish has this morning informed me that he is in distress being ill and as there is no work for his boys they must come home and himself too except he has some assistance from you.   [PAR 511/35/1/271]
Note: During the quarter ending 25 June 1827 Robert Wheeler is recorded by the Winchelsea overseers as having received an allowance of 1s 7d per week.[17]

677 Sep 1841 *Account submitted by the overseers of Winchelsea to the Rye Union*:
[includes inter alia] September 11 R Wheeler to hospital: £1; [September] 14 R Wheeler from hospital: £1. [*Endorsed*] settled – George Blackman.

[PAR 511/35/1/364]

1 PAR 511/1/2/1   2 PAR 511/1/5/1   3 PAR 511/31/1/12 f.44   4 PAR 511/31/1/13 16 Sep 1825   5 ibid QE Dec 1825   6 PAR 511/12/3 13 October 1826   7 PAR 511/31/1/13 QE Mar 1828   8 PAR 511/1/5/1   9 PAR 511/37/7/29   10 PAR 511/31/1/16   11 ibid QE Mar 1835   12 G 8/1a/2 f.237 et seq   13 G 8/1a/3 ff.382-3 et seq   14 AMS 2329   15 PAR 511/31/1/11   16 PAR 511/31/1/13   17 PAR 511/31/1/15 f.19

Thomas Wheeler

678 *As a result of* (**679**) *Winchelsea sent Joseph Mills £4 7s 6d to be used in supporting Thomas Wheeler.[1] A casual payment of five shillings was allocated by the select vestry the following month,[2] and a further entry in the overseers' accounts reads, 'casual pay Thomas Wheeler sick 19s'.[3] Between his return to Winchelsea* (**680**) *and March 1830 he received casual payments usually of 2s 6d.[4]*

679 27 Jun 1828 *Letter from Joseph Mills, Rye, assistant overseer to [David] Laurence, Winchelsea, [assistant] overseer*:

[Thomas] Wheeler, your parishioner has applied to the overseers of this parish for some assistance. He is very old and stands in need of some medical attendance and as he has done nothing to gain a settlement in this parish you cannot wish to put us to the expense of removing him to Winchelsea, but take him without an order.

[PAR 511/35/1/318]

680 28 Jun 1828 *Removal order made by Nathaniel Porter and William Watson, justices of the peace for Rye to the churchwardens and overseers of the poor of that part of the parish of Rye which lies within the Liberty of the Ancient Town of Rye*:

Whereas complaint hath been made to us that Thomas Wheeler lately intruded and came into the said part of the parish of Rye and is become chargeable to the same, we upon examination of the [evidence] upon oath do adjudge this to be true and also adjudge the place of last legal settlement of Thomas Wheeler to be Winchelsea. These are therefore in His Majesty's name to require you to remove and convey him to Winchelsea and him deliver, together with this our order or a true copy thereof, to the churchwardens and overseers of the poor there who are hereby required to receive and provide for him according to law.

[PAR 511/32/3/57]

1 PAR 511/31/1/13 QE Jun 1828   2 PAR 511/12/3 11 Jul 1828   3 PAR 511/31/1/13 QE Sep 1828   4 PAR 511/12/3

John Whiteman

681 *During the four years before the date of (**682**) John Whiteman had been put out to service as a parish pauper in the households of John Tilden the magistrate, of Joash Jones the butcher, and of George Bray a Guestling farmer, all of whom feature elsewhere in this volume.[1] When his wish to go to sea was known, together with the arrangements proposed (**682**), Winchelsea parish, possibly through the influence of John Tilden, took considerable trouble over his case. Whiteman was granted the sum of £1 18s 6d as a casual payment 'to fit him for sea',[2] an amount which might well have been adequate to purchase the items suggested by Thomas Stephens (**682**). In addition to this the parish allowed him the cost of a shirt and of having his ½ boots repaired.[3] Clearly he soon became eager to remain at sea under Captain Stephens for on 22 March 1824 the parish vestry paid him £3 'to put him apprentice to T W Aylward'.[4] However, by 1827 he seems to have returned to Winchelsea for the select vestry 'Resolved that J Whiteman be allowed five shillings as a casual relief',[5] and in 1833 casual payments include, 'Mrs John Whiteman for her child five shillings'.[6] No record of either the marriage or of the child's birth appear in the parish registers.*

682 13 Nov 1823 *Letter from Captain Thomas Stephens, Rye, to the parish officers of Winchelsea*:

I am requested by John Whiteman to say what might be necessary in respect of clothing for him for a trial voyage. After questioning him regarding what he has I think that a jacket and trousers, two pairs of flannel drawers, a hat or cap, a pair of shoes, a bed sack and a pair of blankets might do for the present. Should he like it and be bound he will want more of course. Mr Thomas William Aylward will be his owner and he who has the honour to address you his master. I expect the ship will sail tomorrow morning.   [PAR 511/35/1/39]

1 PAR 511/12/1 f.237; PAR 511/12/2 ff. 13, 27   2 PAR 511/31/1/13 Sep 1823-Feb 1824   3 PAR 511/12/2 1 Jan 1824   4 PAR 511/31/1/12 f.106   5 PAR 511/12/3 9 Feb 1827   6 PAR 511/12/2 24 May 1833

Stephen Whiteman

683 *Stephen Whiteman was two years older than his brother John* (**681-682**) *and was 19 at the time it was proposed he follow his brother by going to sea as an apprentice* (**686**).[1] *Before this and after being put out as a pauper to the households of John Eagles and George Harrod* (**684-685**), *John Edward Wright also agreed to take him into service 'the parish to give one shilling a week and one pound for clothes'.[2] A year later he went back to George Harrod ' at one shilling a week, the parish to wash, mend and clothe him'.[3] This unpredictable lifestyle at the whim of the overseers understandably left him wanting something more permanent* (**686**) *and he seems to have done well* (**687**). *To facilitate this change the parish, on 28 Jun 1824, allowed him 'twenty shillings to go to sea'[4] and the overseers' accounts confirm the note on* (**686**) *by recording the payment of £2 on 20 August 1824.[5] This was confirmed by the select vestry a week later when it was resolved, 'that Stephen Whiteman be allowed two pounds having bound himself apprentice to Mr F Carder for four years'.[6] He appears no further in the parish records.*

684 24 Feb 1820 *Minute of the Winchelsea parish vestry*:
It is agreed for Mr John Eagles to employ Stephen Whiteman from Lady Day 1820 to Lady Day 1821 at 3s per week.   [PAR 511/12/1 f.237]

685 5 Apr 1821 *Minute of the Winchelsea select vestry:*
Resolved that Mr [George] Harrod agrees to take Stephen Whiteman from Mr Eagles, the parish to allow him one shilling a week and clothe him.
[PAR 511/12/2 f.11]
Note: Among other action taken in fulfilling the parish's obligation to clothe Whiteman the select vestry resolved on 2 May 1822, 'to allow Stephen Whiteman 1 round frock, 1 hat and a suit of clothes'.[7]

686 16 Aug 1824 *Letter from Nathaniel F Carder, London to [the overseers of Winchelsea]*:
In compliance with Stephen Whiteman's request to acquaint you when bound apprentice to me, you promised him a remittance of a few pounds. [I] have now to inform you [I] have this day bound him for four years and am glad to say he bids fair to make a sailor and appears to be a good tempered fellow. What money you think proper of sending him you might relay shall be carefully laid out in clothes for him, of which he is very bare. PS Please to direct for me at Mr Joel Ray's, ship

agent, George Lane, Lower Thames Street, London. I shall thank you to answer this by return of post as we leave in a few days.

[*Endorsed*] Sent him £2 Aug 20 [18]24.   [PAR 511/35/1/104]

687 4 Jun 1825 *Letter from Nathaniel F Carder, London to C[harles] Arnett, Winchelsea, guardian of the poor*:

I request you will have the goodness to inform Stephen Whiteman, an apprentice of mine who has lately been very unwell, ([I] was obliged to leave him in the hospital at St Michael's Island [?Isle of Man]) that I am now arrived in London. Please to desire him to set off immediately for London and apply to Mr Joel Ray, George Lane. My stay here will not be above five or six days. I trust you will excuse this liberty, not knowing Whiteman's address. I am pleased to acquaint you the lad behaves very well and I think will make a good sailor.

[PAR 511/35/1/175]

1 PAR 511/1/1/4   2 PAR 511/12/2 14 Feb 1822   3 ibid 13 Feb 1823   4 PAR 511/31/1/12 f.106   5 ibid   6 PAR 511/12/2 27 Aug 1824   7 PAR 511/12/2 f.26

George Willard

688 *George Willard, born 1796, the illegitimate son of Mary,[1] was, at the time of his request noted in (689) receiving the sum of 2s 6d in casual relief quite regularly, in fact he had done so the previous week.[2] This continued during the following quarter when his entry reads 'casual pay George Willard £1 12s 6d'.[3] Later that year he was given work by the surveyors of the highways at 1s 8d per day.[4] Casual payments continued during that employment and afterwards. On 27 March 1835 the public vestry resolved 'that George Willard receive 3s 6d in meat and flour – sick.[5] The following month he was paid 2s 6d for 'laying out G Easton'.[6] This was George Easton who had died aged 18.[7] In c.1836 George Willard was among Winchelsea's able-bodied poor.[8] Three years later the whole family were admitted by the Rye Union guardians to Brede workhouse.[9] They left after five months and George resumed work on the Winchelsea highways this time at two shillings a day.[10] He must again have been ill in 1840 for on 19 April in that year Edward Sladen Banks, the Winchelsea surgeon, submitted a note to the overseers stating, 'George Willard requires half a pound of mutton and a pint of porter daily'.[11] No record has been found that the overseers responded by making this allowance. At the time of the 1841 census he was entered as an agricultural labourer living in Cook Street (Barrack Square), Winchelsea, with his wife Mary 41 and children Frederick 10, Daniel 7 and Mary 1. Their son George junior aged 13 was working at The Castle Inn as a potboy – see appendix A35.*

689 19 Nov 1830 *Endorsed upon a letter from Mrs Hannah Francis, Brighton, to Joseph Bigg, Winchelsea, grocer, are notes concerning payments made to paupers and requests received*:

[inter alia] George Willard [asks] 2s 6d.   [PAR 511/35/1/341]

Note: On 6 November 1830 Winchelsea had made Willard a payment of 2s 6d.[12]

1 PAR 511/1/1/4   2 PAR 511/12/3 12 Nov 1830   3 PAR 511/31/1/13 QE Mar 1831   4 PAR 511/40/1/8   5 PAR 511/12/2   6 PAR 511/12/2 23 Apr 1835   7 PAR 511/1/5/1   8 PAR 511/37/7/29   9 G 8/19/4   10 PAR 511/40/1/9   11 PAR 511/37/7/27   12 PAR 511/31/1/15 f.39

John Willard

690 *The cross placed against John Willard's name in* (**691**) *suggests that any request he made would not be granted. However, on the same date the select vestry 'resolved that John Willard be allowed 1 pair shoes and a new hat'.[1] It may well be that he was a workhouse boy at the time of this clothing grant for he was admitted there in 1825.[2] Just after the Rye Union guardians were advised of his circumstances* (**692**) *they arranged for him to be given work on the Winchelsea highways with pay of two shillings a day.[3] John Willard remained in Winchelsea where he is recorded between 1847 and 1849 as a pauper excused payment of the poor rate.[4]*

691 19 Nov 1830 *Endorsed upon a letter from Mrs Hannah Francis, Brighton, to Joseph Bigg, Winchelsea, grocer, are notes concerning payments made to paupers and requests received*:
[inter alia] John Willard [entry marked] X.   [PAR 511/35/1/341]

692 16 Nov 1840 *Minute of the guardians of the Rye Union records payments of outdoor relief including*:
To John Willard aged 24 years belonging to Winchelsea parish having a wife and two children the eldest 1½ years, the youngest 3 months. He has been out of employment during the last fortnight; he has no permanent master and as an agricultural labourer does not obtain more than 2s per day. [*Allowed*] 2s and 2 galls flour.   [G 8/1a/3 f.297]

1 PAR 511/12/3 19 Nov 1830   2 ibid 19 Aug 1825   3 PAR 511/40/1/9   4 PAR 511/12/2

William Willard

693 *There were two William Willards with families in Winchelsea during the period covered by this volume, both receiving regular poor relief. The overseers' books make no distinction between payments made to them. They can be separately identified only by the removal of one of them from Guestling to Winchelsea* (**694**), *the names of their children entered in the appropriate records and by the residence of the other family in accommodation paid for by the parish at Moneycellar Houses (now known as Moneysellers). The problem is confounded by the fact that both had wives named Ann. It is William Willard of Moneycellar House, the father of John* (**690-692**), *who features in* (**695-701**). *A family listing made by the overseers in 1825[1] confirms that John was in the workhouse* (**690**). *His three sisters remained at home. As* (**696**) *makes clear, the whole family had earlier been workhouse inmates. One of the William Willards was quite often paid for breaking stones.[2] Another entry shows a payment of 1s 6d for killing a hog.[3] The recipient of those payments is unidentified but the William Willard junior who began receiving relief in 1830[4] was the oldest son of the family formerly of Guesting – see* (**694**) *and was paid weekly amounts varying between 3s 6d and 6d, the amount he was receiving in 1835 when surviving records cease.[5] More information is available about William Willard of Moneycellar Houses and his family because, despite the parish's earlier persistent and apparently eventually successful attempts to evict them, by the time of the 1841 census they had returned. Their census entry shows that William aged 55, agricultural labourer, was living there with Ann 50, and their children Mary 20,*

Hannah 18 and Ann 11. Their son John, 25, was also living with them with his own family,
his wife Charlotte, 25, and their children Charlotte 3 and George 11 months. The William
Willard of (**702-703**) *might by then be any one of the three.*

694 8 Jan 1811 *Removal order made by E J Curteis and Charles Lamb, justices*
of the peace for the county of Sussex to the churchwardens and overseers of the
parish of Guestling:
Whereas complaint has been made to us that William Willard and Ann his wife
and their one child viz. William aged about eleven months lately intruded and
came into the parish of Guestling and are actually become chargeable to the same,
upon due proof made thereof as well as upon the examination of William Willard
[we] do adjudge the place of legal settlement of William Willard his wife and
child to be the parish of St Thomas the Apostle, Winchelsea. [We] therefore in
His Majesty's name require you on sight hereof to remove and convey them to
Winchelsea and them deliver, together with this our order or a true copy thereof,
to the churchwardens and overseers of the poor there who are hereby required to
receive and provide for them according to law.   [PAR 511/32/3/22]

695 26 Sep 1822 *[Copy] notice of the churchwardens and overseers of the poor of*
Winchelsea to Mr George Bray [of Winchelsea]:
We, the undersigned, being churchwardens and overseers of the poor of the parish
of St Thomas the Apostle, Winchelsea, do hereby give you notice that Thomas
Edwards and William Willard, paupers of the said parish, will quit possession of
the messuages or tenements now in their occupation, and rented by the parish
officers for the time being, at Lady-Day next or at the expiration of the year's
tenancy if it should not end at Lady-Day and that we will deliver up the possession
thereof to you at that time.   [PAR 511/37/3/20]
Note: For Thomas Edwards see (**238-244**).

696 6 Nov 1823 *Minute the Winchelsea public vestry*:
Resolved that William Willard and family be taken into the house.[PAR 511/12/2]

697 15 Mar 1824 *Notice issued by the churchwardens and overseers of Winchelsea*
to George Bray, landlord:
We hereby give you warning of quitting that part of the Moneycellar Houses now
in the occupation of Thomas Edwards and that part lately occupied by William
Willard on or before Michaelmas next of which be pleased to take notice.
                    [PAR 511/37/3/26]

698 [24] Sep 1825 *Copy notice of the churchwardens and overseers of the poor of*
Winchelsea to Mr George Bray, landlord:
We hereby give you warning of quitting those two houses now in the occupation
of Thomas Edwards and William Willard on or before Lady-Day next of which be
pleased to take notice. [*Endorsed*] Copy of notice delivered to Mr George Bray,
Sept 24 1825, by me [*mark of*] John Chester.   [PAR 511/37/3/31]

699 13 Feb 1826 *Copy notice of the churchwardens and overseers of the poor of Winchelsea to Mr George Bray, landlord*:
We hereby give you warning of quitting all that part of the Moneycellar House and premises now in the occupation of Thomas Edwards and William Willard on or before Michaelmas next of which be pleased to take notice.
[Endorsed] Delivered same day *[mark of]* John Chester *[initials of]* Charles Arnett   [PAR 511/37/3/33]

700 11 Aug 1826 *Copy notice [of the Winchelsea overseers] to Thomas Edwards and William Willard:*
We hereby give you notice to quit that house and premises now in your occupation on or before this day month.
[Appended note] Served the 11th day of August 1826 by me, Henry Tilden.
                                                                        [PAR 511/37/3/17]

701 16 Sep 1826 *Appearance of Charles Arnett, assistant overseer, before Henry Powell and John Tilden, justices of the peace for Winchelsea*:
[Information] against Thomas Edwards and William Willard for unlawfully retaining possession of the[ir] houses and premises after due notice from the churchwardens and overseers or a major part of them.
23 Sep 1826 *[At a further hearing before the same magistrates]* Time given until Tuesday the 26th at 12 o'clock when they [were] to appear before the above two justices of the peace if they did not previously give up possession to the assistant overseer.
26 Sep 1826 *[At a further hearing]* the parties appeared again as they had not given up possession and a warrant granted against each to break open the house of each and forcibly to remove the goods.
[Notes of the outcome] Thomas Edwards hired the house he occupied of George Bray for the ensuing year. Willard's goods were removed by the constables.
                                                                        [WIN 237A]
Note: On 28 September 1826 a warrant was issued stating that the town constables were 'empowered, in the day time, to break open and enter into the dwelling house of William Willard and to take and remove the goods and chattels so that possession of the house may be had by the assistant overseer.' [6]

702 21 Jul 1841 *Account of the overseers of Winchelsea – December 1840 to March 1841*:
[inter alia] To William Willard, pauper, by order of R[ichard] Stileman Esq: 2s 6d.   [PAR 511/35/1/363]

703 27 Oct 1841 *Bill from W[alter] Fuller to the parish officers of Winchelsea*:
July: Relief ordered by Mr [Richard] Stileman to be given to William Willard: 2s
6d.
[*Endorsed*] Received for W[alter] Fuller [by] George Blackman.

[PAR 511/35/1/370]

1 PAR 511/31/1/15 f.20   2 PAR 511/31/1/13 e.g. QE Jun 1827   3 ibid QE Dec 1828   4 ibid QE Mar
1830   5 PAR 511/31/1/16   6 PAR 511/37/3/24

Gilbert Wood

704 *Winchelsea's earliest reference to Gilbert Wood was in 1813 when he was included
in a local militia liability list as 'servant to Edwin Dawes'.[1] In fact he was a footman.[2]
The reason that he was supplied with goods from the workhouse and additional items
purchased for him (705) is not clear. Three days after the date of the letter from Woolwich
(706) the select vestry resolved 'that Gilbert Wood, late servant of Edwin Dawes Esq,
(having become chargeable to the parish of Woolwich in the county of Kent) be allowed
one pound as a casual relief.[3] The settlement examination included in (706) confirms that
he had a wife and three children. For three years he lived without recorded relief from
Winchelsea. In 1830 he was given work on the highways at 1s 6d per day[4] but during that
employment he also received varying amounts in support of his family.[5] He received a
weekly allowance of 2s 9d reducing to 2s between March 1831 and October 1835.[6] When
his wife became ill Wood was allowed five shillings as a casual payment and Mrs [Mary]
Broadfoot and Elizabeth Alce were both paid five shillings by the parish for nursing her.[7]
It was Wood himself who was ill in 1834 when the public vestry resolved 'that Gilbert
Wood be allowed, 'till the doctor says he is able to work, 5s per week extra'.[8] In May
1839 the whole family were admitted by the Rye Union guardians to the Brede workhouse
where they stayed for three months.[9] Gilbert Wood was then given further employment on
the Winchelsea highways. His last recorded income from that work was on 18 December
1841.[10] It was a posthumous payment to his widow for he had died the previous day and
was buried at St Thomas's four days later.[11] The inquest jury recorded a verdict of death by
natural causes.[12] It has to be said that the prejudices and attitudes of those hearing the case
would have made it most unlikely that a complaint by a pauper woman such as Margaret
Wood against a Rye Union official, the medical officer, (707-709), would have been upheld.
Nevertheless the matter was given a good airing. Although the applicant's first name is
not known, it is quite possible that Gilbert Wood, during the last year of his life, hoped to
emigrate to New Zealand and sought financial help from Winchelsea (967).*

705 [28 Nov 1826] *Entry in the inventory book of the Winchelsea workhouse*:
List of goods had by Gilbert Wood: 1 bedstead, 1 flock bed, 3 blankets, 1 chaff
bed, 2 rugs, 1 bolster and 1 pillow, 1 pair of sheets. Goods bought of Fullers for G.
Wood's use: 1 bedstead, 1 square table, 1 washing table, 4 chairs, 1 water crock,
1 stool, 1 fender, 1 gridiron, 1 saucepan, 1 candlestick, tin can, 1 bowl, 1 teapot, 1
tea cup and saucer.   [AMS 2331]

706 21 Aug 1827 *Letter from W Stripe, Woolwich, [Kent], vestry clerk, to the overseers of Winchelsea*:

I am desired by the overseers of the poor of this parish to transmit the annexed examination of Gilbert Wood, a parishioner of yours, and to state his desire not to be removed home if it be possible. He has been ill which threw him out of employ and his desire is that he may be relieved until he obtains another situation and if you request it this parish will relieve him with such sum as you may deem proper under his circumstances. He has been relieved and we [a]wait your reply in order that we may determine how much. The reason why this has not been sent e'er this is the overseer of this parish had laid the examination aside and forgot it.

[*Endorsed*] 10 Aug 1827 *Settlement examination of Gilbert Wood now residing in the parish of Woolwich, Kent*: He never rented a house of £10 a year or 4s a week; about fifteen years ago, being a single man, he hired himself to [Edwin] Dawes of Winchelsea, Esq for a year at 16 guineas a year wages and he served him for three years and upwards; he has not done any act to gain a settlement since to his knowledge and he has a lawful wife named Margaret and three children John (6 years), Mary (3 years) and Sarah (9 months).   [PAR 511/35/1/294]

707 21 Dec 1840 *Minute of the guardians of the Rye Union*:

A report having been made at this meeting of an aggravated want of attention on the part of Mr [Edward Sladen] Banks, the medical officer, in the case of a child of Gilbert Wood of Winchelsea having a broken arm, it was resolved that the clerk do inform Mr Banks thereof and further resolved that at the next meeting of the board such report be taken into consideration and that Mr Banks be requested to attend thereat. Ordered that the clerk do send Mr Banks a copy of the above resolution. Ordered that the clerk request the attendance of Mrs Wood, the mother of the child above alluded to, at the next meeting of the board to state the particulars of the inattention of Mr Banks.   [G 8/1a/3 f.336]

708 28 Dec 1840 *Minute of the guardians of the Rye Union*:

Resolved that the consideration of the report made at the previous meeting of the inattention of Mr Banks in the case of the child of Gilbert Wood of Winchelsea having a broken arm be adjourned to the next meeting of the board in consequence of Mrs Wood not being able to attend (as requested) at this meeting and the father of the child who, being present, was not able to give such information on the case as enabled the board to proceed with the inquiry into the alleged inattention of Mr Banks. Ordered that the clerk request Mr Banks and also Mrs Wood to attend at the next meeting of the board for the purpose of making their statements relating to the report alluded to.   [G 8/1a/3 f.342]

Note: Mr Banks later attended this meeting and made his statement but agreed to repeat it at the next meeting.[13]

709 4 Jan 1841 *Minute of the guardians of the Rye Union*:
At this meeting Mr Banks and Mrs Wood attended as requested and of whom respectively inquiries were made relating to the report of 'an aggravated want of attention on the part of Mr Banks the medical officer in the case of the child of Gilbert Wood of Winchelsea having a broken arm'. This board is of the opinion that there had not been such an aggravated want of attention on the part of Mr Banks as is referred to by such report.   [G 8/1a/3 ff.348-9]

1 WIN 1732   2 WIN 1733   3 PAR 511/12/3 24 Aug 1827   4 PAR 511/40/1/5 20 Feb 1830 et seq 5 PAR 511/31/1/13 Mar 1830-Mar 1831   6 PAR 511/31/1/16   7 PAR 511/12/2 3 Jun 1831   8 PAR 511/12/2 12 Nov 1834   9 G 8/19/4   10 PAR 511/40/1/9   11 PAR 511/1/5/1   12 DAP Box 70/1   13 G 8/1a/3 ff.342-3

David Woodzell (Woodsell)

710 *The Winchelsea records indicate that, at the time of William Woodhams' letter* (**712**), *David Woodzell was living at Playden with his wife and two children. It was there, presumably, that Woodhams could offer work. Winchelsea payments to David Woodzell ceased at the beginning of this employment but were very soon resumed when he, like his wife earlier* (**711**), *became ill.[1] After various casual payments the select vestry resolved on 11 June 1829 'That David Woodzell have nine shillings per week while he is sick'.[2] That was a generous allowance, perhaps too generous to be sustained for the following month it was decided 'that David Woodzell be taken into the [work]house with his wife and family'.[3] He died in 1831 and was buried in Winchelsea.[4]*

711 18 Apr 1828 *Minute of the Winchelsea select vestry*:
Resolved that David Woodzell be allowed the parish doctor and 5s for a nurse for his wife.   [PAR 511/12/3]

712 27 Jun 1828 *Letter from William Woodhams, Udimore, to the parish officers of Winchelsea*:
I shall have no objection to finding David Woodzell work, his living in a cottage of mine to be handy to his work, on the parish of Winchelsea sending me acknowledgement of his being a parishioner of theirs and that they will relieve him as such. I shall be oblige[d] to you to return me your sentiments on the subject. I have another person wish the place.   [PAR 511/35/1/317]
Note: If the Winchelsea overseers wrote to William Woodhams acknowledging Woodzell as their parishioner, no copy of the document survives. However, it seems likely that the offer of work was taken up and Winchelsea certainly continued to support Woodzell with casual allowances of both cash and flour.[5]

1 PAR 511/31/1/13 QE Sep 1828   2 PAR 511/12/3   3 ibid 23 Jul 1829   4 PAR 511/1/5/1   5 PAR 511/31/1/15 f.32

Katharine Wright

713 *No mention of Katharine Wright's case, apart from these two letters, has been found in the Winchelsea records.*

714 20 Sep 1827 *Letter from Colonel F[ielding] Browne, Winchelsea to [Charles] Arnett, [Winchelsea assistant overseer]:*
Miss Wright has again made application to the magistrates respecting her parish matter and as we, the magistrates, are desirous of getting it settled as far as we are concerned, it will be necessary you should be here for that purpose as early today as you can make it convenient.   [PAR 511/35/1/297]

715 21 Sep 1827 *Letter from Katharine Wright, New Inn, [Winchelsea] to the chairman of the select vestry, Winchelsea:*
I have been advised that as I am deserted by my father, Mr Wright, and having no means myself of gaining a livelihood and the proper course for me to pursue is to apply to the parish vestry who are to direct their officers to take me before the magistrates in petty sessions for the purpose of obtaining an order of maintenance on and from my father. I shall be in attendance in the hope that the vestry will favour me with an audience.   [PAR 511/35/1/298]

Unidentified paupers

716 *No further information has been found about those who are the subject of this letter.*

717 Mar 1826 *Letter from Thomas Bonds, Winchelsea to [?George] Bray:*
I have seen the lads – the one that has been to sea says that he has agreed to go to Mr B and therefore think you know better. Settle that point first. I shall be at my ?barge on Sunday if you can come.   [PAR 511/35/1/212]

Requests for the services of Winchelsea paupers

718 *The following letters, with the exception of (728), while adding nothing to the available knowledge about individual paupers featured in this volume, admirably demonstrate the attitudes of those to whom paupers were 'put out' usually as a way of reducing poor rate expenditure.*

719 17 Apr 1824 *Letter from G L Stidolph, 6 Wellington Place, Hastings to C[harles] Arnett, Winchelsea, assistant overseer:*
We are in want of a girl about 14 years of age to raise a child and make herself useful and, understanding by persons that have been supplied by you with useful girls, that you could send us one that you can recommend; should therefore be glad to have one as soon as possible. [I] will thank you to send word by return of posts if we can have a girl of the above description and what you give with them per week

and when we might have one. The principal [duty] will be to take care of a child at our lodging house as we have lodgers to attend to ourselves at present.

[PAR 511/35/1/76]

720 29 May 1824 *Letter from Thomas Milles, [East] Guldeford to [the overseers of Winchelsea]*:

Some time since your parish applied to me to take some labourers. I propose sending 2 pairs of oxen and 2 carts to carry some ditching stuff, say about 1000 loads. If you have 2 men or 1 man and a stout lad I can take them in the course of a week. Please reply by first post. If you have any man say your terms.

[PAR 511/35/1/87]

721 10 Jun 1824 *Letter from Thomas Milles, Combwell, [Goudhurst, Kent] to [the overseers of Winchelsea]*:

I have been to [East] Guldeford this day, first having seen the men at ?Sleath's request to know if it will be convenient for you to send them; the carts were sent on Monday last. If it should not be convenient to you to do as you have proposed have the goodness to drop me a line by return of post addressed as above.

[PAR 511/35/1/89]

722 9 Sep 1825 *Letter from Benjamin Page, 6 Caroline Cottages, Hastings to [the overseers of Winchelsea*:

This note requires of the parish officers if there should be any girls that is a burden to the parish from 12 to 15 years of age that is capable of taking care of a child and likewise necessary uses about the house such as cleaning of knifes and forks, lighting fires etc for the winter as the general terms begin at Michaelmas and what conditions you put them out upon. They must be honest as there is several temptations at times as I am in the habit of taking lodgers during the summer season.   [PAR 511/35/1/193]

723 8 Apr 1826 *Letter from William Woodhams, Udimore to [Charles] Arnett, Winchelsea, assistant overseer*:

If you have a boy in the house man enough to send crows I [would] wish him go with my people this morning and I wish him to continue going every day till I let you know. In sending one you will oblige.   [PAR 511/35/1/215]

724 10 Mar 1827 *Letter from Colonel Fielding Browne to [Charles] Arnett, [Winchelsea, assistant overseer]*:

I should wish that William may come up here tomorrow morning. We want him to do little jobs in assisting the servants as one of them has left us today and we have not yet replaced her and as I do not wish that he should lose any advantage of learning, if you will send his book with him, I will examine him in his lessons.

[PAR 511/35/1/262]

Note: The subject of this letter was William Bacon. Col Browne, initially, paid two shillings a week for William's labour.[1] The arrangement was later changed so that the colonel, an influential Winchelsea Corporation member, in return for providing the boy with lodging and clothing, received two shillings a week from the parish.[2]

725 16 Mar 1827 *Letter from William Campbell, Hastings to C[harles] Arnett, Winchelsea, [assistant overseer]*:
A neighbour of mine wished me to write to you to inform him if you have a girl of about 12 or 13 years of age to put out at Lady Day and the terms that you will agree to. He wishes an answer as soon as convenient. The person that wants a girl is Mr Day, grocer, close by Clark's baker – you may write either [to] him or me as you please. My respects to Mrs Arnett and self. Hoping you are both in good health.
[PAR 511/35/1/264]

726 3 Apr 1827 *Letter from William Campbell, Priory, Hastings to C[harles] Arnett, Winchelsea, [assistant overseer]*:
I received yours and mentioned to Mr Day and the terms he proposes are 1s per week and you to clothe the girl or allow him 30s per year and him to clothe her. He wishes for a good honest sturdy girl. He wishes for an answer as soon as convenient. Hoping you are all well.
[PAR 511/35/1/270]

727 12 Sep 1827 *Letter from James Cox, 1 Great Bourne Street, Hastings, town crier, to the overseers of Winchelsea*:
The present is to enquire if you have a good girl about 13 or 14 that you wish to put out to service as Mrs Cox is in want of one. If you have one you think will answer you will much oblige by sending one as soon as possible who we will take a month upon trial and if she answers the purpose will agree to take her for a year under such proposals as you may think proper to make. In so doing you will much oblige. PS If you have not one pray send an answer immediately.
[PAR 511/35/1/296]

728 26 Mar 1829 *Minute of the Winchelsea select vestry*:
Resolved that Mr Joseph Dixon of Sunderland has undertaken to apprentice two boys of this parish to the sea service on the following conditions viz: that the parish should fit them out well with necessary sea clothing, bed and bedding; that he will bind them for 6 years at £40 wages and 12s a year for washing. [Further resolved] that the parish officers be directed to peruse the above necessaries for George Perigo and Francis Saunders, the former aged 16 years and 10 months and the latter 14 years and 9 months who are desirous of entering the sea service and that they be forwarded to Sunderland by sea by the earliest opportunity.
[PAR 511/12/3]

Notes 1. George Perigo was a member of the Winchelsea pauper family of John Perigo who are not featured in this volume. The only mention found of relief paid directly to George is that, in January 1826, he was provided with six yards of flannel which cost 9s 6d[3] and the parish paid 4s 4d for his schooling for six months (**770**).

2. Francis Saunders was one of the children of Thomas and Elizabeth Saunders – see (**488**). His only noted direct allowance is that on 1 April 1824 the parish paid for him to have a new pair of shoes.[4]

729 16 Nov 1830 *Letter from William French, Landgate, Rye, baker to [David] Laurence, Winchelsea, [assistant] overseer*:

As I have not received any answer respecting of a boy that Mrs French [came] to see you about, if you will let me know by the return of post if you have got one to suit me I will thank you to send him for me to see him. If not, send me word that I may get another. And by doing so you will much oblige.   [PAR 511/35/1/343]

Note: A William French, of Guestling and later Rye, was the father of Lucy Barnes's illegitimate child – see (**55-61**) but no evidence has been discovered to suggest that this is the same William French.

1 PAR 511/12/3 15 Mar 1827   2 ibid 2 May 1828   3 PAR 511/31/2/129   4 PAR 511/12/2

The Barrack Houses photographed in 1912

Despite the date of the photograph and the presence of the postman the scene is
highly reminiscent of the time when these houses were occupied by the poor.
Reproduced by permission of Melvyn Pett with acknowledgement to
The Francis Frith Collection

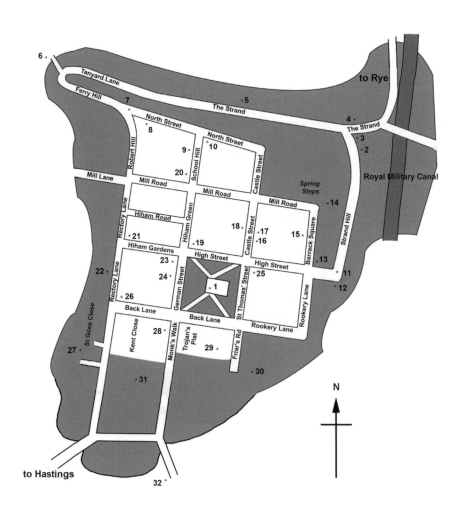

Map of Winchelsea

Based, with permission, on a map originally created by Melvyn Pett

Key to Winchelsea Plan opposite

1	St. Thomas's Church
2	Winchelsea Workhouse (now Strand Guest House)
3	Apple Tree Wick
4	The Old Malt House
5	The Tanyard/Pear Tree Marsh
6	Ferry House
7	Pipewell Gate
8	Moneycellar/Moneyseller House
9	school
10	The Five Houses
11	Strand Gate
12	The Lookout
13	The Retreat
14	Cooks Green
15	The Barrack Houses
16	town well
17	The Armoury (formerly The Bear)
18	The Castle Inn (now Old Castle House)
19	Court Hall (Guildhall)
20	Pound Cottage
21	Paradise
22	Blackfriars Barn
23	New Inn
24	Rose Cottage
25	Firebrand
26	The Oast House
27	The Old Rectory & St Giles's Churchyard
28	Mariteau House
29	Monday's Market
30	Greyfriars (The Friars)
31	Wall Field
32	road to New Gate

Notes:

1. For most of the period covered by this volume the town pound, where animals found wandering in the street were taken, was not at the present site of Pound Cottage but in the north-east corner of the Mariteau House plot.
2. The spelling Hiham, currently in use, was formerly Higham.
3. The road now called Barrack Square was also known as Factory Square (after the cambric factory which was once there), Cook Street because it led to Cooks Green, and, simply, The Square.
4. Strand Hill was also known as Tower Hill.

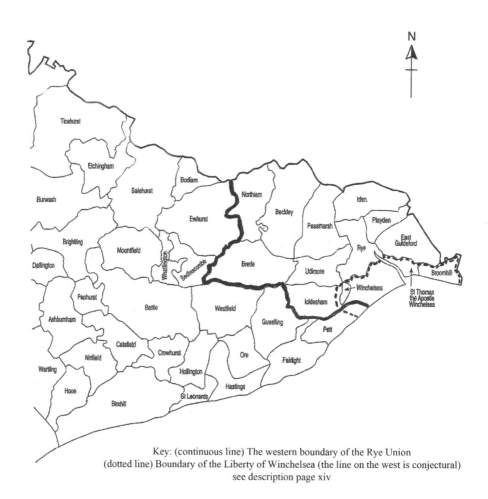

Key: (continuous line) The western boundary of the Rye Union
(dotted line) Boundary of the Liberty of Winchelsea (the line on the west is conjectural)
see description page xiv

The pre-1894 parishes of Eastern Sussex

from *An Historical Atlas of Sussex* (1999)
edited by Kim Leslie and Brian Short
reproduced by kind permission of the editors

Part II Topics

Preface

As this project developed and it became part of editorial policy that all the original letters (PAR 511/35/1/1-371) should be included, it was clear that their important subject matter included not only the affairs of the individual paupers who feature in Part I but also other more general topics relevant to the poor and the parish officers responsible for them.

Research similar to that undertaken for each pauper has revealed much documentary evidence used here to elaborate these topics: the Winchelsea workhouse (**730-800**); the administration of the parish (**801-859**); the revaluation of poor rate assessments (**860-880**); poor rate payment collection and general legal costs (**881-910**); parish tithes (**911-951**); emigration (**952-971**); and Winchelsea's inclusion within the Rye Poor Law Union (**972-998**).

As is explained briefly at their commencement, the amount of available material about the first two of these, the workhouse and parish administration, was too great to present in purely chronological order. Clarity required it to be divided in order to create sub-topics and separate sections consisting of closely related items. That is how they appear in this final arrangement. The documents in these sections speak for themselves except that it has been possible to include in the note following (**771**) an important development in Rye Union workhouse provision after 1840, namely that part of the Winchelsea Barrack Houses was adapted for Union workhouse use. Further information about Winchelsea's original workhouse is also available from the findings of Sir Frederick Morton Eden (see Select Bibliography and also p. xxi-xxii). He wrote of the situation in 1795, 'The number of poor in the parish poorhouse is 15 of whom 8 are children. The house is a very small one. No work is carried on within but a few paupers occasionally earn a little from driving the plough, watching new sown fields etc.'

It is perhaps also necessary to add background information on the overseers' relationship with Winchelsea's courts (**841-845**). The divided responsibility between the overseers, particularly the salaried assistant overseer, and the magistrates in so small a community clearly tended to create friction. The overseers had to refer constantly to the court on matters such as discipline, settlement, removal and tenancy. The index in itself illustrates how many times Charles Arnett appeared during his years in Winchelsea and, since this volume concerns only half of the Winchelsea paupers of the period (see Appendix B1) there is no doubt that he would have been required to attend court even more frequently. Although a large number of those appearances were at Arnett's request, he must have felt inhibited by this restriction on his authority to act. The principal cause of the dispute detailed in (**841-845**) was the cost of such constant referrals, particularly the cost of the attendance of the magistrates' clerk, a function performed ex-officio by the Corporation's town clerk who was a solicitor living and working in Rye. His court work therefore incurred time and travelling costs. Unfortunately the same person was usually the solicitor who acted when required on behalf of the parish. It was doubt over in which capacity he was dealing with this court work which created the dispute which features here and the arguments repay close examination.

The inclusion of parish tithes as a topic in Part II is dictated by the content of the letters, despite seeming largely unrelated to a study of the Poor Law. However, while most of (**911-951**) concern disputes with the rector and parish administration related to the assessment of tithes due from properties, (**942**) and (**943**) bring starkly into focus the fact that some Winchelsea residents, including paupers, were still being pursued through the courts for tithe payments as late as 1827.

The sections on the revaluation of poor rate assessments, parish tithes, emigration and the Rye Poor Law Union have their own separate introductory information at **860, 911, 952** and **972** respectively.

The Workhouse (Poorhouse)

730 *The Winchelsea workhouse was situated in the buildings which are now The Strand Guest House at the foot of Strand Hill. The date on which it began to serve this purpose for the Winchelsea community is not known. The building was eventually sold into private ownership in 1840* (**792-796**) *Unfortunately, of the records kept by the workhouse officials, only an inventory dated 11 April 1831 survives – see* (**760**). *The many documents related to the workhouse and its administration which exist within other Winchelsea records and within the minutes of the guardians of the Rye Union have, for convenience, been subdivided by subject below. An important account of the workhouse in the mid- 1830s is at* (**761-762**).

The Workhouse – repairs to and extension of the building

731 4 May 1800 *Minute of the Winchelsea public vestry*:
At this vestry which was summoned on Sunday last for the purpose of taking into consideration the state of the parish and the necessary repairs and alterations of the poorhouse. It is agreed [that] the parish house being too small for the purpose and incapable of containing the number of poor that the parish officers might find convenient to place in it (to the great increase of the public expenses) it is thought expedient and the churchwardens and overseers are hereby empowered to accede to the proposal of Thomas Marten and Richard Denne Esquires to purchase of them the house now inhabited by [*blank*] Tileman for the sum of forty-two pounds. [Further agreed that] whereas a survey has been taken of the poorhouse which is found to be in very bad condition, and an estimate has been made in consequence of the expense of repairing it and of making a convenient communication with the

house adjoining now purchased by the parish, which estimate amounts to about £80 to be raised in addition to the usual supplies and whereas the poor's rates are greatly burdened by the necessary allowance in consequence of the high price of corn and other provisions, it is further agreed that the sum of £125 be borrowed on the credit of the parish for the purchase and repairs of the aforesaid premises and that the debt and interest be discharged within the term of five years at the farthest from this day. The churchwardens and overseers are therefore empowered to borrow the sum above-mentioned and to give their security on account of the parish.   [PAR 511/12/1 folios 114-116]

Note: The building purchased as a result of this minute was that once known as Crowsnest (also Hillside Cottage) which now remains an integral part of Strand Guest House.[1]

732 30 Apr 1815 *Minute of the Winchelsea parish vestry*:
At a vestry held this day it is agreed that Mr [James] Griffiths of Bexhill, surveyor, do take a survey of the poorhouse and make a written statement of the state thereof, whether advisable to repair it and to give an estimate of the expense.
                                                          [PAR 511/12/1 f.199]

733 9 Jul 1815 *Minute of the Winchelsea parish vestry*:
[Resolved] at a vestry held this day to take into consideration an estimate made by Mr Griffiths of work necessary to be done to repair the workhouse at Winchelsea which estimate amounts to the sum of £151. It is agreed that the repairs should be immediately begun and the money borrowed to be repaid by yearly instalments of £50 until the whole is paid off.   [PAR 511/12/1 f.199]

734 9 Oct 1823 *Minute of Winchelsea public vestry*:
At a vestry held this day pursuant to public notice it is resolved that a committee consisting of Mr [Henry] Powell, Mr [George] Stace, Mr [Richard] Stileman, Mr [Edward] Jeakens, and Mr [William] Sargent be appointed with power to have a plan made out for a new building in addition to the present poorhouse and on the ground belonging to the parish and to get an estimate of the same from some independent and indifferent [*i.e. disinterested*], experienced person and to lay the same before a vestry with such observations as suggest themselves on the subject.
                                                                [PAR 511/12/2]

735 31 Mar 1825 *Minute of the Winchelsea parish vestry*:
Resolved that Mr W[illiam] Chatterton having offered a messuage, garden and premises near the workhouse for £100, such offer to be taken into consideration at the next public vestry.   [PAR 511/12/2]

736 7 Apr 1825 *Minute of the Winchelsea public vestry*:
Resolved that Messrs [Richard] Stileman, [John Edward] Wright and [George] Stace be appointed as a committee to examine into the state of the poorhouse and report to a public vestry if it requires any addition or alteration and in case they

should be of opinion that an addition is necessary to report on the expediency of purchasing the house belonging to Mr William Chatterton or altering the present.

[PAR 511/12/2]

737 19 Apr 1825 *Valuation by James Blackman, land and building surveyor, Rye*:
A valuation of a messuage or tenement and garden situated at Winchelsea at the back of the poorhouse between that and the road leading to Rye, consisting of a timber and [tile deleted, correction illegible] building, two rooms and a [?an outhouse] with a garden, amounts to the sum of seventy nine pounds ten shillings. £79 10s 0d.   [PAR 511/13/3]

738 21 Apr 1825 *Minute of the Winchelsea public vestry*:
Resolved that the parish officers be authorised to treat with Mr William Chatterton for the house and premises as offered by him and not to give more than £80.

[PAR 511/12/2]

739 27 Apr 1825 *[Record of a public meeting held at the vestry room]*:
We the undersigned inhabitants and occupiers of the parish do hereby consent and agree to purchase the house now in the occupation of Thomas Wimble, situate near the present poorhouse at the sum asked for the same viz £80 by Mr [William] Chatterton who as mortgagee is authorised and empowered to sell it, as agreed upon at a general vestry.   [PAR 511/12/2]
Note: The resolution is followed by 32 signatures including, unusually, two women – Elizabeth Hollingberry, wife of John Hollingberry overseer and churchwarden, and Mary Denne, wife of Richard Denne owner of Mariteau House. John Hollingberry also signed. Richard Denne was not present.

740 31 Mar 1826 *Copy resolution of the Winchelsea parish vestry*:
It was agreed that the parish should pay to Mr Chatterton the above amount of purchase (viz forty pounds at Christmas 1826 and forty pounds at Christmas 1827, the parish to take possession at Midsummer 1826; after that time the purchase money unpaid to remain at the interest of £5 per cent with a note of hand from the present parish officers. The expense of conveyance and making good title to be paid one moiety [half] by Mr William Chatterton and the other moiety by the parish.   [PAR 511/13/4]
Note: The property purchased from Mr Chatterton was that now known as Apple Tree Wick beside the A.259. It became part of the former workhouse but is now again in separate ownership.

741 6 May 1826 *Letter from Weeden Dawes [solicitor], Rye to [Charles] Arnett, Winchelsea, assistant overseer*:
My partners have put into my hands (being a parishioner of Winchelsea) the draft of a conveyance handed to them by Mr Miller, a professional gentleman of this town, to peruse on behalf of several gentlemen made parties thereto, for my

perusal and I find it to be a conveyance of a house at Winchelsea to yourself in trust for the use of the poor. As I and my partners have for many years been the solicitors for the parish in their several matters relating to the parish requiring the assistance of professional gentlemen I beg leave to ask if anything has occurred in the conduct of either of us to induce the parish to transfer their confidence to another professional gentleman. If that should be the case I and my partners feel from the long intercourse that has subsisted between us, particularly with myself, that if we have given the parish cause to change their professional adviser, that we should have had the same communicated to us and I hope the parish will indulge us with the reason for inducing them to transfer their parish business to another. I, as a parishioner, wish to be informed who has examined the title on behalf of the parish to the property about to be conveyed. [PAR 511/35/1/224]

Note: No response to this letter has been discovered.

1. see Martins p.137

The workhouse – matters affecting the inmates

742 29 Dec 1766 *Minute of the Winchelsea public vestry*:
At a vestry holden this day it is ordered that the parish officers do have the poor of the parish inoculated by Mr Slaughter at the rate of five shillings and threepence each, the expenses not exceeding fifteen pounds and fifteen shillings and that the [poor]house is the place appointed to receive them. [PAR 511/12/1 f.27]

Notes: 1. This document pre-dates the period covered by this volume but is published to illustrate that Winchelsea was very early taking action to inoculate the poor against smallpox. They all had to go to the workhouse for the procedure and non-inmates had to remain there because at that time it was believed that, for some time after inoculation, a person was infectious.[1]

2. In 1814 a Mr R Henderson submitted to the overseers an account for vaccinating 11 children of the parish including three who were in the workhouse. He charged 2s 6d per child.[2]

3. See also (**813**).

743 4 May 1800 *Minute of the Winchelsea public vestry*:
Resolved that J Ceinon being affected with a cancerous disorder which is too offensive for his residence in the poorhouse, the byelaw of the 31 March 1796 shall in this instance be suspended and his rent be paid by the parish.

[PAR 511/12/1 f.115]

Note: Nothing has been discovered about the nature of Ceinon's affliction or the property rented for him. It is, however, recorded that Jean Baptiste Ceinon was buried at St Thomas's on 25 January 1804.[3]

744 16 Jun 1811 *Minute of the Winchelsea parish vestry*:
It is unanimously agreed that the parish officers are to put out the paupers of the poorhouse to any householders in the parish or elsewhere to keep, clothe etc as they shall think proper to agree for. [PAR 511/12/1 f.177]

745 15 Jun 1820 *Minute of the Winchelsea select vestry*:
Resolved that clothing be allowed to the inmates of the workhouse and six pairs of sheets for the use of same.   [PAR 511/12/2 f.1]

746 13 Jul 1820 *Minute of the Winchelsea select vestry*:
Resolved that the old people of the poorhouse have cheese provided for breakfast.
[PAR 511/12/2 f.2]
Note: The decision that cheese should be provided for breakfast was later varied by a resolution that this provision should be 'once a day'.[4]

747 27 Jul 1820 *Minute of the Winchelsea select vestry*:
It being understood that some of the paupers who are allowed flour have taken bread instead of it and have refused this unless quite new, it is therefore resolved that in future they be supplied with flour instead of bread.   [PAR 511/12/2 f.2]
Note: Many workhouse expenses in support of the inmates are recorded. A fairly typical example is dated within the quarter ending 25 March 1821: '13 weeks yeast at 6d per week 6s 6d; 11 weeks schooling 6 children at 6d per week 5s 6d; 1 dozen of brooms 1s; for cutting 7 boys' hair 7d; for sand and matches 6d; 2 pairs breeches for John Whiteman 8s; for 13 weeks bedding at 1s 2d per week 15s 2d.' [total] £1 17s 3d.[5]

748 28 Jun 1824 *Minute of the Winchelsea select vestry*:
Resolved that Charles Arnett, assistant overseer, be empowered to procure straw for the purpose of setting the children of the parish to work.   [PAR 511/12/2]
Note: The straw is most likely to have been for plaiting needed for the making of hats (see also **547**).

749 8 Jul 1824 *Minute of an adjourned meeting of the Winchelsea select vestry*:
Resolved that Charles Arnett be authorised to agree with Bates for a term to instruct the children of this parish to plait grass etc. at [*blank*] per week.   [PAR 511/12/2]

750 5 Nov 1824 *Minute of the Winchelsea select vestry*:
Resolved that Edward Bennett be taken before the magistrates for his bad conduct in the workhouse, it being the wish of the select vestry that he be punished.
[PAR 511/12/2]

751 2 Apr 1831 *Minute of the Winchelsea parish vestry*:
That the parish having agreed to break up the establishment of the poorhouse, that David Laurence be allowed to see the poor persons in the house and make such arrangements he can with them and report same to the next vestry.[PAR 511/12/2]

752 7 Apr 1831 *Minute of the Winchelsea parish vestry*:
[*following David Laurence's report – see* (**751**)] [Resolved] that Joseph Claise be allowed 3s per week to go from the poorhouse; that Thomas Chester be allowed 3s per week and find himself board etc and be allowed the use of one room in the

poorhouse; that Joseph Bailey be allowed 5s per week for himself and son and to live with Chester; that Mrs Clandenbold be allowed 4s per week and the use of one room in the house; that Mrs Martin be allowed 4s per week and the same terms as Mrs Clandenbold; that Mrs Hoad take her two children from the house and be allowed 2s 3d per head; that Henry Tilden be allowed 6s per week as beadle and he keep himself. [PAR 511/12/2]

Note: Henry Tilden's six shillings per week was paid regularly from this time until his death in 1835 aged 77.[6] He received a pauper's funeral with the parish paying 2s 6d for his laying out and thirteen shillings for 'bearers and washing and cleaning'.[7]

1 Crook (2006) p.23   2 PAR 511/31/2/120   3 PAR 511/1/1/4   4 PAR 511/12/2 f.13 dated 3 May 1821   5 PAR 511/31/2/134   6 PAR 511/31/1/16; PAR 511/1/5/1   7 PAR 511/31/1/16 QE Mar 1835

The workhouse - administration

753 20 May 1804 *Minute of the Winchelsea public vestry*:
We do hereby agree with Thomas Harriott to take charge of the poor in the workhouse from the 24th of June next to Lady Day following at the rate of £15 per annum.
[*endorsed*] I do hereby agree to take charge of the poor in the workhouse on the above terms.
[*signature of*] Thomas Harriott [PAR 511/12/1 f.141]

754 3 Oct 1815 *Letter from office of the Secretary of State, Whitehall, [London] to J[ohn] E[dward] Wright, Winchelsea*:
I herewith return you the printed schedule marked 'A' forwarded by you in pursuance of the provisions of the Act of George III 55 c47 relative to the expense and maintenance of the poor. As you will perceive upon referring to the second clause of that Act that it is required that the schedule in question should be certified and signed by the governor of the workhouse or house of industry (as the case may be) or else that it should be expressly stated that there is no workhouse or house of industry and as the schedule forwarded by you is definite in this particular, I have to require it may be amended and forthwith returned addressed to the Secretary of State. [PAR 511/35/1/4]
Note: The response has not survived among these records.

755 24 Apr 1816 *Insurance policy No 14699 taken out with the Invicta Kent Fire Office by the churchwardens and overseers of the poor of Winchelsea for the Winchelsea workhouse*:
[*Described as*] A dwelling house only, brick plaster and tiled at Winchelsea in their own tenure [for a sum] not exceeding one hundred pounds. Household furniture therein not exceeding £100. Annual premium 5s 6d plus duty 6s: total 11s 6d.
[PAR 511/37/7/2]

756 6 Apr 1820 *Minute of the Winchelsea public vestry*:
It is agreed for Master and Mrs [John] Sinden to be governor and governess of the poorhouse. [PAR 511/12/1 f.238]
Note: See also (**505**).

757 29 Aug 1823 *Letter from Nicholas Wratten, Tenterden [Kent] to [George] Hill and [Joseph] Bigg, Winchelsea, overseers*:
In consequence of your public notice for a master and matron of your workhouse I beg leave to apply for the same and refer you for a character both of my wife and myself to J[ohn] B[utler] Pomfret Esq, Tenterden and [Richard] Stileman Esq, Winchelsea.
[*endorsed*] Witnesses – Richard Cooper, William Colvin, Tenterden.
[PAR 511/35/1/20]

758 1 Sep 1823 *Letter from William Watson, Rye to the overseers of Winchelsea*:
John West (the bearer hereof) having informed me that he has made application to be appointed master of the poorhouse at Winchelsea and that it is necessary for him to produce testimonials of his good conduct, I beg to say that I believe him to be a sober, honest and civil man and very trustworthy. I have known his wife also many years and believe her to be a steady, honest, industrious woman.
[PAR 511/35/1/21]
Note: Dive Milliner was another applicant (**396**). Charles Arnett (**1-26**) was the successful candidate (**3**).

759 24 Jun 1824 *Minute of the Winchelsea select vestry*:
Resolved that two members of the select vestry do attend at the workhouse weekly or at any time they please to appoint. [PAR 511/12/2]

760 11 Apr 1831 *Workhouse inventory of areas and rooms in general use*:
Outdoors: 2 water butts with brass taps and holders, 1 grindstone, 1 hog trough, 1 hog tub.
Little room: 1 cupboard, 1 stove, 1 poker, 1 sifter, 1 table and chairs.
Kitchen: 1 long table, 1 small table, 4 stools and 1 clock, 4 chairs, a grate, poker tongs and fire shovel, 3 tin and 1 earthen pots, 1 box and 2 flat irons, 1 gridiron, pothooks and 1 pair of bellows.
Passage: 1 scythe, 2 thistle spuds [for rooting up thistles], 1 prong, 1 rake.
Workshop: 1 old chair, 1 pair of garden shears, 2 tables, 1 mash tub, 2 keelers and one washing trough, 1 hog rail, 1 hand bill, 1 slop pail, 2 clothes horses, 2 baskets, 1 trug and 1 cinder sieve.
Pantry: 2 stalders, 1 hog form, 5 crocks, 1 milk pan, 2 dishes, 1 bowl, oil pot can and lamp, 1 cutting knife, 1 cutting board, 1 table, 1 chest, 1 basket, 4 brine tubs, 2 pairs of scales and beams, 1 drawer, 1 lantern, 1 hammer, 4 white plates, 1 yeast can, 2 table cloths, 5 towels.
Wash-house: 1 flour bin, 1 bunter, 1 skupet, 2 tables, 1 dresser, 1 stalder, 1 suet

board, 7 dishes, 5 trenchers, 1 tray, 2 tin hand dishes, 1 pair of scales [with] beam and two weights, 2 oven peels and one slice, 2 iron saucepans, 1 frying pan, 1 Dutch and 1 cheese oven, 2 keelers, 2 brushes, 2 copper and 1 iron boilers, 1 skimmer, 1 ladle and 1 flesh fork.

Landing place: 1 warming pan, 1 table, 1 ironing cloth, 1 hair broom, dustpan and brush. [AMS 2331]

Notes: 1. Keelers – vessels for cooling liquids; stalders – frames for casks to stand on; bunter – a machine for cleaning corn; skupet – a spade used for trenching.

2. For the contents of Mary Clandenbold's room see (**133**).

761 [c.1834] *fragment of a return requiring information about the Winchelsea workhouse*:

There are no rules or regulations in writing. The poorhouse is frequently visited and the verbal instructions from time to time given to the mistress being duly attended to and the inmates being few in number and no work of any kind being done in the house or by the inmates (except occasional outdoor work on the roads) it has not appeared necessary to have any written rules. We can conscientiously state that the poor have not to our knowledge or belief any cause of complaint.

[PAR 511/37/7/28]

762 [c.1834] (see date below) *Answers to a questionnaire concerning the management of the poorhouse and the numbers of able-bodied and infirm poor*:

Question 4: The parish of St. Thomas the Apostle, Winchelsea maintains a poorhouse. Until 1831 indoor paupers were maintained as a family in the house, the housekeeping was then given up and the indoor paupers have since been allowed a certain sum per week for their respective maintenance. The alteration has proved beneficial to the parish by a considerable reduction in the rates.

Questions 7 & 8: There are four indoor paupers who are old and infirm and are allowed a weekly sum of 4s each out of which they maintain themselves. There are also two lads who are able to earn enough to maintain themselves but are lodged in the house and there is a little child for whom 2s a week is allowed. And besides these there is a family consisting of husband, wife and three children – the husband can only partially support his family and the wife is allowed 4s per week to act as mistress in superintending the poorhouse and she has 2s per week allowed in coals and candles and the three children are allowed to lodge in the house. Occasionally a sum is allowed to the indoor paupers for clothing. £20 per annum is allowed to a surgeon and apothecary for attendance on the paupers of the parish and medicine. The amount of money expended for the relief of the indoor paupers for the year ending Lady Day 1834 is £ [*blank*].

Question 9: Able-bodied men having three children are allowed the price of half a gallon of flour per week. For a fourth child the price of an additional gallon and for a fifth child the price of an additional half gallon and so on for any other child and occasionally when the children go to service some allowance is made in the purchase of clothing for them. Casual relief is occasionally given to able-

bodied men in the winter when out of employ, sometimes in work on the roads and sometimes in money without employment. The relief in money is after our fixed rate but varies from 2s to 9s per week according to the circumstances of the pauper's family.   [PAR 511/37/7/32]
Note: It seems most likely that the above two documents were submitted in response to inquiries received from the commissioners reporting in connection with the Poor Law Amendment Act.

The workhouse – supplies of goods and services

763 4 Nov 1823 *Letter from Thomas Marley, Rye to [Charles] Arnett, Winchelsea*:
I was in company with Mr Dunaway yesterday. He was saying that you was in want of some person to make some clothes for folks that you have under your care. I should be glad to make them for you if you are not provided. I have made a great deal for our poorhouse and will make at the same price as I have ours.
                                                        [PAR 511/35/1/37]

764 6 Nov 1823 *Minute of the Winchelsea public vestry*:
Resolved that the following bills [for supplies to the parish, particularly the workhouse] be allowed: [inter alia] John Woods, grocery etc. £20 7s 7d and clothing etc. £36 17s 9d; Charles Hill, shoes etc. £15 17s 8d; William Sargeant, flour £59 15s 1d; Henry Barham, clothes etc. £4 6s 9d; William Chatterton, flour £31 8s 11½d; Fuller & Alce, carpentry etc. £4 17s 8¼d.   [PAR 511/12/2]

765 17 Jul 1824 *Letter from Joash Jones, Winchelsea, [butcher] to [Charles] Arnett, assistant overseer*:
Having a sum of money to pay to Mr Standen (bailiff) this evening I should be very much obliged to you to send by my son the balance from my bill deducting my payments. If you call I will give you [a] receipt on stamp at any time.
                                                        [PAR 511/35/1/97]
Note: Jones was a butcher supplying the workhouse.

766 2 Sep 1824 *Letter from Thomas Veness, Winchelsea to [Charles] Arnett, Winchelsea [assistant overseer]*:
I will thank you to let me have the sum of five pounds today for I have some money to pay to a man today and I look for him at two o'clock and if you will do me that favour you will much oblige.   [PAR 511/35/1/108]
Note: Veness was a butcher who was owed money for supplying the workhouse.

767 9 Nov 1824 *Letter from Robert Alce, Rye to [Charles] Arnett, [Winchelsea assistant overseer]*:
I will thank you to favour me with a line if you cannot make it convenient to come over this morning as the coals will be nearly out today. The master says they are the best coals that he has seen in Rye this summer. I will send you over any quantity you think proper by Mr Hunter or any other carrier.   [PAR 511/35/1/132]

768 18 May 1825 *Letter from Charles Poile on behalf of Charles Pilcher, Rye to C[harles] Arnett, Winchelsea, [assistant overseer]*:
Pray to inform you I have arrived a most excellent cargo of Newcastle coals (Earsden Main). Shall be obliged to send over on Friday and Saturday next.
[PAR 511/35/1/172]

769 26 Apr 1826 *Letter from Robert Alce, Rye to [Charles] Arnett, Winchelsea, [assistant] overseer*:
I have a cargo of very good coals that will give you great satisfaction. She will be delivering all the week. If you should come to Rye today I shall take it a favour if you will call on me.   [PAR 511/35/1/220]

770 3 Jul 1826 *Receipted account submitted by Charles Arnett, assistant overseer, to Winchelsea parish headed 'House etc'*:
Xmas boxes to boys and girls: 4s 6d; 6 yards flannel for G[eorge] Perigo at 1s 7d: 9s 6d; 2 quarters schooling [for Perigo] to Xmas: 4s 4d; Mrs Pitt one day: 1s; Fish 6d, wood ashes 3d: 9d; chaff for beds: 3s 9d; keeler and boiler:£1; Henry Willard: 1s; fish 1s, yeast 10s 10d: 11s 10d; Mrs Pitt nursing Mrs Clark: 5s; washing 8 days: 8s; Mrs Pitt 4 days: 4s; [total] £3 13s 6d.   [PAR 511/31/2/129]
Note: keeler = a vessel for cooling liquids; a shallow tub used for household purposes

The workhouse – sale of the building

771 *The sometimes rather repetitive nature of the following documents is caused largely by Winchelsea's reluctance to sell the workhouse building and to hold the required meeting to formalise the sale, or at least to persuade people to attend such a meeting. The resulting delays provoked the persistent efforts of the guardians of the Rye Union to persuade the Poor Law Commissioners to authorise the appropriate procedures. In 1836, the belief that the purchase price would accrue to the parish, made it quite easy to obtain a majority in favour (773). However the Poor Law Amendment Act had transferred ownership to the guardians of the Rye Union whose funds, once expenses had been paid (798), alone benefited (800) despite in theory reducing Winchelsea's required contribution. There was an important development within the Rye Union at the time of the eventual sale of the Winchelsea workhouse to Richard Stileman (796). The guardians, informed that the union workhouses were in a poor state at the same time that the number of applicants for relief was increasing, agreed that additional accommodation was urgently needed and that therefore 'a suitable house or houses should forthwith be hired within the union'.[1] By 24 November 1840 a house in Factory Square [Barrack Square], Winchelsea belonging to Richard Stileman had been inspected and considered in every respect suitable. About £20 would be needed to carry out necessary alterations. The guardians' minute book includes a description and plan of the property. There were four rooms on the ground floor, four rooms on the first floor and an attic in which the children could sleep. It was resolved to rent this building and Mr Stileman who was present at the meeting offered it at a rental of £6 for six months. This was accepted.[2] It would be used for girls to be transferred from Rye workhouse.[3] Alterations to the building were agreed 'excepting as to the furnaces required in case the washing clothes is to be done there, it being deemed for the present expedient* *not to decide upon that matter'.[4] By Tuesday 29th December 1840 all was ready and girls between the ages of seven and sixteen were moved there from Rye.[5] Mr and Mrs G Parsons had been offered the positions of master and mistress[6] and other union staff were sent to assist them. It is not known how long the building remained in this use.*

772 27 Jul 1836 *Minute of the Winchelsea parish vestry*:
Resolved that a public meeting shall be called in the vestry room on Thursday evening August the 4th at 8 o'clock for the purpose of taking into consideration the propriety of selling the parish poorhouse.   [PAR 511/12/2]

773 4 Aug 1836 *Minute of the Winchelsea parish vestry*:
At this meeting it was moved by Mr [David] Manser and seconded by Mr [Richard] Stileman that it is expedient that the poorhouse belonging to this parish should be sold. On the question being put the following voted for the motion: Mr [David] Manser, Mr [Richard] Stileman, Mr [George] Blackman, Mr [Charles] Hill, Mr [George] Haisell, Mr [Henry] Farncomb, Mr W Noon, William Bennett, Henry Barham, and Charles Jones. Against the motion: Mr [Jacob] Holt, Stephen Laurence and David Laurence. Resolved that the poorhouse be sold by public auction and [agreed that] not less than £175 be taken for the above house.   [PAR 511/12/2]

774 7 Oct 1839 *Minute of the guardians of the Rye Union*:
Ordered that the clerk request the parish officers of Winchelsea to apply to the guardians that the Poor Law Commissioners be requested to order sale of the Winchelsea parish property [the workhouse] and that the clerk state in such letter if they, the parish officers, neglect to take the necessary steps for the sale of the property they will be required to account for such rents as the property might be let for.   [G 8/1a/3 f.32]

775 11 Nov 1839 *Minute of the guardians of the Rye Union*:
At this meeting was received a request from the parish officers and some of the inhabitants of Winchelsea to the guardians to apply to the [Poor Law] commissioners to order sale of the Winchelsea property [the workhouse]. Resolved that such application be made to the commissioners for the purpose and the form prescribed by them was accordingly signed by the guardians at this meeting. [G 8/1a/3 f.50]

776 18 Nov 1839 *Minute of the guardians of the Rye Union*:
At this meeting Messrs [J C] Langford, Samuel Selmes, David Smith junior and John Vidler signed the request to the Poor Law Commissioners to order the sale of the Winchelsea property [the workhouse] and, there being a majority of the guardians of the union to [make] such request, ordered that the same be forwarded to the Poor Law Commissioners.   [G 8/1a/3 f.54]
Note: At the following meeting the Poor Law Commissioners requested information about the property. This request was forwarded to Winchelsea. Winchelsea's reply (of which no details are given) was later forwarded to the Poor Law Commissioners.[7]

777 6 Jan 1840 *Minute of the guardians of the Rye Union*:
[A] letter dated the 1ˢᵗ inst from the Poor Law Commissioners was read requesting that the deeds relating to the property proposed to be sold by the parish of Winchelsea may be forwarded to them. Ordered that the clerk request the parish officers to forward to him such deeds for the purpose of transmitting them to the Commissioners. [G 8/1a/3 f.86-87]
Note: On 20 Jan 1840 the deeds were received by the guardians and forwarded.[8]

778 14 Feb 1840 *Order issued by the Poor Law Commissioners for England and Wales to the Rye Union and to the churchwardens and overseers of the parish of Winchelsea in the Rye Union and to all others whom it may concern*:
We, the Poor Law Commissioners, in pursuance of a request from the guardians of the poor of the Rye Union made in pursuance of an application in that behalf from a majority of the parish officers and some of the inhabitants of the parish of Winchelsea do hereby order you, the churchwardens and overseers of the parish of Winchelsea within twenty-one days from the receipt hereof, duly to give notice of and convene a meeting of the ratepayers of the said parish and owners of property therein entitled to vote ... for the purpose of obtaining the consent of such a meeting to the guardians of the poor of the Rye Union selling a freehold house and garden [the workhouse] in Winchelsea ... [PAR 511/38/5/1 Part 1]

779 17 Feb 1840 *Minute of the guardians of the Rye Union*:
A letter dated the 14ᵗʰ inst from the Poor Law Commissioners was read accompanying [an] office copy of their order to the parish officers of Winchelsea to convene a vestry meeting of the parishioners of that parish to consent to the guardians selling their parish property. The title deeds of the property were also received. Ordered that the clerk direct the parish officers of Winchelsea to serve the occupants with notice to quit the premises as early as practicable so that no delay may arise in completing the intended sale thereof. [G 8/1a/3 f.110]

780 18 Feb 1840 *Letter from Henry Edwards Paine, clerk of the Rye Union to the parish officers of Winchelsea*:
As the Poor Law Commissioners have issued an order, copy of which I presume you have, for you to convene a meeting of the parishioners of Winchelsea to consent to the sale of the Winchelsea parish property by the guardians, I am directed to request that you will without delay give the occupiers of the property notice to quit so that no unnecessary delay may arise when the property shall be sold for the want of possession in completing the purchase. [PAR 511/38/6/1]
Note: A copy of this order dated 14 February 1840 and signed on behalf of the Poor Law Commissioners by J G S Lefevre and G C Lewis is available in the records of Winchelsea Corporation.[9]

781 27 Feb 1840 *Minute of the Winchelsea public vestry*:
A public vestry meeting was holden pursuant to public notice [given 22 Feb] for

the purpose of giving the consent of such meeting to sell the poorhouse but no
ratepayers attended such meeting.   [PAR 511/12/2]
Note: Further orders for the convening of meetings to approve the workhouse sale but
with no decision taken, were issued on 14 May 1840 and 9 Jul 1840.[10] The sale, to be
undertaken by the guardians of the poor of the Rye Union within three months, was
eventually authorised by the Poor Law Commissioners on 22 Aug 1840 – see (**790**).[11]

782 9 Mar 1840 *Minute of the guardians of the Rye Union*:
Ordered that the clerk request to be informed by the parish officers of Winchelsea
whether they have held the necessary vestry meeting of that parish to consent to
the sale by the guardians of the Winchelsea parish property and also to request that
the resolution of such meeting if it had been held may be forwarded to the clerk for
transmission to the Poor Law Commissioners.   [G 8/1a/3 f.126]

783 23 Mar 1840 *Minute of the guardians of the Rye Union*:
At this meeting the clerk produced a certified copy of the notice given by the
parish officers of Winchelsea to convene a meeting of the parishioners of that
parish to consent to the sale of the Winchelsea parish property, [the workhouse],
pursuant to the order of the Poor Law Commissioners but it appeared that, there
being no ratepayers but parish officers present at the time and place for the holding
of such meeting, no resolution was passed and, as the time was past within which
by the order of the commissioners another similar meeting can be convened [it
was] resolved that the clerk inform the commissioners of the before-mentioned
circumstances and request them again to order a meeting of the parishioners of
Winchelsea to consent to the sale of the Winchelsea parish property.
                                                            [G 8/1a/3 ff.136-137]

784 27 Apr 1840 *Minute of the guardians of the Rye Union*:
An office copy order of the Poor Law Commissioners dated the 23rd inst was read
directing the parish officers of Winchelsea within 21 days of the receipt of such
order to convene a meeting of the ratepayers and owners of property in that parish
for the purpose of obtaining the consent of such meeting to the guardians selling
the Winchelsea parish property.   [G 8/1a/3 f.162]

785 18 May 1840 *Minute of the guardians of the Rye Union*:
It appearing from a paper giving a form of notice of vestry meeting of the
parishioners of Winchelsea on the 14th inst to consent to the sale of the Winchelsea
parish property [the workhouse], that no ratepayers being present at such meeting
no resolution was passed respecting such property and this being the second
meeting called with similar result it was ordered that the clerk inform the Poor Law
Commissioners thereof and request to be informed what course should be taken by
the guardians to proceed to a sale of the parish property.   [G 8/1a/3 ff.178-9]

786 1 Jun 1840 *Minute of the guardians of the Rye Union*:
A letter dated the 28th ult from the Poor Law Commissioners was read stating they would issue another order for the purpose of obtaining the consent of owners and ratepayers to the proposed sale of the Winchelsea parish property on hearing that there is a probability of the parish giving their consent to such sale. Resolved that the commissioners be again requested to issue another order for the purposes above stated but such order to be delayed being issued until next week. [G 8/1a/3 f.184]
Note: The order was subsequently issued as reported to the guardians on 29 June[12] and has survived within the Winchelsea Corporation records.[13]

787 16 Jul 1840 *Meeting of the ratepayers and owners of property in Winchelsea, chairman Richard Stileman*:
It was resolved by a majority of ratepayers and owners present in person or as respects owners [entitled to vote] by proxy at such meeting[s] that this meeting do consent to the guardians of the poor of the Rye Union selling the premises described in the margin hereof [a freehold house and garden] under provisions of an act passed in the 6th year of the reign of His late Majesty, William IV, entitled 'An Act to facilitate the conveyance of workhouses and other property of parishes and of incorporations or unions of parishes in England and Wales in such manner and subject to such rules, orders and regulations touching such sales', the conveyance of such property and the application of the produce arising therefrom for the permanent advantage of this parish as the Poor Law Commissioners shall in that behalf direct. Voted for the resolution: Richard Stileman, John Beaumont, Henry Barham, Walter Fuller. Voted against the resolution: none. [PAR 511/12/2]

788 [no date c.16 Jul 1840] *Form of request, submitted by the parish of St Thomas the Apostle in Winchelsea, asking the Rye Union to apply to the Poor Law Commissioners to order the sale of the former workhouse*:
We the undersigned majority of the parish officers and we, the undersigned inhabitants of the parish of St Thomas the Apostle, Winchelsea request you to apply to the Poor Law Commissioners for England and Wales for sanction to the sale of the undermentioned premises belonging to the parish: House and Garden. The said premises cannot conveniently be used for the purposes of the [Rye] Union and the sale thereof will be of permanent advantage to the parish. The premises are estimated to be of the value of [*blank*] and yield an approximate rent of: nothing. [*the only signature is that of*] Richard Stileman.   [PAR 511/38/5/1 Part 1]
Note: This is a pre-printed form which suggests that Winchelsea would benefit from the sale which was not the case.

789 27 Jul 1840 *Minute of the guardians of the Rye Union*:
At this meeting was produced [a] certified copy of the resolution of ratepayers and owners of property present at a meeting at the vestry room at Winchelsea on the 16th inst consenting to the sale by the guardians of the Rye Union of the Winchelsea parish property [the workhouse]. Ordered that the same together with a copy notice

of such meeting and certificate thereof by the parish officers of Winchelsea be forwarded to the Poor Law Commissioners and that they be requested to issue their order for sale as stated in such resolution. [G 8/1a/3 f.222]

Note: A meeting on 17 Aug 1840 ordered the clerk to remind the commissioners that the consent was awaited.[14]

790 24 Aug 1840 *Minute of the guardians of the Rye Union*:
An office copy order of the Poor Law Commissioners dated the 22nd inst was read directing the guardians of the Rye Union within three calendar months from the receipt of such order to proceed to the sale of the Winchelsea parish property [the workhouse] by public auction or by private contract as the guardians may deem expedient subject to such conditions of sale as the circumstances of the case may require. The money to arise by such sale it was ordered to be paid to the treasurer of the union and an account to be opened in the union ledger entitled 'Winchelsea Parish Property Account' and the purchase money to be placed to the credit of such account. Resolved that the sale of such property be by public auction and that Mr Robert Alce of Rye be employed as the auctioneer. Ordered that the clerk take the necessary steps for, and to see to, the disposal of such property on behalf of the board, according to the directions of such order of sale for which purpose it was further ordered that the clerk write to the parish officers of Winchelsea and request them without delay to forward to him the title deeds relating to such property.

[G 8/1a/3 ff.232-233]

Note: At the next meeting the guardians requested the parish officers of Winchelsea to fix a time and place for the auction.[15]

791 24 Sep 1840 *Letter from Henry Edwards Paine, clerk of the Rye Union to the parish officers of Winchelsea*:
I shall be obliged by your informing me before Monday next what in your opinion is the value of the Winchelsea parish property [the workhouse] that the same may be submitted to the board of guardians next Monday and as well to take the necessary precaution at the time the property is offered for sale that it is not disposed of at an improper price. [PAR 511/38/6/1]

792 28 Sep 1840 *Minute of the guardians of the Rye Union*:
A letter from Mr W[alter] Fuller, one of the overseers of Winchelsea, (dated the 28th inst) was read stating that he had consulted with several of the ratepayers of that parish and they, with himself, are of the opinion that the workhouse ought not to be sold for a less sum that £100. Resolved that such workhouse, being the Winchelsea parish property, and to be offered for sale by auction on the 1st October next be put up at the sum of £98. [G 8/1a/3 f.261]

793 5 Oct 1840 *Minute of the guardians of the Rye Union*:
The clerk reported that the Winchelsea parish property was offered for sale by auction on the 1st inst at The New Inn, Winchelsea and that the property was put up

at £98 pursuant to the directions at the last meeting of the board but there being no bidding on that sum the property was not then disposed of, after which the property was disposed of by the clerk to Mr Henry Bennett on behalf of Mr Richard Stileman for the sum of £100 which sale by the clerk by private contract was confirmed at this meeting.   [G 8/1a/3 ff.270-271]

794 9 Nov 1840 *Minute of the guardians of the Rye Union*:
At this meeting the chairman affixed the common seal of the union to the conveyance to Mr Richard Stileman of the Winchelsea parish property purchased by him at the sum of £100.   [G 8/1a/3 f.291]

795 16 Nov 1840 *Minute of the guardians of the Rye Union*:
Mr Richard Stileman having paid the sum of £100 to the treasurers, the amount of his purchase money [for] the Winchelsea workhouse and premises, such sum to be placed to the credit of an account to be opened in the ledger to be called 'The Winchelsea Parish Property Account' and the treasurers to be debited therewith.
                                                                       [G 8/1a/3 f.300]

796 21 Dec 1840 *Minute of the guardians of the Rye Union*:
A letter dated the 19ᵗʰ inst from the Poor Law Commissioners was read stating that the conveyance to Mr R[ichard] Stileman of the Winchelsea parish property had been sealed and registered and returned to Messrs Dawes & Son (of London) from whom they had received it and it was ordered that the old title deeds relating to the property, in the possession of the clerk, should now be handed to Mr Stileman.
                                                                       [G 8/1a/3/f.335]

797 21 Dec 1840 *Minute of the guardians of the Rye Union*:
Resolved that the clerk request the Poor Law Commissioners to order the appropriation of the sale produce of the Winchelsea parish property towards the liability of that parish of the union building expenses.   [G 8/1a/3 f.337]

798 28 Dec 1840 *Minute of the guardians of the Rye Union*:
A cheque on the Winchelsea parish property account with the treasurers was signed to Manser and Jenner for £4 11s 8d law expenses etc on the sale of the Winchelsea parish property with which that account is to be debited.   [G 8/1a/3 f.345]

799 11 Jan 1841 *Minute of the guardians of the Rye Union*:
A letter from the Poor Law Commissioners dated the 8ᵗʰ inst was read requesting to be informed the amount of the liability of the parish of Winchelsea to each of the different loans which had been borrowed by the guardians for the union's building expenses previous to the commissioners authorising the appropriation of £92 18s 4d towards payment of the share of that parish to such loans, such sum being the net produce on the sale of the Winchelsea parish property. Ordered that the clerk furnish the commissioners with the required information.   [G 8/1a/3 ff.354-5]

800 8 Mar 1841 *Minute of the guardians of the Rye Union*:

At this meeting the clerk produced [an] office copy order of the Poor Law Commissioners dated 27th February last directing the appropriation of £92 18s 4d, the net produce of the sale of the Winchelsea parish property towards the share of that parish of the union building expenses.   [G 8/1a/3 f.394]

1 G 8/1a/3 f.299   2 ibid ff.304-305   3 ibid f.308   4 ibid ff.314-315   5 ibid f.343   6 ibid f.315   7 ibid ff.55,61   8 ibid f.95   9 WIN2231   10 PAR 511/12/2   11 PAR 511/38/5/1 Part 1   12 G 8/1a/3 f.203   13 WIN 2232   14 G 8/1a/3 f.230   15 ibid f.238

Administration of the parish

801 *Here, as with the documents about the workhouse above, the section has been sub-divided to bring together as far as possible, separate topics covered. As elsewhere, documents pre-dating the period covered by this volume are included to illustrate how matters were dealt with before 1790 and how problems developed during earlier years.*

Administration of the parish - management of the poor

802 7 Aug 1761 *Letter from Elizabeth Cooper, Canterbury, [Kent] to the parish officers of Winchelsea*:

Your poor parishioner that you sent me has got a most dreadful leg indeed and will want a prodigious deal of attendance to make a sound cure of it which I hope she will have. If not the trouble I have will be of no charge to you. If I cure her it will cost you four guineas for the same and five shillings per week for her board. Gentlemen, according to your desire I have taken her into the house by reason of the smallpox. As to the small pox it has been in Canterbury but very little and that a very favourable sort. I have had above three score patients this summer and have not had one of them catch it, but if she should be taken with it she must be put out of the house. I will do the utmost of my endeavour to get her well and send her home.

[*postscript*] Gentlemen, I wish you could contrive to send her a great many white linen rags for she will want a prodigious many. Please to send them to Mr Luxford's at Rye and he will bring them to Mr Brown's at Hythe and Mr Brown will bring them to me on Monday next.   [PAR 511/35/1/1]

Notes: 1. This letter was written forty-five years before the period covered by the main body of correspondence on which this volume is based. It is likely to have been retained by Charles Arnett as a curiosity even in his own day.

2. 'The house' was most likely the Canterbury poorhouse but could have been Mrs Cooper's home.

803 3 Apr 1782 *Minute of the Winchelsea public vestry*:

It is agreed at this meeting that Mr Abraham Kennett do take the poor at one hundred and seventy-five pounds per annum, to commence from the first day of June next for one year according to the same agreement as the late contractor.

                    [PAR 511/12/1 f.68]

Note: No record has been found of the agreement entered into by 'the late contractor'.

804 24 Apr 1783 *Minute of the Winchelsea public vestry*:
It is agreed at this meeting that Mr Abraham Kennett do take the poor at the sum of one hundred and seventy [five] pounds for the year ensuing to commence from the first day of June next and he does agree to indemnify the parish from all expenses whatsoever except suits at law and that the next contractor shall not be obliged to take more than ten dozen of mops.    [PAR 511/12/1 f.71]
Note: Nothing has been found within the available documents to suggest why the number of mops was so significant. It has been suggested to the editor that the word might refer to fish and OED indicates that this is a possibility. However, it seems much more likely that the word has its usual use. Nevertheless an extensive search of the available overseers' accounts and vouchers has revealed no other mention of mops.

805 17 Nov 1784 *Minute of the Winchelsea public vestry*:
At a special vestry held by adjournment it is ordered that all persons laying on their own lands and not belonging to this parish be immediately removed to their respective places where they belong. The parish do likewise humbly recommend it to the magistrates of this Corporation to take some active steps for the discouragement of bastardy at present a growing evil and likely to ruin the parish.
[PAR 511/12/1 f.74]
Note: Four bastardy examinations were taken by the Winchelsea magistrates during the fifteen months prior to this minute and another three during the following twelve months.[1]

806 30 Mar 1785 *Minute of the Winchelsea public vestry*:
I, George Mugliston, do agree to take the poor at the sum of one hundred and ninety four pounds for the year ensuing to commence from the 1st day of June next and I do agree to indemnify the parish from all expenses whatsoever except suits at law and that the next contractor shall not be obliged to take more than ten dozen of mops and the wearing apparel to be approved at the expiration of the above term.
[PAR 511/12/1 f.76]
Notes: 1. This arrangement was renewed for three years, still at £194 per annum, on 20 Apr 1786[2] and for another three years on 17 April 1789.[3]
2. The confidence placed in Mugliston by this appointment did not prevent his being brought before the Winchelsea quarter sessions on 1 April 1788 accused of setting up as a butcher in the town without undergoing a proper apprenticeship.[4]

807 20 Apr 1786 *Minute of the Winchelsea public* vestry:
The committee appointed to superintend the care of the poor are: the rector of Winchelsea, the churchwardens and overseers for the time being, Mr Thomas Fuller, Mr [Joash] Adcroft, Mr [Thomas] Marten, Mr [Septimus] Stonestreet, Mr [Richard] Lamb, George Stace [senior], Mr [Richard] Denne, any three of them to form a quorum   [PAR 511/12/1 f.77]

808 26 Apr 1791 *Minute of the Winchelsea public vestry*:
At the above vestry it is agreed to allow Mr George Mugliston [an extra] twenty-five pounds in consequence of an additional number of poor persons becoming

chargeable from Mr Nouvaille's manufactory breaking up.   [PAR 511/12/1 f.88]
Notes: 1. Mr Nouvaille's crêpe manufactory had operated in Winchelsea in what are now
the Barrack Square houses and elsewhere since at least 1767 when the lease was taken
over from a failed cambric manufactory for which the block had been built as recently as
1763. The generally accepted date on which the business moved to Norwich is 1810.[5] This
document suggests that there had been considerable problems long before that.
2. No record has been found of payments made to the poor by either Abraham Kennett or
George Mugliston under the above arrangements.

809 3 May 1792 *Minute of the Winchelsea public vestry*:
At a public vestry held this day by the churchwardens, overseers and other
inhabitants of the parish it is agreed that the poor are not to be put out to any person
for one year from the first day of June next and that the overseers, assisted by a
committee of the following eight persons, viz: the Rev D[rake] Hollingberry, Mr
[John] Luxford, Mr [Richard] Denne, Mr Richard Lamb, Mr [Thomas] Marten, Mr
Thomas Fuller, Mr Charles Stephens and Mr Richard Stileman do agree to take the
management of the poor.   [PAR 511/12/1 f.91]

810 31 Mar 1796 *Minute of the Winchelsea public vestry*:
Application being made by Thomas Haisell on account of his unfortunate son
subject to epileptic fits it is resolved after due deliberation that instead of removing
him to the poorhouse out of the immediate attention of his parents, Thomas Haisell
shall be paid two guineas quarterly towards the wages and maintenance of a proper
person to attend upon his son and that the sum of £2 12s 0d be allowed him for the
discharge of his year's wages due Lady Day last.   [PAR 511/12/1 ff.101-102]

811 24 Oct 1799 *Minute of the Winchelsea public vestry:*
At a public vestry held this 24th day of October 1799 in consideration of the poor of
this parish towards allowing them a part of their gristing [their ground corn] owing
to the dearth and scarcity of corn and the allowance to be given [inter alia] to the
under-mentioned persons: Stephen Bennett, Edward Field, James Burwash, Widow
Clandenbold, Thomas Oyler, William Bailey, John Chester. And the allowance to
be paid by the overseers weekly till the price of corn gets lower and then a vestry
to be called and the alteration to be made as the [principal] of the inhabitants shall
think proper.   [PAR 511/12/1 f.110]

812 13 Nov 1809 *Minute of the Winchelsea public vestry*:
Resolved that as the paupers of this parish appear in clothes superior to their
dependant situation, no relief shall be extended to those who shall for the future
appear or cause their families to appear in clothing superior to such as is allowed
by the parish and that parochial relief be granted as much as possible in parish
clothing.   [PAR 511/12/1/f.167]

813 6 Apr 1819 *Minute of the Winchelsea public vestry*:
It is agreed for Mr [Francis] Bellingham to inoculate the poor of this parish for the smallpox including the necessary preparation and attendance for the sum of eighteen pounds.   [PAR 511/12/1 f.231]
Note: See also (**742**)

814 4 Mar 1824 *Minute of the Winchelsea public vestry*:
Resolved that no boy or girl shall be consigned capable of leaving their service without being discharged by a magistrate.   [PAR 511/12/2]

815 4 Feb 1826 *Letter from [Richard] Stileman, [The Friars, Winchelsea] to [Charles] Arnett, [Winchelsea, assistant overseer]*:
When you settle with the road men this evening you will tell them I shall not want any men next week excepting George Edwards and T[homas] Fisher and that after next week they must find other work.   [PAR 511/35/1/205]

816 23 Jun 1834 *Minute of the Winchelsea public vestry*:
Resolved that the poor of this parish being labouring men be allowed ½ gallon flour for the third child, 1 gallon for the fourth and ½ gallon for the fifth.
                                                                      [PAR 511/12/2]

1 PAR 511/34/1/28-33, 47-48   2 PAR 511/12/1 f.77   3 ibid f.83   4 WIN 61 f.92r; WIN 264   5 Pratt 2005 pp.221-222

Administration of the parish – financial supervision

817 4 Apr 1774 *Minute of the Winchelsea parish* vestry:
At a vestry holden this day it is agreed to allow the overseers one guinea per year for making the books and keeping the accounts and the churchwardens half a guinea per year for keeping their accounts and making out the usual books.
                                                                      [PAR 511/12/1 f.48]

818 21 Mar 1790 *Minute of the Winchelsea public vestry*:
At the above vestry Mr Richard Maplesden one of the overseers informs this vestry that having taken a review of his accounts finds that he has more than a sufficiency of money in hand to pay all bills and other expenses relative to the poor of this parish during the time he is in office.   [PAR 511/12/1 f.85]

819 31 March 1796 *Minute of the Winchelsea public vestry*:
[Resolved that] Mr [Richard] Denne, Mr [Thomas] Fuller, Mr [Thomas] Easton and Mr [Edward] Jeakens be allowed half of their respective arrears of the taxes which, after using their utmost endeavour, they have found it impossible to collect. But all parish officers are in future to take notice that no allowance shall be made for taxes uncollected unless they have applied to the magistrates for a summons. [Further

resolved] that persons taking and occupying houses at their own discretion without consulting the parish officers shall be responsible for all taxes and assessments as well as rent.   [PAR 511/12/1 ff.101]

820 15 April 1801 *Minute of the Winchelsea public vestry*:
At a public meeting held this day at The Bear the overseers are empowered to borrow the sum of six hundred pounds to pay off the debt due on account of this parish for the last year ending at Easter 1801.   [PAR 511/12/1 f.126]
Note: The Bear is now a private house known as The Armoury.

821 6 Apr 1804 *Minute of a Winchelsea parish meeting:*
At this meeting Mr Walter Fuller, the overseer who keeps the books and accounts being very ill and confined to his bed we adjourn to Thursday the 19th instant in order to settle the accounts and we do appoint the following people to attend to examine the same: Rev [Drake] Hollingberry, Richard Denne Esq, Mr George Stace, Mr Richard Lamb, Mr Thomas Marten junior, Mr Richard Maplesden, Mr George Bray.   [PAR 511/12/1 f.139]
Note: Because of Fuller's illness examination of the accounts was further deferred on 19 April, and 3 May.[1] No further reference to the matter has been found.

822 4 Apr 1816 *Minute of the Winchelsea public vestry*:
Agreed that the overseers for the ensuing year are required to call a vestry to examine and pass their quarterly accounts and to produce quarterly statements of all disbursements and a balance drawn within seven days after each quarter day.
                                                                    [PAR 511/12/1 f.208]

823 8 Jul 1818 *Letter from Thomas Pain, Dover [Kent] to the mayor of Winchelsea*:
I beg leave to acknowledge receipt of the sum of £1 14s 4½d being the proportion of the sum of £150 raised within the Cinque Ports for the relief of poor debtors in the gaol of Dover Castle due from the town of Winchelsea.   [PAR 511/35/1/8]

824 9 Feb 1819 et seq *[Edited] account submitted to the parish officers of Winchelsea by Dawes & Co [of Rye, parish solicitors]*:
9 Feb 1819 Attending Mr [Edward] Jeakens advising in consequence of Mr [John] Tilden's refusal to sign a poor rate on the ground that it was unfairly made and writing to Mr Tilden explaining to him that he had no option and referring him to cases for his satisfaction: 13s 4d.
10 Feb 1819 Attending Mr Tilden in consequence of our letter to him when he undertook that the book should be allowed: 6s 8d.   [PAR 511/31/2/131]
Note: Each occasion on which the poor rate was authorised, collected and recorded was referred to as 'a book' because of the book in which such entries were made.

825 14 Nov 1822 *Minute of the Winchelsea select vestry:*
Resolved that the wages of men employed on the road[s] do not exceed one shilling
per day. [PAR 511/12/2 f.34]

1 PAR 511/12/1 ff.140-141

Administration of the parish – cost of providing poor relief

826 18 Apr 1781 *Minute of the Winchelsea public vestry*:
Mr George Stace, Mr Thomas Fuller, Mr Burford Jeakens, Mr Robert Clark and Mr
John Stevenson or any three of them are hereby appointed a committee to examine
into the number of the poor that receive relief from this parish and to consider what
they will cost yearly to maintain for the space of three years next ensuing and make
their report thereof to the next vestry. [PAR 511/12/1 f.64]
Note: No mention of this report appears subsequently.

827 3 Oct 1786 *Return made to parliament by the rector and churchwardens on
behalf of the parish of St Thomas the Apostle, Winchelsea*:
No charitable donations have been given for the benefit of poor persons with the
parish of St Thomas the Apostle, Winchelsea either by deed or will that we know of
or believe. [*signed*] D[rake] Hollingberry, rector, Richard Stileman, Robert Alce,
churchwardens.
[*Endorsed*] [same date] The above-named were sworn to the truth of the above
return before two of His Majesty's justices of the peace for Winchelsea. [*signed*]
Joash Adcroft, mayor, Thomas Marten, justices, H[enry] Waterman, town clerk.
[PAR 511/37/7/33]

828 14 Apr 1803 *Minute of the Winchelsea [Public vestry]*:
It appears to this meeting that a permanent overseer or parish clerk would be
greatly beneficial to the inhabitants of this parish and the same is ordered to be
further considered. [PAR 511/12/1 f.133]
Note: Four days later George Harrod and Charles Terry were paid £10 each 'for their great
attention to the management of the poor of the parish.[1]

829 2 May 1803 *Minute of Winchelsea public vestry*:
Whereas it has been found of advantage in many parishes to appoint a guardian of
the poor who shall attend to the public expenditure in a more accurate way than
can be expected of the overseers it is the opinion of this vestry that the experiment
shall be made for one year in the parish of Winchelsea and that Mr W[alter] Fuller
is hereby appointed to this office which he agrees to accept with a salary of £15 and
all necessary expenses incurred out of the parish. [PAR 511/12/1 f.134]
Notes: 1. The title 'Guardian of the Poor' was in fairly general use in parishes well before
it was adopted by the Poor Law Amendment Act of 1834 for those elected to manage Poor
Law Unions.
2. The £15 per annum remuneration for the 'acting overseer' was still being paid in 1809.[2]

830 21 Mar 1822 *Minute of Winchelsea public vestry*:
Resolved that notice be given to landlords where the parish pay rent that each tenant pay his own in future. [PAR 511/12/2 f.22]

831 30 Aug 1822 *Return by William Sargent and David Laurence, churchwardens, and John Woods and Henry Barham, overseers, to the Clerk of the House of Commons*:
[In response to an order of the House of Commons dated 10 July 1822] to make a return of the amount of money levied in the year ending 31 Mar 1822 for maintaining the poor of Winchelsea.
[*Return details noted on the reverse*]
Parish rates: Total amount of money levied £1078 9s 2d; total amount of money expended £1157 4s 10½d; amount of money paid for any purpose or purposes other than the relief of the poor £13 6s 10½d; remainder expended on the relief of the poor £1143 18s 0d.
[*Response to questions*]
Has any select vestry been formed [under] the Act of 59 Geo III c12? Yes.
Has any assistant overseer been appointed by virtue of the Act 59 Geo III c12?
Yes. [PAR 511/35/1/13]

832 [Apr] 1824 *Return to the House of Commons of the money levied for the relief of the poor:*
Copy order from the House of Commons. The different sums as collected and expended [on the poor of the parish] from April 1823 to April 1824. Total amount of money collected: £1543 6s 9d. Total amount expended: £1439 6s 11½d. Amount expended for other purposes: £346 2s 6d. Amount expended on the poor: £1093 4s 5d. [PAR 511/35/1/151]

833 8 Jul 1824 *Minute of the Winchelsea select vestry*:
Resolved that this parish do contract for meat and shoes for the paupers of this parish (and that the first offer be made to the trade and inhabitants of this parish) from 16 July to Michaelmas next. Tenders to be delivered to the assistant overseer on Thursday next. [PAR 511/12/2]

834 16 Jul 1824 *Minute of the Winchelsea select vestry*:
Resolved that Thomas Veness do supply the parish in good beef and mutton at 2s 10d per stone from this day to the 29th day of September next inclusive agreeable to tender [and] that Charles Hill do supply the parish in good strong ½ boots and shoes agreeable to tender. [PAR 511/12/2]
Note: In October of the same year similar contracts were entered into with George Martin for boots and shoes, William Sargent for flour and Joash Jones for beef.[3]

835 25 Mar 1825 *Letter from Messrs Meryon and Holloway, Rye to the overseers of Winchelsea*:
This being Lady Day we have taken the liberty of sending in your account.
[PAR 511/35/1/163]

836 7 Aug 1825 *Return to the House of Commons of the expenditure on the poor for the year 25 Mar 1824 to 25 Mar 1825*:
Amount of money levied £990 1s 1d. Total amount of money expended £1093 17s 3¾d. Deduct the amount of money paid for any purpose other than relief of the poor £138 6s 5d. [Total expended on the poor] £955 13s 10¾d.
[*Appended*] Sent another December 7th 1825 as the Clerk of the House of Commons says they have not received it. [PAR 511/35/1/187]

837 25 Jan 1827 *Letter from Messrs Meryon and Holloway, solicitors of Rye to [Charles] Arnett, Winchelsea, [assistant overseer]*:
We have, as you will see, taken the liberty of adding another firkin [ie fourth] to your account as that closes at the end of the year. Trusting that this slight addition will not be disapproved by your parish. [PAR 511/35/1/258]

838 30 Jun 1827 *Circular from the secretary of state, Whitehall, [London] to the churchwardens and overseers [of Winchelsea]*:
The king having been pleased to comply with the prayer of an humble address presented to His Majesty in pursuance of a resolution of the House of Commons dated the 19th instant, for returns from each parish or place maintaining its own poor in the counties of Sussex, Suffolk, Hertford, Hereford, Westmoreland, Cumberland, Salop and Cardigan (as far as the same can be made out) of the number of able-bodied persons relieved in any way from the poor rate in the year ending 25 March 1827, with a summary of the whole in each county … I am directed by Mr Secretary Sturges Bourne to desire that you will prepare the above returns agreeable to the enclosed form as far as relates to your parish or place and transmit the same to me with as little delay as possible in order to their being laid before the House of Commons accordingly. [PAR 511/35/1/287]
Note: William Sturges Bourne was persuaded, rather against his will, by George Canning to succeed Robert Peel as Home Secretary in April 1827 when Lord Liverpool's long-term government fell. Sturges Bourne served in that office only until July of that year. Nevertheless it must have been he who declined to commute John Eagles' death sentence.[4] (see (**188-189**)). It is perhaps relevant to note here that in 1817 he had been chairman of a parliamentary select committee which produced a report highly critical of the then existing system of poor relief.[5]

839 25 Mar 1830 *Account submitted and receipted by G[eorge] Haisell, hairdresser*:
To a quarter's shaving and hair cutting [for parish paupers]. Thomas Chester 2s 6d; Henry Tilden 2s 6d; Joseph Claise 2s 6d; Joseph Bailey 2s 6d; Master Woodval [Woodzell] 2s 6d; Isaac Burvish [Isaiah Burwash] 1s; Thomas Bennett 1s; cutting the children's hair 2s 4d [Total] 17s 6d. [PAR 511/31/2/162]

840 31 Mar 1830 *Circular from George Forwood, secretary of the committee of the select vestry, Liverpool, to the churchwardens and overseers of Winchelsea*:
This letter seeks support for a petition to the House of Commons concerning the

'Bill to declare and amend the law relating to the employment and payment of able-bodied labourers from the poor rates and for the better rating of tenements under a certain annual value'.   [PAR 511/35/1/328]

1 PAR 511/12/1 f.145   2 AMS 2329 1808/1809   3 PAR 511/12/2   4. Fisher [Ed] Vol 7 pp.340-348
5 Hilton p.592

Administration of the parish – overseers' relationship with Winchelsea's courts

841 13 May 1820 *Application for legal advice made by the churchwardens and overseers of Winchelsea to Frederick Pollock, 18 Sergeants Inn, [London]*:
The parish officers of Winchelsea – it being a corporate town in all matters requiring the assistance and interference of magistrates – are obliged to apply to those of the Corporation who refer all such matters to the town clerk who is an officer appointed by the Corporation with a fixed salary and who resides about 3 miles from Winchelsea. During the last 12 months on all occasions when these magistrates have been called upon for their assistance by the parish officers they have been so desired to send and accordingly they, the parish officers, have sent to the town clerk and required his attendance at Winchelsea. The town clerk is also the attorney employed constantly by the parish. In this attorney's bill of last year, presented at the Easter meeting, the following demand is repeatedly made upon the parish: 'for journey to Winchelsea to attend on and advise the magistrates: one guinea'. It is to be observed that no attorney lives in Winchelsea or nearer than the town clerk. With this demand the parish refuses to comply concerning that as the magistrates have no power to act beyond the liberties of the town it is a duty incumbent upon them to require the attendance of their officers within those liberties and [they] are liable for any expenses that may be incurred over and above the customary fee allowed to the magistrates' clerks vide 26th Geo II Chap 14 and that if the parish officers are obliged to comply with this demand upon a similar principle, would they be compelled, should this Corporation think proper to appoint as their clerk an attorney resident in London, to send him and defray his expenses to Winchelsea whenever his attendance might be wanted. Upon this statement of fact the following questions arise:
Is it the duty of the magistrates or the parish officers to send and require the attendance of the town clerk? In either case can any other demand be made upon the parish than the customary fee to magistrates' clerks? Must the charges in the present bill upon the parish be complied with? And if so what steps must be taken to avoid a liability to those charges in future?
[*Response*]
I am of the opinion that it is not the duty of the parish officers but of the magistrates to send for the town clerk for it is the magistrates who require his attendance. Whether the magistrates if they send for the town clerk are bound to pay more than the customary fee I am not able to say as I do not know how far it is the duty

of the town clerk to attend the magistrates' call on these occasions. But I think the parish officers are not liable generally beyond the customary fee to magistrates' clerks. On the present occasion there may be some doubt because the town clerk, being also the attorney to the parish officers, may insist that he attended in the latter character, and if he can so insist the present bill must be complied with and not otherwise. In future when the magistrates are called upon to act officially the parish officers should protest against the town clerk being sent for on their account and at their suit and should insist upon the magistrates being attended by a clerk who will act for the usual fee. [PAR 511/35/2/4]

Note: For the initial resolution which led to the submission of the above see (**847**).

842 18 May 1820 *Minute of the Winchelsea select vestry*:
Counsel's opinion having been received and read relative to certain charges contained in the bill of Messrs Dawes and Co for attendance on and advising magistrates it is resolved that the overseers shall henceforth on all future applications to the magistrates on parish business refuse to send for the town clerk and or incur a liability to any other expenses than the usual and legal fees due to magistrates' clerks. [PAR 511/12/1 f.243]

843 16 Nov 1820 *Minute of the Winchelsea general [public] vestry*:
It is resolved that the magistrates of this town having refused to take the examinations of John Pearce and Abraham Morris in order to [obtain] their removal to their several parishes unless they have the assistance of their town clerk or some other attorney for whom they refused to send on the alleged ground that it is the duty of the parish to procure the attendance of the said clerk or other attorney whereby the said paupers remain chargeable to the parish, the parish officers be instructed to apply to Mr Thomas Dawes, attorney-at-law, of Angel Court, London, to institute such legal proceedings as shall be deemed necessary to redress the aforesaid grievance and protect the parish from similar inconvenience in future.
[PAR 511/12/1 f.245]

Notes: 1. The bill which provoked the above dispute (**841-843**) has not been traced. The town clerk served as magistrates' clerk to the courts then operating in Winchelsea. The same individual was also solicitor to the churchwardens and overseers of the parish of St Thomas's. Hence the problem here in obtaining a ruling as to which he was serving on any particular occasion. At a sitting of the Winchelsea quarter sessions of the peace held on 18 October 1825 it was, 'Ordered that the following table of fees be taken by the town clerk and that the same be presented to His Majesty's justices of assize for their approbation'. It is an extremely detailed list containing no fewer than 125 potential charges for specific aspects of the town clerk's work. As it is dated five years after the above dispute it may well not be directly related to it.[1]
2. The settlement examinations of Pearce and Morris were eventually taken on 12 December 1820.[2] Their removal orders, Pearce to Littlebourne, Kent and Morris to Fairlight, are dated the same day.[3]

844 17 October 1822 *Minute of the Winchelsea select vestry*:
Resolved that a meeting be holden by the different parish officers of the different parishes within the Liberty of the Ancient Town of Winchelsea at the Vestry Room 24th inst to take into consideration the manner of making returns of public rates to the justices at their adjourned sessions.   [PAR 511/12/2 f.33]
Note: The Liberty of Winchelsea consisted of the parish of St Thomas the Apostle, Winchelsea, together with parts of the parishes of Icklesham, Pett and Broomhill.

845 [31 Mar 1823] *Letter from H[enry] Brougham, Lancaster to H[enry] Powell, Winchelsea*:
I understood that the case was only wanted in time for 6th of April and am sorry on coming here today to find it was desired on or before the first. I had answered it at York but by an accident it was not sent away.   [PAR 511/35/1/14]
Notes: 1. Henry Brougham, later Lord Chancellor, was, between 1815 and 1830, Winchelsea's longest continuously serving MP. His advice as a barrister had been sought regarding the settlement of Richard Field. Richard's father, Edward Field, had arranged with Richard Denne of Winchelsea for his son to serve as a labourer on Denne's farm at Udimore. He served for a year and then later for a short extra period but was never apprenticed. Brougham's opinion was that Richard Field had not acquired a settlement in Udimore.[4]
2. The place of origin of this letter is explained by the fact that Brougham, following his successful and highly publicised defence of Queen Caroline in the House of Lords, had been disappointed by a lack of success in other respects in the Commons and had 'returned to the northern legal circuit'.[5]

1 WIN 61D ff.33-38   2 PAR 511/32/4/186 & 187   3 PAR 511/32/2/71 & 72   4 PAR 511/35/2/6   5 Bew p.494

Administration of the parish – general

846 *The following documents do not seem to fit any of the other categories within this section.* (**859**) *with its references to 'man found in pond' is an example of the curious matters with which parish officers sometimes had to deal.*

847 12 Apr 1820 *Minute of the Winchelsea public vestry*:
At a vestry held this day in pursuance of public notice it is resolved that it is expedient to appoint a select vestry to manage the affairs of the parish and that public notice be given that a vestry will be held on Thursday the 27th inst for appointing such select vestry. It is likewise resolved that counsel's opinion be obtained relative to certain charges for attending the magistrates of Winchelsea contained in a bill on this parish presented by Messrs Dawes and Co. In order thereto the parish officers are desired to prepare a case and transmit the same to Mr T[homas] Dawes in London and to report the result thereof. [PAR 511/12/1 f.240]
Note: For the latter part of this minute see also (**841-843**) above.

848 27 Apr 1820 *Minute of the Winchelsea public vestry*:
At a vestry holden this day pursuant to public notice for the purpose of appointing a select vestry to manage the affairs of the parish, the following persons were duly proposed and elected members of the select vestry: Rev^d D[rake] Hollingberry, Richard Stileman, John Hollingberry, John E[dward] Wright, William Sargent senior, Richard Maplesden, Edward Jeakens, Thomas Hoadley, James Holt, George Hill, John Woods, David Laurence, F[rancis] Bellingham, Henry Barham, William Sargent junior, Joash Jones, Richard Osborne, Walter Fuller, Robert Alce, Thomas Winstone .   [PAR 511/12/1 f.241]

849 23 May 1824 *Letter from W Brazier, Rye to C[harles] Arnett, Winchelsea, [assistant overseer]*:
In answer to yours of this morning I am not yet sworn into [the] office of churchwarden of this parish [n]or do I expect it 'till the day of the visitation at Hastings which I understand is fixed for the 22nd of next month.
                                                                 [PAR 511/35/1/85]

850 17 Sep 1824 *Letter from David Taylor, Rye to [the overseers of Winchelsea]*:
I will thank you to say whether you wish for a long folio foolscap book or a broad folio one. The broad folio is the foolscap sheet in the usual state, the long folio is when the sheet is opened and doubled longway. Will not a time and a half book be very thin either way, the binding being in calf it could be a saving of expenses to have it thicker. I merely mention this for your consideration. On hearing from you I will attend to your directions immediately. [*Endorsed*] D Taylor, Rye about pauper list book.   [PAR 511/35/1/110]
Note: This letter must refer to the purchase of PAR 511/31/1/14 (see introduction p.xx) which Charles Arnett brought into use on 30 September 1824.

851 5 Oct 1824 *Letter from Thomas Fuller, Icklesham to [Charles] Arnett, Winchelsea assistant overseer*:
I received yours and as you have ordered a coffin and an inquest to be taken on the body I will thank you to send the coffin down to the spot and take the corpse to Winchelsea and I will go and speak to Mr Richards about burying it and will get him to be there about two or three o'clock tomorrow. If that time should not suit him to attend I will send you another note tomorrow morning [informing you] what time will suit him.
[*Endorsed*] Relative to dead body found off Nook Point.   [PAR 511/35/1/116]
Note: At this time Revd Thomas Richards was serving as both vicar of Icklesham and curate of Winchelsea.

852 6 Oct 1824 *Letter from Thomas Fuller, Icklesham to [Charles] Arnett, Winchelsea assistant overseer*:
I have seen Mr Richards and he is going from home tomorrow, therefore he cannot be at Winchelsea till four or half-past to bury the corpse and he wished me to

inform you that it will be necessary that he should have a warrant from the coroner to authorise him to bury the corpse in the churchyard. I will thank you to speak to the coroner and get one and [send] to Mr Richards before the corpse is brought to the ground.   [PAR 511/35/1/117]

853 1 Jun 1825 *Letter from David Taylor, Rye to [Charles] Arnett, [Winchelsea, assistant overseer]*:
I shall be much obliged by your sending me patterns of the two books you wish for as I shall be writing to town tomorrow. If these books will be required annually I will take care in future to keep the patterns.   [PAR 511/35/1/174]

854 20 Jun 1825 *Letter from Thomas Milles, Combwell, [Goudhurst, Kent] to C[harles] Arnett, Winchelsea, assistant overseer*:
I shall be at William Bentley's [in East] Guldeford, tomorrow between the hours of 12 and 2 if it is convenient for you to be there I can do anything you wish.
                                                                                              [PAR 511/35/1/178]

855 25 Nov 1825 *Letter from T Westover, Icklesham to C[harles] Arnett, Winchelsea, assistant overseer*:
I am very sorry to disappoint you but cannot prevent it as it is inconvenient for the Rev [Thomas] Richards to be at Winchelsea this day. We therefore shall tomorrow at two o'clock in the afternoon without fail.   [PAR 511/35/1/201]

856 23 Oct 1827 *Letter from Samuel Selmes, Beckley, to [Charles] Arnett, Winchelsea, [vestry clerk]*:
Not being able to attend Thursday I beg to say as the parish concerns appear to me to be going on well I trust no one will wish to alter a good system.
                                                                                              [PAR 511/35/1/302]

857 28 Jun 1831 *General quarter sessions of the peace held at The Court Hall, Winchelsea before William Lipscomb, deputy mayor, Joseph Hennah, John Tilden and Fielding Browne, jurats and justices*:
At this sessions the overseers of the poor delivered upon oath [the following figures required for the 1831 census]: Within the town and parish 143 inhabited houses occupied by 172 families, 5 houses uninhabited; that 45 families are chiefly employed in agriculture, 40 in trade and 37 not coming under these heads; 363 males and 409 females making a total population of 772 and a decrease of persons upon the return of population made in 1821.   [WIN 61D f.87]

858 30 Mar 1837 *Minute of the Winchelsea [public] vestry*:
Resolved that Richard Stileman Esq and Mr William Sargent be elected surveyors of the highways for the year ensuing.   [PAR 511/12/2]

Winchelsea Court Hall, 1850

The court sat on the upper floor; the prison was below

859 21 Jul 1841 *Account of the overseers of Winchelsea from 25 Dec 1840 to 25 Mar 1841*:
[Inter alia] 15 March to man found in pond: 1s; refreshment for man found in pond: 1s; postage and stationery 2s 6d; journey to audit 1s 3d; paid to E[dwin] N[athaniel] Dawes [town clerk] for overseers' appointments 8s 6d.

[PAR 511/35/1/363]

Revaluation of poor rate assessments

860 *The documents published as (**861-864**) provide an outstanding example of how really local government could work, if in conscientious hands, at the beginning of the nineteenth century. It was the responsibility of the parish vestry, not only to collect the poor rates but also to ensure that the liability for payment was fairly allocated. It should be remembered that all those mentioned in these documents were volunteers acting in the public interest. As (**862**) shows it was the professionals who let the parish down and the work went on without them. The account of how the revaluation was set up, the rules applied, appropriate committees established, a timetable laid down, and the result displayed for all to see repays careful examination. Even after the delay caused by the unavailability of the professional advisers the revised complex assessment which had required much detailed work was available within just over three months (**863**). The fact that it was quashed on a technicality (**864**) and a substitute was provided exclusively by professionals reduces in only a minor way the value of the purposeful effort involved. The reader may assess the detail and complexity of the work by examining appendix D1 where the revaluation is transcribed. These, of course, were the days when national government provided only general legislation which was interpreted and acted upon on the initiative of local officials and with considerable variations between parishes.*
*A comparison between the work of the overseers and leading citizens (appendix D1) and that of the professionals which replaced it after Jeremiah Curteis's objection (**864, 865-866**) and appears, dated 21 June 1801, immediately afterwards in the account book, shows very little material difference. The total to be paid on the equivalent demand of four shillings in the pound was almost exactly the same, £250 10s 0d compared with the earlier £250 15s 6d. The obligation of the rector who was mentioned in the grounds for objection was reduced by £1 18s 0d and the amount to be paid by Jeremiah Curteis, the objector, was increased by £3 16s 6d. Indeed, the principal change was organisational, the names of those liable being listed, at least for the majority of entries, in alphabetical order rather than in the rather haphazard arrangement which had developed over the years. There is no mention of the rector being taxed on the tithes he has received – the reason for the objection. (see also the introduction to Appendix D)*
*Other revaluations referred to in this sequence of documents took place in 1809 (**868**), 1823, (**869**), an 1837 revision (**875**) which was substantiated in 1838 (**877**) and 1846 (**880**). An 1825 poor rate assessment based on an 1824 revaluation is published as appendix D2.*

861 9 Nov 1800 *Minutes of a public vestry meeting of the parish of St Thomas the Apostle, Winchelsea, held 'for the declared purpose of considering the present rate of taxation'*:
It is agreed that the complaints of several occupiers of land in this parish are neither

vexatious nor unfounded and that the difference between new and old rents is so considerable that it ought to be adjusted. Resolved therefore that a survey be taken of all the land and houses in the parish of Winchelsea and that a fair and equitable rate of taxation be adopted according to their respective value as exactly as the same can be ascertained. Adjourned to Sunday next.

16 Nov 1800 *Minutes of the adjourned vestry meeting*:

The method of taking a valuation by two indifferent [*i.e. disinterested*] persons having failed to give satisfaction in a neighbouring parish from their want of an intimate knowledge of the comparative value of houses and there being a sufficient number of respectable inhabitants in Winchelsea fully competent to [undertake] the valuation of both land and houses, it was resolved that the following arrangements be adopted as most likely to ensure to this parish an equal, fair and satisfactory taxation:

1) Two committees are appointed, the one to be denominated the committee of assessment, the other the committee of appeal.

2) The committee of assessment shall be composed of the following persons: Mr [Robert] Clark, Mr [Thomas] Fuller, Mr W[alter] Fuller, Mr [Abraham] Kennett, Mr [William] Sargent, Mr [George] Tilden with the assistance of [*as professional advisers*] Mr Blackman of Hooe and Mr Griffiths of Battle at the request of Mr Arkcoll and Mr [Walter] Thorpe.

3) The committee of appeal shall be composed of the following: Mr [Richard] Denne, Mr [Revd Drake] Hollingberry and Mr [Thomas] Marten.

4) The first meeting of the commissioners of assessment shall be held on Monday the 1st day of December 1800 at the vestry room with power to adjourn their sittings to any place at their own pleasure from day to day subject, however, to this express condition: that a complete schedule of the proposed taxation shall be prepared and affixed to the church door on Sunday the 14th of December, signed by all the members of the committee.

5) Copies of this schedule shall be sent on Monday the 15th day of December to the commissioners of appeal and to Jeremiah Curteis of Rye and William Shadwell of Hastings Esquires [*major owners of land in the parish*] together with a notice agreeable to the following regulation.

6) Such persons as are dissatisfied with this assessment shall signify to the commissioners of appeal or one of them in writing as to [in] what particulars they are or consider themselves to be aggrieved within six days from the 15th day of December and the commissioners shall give them six days' notice of the time and place at which they are to attend for redress.

7) The commissioners of appeal shall meet at the vestry room with power to adjourn to any other place more convenient on Monday the 22nd day of December to receive such appeals as shall have been directed to them or one of them and after sending answers to the appellants they shall adjourn to the day appointed for hearing the first appeal and continue their sittings as circumstances may require.

8) No appeal shall be heard against the whole assessment but only against such

changes as immediately affect the appellant.

9) On all appeals heard the commissioners of appeal or one of them shall be confronted with the appellant in order to support their assessment.

10) Both committees shall be deemed private [so] that a serious and minute investigation of all circumstances may take place with the least interruption possible.

11) Any member of either committee who has an interest in the article under consideration shall have liberty to explain himself and then shall withdraw if required.

12) As soon as all the appeals are determined the amended schedule of assessment shall be affixed to the church door signed by all the members of both committees.

13) No deviation shall afterwards be made from this schedule of assessment without an alteration of circumstances and it shall be supported by the parish against any appeals made to the quarter sessions and be further supported if necessary in the court of King's Bench.

14) All appeals shall be heard and determined before the 9th day of January 1801 and the amended schedule shall be published as before directed on the Sunday following.

Mr Denne, Mr Fuller and Mr Kennett are requested to attend and assist Mr Blackman in the survey which is here directed to be taken of the Camber and home lands and Mr Walter Fuller, Mr Clark, Mr [William] Sargent [senior] and Mr [George] Tilden are requested to attend to assist Mr Griffith in the survey of the houses at the town of Winchelsea and (if thought necessary) on the Camber land and a valuation shall be made and a rent affixed to all houses though they may be at present inhabited by paupers. This survey must necessarily be completed before the 1st day of December, being the day on which the committee of assessment is appointed to hold its first session.

The churchwardens are desired to provide such accommodation as may be wanted and to satisfy the surveyors and others concerned, if demanded, for their time and trouble which charge, as far as it is reasonable, shall be allowed in their next account.   [PAR 511/12/1 ff.118-121]

862 30 Nov 1800 *Minutes of a meeting of the public vestry of the parish of St Thomas the Apostle, Winchelsea to consider further the re-assessment of the taxation of property within the parish*:

On a report made by Mr [Walter] Fuller that Mr Blackman declines attending without another surveyor:

Resolved that Mr Denne be added to the committee of assessment and as he is so obliging as to accept this nomination the committee is considered as fully competent without the assistance of any other person and they or any five of them have full authority to proceed in this valuation.

Resolved that Mr Denne's services being otherwise engaged the committee of appeal do consist of Mr Marten and Mr Hollingberry with power to call Mr

Blackman, Mr Griffiths or any other person whom they think proper to their assistance in which case all appellants will have the benefit of their judgement if necessary and if not their expense will be spared.

As from unavoidable delays the gentlemen concerned in the committee of assessment have not as yet been able to qualify themselves for acting by taking a view of the land and houses: Resolved that the first day of their meeting be postponed to Dec 9th and the return to Jan 4th 1801 – that copies of the schedule of assessment be sent the day following as before directed; that the first sitting of the committee of appeal shall be on Jan 20th and that all appeals be heard and decided, if possible, before the 1st day of February 1801. [PAR 511/12/1 f.122-123]

863 22 Feb 1801 *Minute of the Winchelsea public vestry*:

At a vestry held this day and which was duly summoned on Sunday last for the purpose of granting a poor cess [*i.e. tax*] it is resolved; that the valuation of land and houses published on the 15th instant by the committee acting under the authority of vestry is approved and that it be taken as the future rate of taxation until a change of circumstances may create a necessity for altering it – the grounds and reasons for which shall always be submitted to and have the approbation of vestry; that an assessment of four shillings in the pound is hereby granted for the relief and maintenance of the poor of the parish; that the public thanks of this vestry be given and they are hereby given to the gentlemen composing the committees of assessment and appeal for the faithful discharge of the duties imposed upon them and for the great care and attention they have manifested to obtain an equal and fair valuation of the land and houses of this parish. [PAR 511/12/1 ff.123-124]

864 14 Apr 1801 *Winchelsea General quarter sessions of the peace held at the Court Hall before Thomas Marten Esq deputy mayor, George Stace and Richard Lamb jurats and justices of the peace for Winchelsea*:

At this sessions Jeremiah Curteis Esq appealed from an assessment bearing date the twenty-second day of February 1801 made for the relief of the poor of the parish of St Thomas the Apostle in the Ancient Town of Winchelsea entitled, 'An assessment made and agreed on by the churchwardens and overseers and other inhabitants of the parish of St Thomas the Apostle in the Ancient Town of Winchelsea at the rate of four shillings in the pound full rents towards maintaining the poor of the parish and defraying all necessary charges thereto belonging' upon the hearing of which appeal the said assessment was quashed for that the rector of the parish was not assessed in the assessment for the tithes of the parish. [WIN 61 f.109]

Notes: 1. The assessment thus objected to was not collected. This resulted in a deficit at the end of the financial year, Easter 1801, of £444 19s 1½d. £600 was borrowed to overcome this problem, £300 from Rye Bank and £300 from Hastings Bank. Despite this, at Easter 1802, the account balance still showed a deficit of £121 5s 2¼d. [1]

2. See also (**820**).

865 3 May 1801 *Minute of the Winchelsea public vestry*:
At a vestry held this day it is agreed to adjourn to Thursday 7th of May next in order to appoint proper persons for the valuation of the parish.   [PAR 511/12/1 f.126]

866 7 May 1801 *Minute of a resumed meeting of the Winchelsea parish vestry*:
At a vestry adjourned from Sunday the 3rd May it is agreed to appoint Mr Henry Kingsnorth of Kenardington [Kent] who is named by Mr Samuel Southerden on behalf of the outdwellers and Mr Thomas Ades senior of Brede, Sussex on behalf of the inhabitants of the town to value the houses and land in the parish of Winchelsea and, if it should happen that any one or both of the above gentlemen should refuse to come, Mr Edward Ades for the outdwellers and Mr W Richardson, appraiser of Lewes, for the inhabitants are appointed. The above gentlemen that are appointed are to propose a third person.   [PAR 511/12/1 f.127]

867 21 Jun 1801 *Minute of the Winchelsea parish vestry*:
At a vestry duly summoned on the preceding Sunday it is agreed to accept of the valuation of Messrs Ades, Kingsnorth and Neeve and a poor book of four shillings in the pound full rents is hereby granted and a church book of one shilling.
                                                                      [PAR 511/12/1 f.127]

868 19 Dec 1809 *Minute of the Winchelsea public vestry held at the New Inn*:
Agreed that Mr Christopher Hoad of Icklesham and Mr Benjamin Blackman of Hooe shall be desired to make a valuation of the lands and houses of this parish, and if either of the gentlemen above-named shall refuse their assistance then a further application shall be made to Mr Edward Ades junior of Sedlescombe and Mr James Griffiths of Bexhill for the same purpose; and if it should so happen that the two gentlemen employed by the parish to make this valuation should differ in their opinion on any given point, it shall rest with them to appoint a third person whose determination shall be final.   [PAR 511/12/1 f.168]

869 13 Feb 1823 *Minute of the Winchelsea parish vestry*:
Resolved that a new valuation of this parish be made and that the following persons be appointed a committee for that purpose: Mr Samuel Selmes, Mr Samuel Southerden, Mr Walter Fuller, Mr David Laurence, assisted by Mr John Neeve of Tenterden.   [PAR 511/12/2 f.37]
Note: This revaluation had taken place and was in operation by the time a rate of six shillings in the pound was demanded on 15 April 1823.[2]

870 18 Mar 1825 *Letter from Weeden Dawes, Rye to the churchwardens and overseers of Winchelsea*:
In the next poor rate and other assessments to be made for the town of Winchelsea I have to beg that you will rate my brother, Mr Thomas Dawes, for the house in which our late brother, Mr Edwin Dawes, resided and the garden and buildings thereto belonging and also the field called Paradise occupied by him and also the

cottage occupied by Nathaniel Benfield and the garden thereto adjoining and that you will rate myself and my brother Thomas Dawes for all the rest of the property for which my late brother Mr Edwin Dawes was rated and assessed in Winchelsea and the liberties thereof.

[*Endorsed*] Copied to the commissioners of the land tax, the surveyors of the highways and to the town clerk of Winchelsea.   [PAR 511/35/1/160]

Note: This request was implemented in time for the next rate demand which is dated 29 March 1825.[3]

871 15 Jul 1825 *Minute of the Winchelsea select vestry*:

Resolved that the Rev^d Mr Dugdell be rated agreeable to the new valuation towards the relief of the poor etc etc.   [PAR 511/12/3]

Note: The Poor Rate assessment of the above date shows that under the new valuation the annual amount on which the rector was liable to pay Poor Rate on his tithes was reduced from £98 10s 0d to £90.[4]

872 2 Mar 1826 *Minute of Winchelsea select vestry*:

Resolved that it having been resolved at a general vestry of this parish held on 23rd December last that the moiety of the expense of the new valuation paid by the rector should be repaid to him by the parish, it is ordered in conformity with such resolution that the said moiety be repaid by the assistant overseer. [PAR 511/12/3]

Notes: 1 A moiety is a half.

2 A reimbursement of £13 10s 0d was made to the rector within the overseers' accounts for March to June 1826.[5]

873 4 Apr 1826 *General quarter sessions of the peace held at The Court Hall, Winchelsea before Henry Powell, deputy mayor, George Stace, John Tilden and Joseph Hennah, jurats and justices*:

At this sessions the Revd John William Dugdell appealed against the existing poor rate and upon the hearing of which and with the consent of the overseers and the several parishioners named in the rate (except Mr [John] Hollingberry to whom notice of appeal was proved to have been served) it is ordered that the sum of ninety pounds at which Mr Dugdell was rated be now reduced to the sum of forty-five pounds.   [WIN 61D f.44]

Note: This order was implemented within the Poor Rate assessment dated 23 June 1826.[6]

874 18 Apr 1828 *Minute of the Winchelsea select vestry*:

Resolved that the Rev^d J W Dugdell be rated at the sum of one hundred and forty pounds instead of forty-five pounds the former rental.   [PAR 511/12/3]

Note: This substantial increase was implemented in the Poor Rate assessment of the same date. It referred to the rector's liability to pay tax on his tithes and later caused a number of disputes. See (**944**) et seq.

875 20 Oct 1837 *Minute of the Winchelsea parish vestry*:
At this meeting it is resolved that Mr William Longley, Mr Samuel Selmes and Mr
J E Langford on behalf of the landowners and Mr D[avid] Laurence, Mr Walter
Fuller and Mr William Chatterton on behalf of the owners of houses be appointed
a committee to revise the present assessment and to assess the property at rack rent
making such deductions as are permitted out of the new act and that Mr Charles
Thorpe be appointed a referee in case the committee cannot agree and that the
committee be requested to proceed forthwith and that notice be given to them by
the overseers.   [PAR 511/12/2]
Note: A rack rent is a rent equal or almost equal to the property's value.

876 29 Mar 1838 *Minute of the Winchelsea public vestry*:
Resolved that until the valuation which is now in progress be completed that
instructions be given to the collector to raise a sufficient sum for present purposes
on the old valuation in equal proportions from such of the ratepayers as shall
consent to advance the same, such sums to be allowed on the first rate under the
new assessment.   [PAR 511/12/2]

877 3 May 1838 *Notice issued by the Poor Law Commissioners for England and
Wales to the churchwardens and overseers of Winchelsea and to the guardians of
the poor of the Rye Union*:
Whereas it has been made to appear unto us by a representation in writing from
the majority of the churchwardens and overseers of the poor of Winchelsea being
one of the parishes comprised within the Rye Union in the counties of Sussex and
Kent that a fair and correct estimate for the purpose of making rates for the relief of
the poor in Winchelsea cannot be made without a new valuation. Now, therefore,
we, the Poor Law Commissioners for England and Wales do hereby in pursuance
and execution of the powers vested in us by an Act passed in the seventh year of
the reign of His late Majesty King William the IV, entitled An Act to Regulate
Parochial Assessments, order and direct that a valuation shall be made of the
messuages, lands and other hereditaments liable to the poor rates in Winchelsea
according to their annual value. And we do hereby declare that the money which
shall be paid for such valuation shall, to the extent of fifteen pounds, be paid by the
guardians of the poor of the Rye Union.   [PAR 511/38/5/1]
Note: An order requiring Winchelsea to contribute £12 6s 4d towards these costs was issued
by the Poor Law Commissioners on 10 September 1838.[7]

878 13 Jun 1840 *Letter from Walter Bearblock of Hainault Hall [Chigwell, Essex]
to Mr W[alter]Fuller, overseer of Winchelsea, Sussex*:
As agent for the rector, I beg to say with respect to your communication of May
30th that I must have a distinct understanding with you and the parish authorities
generally on the subject of the assessment of the rector to the poor rate. A more
glaringly unjust assessment as it at present stands I never saw. Of course, as
the present rate has been allowed by the justices it must be paid but it may be

appealed against and unless I receive <u>without the least delay</u> an assurance that the sum which the rector shall have been overcharged in the present rate, as shall be discovered in the future assessment, shall be returned to him in the next rate. I shall undoubtedly appeal against the rate now in collection and for which appeal I am now in preparation. I shall expect your reply within two posts. I have to request payment by the overseers of the sum of £1 10s 0d for a year and a half's tithe of the poorhouse to Lady Day last and as this has been repeatedly applied for it will be my duty to proceed for recovery of the same unless it be paid into Mr West's account at the Hastings Bank within five days from this date.   [PAR 511/38/6/1] Note: Winchelsea's Poor Rate books dating between May 1839 and May 1842 have not survived.

879 1 Aug 1840 *Letter from Walter Bearblock of Hainault Hall [Essex] to Mr W[alter] Fuller, overseer, Winchelsea:*
In noticing your last communication on this subject [Winchelsea's poor rate assessment] I beg once more distinctly to state that I have been desirous to show by my correspondence with you that I am unwilling to put the parish to expense by an appeal if they will meet the matter fairly and assess the rector justly and equally, assessing the lands and houses in the parish, to use the words of the act, 'upon an estimate of the net annual value of the several hereditaments; that is to say of the rent at which the same might reasonably be expected let from year to year'. Now I say no person acquainted with Winchelsea can be so hardy as to assent on going through the assessments that all the hereditaments or anything like all are put at the value as set out in the above extract from the act. On this point alone, therefore, independent of any other points of invalidity of which I may avail myself, the assessment is 'unequal, unfair and incorrect' and I must repeat that unless the assessment for the purpose of the next rate be more according to the true intent and meaning of the act I shall, on behalf of the rector, appeal against the same. Surely it is unnecessary for me to disclaim all feeling of hostility. I have evidently a duty to perform as the rector's agent which I must not forgo.   [PAR 511/38/6/1]

880 26 Feb 1846 *Minute of Winchelsea public vestry:*
Rev^d Mr West, the rector, having given notice of his intention to appeal against the poor rate assessment and the meeting feeling it is necessary that the parish should be prepared with a proper valuation of all the land and houses by some competent person. Resolved that Mr Barnes the land surveyor of Staplehurst be requested to value the parish and be prepared to support such valuation in court if necessary.
[PAR 511/12/2]

1 PAR 511/31/1/13   2 ibid   3 AMS 2329   4 PAR 511/31/1/13   5 ibid   6 ibid   7 PAR 511/38/5/1 Part 1

Poor rate payment collection and general legal costs

881 20 Oct 1817 *Letter from Weeden Dawes [solicitor], Rye to Edward Jeakens, Winchelsea*:
[John] Fisher has handed me the fifty pounds you paid him on Tuesday with five pounds interest. This is all the money that has been received as I dare say you understand. [PAR 511/35/1/7]

882 12 Jan 1824 *Letter from Thomas Milles, Combwell, [Goudhurst, Kent] to the overseers of Winchelsea*:
In reply to your letter received some time since I beg to inform you 'tis my intention of being at Rye in the course of a week. I will then pay at Rye Bank your demand on me, say £24, for poor rate. [PAR 511/35/1/47]

883 19 Feb 1824 *Letter from Weeden Dawes [solicitor], Rye to [David] Laurence, Winchelsea*:
Enclosed I send you an account of the debt owing by the parish of Winchelsea and their note to me. When convenient I should like to receive the amount but at any rate I shall hope to receive the interest due. [PAR 511/35/1/61]
Note: The account and note are no longer with the letter and have not been traced elsewhere.

884 10 Mar 1824 *Letter from Messrs Dawes and Company [solicitors], Rye, to the parish officers of Winchelsea*:
The amount of our bill is £65 9s 6d. You shall have it sent to you in a day or two as soon as it is copied fair. [PAR 511/35/1/67]

885 25 Apr 1824 *Letter from Thomas Milles, Combwell, [Goudhurst, Kent] to [Charles] Arnett, Winchelsea, [assistant overseer]*:
Your letter duly came to hand. Beg to inform you [I] intend being at Winchelsea in due course of this week [and] will then discharge the taxes due from me to the parish of Winchelsea. [PAR 511/35/1/79]

886 21 Sep 1824 *Letter from Thomas Veness, Winchelsea to [Charles] Arnett, Winchelsea [assistant overseer]*:
I will thank you to let me have three weeks payment today as I have a form of offering to pay and you will much oblige. [PAR 511/35/1/111]

887 5 Oct 1824 *Letter from H Fryman, Rye to [Charles] Arnett, Winchelsea, [assistant overseer]*:
I beg leave to acquaint you that we have for you £24 from Mr [Thomas] Milles of [Combwell], Goudhurst and at any time you like to come over I will pay you.
[PAR 511/35/1/115]

888 11 Mar 1825 *Letter from Thomas Milles, Combwell, [Goudhurst, Kent] to [Charles] Arnett, Winchelsea, [assistant overseer]*:
£16 parish and £4 church rate were paid the 25th ultimo at Mr Fryman's, Rye, to your account. [PAR 511/35/1/159]

889 25 Aug 1825 *Letter from Thomas Veness, Hastings to [Charles] Arnett, Winchelsea, [assistant overseer]*:
I think I shall be at Winchelsea this afternoon and I shall see you for I have some bills that I should wish you to get for me if you will for they will be likely to pay you as you are in the place and I shall see you and will consult about it. [*Endorsed*] Thomas Veness poor rates. [PAR 511/35/1/192]

890 6 Oct 1825 *Letter from William Thorpe, Hastings, to [Charles] Arnett, Winchelsea, [assistant overseer]*:
I only returned home last evening. I enclose you a cheque for £46 12s 10d viz: poor rate £27, procurations £1 12s 10d, poor rate £18 [total] £46 12s 10d for which you will please return me receipts by the bearer. [PAR 511/35/1/196]

891 18 Nov 1825 *Letter from Thomas Milles, Combwell, [Goudhurst, Kent] to [the overseers of Winchelsea]*:
Above I hand your cheque totalling £23 6s 11d as below stated. I should have remitted you before but waited [Samuel] Selmes' report respecting the charge on the rector for tithes. Land tax £4 6s 11d, church tax £3, poor tax £16 [total] £23 6s 11d. [PAR 511/35/1/200]

892 27 Mar 1826 *Letter from Messrs Dawes and Company, [solicitors], Rye, to [the overseers of Winchelsea]*:
We beg leave to hand you our bill for the present year amounting to £22 10s 8d and remind you that the bill ending Lady Day 1824 amounting to £65 9s 6d and the one for the last year amounting to £11 19s 4d are both unpaid. [PAR 511/35/1/211]

893 5 Apr 1826 *Letter from Thomas Milles, Combwell, [Goudhurst, Kent] to C[harles] Arnett, Winchelsea, [assistant overseer]*:
I have directed [William] Bentley of [East] Guldeford to pay you £32 6s 9d on my account. [PAR 511/35/1/213]

894 6 Apr 1826 *Letter [from his wife on behalf of] William Bentley, [East] Guldeford to [Charles] Arnett, Winchelsea [assistant overseer]*:
[Thomas] Milles' servant was at [East] Guldeford with sheep and Mr Milles sent the money that was due, sir, but my husband is so very busy that he cannot come today or tomorrow but if you can tell me where we can leave it, sir, for you I will do it. [PAR 511/35/1/214]

895 11 Apr 1826 *Letter from Charles Taylor for Messrs Curteis and Company, Rye Bank, Rye to C[harles] Arnett, Winchelsea, [assistant overseer]*:
We have received £23 0s 0d to pay Mr [John] Maplesden's bill drawn by Brazier and Company and due today but the said bill was made payable in London at Willis and Company's which is negotiated to a London house by Messrs Brazier & Company. We have seen Mr Blundell who will write to the house today and desire them to present it again for payment. We have not returned any change as there will be an expense on the bill being dishonoured and we cannot tell what till the bill is returned to us which will be on Tuesday next. We learn from Mr B[lundell] the bill was drawn for £22 9s 0d. If this is not right pray let us know as we must write today and desire Willis and Company to pay the same. The money should have been sent yesterday with the particulars of the bill and all expenses would have been saved and trouble prevented. Excuse this scrawl written in a great hurry.

[PAR 511/35/1/216]

896 27 Jun 1826 *Letter from Messrs Dawes and Company, Rye to [the overseers of Winchelsea]*:
On the other side we send you our bill on the parish since last Lady Day as requested. We beg to call your attention to our former bills not paid. The deeds relating to the house bought by the parish have not yet been seen.

[PAR 511/35/1/232]

Notes: 1. This bill is not 'on the other side' and has not been traced.
2. The 'house bought by the parish' is now known as Apple Tree Wick – see (**740**).

897 23 Oct 1826 *Letter from William Bentley, [East] Guldeford to [Charles] Arnett, Winchelsea, [assistant overseer]*:
I have not seen Mr [Thomas] Milles for some time. Neither have I had any money handed to me, sir, for you. [I] expect to hear from him but he has removed from Combwell to Goudhurst town for a few weeks and then he is going to remove again later. But, sir, I don't know anything about Mr Weston's account. I am not looker [a shepherd] to Mr [Samuel] Southerden.   [PAR 511/35/1/245]

898 3 Nov 1826 *Letter from Joseph Mills, Rye, assistant overseer to [Charles] Arnett, Winchelsea, [assistant] overseer*:
Mr [Samuel] Selmes wished me to write to you to know the determination of your vestry respecting the rates due from your parishioners in this parish and if it would be agreeable for you to pay our parishioners and I pay yours in this parish and balance the account at the end of the year.   [PAR 511/35/1/248]

899 14 Jan 1827 *Letter from Thomas Milles, Bustan, Hunton, near Maidstone, [Kent] to [Charles] Arnett, Winchelsea, [assistant overseer]*:
I have directed payment of tithe and poor rate to be forwarded to Winchelsea.

[PAR 511/35/1/255]

900 15 Jan 1827 *Letter from Thomas Allwork, Hastings to the overseers of Winchelsea*:
I have this day paid to Messrs Smith Gill and Company whom I have directed to pay the same to Messrs Curteis & Co the sum of £39 2s 0d for tithe and poor rate due to your parish for Thomas Milles late of Combwell, Goudhurst.

[PAR 511/35/1/256]

901 27 Mar 1827 *Letter from Thomas Milles, Bustan, Hunton, [Kent] to [Charles] Arnett, Winchelsea, [assistant overseer]*:
Enclosed I hand you a cheque value £15. [PAR 511/35/1/268]

902 29 Mar 1827 *Letter from Joseph Mills, [assistant overseer], Rye, to [Charles] Arnett, Winchelsea, [assistant overseer]*:
The rates to this parish are as under: Field, Benjamin 6 rates from March 1826 to March 1827 at 4s 6d: £1 7s 0d; summons for it: 3s; warrant of distress: 3s; Cogger, Thomas 6 rates from March 1826 to March 1827 at 2s 3d: 13s 6d; Relfe, James 6 rates from March 1826 to March 1827 at 3s 9d: £1 2s 6d; [total] £3 9s 0d.

[PAR 511/35/1/269]

903 28 Jul 1827 *Letter from Thomas Milles, Bustan, Hunton, [Kent] to C[harles] Arnett, Winchelsea, [assistant] overseer*:
I have received your letter – intend being at [East] Guldeford next week – will then pay my account. [PAR 511/35/1/291]

904 16 Aug 1827 *Letter from William Bentley, [East] Guldeford to [Charles] Arnett, Winchelsea, [assistant overseer]*:
If you please to call or send to Mr Fryman there is some account left for you from Mr Milles. [PAR 511/35/1/293]

905 13 Oct 1827 *Letter from John Sloman, Udimore to [Charles] Arnett, Winchelsea, [assistant overseer]*:
I have this time sent you a cheque [for] the amount but I will thank you next time not to be in a particular hurry. As the land tax is not required to be paid in the November [it] would be an opportunity to have paid it ere that time

[PAR 511/35/1/300]

906 23 Oct 1827 *Letter from Thomas Milles, Bustan, Hunton, [Kent] to C[harles] Arnett, Winchelsea, [assistant overseer]*:
Your letter came to hand this morning the contents of which give me great satisfaction. As a proof you may rely on my support should it be necessary. My account with Winchelsea shall be paid when at [East] Guldeford next which will be in a fortnight. [PAR 511/35/1/301]

907 10 Nov 1827 *Letter from William Bentley, [East] Guldeford to [Charles] Arnett, Winchelsea, [assistant overseer]*:
If you please to call at Mr Fryman, Market Street when you come to Rye, [Thomas] Milles has left his money, sir, that is due to you, for one £4 6s 9d, for one £8 0s 0d, [total] £12 6s 9d. [PAR 511/35/1/303]

908 12 May 1828 *Letter from Thomas Milles, Hunton, nr Maidstone, [Kent] to David Laurence, Winchelsea, [assistant overseer]*:
I hand you a cheque value £23 1s 1d which includes payment of land tax: Poor [rate] £12, H W [?highways] £4, G[round] R[ent] £2 13s 4d, L[and] T[ax] £4 7s 9d, [total] £23 1s 1d. [PAR 511/35/1/313]

909 5 Feb 1831 *Letter from Thomas Milles, Hunton, [Kent] to [David] Laurence, Winchelsea, [assistant overseer]*:
In answer to your letter [I] have to say I shall be at [East] Guldeford next week and will direct [William] Bentley to pay your demand on me. [PAR 511/35/1/358]

910 4 Oct [1841] *Receipted bill to the overseers of Winchelsea*:
Collection fee for the quarter ending 24 Jun 1841: £95 5s 7d at 4d: £1 11s 5d; £45 19s 8d at 8d: £1 10s 8d; stationery: 1s. [total] £3 3s 1d. [*Endorsed*] Received – 4 October [*signed*] James Richardson. [PAR 511/35/1/366]
Note: James Richardson had been appointed by the Rye Union to collect poor rates in Winchelsea and elsewhere.[1] For the Beckley District which included Winchelsea he also served as registrar of births and deaths,[2] under the registration system introduced by parliament in 1837.

1 G 8/1a ff. 354, 356-357   2 ibid f.252

Parish Tithes

911 '*Tithe was a most irksome and unpopular tax.*'[1] This was certainly the case in Winchelsea. Tithes had been imposed on the agricultural community for many centuries. The editor's source states, somewhat bizarrely, that this began in about the year 764 when King Offa of Mercia 'gave unto the church the tithes of all his kingdom ...... to expiate for the death of Ethelbert, King of the East Angles, whom, in the year preceding he had caused basely to be murdered.'[2] More modern historians do, however, confirm, without being so precise, that tithes had been in existence for at least a thousand years before the passing of the Tithe Redemption Act in 1836.[3] Tithes were originally and for many centuries collected in kind under complex, frequently disputed, arrangements. Tithe collectors would go round annually in carts collecting items due to the clergy worth one-tenth of the value of tithe-payers' produce. This being impractical in a case such as milk arrangements were made for equivalent payments in cash. For example, it was considered that a fair agreement for milk was one pound per annum for every cow kept.[4] A system of commutation for cash developed over the centuries until it became almost universal. It had certainly happened in Winchelsea by the beginning of the following sequence of correspondence (**912**) at which time the rector was required to pay poor rate on tithe payments recorded as worth £98 10s *per annum.*[5] *This figure is shown as comprising 'Rectorial and Vicarial tithes' which were more generally known as great and small tithes. W E Tate explains these terms, 'Great tithes included those of corn, hay and wood; all other tithes are generally 'small'. The general but by no means invariable custom was that where there was both rector and vicar, whether the rector was a cleric or a layman, the rector took the former tithes, the vicar the latter ones'.[6] In Winchelsea, of course, both were due to the rector.*

*The majority of the documents included below (**915-938**) concern the problem of arranging the work of those who were charged with re-assessing the tithe payments due from Winchelsea residents, the reports of their findings and the bills they submitted for this service. Clearly no agreement was reached (**941**) and in 1827/1828 individuals were still being pursued through Winchelsea's courts for tithe payments due to the rector (**942-943**). After the passing of yet another thirteen years, the guardians of the Rye Union and the Winchelsea overseers were still receiving demands for an annual tithe payment on the former Winchelsea workhouse (**946, 950-951**). In engaging Walter Bearblock of Hainault Hall in Essex as his agent in this and other aspects of the problem, Rev[d] James John West, Rector of Winchelsea, seems to have obtained expert representation. A handwritten note on the title page of the Sussex Archaeological Society's copy of New Treatises on the Laws Concerning Tithes (see bibliography) says 'Bearblock's Treaty on Tithes, 1828, is now the best'. The unfortunate impact of such a tax, particularly as it applied to the less wealthy in society, caused great resentment, a fact highlighted by Henry Brougham when he wrote in 1834, 'Nothing has a more direct tendency to excite hatred and contempt towards the [clergy] and towards their sacred office'.[7]*

912 16 Apr 1823 *[Edited] account submitted by Messrs Dawes & Co of Rye to the parish officers of Winchelsea:*

Attending Mr [John] Woods and Mr [William] Sargent conferring with them respecting the rating [of] Mr [J W] Dugdell for his tithe according to the valuation of the land only, the houses not having been valued and advising them so to do but inasmuch as it appeared no notice had been given to dissolve the composition recommended them to pay his tithe or otherwise we considered he would recover back by action against them individually under the contract for composition; 6s 8d   [PAR 511/31/2/144]

Note: On 26 June 1823 the parish vestry resolved 'that Rev[d] Dugdell's poor rates are not to be collected,[8] and during the period February/March 1824 the overseers' accounts show a payment of £29 11s 0d marked 'Mr Dugdell's poor rates'.[9] The situation is further confused by the fact that during the quarter ending the following September the accounts show that the parish sought the repayment of exactly the same amount.[10]

913 11 Jul 1824 *Public notice issued by C[harles] Arnett, Winchelsea, assistant overseer:*

The inhabitants and occupiers in this parish are requested to meet on Thursday the 22nd instant in the vestry room at eleven o'clock in the forenoon to enter into arrangements with the rector for a fresh composition in lieu of tithes, and to consult on the propriety of a revaluation of the parish for that purpose. [PAR 511/35/1/96]

914 22 Jul 1824 *Minute of the Winchelsea general vestry*:
[The meeting was called] for the purpose of considering the propriety of a composition with the rector in lieu of tithes etc. Resolved that the following propositions made by the Revd J. W. Dugdell [rector] to the parishioners of the parish of St Thomas the Apostle, Winchelsea be agreed upon: that the parishioners shall name one competent and disinterested person and Mr Dugdell another and that these two shall name a third before they begin to act; that these persons shall value the tithe of the land and fix the rental upon which the houses and gardens are to be tithed regarding in such valuation and rental the previous determination of the parish whether or not the tithes are to be rated to the poor; that if it be the wish of the parish for the tithe to be rated, the sum at which the same are to be assessed shall be left to the persons appointed to value who, on deciding such amounts, are to regard the proportionate value of the tithe as compared with the proportionate value of the other taxable property in the parish so that the tithes do not become rated at a nearer approach to the actual value than such other property shall appear to be; that if the tithes are not to be rated the rector is willing that the new composition shall take effect from last Michaelmas otherwise the new composition to take effect from next Michaelmas; that the expense of the valuation shall be borne, one moiety [half], by the rector and the other moiety by the parish. [Further resolved] that the parish be revalued and that Mr Henry Hoad of Brightling be appointed by the parish against Mr Murton who is appointed by the Rev^d J W Dugdell; that all persons who hold land etc in the parish shall forthwith send to Richard Stileman and Mr Walter Fuller the maps of their several estates that by them they may be examined and those who have not maps are to be admeasured by Mr Fuller who is fully empowered by the vestry so to do.
[*Footnote*] [Further resolved] that the tithes under the new composition be rated to the relief of the poor.   [PAR 511/12/2]

915 19 Aug 1824 *Letter from Harry Hoad, Brightling, to Samuel Selmes, Beckley*:
I have this day received a letter from Mr Murton respecting the Winchelsea tithes. He has fixed to meet at Ashford on the 14th of September in order to appoint a third person. [I] am fearful I shall not be able to meet him until after Michaelmas and have written to him to that effect. We shall be very busy at that time and moreso in consequence of changing my situation. Should the business require to be done before Michaelmas I hope you'll appoint some other person. [PAR 511/35/1/105]

916 Sep 1824 *Draft notice of public vestry meeting issued by the Winchelsea churchwardens and overseers*:
The inhabitants and occupiers in this parish are requested to meet on Thursday the 22nd instant in the vestry room at eleven o'clock to enter into arrangements with the rector for a fresh composition in lieu of tithes; and to consult on the propriety of a revaluation of the parish for that purpose.   [PAR 511/35/1/113]

917 17 Oct 1824 *Draft notice of public vestry meeting – prepared by C[harles] Arnett, assistant overseer*:
Notice is hereby given that a vestry will be held on Thursday the twenty-first instant at eleven o'clock [in the vestry room] to appoint a person to value the tithes on the part of the parish in case [Harry] Hoad declines acting.   [PAR 511/35/1/120]

918 24 Oct 1824 *Letter from Harry Hoad, Place Farm, Northiam to Richard Stileman, Winchelsea*:
No doubt you will think me neglectful in not answering yours before this. Having removed from Brightling to Northiam and yours being mis-sent to London has been the cause. I am sorry that my health will not allow me to attend to the business as I am most earnestly requested by the faculty to remain still for some time. I hope this will be a sufficient excuse and that you will appoint someone else. [I] have written to Mr Murton to the effect this morning.   [PAR 511/35/1/122]

919 28 Oct 1824 *Letter from Samuel Selmes, Beckley to C[harles] Arnett, Winchelsea, [assistant] overseer*:
I am sorry I have not been able to attend neither of your meetings. The first I was from home and now I am not well. If you wish me to attend at any particular time I will thank you to give as much notice as you can. Be so good [as] to state this to Mr [Richard] Stileman.   [PAR 511/35/1/125]

920 30 Oct 1824 *Letter from Robert Wiltshire, Hurst Green to Richard Stileman, The Friars, Winchelsea*:
I received your letter and am sorry to say I cannot comply with your request [to re-value the parish] as my engagements are more than I am able to fulfil for a long time.   [PAR 511/35/1/126]

921 7 Nov 1824 *Notice published by C[harles] Arnett, Winchelsea, assistant overseer*:
Notice is hereby given that a public vestry will be held at the vestry room on Thursday next the 11th instant at 10 o'clock in the forenoon to fix on some person to value the parish in order to [provide] a new composition in lieu of tithes in the place of Harry Hoad who has declined action.   [PAR 511/35/1/130]

922 11 Nov 1824 *Minute of the Winchelsea public vestry*:
Resolved that Mr Thomas Pain Hilder be written to for the purpose of valuing the parish on account of the parishioners and if he declines acting Mr Clark Howland be applied to; that if the above two gentlemen decline acting Messrs Walter Fuller and William Chatterton be deputed by this vestry to find a proper person and report the same to the vestry.   [PAR 511/12/2]

923 11 Nov 1824 *Copy of letter from C[harles] Arnett, Winchelsea to [Clark] Howland, Aldington, [Kent]*:
At a meeting of the occupiers and inhabitants of this parish held this day it was resolved on the recommendation of several gentlemen 'that Mr Clark Howland of Aldington be applied to as a fit and proper person to value the parish on behalf of the parishioners' against Mr Murton who is appointed by the rector – in order to a composition in lieu of tithes. If you, sir, can undertake the above you will please inform me per return of post and you will be furnished with further instructions.

[PAR 511/35/1/134]

924 15 Nov 1824 *Letter from Clark Howland, Orlestone, [Kent] to [Charles] Arnett, Winchelsea, vestry clerk*:
I have just had your letter this evening respecting to valuing the parish of Winchelsea in the county of Sussex to meet Mr Murton to value the parish in respect of a composition in the regard of tithes. I will undertake to do it with great pleasure according to the best of my judgement. Please to let me know when as I am very much engaged in the valuing business. [PAR 511/35/1/135]

925 21 Nov 1824 *Notice by J[ohn] Hollingberry, J[ohn] E[dward] Wright and C[harles] Arnett, assistant overseer*:
Notice is hereby given that a public vestry will be held at the vestry room on Thursday next the 25th instant at 10 o'clock in the forenoon concerning the appointment of a person to value the parish agreeable to the decision of a former public vestry. [PAR 511/35/1/138]

926 23 Nov 1824 *Letter from Samuel Selmes, Beckley to [Charles] Arnett, Winchelsea, [assistant] overseer*:
I am afraid I shall not be able to attend your vestry Thursday. I should recommend to the parish to name Mr [Clark] Howland who is a man of experience and judgement. If the parish wish I would write to him for them. I think I can get him to do it. I dare say he knows Mr Murton intimately as they must have fallen together.

[PAR 511/35/1/139]

927 25 Nov 1824 *Minute of the Winchelsea public vestry*:
Resolved that Mr Clark Howland of Orlestone in the county of Kent is, by this public vestry, appointed as a fit and proper person to value this parish on account of the parishioners in order to a composition in lieu of tithes. [PAR 511/12/2]

928 31 Mar 1825 *Minute of the Winchelsea public vestry*:
Resolved that the assistant overseer [Charles Arnett] do write to the Rev^d Mr Dugdell and state to him that it is the desire of this vestry that he do appoint Mr Murton forthwith to meet Mr Clark Howland to proceed upon the valuation of the tithes of this parish and that he would be good enough to inform the assistant overseer the result of his application pursuant to this request. [PAR 511/12/2]

929 18 Apr 1825 *Letter from the Rev^d J[ohn] W[illiam] Dugdell, Preston [Kent] vicarage to [Charles] Arnett, Winchelsea, [assistant overseer]*:
I wrote to Mr Murton immediately upon receiving your letter dated March 31st requesting me to appoint him to meet Mr Clark Howland for the purpose of valuing the tithes of Winchelsea. Mr Murton has been suffering under a severe fit of the gout for the last ten weeks and is still so unwell as to render it utterly impossible for him to meet Mr Howland at present. Nor is he able to say when it would be in his power to undertake the business. Under these circumstances he recommended me to appoint someone in his stead and I intend to put the business into the hands of Mr [John] Partridge of Canterbury whom I shall see upon the subject next Saturday and will desire him to communicate with Mr Howland in order to fix a time for their meeting at Winchelsea. [PAR 511/35/1/166]

930 13 May 1825 *Letter from Clark Howland, Orlestone, [Kent] to Charles Arnett, Winchelsea, vestry clerk*:
I write to inform you that I have received a letter from Mr [John] Partridge of Canterbury to inform me that he is going to meet me at Winchelsea respecting valuing the tithes of that parish and please to turn over and there I send you a copy of this letter. Please to inform me whether the parish still think of my doing it and whether they wish me to come to Winchelsea to meet the gentlemen of that parish before Mr Partridge and I come together if the parish have any instructions to give me that they don't wish Mr Partridge to see. Please to answer my letter [as] soon as convenient.
[*Endorsed*] *Copy letter from John Partridge, Canterbury to Howland*:
I have had a clergyman of the name of [the Revd John William] Dugdell write [to] me with a request of meeting you at Winchelsea relative to a valuation of the tithes of that parish. It is rather further from home than I like to go but I have consented upon knowing that you are to meet me. He further informs me that before we go into business that we are to appoint a third man and for the doing which we had better some day meet at Ashford market for that purpose. But I have informed him that I cannot possibly go there before the latter end of this month as I have some large falls of timber this year which lies wide. As you are on the part of the parish he rather wished you to inform them that he had made an appointment of a person on his behalf. [PAR 511/35/1/171]

931 1 Jun 1825 *Letter from Clark Howland, Orlestone, [Kent] to Charles Arnett, Winchelsea [vestry clerk]*:
Just as I had [to] write to you on the 27th May to say that Mr [John] Partridge and myself were going to meet on the 1st day of June I received a letter from him to have the business put off until Wednesday morning the 8th June when I shall be glad for you to meet us at The George in Rye at 9 o'clock on that day with your instructions and you or someone else to go with us to show us the land that lies near Mr [Samuel] Southerden's at Camber etc as we may go there on that day if it

is convenient. Please to let Mr [Samuel] Selmes know that we are coming on that day. Possibly he may wish to see me before we begin the business.

[PAR 511/53/1/173]

932 10 Jun 1825 *Notice from Clark Howland, St George's Place, Canterbury, [Kent], John Partridge and F[rancis] Whitfield:*
We have requested the parish officers of Winchelsea will send us an admeasurement of Cooks Garden and the occupied places and a copy of the last rate of the parish.

[PAR 511/35/1/176]

933 13 Jun 1825 *Letter from Clark Howland, Orlestone, [Kent] to Charles Arnett, Winchelsea, vestry clerk:*
I write to inform you that Mr [John] Partridge, Mr [Francis] Whitfield and myself intend to meet next Monday the 20th of this month at the Saracen's Head Inn, Ashford to settle your parish business and as I very much wish to see you please to meet me at the Woolpack Inn, Tenterden next Friday the 17th instant at 3 o'clock in the afternoon to have some talk with you on the business that I may be prepared to meet them on the business. Please to bring your assessment book with you that I may make a remark or two from it. I should like to know how your parish has been assessed and tithed lately.   [PAR 511/35/1/177]

934 14 [?Jun] 1825 *Minute of the Winchelsea public vestry:*
[Meeting convened] pursuant to the public notice given for the purpose of laying the new valuation of the tithes of this parish before the inhabitants when it was resolved that the new valuation has been laid before the public vestry.

[PAR 511/12/2]

Note: The survey and valuation list compiled by Clark Howland, John Partridge and Francis Whitfield survives.[11]

935 12 Jul 1825 *Letter from John Partridge, Canterbury, [Kent] to C[harles] Arnett, Winchelsea, assistant overseer:*
On looking over my rough draft of survey I fear we have made an error in folio 3 in having carried out in the rental against George Stace's name £52 15s 0d instead of £24 15s 0d, stable &c £3 [total] £27 15s 0d it should stand. That error in the rental does not affect the tithe. I enclose the bills for Messrs Howland, Whitfield and self, copies of which are sent to Revd [John William] Dugdell. It was the wish of those two gentlemen that I should forward them.
[*Endorsed*] £13 12s 10d, £24 8s, £24 8s [total] £82 8s 10d, divided by two [equals] £41 4s 5d.   [PAR 511/35/1/180]

936 [12 Jul 1825] *The expenses and charges of John Partridge for the survey of Winchelsea tithes:*
7 June expenses to Winchelsea, horse and self, 10s; 8 June expenses to Rye horse and self, £1 7s 6d; 9-10 June expenses at Winchelsea horse and self, £2 7s 6d, at

Ashford on return, horse and self 14s; 20 June expenses setting and arranging the accounts, 18s 6d, 2 stamps £1 10s 4d; 5 days on survey and making out accounts £26 5s; total £33 12s 10d, less £1 15s gives £31 17s 10d plus the attendance of Messrs [Charles] Arnett and [Walter] Fuller in the tavern charges, £12 4s [total] £44 1s 10d. [PAR 511/35/1/181]

937 25 Jul 1825 *Letter from the Rev^d J[ohn] W[illiam]Dugdell, Preston vicarage to [Charles] Arnett, Winchelsea, [assistant overseer]:*
I received your letter dated the 15th instant respecting the poor rate etc and will write to Mr [William] Thorpe who has, or is about to receive, money on my account, and will request him to pay to you the amount of the poor rate and also the procuration for the years 1824 and 1825, making in all £28 12s 10d. But in charging me to the church rate you have committed a mistake, the tithe not being liable to any such charge. [PAR 511/35/1/186]
Notes: 1 Dugdell's claim that he was being required to pay church rate on his tithe income is confirmed by the churchwardens' church rate accounts.[12]
2. William Thorpe was a Hastings solicitor and coroner for the Hastings Rape. He must also have been acting on Mr Dugdell's behalf in (**890**). He became Mayor of Hastings in 1836 but was removed during his term of office for bankruptcy.[13] He appears, however, to have remained on the Hastings bench after this removal – see (**374-375**)
3. The word procuration in this context would seem to refer to the cost of employing an attorney or representative. OED

938 16 Aug 1825 *Letter from F[rancis] Whitfield, Ashford, [Kent] to [Charles] Arnett, Winchelsea, [assistant] overseer:*
I shall be much obliged to you paying the amount of my bill into the Rye Bank to be placed into the account of Thomas Bayden of Brookland. I will send you a receipt by the first opportunity. [PAR 511/35/1/190]

939 8 Oct 1825 *Letter from William Curteis, Heronden, Tenterden, [Kent] to [Charles] Arnett, Winchelsea, assistant overseer:*
I understand from Mr [Samuel] Southerden that the new measurement and valuation of the land in his and my uncle J[eremiah] Curteis's occupation was made by some individuals not professional men and that such measurement and valuation has not been general throughout the parish. To such a partial proceeding we feel ourselves bound to object. I now apply to have such valuation set aside and the rate thereon that has just been paid returned. We are ready to produce maps and have the land measured and valued by a proper person provided such measure and value is carried throughout the whole parish. Otherwise we shall appeal. [PAR 511/35/1/197]

940 23 Dec 1825 *Minute of the Winchelsea public vestry:*
[Called] pursuant to public notice for the purpose of considering the propriety of adopting either of the two propositions made to the parish on Friday last the 16th

instant by the Rev^d Mr Dugdell relative to his tithes. Resolved that having read Mr Dugdell's statement it is considered advisable that the rates paid by the rector during the last year shall be refunded and the old composition be returned to and in all respects acted upon till due notice to determine the same be given by one party or the other (viz) by the rector or the parishioners and that the moiety [half] of the expense of the new valuation paid by the rector be repaid to him by the parish and we [the undersigned] therefore subscribe to the above measure and earnestly request the inhabitants and occupiers generally to do the same. [Further] resolved that the vestry clerk be instructed to write to Rev^d Mr Dugdell [about] the proceedings of this meeting with a copy of the resolution.   [PAR 511/12/2]
Note: Payment to Mr Dugdell of £44 1s 0d, his half of these expenses, is included in the overseers' accounts for the quarter ending March 1826.[14] This repayment was authorised by the parish vestry on 2 March 1826.[15]

941 13 Jan 1826 *Minute of a Winchelsea public vestry*:
Resolved that inadverting to the agreement signed by many of the inhabitants in consequence of the recommendation of the public vestry held on 23rd day of December last; this meeting regrets that several inhabitants and occupiers refuse to join in that agreement and they therefore resolve that a copy of the following letter which the vestry clerk is to offer to the inhabitants for signature be forwarded to the rector, the Rev^d Mr Dugdell:
Sir, In consequence of a resolution of the vestry today a copy of which will be forwarded to you by the vestry clerk, we beg to state that we are much concerned that there should exist any difficulty between yourself and the parish relative to your tithes, it is a subject in which a vestry as such cannot interfere so as to bind the parish, however they may be inclined to offer their advice to the parishioners in general, it is therefore out of the power of the inhabitants in vestry to remedy the inconvenience in which you are placed. We the undersigned however to show our desire that you should experience no loss from us, beg to state that we are ready to pay or receive, as the case may be, the difference between the old and the new composition from Michaelmas 1824 to Michaelmas next and also to pay to you such a proportion of the rates paid by you upon the new composition and of the sum of [*blank*] paid as your share of the expense of the late valuation, as our respective rates bear the whole rate.   [PAR 511/12/2]

942 3 Oct 1826 *Information given before Henry Powell and John Tilden, justices of the peace for Winchelsea by Revd J. W. Dugdell, rector of St Thomas's Winchelsea*:
against Benjamin Boots, Sarah Buttenshaw, William Leonard, Thomas Edwards, Mary Woodhams, George Martin, Thomas Skinner [and] Thomas Hoad the elder for refusing to pay to him the tithes due at Michaelmas 1825. Martin ordered to pay the tithes and expenses on the 9th [*marked* paid]; Buttenshaw ordered to pay the tithes and expenses on the 30th [*no payment recorded*]; Boots – warrant granted [*marked*

paid]; Woodhams – warrant granted [*no payment recorded*]; Edwards, Leonard and Skinner ordered to pay the tithes and expenses on the 9th [*marked* paid]; Hoad ordered to pay the tithes and expenses on the 30th [*no payment recorded*]

[WIN 237A]

943 10 Sep 1827 *Appearance before Henry Powell, Joseph Hennah, and Fielding Browne, justices of the peace for Winchelsea, of Charles Arnett, assistant overseer, as agent for Rev*d *J W Dugdell, clerk, of the parish of Preston in the county of Kent and rector of the parish of St Thomas the Apostle, Winchelsea*:

[*Charles Arnett*] humbly complaineth that the Revd Mr Dugdell by the space of twenty days before the date hereof did demand of Benjamin Boots, labourer, John Daniel, shoemaker, Samuel Easton, shoemaker, Thomas Hoad the elder, labourer, Stephen Laurence, painter, William Leonard, sawyer, [and] Thomas Morris, labourer, all of Winchelsea, the small tithes offerings oblations and obventions justly become due within two years now last past from Benjamin Boots 6s 1½d, John Daniel 18s, Samuel Easton 4s, Thomas Hoad the elder 19s 7d, Stephen Laurence 9s, William Leonard 7s, Thomas Morris 4s, unto him, [the Revd J W Dugdell] and that the [*above-named*] did upon the said demand refuse and doth yet refuse to pay or compound for the same or any part thereof. Revd Mr Dugdell therefore prayeth such redress in the [evidence] as to you shall seem meet and to the law doth appertain.

[*Appended note*][same day] Summons against the seven defaulters [issued by the same magistrates].   [WIN 237A]

Notes: 1. Stephen Laurence, a glazier by trade, at this time receiving poor relief for his large family, became a town constable in 1835,[16] served on the quarter sessions grand jury in 1840[17] and was enumerator for the Ferry, Strand and Camber areas in the 1841 census.
2. oblations – offerings; obventions – fees due occasionally. OED

944 15 Apr 1830 *Letter from the Rev James John West, Winchelsea, curate, to [?the overseers of Winchelsea]*:

As nothing is yet settled about the tithes of this parish between the Rev H[enry] S[anders] Mortimer and his parishioners, the Rev J J West is requested by the rector to state that in paying the poor's rate which amounts to £24 19s 7d he begs it to be understood that the quantum of rates already paid – as well as the above named sum – must be taken into the account whenever any agreement with regard to the tithes is entered into.   [PAR 511/35/1/330]

945 4 Feb 1836 *Public vestry meeting of the parish of Winchelsea*:

held at the vestry room on Thursday 4th February [1836] for the purpose of taking into consideration the report of the committee deputed to examine the rating upon the tithes and that Richard Stileman Esq be deputed to write to Mr [Thomas] Bellingham.   [PAR 511/12/2]

946 16 Dec 1839 *Minute of the guardians of the Rye Union*:
A letter dated the 6th inst from Samuel Cloud of Winchelsea was read, requesting, as the agent for the rector of Winchelsea, payment by the guardians of £1 being the tithe for the poorhouse of the parish due September 29th 1839. Ordered that the clerk reply to such letter and state that the guardians do not consider themselves liable to pay such sum. [G 8/1a/3 f.67]

Notes: 1. Subsequently Cloud claimed that this tithe had been paid for the last two years.[18] The guardians denied all knowledge of such payments having been made. They were probably right for it was Winchelsea parish which had paid the poorhouse tithe of £1 to the rector until December 1838[19] and it was still being demanded from the parish in 1840 – see (**878**).
2. Tithe on the building is recorded as being paid in 1820 at a higher rate of £3 7s 0d.[20]
3. Tithe payments, at a rate of twelve shillings per annum were being paid at least by 1786.[21]

947 23 May 1840 *Letter from Walter Bearblock of Hainault Hall, Chigwell, Essex to the overseers of Winchelsea*:
In order to prevent future trouble and expense I, as agent of the Rev[d] J[ames] J[ohn] West, rector of the parish of St Thomas the Apostle in the Ancient Town of Winchelsea, beg to call your attention to the present most unequal and therefore unjust assessment of the rector to the poor rate and to inform you that in the event of the present excessive assessment of the tithes being persisted in, and another rate being demanded of the rector upon such assessment I shall be compelled in justice to appeal against the same. [PAR 511/38/6/1]

948 [n.d. c1840] *Unsigned file copy letter from the parish officers of Winchelsea to [Walter Bearblock of Hainault Hall, Chigwell, Essex] agent of Rev[d] J[ames] J[ohn] West, rector of Winchelsea*:
The parish officers of Winchelsea [have] consulted with some of the principal ratepayers on the subject of the complaint made by you as agent to Mr West of the inequality of the present assessment on the tithe. We beg in reply to state that it appears to us to be fairly rated in proportion to other properties in the parish. As, however, we understand that the mode in which tithes shall in future be assessed is likely to be settled by act of parliament we hope you will not think it necessary to put the parish to expense by litigation as we shall be ready to alter the assessment if the justice of the case requires it as soon as the intended measure is passed or make such deductions from the next rate as may be proved to be unfairly or unequally levied in proportion to the general assessment of other property in the parish. P.S. A vestry meeting is convened for Thursday next to take into consideration your claim for tithe on the late poorhouse at Winchelsea. [PAR 511/38/6/1]

949 [n.d. c1840] *Unsigned file copy letter from the parish officers of Winchelsea to [Walter Bearblock of Hainault Hall, Chigwell, Essex] agent of Rev[d] J[ames] J[ohn] West, rector of Winchelsea*:
We have to acknowledge your letter of the 9th instant. Since our last communication

to you we have received the circular of the Poor Law Commissioners' directions as in what manner to assess the tithes and we are totally unable to comprehend how your statement of unfair rating as regards the assessment of the tithes can in any way be substantiated. We believe you will find the land throughout highly rated and the houses fairly so. If there are exceptions and they are pointed out they will be willingly put right but we are sorry to say we believe your estimate of their value will prove as erroneous as that you set on the land and we firmly believe if the whole valuation should again be revised, which is hardly necessary after the various [?amendments] it has lately experienced, that it will be found the rector does not stand rated as high as in strictness he might. Under these circumstances and with these impressions we cannot hold out any hope of alteration by lowering the rector's assessment.   [PAR 511/38/6/1]

950 8 Jul 1840 *Letter from Walter Bearblock of Hainault Hall [Chigwell, Essex] to Mr W[alter]Fuller, overseer of Winchelsea, Sussex*:
The parish officers, who have hitherto paid the rector £1 a year tithe, are the tenants of the poorhouse not the paupers therein as you intimate. I must again therefore require payment of the tithe already demanded and it will be my duty as surely you must see to proceed for recovery of the same in the event of its being still withheld.   [PAR 511/38/6/1]

951 16 Jul 1840 *Minute of the Winchelsea public vestry*:
A public meeting was holden pursuant to public notice in the vestry room on Thursday 16th July for the purpose of taking into consideration the payment of the tithe on the house late the poorhouse. Resolved that the parish officers are not liable to the demand made upon them for tithe on the house in question.
                                                   [PAR 511/12/2]

1 Evans 1976 p.16   2 Cunningham 1765 p.4   3 Kain and Prince p.6   4 Cunningham - handwritten flyleaf note   5 PAR 511/31/1/13 15 Apr 1823 et seq   6 Tate p.135   7 Evans 1976 p.109   8 PAR 511/12/2 26 Jun 1823   9 PAR 511/31/1/13 Feb-Mar 1824   10 ibid   11 PAR 511 37/2/1b   12 PAR 511/9/1/3 10 Jun 1825   13 Hunnisett p.xxi; Baines p.29   14 PAR 511/31/1/13   15 PAR 511/12/3   16 Win 61b   17 WIN 61D f.154   18 G 8/1a/3 f.89   19 PAR 511/31/1/16   20 PAR 511/31/2/134   21 PAR 511/31/2/61

Emigration

952 *It was, as these documents demonstrate, clearly in the interests of parishes and unions to encourage paupers receiving relief to emigrate thus reducing the local burden. Nevertheless, supporting financial investment was limited and numerous controls and conditions were applied (**958**). It is likely but by no means certain that Wood and Martin (**967**) were Gilbert Wood (**704-709**) and William Martin (**376-389**). For the most detailed example in this volume of a family seeking to emigrate see Samuel Easton (**221-224**). With the same motive, the guardians of the Rye Union considered actively encouraging resident families to move to 'manufacturing districts' where work would be more readily available. See (**982**)*

953 24 May 1828 *Letter from Musgrove Tomkin, Wittersham, overseer, to the overseers of Winchelsea*:
Mr [John] Fisher of Rye office informs me that you are wishing to join some parish who is sending families to America. We are now arranging with a captain in the same channel as Benenden and Sandhurst was sent. If you would like to join us someone had better come over this afternoon or the morrow before twelve o'clock as we expect an answer by post tomorrow from London. If you think of joining us I wish you to make out a list of folks in the following way: Thomas Martin and wife; children 14 years and above – Sarah; [children] 7 years and under 14 – Charles; [children] under 7 – Ann. Every family in the like manner.   [PAR 511/35/1/282]

954 8 Jan 1838 *Minute of the guardians of the Rye Union*:
A letter dated the 5th instant from Mr Tufnell, assistant poor law commissioner [for Kent and Sussex], was read accompanying certain papers respecting the emigration of paupers to Australia in which letter it is stated among other matters that the Poor Law Commissioners would sanction the charging to the out-relief the expense of conveying the emigrants to the place of embarkation (which must not exceed 3d per mile for adults and 1½d per mile for children under 7 years) as well as the cost of a small quantity of clothes and that the charge might be done without application for permission to individual parishes and vestries.   [G 8/1a/2 f.96]

955 22 Jan 1838 *Minute of the guardians of the Rye Union*:
The clerk was ordered to get printed 150 copies of a notice that the government agent (who attended the meeting of this day) for persons desirous of emigrating to New South Wales was in the town [of Rye] to whom application might be made by persons desirous of emigrating to the above colony and it was ordered that the relieving officers put up and distribute such notices in their several districts.
                              [G 8/1a/2 f.106]

956 [Mar 1838] *Public Notice given by the parish authorities of Winchelsea*:
Notice is hereby given that a meeting ...... will be held at the Court Hall in [this] parish on Thursday the 15th day of March next at 11 o'clock in the forenoon for the purpose of considering whether any and what sums of money not exceeding half the average yearly poor rate for three years now last past shall be raised or borrowed as a fund for defraying the expenses of emigration of poor persons having settlements in the parish and being willing to emigrate and giving directions for raising or borrowing of such sums ...... [*signatures of*] J[ames] J[ohn] West, [rector], David Laurence, churchwarden, George Blackman and Robert Sharps, overseers.
                              [PAR 511/38/5/2]

957 19 Apr 1838 *Minute of the Winchelsea public vestry*:
Resolved that this vestry having, pursuant to notice duly given, taken into consideration whether any and what sums of money should be raised or borrowed

as a fund for defraying the expenses of emigration of poor persons having settlements in this parish and being willing to emigrate; and some of the poor persons having settlements in this parish having attended this vestry and being desirous to emigrate to Australia, this vestry are of opinion that it is proper to raise a sum of twenty five pounds for the purposes of such emigration and that the same be borrowed in pursuance of the Poor Law acts.   [PAR 511/12/2]

958 26 May 1838 *Letter from J. W. Parham, assistant secretary at the Poor Law Commission office, Somerset House to the clerk and overseers of the parish of St Thomas the Apostle, Winchelsea*:

The Poor Law Commissioners for England and Wales have to transmit to you herewith an order confirming the resolution of the ratepayers and owners of the parish of St Thomas the Apostle, Winchelsea as to borrowing the sum of £35 for the purpose of emigration and the commissioners have to request your particular attention to the conditions at the foot of this order. A list of the emigrants on the enclosed form should be sent to this office.   [PAR 511/38/5/2]

Notes: 1. The list of emigrants has not survived in the parish records.

2. The order referred to above is dated 25 May 1838 and the conditions to which particular attention was required were:

(i) The parties emigrating shall go to some British colony.

(ii) The churchwardens and overseers may expend not exceeding three pence a mile in conveying each person above seven years of age to the port of embarkation; and each child under seven years three halfpence.

(iii) The churchwardens and overseers may give to each emigrant clothing to the value of one pound if the place of the parties' destination be not eastward of the Cape of Good Hope and to the value of two pounds if the place of their destination is to be eastward of the Cape of Good Hope.

(iv) If the cost, or any part thereof, of conveying the parties from the port of embarkation to the port of discharge, shall be defrayed from the fund above directed to be provided, a contract, to be approved by the Poor Law Commissioners, shall be entered into for conveying them to such port of discharge.

(v) If no part of the cost of conveying the parties shall be defrayed from the fund and no provision be made for their maintenance on arrival at their place of destination, a contract to be approved by the Poor Law Commissioners shall be entered into for giving them money on their arrival, according to the following scale: To each person exceeding fourteen years of age £1; exceeding seven years and not fourteen years 10s; not exceeding seven years 6s 8d.

(vi) If no part of the fund above directed to be provided shall be expended [as in 4 and/or 5 above] the churchwardens and overseers shall transmit to the Poor Law Commissioners within ten days after all the parties shall have embarked, a list containing the names, ages, occupations and places of destination of the said parties.

(vii) Every contract entered into [under 4 or 5 above] shall be registered at the office of the Poor Law Commissioners for England and Wales previous to the day on which the parties shall embark.

3. On 28 May 1838 the Rye Union guardians passed a formal resolution authorising the parish officers of Winchelsea to borrow the sum of £25 'for emigration purposes'.[1]

4. As a result of the permission granted by both the Poor Law Commissioners and the Rye Union, the sum of £25 was borrowed from Richard Stileman of The Friars on the security of its repayment from the parish rate. The interest terms were five percent per annum by five annual instalments of five pounds. The churchwardens and overseers of the poor who executed the indenture on behalf of the parish were Samuel Cloud, David Laurence, William Fuller and Henry Barham. Their signatures were witnessed by Charles Hill. The indenture is dated 6 December 1838 and was approved and registered by the Poor Law Commissioners on 12 January 1839.[2] Receipt of the loan money is recorded in the overseers' accounts for the quarter ending 25 December 1838.[3]

959 6 Aug 1838 *Minute of the guardians of the Rye Union*:
A letter dated the 1st inst from T F Elliott Esq emigration agent-general was read intimating that government intended to allot two ships in October next for the conveyance of emigrants from Kent and Sussex to New South Wales and the clerk was ordered to request to be informed how many families from this union it is possible may be taken in one or both of the ships. [G 8/1a/2 f.213]

960 13 Aug 1838 *Minute of the guardians of the Rye Union*:
A letter dated the 7th inst from T F Elliott Esq was read stating that he could not pledge himself as to the number of families as emigrants to New South Wales which can be taken from this union in the government ships but there will be no desire to stint the number of persons who are eligible for a free passage.
[G 8/1a/2 f.217]

961 4 Feb 1839 *Minute of the guardians of the Rye Union*:
Numerous applications having been made to several of the guardians to know whether there will be ships shortly provided for the conveyance of emigrants to New South Wales, it was resolved that public notice be given by placards throughout the union that persons desirous of emigrating to that colony are directed to make applications to the clerk before 1st March next and the clerk is requested to report such applications to Mr Tufnell and also to submit the names of such applicants to Mr Marshall who is shortly expected to visit the neighbourhood to select emigrants and those applicants who may be rejected by Mr Marshall that he, Mr Tufnell, will then ascertain whether any government ships can be allowed to take out to the colony all or any of those persons who may not be taken in Mr Marshall's ship.
[G 8/1a/2 f.305]

962 8 Apr 1839 *Minute of the guardians of the Rye Union*:
A letter from Mr Elliott, emigration agent general, giving information that Dr Inches will be at Rye on the 15th instant to select emigrants to New South Wales. Ordered that the relieving officers inform the several eligible candidates thereof and request their attendance at the register office by 10 o'clock in the forenoon.
[G 8/1a/2 f.341]

963 22 Jul 1839 *Minute of the guardians of the Rye Union*:
A letter dated the 18th inst from Mr T F Elliott, emigration agent general, was read stating that government intended to send out a ship in October next with emigrants to New South Wales and it was resolved that the clerk get printed 100 copies of a notice that persons residing in the union desirous of emigrating are requested to apply to him on or before the 12th August next for a free passage.

[G 8/1a/2 ff.405-406]

964 1 Apr 1841 *Minute of a meeting of Winchelsea ratepayers and owners of property*:
Resolved that the churchwardens and overseers of the poor shall and they are hereby directed to raise the sum of thirty pounds as a fund for defraying the expenses of emigration of poor persons having settlements in this parish and being willing to emigrate to be paid out of the rates raised or to be raised for the relief of the poor in this parish and to be applied under such titles, orders and regulations as the Poor Law Commissioners shall in that behalf direct.   [PAR 511/12/2]

965 May 1841 *Receipted bill for £12 from H[enry] E[dwards] Paine [clerk to the guardians of the Rye Union] to the parish officers of Winchelsea*:
Share of expenses on journey to London to see the Poor Law Commissioners respecting the payment of passage, clothing and other monies for the emigration of numerous poor persons to Sydney and New Zealand belonging to Beckley, Peasmarsh, Winchelsea and Northiam parishes (there being in some cases no order issued for such expenditure and in other cases no contract under the order issued for such payments) as has been arranged under urgent circumstances by the parish officers and guardians. The secretary of the commission, Mr Lumley, assured me that the payment agreed to be made wherever an order for emigration had been issued would be allowed for such parishes although not agreeable to the strict letter of such orders.   [PAR 511/35/1/362]

966 14 May 1841 *Public notice issued by Nathaniel Benfield, churchwarden, Richard ?Offord and George Blackman, overseers*:
Notice is hereby given that there will be a public vestry holden in the Vestry Room on Tuesday May 18th inst at eleven o'clock in the forenoon to take into consideration the propriety of several families emigrating.   [PAR 511/13/20]

967 1 Jun 1841 *Letter from Henry Edwards Paine, clerk to the Rye Union, to the parish officers of Winchelsea*:
I am directed to enclose for your perusal the letter from the Poor Law Commissioners and copy letter to them from Wood and Martin respecting their wish to emigrate to New Zealand by assistance from the parish of Winchelsea but as the board of guardians are not sufficiently informed upon the matters referred to in such letter to reply to that of the commissioners I am directed to request that you will furnish me with such observations upon the applications of Wood and Martin as you consider necessary to state to the commissioners in reply to their letter.   [PAR 511/38/6/1]

968 13 Sep 1841 *Note appended to a letter about Elizabeth Taunton from Henry Edwards Paine, clerk to the Rye Union, to [George] Blackman, overseer of Winchelsea*:
If in your communicating to [George] Blackhall that he cannot have more assistance, he states that he will not be able to emigrate please let me know [so that] his place may be applied for by someone else – the deposit [of] £1 has been remitted to Messrs Carteret Bonnet who will not of course return it.

[PAR 511/38/6/1]

969 [26 Sep 1841] *Letter headed 'Rye, Sunday morning' from Henry Edwards Paine, clerk to the Rye Union, to [George] Blackman, Winchelsea*:
I enclose your letter for G[eorge] Blackhall which you will have the kindness to forward to him today if possible. I believe he is to be married today, I having for him order to embark in the ship at Gravesend. I cannot get him and his wife taken there for less than 25s. 12s 6d I have paid to Mr Thomas for Blackhall's wife and if you can manage to get the 12s 6d instead of 10s for him and pay Thomas it will be of great help to Blackhall who from being obliged to have an extra day at Gravesend previous to embarkation will want every shilling he has to afford him although he will not it is true be at that much expense at Gravesend the arrangements of the parties here obliges them to leave a day earlier than necessary for going on board the ship and therefore I wish Blackhall to get this letter today if possible as from what I told him yesterday he supposes he will not leave until Thursday – you had better send a lad with the letter and charge the expense. In haste.

[PAR 511/38/6/1]

Note: No record of George Blackhall's marriage at this time appears in the St Thomas's church registers.[4]

970 28 Sep 1841 *Receipt*:
The overseers have paid me twelve shillings and sixpence for expenses of conveyance to Gravesend. [*signature of*] George Blackhall.   [PAR 511/38/6/1]

971 28 May 1849 *Minute of Winchelsea public vestry*:
Resolved that the churchwardens and overseers shall and they are hereby directed to raise the sum of three and not exceeding five pounds as a fund for defraying the expenses of [name of John Stevenson inserted here] poor persons having a settlement in this parish and being willing to emigrate to be paid out of the rates raised or to be raised for the relief of the poor in this parish and to be applied under such rules, orders and regulations as the Poor Law Commissioners shall in that behalf direct.   [PAR 511/12/2]

1 G 8/1a/2 f.180   2 PAR 511/38/5/2   3 PAR 511/31/1/16   4 PAR 511/1/3/2

Rye Poor Law Union

972 *The Poor Law Amendment Act of 1834 removed from parishes the responsibility for administering the poor law and placed it locally in the hands of elected poor law unions which were required to act under the direction of a brand new national body, the Poor Law Commissioners. Winchelsea was placed within the Rye union of parishes together with Rye, Beckley, Peasmarsh, Icklesham, Iden, Brede, Playden, Udimore, [East] Guldeford, Northiam and Broomhill,[1] each community being entitled to representation on the board of guardians. On the day before the first meeting of the Rye Union (**974**) the Winchelsea public vestry resolved unanimously 'that David Manser Esq be elected guardian of the poor for this parish'.[2] On 8 September 1835 the guardians of the Rye Union to which Manser had been elected, thinking in a way somewhat contrary to the intention of the Act, acknowledged that this was an unwieldy area to administer as a single unit and divided the union into four districts of which Winchelsea was to be in District 3 together with Icklesham, Udimore and Brede.[3] Nevertheless the provision of workhouses was centralised with three existing premises 'appropriated for the use of the union': Rye for the aged and infirm, Brede for the able-bodied and Northiam for the children. Under this arrangement it was estimated that Rye workhouse would need to accommodate eighty paupers, with Brede and Northiam taking two hundred each.[4] Winchelsea resented the removal of this responsibility and its attitude to the requirements of the union was, initially at least, uncooperative. When a return of how many aged and infirm paupers from each parish were likely to enter Rye workhouse Winchelsea failed to respond. The guardians' minute book entry reads 'Winchelsea (supposed) 4 men 4 women'.[5] Payments towards union expenses were soon being regularly demanded. On 5 October 1835 Winchelsea was required to pay £20 within the following week. It failed to do so but eventually, and no doubt reluctantly, paid up by 19 October.[6] Things got worse. A year later Winchelsea was declared to be 'considerably in arrears' in union payments and legal proceedings for recovery were authorised.[7]*

*It was the intention of the Poor Law Amendment Act and, initially at least, of the guardians of the Rye Union that poor relief payments within the union should be greatly reduced by supporting only those who were in the workhouses and nobody else. A proposal to this effect first appears in the guardians' minutes on 21 March 1836 when it was resolved 'that no out-relief be given to any pauper of the union except in cases of old age.' The following week the age of 70 was specified but by 11 April the guardians had to admit that the condition of the union workhouses made it impossible to implement the resolution.[8] Some attempt to take action was made on 11 July that year when it was resolved that 'one gallon of flour be deducted from the amount allowed to able-bodied paupers from Monday next'[9]. The matter surfaced again without any initial progress early in 1837 (**983**) but following that some action was proposed (**984**). It would seem that this was ineffective in the longer term for on 28 August 1840 the Poor Law Commission issued a directive prohibiting the granting of outdoor relief. The Rye Union appealed and made a detailed submission, including reporting the current failure of the hop crop in the area, as to why this could not be implemented. An assistant poor law commissioner, Mr Tufnell, was sent to sort things out and he allowed postponement of the requirement subject to conditions.[10] No further mention of the matter has been found within the period covered by this volume. Note: Edward C Tufnell was author of the* Second Annual Report of the Poor Law Commissioners *published in 1836. As an assistant commissioner his particular responsibility was for Kent and Sussex. See also (**954**) and (**961**).[11]*

973 10 Sep 1834 *Minute of the Winchelsea public vestry*:
The questions sent by the Poor Law Commissioners were considered and answers agreed to. Until the regulations come down from the commissioners the overseers are empowered by this vestry to give relief as before. [PAR 511/12/2]

974 29 Jul 1835 *Minute of the first meeting of the guardians of the Rye Union held at The Workhouse, Rye*:
[Resolved] to adjourn this meeting to Friday the 7th day of August next at 10 o'clock in the forenoon without proceeding to the election of a chairman or vice-chairman or to any other business of the union in consequence of the doubts which exist as to the power of the magistrates of the boroughs of Rye and Winchelsea to act as ex-officio guardians of the union. [G 8/1a/1 f.1]
Note: At subsequent meetings no mention is made of this problem but the names of the then Winchelsea magistrates do not appear in the guardians' attendance records. Richard Stileman attended on 11 Jan 1836 with 'ex-officio' beside his name and regularly later without the qualification 'ex-officio'.[12] However, at that time he was serving as a county magistrate, and was not a member of the Winchelsea bench.

975 8 Sep 1835 *Minute of the guardians of the Rye Union*:
[Resolved] that the guardians direct the overseers of their respective parishes to continue relieving the poor as heretofore till that duty is transferred to the paid officers [of the union] in compliance with the circular of the Poor Law Commissioners. [G 8/1a/1 f.8]

976 5 Oct 1835 *Minute of the guardians of the Rye Union*:
[Resolved that the clerk be required] to direct the overseers [of constituent parishes] to desist from giving any further relief after the 10th instant as the relieving officers will then undertake that duty. [G 8/1a/1 f.19]

977 12 Oct 1835 *Minute of the guardians of the Rye Union*:
It was resolved that for the present week the relieving officers in their several districts give the same amount and description which the overseers of each parish have done the preceding week. [G 8/1a/1 f.22]

978 2 Feb 1836 *Entry in the inventory book of the Winchelsea workhouse*:
Furniture sent from the Winchelsea poorhouse for the use of the [Rye] Union by request of the guardians: 1 long deal table on 3 trestles, 2 long [*illegible*], 1 feather bed and bolster, 1 chaff bed and bolster, 2 empty ticks [pillowcases], 2 pairs of blankets, 1 pair of sheets, 2 rugs, 4 bedsteads. Copy of the above sent with them. [AMS 2331]
Notes: 1. On 7 March 1836 the Rye Union guardians drew a cheque for £5 16s 0d 'for furniture and effects as per valuation'.[13]
2. On 22 February 1836 the Rye Union guardians resolved, 'that oak coffins should be advertised for to supply the whole Union from the 25th day of March next for one year'.[14]

979 21 Mar 1836 *Order issued by the guardians of the Rye Union to the overseers of Winchelsea*:

You are hereby authorised and directed to pay to Messrs Pomfret and Co, treasurers of the Rye Union, on or before the 25th of March 1836 at Rye the sum of twenty pounds from the poor rates of Winchelsea towards the relief of the poor thereof and towards defraying such proportion of the general expenses of the union as is lawfully chargeable to Winchelsea and you shall take the receipt of Messrs Pomfret and Co for the said sum.

PS The above order must be complied with punctually to enable the guardians to meet the demands against the union and in default of its payment by the time appointed they will be obliged to enforce the payment thereof as provided by the Poor Law Amendment Act.   [PAR 511/38/3/3]

Note: Another order, in the same terms, for the payment of £90 19s 0d by the 30th of April 1836 was issued on 11 Apr 1836.[15]

980 20 Apr 1836 *Minute of Winchelsea public vestry*:

Resolved that a rate be granted for the relief of the poor of 2s in the pound in lieu of the rate granted March 31st, that rate not being sufficient to meet the demand of the board of guardians.   [PAR 511/12/2]

Note: On 24 May 1836 the clerk of the Rye Union was directed to write to the overseers of Winchelsea requiring the immediate payment to the treasurer of their contribution.[16]

981 5 Dec 1836 *Minute of the guardians of the Rye Union*:

It was ordered that if any pauper misbehave himself or break any of the rules and regulations of the workhouse the master shall reduce the diet of any such individual to bread and water for the space of 24 hours for the first offence.

[G 8/1a/1 f.278]

982 16 Jan 1837 *Minute of the guardians of the Rye Union*:

It was moved by Mr [Richard] Stileman and seconded by Mr Samuel Selmes and resolved unanimously that the thanks of this board be presented to Mr Ralph Collyer for the trouble taken by him in accompanying Messrs Spencer Larkin and Henry Catt to the manufacturing districts for the purpose of inquiring into the state and condition of the labourers there to ascertain how far the migration thither of families belonging to this union would be advisable and also for the care and attention which had been bestowed by him in drawing up his report. It was also resolved that the report be printed and 200 copies circulated throughout the union.   [G 8/1a/1 f.305]

Note: 23 Jan 1837: Spencer Larkin had been appointed master of Udimore School and was loaned £4 to allow him to obtain the necessary qualifications, the money to be repaid at £1 per quarter.[17]

983 30 Jan 1837 *Minute of the guardians of the Rye Union*:

The clerk was directed to write to the guardians not present at this meeting

requesting their attendance on Monday next to discuss the propriety of taking off
the out-relief for all able-bodied paupers.   [G 8/1a/1 f.311]
Note: On 6 Feb 1837 the debate re discontinuation of out-relief was postponed to 20 Feb.
No resolution was passed on that date.[18]

984 20 Mar 1837 *Minute of the guardians of the Rye Union*:
Resolved that permanent relief be discontinued to all paupers having less than six
children unless in cases of sickness or where otherwise disabled. [G 8/1a/1 f.339]

985 3 Jul 1837 *Letter from Joseph Mills, auditor of the Rye Union, to the parish
officers of Winchelsea*:
I hereby inform you [that] I shall audit the accounts of the several parishes in the
Rye Union at the Board Room, Rye Workhouse on Wednesday the 12th instant at
10 o'clock in the forenoon at which place you will attend and produce your books
and vouchers for the quarter ended 24th June last.   [PAR 511/38/6/1]

986 13 Sep 1837 *Letter from Joseph Mills, auditor of the Rye Union, to Mr.
[George] Blackman, overseer, Winchelsea*:
I have not seen Mr Marten to [know] if Mr Jones has arranged with your parish
but as you are one of the overseers since the 25th March you must account for the
quarter ending 24th June which must be done immediately or I must return you as
not having complied with the order of the Poor Law Commissioners which will
be of serious consequence to you and the other overseer and the churchwardens
too. P.S. Do make out an [*illegible*] account that I may enter it in your parish book
which I have.   [PAR 511/38/6/1]

987 26 Mar 1838 *Order from Joseph Mills, auditor of the Rye Union to the
churchwardens and overseers of Winchelsea*:
Take notice you are hereby required to appear before me at Rye Workhouse on
Wednesday the 4th day of April at the hour of ten in the forenoon then and there to
render to me as directed by the 47th section of the Poor Law Amendment Act a full
and distinct account of all monies, matters and things committed to your charge or
received, held or expended by you on behalf of the parish of Winchelsea and also
to make out and present a quarterly statement of receipts and payments according
to the form numbered 4 in schedule A in the orders for keeping the accounts of
this union issued by the Poor Law Commissioners, bearing date the [*blank*] day of
[*blank*] 1836; and further, if thereunto required, to verify on oath or by declaration
the truth of such accounts and quarterly statement as directed by the said statute
and regulations.
[*Appended*] In order that you may not incur the penalties by non-compliance with
the above notice your attention is directed to the following extracts from the order
issued by the Poor Law Commissioners for the keeping, examining and auditing
the accounts and also the 98th, 47th and 13th sections of the Poor Law Amendment
Act.   [PAR 511/38/5/1 Part 1]

Note: The appended extracts require the parish officers to submit a quarterly statement of receipts and payments; to make out at the end of the Michaelmas quarter every year a terrier of the lands and tenements held by the parish and inventory of stock, monies, goods and effects belonging to the parish; to produce to the auditor the register of parish apprentices and all other books kept by the parish officers; to ensure that no bill or demand exceeding 40s shall be paid unless it has been allowed by two overseers or by one churchwarden and one overseer of the parish and confirmed by their signatures on the bill; to submit all bills etc for examination at the time of the audit; to require the parish officers to attend the audit and produce all the relevant books and vouchers. ... The document then lays down the regulations which the auditor must follow and concludes with the penalties to be incurred by parish officers for non-compliance with the regulations, namely a fine not exceeding £5 for the first offence, not exceeding £20 and not less than £5 for a second offence, not less than £20 for a third and subsequent offences and to be liable to suffer imprisonment with or without hard labour according to the decision of the courts.

988 10 Apr 1838 *Letter from H[enry] Holt of the R[ye Union] office to the overseers of Winchelsea*:
I am directed by the Board [of Guardians] to inform you as overseers of the parish of Winchelsea to prepare a cart or conveyance to remove all bodies of paupers that die in or out of the house within the union belonging to the parish of Winchelsea when notice [is] given by the master of the house or relieving officer so that the bodies may be buried in their own parish. <u>You will prepare the same immediately.</u>
[PAR 511/38/6/1]
Note: Holt was acting on a resolution of the guardians' meeting held the previous day.[19]

989 16 Apr 1838 *Minute of the guardians of the Rye Union*:
The declaration of the parish officers of Winchelsea of the necessity of a new valuation of that parish for the purposes of the Parochial Assessments Act, and their request to be allowed to spend a sum to the extent of £15 in making such valuation were produced at this meeting and ordered to be forwarded to the Poor Law Commissioners. [G 8/1a/2 f.161]
Note: On 3 May 1838 the Poor Law Commissioners authorised this revaluation and agreed that the Rye Union should pay £15 towards the cost.[20]

990 20 Jul 1838 *Letter from Henry [Edwards] Paine, clerk to the Rye Union [to the parish officers of Winchelsea]*:
By the 95th section of the Poor Law Amendment Act it is enacted that if any overseer or other person shall disobey the legal order of the guardians such persons may be fined £5 for every such offence. The [Rye] Board of Guardians have therefore directed me to request that you will immediately pay all monies now due and also that you punctually pay all monies to become due from you by virtue of any order or request of this board as in the event of your neglecting to do so the board have resolved to adopt the necessary proceedings to enforce payment of the fine to be incurred by such neglect. [PAR 511/38/6/1]

991 8 Apr 1839 *Minute of the guardians of the Rye Union*:
Ordered that the clerk write to the parish officers of Brede, Winchelsea, Icklesham and Udimore and direct that, during the inability of Mr Henry Holt from illness to attend to the orders and relief relating to the poor belonging to such parishes, they will attend to and see that the several orders are properly administered – more especially those orders relating to the sick poor belonging to these parishes. Also Messrs Hall and Sheather were ordered to assist in the dispensing of relief in Mr Holt's district. [G 8/1a/2 f.342]
Note 1. Jeremiah Hall and William Sheather were the relieving officers for the other two districts within the union.
Note 2: The guardians were informed on 7 May that Henry Holt had died. He was replaced temporarily by Mr W F Clark of Rye and later by James Richardson, already collector of the rates for the district.[21]

992 25 Jun 1839 *Letter from Henry Edwards Paine, clerk to the Rye Union to the overseers of Winchelsea*:
At a meeting of the Board of Guardians of the Rye Union on the 17th instant a resolution was passed for discontinuing the separate parochial accounts of each parish in the union with the bankers from the 24th of June and that in future all monies received by you or the collectors of rates be paid to the treasurers of the union into one account to be kept by them and that I keep the several accounts of receipts and payments hitherto received and made by the parish officers, such account to be open to inspection by you and other persons interested therein. This resolution I am directed to inform you has been approved by the Poor Law Commissioners and at the meeting of the board yesterday a resolution was passed upon which an authority was signed to Messrs Pomfret & Co requesting them to close your account with them and the balance (if any) due they were directed to transfer the amount to the 'Union Parochial Account' from which account monies can only be drawn by cheques signed by a [member of the] Board of Guardians and countersigned by the clerk of the union. By this means the future receipts from rates or other sources as also the payments required on account of your parish will be brought under the notice of the board. Therefore every account on your parish whether for constables' charges, county rates and other matters the commissioners recommend you should forward to the Board of Guardians who will immediately order them to be discharged if found correct thus saving the necessity of your keeping an account at all. Whenever an account on your parish is delivered by you, be pleased to forward the same by one of the relieving officers with as little delay as possible first making a note at the foot of such account that it has been inspected by you. [*Appended note*] Whenever you make a payment to the treasurer send me information of the amount of such payment and from what source you received the monies. [PAR 511/38/6/1]
Note: Only at this point in the records do we find the numbers of Winchelsea poor being cared for or assisted by Rye Union. In the Union workhouses were 6 men, 5 women and 17 children. Despite the original intentions of the Poor Law Amendment Act, 10 men and 11 women were still receiving outdoor relief.[22]

993 13 Jan 1840 *Minute of the guardians of the Rye Union*:
A letter dated the 8th inst from the Poor Law Commissioners was read stating that their privilege of franking and receiving letters free has been abolished by the new Post Office Regulations and requesting pre-payment of all letters to them, the expense whereof it was ordered for the present quarter be charged to the establishment account. [G 8/1a/3 f.91]

994 27 Jan 1840 *Minute of the guardians of the Rye Union*:
A circular letter dated the 20th inst from J Ryland & Co read at this meeting containing particulars and drawings of Herbert's Patent Domestic Flour Engine was ordered to be deposited with the union papers in case the guardians shall at any time consider the propriety of having such engine to be worked by inmates of the workhouses. [G 8/1a/3 ff.98-99]

995 26 Mar 1840 *Minute of the Winchelsea public vestry*:
Resolved that William Longley be appointed guardian to the Rye Union for this parish. [PAR 511/12/2]

996 Sep 1841 *Receipt from G[eorge] Blackman, overseer of Winchelsea to Rye Union*:
To six claimants for voting list 6 shillings.
[*Endorsed*] Winchelsea parish G Blackman receipts: claims to vote 6 shillings.
[PAR 511/35/1/365]
Note: The endorsement on this receipt may be misleading. According to the terms of the 1832 Reform Act, the charge of one shilling applied not to those applying to vote but to those requiring to be provided with a copy of the voting list. However, when Richard Stileman applied in 1836 to the Winchelsea overseers to be included in the list of those eligible to vote in the Eastern Division of Sussex, his letter is marked 'one shilling – paid'.[23]

997 25 Jan 1849 *Minute of Winchelsea public vestry*:
The parish officers in obedience to the call of the guardians [of the Rye Union] have made a rate of 1s 1d in the pound under protest of Revd J J West, Mr Jacob Holt and Mr Basil Kennett. [PAR 511/12/2]

998 14 Jul 1849 *Notice of a Winchelsea public vestry*:
The churchwardens and overseers of the poor of the parish of St Thomas the Apostle, Winchelsea do hereby give notice that a public vestry will be held at the vestry room on Thursday the 19th day of July at 2 o'clock in the afternoon for the purpose of examining the overseers' accounts, to make a parish rate and to consider the necessity of altering and improving the drainage of the town in High Street, also the guardians of the poor will explain to the vestry in what manner the sums raised by the poor rate assessment are applied. [PAR 511/12/2]

1 G 8/1a/1 f.29   2 PAR 511/12/2   3 G 8/1a/1/ff.5-6   4 ibid f.9   5 ibid f.13   6 ibid ff.19, 21, 24   7 ibid f.231   8 ibid ff.128, 139, 146   9 ibid f.205   10 G 8/1a/3 ff.237, 250-252, 272-273   11 Hilton p.593n; Fowler p.25   12 G 8/1a/1 f.72 et seq   13 ibid f.115   14 ibid f.107   15 PAR 511/38/3/3   16 G 8/1a/1 f.174   17 ibid f.308   18 ibid ff.314, 319-324   19 G 8/1a/2 f.156   20 PAR 511/38/5/1   21 G 8/1a/2 ff. 354, 356-357   22 ibid f.403 15 July 1839   23 2W^{m}IV Cap 45 Clause 47; PAR 511/38/7/1

Appendix A: Leading Winchelsea Residents and Officials

Biographical information about those who feature in the published documents:

These mini-biographies of fifty leading Winchelsea residents of the period 1790-1841 include mayors, deputy mayors, rectors, churchwardens, magistrates (jurats), town clerks, overseers, landowners, shopkeepers and constables. Under the legislation in force at the time, on them fell the responsibility in their various capacities for providing assistance to the poor through the poor rate and for enforcing statutes relating to the poor. The jurats were elected by the members of Winchelsea Corporation to serve as justices of the peace on the town's bench. The mayor and deputy mayor were ex-officio although, with the mayor frequently nominated by the patron from persons living outside the town, the responsibility of acting as chairman of the Winchelsea bench was normally exercised by the deputy mayor.

It may be of interest to know that we believe the office of jurat to exist in the twenty-first century only in Winchelsea and the Channel Islands. In Winchelsea they no longer have a legal function but are the mayor's assistants; in the Channel Islands their real legal responsibility continues.

The information which is not specifically referenced about the offices held by the residents included below has been drawn, in the case of rectors, churchwardens and overseers of the poor, from the minutes of the public and select vestries in the three volumes PAR 511/12/1-3. Appointments to the offices of mayor, deputy mayor, jurat, chamberlain, sergeant-at-mace and constable were made by the Corporation. The relevant dates have been extracted from the Corporation's Court Books of Hundreds and Assemblies, particularly WIN 61, 61AA and 61B.

Some details also draw on the editor's extensive researches into Winchelsea's history and people.

1. Robert Alce senior (overseer 1815-16, 1818-20, 1822-23, 1829) was a carpenter.[1] His father, also Robert, was a Winchelsea miller who was at one time churchwarden (**827**). Robert senior married Mary Ollive on 7 May 1789.[2] Their first son, Robert junior, born the following year[3] also became a carpenter. Father and son later worked together in a company, Fuller and Alce, which, among its contracts, carried out maintenance work for the Corporation on the town pound[4] and the workhouse (**764**). They also made coffins for the local undertakers.[5] Robert Alce senior, with many others, was made a freeman of Winchelsea in 1834 to ensure the future of the Corporation.[6] The 1841 census shows him aged 83 living in Cook Street (Barrack Square) with Mary, 79, their second son Thomas, a tailor, and a servant, Cecilia Field. It seems that the Robert Alce of Rye who supplied coal to Winchelsea workhouse (**767, 769**) and was appointed auctioneer for its sale (**790**) was not a relation, or at least not a member of the immediate family.

1 WIN 61AA 7 Jul 1807 (6th quarter)   2 PAR 511/1/1/4   3 ibid   4 WIN 61D f.2   5 PAR 511/31/2/148
6 WIN 61B

2. Henry Barham (overseer 1817-18, 1820-22, 1824-30, 1832, 1837, 1839-40), a Winchelsea tailor, and his wife Maria had ten children baptised in Winchelsea between 1816 and 1833[1] of whom four died young.[2] Henry Barham served as a Winchelsea constable between 1814 and 1818.[3] In his professional capacity he frequently undertook work for the parish both supplying and mending clothes (**764**).[4] He served as foreman of the Winchelsea grand jury at the Winchelsea quarter sessions in 1829 during which proceedings he pressed a complaint against his fellow overseer, Joseph Bigg, for encroaching on a right of way by enclosing highway land.[5] In 1834 he was, like Robert Alce senior, one of those made a freeman to ensure the Corporation's future.[6] Later he was elected as one of the surveyors of the highways.[7] The 1841 census shows him aged 50 and living in Cook Street (Barrack Square) with his wife Maria also 50, Arthur 24, a tailor like his father, Caroline 15, Emily 10 and Albert 8.

1 PAR 511/1/2/1   2 PAR 511/1/5/1   3 WIN 61AA   4 also PAR 511/31/2/119, 130   5 WIN 61D f.?
6 WIN 61B   7 PAR 511/12/2 2 Sep 1835

3. Joseph Bigg (overseer 1823-25, 1828-30) was a Winchelsea grocer and haberdasher who frequently supplied the workhouse with such items as butter, salt, pepper, vinegar, oatmeal, shirt buttons, pins, thimbles, thread etc.[1] When being owed money for these supplies he seems to have been in the habit of deducting the amount of his due poor rates from his bill.[2] He was, for a time at least, the parish's regular supplier of flour for which he was contracted to charge 15½d per gallon of a quality equivalent to the sample he had provided.[3] In 1829 he was 'presented' [charged] by the Winchelsea grand jury with enclosing highway land.[4] See also Henry Barham above.

1 PAR 511/31/2/132   2 ibid   3 PAR 511/12/3 30 Sep 1825   4 WIN 61D f.75

4. George Blackman (overseer 1831-32, 1837, 1839-41) was, like Joseph Bigg, a Winchelsea grocer. He and his wife Sarah had three children baptised in Winchelsea between 1830 and 1833.[1] As with many others who feature in this appendix he was made a freeman in February 1834 when the future of the Corporation was assured by multiple appointments.[2] It was after his second appointment as overseer of the poor in 1837 that he became, as documents in the main text show, principally responsible for liaison between Winchelsea and the Rye Union. He died in 1869 at the age of 73.[3]

1 PAR 511/1/2/1   2 WIN 61B   3 PAR 511/1/5/1

5. George Bray (overseer 1797-1814, 1816-17, 1825) had a farm at Guestling where he was the dissatisfied employer of Thomas Bennett (**65**). During his early years as an overseer he took a major share of the responsibility and in 1804 was one of those appointed to conduct an examination of the overseers' accounts.[1] The following year he was, together with George Harrod, rewarded by a payment of £10 for his attention to duty.[2] He served as foreman of the grand jury,[3] and is listed in the 1807 record of Winchelsea Corporation's queen's dues as paying the fairly substantial amount of three shillings for 'a house and garden formerly Abraham Kennett's'.[4] Most importantly within this volume George Bray was the owner of property, particularly Moneycellar House, in which Winchelsea paupers lived and for which the parish paid the rent at least until eviction was proposed (**240, 242-244, 695, 697**).

1 PAR 511/12/1 f.139   2 AMS 2329 1805/1806   3 WIN 61 f.121   4 WIN 61AA 7 Jul 1807 (5th quarter)

6. Fielding Browne (jurat 1827-1835, deputy mayor 1830) was, during his time as a justice of the peace, a conscientious and active member of the Winchelsea bench. In 1825 he is recorded in the parish register record of the burial of his infant son Robert Henry as 'Lt Col Fielding Browne CB'.[1] Whether these letters indicate the distinction which we would associate with them today the editor has not discovered but it seems extremely unlikely; they do not appear after any further entry of his name. By 1827 he is recorded as 'Colonel of the 40th Regiment of Foot'. Three years later his fortunes seem to be in decline for he becomes 'Late Colonel of the 40th Regiment of Foot now ½ pay Rifle Brigade'.[2] In 1830, at the time he was deputy mayor, he paid the poor rate on a house and garden with an annual value of £11 5s 0d which suggests a residence appropriate to his rank. He was also the owner of 'The Cliff Field'[3] and was among those who took into their households Winchelsea paupers. The boy allocated to him was William Bacon and the arrangement was that Browne would 'find him in board lodging and clothing ... and that the parish do allow Colonel Browne two shillings a week'.[4] See also (**724**). The parish registers reveal a sad story about the colonel and his wife Lucy. They were clearly anxious to have a son with his father's Christian name. Between 1826 and 1836 were buried in Winchelsea three boys called Fielding Browne aged 5, 'an infant' and aged 5 again.[5] Two of their children, Charlotte and Montague, feature among parish baptisms but not burials which suggests that they survived.[6]

1 PAR 511/1/5/1   2 PAR 511/1/2/1   3 PAR 511/31/1/13 15 Jan 1830   4 PAR 511/12/3 2 May 1828
5 PAR 511/1/5/1   6 PAR 511/1/2/1

7. Henry Pearch Butler (town clerk 1822-1826), a Rye solicitor, took office on the resignation of Weeden Dawes 'on account of his health'.[1] Butler was almost immediately required to precept for a county rate. This form of taxation falls outside the scope of this volume but was yet another burden upon the ratepayers of Winchelsea. However, its impact was reduced because it was shared with those parts of Icklesham, Pett and Broomhill which fell within the Liberty of Winchelsea.[2] Unfortunately Butler had no idea how to implement the necessary procedure so John Woods put him in touch with John Tompsett, town clerk of Hastings. Tompsett invited Butler to come to Hastings for a consultation. In response Butler wrote 'I would with the greatest alacrity could I do so but I really cannot by reason of the scurvy which broke out in my right leg the week after Easter [and] has occasioned me to be very lame ever since [so] that I cannot now without the greatest pain and torture get about my house.'[3] Tompsett rose to the occasion by sending appropriate documents as examples and the rate was raised as required. Henry Pearch Butler, son of Richard and Susannah, was baptised at St Thomas's on 25 January 1761.[4] His burial does not feature in the parish registers but a poor rate assessment dated 15 January 1830 lists a house and garden with an annual value of £3 belonging to 'H P Butler (the late)'.[5]

1 WIN 61AA 8 Apr1822 2 WIN 61 ff.135-138 3 WIN 1561 4 PAR 511/1/1/2 5 PAR 511/31/1/13

8. William Chatterton was included in the 1803 militia return as a 'waggoner' (appendix C3). By the time he was in a position to sell property for the extension of the workhouse (**735-740**) he was in business as a miller and major supplier of flour to the parish, frequently receiving considerable payments for specific orders.[1] Later he was awarded a general contract[2] although in 1830 half the contract was transferred to James Clarke on a temporary basis.[3] At his marriage at St Thomas's by licence issued on 5 February 1829[4] he was described as 'widower of Rye'. Beyond his usual trade, on one occasion he was paid £8 8s 3d for 'hog meat'.[5] William Chatterton was among the many new freemen appointed in February 1834 to ensure Winchelsea Corporation's future.[6]

1 e.g. PAR 511/31/1/13 QE Sep 1824 2 PAR 511/12/3 5 May 1826 3 ibid 3 Dec 1830 4 PAR 511/2/2/6 5 PAR 511/31/1/13 QE Mar 1825 6 WIN 61B

9. Jeremiah Curteis of Rye and Tenterden owned substantial amounts of land within the Liberty of Winchelsea for which he paid considerable sums in poor rate. In August 1800 he is recorded as being taxed on 'part of Camber Land and Point House' (Rye Harbour) with an annual value of £112.[1] By February 1801, the assessment to which he objected (**864**) because the rector was not paying poor rate on his tithe income, Curteis's land value had been increased to £128 18s 6d (appendix D1). In 1825 he had over 102 acres valued at £93 10s 0d, mostly described as 'oatlands' – presumably arable (appendix D2). Edward Jeremiah Curteis of Wartling who sat as a county magistrate hearing cases related to Icklesham and Iden – e.g. (**140, 640**) and was a visiting JP at Battle House of Correction[2] was his son.[3] Jeremiah died in 1806 and is buried at Tenterden. Edward Jeremiah erected a mural monument in Wartling Church in memory of his parents.[4] William Curteis's objection in 1825 (**939**) to the measurement and valuation of his 'uncle Jeremiah's' land must refer to Edward Jeremiah who would in normal circumstances have inherited from his father. This possibility is to all intents and purposes confirmed by an entry in the churchwardens' accounts for the church rate dated 7 March 1808 where this land is clearly shown as the property of E J Curteis although a later entry has him as 'Edward Jeremy'.[5]

1 AMS 2329 2 QO/EW/48 20 Oct 1828 3 Llewellyn 2011 p.xxi 4 ibid 276B 5 PAR 511/9/1/3

10. Edwin Dawes was a leading Winchelsea resident and member of a family long connected with the town. In 1800 he is recorded as owning a house with an annual value of £8 and the Pewes Field valued at £10. He was a regular employer of Winchelsea pauper boys including Robert Wheeler (**667-668**). He also made a number of payments for the work of boys who were not members of his household but employed on a casual basis.[1] He employed Gilbert Wood as a footman (**704**) and Nathaniel Benfield as a groom.[2] In 1821 when the select vestry was established to manage the poor of the parish he was one of the first members.[3] He died in 1824 at the age of 75.[4]

1 PAR 511/31/1/10 2 WIN 1728 3 PAR 511/12/2 f.12 4 PAR 511/1/5/1

11. Thomas Dawes was also a leading Winchelsea resident who, like so many of his family, had a legal career, in his case as a barrister, described in (**843**) as 'attorney-at-law'. He was principal of a London firm, Dawes and Co, to which the parish sometimes referred when requiring specialist advice e.g. (**843, 847**). Appendix D2 includes his major Winchelsea landholdings and those owned jointly with his brother Weeden. He it was who, with David Laurence, conducted a major investigation into the parish's financial situation at the time of Charles Arnett's appointment as assistant overseer (**17**). In 1826 Thomas Dawes was elected to be a member of the select vestry[1] and, like his brother, was among those appointed freemen in February 1834 to ensure the future of the Corporation.[2] The townspeople, particularly the children, became warmly appreciative of his beneficence when in 1851 he paid for the building of the town well which stands in Castle Street. It was the only public facility available within the main town area, until that time all water for those who did not have wells in their gardens had to be carried from the foot of the hill.[3]

1 PAR 511/12/3 28 Mar 1826   2 WIN 61B   3 Pratt 1998 p.60

12. Weeden Dawes (town clerk 1819-1822) was, in common with all Winchelsea's town clerks of this period, a Rye solicitor. Henry Pearch Butler's predecessor, he retired citing ill-health having acted for the parish during much of the time that John Woollett, his partner in the firm of Woollett and Dawes, was the town clerk in office (1798-1819), first featuring in these pages in 1815 (**52**). Together with his brother Thomas he owned a considerable amount of valuable property in Winchelsea – see appendix D2. He and his twin sister Elizabeth were baptised at St Thomas's on 13 November 1768[1] when his father, Nathaniel, was himself serving as town clerk. Appreciation of Weeden's service to the town and parish was recorded in the books of the Corporation.[2] In February 1834 he was among the many new freemen appointed to ensure Winchelsea Corporation's future.[3]

1 PAR 511/1/1/2   2 WIN 61AA 8 Apr 1822   3 WIN 61B

13. Richard Denne, owner of Mariteau House, was heavily involved in the administration of the parish during the earlier part of the time covered by this volume. He was one of those appointed to manage the poor in 1786 (**807**) and 1792 (**809**), examined the overseers' accounts when necessary – e.g. (**821**) and, although eventually unavailable, was elected a member of the re-assessment committee of appeal in 1800 (**861-862**). On one occasion he was accused of digging a dangerous ditch opposite his Mariteau home and ordered to erect a fence within one month.[1] His extensive property included Pound Piece – see appendix D2. The Pound, to which stray animals were taken, was within the area of the Mariteau garden. Richard Denne appears to have had no major objection to this but soon after his death at the age of 69 in 1819[2] his family allocated land to Winchelsea Corporation to which The Pound could be moved.[3] It was then established in School Hill and is now the site of Pound Cottage and an electricity sub-station, the sub-station still being the freehold property of the Corporation.[4]

1 WIN 61 ff. 117-117r   2 PAR 511/1/5/1   3 WIN 129   4 WIN 2359/7/5/1

14. Revd John William Dugdell (rector 1822-1829) was the vicar of Throwley near Preston in Kent and an absentee rector of Winchelsea. He principally features in this volume through his disputes with the parish over his liability for poor rate (**871, 873**) and the income from his tithes (**912, 914** et seq). To carry out his duties at Winchelsea Mr Dugdell appointed Rev[d] Thomas Richards, Vicar of Icklesham, as his curate. No doubt grateful for the additional income, Mr Richards did as well as he could as is evidenced by the parish registers, but, having to share his time with Icklesham, was only able to take one Winchelsea service each Sunday. This failure to provide what was known as 'double duty' in order to enable all Winchelsea parishioners to attend a service on Sundays caused the parish to complain strongly to Mr Dugdell and to seek the support of the Bishop of Chichester.[1] (see also pp.xxiii-xxiv)

1 PAR 511/12/2 13 Jan 1826

15. Walter Fuller senior (overseer 1795, 1797-1805, 1807-1811, 1815, 1819, 1822, 1826-1828) was a carpenter who took a conscientious part in the administration of the parish, particularly in assuming responsibility for sorting out the accounts which had been somewhat carelessly kept (**829**). He was an extensive property owner including rooms in The Square (Barrack Square) which were rented by the parish for the use of paupers – e.g. (**80, 488**) but many of which were empty in 1825 – see appendix D2. He also served as Corporation treasurer[1] and was a town constable between 1802 and 1808.[2] He married Lucy Amon on 26 January 1796.[3] Their oldest son, Walter junior, was baptised at St Thomas's in December of that year and seven more children were born between then and 1813.[4] Walter Fuller was also a regular employer of Winchelsea paupers such as Robert Broadfoot (**173**), William Fisher (**262**) and Thomas Mitchell who was taken from his household into the workhouse[5] not long before Fuller's death aged 63 in 1829.[6]

1 WIN 855   2 WIN 61AA   3 PAR 511/1/1/4   4 ibid; PAR 511/1/2/1   5 PAR 511/12/3 15 Jan 1829
6 PAR 511/1/5/1

16. Walter Fuller junior (overseer 1830-1833, 1835, 1837, 1839-41) took up his father's trade as a carpenter and many of his father's former duties, adding more. He became a town constable in 1830,[1] was Winchelsea Corporation's chamberlain between 1834 and 1844[2] assuming in that capacity the Corporation treasurership, was appointed vestry clerk at a salary of £15 per annum in 1835[3] and in 1841 was the census enumerator for the Winchelsea town area. Either he or his father considerably expanded the family property ownership. By 1830, quite apart from his own shop, house and land, he was paying the poor rate on 9 rooms in The Square and had a further 42 rooms unoccupied.[4] In February 1834 he was one of those appointed freemen to ensure the Corporation's continued existence.[5] According to the Tithe Map, the property he occupied in 1842 included Barn Plat, now known as Blackfriars Barn.[6] The entry which he wrote for himself and his family in the census return shows him aged 40 and living in Castle Street with his wife Cecilia also 40 and their children Cecilia 12, Walter 10, and Richard 8. At the Easter Monday mayoring in 1867 a vote of thanks was recorded to 'Mr Walter Fuller on his resignation for his services as [Corporation] treasurer during the last thirty-eight years'.[7]

1 WIN 61B   2 ibid   3 PAR 511/12/2 8 Apr 1835   4 PAR 511/31/1/13 15 Jan 1830   5 WIN 61B   6
TD/E 90/1/2 ..7 WIN 61B f.147

17. George Haisell, father of Sarah (**321-325**), was the Winchelsea barber who frequently charged the parish for cutting the hair of the paupers – e.g. (**97, 839**). The poor rate assessments for both 1825 (appendix D2) and 1830[1] show him occupying a house and garden valued at £2 but excused payment on account of poverty, although his work seems to have provided him with a living, if a less than adequate one, because no direct poor law relief paid to him has come to light. His straitened circumstances did not prevent him playing a full part in Winchelsea's affairs for he was appointed as town constable on fifteen occasions between 1831 and 1850 and as town or common sergeant in 1835-1836.[2] He was a member of the Winchelsea quarter sessions grand jury in 1840.[3]

1 PAR 511/31/1/13 15 Jan 1830   2 WIN 61B   3 WIN 61D f.154

18. George Harrod (overseer 1799-1814, 1816, 1821, 1823-1825), sometime employer of William Blackhall (**87**), was proprietor of the New Inn, Winchelsea[1] who, as an example of the services he provided on the parish's behalf, submitted in 1821 an account to the overseers for 'wine, spirits, tobacco etc', for 'breakfast, dinner, beer, supper and lodging at 4s 4d a day' for a guest whose expenses the parish was meeting and 'for poor men breakfast and beer 1s 7d'.[2] During the period before Winchelsea had a paid official as assistant overseer, George Harrod took a considerable lead. In 1803 he was rewarded, together with Charles Terry, with a payment of £10 'for their great attention to the management of the poor of the parish'.[3] The following year he, again with Terry, took considerable trouble compiling the parish's disbursements and receipts accounts,[4] and continued the same task in co-operation with George Bray.[5] For a considerable majority of years between 1798 and 1829, Harrod was also a town constable.[6] He served on the quarter sessions grand jury in 1823[7] and was among the many freemen appointed in February 1834 to ensure the Corporation's future.[8] He died in 1837 aged 72.[9]

1 PAR 511/12/1 f.182   2 PAR 511/31/2/134   3 PAR 511/12/1 f.145   4 AMS 2329 E1804-E1805]   5 ibid E1805-E1806   6 WIN 61AA; WIN 99 et seq   7 WIN 61D f.10   8 WIN 61B   9 PAR 511/1/5/1

19. Joseph Hennah (jurat 1821-1858; deputy mayor 1828, 1832, 1853; mayor 1836, 1844-1849) Apart from his long and conscientious service as a Winchelsea magistrate, of which there is much evidence in these pages, as the deputy mayor in office he was the senior person persuaded by John Tilden to form a quorum for the February 1834 Assembly[1] which guaranteed that Winchelsea Corporation would have a future. The 1842 Tithe Map shows him with a garden between Rectory Lane and German Street on land which was the freehold of the Corporation.[2]

1 WIN 61B   2 TD/E 90/1/2

20. Charles Hill was one of Winchelsea's most loyal and conscientious servants. He was an unpaid town constable between 1825 and 1850 and the mayor's sergeant-at-mace between 1828 and 1850, relinquishing both posts only in 1842 when he was, for just one year, pound driver.[1] As mayor's sergeant he drew a small salary and expenses but his principal civic income was as the town gaoler. To this position he was appointed in 1828,[2] serving until 1850[3] and receiving £25 per annum plus expenses throughout that time. By profession he was a shoemaker who was frequently engaged to supply the parish.[4] His varied service, recorded in this volume, included giving evidence against Thomas Bennett

(**73**) and Stephen Field (**253**), travelling to carry out arrests such as those of Samuel Easton in London (**215**) and William Foster in Liverpool (**271**) and apprehending 'rogues and vagabonds' such as Ann Stevens (**530**). The respect in which he was held is illustrated by his being invited to witness the signatures on a mortgage document (**958**). By far the most embarrassing moment in Charles Hill's long career must have been having to deal with a drunken and uncooperative magistrate. This was on the evening of 9 June 1826 when an election ball was held in the Court Hall with invitations going only to the gentry of the town with some distinguished visitors from elsewhere. George Stace junior was one of the eleven eligible freemen (a 100% turnout) who had cast his vote at the election of two MPs to the House of Commons in the morning. Stace seems to have spent the rest of the day in the New Inn, possibly on the proceeds of the payment he had received for voting as required by the borough patron. When Stace returned to the Court Hall in an inebriated state he found a crowd of uninvited Winchelsea residents noisily demanding admission. He supported their demand, forced his way into the room and became involved in a fight. Charles Hill was ordered to restrain him and it was Hill who was most frequently in the witness box at the ensuing inquiry held into the events of that day by Stace's fellow magistrates.[5]

1 WIN 61B   2 WIN 61D f.65   3 WIN 629   4 e.g. PAR 511/12/2 16 Jul 1824   5 WIN 237A 12 Jun 1826

21. George Hill (overseer 1815-1816, 1823-1830) was one of the overseers delegated to collect the poor rate after Charles Arnett's suspension (**19**), was contacted by Sarah Cole seeking assurances about her brother (**152**) and in 1823 signed the advertisement for a master and mistress for the workhouse (**757**). Apart from these occasions he features little in the records except that the 1842 Tithe Map shows him occupying a garden in Quarter 14 between Rectory Lane and German Street, part of land which was the freehold of Winchelsea Corporation.[1] The 1841 census shows him as aged 78, of independent means, and living in German Street with one servant, Mary Bennett, in his household. His age relative to that of Charles (he was 28 when Charles was born)[2] suggests that he could have been Charles's father but nothing else has been found to connect the two.

1 TD/E 90/1/2   2 PAR 511/1/5/1

22. Revd Drake Hollingberry whose appearances in these pages include being employer of Stephen Sinden (**516**) and a member of the 1801 committee of appeal (**861**) was an important figure in the parish for he was rector of St Thomas's between 1767 and 1822. Throughout the vast majority of his time as rector he was also chancellor of the Diocese of Chichester, a legal appointment. Despite this preoccupation elsewhere he took a deep interest in his parish and its people and was greatly respected. The parish registers illustrate this commitment for he was seldom unavailable to officiate at baptisms, marriages and burials. His entries and his signature constantly appear. He was buried in his parish churchyard on 5 January 1822 at the age of 80.[1]

1 PAR 511/1/5/1

23. John Hollingberry (churchwarden 1826, overseer 1824-1825), son of Drake and Elizabeth, was baptised by his father on 23 June 1780.[1] For a time he served as an officer in the Sussex Militia.[2] He was a regular employer of Winchelsea pauper boys[3] including Stephen Sinden (**516, 520**). He was among those appointed to the freedom in 1834 to ensure the future of Winchelsea Corporation.[4] At the time of his death in 1844 at the age of 63 he was living in Hastings.[5]

1 PAR 511/1//1/2   2 PAR 511/1/2/1 6 Sep 1814   3 e.g. PAR 511/31/1/13 QE Mar 1827   4 WIN 61B
5 PAR 511/1/5/1

24. Jacob Holt was a bricklayer who also acted as an undertaker within the parish (**237, 260, 625**). He served as a town constable between 1814 and 1821[1] and again in 1824.[2] He often did bricklaying and repairs for the parish, for example in 1821 he charged £20 4s 1d for work at the poorhouse.[3] He was a regular member of the public vestry – e.g. (**672**) and the quarter sessions grand jury,[4] was among those appointed freeman in February 1834 to ensure Winchelsea Corporation's future[5] and from 1839 was often chairman of the public vestry.[6] Jacob Holt had a twin brother Esau, another bricklayer (both following their father James into that trade). Esau's career in the town was far less distinguished, he and his wife Elizabeth being eventually removed as paupers to St Mary in the Castle, Hastings in 1847.[7] The census records for the twins illustrate the danger of taking census ages of that time, permitted to be rounded up or down to the nearest five years, too literally. They were baptised together on 3 December 1785.[8] In 1841 Jacob was listed as living with his family in Higham Green *aged 50*, Esau with his family in Cleveland Road (Friars Road) *aged 55*.

1 WIN 61AA 2 WIN 61B 3 PAR 511/31/2/132 4 e.g WIN 61D f.154 5 WIN 61B 6 PAR 511/12/2
7 PAR 511/32/2/107 8 PAR 511/1/1/2

25. Edward Jeakens (overseer 1806-1813, 1815, 1821-1822, 1824-1825) These pages provide ample evidence that Edward Jeakens, tanner, father of Burford – see (**344**) – played a leading part in the management of parish affairs in the time before the appointment of Charles Arnett as the first professional assistant overseer. As a few examples, he represented the parish in dealing with the cases of Hannah Francis (**275-276**), Dive Milliner (**393-394**) and Elizabeth Watson (**647**), was a poor rate collector (**819**) and was appointed to the first select vestry (**848**).

26. Thomas Sylvester Keene see (**151**)

27. Richard Lamb (jurat 1781-1811, mayor 1790, 1792) features in these pages – e.g. (**114, 159, 864**) – as a Winchelsea magistrate. He was married at St Thomas's to Sarah Gurley on 2 November 1784[1] and their daughter Elizabeth was baptised there the following month.[2] In the same year he is described in the Winchelsea Corporation records as 'one of His Majesty's riding officers'.[3] His wife died in 1803.[4] In 1805 Lamb indemnified Winchelsea parish against any expense arising from the birth to Ann Buck of an illegitimate daughter 'of which he is the father'.[5] On the same date, 28 March 1805, Thomas Marten the elder gave a similar undertaking in respect of William, the illegitimate son of Richard Lamb's daughter Elizabeth.[6] The complete record of the payment of the queen's dues, made in 1807, shows Richard Lamb living at Firebrand, formerly owned by the Martens.[7] Richard Lamb remarried in 1808.[8] The Lamb family were prominent in Rye for many years. Whether Thomas, William or Charles, all of whom appear in this volume as magistrates for Winchelsea, Rye or Sussex, were members of Richard's family is not known to the editor but it seems very likely.

1 PAR 511/1/1/2 2 ibid 3 WIN 61 f.90r 4 PAR 511/1/1/4 5 PAR 511/34/3/11 6 PAR 511/34/3/10
7 WIN 61AA 7 Jul 1807 (13th quarter) 8 PAR 511/1/1/6

28. John Haddock Lardner (town clerk 1826-1848) who, for example, investigated the cases of Ann Easton (**197-198**) and Samuel Easton (**205, 220, 224**), was a partner in the Rye solicitors, Dawes, Lardner and Fisher. He was a first cousin of Edwin Nathaniel Dawes who succeeded him as town clerk in 1848, to be succeeded in turn in that office by his son, Walter Dawes (1876-1930) and grandson Edwin Plomley Dawes (1930-1961); a remarkable record of service to Winchelsea made even more remarkable by the fact that Edwin, Thomas and Weeden Dawes – see above – were members of the same family.

29. David Laurence (overseer 1814-1816, 1818-1820, 1824, 1826-1830, 1833; churchwarden 1823, 1834-1836, 1838-1841; assistant overseer 1828-?). After what they saw, despite his good results, as the unsuccessful employment of Charles Arnett, an outsider, as Winchelsea's salaried assistant overseer, the churchwardens and overseers decided to turn to one of their own. David Laurence, the detailed requirements of whose office are published as appendix E1, was engaged, despite the absence of Arnett's responsibility as workhouse master, at the still ungenerous salary of £20 per annum (**22**). Laurence was a local carpenter who was recorded in Winchelsea's militia return of 1809 as being aged 25 and having at that time two children[1] and therefore liable for service. He had married Sarah Barnard in 1806[2] and their eventual family of seven children, two of whom died in infancy, were baptised at St Thomas's.[3] Laurence served as a Winchelsea constable between 1811 and 1813.[4] From the time of his first appointment as an overseer he became, unlike many of his colleagues, actively involved in parish affairs, for example delivering the bastardy order to John Eagles (**168**) and giving evidence against him (**178**), dealing with the cases of Gilman (**320**) and William Martin (**378**) et seq, and seeking the arrest of Bourne Russell (**642**). He served as chairman of the select vestry and was among those opposing the sale of the workhouse (**773**). His work as assistant overseer after 1828 is constantly evident in these pages. The detailed list of his responsibilities (appendix E1) indicates clearly the demands of the post. No similar document has survived drawn up at the appointment of his predecessor. David Laurence was among the many new freemen appointed in February 1834.[5] The 1841 census, using the enumerator's authority to show ages to the nearest five years, shows David Laurence as aged 50 (he was 56)[6] living in Tower Hill (Strand Hill) with his wife Sarah, 60 (she was 57),[7] and children George and Harriett who were both recorded as aged 25 despite the fact that George was three years older than Harriett.[8] David Laurence died in 1848 at the age of 63.[9]

1 WIN 2359/3/1   2 PAR 511/1/1/4   3 ibid; PAR 511/1/2/1; PAR 511/1/5/1   4 WIN 61AA   5 WIN 61B   6 PAR 511/1/5/1   7 ibid   8 PAR 511/1/1/4; PAR 511/1/2/1   9 PAR 511/1/5/1

30. William Lipscomb (jurat 1827-1834, deputy mayor 1831, mayor 1832) appears in this volume as a Winchelsea justice of the peace. Although apparently never a resident, he was recruited to Winchelsea Corporation by the Duke of Cleveland whose tutor he had once been.[1] The duke was at the time patron of Winchelsea's two parliamentary seats and thus controlled membership of the Corporation.[2] Lipscomb has the dubious distinction of having Winchelsea's shortest term of office as mayor – he served for just two weeks.[3] He was, however, one of those who responded to John Tilden's appeal for support in ensuring the future of the Corporation by attending to create a quorum at the Assembly which appointed many new freemen in February 1834.[4]

1 Pratt 1998 p.44   2 ibid   3 WIN 61B ff.44-45   4 ibid

31. William Longley was a resident, first of Lydd and later of Camber. His move to Camber may well have been as a result of his marriage at St Thomas's on 13 September 1828 by licence issued four days earlier[1] for his first wife was Mary Southerden.[2] However, no direct evidence has been found that she was a daughter of Samuel who lived there. Longley remarried in 1834 as a widower.[3] He was among those made freemen in February 1834 to ensure Winchelsea Corporation's future[4] and was in 1840 elected to represent Winchelsea as one of the guardians of the Rye Union (**995**). In the 1841 census he is recorded as a farmer living in Camber with his second wife, Jane née Holder.

1 PAR 511/2/2/5   2 PAR 511/1/3/1   3 ibid   4 WIN 61B

32. Richard Maplesden was a grocer and draper with premises in German Street. He was frequently appointed overseer and in 1816 was serving as churchwarden. His career in parish affairs had an unfortunate start when, in 1795, he was fined twenty shillings for failing to attend the Winchelsea quarter sessions as a member of the grand jury.[1] However, he seems to have learned his lesson for two years later he appeared promptly in court for the same duty.[2] In 1803 he and his son, Richard junior, were both sworn in as extra constables, presumably in response to the threat of invasion.[3] In the same year Richard senior, despite being 52 and well over the required age, volunteered to serve in the local militia as a rifleman, offering his services 'if it is felt proper' (appendix C2). During the French revolutionary and Napoleonic wars, when Winchelsea was a busy garrison town, Richard Maplesden issued his own token coins which could be used at his shop and elsewhere.[4] By 1841 such enterprise had left him sufficiently well-off to be described as 'independent' in the census. He was then living with his wife Ann at Rose Cottage (German Street) and died two years later at the ripe old age of 91.[5]

1 WIN 61 f.98r   2 ibid f.101r   3 ibid f.112r   4 Pratt 2005 p.216   5 PAR 511/1/5/1

33. Thomas Marten was one of a leading Winchelsea family whose members served as mayors of the town between 1680 and 1795. Their home was Firebrand in the High Street. The Thomas Marten who features fairly extensively during the early years covered by this volume as deputy mayor and justice of the peace was known by those compiling the records as Thomas Marten the elder. He served on the committee of appeal for the 1800 poor rate revaluation (**861**) and was sitting as a magistrate when that revaluation was quashed (**864**). He is also notable for having to indemnify the parish against costs arising from the birth of Elizabeth Lamb's son[1] (see also entry for Richard Lamb above). Thomas Marten junior was, in 1800, 'supervisor of His Majesty's Riding Officers in the service of His Majesty's Customs at the Port of Rye'.[2] He died in 1805 but the parish register does not give his age.[3] Thomas Marten the elder died in 1807, two years after his son, while still in office as deputy mayor and jurat. Once again no age is given in the register.[4]

1 PAR 511/34/3/10   2 WIN 61 f.106r   3 PAR 511/1/1/4   4 ibid

34. Thomas Milles farmed at East Guldeford (**894, 903**) and was liable for the Winchelsea poor rate because his land, or part of it, lay within the Liberty of Winchelsea. He was, for example, registered in 1830 as an 'outdweller' liable to pay the sum of £14 on more then 59 acres of land with an annual value of £80.[1] For the same 59 acres in 1825 see appendix

D2. Milles lived at Combwell, Goudhurst but later moved to Buston in Hunton in Kent. He was an occasional employer of Winchelsea labourers (**720-721**) and seems often to have been tardy in meeting his liability to the parish – e. g. (**885, 887, 888**)

1 PAR 511/31/1/13 15 Jan 1830

35. Richard Osborne was licensee of The Castle in Castle Street (**627**), now Old Castle House. He stood surety for William Martin (**15**) when he was in trouble for assaulting Charles Arnett. Osborne married Maria Went in 1816[1] and they were the employers of Hannah Turk (**626**). His wife died in 1829. In earlier years the militia return of 1809 shows him as a carpenter aged 18 and liable for service.[2] In 1830 he was owner of a house, stables and land with a considerable annual value of £13 5s 0d.[3] See also 1825 (appendix D2) which adds that his land included Chapel Field and Float Field. In February 1834 he was one of those appointed a freeman of Winchelsea to save the Corporation[4] and in 1836 was appointed an overseer of the poor.[5] The 1841 census shows him resident at The Castle with his daughter Ann aged 14, a female servant named Ann Holt and George Willard aged 13, potboy. By 1843 the respect in which Richard Osborne was held is evidenced by his fairly regular appointment as chairman of the public vestry.[6]

1 PAR 511/1/3/1   2 WIN 2359/3/1   3 PAR 511/31/1/13 15 Jan 1830   4 WIN 61B   5 WIN 61D f.120   6 PAR 511/12/2

36. Rev[d] Thomas Richards was Vicar of Icklesham. He assisted Winchelsea parish by acting there fairly frequently during the declining years of Drake Hollingberry and was appointed Winchelsea's curate by the new rector, Rev[d] J W Dugdell. The baptisms of three of Thomas Richards' children, Thomas junior and the twins James and Elizabeth, although undertaken by their father at Icklesham, are recorded in the Winchelsea register.[1] Thomas and Eliza's third son, Richard Hollingberry Richards, named for the then rector, was baptised in 1819 by his father at Winchelsea but lived only for just over a month.[2] Eliza Richards probably died in childbirth for she was buried on 5 July 1819, the day before the baptism of their son.[3] Both their surviving sons became clergymen.[4] Richards himself was buried at Icklesham where 'his remains lie beneath the communion table in Icklesham church'.[5] Thomas Richards took an active part in Winchelsea parish affairs (**305, 371, 851-852**), was recorded in 1825 as an outdweller paying the poor rate on the Winchelsea churchyard. (see appendix D2) and was elected to the select vestry in 1826.[6]

1 PAR 511/1/2/1   2 ibid; PAR 511/1/5/1   3 ibid   4 Cooper 1850 p.139   5 ibid   6 PAR 511/12/3 28 Mar 1826

37. Henry Powell (jurat 1818-1828, deputy mayor 1823-1826) was, perhaps, one of Winchelsea's most conscientious magistrates during the period covered by this book. A Winchelsea resident taxed on the ownership of two houses – see appendix D2 – he was never appointed mayor but, while deputy, undertook mayoral duties on behalf of absentees. A strong supporter of Charles Arnett and his work (**1**) Powell's regular appearances on the bench are well illustrated by cases in which Arnett was involved where he sat alone (**6, 8**) and with others (**13-15**). He appears regularly elsewhere and his complaint about the inefficiency of the beadle (**110**) suggests that John Chester replacing Henry Tilden in that office had not improved the situation. Henry Powell's court duties ended only on his death in 1828 at the age of 78.[1]

1 PAR 511/1/5/1

38. William Sargent senior (churchwarden 1795-1802, 1804-1814, 1818-1822) was a miller who was supplying the parish with flour by 1802/3.[1] Later he submitted substantial bills for the same service, for example for £51 12s 0d between March and September 1820.[2] He had served as a quarter sessions grand-juryman in 1797.[3] William Sargent appears in the record of liability for the queen's dues in 1807 as paying 4d for 'a chimney plot' and 4d for a stable, both in quarter 13.[4] He was appointed to the first select vestry in 1820 (**848**). A poor rate assessment made in 1830 shows his house as having an annual value of £1[5] which is very low for someone with the status in the community suggested by his being churchwarden. He died in 1833 aged 78.[6]

1 PAR 511/31/1/9   2 PAR 511/31/2/131   3 WIN 61 f.101r   4 WIN 61AA 7 Jul 1807   5 PAR 511/31/1/13 15 Jan 1830   6 PAR 511/1/5/1

39. William Sargent junior (overseer 1812-1815, 1819-1822, 1824; churchwarden 1829-1833), son of William senior and his wife Judith was baptised at St Thomas's on 21 June 1785.[1] He succeeded his father as a miller and in that capacity also supplied the parish. In June 1824 the select vestry, to which he had been appointed on the same day as his father (**848**), resolved 'that William Sargent junior do supply the parish with flour according to sample approved at one shilling and threepence per gallon from 1 July to 1 October next'.[2] When that arrangement ran out he tendered to continue at the fixed price of 9s 11d a bushel. His tender was accepted.[3] As an overseer he was involved in drawing up plans for extending the workhouse (**734**). Later he was elected as one of the surveyors of the highways (**858**). With many others, he was made a freeman of Winchelsea in February 1834[4] and by the following year he had successfully tendered to the guardians of the Rye Union to supply flour for out-relief in the parishes of Winchelsea and Icklesham at 8s 2d 'per gallon'.[5] In 1841 William Sargent junior was aged 55 and living in the High Street with his daughter Elizabeth, 20, his wife having pre-deceased him. He died in 1859 aged 74.[6]

1 PAR 511/1/1/2   2 PAR 511/12/2 28 Jun 1824   3 ibid 12 Oct 1824   4 WIN 61B   5 G 8/1a/1 f.25   6 PAR 511/1/5/1

40. Samuel Selmes was a substantial landowner in the Camber area, paying poor rate to Winchelsea on land valued at £57 10s 0d – see appendix D2. (**369**) suggests that he was an overseer in Rye. He was appointed to the Winchelsea 1837 revaluation committee on behalf of the landowners (**875**) by which time he had been a regular and leading member of the guardians of the Rye Union since that body's formation.[1] and by 1837 was serving as vice-chairman.[2]

1 G 8/1a/1 f.4   2 ibid f.353

41. Samuel Southerden lived and farmed at Camber where he was a substantial landowner paying Winchelsea poor rate on land valued at £85 in 1794[1] a figure which had risen to £120 by 1825 – see appendix D2. He was a regular employer of Winchelsea men such as, in this volume, William Coleman (**157**), William Morris (**403**), Richard Richardson (**472, 475**) and William Selden (**497**). Samuel Southerden, as a resident living within the Liberty, played a full part in parish affairs, being appointed to the revaluation committee in 1823 (**869**) and elected to the select vestry in 1826. He and his family do not feature in the Winchelsea parish registers but the fact that he had died by 1830 is indicated by his poor rate assessment for January that year being made out to 'Samuel Southerden executors'.[2]

1 AMS 2329 24 May 1794   2 PAR 511/31/1/13 15 Jan 1830

42. George Stace senior (jurat 1782-1816; deputy mayor 1809, 1811, 1813, 1815; mayor 1794) had a unique Winchelsea record for he served in every one of the Winchelsea Corporation's surviving offices, except that of town clerk. After his first appointment as sergeant-at-mace in 1769[1] he became chamberlain, freeman, jurat and served one year as mayor in 1794.[2] The queen's dues record compiled in 1807 shows him paying 6½d for a house and garden in quarter six.[3] This property is now known as The Retreat. In this volume Stace senior features during the later years of his time as jurat and justice dealing with such matters as the John Eagles bastardy order (**168**), Isaac Hearnden's failure to produce some weights and measures (**327**) and Bourne Russell's bastardy order (**644**). At the annual mayoring ceremony in 1816 he produced, to general surprise, the original document which lists holdings transferred by the crown to Winchelsea in 1586. It is generally, but inaccurately because it is not a charter, known as Queen Elizabeth's Charter. How it came to be in Stace's possession, and quite unknown to other Corporation members remains a mystery.[4] The members of Winchelsea Corporation, however, have every reason to be grateful to Stace because the document remains one of their prized possessions, now held at East Sussex Record Office[5] with a framed copy of the first sheet displayed in the Court Hall Museum. George Stace senior died on 9 August 1816 only four months after producing the 'charter'.[6]

1 WIN 61 f.138r   2 WIN 96   3 WIN 61AA 7 Jul 1807   4 Pratt 1998 p.49   5 WIN 2359/1/1   6 PAR 511/1/5/1

43. George Stace junior (jurat 1814-1826; deputy mayor 1818, 1820, 1821) was in the local customs service at the age of 27 in 1803 (see appendix C3). He joined his father on the Winchelsea bench in 1814 and served with him for the next two years. Between 1816 and the time of his death in 1826 aged 50[1] he was extremely conscientious and regular in his attendance at court as frequent references in this volume demonstrate. The one blemish on his record took place at the 1826 post-election ball (see Charles Hill above) and, as he died only two months after that incident, he hardly had time to redeem himself. George Stace junior was married to Susannah Austen of Rye at St Thomas's on 30 January 1816. The March 1825 poor law assessment shows his property holding to include a house and garden valued at £9 (The Retreat inherited from his father) together with Little Monday's Market and Newgate Field (see appendix D2). The 1842 Winchelsea Tithe Map shows Little Monday's Market as being among the property of 'Sarah Stace'.[2] This must surely refer to George's widow, Susannah, although she did have a daughter Sarah.[3] Had he survived until 1841 George would no doubt have been recorded in the census as independent, as was his widow.

1 PAR 511/1/5/1   2 TD/E 90/1/2   3 PAR 511/1/2/1

44. Richard Stileman (jurat 1837-1844, deputy mayor 1837, 1840, 1842; mayor 1838, 1839, 1841, 1843, 1844) who made representations on behalf of Philadelphia Tree (**624**) and against Richard Richardson (**476**), who lent £25 to help finance emigration from his parish (**958**) and who bought the old workhouse (**796**) was Winchelsea's leading citizen for many years. His principal legacy to the town is the property now known as Greyfriars, formerly The Friars which, in 1819, he commissioned the architect J B Rebecca to build as the Stileman family home. In the process part of the medieval Greyfriars monastery was replaced, although the ruins of its chapel survive in the grounds as one of the most important Franciscan remains in the country. Richard Stileman inherited his wealth from his father, another Richard, and the 1809 militia return for Winchelsea describes him as 'aged 22, gentleman'.[1] His earliest public service was as a county magistrate, sitting, usually on his own at his home, and keeping, in his own hand, records of the complaints he heard from residents of parishes in the surrounding area.[2] Sometime after the passing of the 1832 Reform Act, however, which removed the town's two parliamentary seats and with them the patron's control of Winchelsea Corporation, Stileman became a jurat and subsequently took a leading role in Winchelsea Corporation. The 1842 Winchelsea Tithe Map shows Stileman's extensive property in the town including the Greyfriars and what was then, and is still, known as Wall Field.[3] He died in office as mayor in 1844, just thirteen days after the death of his wife.[4]

1 WIN 2359/3/1   2 AMS 6192/1-2   3 TD/E 90/1/2   4 PAR 511/1/5/1

45. John Tilden (jurat 1823-1837; deputy mayor 1827, 1829, 1834, 1836; mayor 1835) appears regularly in these pages as a Winchelsea magistrate, featuring notably, for example, dealing with attacks on Charles Arnett (**14-15**) and the corporal punishment of Thomas Bennett (**74**). The 1809 militia return for Winchelsea describes him as 'aged 18, gentleman, cripple, exempt'.[1] Nothing has been discovered to clarify the term cripple. Two years later he was included as 'gent, infirm'.[2] The only clue available about John Tilden's occupation is that he is recorded as being paid for supplying potatoes to the parish.[3] He was for a time the employer of John Whiteman (**681**). According to the March 1825 poor rate assessment he was occupying a house with the substantial annual value of £7 15s 0d (see appendix D2) where, no doubt, he was joined the following year by his wife Harriett whom he married at St Thomas's on 24 April 1826.[4] Whatever may have been the nature of his infirmity, it was John Tilden's determined persistence which ensured that, after the 1832 Reform Act came into force, Winchelsea Corporation continued in existence together with its judicial and local government responsibilities (see p.xxiv)

1 WIN 2359/3/1   2 WIN 1731   3 e.g. PAR 511/31/1/13 QE Mar 1825   4 PAR 511/1/3/1

46. Rev[d] James John West (curate 1829-1831; rector 1831-1872) played a full part in parish life (e.g. **956, 997**) and frequently in his earlier years in Winchelsea took the chair at select vestry meetings,[1] but nevertheless engaged a distinguished and probably expensive agent to act on his behalf in his dispute with the parish over his tithes (**947-949**). During his long incumbency West became a controversial figure in the parish and alienated a large number of his congregation. David Laurence, when churchwarden in 1840, registered a strong complaint with the Bishop of Chichester about the rector's Calvinist views. Also, the behaviour of the rector's family in the town did nothing to endear him to his parishioners. West's preaching, however, while not appreciated in Winchelsea, particularly because it could be scornful about the behaviour and attitudes of Winchelsea people, drew large and appreciative congregations when he preached in London where he was greatly esteemed by the Calvinist Independents.[2] During his early years in Winchelsea West had to seek diocesan approval to live in Hastings.[3] There was no rectory (described in the documents as 'Glebe house') because it had been pulled down soon after the death of Drake Hollingberry.[4] Nevertheless West was travelling from Hastings to fulfil his duties in person which was seen as a great improvement by his parishioners for the previous two rectors had been absentees. A new rectory (now the Old Rectory in Rectory Lane) was built about 1845 when the residence permissions cease.

1 PAR 511/12/3   2 Pratt 1998 pp.110-115   3 PAR 511/5/1/1-6   4 Pratt 1998 p.112

47. William Woodhams was a resident of Udimore and, as an 'outdweller', a Winchelsea landowner. He was elected to the Winchelsea select vestry in 1826.[1] In 1825 his land in St Thomas's parish included, Ferry Marsh, Morley's Marsh, Cliff Gill and part of Roundle Field (see appendix D2). In 1828 the parish reduced his liability 'in consequence of ½ an acre of land having been taken for public works'.[2] Woodhams' concern about parish matters is expressed in his letters to the overseers, for example his opposition to action being taken against Charles Arnett (**25**) and to money being granted to Samuel Easton (**223**). As he was a Udimore resident the Winchelsea parish registers make no mention of him but the poor rate assessment for 15 January 1830 refers to 'William Woodhams (the late, executors [of])'.[3]

1 PAR 511/12/3 28 Mar 1826   2 ibid 18 Apr 1828   3 PAR 511/31/1/13

48. John Woods (overseer 1812-1814, 1817-1818, 1822) had his occupation recorded as 'grocer' both in Winchelsea's 1811 militia return[1] and in the parish registers. However, haberdashery seems to have been his speciality for in 1820 receipts show that he had supplied the parish with 'shrouds, calico, cotton, fustian, nankeen, handkerchiefs, shawls, buttons etc.'[2] He also made hats which he sold to the parish officers for Winchelsea paupers such as William Willard, Robert Broadfoot, John and Stephen Whiteman and Thomas Bennett[3] and to Winchelsea Corporation for the mayor's sergeant and the town sergeant.[4] Hats for paupers cost 2s 6d, the Corporation, however, paid £5 15s 3d for the two hats for their officers. Woods served as a town constable during his first term as an overseer.[5] In the latter capacity he took a leading part, for example, in the cases of Mary Clandenbold (**115-116** etc) and John Eagles (**174-175** etc). The parish burial register indicates that by 1824 he had moved to Hastings for his infant daughter was buried at St Thomas's on 14 November 1824, the entry reading, 'Woods, Mary Jane, daughter of John and Charlotte of Hastings'.[6]

1 WIN 1731   2 PAR 511/31/2/134   3 ibid   4 WIN 618   5 WIN 61AA   6 PAR 511/1/5/1

49. John Woollett (town clerk 1798-1819) was a partner in the Rye solicitors of Woollett & Dawes who acted for Winchelsea in legal matters including bastardy cases (**84, 400, 645**). Despite Woollett's name appearing in those documents, it was Weeden Dawes who undertook most of the work (see his entry above). As town clerk Woollett is noteworthy for having, on taking office, drawn up a complete new record of the oaths, many of them still used, taken by various office holders at the annual Easter Monday mayoring ceremony. This document, entirely in his hand, survives within the Winchelsea archives.[1]

1 WIN 2359/3/5

50. John Edward Wright (overseer 1807-1810, 1815-1817, 1823; churchwarden 1811) also served Winchelsea Corporation as chamberlain from 1809 until succeeded by Walter Fuller in 1834.[1] This office was an important one involving representing and enforcing decisions of the Corporation and acting as its treasurer. One of his trickiest tasks must have been, in 1820, to require, on behalf of the corporation, Richard Stileman, a formidable and dominant figure in the town, to take down fences with which he had enclosed land at Monday's Market and near the New Gate without the Corporation's permission.[2] The surviving documents are not clear as to whether or not Wright succeeded but it seems likely that he did for, despite his eminence, Stileman was not a corporation member at that time (see 44 above). Preoccupation with his duties as chamberlain did not prevent Wright from playing a leading part in parish life as these pages show. For example, he was a strong supporter of Charles Arnett and stood surety for him on his move to Bexhill (**1**), inquired into the case of Lucy Barnes (**53**), was appointed to the committee inquiring into the condition of the poorhouse (**736**) and was elected to the first select vestry (**848**). In 1825 he was the owner of a house and garden with an annual value of £11 5s 0d (see appendix D2), a substantial amount. He was also the owner of a shop, annual value fifteen shillings. No evidence has been found as to the trade Wright might have carried on at the shop or, indeed, whether it was rented out.

1 WIN 618; WIN 61B   2 Pratt 1998 p.57; WIN 2035

Appendix B: The Poor

B1 This list includes all those not featured in Part I who have been noted as having received poor law relief from the Winchelsea authorities between 1790 and 1841. The length of the list alone emphasises the extent of Winchelsea's problem providing for its poor during this time. These names do not appear in the letters which form the basis of this volume but they have been extracted from the overseers' account books AMS 2329 and PAR 511/31/1/11-16 and from the vestry minutes PAR 511/12/1-3. For details of these volumes see Primary Sources in the introduction (p. xxxiii). While not appearing in the main text, some of these names are included in Appendices C2(b) and C3(d) which relate to both voluntary and compulsory military recruitment and in Appendices D1 and D2 which list poor rate assessments.

Adams, Caroline
Adams, William
Alce, John
Atfield, John
Atfield, George
Attwell, George
Attwood, John
Baker, Job
Baker, Judith
Baker, Philadelphia
Baker, Zebulon
Bennett, Benjamin
Booth, Thankful
Bourner, James
Bragg, Mary
Bragg, Richard
Brisenden, Ann
Brisenden, Mary
Burkenstock, Jane
Burkenstock, Henry
Buttenshaw, Henry
Care, Jane
Care, Mary
Chart. James
Chasmar, William
Cockburn, James
Coleman, Charles (alias Leaver)
Crittenden, Mary
Dew, Mary
Duffy, James
Edwards, Mary
Eldridge, Mary
Eldridge, Richard
Field, Emmy
Field, Richard
Gurr, John
Harvey, Mariah
Harwood, Thomas
Hill, James
Hoadley, Elizabeth
Hoadley, Mary
Holt, Mary

Holt, Richard
Jeakens, George
Knight, Elizabeth
Lamb, Joseph
Lavender, Mary
Lowes, Ann
Lowes, Martha
Martin, John
Masters, John
Mays, William
Miles, James
Miles, Richard
Mitchell, William
Neeves, James
Neeves, John
Noakes, Mary
Ockenden, William
Packham, Mary
Payne, Hannah
Perigo, Judith
Pim, John
Pitt, William
Relfe, William
Richardson, Constant
Sargent, Lewis
Saxby, John
Seager, Mary
Seere, William
Sinden, Delia
Skinner, Thomas
Stephens, Rachel
Stephenson, Thomas
Stevenson, Henry
Vinall, Elizabeth
Vinall, Henry
Wenham, Lucy
Wimble, James
Woodhams, Elizabeth
Woodliff, Thomas
Woodman Sims, Maria
Young, George

B2 Parishes in Sussex and elsewhere with which paupers featured were associated:

The following list indicates all the parishes other than Winchelsea with which paupers featuring in Part I were connected. All parishes are in Sussex except where otherwise stated and present London boroughs have been included within their former counties.

Joseph Bailey (Bayley)	Rye
Lucy Bailey (Bayley)	Lydd, Kent
Mary Bailey	Stone-in-Oxney, Kent
Richard Bailey (Bayley)	West Malling, Kent
Stephen Bailey (Bayley)	Lydd, Kent
Lucy Barnes (formerly Stonestreet)	St Clement's, Hastings
Thomas Bennett	West Malling, Kent
Robert Broadfoot	Newchurch, Kent
Frances Butler	Battle & Brighton
John Chester	Beckley
Mary Clandenbold	Canterbury, Kent (Borough of Northgate, Borough of Staplegate, parish of St Alphage)
Cornelius Clarke	Icklesham
Thomas Clarke	Icklesham
Thomas Cogger	Rye
James Crowhurst	Wartling & Rye
William Cutbeard	New Romney, Kent and St Giles's, London
John Eagles	St Saviour's, Southwark, Surrey
	Minster and Sheerness, Isle of Sheppey, Kent
	Milton (near Sittingbourne), Kent
Mercy Eastman	All Saints & St Clement's, Hastings
	Sheerness, Kent
Ann Easton	Holy Trinity, Hastings & New Romney
Samuel Easton	Upton, West Ham, Essex
William Edwards	Snargate, Kent
Benjamin Field	Rye
Thomas Foster	Tovil, near Maidstone, & East Farleigh, Kent
Hannah Francis	Rye, Battle & Brighton
---- Gilman	Chatham, Kent
Joseph Hoad	Boulogne-sur-mer, France
Burford Jeakens	Battle
George Jenkins	Lewisham, Kent
Lucy Kite, née Vennall, formerly May	Arbroath, Scotland
Thomas Lancaster	Rye & Rye Foreign
William Martin	Icklesham
---- Middleton	Patrixbourne, Kent
Dive Milliner	Ramsgate, Kent
William Morris	Guestling, Fairlight, Ore
John Nash	Hawkhurst, Kent
Eliza Oyler	Hooe
Lucy Oyler	Hastings
Joseph Parsons	Stalbridge, Dorset

Ann Ralph	Playden
James Relfe	Rye
Mary Relfe	Iden & Rye
	Brookland & Ivychurch, Kent
Joseph Ronalds	Hambledon, Hampshire
Elizabeth Saunders	St Clement's, Hastings
Mary Saunders	Hastings
John Simmons	Hythe, Kent & Hoxton, London
John Sinden	Guestling
Stephen Sinden	Rye
Ann Stevens	Hastings
Susannah Stevenson	St Clement's, Hastings
Elizabeth Taunton	Canterbury & Walmer, Kent
Elizabeth Tilden	Dover, Kent
Mary Tilden	Dover, Kent
Hannah Turk	Playden
Richard Unicume	Cranbrook & Rolvenden, Kent
Ann Vinall	Brookland, Kent
Elizabeth Watson	Iden
James Weller	Wittersham, Kent
Gilbert Wood	Woolwich, Kent
David Woodzell	Playden

Appendix C
Naval and Army Recruitment

C1 Naval Recruitment 1795

While the life of Winchelsea's people generally proceeded unaffected by national events, the impact of the Revolutionary and Napoleonic wars with France was a major exception. Prime Minister William Pitt, whose earlier initiatives had ensured that naval vessels were ready for such an emergency, remained deeply concerned about the required level of recruitment to ensure they were adequately manned. Norman Longmate[1] quotes Pitt as informing the House of Commons, 'Our navy is the national defence of this kingdom in case of invasion. In this department, however, little remains to be done; our fleet at this moment being more formidable than at any former period of our history.' He proposed to keep the navy up to strength 'by a levy of 15,000 men from the different parishes for the sea service', in effect conscription, with each parish submitting its quota of 'unemployed or ne'er-do-wells'.

Winchelsea's less than patriotic reluctance to provide even one 'unemployed or ne'er-do-well' man is indicated by the documents below. The key to that reluctance almost certainly lies in the detail of C1(e) which emphasises that anyone guilty of smuggling should be among the enforced recruits. There is little doubt that the constables ordered to implement the requirements of the Act were smugglers themselves and the magistrates probably benefited knowingly from 'the trade'.

1 Longmate, Norman, Island Fortress (2001) p.217

C1(a) 20 Mar 1795 *Minute of the Winchelsea parish meeting*:
At a meeting of the parishioners of Winchelsea on Monday the 20th day of March in the year 1795 to take into consideration so much of an act entitled An Act for Raising a Certain Number of Men in the Several Counties of England for the Service of His Majesty's Navy as respects the raising of one man to be found by this parish it is ordered that the churchwardens and overseers do immediately offer such reward, not exceeding £20, as to them shall seem proper and necessary for finding one man to be approved of by such regulating officer as shall be appointed by the government for this district. [PAR 511/12/1]

C1(b) 26 May 1795 *The first Petty Sessions holden in and for the Ancient Town of Winchelsea in the County of Sussex on Tuesday the 26th day of May in the year of our Lord 1795 before Thomas Marten Esq, mayor, Richard Lamb and George Stace, jurats and justices of the peace of and for Winchelsea for putting in execution a certain Act of Parliament made and passed in this present session of Parliament* *for enabling the magistrates in the several counties in Great Britain to raise and levy under certain regulations such able-bodied and idle persons as shall be found within the said counties to serve in His Majesty's navy.*

The act being read the mayor and jurats appointed Henry Waterman their clerk to attend their meetings to transact such business as shall belong to him by virtue of the said Act and issue their precepts to the constables of Winchelsea requiring their attendance at the next succeeding sessions to be holden at the Court Hall in and for the said town on Monday the first day of June next at ten o'clock in the forenoon to receive instructions for carrying the Act into execution and give notice to the Secretary of the Admiralty of the time and place appointed for holding such sessions. Adjourned to 1st of June. [WIN 2019]

C1(c) 27 May 1795 *Letter from Evan Nejean of the Admiralty Office to Thomas Marten, mayor of Winchelsea*:

In return to the letter signed by you and other magistrates at Winchelsea of yesterday's date I am commanded by my Lords Commissioners of the Admiralty that they have directed Captain Ballard to attend at the sessions to be held there on the day appointed to receive the man that may be levied for that part of the county of Sussex. [WIN 2021]

C1(d) 1 Jun 1795 *The second petty sessions holden by adjournment in the Court Hall in and for the town of Winchelsea on Monday the 1st day of June 1795 before Thomas Marten Esq, mayor, Richard Lamb and George Stace, jurats and justices*:

The constables appeared pursuant to the precepts and received instructions and warrants under the hands of the mayor and jurats to search for and apprehend within Winchelsea all such men who shall appear to them to be within any of the descriptions in the Act mentioned to bring such men so apprehended before the magistrates at their next petty sessions here to be holden to be examined and dealt with according to the directions of the Act. Adjourned to the 9th of June. [WIN 2019]

C1(e) 1 Jun 1795 *To the constables of the Ancient Town of Winchelsea in the county of Sussex and also the overseers of the poor of the parish of St Thomas the Apostle within the town of Winchelsea and to every of them*:

By virtue and in pursuance of an Act of Parliament made and passed in this present session of Parliament for enabling the magistrates in the several counties in Great Britain to raise and levy under certain regulations such able-bodied and idle persons as shall be found within the said counties to serve in His Majesty's navy, we, His Majesty's justices of the peace for the town of Winchelsea do hereby require and command you, the constables and overseers of the poor and every of you forthwith to make a general search throughout Winchelsea and the limits thereof for all able-bodied, idle, disorderly persons who cannot upon examination prove themselves to exercise and industriously follow some lawful trade or employment or to have some substance sufficient for their support and maintenance and also all men who shall have offended against any law in force at the time of passing this Act by virtue whereof they shall be or be liable to be deemed or adjudged to be idle disorderly persons or rogues and vagabonds or incorrigible rogues and punishable as such respectively. And also all men who shall be adjudged to be guilty of illegal landing, running, unshipping, concealing, receiving or carrying prohibited goods, wares or merchandises or any foreign goods liable to the payment of the duties of customs or excise, those same duties not having been paid or secured, or of embezzling any naval stores, the property of His Majesty, or of aiding or assisting in any of the offences before mentioned. And all such men as you shall find within the Town and Liberty who are or shall appear to you to be within any of the descriptions aforesaid, we, the justices, do hereby command and require you, the constables and overseers, to convey and bring before us at the Court Hall in Winchelsea on Tuesday the ninth day of June instant at ten o'clock in the forenoon on the same day to be examined and dealt with pursuant to the directions of the said Act of Parliament and be you yourselves there present to make a return of this warrant and how you have executed the same hereof fail not at your peril.

Given under our hands and seals at Winchelsea this 1ˢᵗ day of June 1795.

[WIN 2022]

Note: The magistrates would have been the same as those above and below but the document here transcribed is a copy and does not contain their names or signatures.

C1(f) 9 June 1795 *The third petty sessions holden by adjournment in the Court Hall in and for the Town of Winchelsea on Tuesday the 9ᵗʰ day of June 1795 before Thomas Marten Esq, mayor, Richard Lamb and George Stace, jurats and justices etc.*

The constables appeared and informed the court that they had not as yet found any person or persons within the meaning of the said Act of Parliament in Winchelsea or the Liberty thereof. Adjourned to the 15ᵗʰ June.

C1(g) 15 Jun 1795 [*Fifth petty sessions before*] *Thomas Marten Esq, mayor, Richard Lamb and George Stace jurats.*
Adjourned to 23ʳᵈ June 1795

C1(h) 23 Jun 1795 [*Sixth petty sessions before*] *Thomas Marten Esq, mayor, Richard Lamb and George Stace jurats.*
[No entry appears against this date]   [WIN 2019]

Note: At this point the court sittings in response to the requirement of the Act cease. No record has been found that, despite the proposed reward with which this record begins, any Winchelsea man was found and sent to serve.

C2 Army Recruitment – militia volunteers 1803

C2(a) During the summer of 1803 the nation was swept by what Prime Minister Addington described as 'an insurrection of loyalty'. Winchelsea's response, quite unlike that for compulsory naval recruitment, was impressive. With Napoleon's troops gathering on the other side of the Channel the traditional first measure to counter an invasion threat was to withdraw the population and all livestock from the coastal areas where enemy troops might land, thus making these areas far less useful in supporting an enemy. Winchelsea's geographical position placed it firmly within the threatened area and below is published a list of those who were prepared to join the military in armed resistance, those who were prepared to dig defensive positions (the pioneers), those who were prepared to implement the evacuation and those who offered to help in other ways or, in several cases 'in any way useful'.

The precept issued by William Pitt as Lord Warden which required the following edited return has not survived within Winchelsea Corporation's archive.

The notes which were appended to the original document have been transferred to the beginning, thus providing further background information.

The list as submitted to the Lord Warden contained no fewer than 175 names. Included here are only those who feature in Parts I and II of this volume and in Appendix B1.

C2(b) *The return of the Mayor and Jurats of the Ancient Town of Winchelsea in the County of Sussex to the precept of the Right Honourable William Pitt, Constable of Dover Castle and Lord Warden of the Cinque Ports, the two Ancient Towns and their Members dated the 15ᵗʰ day of July 1803 directed to the Mayors and Jurats of the Towns and Ports of Hastings, Sandwich, Dover, Romney and Hythe, of the Ancient Towns of Rye and Winchelsea, of the Towns of Fordwich, Faversham, Folkestone, Tenterden and Deal and to the Bailiffs and Jurats of the Towns of Lydd, Seaford and Pevensey so far as relates to the Ancient Town and Parish of Winchelsea.*

[*signed*] Thomas Marten, Deputy Mayor

Those whose names are marked with a ˣ have more than one child born in lawful wedlock and under ten years of age.
Besides the [following] there are one hundred and fifty boys under 15 years of age and three hundred and seventy-six women and girls all of whom it is expected will be incapable of removing themselves in case of danger.
From the list of the inhabitants it will be seen how many have offered to enrol themselves as riflemen and it will also be seen how many have offered themselves as pioneers [i.e. in this context, labourers] and each [pioneer] will be prepared with a saw, axe, mattock or spade or some other useful tool. The pioneers will propose their leader to the Deputy Lieutenant when chosen.
There are not any aliens or quakers in the Town or Parish.

Names	Professions	Ages	Services willing to engage in
Thomas Fuller	farmer	44	conductor of sheep
Richard Denne	esquire	52	in any way useful
Thomas Easton	maltster	46	conductor of waggons with women and children
Richard Maplesden	shopkeeper	52	Rifleman if thought proper
Edwin Dawes	gent	54	enrolled as a volunteer in the ward of Broad Street [London] in which he principally resides His 4 horses and carts [at Winchelsea] will be at the public service
James Bray	gardener	44	stock driver
Stephen Laurence	looker [shepherd]	64	driver of sheep
Charles Suters	labourer	45	Constable
ˣThomas Marten jnr	supervisor of the customs	36	in any way useful
ˣThomas Oyler	labourer	44	will serve with his cart and horse
Revᵈ Drake Hollingberry	chancellor of the diocese	60	in any way useful
ˣSimon Graddon	excise officer	36	cattle driver
Abraham Kennett	yeoman	55	guide to cattle drivers
William Sargent snr	miller	47	Rifleman
Burford Jeakens	tanner	73	
George Harrod	innkeeper	37	Constable
Richard Stileman		15	at school in Chelsea
Thomas Marten [snr]	esquire	70	
Thomas Stephens jnr	riding officer	51	driver of cattle
George Stace	esquire	60	conductor of stock
Richard Lamb	ditto	56	in any way useful
Charles Terry	yeoman	55	conductor of waggons and in any way useful
ˣRichard Richardson	labourer	26	Rifleman
ˣJames Hoad	tailor	28	ditto
ˣJames Bourner	labourer	45	in any way useful
ˣWilliam Ockenden	ditto	38	Rifleman
John Alce	shoemaker	48	ditto
ˣJohn Stevenson	labourer	44	Rifleman
ˣThomas Keen[e]	shoemaker	35	ditto
William Leonard	labourer	16	ditto
ˣJoseph Parsons	ditto	28	ditto
Daniel Edwards	ditto	58	stock driver
Thomas Chester	ditto	50	ditto
ˣJoseph Claise	ditto	33	Rifleman
ˣJames Clarke	miller & baker	33	Baker
ˣThomas Hoad	tailor	26	Rifleman
Richard Edwards	labourer	29	ditto
George Tilden	farmer		in any way useful
Robert Alce	carpenter	45	Pioneer

Joseph Hoad	tailor	53	Rifleman
Isaac Hearnden	carrier	31	Pioneer
Stephen Bennett	labourer	53	driver of sheep
Joseph Bailey	seaman	30	sea fencible
Thomas May	shoemaker	50	driver of sheep
ˣThomas Parsons	labourer	30	waggon driver
Henry Tilden	ditto	49	driver of stock
James Relfe	bargeman	46	will assist with his barge
Samuel Southerden	farmer	45	conductor [of] stock drivers
John Neeves	labourer	18	driver of a waggon
John Easton	ditto	17	Rifleman
Richard Maplesden jnr	shopkeeper	20	ditto
John Jenkins	shoemaker	54	Constable
Joel Benfield	servant to Mr Dawes	27	driver of sheep
Robert Sharps	ditto	25	Rifleman
George Bray	farrier	37	conductor of cattle drivers
William Sargent jnr	miller	18	Rifleman
William Blackhall	servant to Mr Harrod	30	driver of waggon
George Stace jnr	riding officer	27	Rifleman
William Willard	labourer	16	stock driver
James May	shoemaker	21	Rifleman
ˣEdward Field	labourer	45	driver of a waggon
ˣJames Burwash	ditto	42	sea fencible
Stephen Field	ditto	20	Rifleman
Joseph Cogger	blacksmith	53	shoeing smith
James Holt snr	mason	49	Pioneer
Esau Holt	ditto	17	Rifleman
John Chester	labourer	47	stock driver
ˣThomas Hoadley	blacksmith	21	Rifleman
Thomas Haisell	peruke [wig] maker	63	Pioneer
George Haisell	ditto	17	Rifleman
ˣZebulon Baker	labourer	37	in any way useful
William Martin	ditto	34	Pioneer
ˣGeorge Jenkins	butcher	32	Rifleman
Walter Fuller	carpenter	37	Constable
ˣSamuel Easton	wheelwright	26	Pioneer
William Chasmar	labourer	28	Rifleman
Edward Jeakens jnr	tanner	27	ditto
Charles Suters	gardener	45	driver of cattle
ˣJohn Attwood	ditto	37	driver of a waggon
Thomas Bennett	labourer	24	Rifleman
James Hill	ditto	22	ditto
Francis Saunders	gardener	63	driver of stock
David Laurence	labourer	18	driver of sheep
Josiah Boots	carpenter	44	Pioneer
William Bailey	labourer	32	Rifleman
Edward Jeakens snr	tanner	53	driver of sheep

John Perigo snr	labourer	52	stock driver
ˣJohn Perigo jnr	ditto	28	ditto
William Leonard	labourer	49	sheep driver
Nathaniel Bragg	ditto	40	Pioneer
William Fisher	pedlar	25	cart driver
James Relfe jnr	bargeman	17	
William Field	labourer	60	Pioneer
John Bennett snr	gardener	40	ditto
John Bennett jnr	labourer	19	Rifleman
Thomas Harwood	seaman	43	
John Jenkins	servant to Mr Luxford	19	driver of waggon – now serving by substitute in the militia
Richard Bragg	collar maker	33	sea fencible

[WIN 1701]

Note: Sea Fencibles were naval personnel liable only for defensive service in home waters.

C3 Recruitment for the Army of Reserve as a statutory requirement 1803

C3(a) Unlike the enthusiastically supported voluntary service of Appendix C2 this requirement was compulsory and consequently resented. That resentment and sympathy for any who might be unlucky in the ballot was shared by the parish authorities who ensured as shown in C3(c) that those prepared to serve as substitutes for any man balloted would be compensated, the money being raised through a charge on those eligible and supplemented from the parish rate. Winchelsea continued to look after its own! A small envelope which has been given the reference WIN 1722 survives within the records of Winchelsea Corporation. This contains the small folded slips of paper on which were written the names of those liable to serve who were to be included in a ballot. Those slips would not have been used to draw the names on the occasion recorded here because, as will be seen in the listing, in this case each eligible man was allocated a number which would have been used in the draw. The abbreviation Excd for excused is entered against the names of those who were declared ineligible to serve. The reason that the parish excused all those with two or more children under 10 is that, if such a father chose to go when balloted, the parish would have been very likely to have to maintain the family. C3(e) shows who was unlucky in this ballot, who went as their substitutes and how much the substitutes were paid. The reason for the discrepancy between those payments is not known.

C3(b) 1 Sep 1803 A letter addressed to the Mayor, Winchelsea, Sussex and signed W Pitt [Lord Warden of the Cinque Ports] requires the mayor's attendance at Dover on 6 September at 12 noon 'for the purpose of apportioning the number of men to be balloted for the Army of Reserve in the respective Cinque Port towns and

members.'   [WIN 1689]
Note: At the initial meeting thus convened, a total of 400 men being required, Winchelsea
was ordered to find five. When the total number was reduced to 280, Winchelsea's allocation
was reduced to three.   [WIN 1690]

C3(c) 27 Sep 1803 *Minute of the Winchelsea public* vestry:
All persons serving in the Winchelsea volunteers and liable to be balloted for the
Army of Reserve shall be indemnified upon paying 10s 6d before the drawing [of
lots] into the hands of the overseer and all other persons liable shall be indemnified
upon paying to the overseer one guinea before the drawing and that the remainder
of the money necessary to be raised for procuring three substitutes charged on this
parish shall be paid out of the parish rate.   [PAR 511/12/1 f.136]

C3(d)
Army of Reserve List made pursuant to the directions of an Act passed in the
forty-third year of the Reign of King George the third [1803] entitled 'An Act to
enable His Majesty more effectually to raise and assemble in England an additional
military force for the better defence and security of the United Kingdom and for the
more vigorous prosecution of the war'.

Name	Rank or Occupation	Infirmity likely to incapacitate from Service	Ground of exemption claimed
Thomas Fuller	farmer	1	Churchwarden
William Chatterton	waggoner	2	
John Neeves	servant		Exc^d under 5 foot 2 inches
Thomas Law	surgeon	3	
William Weller	footman		Exc^d rupture
George Stace jnr	riding officer	4	
Thomas Hoadley	blacksmith		Exc^d 2 children under 10
James Hoad	tailor		Exc^d 2 children under 10
Solomon Suters	carrier	a cripple	
Thomas Ridley	servant	5	
Haines Bragg	grazier	6	
Joseph Bailey	labourer		Exc^d Sea Fencibles & seaman
John Tree snr	carpenter		Exc^d 2 children under 10
John Tree jnr	ditto		Exc^d Under 18 years
John Bennett jnr	labourer	7	
James Drury	carpenter		Exc^d 3 children under 10
John Hills jnr	servant	8	
Henry Valler	gardener	9	
James May	shoemaker	10	
Edward Apps	ditto	11	

Name	Occupation	No.	Notes
Needler Baker	brickmaker		Exc^d
Zebulon Baker	labourer		Exc^d 4 children under 10
Robert Clark jnr	baker	12	
Joseph Leonard	clocksmith	13	
John Standen	servant	14	
Richard Edwards	labourer	15	*Entry deleted and marked '[?] omitted'.*
William Edwards	ditto	16	
John Bennett snr	gardener	17	Once drawn in the Sussex Militia & found substitute
Robert Jenkins	butcher	18	Exc^d 4 children under 10
William Fisher	peddler	19	
Robert Moon	coachman		Exc^d 4 children under 10
Sion Baker	labourer	20	
John Attwood	gardener		Exc^d 3 children under 10
Thomas Hoad	tailor		Exc^d 2 children under 10
William Williams	labourer		Exc^d seaman & Sea Fencibles
John Perigo	ditto		Exc^d 2 children under 10
James Clark	miller		Exc^d 4 children under 10
William Bailey	labourer		Exc^d 3 children under 10
James Relfe	bargeman		*Entry deleted and marked '[?] and not of age'*
Richard Larkins	labourer		Exc^d 5 children under 10
Thomas Tickner	ditto		*Entry deleted & marked '45 years of age'* Exc^d 3 children under 10
Thomas Parsons	ditto		Exc^d 2 children under 10
John Tibbs	schoolmaster	21	
John Attwell	bricklayer		Exc^d 4 children under 10
William Hunt	tailor	22	
James Dengate	shoemaker		Exc^d an apprentice
James Cochran	labourer		Exc^d 3 children under 10
Joseph Claise	ditto		Exc^d 3 children under 10
Thomas Keene	shoemaker		Exc^d 2 children under 10
James Tutt	seaman		Exc^d belongs to a revenue cutter
Joseph Parsons	labourer		Exc^d 2 children under 10
John Stevenson	ditto		Exc^d 3 children under 10
Edward Jeakens jnr	tanner	23	
William Ockenden	labourer		Exc^d 4 children under 10
Thomas Sanders	ditto	24	
Thomas Bennett	ditto	25	
Richard Richardson	ditto		Exc^d 3 children under 10
Nathaniel Bragg	ditto		Exc^d 4 children under 10
Luke Leadbeater	ditto	26	
Thomas Whiteman	timber carrier	27	Exc^d 4 children under 10
Thomas Grinfield	lodger	28	
George Haisell	barber	29	
Richard Maplesden jnr	shopkeeper	30	
Simon Graddon	excise officer		Exc^d 4 children under 10

Name	Occupation	No.	Note	Exemption
William Sargent jnr	miller	31		
George Jenkins	butcher			Exc^d 4 children under 10
Isaac Hearnden	carrier	32		
Thomas Seere			subject to fits & a cripple	
William Martin	labourer	33		
Joseph Weller	ditto			Exc^d discharged from the militia unfit for service
William Adams	ditto		lost one eye & one thumb	
Richard Lamb	carpenter	34		
Thomas Oyler	labourer			Exc^d 3 children under 10
George Dawes	gentleman	35		
Joel Benfield	groom	36		
Robert Sharps	footman	37		
Richard Bragg	collar maker			Exc^d 2 children under 10
Stephen Laurence jnr	glazier		lame & an apprentice	Exc^d
David Laurence	labourer	38		
George Bray	farrier	39		
Richard Bray	ditto	40		
James Bray	gardener	41		Exc^d 2 children under 10
John Elliott	shopkeeper	42		
James Holt jnr	bricklayer			Exc^d infirm
Richard Miles	labourer			Exc^d 4 children under 10
Stephen Field	ditto	43		
Thomas Marten jnr	Superintendent of the Custom House, Port of Rye	44a		
William Lacy	labourer	44b		Exc^d [?omitted]
William Chasmar	ditto	45		
James Burwash	ditto			Exc^d 3 children under 10
Benjamin Bennett	gardener	46		
William Blackall	servant	47		
Edward Field	labourer			Exc^d 2 children under 10
John Baker	glazier	48		
Samuel Easton	wheelwright	49		Exc^d 2 children under 10
John Alce	shoemaker	50		

[WIN 1720]

C3(e) Those of the above who were selected when lots were drawn were Richard Lamb, William Sargent junior and Robert Sharps. Payments to their substitutes are recorded in a document dated 12 October 1803 as being made by the parish from the sums collected. The substitutes were respectively, Thomas Smith who received £7 17s 6d, Phillip McKee and Thomas Horsee who both received £10 10s 0d.

[WIN 1726]

Appendix D
The Poor Rate

The necessity of financing support for the poor from the poor rate and the fact that everything had to be done within each parish, created an enormous amount of work for the responsible overseers. These examples, dated 1801 and 1825, are extracted from several volumes of overseers' accounts[1] to illustrate this complexity and the demanding requirements of the necessary book-keeping. The rate was collected three or four times a year and the lists painstakingly prepared on each occasion. In these examples the rents on the left represent the assessed annual rental value of each property and the figures on the right the amount collected as a result of the levy resolved by the vestry and approved by the magistrates; four shillings in the pound in both cases. This was the usual amount; sometimes it was six shillings in the pound but only occasionally less than four. There is no indication in the 1801 example of either property or persons excused payment. These may merely have been left out of the account book. Here, too, the listing seems haphazard. In fact the gentry are listed first, those considered to be of reasonable other status such as jurats come next and lesser persons at the end. However, by 1825 when the ledgers had been placed in a better organised mostly alphabetical order of those liable, empty property and paupers excused are included in the record. Also added in this latter example are the areas in acres, rods and perches of assessed land. The abbreviation OH stands for Old Harbour and refers to property in approximately the area now occupied by the village of Camber. It will be noted in both cases that, as shown in the left-hand column, land was much more heavily assessed than buildings and that non-resident landowners (recorded as Out Dwellers) paid a very substantial proportion of the rate. Although the recording methods differ, there is almost no difference between the total amounts collected at four shillings in the pound, despite the fact that these examples are almost a quarter of a century apart.

The 1801 assessment was made as a result of an outstanding example of local management (**861-863**) but never implemented because of the objection of Jeremiah Curteis (**864**). This is recorded, without mention of his name, at the end of Appendix D1. It is clear that the assessment of incumbents for the payment of poor rate on their tithe income caused disputes in many parishes[2]. The strange thing about the situation in Winchelsea is that, despite Curteis's objection being upheld, no action was taken to charge the then rector, Revd Drake Hollingberry in this way. The first charge of that nature was required of the Revd J W Dugdell, more than twenty years later in April 1823 and is the subject of (**912**). No documentary evidence has been found to explain this delay. Perhaps it can be assumed that the difference in treatment, if not as a result of legislative requirements, was a local initiative arising from the fact that, while Hollingberry was a deeply respected long-serving resident, Dugdell was an absentee whose arrangements for the parish cause considerable resentment.

The documents are reproduced here exactly as they appear in the account books. For example, in D1 there are no details of property occupied between the names of Widow Chester and William Seere, or of land owned by the named out dwellers between Hugh Whistler and Jeremiah Curteis.

1 AMS 2329; PAR 511/31/1/11-16   2 see particularly Evans 1976 pp.31-32

D1 Assessment of the Parish of St Thomas the Apostle, Winchelsea
22 February 1801

An assessment then made and agreed on by the churchwardens and overseers and other inhabitants of the parish of St Thomas the Apostle in the Ancient Town of Winchelsea aforesaid at the rate of four shillings in the pound agreeable to valuation towards maintaining the poor of the said parish and defraying all necessary charges thereto belonging.

Rent			Owner	Property	Payment Due		
£	s	d					
10	0	0	Richard Barwell Esq	part of house	2	0	0
35	10	0		for the houses in the Square	7	2	0
15	10	0		for the Five Houses	3	2	0
3	0	0		for the Moneyceller Houses		12	0
2	0	0		for a part house occd by Widow Martin		8	0
4	0	0		for a house occd by William Burden		16	0
2	0	0	Revd Mr Simpkinson	part house		8	0
2	0	0	Revd Mr [Thomas] Raddish	ditto		8	0
2	0	0	Mr [John] Lyne	ditto		8	0
2	0	0	Charles Graeme Esq	Summer House		8	0
8	0	0	Leaver Oliver Esq		1	12	0
3	0	0	Isaac Coffin Esq	part house		12	0
2	10	0	Mr [Alexander] Tulloch	ditto		10	0
2	10	0	Mr [George] Knight	ditto		10	0
10	0	0	Arthur Balfour Esq		2	0	0
2	0	0	Barwell Brown[e] Esq	part of Miss [Mary] Lamb junior's house		8	0
3	10	0	John Shakespeare Esq	part of Miss [Mary] Lamb senior's house		14	0
3	10	0	J[onathan] P[erry] Coffin Esq	part ditto		14	0
3	0	0	Thomas Marten Esq	for the Paradise, Bowling Green, cliff etc		12	0
4	0	0		for a malthouse occd by Thomas Easton		16	0
2	0	0		by John Chester		8	0
25	0	0	Richard Denne Esq	house	5	0	0
3	15	0		for 2½ acres land, Pound Piece & lodge		15	0
13	0	0		for the King's Green	2	12	0

44	10	0	Captain Aylmer	house & land	8	18	0
25	0	0	Revd [Drake] Hollingberry	house	5	0	0
14	17	6		for the Chestnut land, barn & lodge	2	19	6
3	2	6		for St Giles's churchyard & garden		12	6
1	10	0	Revd Mr Hollingberry	for the Glebe garden, yard & stable		6	0
10	0	0	Mr [Edwin] Dawes	house	2	0	0
3	0	0	Mr [Richard] Butler	part house		12	0
11	0	0		for Pewes field and part of Pewes pond	2	4	0
2	15	0		for the two acre field and lodge		11	0
15	0	0	Mr [Richard] Stileman	house etc	3	0	0
9	7	6		for the Holyrood, part of Pewes & lodge	1	17	6
1	0	0		for the Frog Marsh & part of Castle Field		4	0
	7	6		for a small garden		1	6
7	0	0	Mr George Stace	house	1	8	0
11	0	0		for Tinker's garden, cliff, field etc	2	4	0
31	15	0	Mr Thomas Fuller	house and land	6	7	0
8	0	0	Mr Richard Lamb	for a house, nursery garden & Horse Pond Piece	1	12	0
	12	6		a stable unoccupied	--	--	
11	0	0	Mr [Thomas] Marten	house etc	2	4	0
3	10	0	Mr Thomas Marten jnr	field		14	0
40	7	0	Mr Burford Jeakens	house and land	8	1	0
10	0	0	Mr Richard Cropper	house	2	0	0
6	10	0		for the Pear Tree Marsh	1	6	0
5	0	0		for a house occd by Thomas Haisell	1	0	0
5	0	0		house occd by James Jones	1	0	0
3	0	0		house occd by Thomas Stephens		12	0
5	10	0	Mr George Bray	house	1	2	0
9	10	0		for the Coney Field and cliff	1	18	0
5	5	0	Mr Thomas Easton	house	1	1	0
13	15	0		land, stable and lodge	2	15	0
7	0	0	Mr William Sargent	house	1	8	0
6	10	0	Mr Walter Fuller	house and shop	1	6	0
3	0	0	Edward Piddlesden	house		12	0
	15	0		the Float Field		3	0
1	0	0	Widow Chester			4	0
2	0	0	William Adams			8	0
1	10	0	Widow Easden			6	0
1	10	0	Joseph Weller			6	0
2	0	0	William Martin			8	0
2	0	0	Thomas Osborne			8	0
3	0	0	Thomas Stephens			12	0
1	10	0	Mr [William] Graddon			6	0
1	10	0	William Burden jnr			6	0
4	0	0	William Seere			16	0
3	0	0	George Jenkins	house		12	0

Poor Rate Assement 22 February 1801 - Continued

1	0	0		a slaughterhouse		4	0
2	10	0	Widow Amon			10	0
1	0	0	Isaac Hearnden	a workshop		4	0
2	0	0	George Martin			8	0
2	0	0	Widow Holt junior			8	0
3	0	0	James Drury			12	0
4	0	0	John Baker			16	0
14	0	0	Richard Maplesden	house & shop	2	16	0
	10	0	Thomas Haisell	a garden		2	0
1	0	0	James Jones	a shop		4	0
5	0	0	Widow Holt senior		1	0	0
2	10	0	Thomas Skinner			10	0
3	0	0	Samuel Easton	house		12	0
1	0	0		shop		4	0
1	0	0	James Trigwell	ditto		4	0
5	0	0	James Holt	house	1	0	0
3	10	0	William Hunt	ditto		14	0
4	10	0	Josiah Boots	ditto		18	0
1	10	0		shop & garden		6	0
10	0	0	Mr George Harrod	house	2	0	0
1	10	0		stable & garden		6	0
5	0	0	Miss Lamb junior	part of a house	1	0	0
3	0	0	Widow Woodhams	house		12	0
4	0	0	Thomas May	ditto		16	0
2	0	0	George Tilman			8	0
4	0	0	The Poor House			--	--
1	10	0	Peter Crinone	house		6	0
1	10	0	Joseph Bayley	ditto		6	0
3	0	0	John Saxby	ditto		12	0
3	0	0	David Howell	ditto		12	0
9	0	0	Mr Richard Ade	house, garden etc	1	16	0
3	0	0	Joseph Hoad	house		12	0
2	0	0	Nathaniel Bragg	ditto		8	0
6	0	0	Robert Alce	ditto	1	4	0
8	0	0	Mr George Tilden	ditto	1	12	0
6	0	0	Edward Jeakens snr	house & garden	1	4	0
1	0	0	William Bayley	house		4	0
2	0	0	James Cockburn	ditto		8	0
7	10	0	Mr Robert Clark	ditto	1	10	0
1	10	0		a field		6	0
6	0	0	Robert Jenkins	house & shop	1	4	0
3	10	0	Thomas Oyler	part of a house		14	0
1	0	0	Mrs Bray	ditto		4	0
1	0	0		a stable		4	0
2	10	0	Thomas Williams	house		10	0
3	0	0	John Jenkins	ditto		12	0
2	10	0	Richard Bragg	ditto		10	0
3	0	0	Widow Tree	house		12	0
3	0	0	John Attwood	ditto		12	0
4	10	0	Charles Suters	ditto		18	0
1	0	0		a garden		4	0
3	0	0	Edward Jeakens jnr	house		12	0
1	10	0	Joseph Cogger	ditto		6	0

2	10	0	Stephen Bennett	ditto		10	0
4	0	0	James Bray	house & garden		16	0
9	0	0	Mr Abraham Kennett	ditto	1	16	0
2	0	0	Thomas Harwood	house		8	0
2	10	0	Edward Field	ditto		10	0
2	10	0	Henry Leadbeater	ditto		10	0
2	10	0	Thomas Parnell	ditto		10	0
7	0	0	John Tree	house & field	1	8	0
				Out Dwellers			
109	10	0	Mr [Samuel] Southerden	house and land	21	18	0
33	10	0	Jeremiah Curteis Esq, Rye	land	6	14	0
48	0	0	Richard Curteis Esq, Tenterden	land	9	12	0
26	0	0	Mr [Hugh] Whistler, Bexhill		5	4	0
100	0	0	Mr Arkcoll & Co, Hastings		20	0	0
63	0	0	Mr [Christopher] Thorpe, Ore		12	12	0
38	0	0	Mr [John] Lansdale, Bexhill		7	12	0
82	18	6	Jeremiah Curteis Esq, Tenterden		16	11	6
12	10	0	ditto	for the Point House and sanded outlands occupied by Mr Southerden	2	10	0
1	10	0	-- Cooke	house		6	0
1	10	0	-- Tickner	ditto		6	0
4	0	0	-- Ralph	house & woollhouse		16	0
				[Total]	250	15	6

28 February 1801   Winchelsea   Examined & allowed
    Thomas Marten, deputy mayor, G Stace [magistrates]
    William Sargent, Thomas Fuller   churchwardens
    Robert Clark, Josiah Boots overseers
    D Hollingberry
    Walter Fuller
    George Tilden

14 April 1801 Easter Sessions
    The above rate upon appeal was quashed.
    [*signed*] Thomas Marten, deputy mayor, G[eorge] Stace

                                      [AMS 2329]

D2   Assessment of the Parish of St Thomas the Apostle, Winchelsea
29 March 1825

An assessment then made and agreed on by the churchwardens, overseers and other inhabitants, members of the select vestry of the parish of St Thomas the Apostle in the Ancient Town of Winchelsea aforesaid at four shillings in the pound agreeable to the late valuation towards maintaining the poor of the parish and defraying all necessary charges thereto belonging.

Rent			Owner	Property	Site/Area/ Occupation	Payment Due		
4	10	0	Alce, Robert senior	house and garden			18	0
1	10	0	Ashdown, widow	ditto			6	0
1	10	0	Amon, widow	ditto			6	0
	15	0	Bennett, Thomas	ditto and garden			3	0
3	10	0	Browne, Barwell Esq	ditto			14	0
4	0	0	Boots, widow	ditto	poor		--	--
3	0	0	Bray, James	ditto ditto			12	0
2	0	0	Bennett, widow (?B)	ditto	poor		--	--
3	0	0	Buttenshaw, widow	ditto	poor		--	--
			ditto	Oast House, Jeakens	poor		--	--
	15	0	Barden, George	House OH	poor		--	--
2	0	0	Barden, George	house and garden			8	0
	15	0	ditto	shop and yard			3	0
2	0	0	Ballard, William	house and shop			8	0
	5	0	ditto	garden			1	0
2	0	0	Butler H P	part house			8	0
1	10	0	Barden, Edward	house and garden			6	0
1	10	0	Bennett, John	ditto			6	0
2	15	0	Baker, John	ditto			11	0
2	15	0	Bigg, Joseph	house, garden and shop			11	0
6	10	0	Blackman, widow	house and garden		1	6	0
2	15	0	Barham, Henry	ditto			11	0
	15	0	Bailey, William	house and garden [in] Square	poor		--	--
2	0	0	Baker Henry (?Z)	house and garden	poor		--	--
	7	6	Broadfoot, widow	part house	poor		--	--
1	0	0	Boots, Benjamin	house and stables			4	0
1	0	0	Baker, Susan	house and garden	OH		4	0
2	5	0	Booth, James	ditto			9	0
8	0	0	Bray, George	ditto		1	12	0
7	10	0	ditto	Pear Tree Marsh	4a 2r 20p	1	10	0
	14	0	ditto	part Castle Field	0a 1r 21p		2	9
2	10	0	Chart M[ary]	house and garden			10	0
1	0	0	Claise, James	house and garden	poor		--	--
5	10	0	Chatterton, William	house, garden and shop		1	2	0
1	0	0	Chester, John	house and garden [in] Square	poor		--	--
1	0	0	Chart, James	house, garden and stable	poor		--	--
	15	0	Clark, James	part house [in] Square			3	0
3	0	0	Clark, widow	house and garden			12	0
1	0	0	Clark, Robert	ditto	occupied by Moulton		4	0
	15	0	ditto	ditto	occupied by Warner		3	0
1	0	0	Cogger, John	house OH	poor		--	--
1	0	0	Cogger, Joseph	house and shop	poor		--	--
98	10	0	Dugdell, Rev J W	rector[ial] & vic[arial] tithes		19	14	0

£	s	d	Name	Property	Area	Notes	£	s	d
			Dawes, Thomas Esq	house and gardens					
			ditto	ditto		occupied by N Benfield			
22	15	0	ditto	Paradise	1a 2r 0p		4	11	0
			Dawes, Weeden & Thomas	Pewes [Marsh]	6a 0r 0p				
				Pewes Slope	3a 0r 0p				
				Reed Bed	2a 2r 0p				
				Fryers Orchard	2a 0r 30p				
				Little Gallows Field	3r 0p				
				Chestnut Land & Barn	9a 2r 29p				
				pt St Leonard's Field	3a 0r 0p				
				Great Mill Bank	2a 1r 0p				
				Two Acres	2a 0r 27p				
59	2	6		White House Field	2a 1r 0p		11	16	6
3	0	0	Daniel, John	house				12	0
			Denne, Mrs	house and garden					
				new stables					
				Upper Two Acres	2a 1r 0p				
				Lower ditto	1a 3r 0p				
				Front Field	2r 30p				
				Thornland	6a 0r 26p				
				Great Gallows Field	3a 1r 0p				
				Ferry Field	1a 0r 0p				
58	0	0		Ferry House and garden			11	12	0
1	0	0	Denne, Mrs	Ferry House Cottage (field)				4	0
8	10	0	Dunk H	house, shop & garden			1	14	0
	15	0	Edwards, Thomas	house		poor		--	--
	15	0	Edwards, widow	part house [in] Square		poor		--	--
1	0	0	Easton, Thomas	house & garden				4	0
1	0	0		house	Pensull	empty		--	--
1	0	0		ditto	Wheeler	empty		--	--
4	0	0		ditto	Miss Easton's	empty		--	--
2	0	0	Easton, Samuel	house and shop		poor		--	--
16	0	0	English	house etc	late Winch	empty		--	--
			Fuller, Walter	house, shop & garden					
				Ferry Marsh	2r 26p				
				Nursery Orchard	2r 0p				
12	0	0		Horsepond Piece	2a 0r 0p		2	8	0
	7	6		1 room [in] Square				1	6
6	0	0		16 rooms ditto		empty		--	--
1	10	0	Fisher, widow	house & garden		poor		--	--
1	10	0	Fuller, John	part house				6	0
1	2	6	Field, Richard	3 rooms [in] Square		poor		--	--
	15	0	Foster, widow	2 ditto		poor		--	--
	15	0	Gill, William	house				3	0
	15	0	Gurr, John	ditto				3	0
12	0	0	Hollingberry, Mrs	house, garden & stables			2	8	0
10	0	0	Harrod, George	house, stable & garden			2	0	0
	15	0		stables				3	0
	15	0		garden				3	0
1	10	0		house	occupied Stevens			6	0
1	10	0		ditto	late Chasmar	empty		--	--
1	10	0		ditto	late	empty		--	--
4	10	0	Hoadley, Thomas	house, shop and garden				18	0
1	10	0	Hoad, James	ditto	[in] Square	poor		--	--
2	0	0	Haisell, George	ditto		poor		--	--

Poor Rate Assement 29 March 1825 - Continued

£	s	d	Name	Property	Note	Status		£	s	d
3	0	0	Hollingberry, John Esq	old churchyard				12	0
3	15	0		house				15	0
2	0	0		ditto	late Blake	empty		--	--
5	0	0	Hoad, Joseph	ditto shop & garden			1	0	0
2	0	0	Hills, James	house & garden				8	0
3	0	0	Hill, Charles	ditto				12	0
1	15	0	Hoad, Thomas snr	ditto		poor		--	--
4	0	0	Hill, George	ditto				16	0
3	10	0	Holt, widow	ditto				14	0
3	0	0	Hearnden, Isaac	ditto	and shop			12	0
	15	0		shop		empty		--	--
1	10	0		house	late Harmer	empty		--	--
1	10	0	Holt, Esau	ditto & garden				6	0
4	0	0	Hennah, Joseph Esq	ditto & 2 gardens				16	0
3	0	0	Holt, Jacob	ditto & garden				12	0
	15	0	Harmer, widow	2 rooms	[in] Square			3	0
7	0	0	Jones, Joash	house, shop and stable			1	8	0
2	10	0	Jones, widow (James)	house				10	0
	15	0	Jones, widow (William)	house				3	0
1	0	0	Jeakens – representatives	stable		)			
6	12	0	[of widow of Edward d.1815]	Cooks Green & cliff	2a 2r 0p	)			
6	0	0		Walnut Tree Field	4a 2r 0p	)			
3	0	0		Cliff Field	2a 1r 0p	) empty		--	--
3	6	8		Tanyard Piece	2a 2r 0p	)			
1	0	0		Shed Piece	3r 0p	)			
2	0	0		Tanyard & buildings		)			
	13	4		hut	occd by Sculthorpe			2	8
1	0	0		house	occd by Bourner	poor		--	--
4	0	0		house & garden	late E Jeakens	empty		--	--
1	0	0	Jeakens, widow	house & garden				4	0
2	0	0	Jenkins, widow	ditto		poor		--	--
1	10	0	Haisell		late Watts H	empty		--	--
1	15	0	Jeakens – representatives	house	Bartholomew	empty		--	--
2	10	0		ditto	Sinden	empty		--	--
2	10	0	Keene T S	house & garden				10	0
1	10	0	Laurence & Osborne	shop & yard	late Boots			6	0
2	15	0	Laurence, David	house & garden				11	0
2	0	0	Leonard W	ditto		poor		--	--
2	15	0	Laurence, Stephen	ditto		poor		--	--
1	10	0	Laurence, widow	ditto		poor		--	--
11	0	0	Malliphant, Mrs	ditto			2	4	0
	15	0	Morris, Thomas snr					3	0
	7	6	Morris					1	6
1	0	0	Mannering, Thomas	house	OH			4	0
1	0	0	Morris, William	ditto	OH	poor		--	--
2	15	0	Maplesden, Richard snr	house & garden				11	0
3	0	0	Maplesden, Richard jnr	ditto				12	0
1	10	0	Martin, William (Harrod's)	ditto				6	0
1	0	0	Morris, Edward	ditto				4	0
1	10	0	Martin. George	ditto				6	0
1	0	0	Martin, William CC	ditto				4	0
	12	6	Needham, William	part School				2	6
1	10	0	Ockenden, William	house	[in] Square	poor		--	--
			Osborne, Richard	house, stable and garden					
				Chapel Field	5a 0r 0p				
				Float Field	2r 20p				
14	10	0		part garden			2	18	0

£	s	d	Name	Property	Note	Status	£	s	d
2	0	0	Perigo, late	house and garden		empty		--	--
4	15	0	Powell, Henry Esq	ditto				19	0
3	10	0		ditto				14	0
1	0	0	Parsons, Thomas	house	OH	poor		--	--
1	10	0	Parsons, Joseph	ditto	[in] Square			6	0
1	0	0	Packham, G	ditto	OH			4	0
1	10	0	Russell, F	ditto	OH			6	0
1	10	0	Sa[u]nders, widow (T)	ditto	[in] Square	poor		--	--
3	10	0	Sheppard, Rev S P	house & garden				14	0
9	0	0	Scott, A MD	house, garden & stable			1	16	0
3	10	0	Suters, Mrs	ditto				14	0
1	10	0		two gardens				6	0
2	0	0	Stevenson, George	house & garden		poor		--	--
9	0	0	Stace, George Esq	ditto			1	16	0
				Little Monday Market	2a 0r 20p				
5	0	0		Newgate Field	2a 0r 0p		1	0	0
2	0	0	Scarth, Thomas Esq	house & garden				8	0
3	15	0	Sargent, William jnr	house, garden & bakehouse				15	0
5	10	0	Stileman, Mrs	house & garden			1	2	0
1	10	0	Smawley, Joseph	ditto	[in] Square			6	0
			Stileman, Richard Esq	ditto					
				Cottage	occd Bragge				
				Saffron Garden	1r 0p				
				Holyrood Field	6a 2r 0p				
				part Pewes	3r 0p				
				part Cliff Field	2a 2r 0p				
				part cliff	2a 0r 29p				
				Tinker's Garden	2a 2r 28p				
				Upper Orchard	1a 3r 0p				
				Lower Orchard	2a 1r 20p				
				Leaping Bar Field	5a 0r 0p				
				Monday Market	5a 0r 6p				
				King's Green	10a 0r 0p				
				Coney Field	8a 0r 0p				
122	10	0		cliff	6a 3r 31p		24	10	0
	12	6		part school				2	6
	10	0		hut	late Watts	empty		--	--
1	0	0	Seere W	house	occd Howell	poor		--	--
1	10	0	Stevens, widow	house and garden		poor		--	--
2	10	0	Stephens, Mistress	ditto	ditto			10	0
1	10	0	Sharp, Richard	ditto	ditto			6	0
2	0	0	Sanders, widow	ditto		poor		--	--
			Southerden, Samuel	house etc					
				Pell Field	28a 0r 0p				
				Pound Fields	8a 0r 0p				
				Hospital Fields	10a 0r 0p				
				Oatlands	30a 0r 0p				
				Barn Field	7a 0r 0p				
				Corner Field	14a 0r 0p				
120	0	0		House Field	27a 0r 0p		24	0	0
3	0	0	Southerden C	house				12	0
2	15	0	Skinner, Thomas	house & garden				11	0
1	5	0	Sinden, John	ditto		poor		--	--
	5	0	Tree, David	shop				1	0
7	15	0	Tilden, John Esq	house & garden			1	11	0
4	0	0	Tilden, Mrs	ditto				15	0
2	0	0	Thornhill, Rev	ditto				8	0
2	0	0	Tulloch, A Esq	ditto				8	0
2	0	0	Vane, Honble [Henry]	ditto				8	0
3	10	0	Veness, Thomas	house & shop				14	0
	15	0		lodge & stables				3	0
3	0	0	Winstanley, John (late)	house		empty		--	--
	7	6	Willard, G	1 room	[in] Square	poor		--	--
1	10	0	Whiteman, Thomas	house	ditto	poor		--	--

Poor Rate Assement 29 March 1825 - Continued

£	s	d	Name	Property	Measure	Status	£	s	d
2	0	0	Woodhams, widow	house & garden		poor		--	--
4	0	0	Winstone. John	ditto				16	0
1	15	0	Winter, Charles	Glebe Gardens				7	0
1	0	0	Wimble, T	house & garden				4	0
2	15	0	Whiteman, William	ditto				11	0
11	5	0	Wright, J E Esq	ditto			2	5	0
	15	0		shop				3	0
1	0	0	Westover, John	house & garden				4	0
1	0	0	Wheeler, Robert	ditto		poor		--	--
	15	0	Willard, William	ditto		poor		--	--
1	0	0	Watson, Jeremiah	ditto	OH	poor		--	--
1	0	0	Weller, James	ditto	OH			4	0
2	0	0	Willson, Richard	ditto				8	0
2	0	0	Waters, W (late)	ditto		empty		--	--
				[Total]			164	5	11
			Out Dwellers						
			Curteis, Jeremiah	2 pieces marsh	32a 2r 0p				
				good Oatlands	28a 0r 0p				
				indifferent Oatlands	12a 1r 0p				
93	10	0		Oatlands,	30a 0r 0p		18	14	0
				Southerden					
1	0	0		house, Burgess				4	0
46	10	0	Croughton, William Esq	marsh land	27a 1r 0p		9	6	0
			Milles, Thomas Esq	Great Piper Field	40a 1r 3p				
				Little Piper Field	10a 2r 27p				
80	0	0		sand bank	9a 0r 0p		16	0	0
			Sloman, John	part Fifty Acres	25a 3r 31p				
				Ten Acres	10a 0r 15p				
56	0	0		Pound Plat	2a 0r 3p		11	4	0
			Stonham, Thomas	part Fifty Acres	24a 0r 7p				
57	0	0		Pell Fields	14a 3r 6p		11	8	0
			Selmes, Samuel	part Fifty Acres	13a 1r 32p				
				Ten Acres	10a 2r 0p				
				Coney Bank	3r 3p				
				Pell Fields	7a 2r 21p				
57	10	0		Wall Fields	7a 0r 19p		11	10	0
			Woodhams, William	Ferry Marsh	7a 1r 13p				
				Morley's Marsh	4a 0r 0p				
				Cliff Gill	1a 1r 0p				
21	10	0		part Roundle Field	2a 0r 0p		4	6	0
3	10	0	Richards, Revd	churchyard	2a 0r 0p			14	0
				[Total]			247	11	11

[signed by]	J Hollinberry	)
	J E Wright	) churchwardens
	G Harrod	)
	Richard Maplesden	) overseers
	C Arnett, assistant	)
	Richard Stileman	) inhabitants, members of
	A Scott	) the select vestry

[*Endorsed*]   **The Ancient Town of Winchelsea in the County of Sussex** to wit
We whose names are hereunder written being two of His Majesty's justices of the peace in and for the said Ancient Town do hereby allow and confirm the aforegoing rate or assessment for the relief of the poor of the parish of St Thomas the Apostle in the said Ancient Town of Winchelsea. Given under our hands this 2nd day of April 1825

Henry Powell
J Tilden

[PAR 511/31/1/13]

Appendix E

Additional Documents

E1 Assistant Overseers' Appointment

This massively detailed document, provided nationally in printed form and with the necessary details (here shown in bold and italicised) filled in locally by the magistrates or their clerk is published as an important example of how central government had started its attempt to standardise and regularise what was being done in parishes in many different ways. Salaried assistant overseers on appointment, certainly if it was their first appointment, must have found it a formidable document in its expectation that their knowledge of the law would extend over such a wide range of duties. No doubt they all did the job in their own way but the basic requirements for dealing with bastardy, removal, settlement, accounting, poor rate collection, financial relief of the poor and book-keeping, described and laid down here, are illustrated throughout this volume in many ways. Although Charles Arnett, on leaving, was accused of failing to present accurate accounts and of owing the parish money, his defence (**24**) was so robust that we have no evidence that either Charles Arnett or David Laurence ever faced the kind of penalties for misconduct which the document also lays down.

David Laurence, to whom this document applies, was a local man, already widely experienced as an elected overseer and as churchwarden, before he undertook this paid employment in the parish. No doubt after what they saw, with no justification that can be discerned from documentary evidence nearly two hundred years later, as the unfortunate experience of employing someone who came from outside the parish, the vestry members felt they would be happier with a Winchelsea man undertaking the work. Nothing has been found to suggest other than that David Laurence fulfilled this trust faithfully and conscientiously.

If documents like this one existed in 1823 when Charles Arnett was appointed, the one referring to him has not survived in the parish records.

To *David Laurence* substantial housekeeper of the *Parish of St Thomas the Apostle in the Ancient Town of Winchelsea in the County of Sussex.*

Whereas at a public vestry of the inhabitants of the parish of *St Thomas the Apostle in the Ancient Town of Winchelsea in the county of Sussex* held at *Winchelsea* the twenty-second day of March pursuant to public notice *David Laurence* an inhabitant householder of the said parish, being a discreet person was duly elected as an ASSISTANT OVERSEER of the POOR of the said parish, to execute all such and the like duties as appertain to or belong to or are incident to the office of the ordinary Overseer of the Poor of the said parish, and at the salary of *Twenty Pounds* per annum. Now we, whose hands and seals are now to set, being two of His Majesty's Justices of the Peace of and for the **Town of Winchelsea** dwelling in or near to the said parish of **St Thomas's the Apostle** do, in pursuance of the statute in that case made and provided, appoint the said **David Laurence** to be Assistant Overseer of the Poor of the said parish of **St Thomas the Apostle** for such purposes as aforesaid and such salary as has been fixed by the inhabitants in the said vestry assembled as aforesaid, which appointment shall continue until the said **David Laurence** shall resign the said office, or until his appointment shall be revoked by the inhabitants of the said parish in vestry assembled. And we do hereby require you forthwith to take upon you the execution of the said office, and for that purpose you, together with the churchwardens and overseers of your said parish for the time being, under the penalty of forfeiting 20s each, are to meet at least once in every month in your parish church, upon the Sunday afternoon, to confer together, consider of, and take order for setting to work the children of all such within your said parish, whose parents shall not be thought able, by you, to keep and maintain them; and also for setting to work all such persons, married or unmarried, having no means to maintain themselves, and using no trade to get their living by; and also for the raising of a convenient stock of hemp, flax, wool, thread, iron and other stuffs for those purposes; and also for the providing of necessary relief for such persons as are lame, old, blind, poor, or unable to work, within your said parish, and for placing out as apprentices such children as aforesaid. To which end you are to raise weekly, or otherwise (by taxation of every inhabitant, parson, vicar, and other, and of every occupier of houses, lands, tythes impropriate [tythes which had passed into lay hands], propriations [acquisitions] of tythes, coal mines, and saleable underwoods, within your parish) such sums of money as shall be sufficient for those purposes, and as shall be allowed of by any two justices of the peace of this county, dwelling in or near your parish. Stat. 43 ELIZ. cap. 2. and 13 & 14 CAR. II. cap.12.

You are to cause public notice to be given in the church, of every rate for relief of the poor, allowed by the justices of the peace, on the next Sunday after the same shall be allowed; no such rate being sufficient to be collected, unless such notice shall be given. And you are to permit every inhabitant of your parish to inspect every such rate at all reasonable times, and on demand to give him or her a copy of the same, or any part thereof, he or she paying at the rate of 6d for every twenty-four names, or otherwise you forfeit £20. Stat. 17 Geo. II.

If any person shall refuse or neglect to pay any monies that he or she shall be legally rated or assessed to, for the relief of your poor, any succeeding overseers may and are required to levy such arrears and therewith reimburse their predecessors. Stat. 17 Geo. II.

All persons occupying houses, lands or tenements, for only part of a year, are to pay their proportionable share of the sums charged thereon, although such persons were not originally rated; the proportion, if disputed, to be ascertained by two or more justices of the peace. Stat. 17 Geo. II.

True and just copies of all rates and assessments, made for the relief of the poor of your parish, are to be written and entered into a book or books provided for that purpose, by you and the overseers and churchwardens of your parish, within fourteen days after all appeals from such rates are determined, and you and they are to attest the same, by putting your names thereto; which book or books are to be, by you and the said churchwardens, carefully preserved in some public or other place, whereto all persons assessed, or liable to be assessed, may freely resort, and are to be delivered over from time to time to all succeeding churchwardens and overseers, as soon as they enter on their offices; and this you and they are to omit, on pain of forfeiting a sum not exceeding £5 nor less than 20s. Stat. 17 Geo. II.

If any person shall give you notice of appeal against a rate, then you are not to collect more of him or her than the premises were assessed at in the then last effective rate, until such appeal is heard and determined. Stat. 41 Geo. III. cap. 23, sec. 2.

You are also to repay the preceding churchwardens and overseers, out of the monies to be collected by you by virtue of your office, all such sums of monies (if any) as they may have advanced or expended for the relief or maintenance of the poor during the time any appeal has been depending, or the time that no rate or assessment has been made, in case the same shall be made appear to be justly due to them. Stat. 41 Geo. III. cap 23. sec. 9.

You, together with the churchwardens and overseers of your parish, may, by the assent of any two justices of the peace aforesaid, bind any such poor children as aforesaid to be apprentices, if a man child, until he attain his age of one-and-twenty years; and if a woman child, until she attain her age of one-and-twenty years, or the time of her marriage: and if the persons to whom they are bound shall refuse to receive and provide for them, and to execute one part of the indentures, they are subject to a penalty of £10 to the poor of your parish: and you may with the like consent bind out boys who are chargeable, and of the age of eight years each, apprentices to chimney-sweepers, till they attain the ages of sixteen years each; but such chimney-sweepers must not have more than six apprentices each. Stat. 28 Geo. III cap. 48. f. 1 and 7.

You, with the churchwardens and overseers of your parish, by leave of the Lord of the Manor, may build on any waste or common within your parish, at the charges of the same, houses or dwelling for your poor, and may place therein inmates, or other poor or impotent persons of your parish. Stat. 49 Eliz. cap. 2. And 8 & 9 Will. III. cap. 30. and 18 Geo. III. cap. 47. And, with the like consent, you may set up or use any trade, only for the setting on work and relief of your poor. Stat. 3 Car. I. Cap. 5.

You, and the overseers and churchwardens of your parish, with the consent of your parishioners in vestry, may purchase or hire houses in your parish; and contract with persons for the lodging, maintaining and employing all such of your poor as shall desire relief; and if any person shall refuse to be lodged in such house, he or she shall be put off the books, and not be entitled to relief. And with consent of one justice of the peace, your parish may join with any adjacent parish in purchasing or hiring a house, for the purposes aforesaid; and you may contract with the churchwardens and overseers of any other parish for the lodging, maintaining and employing of your poor. Stat. 9 Geo. I. c.7.

You are to take care that there be kept in your parish a book wherein the names of persons in your parish who receive collection, pay or relief, shall be registered, with the day and year when they were admitted, and the occasion which brought them under the necessity; and yearly in Easter week (or as often as shall be thought convenient) your parishioners shall meet in vestry, before whom the books shall be produced, and all persons receiving collections or relief shall be called over, and the reason of their taking relief examined and a new list made of such as they think fit to receive collection or relief; and no other person is to be allowed collection at the charge of your parish but by order under the hand of some justice of the peace residing in or near the same, or by order of the justices in quarter sessions (except in cases of pestilential diseases, plague or smallpox, and for such families only as are infected, AND ALSO UPON ANY SUDDEN AND EMERGENT OCCASIONS); and if such justices shall order relief for any poor persons as aforesaid, you are to enter into the said books such person's name as one of those who is to receive collection, as long as the cause of such relief continues. And you are to pay no weekly or other payments, under pretence of extraordinaries, to any poor person whatsoever whose name is not registered as aforesaid, unless by such order, or except as aforesaid; or unless it is to any industrious poor person or persons, at his or her homes or houses under the circumstances of temporary illness or distress, or under any order of any of his majesty's justices of the peace, as now, under these circumstances, they may be relieved at their own homes, by Stat. 36 Geo. III. cap. 23. And if you charge any monies as paid contrary hereto, you forfeit £5 to the poor of the parish. (Stat. 3 & 4 Will. and Mar. cap. 11. and 9 Geo I. cap. 7.) And in consequence thereof you are not to bring to the account of your parish any money given to the soldiers or sailors, although they have proper passes or certificates (for these are to be relieved by the treasurers of the respective counties through which they pass, by Stat. 43 Eliz. cap. 3.) nor any monies given to any other persons travelling with passes or pretended passes, or to any persons begging for losses by fire, or any other pretence whatever, under the said penalty of £5.

And if any person coming to settle in your parish shall become actually chargeable thereto, you may then, and not before, take them before two justices of the peace, to be examined and removed to the place of their last legal settlement; and in case they should be sick or ill, at such time the justices may suspend the removal of them, and the parish officers must pay the expenses occasioned by such suspension. Stat. 35 Geo. III. cap. 101. And if you refuse to receive any person that shall be removed from any other parish or place to your parish, by warrant under the hands and seals of two justices of the peace you incur a penalty of £5.

Any persons coming to inhabit in your parish, not having a lawful settlement there, who shall have been convicted of larceny, or any other felony, or be by law deemed a rogue, vagabond, idle or disorderly person; or who shall appear to any two justices, to be a person of evil fame, or a reputed thief; and every unmarried woman with child; shall be considered as actually chargeable; and not bringing any certificate of his or her being settled elsewhere, nor giving security for the discharge of your parish, you ought to make complaint thereof to some two justices of the peace of this county, in order to the examination and removal of such person to the place of his or her last legal settlement. Stat. 35 Geo. III. c. 101. f. 5 & 6.

You are also, within four days after the end of your year, and after other overseers are nominated, to yield unto such two next justices of the peace, as aforesaid, a just, true and perfect account of all sums of money you received, or rated and assessed and not received, and also of all goods, chattels, stock and materials in your hands, or in the hands of any of the poor of your parish in order to be wrought; and of all monies paid by you, and of all other things concerning the said office. And you are further required, within fourteen days after other overseers shall be nominated and appointed to succeed you, to deliver to such succeeding overseers one other such account as aforesaid, fairly entered into a book or books to be kept for that purpose, signed by you and the overseers and churchwardens; and also to pay and deliver over all such sums of money, goods and chattels and other things, as shall be in your hands, unto such succeeding overseers; which account is to be verified upon oath (or by the affirmation of persons called Quakers) before one or more justices of the peace. And if you, or your said overseers and churchwardens, shall refuse or neglect to do as before required, every person so refusing or neglecting, is liable to be committed to the common gaol. The said book or books to be from time to time carefully preserved by you and the churchwardens and overseers of the poor of your parish in some public or other places; and all persons assessed, or liable to be assessed, are to be permitted to inspect the same at all reasonable times, and to have copies thereof, paying for the same. Stat. 43 Eliz. cap. 2. 17 Geo II. 50 Geo. III. cap 49.

Parish officers are to verify their accounts before two or more justices, at a special session within the fourteen days specified by 43 Eliz. and 17 Geo. II. which justices may strike out and reduce charges in such accounts, noticing the same at the foot of each. And if within the above-mentioned time overseers refuse to pay the balance of money to their successors, such successors may obtain the same by distress warrant of two justices; if no distress, the offender is to be committed until the same is paid. Parish officers may appeal to the next sessions, first paying the balance due, and entering into recognizance with sureties to try the appeal. 50 Geo. III. cap 49. sec. 1 and 2.

And you are hereby also required at some petty sessions or monthly meeting of His Majesty's justices of the peace of the *said town* to be holden for the *said town* on the twenty-fifth day of March next ensuing the date hereof, or within fourteen days afterwards, to deliver in unto the said justices, for their better information in appointing other overseers to succeed you, a list in writing of a competent number of the most sufficient householders of your parish as shall be made choice of at some public meeting of your parishioners or inhabitants for that purpose. 54 Geo. III. cap. 91.

And you and the overseers and the said churchwardens of your said *parish* are not to fail of your duties in the execution of the said office of overseer, and assistant overseer, as you will answer the same at your respective perils.

GIVEN under our hands and seals this *twenty-seventh* day of *March* in the *Ninth* year of the reign of our sovereign lord *George the Fourth* by the grace of God of the United Kingdom of Great Britain and Ireland King, Defender of the Faith, and in the year of our lord one thousand eight hundred and *twenty-eight*.

John Tilden   J. Hennah

[PAR 511/37/1/2]

 E2 *The Times* **13 June 1835 page 6 Issue 15815 column A**

In this article we find, rather surprisingly, that in 1835 a labourers' union existed in Winchelsea, formed for the specific purpose of increasing agricultural labourers' wages and prepared to resort to violence when unsuccessful. The quoted subscription figure of two shillings a week seems very high when the members were only receiving two shillings and threepence a day. It could be that other more fortunate workers were supporting those less well-paid. *The Times* refers to the dissatisfaction 'of the labouring classes' with changes in poor relief provision made as a result of the 1834 Poor Law Amendment Act. These provisions were no doubt well-known to Winchelsea workers but they had not come into force in the town by the date of the article because the first meeting of the Rye Union was not held until more than six weeks after the Winchelsea violence (**974**) and the Winchelsea authorities were currently acting under an instruction to 'give relief as before' (**973**). Although more than one Mr Smith farmed in the area at this time, the one most likely to have had a sufficient workforce and to have been the victim of the attack described in the final paragraph was Jeremiah Smith of Wickham Farm. He later became a leading member of the guardians of the Rye Union. Although the Winchelsea incident appears only at the end, the whole text of

The Times report is included here for the very considerable insights it provides into policing investigation as carried out in the countryside before the establishment of county forces.

This report was traced by the present editor through the reference to it on page 284 of *Captain Swing* by Eric Hobsbawm and George Rudé.

AGRICULTURAL DISTURBANCES IN SUSSEX
(From a Correspondent)

In consequence of complaints received about three weeks back by the Commissioners of Police from the Earl of Chichester, Mr. Chambers, a county magistrate, and other extensive landholders in the eastern division of Sussex, stating that numerous wanton outrages were continually being committed, in the dead of the night, upon farming property, particularly in the destruction of sheep, when left in the pastures, the Commissioners sent down John Hall and Thomas Ryan, two intelligent and experienced policemen of the A division with orders to remain so long as the magistrates there might require their services. These men have only just returned from this duty, and, in the course of performing it, had recourse to various disguises. Sometimes Hall appeared as a gentleman on a visit to the country; at others with the smockfrock and ordinary dress of a farming servant. Ryan for the most part was dressed as a sailor, and under these and various other disguises they visited every part of the east division of Sussex. They first proceeded to Stanmer, near Brighton, where Hall saw the Earl of Chichester, who, after giving a general account of the system of outrage that prevailed, referred him to Mr. Thomas, an active magistrate for the county, living at Railton House near Eastbourne. Mr. Thomas swore in both Hall and Ryan as special constables for the eastern division of the county, and then despatched them to make inquiries where outrages had been most recently perpetrated.

The officers learnt that scarcely a night had passed, previously to their being sent for, without some farmer in that part of the county finding one or more, but generally only one, of his sheep stuck through the neck, and, left in the field to die a lingering death. It was evident that a rankling feeling of discontent, and a diabolical spirit of revenge, prevailed over a large portion of the peasantry. The object in almost every instance was merely to destroy, for scarcely ever was the carcass of the slaughtered sheep carried away. Two causes appear to have been in operation to produce this dreadful state of society – the one the formation of labourers' unions at Rye, Eastbourne and Winchelsea, the men belonging to which paid to the fund 2s. per week, and the main avowed object of their association was compelling the farmers to advance the rate of pay of their day labourers from 2s. to 2s. 6d. per day. This was firmly, and in the end successfully, resisted. The other cause was the general dissatisfaction of the labouring classes with the changes which the New Poor Law Bill had produced in the mode of granting parochial relief. The operation of the latter cause was strikingly exemplified by the fact that the majority of the night attacks was made on the property of those farmers who as guardians, churchwardens, or overseers took an active part in the administration of the poor laws.

Acting under the instructions received from Mr. Thomas, Hall first proceeded to the farm of Mr. John Pagden, a guardian of the poor, living near Willingdon, who he found had several sheep stuck and left to die. The manner in which they were stuck in the neck seemed to show the act had not been committed by a practised slaughterer, for it left the poor animal to slowly bleed to death, it often living, or rather lingering for hours afterwards. At the farm of Mr Henry Pagden near Alfriston, an attempt had been made a short time previous to destroy the barn and stacks, to a pert of which fire was set, but was happily discovered so early as to prevent any serious consequences. Several sheep had likewise been killed on this farm. Mr Chambers, the magistrate, had also had much wanton damage done upon his farm. Several other cases were referred for the examination of the officers, but in all the cases the farms were of great extent, and as it was in the open downs and other outlying parts of the farms the mischief had been done, and that in the secrecy of the night, it was found impossible to find conclusive evidence, although various parties were apprehended on suspicion, and some who could give no good account of their mode of life, held to bail, and in default of finding it, sent to prison; some few, on finding the stir making, disappeared.

Under the directions of the magistrates the officers, during their stay, succeeded in organising an efficient local police force which was readily formed by the farmers and their head servants and had the effect of repressing further outrages. Its efficiency was proved by Hall himself being, while pursuing his nocturnal espionage, twice apprehended by parties of this nocturnal patrol. While thus engaged, the officers were suddenly called off to a fire which broke out last Saturday week at Sutton near Seaford. The fire broke out in the adjoining barns of Mr Buckwill and Mr Horne, about half-past nine o'clock on the Saturday night. The evidence is most conclusive that it was the work of an incendiary, for it was proved to have broken out in three different places, and at each the irruption of flames was preceded by a loud explosion. It is evident a slow burning fuse must have been attached to the combustible material, so as to allow the perpetrator ample time to retire. The property destroyed consisted of 700 bushels of potatoes, two loads of wheat and two pigs. The most diligent inquiry was made but unfortunately without any beneficial result.

At Winchelsea the officers were called upon to examine the premises of Mr Smith upon whose life a most daring attempt was made. Mr Smith is the most extensive farmer in that neighbourhood, and had resisted the attempt made by his labourers to obtain an advance from 2s 3d to 2s 6d per day; on which they all struck. A few nights after some gravel was thrown at his bedroom window obviously with the intention of drawing him to it to see what was the matter, for immediately afterwards a gun was discharged at the window, the bullet from the barrel of which has lodged in the opposite wall and there are besides the marks of upwards of 100 small shots. A reward of £400 has been offered for the discovery of the author of this diabolical attempt.

Index of Persons

No attempt has been made in this index to separate references to people of the same name. Where this information is available, the documents make it clear through such indications as senior or junior, the elder or the younger.
Bracketed numbers indicate two persons of the same name in different families.
* indicates two people of the same name within the same family.
All occupational designations are for Winchelsea unless otherwise stated.
This index does not indicate when a person receives two or more mentions within the same document.
W = Winchelsea

Adams, Caroline B1
  William B1 C3(d) D1
Adamson, Dr 71
Adcroft, Joash 807; as mayor 827
Ade, Richard D1
Ades, Edward 866 868
  Thomas 866-867
Alce, Elizabeth 704
  John B1 C2(b) C3(d)
  Mary née Ollive A1
  Robert*, carpenter/miller 399 848 A1-2
    C2(b) D1,2; as overseer 101 278 410
    555-558; as churchwarden 827
  Robert, coal merchant of Rye 767 769
    A1
  Thomas A1
  see also Fuller & Alce
Alexander, Sir William 10 331
Allen, Captain, of Dover 620
  William xvi
Allwork, Thomas, of Hastings 900
Almond, Mr 538
Amon, Joseph 541
  Lucy – *see Fuller*
  widow D1,2
Apps, Edward C3(d)
  Mr 107
Arkcoll, Mr 861
  & Co of Hastings D1
Arnett, Charles, assistant overseer, W
    xiii xiv xix-xxi xxvi-xxvii 416 467
    478 509 936 A37 A50; account

submitted by 210n 770; accounts of
xx 1 11 17 19-20 22-26; appearances
before magistrates xx 6 8 13-14
16 58 61 66-67 69 72-73 86 89-90
201 210 233 244 258 271 332-333
383 385 387 402 404 457 510 527
529-530 632 653 701 943 A37;
appearances before quarter sessions
418; appointment of 1-5 11 758n
A11 A25; as assistant overseer 12
18 34 59 152 191 242 256 304
592 604 631 748-749 802n 850n
928 D2; as governor/master of the
workhouse 1 525-526 528 770 A29;
as schoolmaster xxi 1; as special
constable 210; as vestry clerk 1
19; conduct at Bexhill 1; death of
xxi; dismissal of 19 22 A21 A29
A47; expense claims of 9n 15n 210
330n 386n; financial advice to 219;
legal advice sought by 18 217 470;
letters from 24 189 406 425 454
923; letters to 9 37 96 98 118-120
122-131 146 148-149 183 187-188
190 211 213-214 216 218-219 231
249 259 272 283-285 288-290 294-
295 301-305 307-311 318 330 359
369 372-373 403 406 411-412 422
424 433-434 448 460 463-466 468
483-484 486-487 495 501 514-515
560-562 571-572 574-581 596 600
603 605-608 633-634 654 672 676

687 714 719 723-726 741 763 765-769 815 837 849 851-856 885-890 893-895 897-899 901-907 919 924 926 929-931 933 935 937-939; notices to quit issued by 88 489 512 674 699; notices of public meeting issued by 913 917 921 925; proposed proceedings against xxi 25-26; violence etc against xxvii 6-10 13-16 72 232 234-235 258 270 326 329-331 333 376 385-386 401-402 627n A35 A45

Mary 1 3 24 372 570 572 574 576-579 725

Mary Ann 1

William Henry 1 570

Artlett, George (or Hartley) 618 620-621

Ashburnham, Rev[d] John 506

Sir William 506n

Ashdown, widow D2

Atfield, John B1

George B1

Atkins, [-] 549

Attwell, George B1

John C3(d)

Attwood, John B1 C2(b) C3(d) D1

Austen, Susannah – *see Stace*

Austin, Mr E of Rye 670 672n

Aylmer, Captain D1

John 165

Harriett 165

Henry 165

Aylward, Thomas William 681-682

Backhouse, J B, JP of Walmer 548

Bacon, William 724

Bailey (Bayley), Elizabeth 32 40 43-44

Jane 27 29

John 40 43 47-49

Joseph* 27-30 35 752 839 B2 C2(b) C3(d) D1

Lucy 31 33-34 43 B2

Mary (2) 27 29 35-39 43 B2

Mr, landlord of Canterbury 572 576 578

Richard 40-43 49 B2

Stephen, labourer of Lydd 31 32n 34 40 43 45-49 B2

William 40 43 49 811 C2(b) C3(d) D1,2

Bains, Captain James 229

Baker, Henry D2

Job B1

John C3(d) D1,2

John, clerk of the guardians of St Mary's Dover 597 601 605

Judith B1

Mary 239

Needler C3(d)

Philadelphia B1

Sir Robert, JP for Middlesex 647

Sion C3(d)

Susan D2

Zebulon B1 C2(b) C3(d)

Balfour, Arthur D1

Ballard, Captain RN C1(c)

William D2

Banks, Edward Sladen, medical officer 688 707-709

Barden, Charles 139

Edward D2

Elizabeth – *see Lowes*

George D2

William 139

Barford, Edmund 545

Barham, Albert A2

Arthur A2

Caroline A2

Emily A2

Henry, tailor 764 773 787 848 958n A2-3 D2; as overseer 381 831

Maria A2

Barnard, Sarah – *see Laurence*

Barnes, Lucy* (formerly Stonestreet) 50-56 58 60 729n A50 B2

Mr, surveyor of Staplehurst 880

Thomas, of Hastings 50 60 539

Barrett, John, overseer of Stalbridge 448

Bartholomew, [-] D2

Barton, Mr 107

Barwell, Richard 623 D1

Bates, [-] 749

Captain 477-478

Bayden, Thomas 938

Beaching, Joseph 426

Mrs P, of Hastings 426-434
Beale, Hannah 232 236
Bearblock, Walter 878-879 911 947-950
Beaumont, John 787; as JP 661
Becher, William xvii
Bellew, Mr 275
Bellingham, James, surgeon of Rye 516
    Francis 813 848
    Thomas Charles, solicitor of Battle 1
      511 945
Belsey, John, of Dover 592 615-617
Benfield, Joel 452 C2(b) C3(d)
    Nathaniel 870 A10 D2; as
      churchwarden 966
Bennett, Benjamin B1 C3(d)
    Edward 750
    Henry 793
    John* 450 C2(b) C3(d) D2
    Mary 450 A21
    Mrs 35 93
    Stephen 811 C2(b) D1
    Thomas* (alias Selden) 40 62-76 145
      208 397 839 A5 A20 A45 A48 B2
      C2(b) C3(d) D2
    widow D2
    William 773
Bentley, William, of East Guldeford 854
    893-894 897 904 907 909
Berens, Joseph 549
Bevill, Simon, assistant overseer Hastings
    534
Bigg, Joseph 76 334n A2-4 D2; as overseer
    207; letters to 78 254 313-315 429
    431-432 494 532 542 559 689 691
    757
Bishop, John, JP for Sussex 156 368
Bitmead, Samuel 87
Blackhall, Amy 80 84
    Ann 87
    Elizabeth 77
    Elizabeth née Haisell 77 80-84 87
    George 80 87 968-970
    Harriett 80 87 340
    Isabella 80 87
    John 87
    Richard 87
    Sarah 77

    Walter 77-79 85 87
    William*, labourer 77 80-84 85n 86-90
      340 A18 C2(b) C3(d)
Blackley, Mrs, of Canterbury 578
Blackman, Benjamin, surveyor of Hooe
    861-862 868
    George 773 A4; as overseer 588-589
      677 703 956 966 996; letters to 664
      968-969 986
    James, surveyor of Rye 737
    Sarah A4
    widow D2
Blake, [-] D2
    George Hayes 321-325
Blundell, Mr 895
Bohanner, Mary 585n
Bolland, William 329
Bonds, Thomas 717
Bontin, Mrs 279
Boorman, Dive 523 528
Booth, James D2
    Thankful B1
Boots, [-] D2
    Benjamin 942-943 D2
    Eliza 91
    Jesse Ann 91
    Josiah*, carpenter 91-93 C2(b) D1; as
      overseer 380 D1
    Mrs 91 93
    widow D2
Bourne, James, churchwarden Snargate
    246
Bourner, [-] D2
    James B1 C2(b)
    Mrs 209
Bragge, [-] D2
    Haines C3(d)
    Mary B1
    Nathaniel 366 C2(b) C3(d) D1
    Richard B1 C2(b) C3(d) D1
Brasselay, James 196
Bray, Charlotte – see Milliner
    George, farmer at Guestling 62 64-65
      237-238 240-242 244 496 681 695
      697-699 701 821 A5 A18 C2(b)
      C3(d) D1,2; as grand jury foreman
      327; as overseer 400; letter from 670;

letter to 717
James 488 C2(b) C3(d) D1,2
Mrs D1
Richard C3(d)
William 23 25 237
Brazier, & Co 895
W, churchwarden of Rye 849
Breeds, B 256
Thomas & Co, of Hastings 263
Brent, John, JP of Canterbury 585-586
Bright, Thomas* 639 650 652 655-656 658
Brignall, Edward 461 463-468
Mrs 33
Brisco, Musgrove, JP for Sussex 135-136
Brisenden, Ann B1
Mary B1
Broadfoot, Mary 94-95 200 704; as widow
D2
Robert 94-96 A15 A48 B2
Sarah 94-95
Brougham, Henry, MP for W 845 911
Brown, Mr, carrier of Hythe 802
Browne, Barwell D1,2
Charlotte A6
Fielding 74 724 A6; as JP, 73-74 449
518 537 714 857 943 A6; as deputy
mayor A6
Lucy A6
Montague A6
Robert Henry A6
Bryant, Mr 415
Buck, Ann A27
Buckwill, Mr E2
Burch, George, overseer of Canterbury 585
Burden, William* D1
Burford, W 546
Burgess, [-] D2
Dr 341
Burkenstock, Jane B1
Henry B1
Burrows, Mark, overseer, Northgate,
Canterbury 119
Burwash, Isaiah 97-98 839
James 811 C2(b) C3(d)
Butler, Edward Sisley 99 102
Frances 99-105 B2
Henry 334-335

Henry Pearch, solicitor of Rye A7
A12 D2; as town clerk of W, 3n 13n
86 175-178 194n 328-329 334 384
385n 527 556; bills submitted by 385
417n; violence against 384
R W, JP of Rye 29
Richard A7 D1
Susannah A7
Buttenshaw, Henry B1
Sarah 942
widow D2
Button, John, overseer of Brookland 637-
638
Cadwell, Mr 569 576
Campbell, William, of Hastings 725-726
Canning, George, Prime Minister 838
Carden, Charles xxvi
Carder, Nathaniel F, of London 683 686-
687
Care, Jane B1
Mary B1
Carman, William 643
Caroline, Queen 845n
Carpenter, Isaac, shoemaker of Hastings
523 525-527
Carteret Bonnet, Messrs 968
Catt, Captain 516
Henry 982
Mrs 462
Ceinon, J 743
Chaffey, Mr 439 443
Chambers, Mr E2
Chapman, Elizabeth, formerly Oyler, *see*
Oyler
Chappell, Harriett, daughter of Elizabeth
Taunton – *see Taunton*
Thomas 553
Chart, Caroline 382n
James B1 D2
Mary 376 382 D2
Chasmar, [-] D2
William B1 C2(b) C3(d)
Chassereau, G, assistant overseer, Brighton
105 299
Chatterton, William, miller 93 161 735-736
738-740 764 875 922 A8 C3(d) D2;
as overseer 339

Chester, John, beadle 106-110 241-242 508
    698-699 811 A37 B2 C2(b) D1,2
    Thomas 30 752 839 C2(b)
    widow D1
Chichester, Bishop of xxiii A14 A46
    Earl of E2
Claise, James D2
    Joseph 752 839 C2(b) C3(d)
Clandenbold, John 111 114
    Mary*, of Canterbury xxviii 111-116
      132-133 562n 570 576n 578 752
      760n 811 A48 B2; letters from 117-
      131; property of 111
Clark, [-], baker of Hastings 725
    James 272 C3(d) D2
    Mrs 770
    Robert 826 861 D1 D2 C3(d); as
      overseer D1
    W F, of Rye 991n
    widow D2
Clarke, Cornelius, agricultural labourer
    134-139 B2
    Hannah 134
    Harriett (2) 134-136 139 143
    Isaac 134
    James 134 143 A8 C2(b)
    Jane 134
    Mary (2) 134 139-140 143
    Sarah (2) 134-137 139 143
    Thomas, ?agricultural labourer 139-144
      B2
    William Henry 139
    Zebulon 139 143
Cleveland, Duke of xxiv A30
Cloke, John, assistant overseer of
    Guestling 397 406
Cloud, Samuel 946 958n
Cochran, James C3(d)
Cochrane, Rev^d R A xxix
Cockburn, James B1 D1
Coffin, Isaac D1
    Jonathan Perry D1
Cogger, [-], carrier 104 344 348-351
    Captain 146 337 339
    Charles 150
    Ellis 62 498 500
    George 150

    John 62 145 498 D2
    Joseph (2) 145-146 C2(b) D1,2
    Mary (2) 145 150
    N, of Rye 145-146
    Thomas* 147-150 902 B2
Cole, John 154
    Sarah née Keene 151-152 154 A21
    William 151-154
Colegate, Mary 112
Coleman, Ann 156
    Charles alias Leaver B1
    Charlotte 155
    Elizabeth 155-156
    John, JP of Dover 614 619
    Thomas, surgeon of Dover 611
    William, agricultural labourer 155-157
      A41
Collings, Richard John, surgeon of W 47-
    48 75
Collins, Sarah 421-423
Collyer, Ralph 982
Colvin, William, of Tenterden 757
Conant, Thomas, JP of London 164
Coningham, Robert, of Brighton 199 201
Cooke, [-] D1
Coomber, Mrs 452
Cooper, Elizabeth, of Canterbury 802
    Richard, of Tenterden 757
    William Durrant xxv
Cornwall, Thomas 100
Corrall & Co (of Maidstone) 42
Cossum, John, JP for Hastings 197 539
Courthope, George, barrister of Temple,
    London 276 370 506
Cousens, John, of Bishop's Waltham,
    Hampshire 481
    Mr 481
Coussins, Henry, relieving officer, St
    Clement's, Hastings 491-492
Cox, James, town crier of Hastings 727
Cramp, Mr 101
Crinone, Peter D1
Crittenden, Mary B1
Cropper, Richard D1
Crossley, Mr 645
Crouch, Mercy, later Eastman 194
    Sally 194

W, JP of Hastings 534
Croughton, William 342 D2
Crowhurst, Ann 159
    James*, of Rye 158-161 B2
Curteis, & Co, bankers of Rye 895 900
    Edward Jeremiah, of Wartling, JP for
        Sussex 140 143 377 640 649 694 A9
    Jeremiah, of Rye 860-861 864 939 A9
        D1,2
    Richard of Tenterden D1
    William, 939 A9
Cutbeard, Mary 164
    William, coachman 162-164 B2
Daniel, John 943 D2
Davies, John, JP for Surrey 184
Dawes, & Co, Rye solicitors, (various
        partners) xxv 567n A28 A49; bills
        submitted by 51 53 56-57 107 203
        205 274-275 329 393 395 400 499n
        549 552 554 556 645-646 665 824
        842 847 884 892 896 912; counsel's
        advice sought by 197 276
    & Co, solicitors of London A11
    & Son, solicitors of London 796
    Elizabeth A12
    Edwin 17 666-668 704 706 870 A10
        A28 C2(b) D1
    Edwin Beresford 522
    Edwin Plomley, town clerk of W A28
    Edwin Nathaniel, town clerk of W xxv
        139 859 A28
    George C3(d)
    Nathaniel A12
    Thomas xxiv 17 843 847 870 A11-12
        A28 D2
    Walter, town clerk of W A28
    Weeden, solicitor of Rye and town
        clerk of W 9 52 54 185 265 329-
        330 549n 626 672 741 870 881 883
        A7 A11-12 A28 A49 D2; account
        submitted by 883
    see also Woollett & Dawes
Day, Mr 725-726
Dean, Samuel, of Hastings, 416-420
Deane, David, JP of Lydd, 49
Dell, George, JP and mayor of Dover, 593
    614

Dengate, James C3(d)
    John 38
Denne, Mary 739n
    Mr 337
    Mrs D2
    Richard 163n 251 731 739n 807 809
        819 821 845n 861-862 A13 C2(b) D1
    William, of London, 163
Dew, Mary B1
Ditch, William, of Iden, carpenter 652
Dixon, Joseph, of Sunderland 728
Doreham, Mr, of Canterbury 583
Drury, James C3(d) D1
    William 635 638
Duffy, James B1
Dugdell, Revᵈ John William, rector xxiii-
        xxiv 22n 871-874 912 914 928-930
        935 937 940-943 A14 A36 D2
Duke, Robert 213
Duly, Philip William, relieving officer,
        Canterbury 584-585 590-591
Dunaway. Mr 763
Dunk, H D2
Dunn, George 543-545
Eagles, Elizabeth 182n
    Frances* née Hobbs 165 182-184 186
        189-191
    Jane 184 191
    John, butcher 165-175 177-183 185-
        189 329 496 506 683-685 838 A29
        A42 A48 B2
Easden, widow D1
Eastman, Mercy, workhouse mistress 192-
        195 B2
    William* 194
Easton, Ann (2), domestic servant 196-201
        A28 B2
    Edward 202
    George 202 688
    Harriett 224
    John 202 226 C2(b)
    Joseph 405
    Mary 202 209 214 217 219 222 224
    Mary Jane 196
    Miss D2
    Neriah 202
    Samuel (2), shoemaker/wheelwright

202-216 218-224 227 943 952 A20
A28 A47 B2 C2(b) C3(d) D1,2; as
constable 68 258n 652
Sarah* 202
Thomas* (2) 202 666 672-673 819
C2(b) D1,2
William 202
Eden, Sir Frederick Morton xxi xxviii
Edmunds, Mrs 155
Edney, Mr, of Bullington, Hampshire 480
Edward I xiii
Edward III xxiv
Edwards Ann 237
Daniel 228-230 C2(b)
Edward 230
Edwin 245
Francis* 237
Frederick 237
George (2), labourer 230-231 259 815
George H, JP of Rye 365
Hannah 237
Hannah née Tilman 232 236
Jane 245
John, of Northiam, 209 225 227
Marianne 232
Maria Jane 232
Mary B1
Mrs/widow 228-229 D2
Richard (2), labourer 6 232-236 245
C2(b) C3(d)
Richard James 232
Thomas (2), labourer/solicitor of
Newenden 217 219 237-244 695 697-
701 942 D2
William (2) 245-246 B2 C3(d)
Eldridge, Mary B1
Richard B1
Elliott, John C3(d)
T F, emigration agent-general 959-960
962-963
William, of Brighton 273 278-284
Emerson, Philip xxi
English, [-] D2
Evans, William, landlord, Queen's Arms,
Southwark 189n
Exall, Joseph, clerk to Tenterden Union
662-664

Fairhall, [-] 55 58
Farncomb, Henry, of Icklesham 135 139
141-142 773
Field, Ann 250 255
Benjamin, of Rye* 247-249 902 B2
Cecilia A1
Edward 811 845n C2(b) C3(d) D1
Elizabeth (2) 247 250
Emmy B1
Harriett 247
Hannah 250
Henry 247
James (2)* 247 250
Jane 250
John (2) 247 250
Judith 250
Richard 845n B1 D2
Robert 247
Sarah* 247
Stephen*, agricultural labourer 250-254
627n A20 C2(b) C3(d)
William 250 C2(b)
Finn, Samuel, of Lydd 396
Finnis, George, JP and mayor of Hythe 503
Nathaniel, JP of Hythe 503
Fisher, Caroline 256 260 340
Eleanor 256 260
George 256 260
John, solicitor of Rye 18 53 183 217
247-248 276 393 395 470 626 881
953
Mrs [William] 257
Thomas 13 16n 85 231 256-260 815
Walter 256
widow D2
William* 260-263 340 A15 C2(b)
C3(d)
Forbes, R W, JP for Kent 409
Forwood, George, select vestry of
Liverpool 840
Foster, [-] 264-265
Charlotte 659 661-662
Hannah – *see Weller*
Jane 89
John, of Rye 206-207 209
Louisa Jane 271
Mrs (2) 264-265 267

Sarah (2) 271 659 661-662
Thomas*(2) 266-269 B2
widow D2
William 13 16n 270-272 A20
Francis, David* 273-276 291 304-305 307
    309 312
    Ebenezer 273
    Hannah, née Knight, of Brighton 78
        254 273-315 532 542 689 691 A25
        B2
    John 273 304-305 311-312
    Mary 273 304-305 312
Freeman, Edward 549
French, Mr 278
    Mrs [William] 729
    William of Guestling & later Rye 50
        55-61 729
    William, baker of Rye 729
Friend, William, vestry clerk, Hambledon
    483-484
Fryman, H, of Rye 887-888 904 907
Fuller, & Alce, carpenters ?705 764 A1
    Cecilia* A16
    John, JP for Sussex 398 ?511 649
    John* (2) 317 409 D2; as overseer 19
        209
    Lucy née Amon A15
    Maria 53n
    Mrs [Walter] 35
    Richard A16
    Sarah 317
    Thomas*(2) 97 316-318 807 809
        819 826 861 C2(b) C3(d) D1; as
        churchwarden D1
    Thomas, JP for Sussex 312
    Thomas, of Icklesham 851-852
    Walter*, farmer xix 17 35 80 94 262
        488 787 821 829 848 861-862 869
        875 914 922 936 A15-16 A50 C2(b)
        D1,2; as corporation treasurer 17;
        as overseer 703 878-879 950; letter
        from 792
    William 958n
Gains, William 514
Gaselee, Mr Justice 189n
German, Mr, of Hambledon, Hampshire
    480

Gilbert, Mr, of Hastings 538
Gill, D, JP for Hastings, 197 534 539
    William D2
Gilman, [-] 319-320 A29 B2
Goble, Richard 139
Godden, Henry 652
?Good, John, JP for Kent 191
Gooding, Joseph 187 190
Goschen, G, JP for Kent 191
Gosley, Thomas, of Rye 452 456
Gould, Mr 388
Goulden, John, of Canterbury 119
Graddon, Mary 112
    Simon 112-114 C2(b) C3(d)
    William D1
Graeme, Charles D1
Green, W J, assistant overseer of Lydd 46
Greigsby, Philadelphia – *see Tree*
Griffith, Mr, barrack master of Bexhill 276
Griffiths, James, surveyor of Battle/Bexhill
    732-733 861-862 868
Grinfield, Thomas C3(d)
Gurley, Sarah – *see Lamb*
Gurr, John B1 D2
Guy, Judith 159
Haddree, Mr 304
Hadly, Mrs 432
Hague, William xviii
Haisell, [-] D2
    Eliza (Sarah) Hayes 322 324
    Elizabeth – *see Blackhall*
    George, hairdresser, 97 322-323 773
        839 A17 C2(b) C3(d) D2
    Sarah 321-322 324 A17
    Thomas 82 810 C2(b) D1
Hall, Jeremiah 991
    John E2
Harman, Joseph 524n
Harmer, [-] D2
    widow D2
Harriott, Thomas 753
Harris, Francis, Lt RN 402n
    Frederick 402n
    Julia 402n
    Samuel, of Stalbridge 441
Harrod, [-] D2
    George, 87 173 478 683 685 828n A5

A18 C2(b) D1,2; as overseer 59 380
A18 D2
Hartley, George – *see Artlett*
Harvey, Mariah B1
Harwood, Thomas, seaman B1 C2(b) D1
Hawes, Mr 511
Hearnden, Elizabeth 326
  George, 13 16
  Isaac, carrier 9-10 326-335 A42 C2(b)
    C3(d) D1,2
  Thomas 326
Heasley, Mr, of Micheldever, Hampshire
  480
?Hedingfield P, JP for Sussex, 143
Henderson, R 742n
Hennah, Joseph D2; as mayor and deputy
    mayor 518 A19; as JP 71 74 76 87
    235 239 325 328 382 404 417-418
    457 527 536-537 621 650 655 661
    857 873 943 E1
Henry VIII xxix
Hickman, George, overseer, Snargate 246
Hilder, Thomas Pain, valuer 922
Hill, Charles, shoemaker 764 773 834 958n
    A20-21 A43 D2; as constable, 73 215
    253 271 530 651
  James, labourer B1 C2(b)
  George, 848 A21 D2; as overseer 19
    101-102 152 278 757 A21
Hills, James D2
  John, servant, C3(d)
Hoad, [-] (2) 307 630
  Christopher, surveyor of Icklesham 868
  Edwin 340
  Elizabeth* 340
  Frederick 340
  George 340
  Harriett 340
  Henry (Harry), valuer of Brightling
    914-915 917-918 921
  James 419-420 537 625 C2(b) C3(d)
    D2
  Joseph*(2), tailor/town sergeant/baker
    172 336-340 544 650 B2 C2(b) D1,2
  Mary Ann 340
  Mercy 340
  Mrs 627 752

  Thomas*, tailor/labourer 80 340-343
    942-943 C2(b) C3(d) D2
  William* 340
Hoadley, Elizabeth B1
  Mary B1
  Thomas, blacksmith 496 666 848 C2(b)
    C3(d) D2; failure to pay worker 675
Hobbs, Frances – *see Eagles*
Hodder, Jane – see Longley
Hodges, Rev[d] Henry, rector of Beckley 107
Hollingbery, Rev[d] Drake, rector xiii xxiii
    305 516 809 821 827 848 861-862
    A22-23 A36 A46 C2(b) D1
  Elizabeth 739n A23
  John 516 520 739n 848 873 925 A23
    D2; as churchwarden D2
  Mrs D2
Holmesbrook, Mrs, of Lewisham, 359
Holt, Ann A35
  Elizabeth A24
  Esau A24 C2(b) D2
  Henry, relieving officer of Rye Union
    988 991
  Jacob, bricklayer, 380 672 773 997 A24
    D2; as undertaker, 237 260 625
  James* 848 A24 C2(b) C3(d) D1
  Mary B1
  Richard B1
  Widow* D1,2
Homersham, William, JP of Canterbury
    567 585
Horne, Mr E2
Horsee, Thomas C3(e)
Horton, Mr, of Milton, Kent 183
Hoskins, Thomas, of Wittersham, butcher,
    388
Howell, [-] D2
  David D1
Howland, Clark, valuer of Aldington/
    Orlestone 922-924 926-933 934n 935
Hubbard, William, churchwarden St
    Mary's Dover 598
Huggard Jemima – *see Unicume*
Hume, Captain William 318
Hunnisett, Dr Roy xi-xii
Hunt, William C3(d) D1
Hunter, Mr, carrier of Rye 767

Mrs, of Rye, 627
William, of Rye, 3 5
Hyde, Henry xxv
Inches, Dr 962
?Jacken, Joseph, JP for Kent 358
Janaway, Mr, solicitor of Hythe 549
Jarrett, Mr 514
Jeakens, [-] D2
    Alfred 344-349 351 353n 354
    Burford* 344-355 367 826 A25 B2
        C2(b) D1
    Edward* 172 251 344 734 819 848 881
        A25 C2(b) C3(d) D1,2; as overseer
        56-57 203 274-276 393-394 411 473
        549 626 645-647 824; expenses claim
        of 647
    George B1
    Jane 349 354
    Mrs [Burford] 348
    Sarah 344-346 349n 353n
    widow(s) 344-345 D2
Jenkins, Elizabeth (2) 165 357-358
    George 356-359 B2 C2(b) C3(d) D1
    Jane 165 167-168 174 178-179
    John* 165 C2(b) D1
    Mary 167-168
    Robert C3(d) D1
    widow D2
Jones, Ann Giles – *see Richardson*
    Charles 773
    James D1
        his widow D2
    Joash, butcher 165 171-172 681 765
        834 848 D2
    Mr 161 986
    widow (of William) D2
Judd, William, of Rye 459
Keene, Sarah *see Cole*
    Elizabeth (Betty) 152
    Henry 152
    Thomas Sylvester*, sergeant-at-mace
        & gaoler 61 91 151 153-154 416 457-
        458 510n A26 C2(b) C3(d) D2
Kemp, Mr 511
Kennett, Abraham xviii 803-804 808n 861
    A5 C2(b) D1; as overseer 117
    Basil 997

Kingsnorth, Henry, valuer of
    Kenardington, Kent 866-867
Kitchenham, John, of London 521
Kite, James 360 363-364
    Lucy née Vennall, formerly May 360-
        365 B2
    Susan 362n
Knapp, Thomas George, clerk of assize 10
    329 331
Knatchbull, Sir Edward xviii
Knight, Elizabeth B1
    George D1
    Hannah – *see Francis*
    Lewis, barrister-at-law of London 513
        516 519-521
    Mrs 308 310-311
    Richard, overseer of Wittersham 409
Lacy, William, labourer C3(d)
Lamb,   Charles, JP for Sussex 694 A27
    Elizabeth A27 A33
    George, of London 536-537
    George Augustus of Iden 549n
    Joseph B1
    Mary* D1
    Richard (2) 807 809 821 A27 A33
        C2(b) C3(d)-(e) D1; as JP 114 159
        545 864 C1(b) (d) (f)-(h)
    Sarah née Gurley A27
    Thomas 366-367; as JP for Sussex 398
        640 A27
    William (2), one of them JP of Rye 469
        A27
Lambert, H, carrier 351 353
Lancaster, Caroline 366 368
    Elizabeth 366 368
    George 366
    Harriett 366 368
    Jane 366
    John* 367n
    Mary Ann 366
    Mrs [Thomas senior] 366
    Rose 367n
    Thomas*, labourer(s) of Rye 366-369
        B2
Langford, J C, Rye Union guardian 776
    J E 875
Lansdale, John, of Bexhill D1

Lardner, John Haddock, solicitor of Rye
    and town clerk of W 28 198 220 224
    406 A28
Larkin, Spencer 982
Larking, John 337-339
Larkins, Richard C3(d)
Laurence, [-] D2
    David xix xxiv 17 76 380 499 773 848
      869 875 958n A11 A29 C2(b) C3(d)
      D2; as assistant overseer 23 222-223
      391 532n 751-752 883 appointment
      22 A29 E1; as churchwarden 381
      831 956 A46; as constable A29; as
      overseer 168 178-179 378 642; letters
      to 28 137 152 154 161 224 267-269
      320 347-355 391 413-415 490 519-
      522 535 569 582-583 658 679 729
      883 908-909
    George A29
    Harriett A29
    John & Mrs, of Rye, 33-34
    Sarah née Barnard 320 A29
    Stephen* 62 635-636 773 C2(b) C3(d)
      D2; as constable 943n
    widow D2
Lavender, Mary B1
Law, Thomas, surgeon, C3(d)
Leadbeater, Henry D1
    Luke C3(d)
Leaver – *see Coleman*
Lefevre, J G S 780
Lennard, William, 93 522n
Leonard, Elizabeth – *see Saunders*
    Joseph C3(d)
    William*, sawyer 942-943 C2(b) D2
Lepper, R, of Chatham 320
Lewis, G C, 780
    Mr, barrack master of Rye 276
Lipscomb, William A30; as mayor A30; as
    deputy mayor 857; as JP 537 620
Liverpool, Lord, Prime Minister 838
Lloyd, Mr 516
Longley, William, of Lydd & Camber 45
    660 875 995 A31
    Jane née Hodder A31
    Mary née Southerden A31

Lowes, Ann B1
    Clifford 370 374-375 552
    Elizabeth, née Barden 370 372-375
    Martha B1
Lowrey, [-] 549
Lucas, Matthew P, JP for Kent, 358
Lulham, Henry, JP of Dover 619
Lumley, Mr, secretary, Poor Law
    Commission 965
Luxford, Capt 87
    John, carrier of Rye, 802 809
    Mr C2
Lyne, John D1
Macket, George, butcher of Sheerness 182
Mailey, [-] 61
Maister, Peter xvi
Malliphant, Mrs D2
Mannering, Thomas D2
Manser, David 773 972
    & Jenner, solicitors, 798
Maplesden, Ann A32
    John 478 895
    Richard* 821 848 A32 C2(b) C3(d)
      D1,2; as churchwarden 380; as
      overseer 818 A32 D2; coinage issued
      by A32
Marley, Thomas, of Rye763
Marshall, George Clough 197
    Mr 961
Marten, Mr 986
    Thomas* 731 807 809 821 861-862
      A27 A33 C2(b) C3(d) D1; as deputy
      mayor 63 83-84 112-114 544-545
      864 A33 C2(b) D1; as JP 82 159 366-
      367 399 827 A33; as mayor C1(b)(d)
      (f)-(h); as overseer 81; letter to 265
    William 399
Martin, & sons, solicitors 407
    Elizabeth 376-381
    George (2) 388-389 523-524 834 942
      D1,2
    Henry 389
    Jane 388-389
    John B1
    Julia née Moon 376 388-389
    Lavinia 388-389
    Mary 376

Mrs 752
Thomas, of Wittersham, shoemaker
    387-388
widow D1
William (?4) 14-15 376-389 397 952
    ?967 A29 A35 B2 C2(b) C3(d) D1,2
Masters, John B1
William, JP and mayor of Canterbury
    585-586
Maude, Daniel xxiv-xxvii
Mauger, Mr, of Iden 627
Maule, [Rev] John, of Dover 598
Mr, of Bath, Somerset 549
Maxsted, John, JP of Lydd 49
May, & Mercer, solicitors of Walmer 549
James*, shoemaker 360-363 C2(b)
    C3(d)
Jane 360 361n 362-363
Lucy – *see Kite*
Mary 274 276
Thomas 364 C2(b) D1
Mays, William B1
McKee, Phillip C3(e)
Meads, F*, of Hastings 261
Meryon and Holloway, solicitors of Rye
    835 837
Middleton, [-] 390-391 B2
Miles, James B1
Richard B1 C3(d)
Milford, S J, JP for Sussex 312
Miller, Mr, of Rye 741
Milles, Thomas, of East Guldeford,
    Goudhurst & Hunton near Maidstone
    xxviii 720-721 854 882 885 887-888
    891 893-894 897 899-901 903-904
    906-909 A34 D2
Milliner, Charlotte née Bray 392
Dive* 392-396 758n A25 B2
James 392
Mills, James, house agent of Brighton 310
Joseph, assistant overseer, Rye 28 149
    249 369 460 676 678-679 898 902; as
    Rye Union auditor 985-987
Millward, Mr 511
Minchinton, W E xviii
Mitchell, Mr, of London 549
Thomas A15

William B1
Moneypenny, Mrs of Rye 627
Robert, JP for Kent, 409
Monk, Thomas xxv
Moon, Julia – *see Martin*
Robert C3(d)
Moore, George, overseer of Stalbridge
    444-447
Mr 161
Morris, [-] D2
Abraham 843
Barnard, agricultural labourer 397-398
Edmund 666 671
Edward D2
Eliza 397 407
Elizabeth (2) 397-399 405n 407 666
    671
George 397 407
Jane 397
Jane Elizabeth 402
Mary 397-398
Mary Ann 397 407
Michael 402
Mrs 400
Sarah* 397
Thomas 943 D2
William* (?3) 7-8 69 397-399 401-407
    541 A41 B2 D2
Mortimer, Rev[d] Henry Sanders, rector xxiv
    944
Moulton [-] D2
Mugliston, George, butcher & poor relief
    provider xviii 806 808n
Muir, [Rev[d]] John, minister, Arbroath,
    Scotland 363
Murton, Mr, valuer 914-915 918 923-924
    926 928-929
Myers, Rev[d] John, vicar of Rye 305
Nares, Edward K, of Newchurch, Kent 96
Nash, Alfred 411-412
Angelina 411-412
Caroline 408
Henshall 411-412
John*, shoemaker of Hawkhurst 408-
    415 B2
Mary née Selman 408 410
William 412

Needham, William D2
Neeve, John, surveyor of Tenterden 867
   869
Neeves, James B1
  Jane *see Parsons*
  John B1 C2(b) C3(d)
Nejean, Evan, of the Admiralty C1(c)
Nevill, Lord 516
Newton, Isaac 485-487
Noakes, Mary B1
  Mr 347 349 351 354
Noon W 773
Nouvaille, Peter, crêpe manufacturer 808
Nutt, John, town clerk of Canterbury 566
Nye, Samuel, of Rye 473-474
Ockenden, William, labourer B1 C2(b)
  C3(d) D2
?Offord, Richard, overseer 966
Oliver, Leaver D1
Ollive, Mary – *see Alce*
Osborne, [-] D2
  Ann A35
  Maria née Went 626-627 A35
  Richard 15 386 848 A35 D2
  Thomas D1
Oxberry, Lord, Cinque Ports Fencibles 87
Oyler, Edward 435
  Eliza 416-417 419-426 435 B2
  Elizabeth, later Mrs Chapman 416 417n
  424-425 435
  Lucy 426-435 B2
  Thomas, labourer/carrier 416-417 435-
  438 811 C2(b) C3(d) D1
Packham, G, of Camber 137 D2
  Martin 403
  Mary B1
Pagden, Henry E2
  John E2
Page, Benjamin, of Hastings 722
Pain, Thomas, of Dover 823
Paine, Henry Edwards, clerk of the Rye
  Poor Law Union 588 591 617 780
  791 965 967-969 990 992
Paley, Dr Ruth 329n
Parham, J W, assistant secretary, Poor Law
  Commission 958
Parker, Thomas, innkeeper 159

& sons, of Lewisham 358
Parnell, Thomas D1
Parsons, Catherine née Summers 439-440
  442
  Charles 440
  George 442 446 449
  James* 439-440 442
  Jane*, mother née Neeves 442 446 449
  Joseph*, labourer 439-449 B2 C2(b)
  C3(d) D2
  Mr & Mrs G
  Philip 442 446 449
  Robert 449
  Simeon 442
  Thomas 397 C2(b) C3(d) D2
Partridge, John, valuer of Canterbury 929-
  933 934n 935-936
Payne, Hannah B1
Pearce, John 843
Peckham, James 549 585
Peel, Robert, as Home Secretary 838
Pennett, Mr, shoemaker of Brighton 307
  309
Pennington, M, JP of Walmer 548
Pensull, [-] D2
Perigo, [-] 238n D2
  George 728 770
  John*, both labourers 408 728n C2(b)
  C3(d)
  Judith B1
Perivell, Mr 62
Perkins, Mr 323
Piddlesden, Edward D1
  Mrs 197
Pierce, John James, JP of Canterbury 567
  585
Pilcher, Charles, of Rye 768
  R 391
Pim, John B1
Pitt, Mrs, nurse 62 629 770
  Rt Hon William 504n C2(a)-(b), C3(b)
  William B1
Player, Peter xxvi
Plomley, F, surgeon of Lydd 47-48
Plummer, William, JP of Canterbury 586
Poile, Charles, of Rye 486 768
Pollock, Sir Frederick 329 841

Pomfret, & Co, treasurers of Rye Union 979 992
  John Butler 757
  Richard Curteis, solicitor of Rye 323
Pope, Peter, assistant overseer of Hawkhurst 411-412
Porter, Nathaniel, JP of Rye 29 150 680
Powell, Henry 1 106 335 734 A37 D2; as deputy mayor 235 239 325 333 343 418 873 A37; as JP, 6 8 13-15 58 61 66-70 72-74 86-87 89 174-176 178-180 194-195 197 199-201 208 210 215 232-234 236 244 253 258 271 322 324 332 334 383 385-389 402 404-405 407 409 417 419-420 442 457 471 480-482 510 516-518 527 529-530 630-631 652-653 655 675 701 942-943 A37 D2; as tax commissioner 328; letters from 110; letters to 343 845; verbal abuse of 328 333-335
Price, Rowland 69
Purdith, Richard, mariner of Deal 553
Purdon, George, churchwarden St Mary's Dover 598
Putland, Samuel 376 378 388
Raddish, Revd Thomas D1
Ralph, [-] D1
  Ann 450-451 B2
Ranking, Robert, mayor of Hastings 375n
Ray, Joel, ship agent 686-687
Rebecca, J B, architect A44
Relfe, Ann 452
  Elizabeth 452
  James*, bargeman of Rye 450 452-461 471 902 B2 C2(b) C3(d)
  Jane 452
  Maria 461
  Mary 450 461-471 B2
  Richard 452
  Thomas 421-422
  William B1
Revell, Mr, of Hastings 481
Richards, Eliza A36
  Elizabeth A36
  James A36
  Richard Hollingberry A36

Revd Thomas*, curate of Winchelsea, vicar of Icklesham xxiii 305 371 851-852 855 A14 A36 D2
Richardson, Ann Giles née Jones 472 477
  Constant B1
  Henry 477
  James 910 991n
  Richard, labourer 472-477 A41 A44 C2(b) C3(d)
  Twosine 477-478
  W, valuer of Lewes 866
Ridley, Thomas C3(d)
Ridout, James, churchwarden, St Alphage, Canterbury 121 125 131
Rix, Benjamin, 40-41 62;
  Jane 40 42 62
Roberts A W, MP 189n
Robinson, W, surgeon of Dover 604 607 610
Robson, Revd William, minister, of Banff, Scotland 362
Ronalds, Elizabeth née Warner formerly Voller 480-482
  Joseph 479-484 B2
  Richard 481-482
  Robert 481-482
Russell, F D2
  Bourne, mariner of Rye 639 641-647 653-654 657 A29 A42
Ryan, Thomas E2
Ryland, J & Co 994
Samson & Leith, solicitors of Walmer 549
Sanders, Mr 329
  Thomas C3(d)
  widow D2
  see also Saunders
Sands, William 485 487
Sankey, Dr, of Dover 602 604
Sargent, Elizabeth A39
  Judith A39
  Lewis B1
  William*, miller 734 764 834 848 858 861 912 A38-39 C2(b) C3(d) C3(e) D1,2; as churchwarden 381 831 D1; as overseer 44 48
Saunders, Amelia 488
  Elizabeth née Leonard 488-493 728n

B2; as widow D2
Francis, gardener 728 C2(b)
Lavinia 488
Mary 493-495 B2
Thomas 488 491 493 728n
Saxby, John B1 D1
Scarth, Thomas D2
Scott, Dr Adam xxiv 77 85 256 334n 341
    452 522 538 540 629 D2; as select
    vestry member D2
Sculthorpe, [-] D2
Seager, Mary B1
Seere, Thomas C3(d)
    William B1 D1,2
Selden, Ann 62-63
    Cordelia 496
    Elizabeth 496
    Thomas – *see Bennett*
    William* 166 169 496-497 A41
Selman, Mary *see Nash*
Selmes, Samuel, of Beckley 369 776 856
    869 875 891 898 915 919 926 931
    982 A40 D2
Shadwell, William Lucas, of Hastings 53
    861; as JP for Sussex 135-136
Shakespeare, John 520 D1
Sharp, Richard D2
Sharps, Robert, footman & overseer 956
    C2(b) C3(d) C3(e)
Sheather, William (2) 57 498-501 991
Sheppard, Revd Samuel Philip JP 382 650
    D2
Shifnor, George 196
Simmons, John 502-504 B2
    Mary Ann 503
    Sarah 503
    William (2) 398n 503
Simpkinson, Rev^d Mr D1
Sinden, [-] D2
    Ann 408
    Delia B1
    Harriett 408
    Jane 513 516 756
    John, beadle 108 505-513 516 756 B2
    D2
    Stephen 513-514 516-521 522n A22-23
    B2

William 516
Sisley, Sherington, of Hastings, 99-100
Skinner, Samuel, overseer of Iden 648
    Thomas 942 B1 D1,2
Slack, Paul xvii
Slaughter, Mr 742
?Sleath [-] 721
Sloman, John, of Udimore 905 D2
Smawley, Joseph D2
Smith, [-] E2
    Ann 461-462
    Atwood 182-183
    David 776
    Gill & Co 900
    Henry, JP of Hastings 491-492
    Henry of W xvii
    John, of Hastings 417
    Mr E2
    Thomas 461 C3(e)
Southerden, C D2
    Mary A31
    Stephen, of Stone-in-Oxney, Kent 35-
    39
    Samuel, farmer, of Camber 142 155
    157 403 472 475-478 496-497 866
    869 897 931 939 A31 A41 C2(b)
    D1,2
Spain, Mr 504
Stace, George* 395 554 734 736 807 821
    826 935 A20 A42-3 C2(b) C3(d)
    D1,2; as mayor A42; as deputy mayor
    171 180 327 A42-43; as JP, 81 83-84
    100 114 167-168 172 179 235 239
    317 325 332 361 387 394 399 409
    418 440 442 480-482 499 529 545
    628 630-631 641-644 647 655 671
    864 873 C1(b)(d)(f)-(h) D1; as tax
    commissioner 328
    Sarah A43
    Susannah A43
Standen, Edward 461 471
    John C3(d)
    Mr 765
Starr, Mr, of Canterbury 549
Stephens, Charles 809
    Jane 94
    Mistress D2

Rachel B1
Thomas, Captain 228-229 681-682
Thomas C2(b) D1
Stephenson, Thomas B1
Stevens, [-] D2
    Ann 523-530 A20 B2
    Elizabeth 202
    widow D2
Stevenson, Elizabeth 531
    Esther 531
    Fanny* 531
    Frederick 534
    George 531-532 D2
    Henry B1
    James 533-534 535n 536
    Jane 531
    John (2) 531 826 971 C2(b) C3(d)
    Joseph 531
    Susannah 533-537 B2
Stickham, Mr, of Sutton Cotton,
        Hampshire 480
Stidolph, G L, of Hastings, 719
Stileman, Mrs D2
    Richard xxiii-xxiv 5 53 209 472 672
        702-703 734 736 757 771 773 787-
        788 793-796 809 848 914 919 945
        958n 974n 982 A44 A50 C2(b) D1,2;
        as churchwarden 380 827; as deputy
        mayor A44; as JP for Sussex 65 156
        368 648 A44; as mayor A44; as select
        vestry member D2; as surveyor of
        highways 858; letters to 93 306 364
        467 511 918 920; letters from 231
        259 476 623-624 815
Stocks, Henry 665
Stonaker, William xvi
Stonestreet, Frances 538
    Harriett 538
    James 538
    Lucy 538
    Lucy, later Mrs Barnes – *see Barnes*
    Septimus 807
    William* 50 538-542
Stonham, David, of Rye 272 291-293 343
        514-516
    Thomas D2
Stripe, W, vestry clerk, Woolwich 706

Sturges Bourne, William, Home Secretary
        838
Summers, Catherine *see Parsons*
Suters, Ann 543
    Charles (?3), carrier 543-544 C2(b) D1
    Mrs D2
    Solomon 543-546 C3(d)
Symonds, Rev[d] Mr, of Boulogne 337
Tapp, Ann née Easton 196-197
Tapsfield, Thomas, overseer of East
        Farleigh, Kent 268
Taunton, Elizabeth*, of Canterbury 119
        129 547-592 968 B2
    Harriett [Chappell] 547 550 553 567
        571 578 585
    James 548 553 567 585-586
    'Old' [Elizabeth senior's father] – *see
        Peckham, James*
Taylor, C J, overseer of Cranbrook 633-634
    Charles 895
    David, stationer of Rye 850 853
    Henry, of Stalbridge, Dorset 443
Terry. Charles, 828n A18 C2(b); as JP, 55
        168 179 327 380 440; as overseer
        A18
    E 495
    Henry (2) of Romney, Kent & Hastings
        396 493-494
Thomas. Mr (2) 969 E2
Thornhill, Rev[d] D2
Thorpe, Charles 875
    Christopher D1
    Mr & Mrs 666
    Thomas 39
    Walter 861
    William, solicitor and JP of Hastings 53
        374-375 890 937
Tibbs, John C3(d)
Ticehurst, Frederick, JP and mayor of
        Hastings 491-492
Tickner, [-] D1
    Thomas C3(d)
Tilden, Elizabeth, of Dover 592-618 B2
    George, 861 C2(b) D1; as JP 55 317
        327 361 380 499 643-644
    Harriett A45
    Henry(2), 1 of Dover, 2 beadle of

Winchelsea 106 243 593 603 607 610 700 752 839 A37 C2(b)

Jane 593 598 601 603-605 607

John xxiv xxvi 681 A19 A30 A45 D2; as deputy mayor 74 A45; as JP 13-15 67-69 71 76 89-90 194-195 197 199-201 208 210 239 244 322 324-325 332-334 383 385-389 405 407 418-420 449 471 510 516-518 621 652 655 675 701 824 857 873 942 D2 E1; as tax commissioner 328

Mary 593 598 603 607 618-622 B2

Mrs D2

Tileman [-] 731

Tilman, George D1

Hannah *see Edwards*

Tobitt. Mr 411

Tomkin, Musgrove, overseer of Wittersham 953

Tompsett, John, town clerk of Hastings 51 A7

Tonge, W S, of Sittingbourne, Kent 188-189

Tree, [-] 506

Benjamin* 623

David, 13 16 253 625 627-628 D2

John* C3(d) D1

Philadelphia 623-624 A44; as widow D1

Trigwell, James D1

Trill, Mr, of Hastings 481

Tufnell, Edward C, assistant Poor Law Commissioner 954 961 972

Tulloch, Alexander, JP 382 D1,2

Tully, William, of Brighton 273 280-290 294-297 301-303 306

Tunbridge, William, of Romney, Kent 396

Turk, Elizabeth 627n

Hannah 625-628 A35 B2

Thomas 627n

Turner, Thomas 68 208

Tutt, James C3(d)

Tyrrell, Elizabeth 450-451

William 450

Unicume, Jemima née Huggard 629-631

Richard 629-634 B2

Valler, Henry C3(d)

Vane, Hon [Henry] D2

Veness, Thomas, butcher 80 766 834 886 889 D2

Vennall, Lucy – *see Kite*

Vidler, A B, JP of Rye 365

J, of Rye 148

John 776

Vinall, Ann 635-638 B2

Elizabeth B1

Henry B1

Mary 635

Voller, Abraham 481 482n

Ann 481 482n

Elizabeth née Warner– *see Ronalds*

John 481

William 481

Walker, Robert, JP of Dover 593

Walsh, John 205 227

Ware, Revd Rex M xiii

Warner [-] D2

Elizabeth – *see Ronalds*

Waterman, Henry, town clerk 827 C1(b)

Waters, Edward, blacksmith of Rye 635

W D2

Watson, Elizabeth 639-644 648-657 A25 B2

Jeremiah D2

Thomas 639 650

William, JP of Rye, 150 469 680 758

William Bourne Russell 639 657

Watt, Job, labourer 70

Watts, [-] D2

H D2

Webster, G, JP for Sussex 140 377

Weeling, John, of Walmer, Kent 553

Weller, Frederick 659 661

Hannah, formerly Foster 659 661 664

Harriett 659 661

James* 659-665 B2 D2

Joseph C3(d) D1

Susannah 659 661

William C3(d)

Wellesley, Dr 197

Wenham, Lucy B1

Went, Maria – *see Osborne*

Wesley, John xxii

West, Rev[d] James John, curate, later rector

xxiv 878-880 911 944 947-949 956
        997 A46
    John 758
Weston, Mr 897
Westover, John D2
    T, of Icklesham 855
Whayman, John xxv
Wheeler, [-] D2
    Harriett 666 671 675
    James 666
    Jane 666
    Maria 666
    Mrs 666
    Robert* (?4 one of Rye) 666-677 A10
        D2
    Thomas 666 678-680
Whistler, Hugh, of Bexhill D1
White, Francis Thomas, of Canterbury,
        115-116 118-119 558-561 562n 563
        570 578
    John 196 199-201
    Mrs [Francis Thomas] 557
Whiteman, Alice 498-499
    Edward 13 16n
    John 681-683 747n A45 A48
    Mrs [John] 681
    Stephen 170 173 683-687 A48
    Thomas C3(d) D2
    William D2
Whitfield, Francis, valuer of Ashford 932-
        922 934n 935 938
Whittick, Christopher 329n
Willard, Ann* (2) 693-694
    Charlotte 693
    Daniel 688
    Frederick 688
    George* (2) 688-689 693 A35 D2
    Hannah 693
    Henry 770
    John 690-693
    Mary* (2) 688 693
    William (2) 237-238 240-244 693-703
        A48 C2(b) D2
Williams, Thomas D1
    William C3(d)
Williamson, J J, churchwarden, St
        Alphage, Canterbury 121 125 131

Willis & Co, of London 105 895
Willson, Richard D2
Wilmot, Robert Montague, JP of Hastings
        375
Wilson, Daniel, naval surgeon 370-371
    James 97-98
    ?T H, surgeon of Rye 160
Wiltshire, Robert, valuer of Hurst Green
        920
Wimble, James B1
    Thomas 739 D2
Winch, [-] D2
Winchilsea, Earl of 504n
Winstanley, John D2
Winstone, John 19 D2
    Thomas 848
Winter, Charles D2
    Mary 519
    Mrs 93
Wood, Benjamin 367
    Gilbert 704-709 952 ?967 A10 B2
    John (2) one an overseer of Wittersham,
        Kent 409 706
    Margaret 704 706-709
    Mary (2) one of London 519 706
    Sarah 706
Woodhams, Elizabeth B1
    Mary 942
    Andrew 94
    widow D1,2
    William, of Udimore 25 223 710 712
        723 A47 D2
Woodliff, Thomas B1
Woodman Sims, Maria B1
Woodroffe, William, tipstaff 10 331
Woods, Charlotte A48
    John (?2), grocer 304 306 637 651 672
        764 848 912 A7 A48; as overseer,
        107 174 179-180 381 831; letters
        from 175-176 206 535; letters to 115-
        116 177-178 428 637
    Mary Jane A48
    Mr 490
Woodzell, David 710-712 839 B2
Woollett, John, solicitor of Rye and town
        clerk of W 84 645 A12 A49
        & Dawes 400 A12 A49

Nicholas, of Sittingbourne, Kent 367
William, of Rye 3
Wratten, Nicholas, of Tenterden 757
Wright, John Edward, overseer and
churchwarden 1 53 683 736 848 925
A50 D2; as churchwarden D2; letter
to 754
Katharine 713-715
Young, Joan 450
George B1
Mr 411
William 450

Index of Places

The name of Winchelsea appears, of course, within almost every document. This index includes only the names of specific places within the town.

Towns and villages are in Sussex unless otherwise stated.

Places which are currently in London boroughs are included within their original counties.

Aldington, Kent 923

Alfriston E2

America 221-223 266 549 953

Arbroath – *see Scotland*

Ashford, Kent 128 915 936 938; market of 930; Saracen's Head 933

Australia 954 957; Botany Bay 187; New South Wales 955 959-963; Sydney 965

Bath, Somerset 87 549

Battle 101-104 194 274 344-345 347-355 505 861 B2; house of correction (gaol) 66 69n A9; magistrates of 323; market 279; petty sessions at 506n 511

Beckley 106 107n 499 501 856 910 915 919 926 965 972 B2; removal order to 316-317

Benenden, Kent 953

Bexhill xxi 1 24 276 732 868 A50 D1; Bell Inn 1

Bishop's Waltham, Hampshire 481

Botany Bay – *see Australia*

Boulogne, France 146 336-339 B2; English chapel of 337

Brede 500-501 866 972 991; workhouse of 139 202 225 227 452 523 688 704 972

Brede, River xiii

Brightling 914-915 918

Brighton 91 104 200 273 291 293 299 311 B2; Albion Street 279 283; assistant overseer of 105 299; Blue Coach Office 280-283 286-288 290 295 301; as Brighthelmston 276 312; Carlton Row 313 315; Crescent Street 309; East Street 284; Edward Street 280-287 289; Egremont Street 304 306 308 311; Essex Street 308 310-311; Gloster Street 290 295 297 301-303; Hereford Street 296; magistrates of 299; Marine Parade 199 201; overseers of 99 287-288; Paradise Street 294; parish officers of 300 305; removal order from 312; Richmond Arms Inn 279; Stanmer near E2; *for residents, office holders and firms see persons index.*

Brookland, Kent 463-466 635 637-638 938 B2; Cheyne Court 468

Broomhill xiv 33 370 844 972 A7

Bullington, Hampshire 480

Calais, France xxi

Camber (also Old Harbour): 155 157 376 397 402 472 475 478 497 659-660 861 931 943n A9 A31 A40 A41 D2; Castle (Winchelsea Castle) 97-98; Coastguard Station xxv; Farm 137 403; Watch House xxvi 402n

Canterbury, Kent xvii 111 129 547 549 570 573 583 591 802 B2; board of guardians of the poor 549n 584-585 590; Borough of Northgate 119 557-563 570 572 576 578 580 B2 Gallery Square 555; Castle Street 583; Little Rose, Borough 116 118; magistrates of 567; president of 565; quarter sessions of 548n 567n; removal orders from 566-567 585 W's appeal against 567; St Alphage parish, Borough of Staplegate 121 125 131 B2; St Augustine's near 548; St George's Place 932; St Mary Bredman parish 585 Jewry Lane 587 removal order from 586-588 590; St Mary's parish, Northgate 567 584-

585; St Mildred's parish 584; Star Yard, Little Douston 583; Sun Street 578; workhouse of 585 587 802; *for residents, office holders and firms see persons index.*

Cardigan[shire] 838

Chart, Kent 388

Chatham, Kent 320 388 516 B2

Chichester, Diocese of A22

Chidham, Hampshire 480

Chigwell, Essex – Hainault Hall 878-879 911 947-950

Christchurch, Hampshire: 199-201

Cranbrook, Kent 629-631 633-634 B2; required return to 634

Crayford, Kent 543 546

Croydon, Surrey 388

Cuckfield xxi

Cumberland 838

Deal, Kent 549-550 552-553 585 620-621 C2(b); Upper 585

Dover, Kent 129 592 612 615-619 622 823 B2 C2(b) C3(d); Castle 823 debtors in gaol of 823; dispensary of 604-605; New Street 594-596 599 602 608-611; St Mary's parish 362n 597-598 601 605 614 619 removal orders from 614 619; St James the Apostle parish 593 removal order from 593; Snargate Street 602 604; Worthington's Lane 622; York Street 615; *for residents, office holders and firms see persons index.*

Droxford, Hampshire 480

Durley, Hampshire 481

East Farleigh, Kent 268 B2

East Guldeford 720-721 854 903 906 909 972 A34

Eastbourne E2

Enchantress, HMS 371

Exton, Hampshire 481

Fairlight 53n 399 405 520 843n B2; Hall 53n

Faversham, Kent C2(b)

Folkestone, Kent C2(b)

Fordwich, Kent C2(b)

France 516

Goudhurst, Kent 897; Combwell 721 854 882 885 888 897 900 A34

Gravesend, Kent 969-970

Guestling 55-56 62 65 397 399 405 516 693 729n A5 B2; Broomham 506n; removal orders from 398 506 693-694; churchwardens and overseers of 398 407 511 694

Guldeford – *see East Guldeford*

Hainault Hall – *see Chigwell*

Hambledon, Hampshire 479-480 482-484 B2; workhouse of 480

Hamsey 196

Hastings xvi 50 100 135 197 215 375 406 417 419 421 488 495 520 533 577 849 889 A7 A23 A46 A48 B2 C2(b) D1 removal order to 192; All Saints parish 194 481 491 B2; bank of 864n 878; Caroline Cottages 722; coroner for Rape 53n 511n 957n; delivery by coach from 279-281 286-287 290 295 301; Great Bourne Street 727; Holy Trinity parish 197 B2 removal order from 539; mayor of 375n 937n; Poor Law Union of 491; Priory 726; St Clement's parish 51 194-195 479-482 488 491 534 B2 removal order from 492; Henbrey's Row, Barrack Ground 491; St Mary in the Castle parish 370 374-375 A24; town crier of 727; Wellington Place 719; *for residents, office holders and firms see persons index.*

Hawkhurst, Kent 408 410-415 B2

Henley-on-Thames, Oxfordshire 87

Hereford, county of 838

Hertford[shire], county of 838

High Wickham, Buckinghamshire 553

Hooe 421-425 435 861 868 B2

Horsham 9-10 329-331; sessions of oyer and terminer at 10 331

Hunton, Kent 899 901 903 906 908-909 A34

Hurst Green 920

Hythe, Kent 502 504 549 802 B2 C2(b); removal order from 503

Icklesham xiv 134-136 139-141 143 371

374 376-381 388 442 449 844 851-852 855 868 972 991 A7 A9 A14 A36 A39 B2; baptisms at A36; removal order to 389; vicar of xxiii 851 A14 A36

Iden xx 3 366 462 541 549 627 639-640 648-650 652 972 A9 B2; removal order from 640 649

Iham, Hill of xiii

?Isle of Man 687

Isle of Oxney, Kent 409

Ivychurch, Kent 467 B2

Kenardington, Kent 866

Kent 371n 877 959 972

Lancaster 845

Lewes 15 220 329 386 866; assizes at 333; house of correction at 67-68 73-74 139 202 208 216 270-272; county quarter sessions at xvi 15 139 195 197 386 407 orders of 317 389

Lewisham, Kent 356-359 B2

Littlebourne, Kent 843n

Liverpool 270-271 840 A20

London xvii 153 185 187 194 202 215 237 260 267 323 329 388 416 421 423 487 504 522n 549 647n 666 669 687 841 847 895 918 953 965 A11 A20 A46; Angel Court 843; Bedford Square 506; Board of Customs 536-537; Bow Street 212-214; Bridewell prison 462; Calvinist Independents of A46; Chelsea C2(b) – Hospital 553 Jew's Row 550 553; George Lane, Lower Thames Street 686-687; Greater Marlborough [Street] 164; Holborn – Barnard's Inn 323 Featherstone Buildings 522; Hoxton B2 Norris Street, Whitmore Road 504; Mary le Bow parish, Middlesex 516; Montague Square 520-521; Newgate prison xi 165 181-182 185 187-188; Old Bailey 189n; Regent Street 152 154; St Bartholomew's Hospital 342 513 522; St Giles's parish 163 B2 Crown Street 162; Sergeants Inn 841; Somerset House 958; Southwark – Bear Lane 182

Pitt's Place 182 Great Guildford Street 182 189n Keppel Street 182 White Street 537; St Saviour's parish 181-182 184-185 188 B2 removal order from 184; St Mary Woolnoth parish 189n; St Martin's Watch House 214-215; Temple 506; Upton, West Ham, Essex 211 213 B2; Wapping, Middlesex 639 647; Wardour Street 549; Whitehall 754 838; *for residents, office holders and firms see persons index.*

Lydd, Kent 31-34 43-49 396 A31 B2 C2(b); assistant overseer of 46; churchwardens and overseers of 49; Recorder of 549n

Maidstone, Kent xx-xxi 41-42 267 269 652 899 908

?Medwich, Kent 388

Micheldever, Hampshire 480

Milton, Kent 183 191 B2

Minster, Isle of Sheppey, Kent 181-182 190 B2

New Romney, Kent 164 197 396 B2 C2(b); Liberty of xiv

New South Wales – *see Australia*

New Zealand 704 965 967

Newchurch, Kent 96 B2

Newenden, Kent 219

Nook Point – *see Rye Harbour*

Northiam 209 225 918 965 972; Place Farm 918; workhouse of 202 533 972

Norwich, Norfolk 808

Old Harbour – *see Camber*

Old Romney, Kent 396

Old Winchelsea xiii

Ore 399 B2 D1

Orlestone, Kent 924 927 930-931 933

Oxney – *see Isle of Oxney*

Patrixbourne, Kent 391 B2

Peasmarsh 366-367 965 972

Pett xiv xvi 50 52-54 398 844 A7

Pevensey C2(b)

Playden 450-451 627 710 972 B2

Preston, Kent xxiii 929 937 943 A14

Ramsgate, Kent 392 395 522 B2

Reading, Berks 87

Rochester, Kent 229
Rolvenden, Kent 630 B2
Romney – *see New Romney*
Romney Marsh, Kent 480-481 549n; St
    Mary's Church 480-481
Rother, River xiii xxv 371n 376
Royal Military Canal xxiii xxvi
Rye 27 34 147 248 272 276 318 336 351
    365-366 371 414 457 471 522 549
    627 635 670 682 737 767 769 771
    882 907 936 955 962 969 972 974
    979 A8-9 A27 A33 A40 A43 A49 B2
    C2(b) C3(d) E2; assistant overseer
    of 28 149 249 369 460 676 679 898
    902; bank of 105 638 864n 882 895
    938; baptisms at 273; coach service
    to/from 9 152 330; George Hotel
    931; Liberty of 29 150 680; lime kiln
    near 456; London Trader Inn 471;
    Market Street 907; marriages at 159
    388; overseers of 666 A40 – see also
    removals to and from; packet [cross-
    channel] service from 337 339; parish
    register of 305; poor rates of 159 366
    460; removals from 150 360-361 365
    469 680; removals to 513 517-518;
    settlements in 247-248 517; vicar
    of 305; workhouse of 43 106 111
    139 226 237 452 547 666 771 972
    974 985 987; see also Rye Poor Law
    Union in subject index and residents,
    office holders and firms in persons
    index.
Rye Bay xiii
Rye Foreign 366 368 B2
Rye Harbour xxiii 371-374; No 28
    Martello Tower 371; Nook Point 851;
    Point House A9 D1
Salop [Shropshire] 838
Sandhurst, Kent 953
Sandwich, Kent C2(b)
Scotland 360; Auchmithie, Arbroath
    363-364 B2; Buckie, Banff 362;
    Jedborough 87
Seaford C2(b) E2
Sedlescombe 405 868
Sevenoaks, Kent 388

Sheerness, Kent 182 187 194 B2
Sittingbourne, Kent 165 188-189 191 367
Snargate, Kent 245-246 B2
South Shields, Co Durham 229
Speenhamland, Berkshire xviii
Stalbridge, Dorset 439-449 B2
Staplehurst, Kent 880
Stone-in-Oxney, Kent 35-37 B2
Suffolk 838
Sunderland, Co Durham 318 486-487 728
Sussex xxv 371n 838 877 959 972 A27
Sutton Cotton, Hampshire 480
Sydenham, Kent 77
Sydney – *see Australia*
Tenterden, Kent 652 656 658 757 869 A9
    C2(b) D1; Heronden 939; Union
    Board of Guardians 660 662-664;
    Woolpack Inn xxi 933
Throwley, Kent A14
Ticehurst 506
Titchfield, Hampshire 481 482n
Tovil, near Maidstone, Kent 267 269 B2
Udimore 25 155-156 223 712 723 845n
    905 972 991 A47; burial at 155;
    school of 982n
Walmer, Kent 548-550 552-554 584 B2;
    removal order from 548 554 585
Wartling 159 A9 B2
West Malling, Kent 40-42 62 B2
Westmoreland 838
Willingdon E2
Winchelsea
    buildings: Apple Tree Wick 740n 896n;
    Armoury, The (formerly The Bear)
    820; Blackfriars Barn (Barn Plat)
    A16; Castle Inn (now Old Castle
    House) 627 688 A35; Chestnut Barn
    D2; Court Hall (Guildhall) xii 74
    114 174-175 178-179 235 239 325
    327 418 518 545 857 864 873 956
    A20 C1 museum A42; Crowsnest
    731n; Ferry House D2; Firebrand
    A27 A33; Five Houses, The D1;
    Friars, The (Greyfriars) xxiii 231
    259 306 364 476 624 815 920 958n
    A44; gaol (house of correction) xiv
    xxv 17 72-74 165 180 239 458 523

530n discharge from 235; Glebe house A46; Greyfriars Chapel A44; Greyfriars (house) – *see Friars, The*; Guildhall – see Court Hall; Hillside Cottage 731n; Lookout, The (Watchhouse) 16n 530; malthouse D1; Mariteau House 739n A13; Moneycellar (Moneyseller) House(s) 77 237 240 242 693 697 699 A5 D1; New Gate A50; New Inn 715 793 868 A18 A20; Oast House D2; Old Malt House, The 134; Old Rectory A46; Pound Cottage A13; Pound Plat D2; Retreat, The A42-43; Rose Cottage A32; St Thomas's Church – *see subject index*; School D2; Strand Gate 16 Strand Guest House 730 731n; Summer House D1; town well A11; workhouse (poorhouse) *see subject index*; Watchhouse *see The Lookout*

fields and land: Barn Field D2; bowling green D1; Castle Field D1,2; Chapel Field A35 D2; Chestnut land D1,2; churchyard D2; cliff D2 Cliff Field A6 D2 Cliff Gill A47 D2; Coney Bank D2 Coney Field D1,2; Cook's Garden 932 Green D2; Corner Field D2; Ferry Field D2 Ferry House Cottage (field) D2; Ferry Marsh A47 D2; Fifty Acres D2; Float Field A35 D1,2; Friars Orchard D2; Frog Marsh D1; Front Field D2; Gallows Fields, Great & Little D2; Great Mill Bank D2; Glebe Garden(s) D1 D2; Holyrood D1 Holyrood Field D2; Horse Pond Piece D1,2; Hospital Fields D2; House Field D2; King's Green D1,2; Leaping Bar Field D2; Monday's Market, A43 A50 D2; Morley's Marsh A47 D2; Newgate Field A43 D2; Nursery Orchard D2; Oatlands A9 D2; old churchyard D2; Orchard, Lower & Upper D2; Paradise D1,2 Paradise Field 870; Pear Tree Marsh D1,2; Pell Field(s) D2; Pewes [Marsh] D1,2 Pewes Field

A10 D1 Pewes Pond D1 Pewes Slope D2; Piper Field D2; Pound, The A1 A13 Pound Fields D2 Pound Piece A13 D1; Reed Bed D2; Roundle Field A47 D2; St Giles's churchyard D1; St Leonard's Field D2; Saffron Garden D2; Shed Piece D2; Tanyard D2 Tanyard Piece D2; Ten Acres D2; Thornland D2; Tinker's Garden D1,2; Two Acres D2; Wall Field(s) A44 D2; Walnut Tree Field D2; White House Field D2

roads etc: Barrack Square (Cook Street/ The Square/Factory Square) 80 89 237 250 397 439 488 688 771 808 A1-2 A15-16 D1,2 cambric and crêpe manufactories in 808; Barrack Yard 419; Castle Street 202 326 A11 A16 A35; Cleveland Street/Road – *see Friars Road*; Cook Street – *see Barrack Square*; Factory Square – *see Barrack Square*; Ferry, The 943n 250; Ferry Marsh A47 D2; Friars Road (Cleveland Street/Road) 94 505 A24; German Street xxii A19 A21 A32; High Street 998 A33 A39; Higham Green A24; Mill Road 165 202 538; North Street 77 202; Rectory Lane xxii A19 A21 A46; School Hill A13; Spring Steps 91; Square, The – *see Barrack Square*; Strand Hill (also Tower Hill) 730 A29; Strand, The 80 134 397 531 666 943n; Tower Hill – *see Strand Hill*;

Winchelsea Beach xxiii
Winchelsea Castle – *see Camber Castle*
Wittersham, Kent 387-388 409 659-660 662 665 B2; removal order to 661
Woodchurch, Kent 528
Woolwich, Kent 549 704 706 B2
York 845

Index of Subjects

W = Winchelsea

apprenticeship xvi 152 154 194 202 228-
229 256 263 304 307 309 313-314
318 344 347-349 354 388 403 409
413 477 485 487 514 516 603 652
681-683 686-687 728 806n 987
assistant overseer 872; appointment of xv
xix 3 19 21 829 831 E1; need for
828-829; remuneration of 3 11 21-
22 829; *see also Arnett, Charles &
Laurence, David in persons index*
banking services xix 41 105 272 577 638
878 882 895 938
Baptists xxii
barrack master xxiii
bastardy xvi xxvii 50-54 56-58 60 80-81
99 165 196-197 321-322 400 416 419
533 552 554 556 625 642 729n 805n
A27 A49; examinations 63 82 100
167 199 417 471 536-537 620 627-
628 635 641 643 650; maintenance
arrears 56-59 61 174-180 499-500
645-647 653 658; maintenance orders
55 58 83-84 168 200-201 255 324
361 382 398 402 420 499 618 621
644 655 A29 A42 representations
against 323; maintenance payments
50 60 99 321 376 416 498 500-501
635 639 653 655-656 account of
657 withdrawal of 651; refusal to
surrender child 654
beadle of W 752 A37; appointment of 106
108-109 397 505 507-508; duties of
110 507; pay of 507 752; uniform
of 507 509-510; *see also Chester,
Sinden, Tilden in persons index*
Black Friars (Dominicans) xvi
Bow Street (police) service 212-214
bread: cost of xviii-xix
cambric manufactory in W xxi
carrier services xxi 128-129 349-351 435
515 802; by coach 279-283 285-287

290 295 301
census returns xiii xiv A43; enumerators
of 943n A16; figures 1831 857;
information from 1841 77 80 94 134
165 202 250 326 397 505 531 538
659 666 688 693 A1-2 A16 A21 A24
A29 A31-32 A35
certificates of residence and settlement 87
119 121 125 131 191 287-288 362-
363 365 376 378-381 399 598 614
619 712
chamberlain of W – *see Corporation of W*
churchwardens of W: xv 817 827 861;
*see also parish officers; see also
Alce, Benfield, Fuller, Hollingberry,
Laurence, Maplesden, Sargent,
Stileman, Wright in persons index*
Cinque Ports Confederation xiv xxvi
xxix 823 C3(b); Fencibles 87 405;
Lord Warden of C2(a)(b) C3(b); *see
also member towns Deal, Dover,
Hastings, Hythe, Lydd, New Romney,
Ramsgate, Tenterden in places index*
coach travel xi 152 215
Coastguard Service – *see customs and
excise service*
constables xii 165 C1(b)(d)(e);
appointment and service of 91 151
202 210 336 397 623 A2 A15-18
A20 A24 A29 A32 A48; expenses
claimed by 68 208 215 416 992;
enforcement action by 232 244 258n
701; magistrates' orders to 6 74 76 81
171 174 178-180 201 233-234 394
642; *see also Hill, Easton, Laurence
in persons index*
coroner xiv xxiv xxv 852
Corporation of W: xii xxiv xxvi xxix 17
326-327 336 456 623 724n 780 786
805 841 A5 A12-13 A21 A27 A30
A42 A44-45 A48 C3(a); archives of

xxv 786n; chamberlain of 114n A16
A50; 'charter' of A42; deputy mayors
of xii 326 *see also Browne, Hennah,
Lipscomb, Marten, Powell, Stace,
Stileman, Tilden*; mayoring ceremony
(Easter Monday Hundred Court) xxv
A16 A42 A49; mayors of xii xiv xvii
xxiv-xxv 823 827 A19 A27 A30 A33
A37 A42 A44-45 C1(b)-(d) (f)-(h)
C3(b); meeting of xxiv; treasurer
of A15-16 A50; *for Corporation
members see also freemen; for
officers see also beadle, gaoler,
highway surveyors, pound driver,
town clerk, sergeant-at-mace, town
sergeant, water bailiff's sergeant*
Court of King's Bench 329n 861
Court of Record 623
courts – magistrates/justices of the peace
xii xiv xxvi-xxvii 24-25 62 274 714
841; corporal punishment ordered
by 66 73; custodial sentences of
50 66-69 69 72-73 151 165 216
232 271 452 457-458 523 530;
examinations conducted by 63 82 87
100 112-113 159 194 197 199 322
388 399 405 417 419 440 442 449
471 480-481 516 536-537 553 620
627-628 630 641 643 650; forfeiture
of goods 244; information/evidence
submitted to 70-71 89-90 112 236
328 334 384 402 675 715 942 *see
also Arnett, Charles – appearances
before magistrates*; orders issued by
6 55 71 76 81 83 168 179 200-201
210 324 361 382 394 398 420 469
482 499 517 523 621 631 642 644
647 655 661; prisoners – treatment
and transport of 68 202 208;
recognisances entered into at 8 15
172 235 333 386 402 418 544-545
652 671; sureties required by 72
courts – quarter sessions xii xxiii 17 73-
74 179 235 245 253 317 389 418
506 548 652 806n 843-844 857 861
C1(b)(d) (f)-(h); affiliation orders
confirmed 325; appeals considered

864 873; as petty sessions 180
715; complaints submitted to 327;
corporal punishment ordered by 74
114; custodial sentences of 74 180
235; fines imposed by 253; gaol fee
payment ordered by 114; grand jury
of xxiii 27 91 114 239 326-327 943n
A2 A5 A17-18 A24 A32 A38; orders
to appear at 81 172 201 235 327 386
544 652; removal order revoked by
518; trials at 114 239 545; *see also
Canterbury and Lewes in places
index*
customs and excise service xiv xxvi 16
112-113 536-537 A27 A33 A43
deputy mayors of W – *see Corporation of
W*
East Sussex Record Office (ESRO) xi
education – *see schools and schooling*
emigration xiv 80 202 221-223 266 336
704 952-971 A44
employment of the poor xxiii 45 403 475
712 718 744; agreement terms with
employers 64 85 94 96-97 135 166
169-170 173 261-262 403 426 432-
433 450 452 461 495 520 524 527
538 540-541 627 636 668 683 724
726-727; as baker 337 339; as carrier
435; as carter 135; as coachman 162-
163; as general labourer 135 340
720-721; as groom 435; as nursemaid
197; as ostler 87; as (inn) potboy
688; as schoolteacher 289 304; at
sea 228-229 256-257 260 263 316
318 405 477-478 485 487 513 516
681-683 686-687 717 728 aboard
Brunswick of Rye 514 *Speculation*
schooner 516 *Prometheus* schooner
516 *Old Peace* collier 620; breaking
stones 62 531 693; failure to pay for
work done 675; in agriculture xiv
xxi 62 64-65 79 87 97 134 262 475-
476 496-497 723 wages xxviii 79
476 497; in bakery 729; in domestic
service xii xvi 32 35 77 80 85 87 94
96 134 164 166 169-170 173 190
194 237 256 261 291 340 367 417

426-434 450-452 461-468 493-495
516 519-521 524-525 527 538 540
547 578 626-627 636 667-668 681
683-685 704 706 719 722 724-727
814 unlawful dismissal from 527;
on licensed premises 159; pay rates
xxi; shortage of work 32 43 79 139
147-148 160 163 237 247 254 337
340 456 560-562 610 622 658 676
692; termination of 494; *see also
highways; for trades of individual
paupers see persons index*
excise service – *see customs and excise*
freemen of W xxiv; appointment of 326
A1-2 A4 A8 A11-12 A16 A18 A23-
24 A29-31 A35 A39; as voters for
parliament A20
gaoler xii 151 239 458 A20
Grey Friars (Franciscans) xvi
health, particularly of the poor 32 43 48
91 93 102 134 138 147 158 160-161
187 209 223 237 267 295 304 320
340 343 374-375 391 410-412 415
441 483 501 526 570-572 574 577
580 583 592 600-608 611 615 623-
624 660 666 676-678 687 706 710;
affliction with dropsy 342n; ague and
fever 546 570; cancer 743; disability
165; epilepsy 810; hospital admission
341-342 522 669 677 expense of 522;
injury 490; insurance 546; medical
attendance xii 46-48 209 310 354 373
391 411 572 577 605 607 610-611
629 679 704 711 762 802 alleged
inadequacy of 707-709 lack of 366;
medical certificates 604-605 607
610-611; mental health 40-42 45 62
75-76; nursing provision 94 155 493
505 603 624 629 666 704 711 770;
rheumatism 610; rupture 216 472-
474; scurvy A7; smallpox xi 46-48
370-371 742 802 inoculation against
742 813; typhus fever 575; *see also
removal orders, suspension of*
highways xxiii; employment on 62 77
134 147 202 230-231 250 254n 256
259 340 376 505 688 690 531 704

761-762 815 825; encroachment
on A2-3 A13; expense of travel on
497; misuse and obstruction of 253;
surveyors of 858 870 A39
hospitals (almshouses) of W xvi-xvii; of
Holy Cross xvii; of St Bartholomew
xvii; of St John xvii
House of Commons xxvi 840 845;
representation of W in xxiv xxvi 623
A20 A30 A44; returns made to 827
831-832 836 838
House of Lords 549n 845n
Huguenots xvii
inquests xxv 496 659 704 851-852
jurats xii xvii xxiv-xxv C1(b); *see also
courts – magistrates*
justices of the peace xix-xx – *see also
courts – magistrates*
king's/queen's dues and town rents A5 A27
A38 A42
lace making xxi
land tax 891 905 908; commissioners of
326 328 870
Liberty of Winchelsea xiv xxiv 374 841
844 A7 A9 A34 A41
magistrates – 974; *see also courts*
Martello Towers xxiii xxvi
mayors of W – *see Corporation of W*
medical services – *see health of the poor*
Methodism in W xxii xxv-xxvi 435
military service xv 165 265 273 276 320
398 435 528 553 704 A6 A23 A32
compulsory liability for C3(a)-(d);
see also Cinque Ports Fencibles
military units xxii
militia returns 163 165 202 435 704 A8
A29 A35 A44-45 A48
monasteries, dissolution of xvi-xvii
monetary values xxviii-xix
Municipal Corporations Act, 1835 xxiv-
xxvi
Napoleonic Wars xxii-xxiii 273; voluntary
service during C2(a)-(b)
naval service xv 322 324 370-371 405
Ordnance, Board of 275n 276
overseers of the poor – *see parish officers*
parish officers (churchwardens and

overseers of the poor) xi xv xvii xix
xxii xxvi 36 66 94 99 151 209 220
225 258 287 299 426 461 476 502
510 512 523 528-529 542 547 549
588 629 676n 683 693 722 731 738
742 744 774-775 777-779 782 788
790 807 809 817 819-820 822 841
844 846-847 857 860 932 950-951
958n 964 973 977 980n 986 989 991
996n 997-998 A29 A48 C1 C3(a);
accounts of xii-xiii 17 24 111 129n
202 209 250 264 266 279n 286n
288n 307n 308n 326 336 349n 353n
366 408 425n 477 498 513 547 555n
558n 574n 580n 603n 631n 669n
678 683 702 804n 820 829 837 859
872n 912 940n 958n 970-971 987n
992 998 A5 A13; accounts submitted
for payment by 105 251 589 631 677
895; accounts submitted for payment
to 51 53 56-57 107 203 205 213
274-275 329 393 395 473-474 499
534 549 552 554 556 645-646 703
824 835 878 886 910-912 965 A18;
appointment of xii xv ; audit and
supervision of accounts 859 987 A5
A13 A15; certificates of residence
issued by xxii 380; legal advice to
220 222 224 841-843; letters from
948-949; letters to 32-33 41-42 44-
46 60 103-105 121 157 160 163
181 185 198 220 225 246 248 263
279-282 286-287 291-293 296-299
323 337 358 378 396 421 423 427
430 443-445 447 451 454 459 462
475 478 497 500 504 546 561 563-
566 568 570 573 590 594-595 597
599 601-602 609-611 615 617 622
638 656 660 662-663 682 686 706
712 720-722 727 758 780 791 802
850 835 838 840 870 882 884 891-
892 896 900 944 947 953 958 967
985 988 990-992 A47; notices of
public meeting issued by 783 916
956 966 998; notices to landlords
of intention to quit property rented
for the poor 88-90 237-238 240-242

673 695 697-699; notices to quit
issued to the poor by 243-244 489
512 674 700-701; orders issued to
76 616 728 778 784 789 975-976
979 987-988; request to for parish
work 218 415; supplies provided
for 165 202 250 326 408 505 850
853 859 A8 A20 A38-39 A45 A48;
see also assistant overseer, beadle,
constables, highway surveyors;
for responsibilities of the parish
officers see also apprenticeship,
bastardy, poor rates, poor relief; for
individual churchwardens see above;
for individual overseers see Alce,
Barham, Bigg, Blackman, Boots,
Bray, Chatterton, Clark, Eagles,
Fuller, Harrod, Hill, Hollingberry,
Jeakens, Kennett, Laurence,
Maplesden, Marten, Offord, Osborne,
Sargent, Sharps, Terry, Woods,
Wright in persons index
Parochial Assessments Act 877 989
Poor Law xi xiii xxvi 504n
Poor Law Amendment Act xiii xix 1834
588 762n 771 829n 957 972 979 987
990 992n E2
Poor Law Commissioners xix 79 588 666
771 774-780 781n 782-790 796-797
799-800 949 954 958 964-965 967
971-973 975 986-987 989 992-993;
notices issued by 877; orders of 778
877; representations to 79
poor, the: bequests in support of xvi-xvii;
provision for xvii
poor rate xii xvii-xviii xix-xx xxii xxv 1
62 91 248 334-335 340 731 838 840
932 944 956 958 964 971 979 980
992 A3 C3(a)(c); assessments of 93n
165 438n 863-864 867 869-871 873n
874 878-879 947–948 A7 A17 A45
A47 A50 D1,2 appeals against 873
880 939; collection of xiv-xv 17 19
439 819 831 876 878 881-882 885
887-891 893-894 897-901 903-910
912 932 992 998 A6 A9 A16 A21
A25 A34-36; failure to pay 332 383

404; liability for A14 A38 A40-41 A43; payments due to Rye 148-149 159 247 249 366 369 460 898 902; payments excused 43 134 250 326 439 531 659 666 690; properties occupied by paupers 861; proposed legal amendments 840; protest against 997; reduction of 24 718 762; refusal to approve 824; revaluations of xiv 860-869 871-877 913 940-941 989 A33 A40-41 costs of 877; valuations 531

poor relief: costs of xix 1 11 754 817-818 820 826 828 831-832 836 839; account keeping 821-822; increase of need for xviii; lack of donations towards 827; provision by officer paid fixed amount 803-804 806 808; supervision by committee 807 809

poor relief – discontinuation or refusal of 111 142 155 189 228 247 256-257 273 296 299 305 336 343 360 364 401 408 472 488 547 561 613 710

poor relief – eligibility for 287-288 343 424-425 445

poor relief – payments: acknowledgements of receipt 41-42 117 129 285 413 415 424 433 571 574 591 595 603; owed by W to other parishes or Rye guardians 226 249 357-358 370 397 503 534 586 590; owed by other parishes to W 663; owed by paupers to third parties 272 459 475; paid by other parishes 105 183 391 441 443-444 447-448 631 634 662 664 706; paid by third parties 289 298 535 656; paid to paupers of other parishes 483-484 633 637-638; reduced 578 580 582; requests for reimbursement submitted by/to third parties 37-39 225 260 273 278-283 286-287 290 295 297 301-303 494-495 631; requested by third parties on behalf of paupers 115-116 119 188 190 291-293 297 337 339 486-487 597 601 615 624; required from parents 453-455 457

poor relief – proposals/threats to return to W through lack of 36 45 126 163 181 185 190 268-269 289 296 298 304-306 311 314 337 349 354 360 364 414-415 421 428 432 459 466 504 546 555 563-565 569 575 580 584 609 622 676 679; requirement to return 189 214 564 613

poor relief – provision by W of: bread 747; broth for the sick 12; clothing and/ or shoes xxviii 27 33 35-36 38-39 77 94-95 97 139 147 153 155 222 226 228 237 252 256 261 366 408 426 450 452 461 472 488 493 496 513 524 538 547 618 666 681 683 685 690 728n 745 762 812 833-834 unauthorised retention of 258; coal 139 155 202 204 472 488 762 corn 436 811; flour 18 44 80 138 202 237 252 340 472 670 688 712 747 762 816 834; food 48; funeral expenses 340 366 610n 625 752n; haircutting 97 839; leather 206-207; meat 472 688 833-834; money 27 30 33 40 43 46 62 77-78 80 91 93-95 99 106 109 111 132 134-135 138-139 142 147 150 153 155 158 162 165 186 192 196 202 204 206-207 209 222 228 230 232 237 243 247 256 260 264-266 273 277 279 294 300 307-308 312 336 338-340 343-347 348 356 360 366 370 373 376 392 397 408 413 415-416 420 425 434 437 439 450 452 462 472 475 477 485 488 490-491 493 498 502 505 513 531 533 535 538 543 547 551 555 558 569 570n 572n 577 592 607 610 612 614 618 623 629 639 666-667 669 676 678 681 683 686 688-689 693 702-704 710 712 752 762 810; intention to withdraw 812; relief after 1834 Act 973 975-977; rent xxii 32 43 88 139 237-238 438 488 505 666 672 695 743 payments stopped 830; unspecified xi-xii 145 250 341 374 376 435

poor relief – requests to W for: a cow xi

502 504; clothing and/or shoes 32-34
36 44 85 98 102 120 152 154 263
288 304 309 314-315 359 364 411
424 427-434 451 465-467 478 497
682 728; continued support 411-412;
corn 44; decision on allowance 352;
dietary provision 160; fireing (wood
and coal) 137 141; flour 44; money
33 101-104 118 120-131 154 163 181
185 187 190 221 223 229 267-269
288-289 291 294-296 304-309 313
347-351 353-356 359 372 410-415
421-423 430 432-433 459 463-464
468 532 542 555 557-566 569-583
594 596 599-600 602-603 608-609
689; rent 45 157 211 310-311 410
475 582-583 608-609; unspecified
137 148 209 343 476 490 546 606
611 622 715; work 254
poorhouse – *see workhouse*
population of W xxi
postal services 121 123 177 181 185 187
189n 267-269 283-284 289 296 308-
310 359 445 519 555 558 565 686
720-721 729 923 953 993
pound driver 397 A20
poverty xxvi; impact of the weather on
xviii
quarter sessions – *see courts.*
queen's dues – see king's/queen's dues
rate in support of gaol 17
Reform Act 1832 xxiv 996n A44-45
registrar of births and deaths 910n
removal orders xii xvi xxii 1 543 617 843;
from W 192 194-195 245 317 389
397 439 479 482 517 552 631 659
661 665 805 A24; appeal against
407; revocation of 518; suspension of
357-358 375 482 503n 534 585-588
590 605 614 631 661-662; to W 29
49 107 136 140 143 150 156 184 188
191 197 274 299 312 357-358 360
361n 365 368 375 377 398 469 492
503 511 534 539 548-549 554 566-
567 584-588 590-591 593 614 616
619 640 649 679-680 694 706 appeal
against 107 548n 567

Rye Poor Law Union (Rye Union) xi
xiii-xiv xix xxvii 704 771 778 788
877 910n 952 961 963 972 982
A4; accounts of 790 798 987 992
submitted by 965 972 submitted
to 589 677 911 946 996; audit of
parish accounts by 985-987; Beckley
District of 910n; building expenses of
797 799-800; clerk of 225 255 707-
708 774 779 782-783 785 789n 790
793 796 799-800 955 959 961 963
965 976 980n 983 991-992; chairman
of 794 974; coffins – provision
by 978n; common seal of 794;
composition of 972; division into
districts 972; flour – provision by 79
692 972 supply to A39; guardians of
xix 79 111 617 688 690 704 730 771
775-776 778 781n 787 790-791 877
958n 972 974 978 979-980 983 990
992 994-995 A31; letters from 588
617 780 791 967-969 990 992; letters
to 591; minutes of xiii 225-227 255
616 692 707-709 774-777 779 782-
786 789-790 792-800 946 954-955
959-963 972 974-977 981-984 989
991 993-994; orders issued by 979
991-992 received by 778; payments
by 27 40 80 134 147 158 505 531
692 702 982n 996; payments due to
990 992; poor rate demands by 980
997-998; potential removal of pauper
families from 982; relieving officers
of 962 977 988 991n; resolutions of
988n; transfer of ownership to 771;
treasurer(s) of 790 798 979 992; vice-
chairman of 974 A40; withdrawal of
relief by 972 983-984; workhouses
in 771 972 981 988 992n inmate
employment 994 inmate punishment
981; *see also workhouses of Brede,
Northiam, Rye*
St Thomas's Church, W xxvi; archives of
xi xiii; baptisms at xxii 1 80 99 111
134 145 196 202 228 237 273 305
322n 340 360 361n 362n 376 382n
389 392 417n 435 461 472 493 496

543 585n 623 625 635 639 650 666
A2 A4 A7 A12 A15 A23-24 A27 A29
A36 A39; burials at xxii-xxiii 1 27
99 111 145 158 182n 192 195n 237
260 273 340 439 442n 461 488 496
610n 625 666 704 710 743n 851-852
A6 A22 A36 A48; church rates 867
888 891 937; churchyard 165 D2;
curate of xvi xxiii-xxiv 305 851n 944
A14 A36 A46; dedication of xxix;
marriages at xxii 53 80 87 145 165
232 273 360 370 392 408 440 472
488 491 585n 623 635 659 969 A1
A8 A15 A27 A29 A31 A35 A43 A45;
parish of xiii-xiv xvii xxiii xxvii 10
24 55 74 81-82 85 100 135 167-168
179 194-195 197 199 200-201 239
253 258 317 322 324 331 357-358
365 368 374-375 380-382 387-389
398 407 420 440 457 480 499 503
517 534 536 548 553 567 621 627-
628 631-632 640-644 649 652 655
661 694 788 827 844 861-862 864
914 958 A47; parish registers of xiii
xxii 1 80 111 192 202 340 344 435
472 488 493 496 537n 623 635 681
969n A6-7 A14 A22 A33 A36 A41
A47 A48; Parochial Church Council
of xxix; rector of xiii xvi xxiii-
xxiv 22 305 807 827 860 864 872
874 878-880 891 911 913-914 916
923 940-944 946-950 956 A9 A14
A22 A36 A46; rectory of xiii A46;
services at xxiii; *see also – tithes*
schools and schooling 289 304 311 724
728n 747 770 982
sergeant-at-mace (mayor's sergeant) 91
151 457 623 A20 A42 A48
settlement xi xxvii 34 43 106-107 147
158 192 203 247 273 275 326 376
409 549 616 635 659 679 956;
examinations xvi 86-87 135 159
182-183 194 197 322 367 374 387-
388 391 395 398n 405-406 440
442 449 480-481 491 516 552-553
585 626 630 662 706 843; Law of
xvi; legal opinions regarding 197;

qualification conditions xvi 18 164
181 211 248 274 276 506 627 706;
*see also certificates of residence
and settlement, emigration, removal
orders*
smallpox – *see health*
smuggling xxv-xxvi 151 371n; Coastal
Blockade Service xxv-xxvi 371n
Sussex Record Society xi-xii
Times, The xv E2
tithes xiv 860 864 874 878 891 899-900
A14 A46; background information
about 911; due to rector 912-913;
failure to pay 942-943; revaluation of
913-917 920-921 923-925 927-937
940-941 944-945 947-949; *see also
workhouse*
town clerk xii xxv 1 14 258 328 510 841
870 A12 A42; disputed costs of 843
847; duties of 843; permitted fees
of 841-842 843n; *see also Butler,
Dawes, Lardner, Waterman, Woollett
in persons index*
town crier of W 74
town sergeant of W xii 336 A17 A48
town rents – *see king's/queen's dues*
transport – *see coach travel, carrier
services, postal services*
vestry clerk 1 19 96 856 924 930-931 933
940-941 A16
vestry, public/parish xv xix xxi xxiii-xxiv
19 24-25 32n 85 221 334-335 408
450 603n 860 A24; chairman of A24
A35; financial report received by 17;
letters to 24-25 223; minutes of xii-
xiii 2-5 17 22 26 30 52 54 64 132 166
169-170 186 193 222 251 261-262
338 379 436-438 524 540 551 623
636 667-669 684 696 731-736 738
742-744 751-753 756 764 772-773
781 803-814 816-822 826 828-830
843 847-848 858 861-863 865-869
875-876 880 914 922 927-928 934
940n 941 951 957 971 964 973 980
995 997; public meeting called by
787; resolutions of 18 62 247 273
336 472 493 496 505 523 618 681

688 704 740 912 972

vestry room 861; meetings in 2 739 772
789 844 861 913 916-917 921 925
945 951 966 998

vestry, select xii 24-25 189 211 217 292
312n 344 352 347 401 406 413 672;
appointment/election of members 831
847-848 A10-11 A25 A36 A38-39
A41 A47 A50; chairman of 476 A29
A46; conduct of meetings 672; letters
to 36 110 476 624 715; minutes of 7
12 19-21 23 92 95 108-109 138 142
153 173 204 212 221 252 257 277
300 336 341 345-346 401 408 453
455 507-509 612-613 651 685 711
728 745-750 759 825 833-834 842
844 871-872 874; parish management
by 856; resolutions of 18 57n 155
158 232 260 266 294n 340 360 366
434n 452 461 472 488 531 582n 592
623 678 681 683 690 704 710

water bailiff's sergeant 623

Winchelsea Corporation – *see Corporation
of Winchelsea*

workhouse of W (poorhouse) xii xiv
xviii xxi-xxii xxvii 4 40 146 189-
190 354 406 412-413 504 525-526
615 723 730 742 744 801 810 D1;
absconding from 547 568; admission
to 1 109 111 139 165 232 256 260
341 356 360 397 416 472 543 613
690 696 710 A15; closure of 111
132 751-752 779-780; compulsory
confinement in 523 531; condition
of A50; contents of 704; damage to
66; discharge from 62 94-95 273
277; employment in 547 748-749;
expenditure account 747n 770; fear
of 605; inmates; provision for 24
745-747 762 punishment of 750;
insurance of 755; inventory of 133
144 705 760 978; master/mistress/
governor of xvi xix-xx 1 141 192-
194 392 505 513 528 754 761-762
A29 appointment of 3 392 396 753
756-758 A21; regulations of 761-762;
repairs to and extension of 731-736

738-741 A8 A24 A39; residence in
2 22 30 77 94 99 102 106 132 194
340 452 454 693 743 762 of Charles
Arnett 4 307-311; sale of building xix
771-789 793-796 A29 A44 by auction
790 792-793 proceeds of 790 795
797-800; supervision of 759 761-762;
supplies and services for 165 230 326
763-764 765n 766n 767-770 A1 A3
A8 A39; theft of clothing from 529;
tithe payments on 878 911 946 948
950-951; title deeds of 777 779 790
796 896; valuation of 737-738 791-
792